PAPERS ON THE POLITICAL ECONOMY OF TANZANIA

Studies in the Economics of Africa

Editors: I. LIVINGSTONE and H. W. ORD

Money and Credit in Developing Africa
ERIC L. FURNESS

Economic Integration: The East African Experience
ARTHUR HAZLEWOOD

Development Economics in Action
TONY KILLICK

Macroeconomics for Africa
CHARLES HARVEY

Papers on the Economy of Tanzania
Edited by: KWAN S. KIM, ROBERT B. MABELE and MICHAEL J. SCHULTHEIS

Papers on the Political Economy of Tanzania

Editors: KWAN S. KIM, ROBERT B. MABELE
and MICHAEL J. SCHULTHEIS

HEINEMANN EDUCATIONAL BOOKS LTD.
NAIROBI • LONDON • LUSAKA • IBADAN.

Heinemann Educational Books Ltd
22 Bedford Square, London WC1B 3HH
P.O. Box 45314, Nairobi . P.M.B. 5205, Ibadan

EDINBURGH MELBOURNE AUCKLAND
HONG KONG SINGAPORE KUALA LUMPUR NEW DELHI
KINGSTON PORT OF SPAIN

Heinemann Educational Books Inc.
4 Front Street, Exeter, New Hampshire 03833, U.S.A.

ISBN 0 435 97440 8

First published 1979

ERRATUM

The publishers regret that the text on pages 208 and 209 has been inadvertently transposed. After page 207 please read text on page 209 followed by page 208.

Printed by Printing and Packaging Corporation Limited,
Likoni Road, P.O. Box 30157, Nairobi, Kenya.

Table of Contents

Biographical Note on Editors

Kwan S.Kim
Associate Professor, Department of Economics, University of Notre Dame, Notre Dame, Indiana, (USA): Associate Professor, Dept. of Economics, University of Dar es Salaam, 1975–77.

Robert B. Mabele
Director and Senior Research Fellow, Economic Research Bureau, University of Dar es Salaam.

Michael J. Schultheis
Senior Research Fellow, Economic Research Bureau, University of Dar es Salaam.

Notes on Contributors

The present position of contributors is indicated: If an individual is no longer in Tanzania, his/her position and years in Tanzania also are indicated.

D. G. R. Belshaw:	*Senior Lecturer, School of Development Studies, University of East Anglia, Norwich, (U.K.); Visiting UNDP/FAO Research Professor, Bureau of Resource Assessment and Land Use Planning (BRALUP), University of Dar es Salaam, and Regional Planning Advisor to Prime Minister's Office, 1975–77.*
Manfred Bienefeld:	*Fellow, Institute of Development Studies, University of Sussex, (U.K.); Research Fellow, Economic Research Bureau, University of Dar es Salaam, 1969–73.*
David Feldman:	*Lecturer, School of Development Studies, University of East Anglia, (U.K.) and Planning Advisor, Ministry of Agriculture, Kenya; Research Fellow, ERB, 1968–70.*
Rayah Feldman:	*Lecturer, School of Development Studies, University of East Anglia; Research Officer (in Tanzania), Institute of Development Studies, University of Sussex, 1968–70.*
Louise Fortmann:	*Occasional Consultant on Rural Development and Regional Planning for FAO, USAID and World Bank; Lecturer, Department of Rural Economy and Extension, Faculty of Agriculture and Forestry, University of Dar es Salaam, 1974–75.*
Manuel Gottlieb:	*Professor of Economics, University of Wisconsin at Milwaukee, (U.S.A.); Visiting Professor, ERB, 1971–73.*
Yukon Huang:	*Associate Professor of Economics, University of Virginia, (U.S.A.); Visiting Lecturer, Department of Economics, University of Dar es Salaam, 1972–74.*
Gerald K. Helleiner:	*Professor of Economics, University of Toronto, (Canada); Director, ERB, 1966–68.*
Goran Hyden:	*Visiting Professor, University of California at Berkeley, (U.S.A.), 1977–79; Professor, Department of Political Science, University of Dar es Salaam, 1975–77.*
Kwan Kim:	*Associate Professor of Economics, University of Notre Dame, (U.S.A.); Associate Professor, Department of Economics, University of Dar es Salaam, 1975–77.*
Ian Livingstone:	*Professor of Development Economics, University of East Anglia, (U.K.); Director, ERB, 1968–71.*
John Loxley:	*Visiting Professor, Department of Economics, University of Manitoba, (Canada), 1977–78; Senior Lecturer, Department of Economics, University of Dar es Salaam, 1969–72.*
Robert B. Mabele:	*Senior Research Fellow and Director, Economic Research Bureau, University of Dar es Salaam.*
Kighoma Malima:	*Associate Professor and Head, Department of Economics, University of Dar es Salaam.*
Adolpho Mascarenhas:	*Director, Bureau of Resource Assessment and Land Use Planning, University of Dar es Salaam.*
Simon Mbilinyi:	*Associate Professor, ERB, on Secondment to the Tanzania Government as Senior Principal Economist, President's Office.*
A. T. Mohele:	*Head of Research Department, Tanzania Rural Development Bank.*
L. A. Msambichaka:	*Research Fellow, ERB.*
C. M. Nyirabu:	*Governor, Bank of Tanzania.*
David Phillips:	*Lecturer, Project Planning Centre, University of Bradford, (U.K.); Economic Advisor to SIDO, 1975–76.*
Robert Rice:	*Professor of Economics, University of Monash, (Australia); Member of Harvard Advisory Group, Ministry of Finance and Planning, Tanzania, 1974–75.*
D. G. Rwegasira:	*Director of Research, Bank of Tanzania; Senior Lecturer, Department of Economics, University of Dar es Salaam.*
J. F. Rweyemamu:	*Professor of Economics, University of Dar es Salaam, on Secondment to Tanzania Government as Personal Assistant to the President, (Economic Affairs).*
R. H. Sabot:	*Economist, World Bank, Washington D.C.; Research Fellow, ERB, 1970–72.*
S. Sumra:	*Lecturer, Department of Education, University of Dar es Salaam.*
Peter Temu:	*Senior Economist UN/ECA, Addis Ababa; Senior Research Fellow and Director, ERB, 1971–73.*
S. M. Wangwe:	*Lecturer, Department of Economics, University of Dar es Salaam.*
David Williams:	*Senior Industrial Economist, World Bank, Washington D.C.; Project Director, Harvard Advisory Group, Ministry of Finance and Planning, Tanzania, 1972–76.*

Foreword

Although the majority of the universities which exist in Africa today are, by and large, a creation of the post-independence era, it is true that they are still very much replicas of the colonial legacies. During the colonial days the University Colleges established in Africa not only offered degrees and followed the curricula of the 'mother' metropolitan institutions, but they also were staffed by people recruited mainly from the respective colonial powers. Indeed, even though the curricula followed were based on those of the metropolitan institution, they were so designed as to provide for the needs of the colonial administration. Thus apart from omitting such important areas as Engineering Education, which is so vital for self-reliance, these institutions were also fed with teaching materials from the metropolis.

Since independence, a number of African countries have tried to establish independent national universities (designated as National High Seats of Learning) to cater for national objectives. But it must be admitted that little has been achieved beyond the establishment of these nuclei. Much of what they do is still very much influenced by what happened and is happening in European and American universities. The textbooks, the standards set for the staff and students and the values attached to the education imparted and the manner of its dissemination are very much conditioned by these older institutions. So much so that up till now we have very little written about ourselves and by ourselves.

In Tanzania, we have attempted to redesign the curricula so that both courses and content conform to the national objectives of building a socialist and self-reliant Tanzania. These efforts still leave something to be desired for the development and teaching of such curricula has continued to rely on overseas textbooks and journals both as teaching and research material source. Yet the reorientation of our educational institutions to contribute to the achievement of national objectives requires as a pre-requisite the production of texts and periodicals oriented to the local situation; thus the appearance of this volume of readings is an important step in the right direction: it is in fact long overdue.

The editors have selected for this volume what they consider the best papers published by the Economic Research Bureau at the University of Dar es Salaam during the first decade of the Bureau's existence. The Bureau sponsors weekly seminars on economic topics during the regular academic year and publishes many of these for wider distribution. Of the nearly 200 seminar papers that the Bureau has published, the 29 papers presented here are intended to provide a comprehensive picture of the Tanzanian economy as it has been evolving. The major features of the economy and the nation's economic policy which are covered here include industrialization, money and finance, rural development, education and planning for development.

As I write these remarks, I am aware of the many changes presently underway and the important implications which they have for the future of the Tanzanian economy. First and foremost, perhaps, is the birth of *Chama Cha Mapinduzi*, which is the result of the merger between TANU and Afro-Shirazi parties. This merger has made the union between the Tanzanian Mainland and Zanzibar more real and its significance is that already considerations are underway to integrate the planning periods of the two entities. Second, the Third Five-Year Development Plan, which aims at introducing fundamental changes in the structure of the Tanzanian economy, particularly in the industrial sector, has recently been approved by the Party and Parliament. The Plan actually started operation in 1976/77. Third, in the other sectors, bolder schemes than those described in the readings have been launched. In particular in the rural sector, villages are now self-governing and their responsibility includes Primary Education, which has been universalised, since November, 1977. This means that this volume to a certain extent is already out of date. But still it is an important step, for it places more permanently on record the economic background to these changes as well as to other changes that will occur. It is thus my hope that the appearance of this volume will act as a stimulus to our teachers, researchers and students to embark on the most urgent question of producing relevant scholarly material to back up the very dynamic efforts of the Party to try and understand our past and present. Such efforts at the same time will assist in the construction of our future on the basis of Socialism and Self-Reliance.

I. M. Kaduma
Vice-Chancellor
University of Dar es Salaam

Preface

The present volume of readings on the Tanzanian Economy represents a collection of papers prepared over the past decade by visiting and faculty scholars for the Economic Research Bureau seminars at the University of Dar es Salaam. On the occasion of the tenth anniversary of the Arusha Declaration, the Bureau has been encouraged to publish such a selection of readings to make more readily accessible to students and researchers this hitherto loosely available research material. Many of these selections have already been tested for their pedagogical effectiveness in classrooms at the University. Others are frequently requested by the international community of economists and scholars interested in Tanzania's unique approach to development and progress.

Although these readings essentially deal with economic conditions and problems specific to the Tanzanian economy, their interest extends far beyond this. Tanzania's model of development is guided by the basic principles of socialism and is widely recognized as relevant to many other developing countries in Africa and beyond. Broadly viewed, the guiding principles of Tanzania's socialist development place priority on social justice, equity and self-reliance. In a low income developing economy, social justice and equity can best be guaranteed in circumstances where the principal means of production are socialized. The achievement of self-reliance and economic independence fundamentally requires the creation of basic industrial structures that utilise domestic resources. At the same time, these principles must incorporate various policy-measures directed to securing self-sufficiency in food, attaining long term material balances within the economy, raising productivity and improving living standards for the majority of the people who obtain their livelihood from the land. Consequently these readings will particularly interest those students of development who seek a model of integrated development that is an alternative to the orthodox model.

Some remarks on the methodology of selecting the articles are in order. The more than 200 Economic Research Bureau papers were grouped somewhat arbitrarily into seven general categories. The initial selection in each section was a joint venture by the following staff members of the Bureau and the Economics Department: R. Mabele and K. Kim, Section 1; S. Curry and O. Brookins, Section II; D. Rwegasira, Section III; S. Wangwe and M. Kuuya, Section IV; K. Kim and G. Kileo, Section V; M. Schultheis, R. Mabele, D. Belshaw and B. Musti, Section VI; and M. Schultheis, Section VII.

The final selection of papers was based on the following general criteria:

(1) they directly relate to some aspect of the development of the Tanzanian economy;
(2) they either represent the results of original research or deal with important policy issues;
(3) they view the problem of development as interdiscipline, reflecting the complexity of society; and
(4) they are relevant to the economic problems and aspirations of Tanzania in the post-Arusha Declaration decade.

Each section is prefaced by an introduction that acquaints the reader with the key issues and themes of the selections. In a few instances the introduction has been expanded to identify or elaborate important issues not covered in the selections. Although the editors have attempted to retain the original manuscripts, they have been forced to shorten and condense some of the longer papers. For this reason, some papers have been partly rewritten and some tables, diagrams, technical derivations and appendices have been omitted. Such editing, however, has sought to be faithful to the substance and theme of the original papers.

The editors wish to express their appreciation to the authors and to those who assisted in the selection and editing. Special acknowledgement is given to S. Curry and D. Rwegasira who have written the introductions to the sections on Planning for Development and Money and Banking, and to O. Brookins, E. Ndungutse, O. Lameck and R. Sutcliffe for special assistance in editing. It is impossible to name the many other persons who have contributed to this project, but we are especially grateful to Mrs. R. Kajumba, who has been involved in the supervision, preparation and typing of the several stages of this manuscript.

Finally, we are indebted to the Rockefeller Foundation for their encouragement and financial support which has facilitated the preparation of this volume.

The Editors
March, 1978

REGIONAL MAP OF TANZANIA
30°
40°
2°
2°
4°
6°
8°
8°
10°
10°
30°
32°
34°
38°
BUKOBA
MUSOMA
MWANZA
MOSHI
ARUSHA
SHINYANGA
KIGOMA
TABORA
SINGIDA
TANGA
DODOMA
KIBAHA
D'SALAAM
MOROGORO
IRINGA
SUMBAWANGA
MBEYA
LINDI
SONGEA
MTWARA
0 200
Kilometres

Section 1

Background to Socialist Development in Tanzania

INTRODUCTION

The broad economic policy of Tanzanian Socialism outlined in the Arusha Declaration of 1967 must be understood in a much wider context than that of the social ownership and control of the means of production. Self reliance, the eradication of absolute poverty, improved standards of living and an equitable distribution of wealth and income, participation in decision-making processes and the organization of farm production on the basis of Ujamaa villages—these are some of the more significant features that characterize Tanzania's unique approach to Socialism.

The readings in this section provide an introduction to understanding the relationships that influence the policies and the institutional forms of Tanzania in the post Arusha period. In the first paper, Professor Hyden analyzes the style of policy-making and the role of polity and power in relation to the ongoing transformation of the society. He suggests that Tanzania has charted a unique type of politics because the foundation for socialism has been laid less by armed revolutionary struggle than by political means. The special role played by the Tanzanian "polity," however, often provides methodological difficulties to both Marxist and non-Marxist social scientists who seek to assess Tanzanian's real progress toward socialist development.

Elsewhere a strong case has been made to support Tanzania's strategy of socialist agricultural development. In the second reading the Feldmans identify the functional linkages that operate among various socio-economic and cultural factors, particularly in the rural communities. They relate these factors to two different farming systems as they attempt to account for the success and failure of cooperative organizations in Tanzanian agriculture. This largely exploratory paper concludes that it is not necessary to take refuse in "unexplainable" residual factors in explaining different patterns of cooperation, and their success or failure. The authors illustrate how patterns of agricultural cooperation are open to economic and sociological analysis, precisely because they are enmeshed in a structure of economic and social variables.

These two papers set the tone for many of the theoretical and methodological issues that are explored in greater detail in subsequent sections.

"We must run while others walk": Policy-Making for Socialist Development in the Tanzania-Type of Polities*

GORAN HYDEN

Introduction

The purpose of this paper is to analyze the style of policy-making that has developed in Tanzania as a result of its efforts at socialist development. It addresses itself critically to the notion that "economy" and "planning" as opposed to "polity" and "power" are the key factors determining the transition to socialism. Although these four variables are all interrelated—and many writers have tackled them together under the concept of "political economy"—few attempts have been made, while treating the issues of socialist transformation, to analyze in their own right factors like "polity" and "power." Political changes follow directly from economic transformation, so the argument usually goes.

The extent to which the economy shapes polity, and vice-versa, will no doubt differ from one society to another. The argument advanced in this paper is that several factors tend to increase the relative importance of the polity in a country like Tanzania. Socialism in Tanzania is not originally a product of a domestic class struggle, but induced primarily by the contradictions at the international level, interpreted and developed as an ideology by one man and finally taken to the people through a mass political organization by what is essentially an emerging bourgeois class. The contradictions involved in this process are bound to produce some unique features, one of which, as we shall argue later, is to reinforce the importance of the polity as a chief determinant of opportunities and limitations in any attempt at transition to socialism.

But it is not only the position of the polity vis-a-vis the economy that changes in this situation. So does the nature of the polity itself. Since the foundation for socialism in Tanzania has not been laid through a revolutionary struggle, it has to be laid by other, notably political means. The revolutionary spirit, if not consciousness, has to be induced by artificial means. By adopting the notion that "we must run while others walk," the impression of a revolutionary atmosphere is created. Every polity change is dramatized so as to make the people feel that the country is making great leaps forward. These features make it possible to talk of a Tanzania-type of polities.

This paper is devoted to a presentation and analysis of Tanzania's policy-making style, here referred to as we-must-run-while-others-walk. The concluding part of the paper will address itself to the difficulties of assessing progress, notably the methodological mistakes often made by social scientists.

POLICY-MAKING FOR SOCIALIST DEVELOPMENT IN TANZANIA

When analysing socialist development in Tanzania observers have invariably compared it to the experience of other more advanced socialist countries. Bienen[1] maintains that because Tanzania still is at a low level of economic development it cannot sustain a Leninist vanguard party, a precondition, according to him, for radical and purposeful change. His analysis of Tanzania in terms of the Soviet model is questioned by Lionel Cliffe in a review of the same book[2]. Because Tanzania's emerging socialism is rural, the country has more to learn from Chinese experience. Like in China, reliance on people and local cadres rather than a state bureaucracy must be Tanzania's strategy, says Cliffe. Writing along similar lines, Saul[3] emphasizes the need to consider the socio-political context of planning; the latter is not purely a matter of economic calculation or improved coordination. In offering prescriptions as to how the contextual variables can be changed, Saul is basing himself on the experience of revolutionary transformations in other countries. While all these points are potentially valid and certainly should be part of any analysis of "transition to socialism", the focus on the comparative experience of other socialist countries has often been pursued at the cost of local factors. And when the latter have been analyzed, more attention has been paid to the economic rather than the socio-political factors[4]. It is in the light of these considerations that we will now return to and develop our argument that the circumstances under which Tanzania has to attempt a transition to socialism puts the polity "in command" and in turn gives rise to a unique mode of policy-making.

THE STRATEGY OF WE-MUST-RUN-WHILE-OTHERS-WALK

One main reason why many Tanzanians believe that they have to "run" rather than "walk" is that their country is one of the 25 poorest in the world and a "late-comer" in the development race. It would be wrong to assume, however, that Tanzania is running only because some other countries are ahead of her. She is not content with watching the backs of her competitors without first knowing where the race is supposed to end. The socialist ideology of ujamaa provides a notion of what is conceived by many people in the country as the ultimate stage of this development race. The President often emphasizes that this race is a long-distance one, full of hurdles that have to be overcome. This approach is aimed partly at holding expectations back, partly at enforcing the need for discipline and restraint. Given the fact that the still undeveloped forces of production do not automatically enforce such discipline and that Tanzania lacks the guerilla warfare conditions that may produce the same effects, ideology and party organization do take on key roles in the efforts to achieve such behavioural transformation. Policies have to be so presented that they have the effect of changing people's

*Excerpted from ERB Paper 75.1; pp. 1–2 and 16–48. The literature on policy-making and planning is reviewed in the first fifteen pages of the original ERB paper.

attitude to life and work. They always have to be put forward in the name of the official ideology so as not to imply a change in direction. Since the implications of this long-distance race are known to only a few Tanzanians, the party has to play the role of the coach, standing by the side to ensure that those involved in the race do not lose their stamina. They must be constantly reaffirmed that it is worth continuing the race.

This strategy or mode of policy-making has at least four main features. The first is the strong urge to do everything and do it at once. The effort is to maximize as many social values as possible through policies which serve to mobilize new resources for their very achievement. This ambition is manifested in the way various programmes and policies are presented as "frontal attacks" (the ujamaa programme), "operations" (recent villagization moves) and "matters of life and death" (current efforts at raising agricultural production). Because the social values rarely are operationalized in advance, the aspiration to maximize is pursued with an explicit or implicit acceptance of the fact that one has to settle for a less ambitious target. In this respect, the approach resembles that of the fisherman who when throwing his net out is aware that while pulling it back some of the catch may escape.

The second feature is that policy-makers often decide without first having obtained full and detailed knowledge of possible consequences of their decisions. They start running and take the consequences as they occur. It resembles the approach which Hirschman[5] has called "the motivation-outruns-understanding" style of policy-making. Full understanding of what can or cannot be achieved with existing resources is not sought as a precondition for making a policy. Instead, the political decision is made first, often under dramatized circumstances, to produce a sense of rapid advance. In this approach ends are allowed to justify means: the ultimate objective is considered so important that the cost of resources to attain it becomes a secondary matter. The Arusha Declaration as well as *Mwongozo* and the *Musoma Resolutions* are cases in point. In the case of the first, Tanzania expressed its readiness to accept a lower economic growth rate per annum in the interest of building socialism. In *Mwongozo* it put human dignity above the specifics of organization efficiency. In the recent *Musoma Resolutions*, Universal Primary Education (UPE) was set for 1977 instead of the previous target year of 1989, leaving the task of working out the implications of this decision to those in charge of implementation.

The third feature of the strategy is the unwillingness of policy-makers to use the past as a source of guidance for the future. Being associated with colonial rule, from which the present leadership seeks a break, the past is to them by and large irrelevant. Dror[6] has identified this inclination as a main feature of policy-making in most developing countries. It is likely to be particularly strong in Tanzania where the desire to break with the past is very explicit. Policy-makers in Tanzania, therefore, are not always trotting on familiar grounds but making frequent moves into the unknown, the assumption being that the right policies are not necessarily those which are chosen from the realm of what is presently known as feasible in economically rational terms. The solution to a given problem is not always found where there is light; it may well be hidden in the dark. Thus, the task of the policy-makers becomes, in Hirschman's terms, that of "zeroing in" on a new policy which would otherwise have been ruled out by the conventional criteria of rational calculation. One case in point is the policy of cooperative development in recent years. The management crises in the cooperative institutions have not been solved by gradual improvements from "within", as proposed, for instance, by the 1966 Presidential Committee of Enquiry but rather tackled by more far reaching structural changes as outlined in the policy of ujamaa villages and related programmes.

The fourth feature of the strategy is that employees in the public sector are compelled to work in a context where public expectations constantly supercede what can actually be attained by the incumbent officers. This situation no doubt makes many public servants feel a sense of anxiety. The President, who makes most top appointments in the public sector, seems to work on the assumption that this state of anxiety or insecurity will produce beneficial results as officers will clamour for more security through improved performance. In this respect, the Tanzanian strategy differs from the findings of, e.g. Blau[7] that initiative occurs only with job security. It is more in line with the view of Gunder Frank[8] who argues that "over-defined" roles, i.e. where role expectations cannot be satisfied by role incumbents, often produce positive results.

THE RATIONALE OF THE STRATEGY

We have argued that this strategy is one way of creating a sense of participation in a radical transformation of a society which is void of the preconditions that have allowed for revolutionary changes in countries like China, Korea and Vietnam. This, however, is not the only reason that justifies the policy-making strategy adopted by Tanzania.

It may be useful to return to the development race analogy. When Tanzania is attempting to run while others walk she is not, like Filbert Bayi, proceeding on a smooth and well-paved track. Running in this context is more like a rough cross-country contest where the problems are not only unknown but all the time pressing themselves on the competitors. Tanzania, like most other developing countries, does not have its development problems, so to speak, at arms' length. Her race is a constant fight against heavy odds, with no or little breathing-space. Bogged down by these hurdles there is rarely time to plan the next move. Under such circumstances it is not only natural but also justified if policy-makers abandon the disposition of routinization implied in planning and instead of extolling the values of efficiency and rationality and gearing their efforts towards results that are measurable in economic terms, seek refuge in the more romantic and youthful risk-taking of the strategy of we-must-run-while-others-walk. There is no doubt that this strategy may cause disorder and discomfort to those who are used to the routinizing tendencies of orderly administration. Yet, as the Chinese have shown, campaigns based on ideological spontaneity in order to make "great leaps forward," have often resulted in the release of productive efforts by the people themselves. There is reason to agree with Green[9] that China's historical circumstances in many respects—revolutionary experience, government organization, tradition of public work, social discipline, etc.—are different. Yet, as Kunz[10] has pointed out, with respect to reliance on ideological spontaneity there exists a close affinity between Tanzania and China. The notion of "we must run while others walk" certainly may be a useful counterforce to the crippling effects on the development efforts by the people that easily follow from too strong dependence on planning and administration[11].

To make bold policy moves into the unknown may be justified particularly in circumstances like those in Tanzania where understanding, due to environmental and other factors, is low. Hirschman[12] concludes that this problem-solving approach becomes harmful only if it is insisted upon after knowledge about the problem has accumulated and progress has been made in tackling it. In such situations a formalized system of planning becomes cumbersome and policies produced under it easily lose their validity, as extensive conclusions have been drawn from incomplete and often unreliable data. Thus, it is not the "optimizing" orientation of the planner, but rather the commitment of the policy-maker to realize an idea or a social value that is important for initial success in development programmes. Compared to planning, ideology is a more crucial variable in this kind of approach to solving development problems. In this context, it would be wrong not to remember Landau's warning[13] that policy-making under conditions of uncertainty can never search for optimal or perfect solutions but most go for reliable ones. This often implies a deliberate reliance on duplication and overlap. Redundant spare resources that can be mobilized in the case of emergency become necessary. It is in this light that some observers have also argued that unspent budgetary appropriations are not a waste, but an asset which can be exploited to satisfy sudden demands arising out of the uncertainty surrounding much of the policy-making in developing countries. Tanzania has experienced this, not the least during 1974 when priorities had to be drastically rearranged following rising oil prices and falling food crop production.

Chambers[14] provides evidence which corroborate the ideas expressed above. The Mwea Irrigation Scheme in Kenya, which was started under circumstances of almost unbelievable ignorance about physical, technical and economic aspects became a success story, partly because of bold initiatives by the policy-makers, partly because of imaginative and effective follow-up. It goes to show, as Chege[15] points out, that inadequate preplanning need not be the paramount precursor of faulty implementation it is always supposed to be.

There are many observers, e.g. Adedeji[16], who express strong reservations against the kind of approaches that Hirschman and Landau advocate. The key assumptions underlying these approaches go contrary to the prevailing notions of development as 'integrated'', "balanced", etc. Yet, a strategy of policy-making that allows for reliance on "moves into the unknown", "ideological spontaneity", "duplication and overlap", etc. does not necessarily imply bungling and blundering. As one economist, Streeten[17], has noted, such a strategy only points to the limitations of the conventional notions of rationality.

Also the prevalence of "overdefined" roles may have its positive effects. The gap between ends and means of roles surrounded by excessive expectations can generate enterprise and initiative, so sorely needed in countries anxious to enjoy rapid social and economic development, argues Gunder Frank[18]. Such situations give the incumbents a substantial range of discretion and permit innovation and adaptation. His conclusion, not very different from that of Hirschman, is that if only there is a single desired direction of change, and it is known, reliance on excessive role expectations is appropriate, say for countries like Tanzania, which try to lift themselves by their bootstraps or run while others walk. Such discretion may not only help to combat the dangers of routinization but also facilitate making new policy moves.

IMPLICATIONS OF THE STRATEGY

The implications of Tanzania's policy-making strategy must also be considered as the point in the direction away from those associated with more conventional policy-making models of capitalist and socialist societies.

Western decision-making models, as shown above, assume that ends-means conflicts are solved prior to the final authoritative decision that turns proposal into official policy. Either it is achieved through the optimizing efforts of professional planning economists or it is arrived at through a process of bargaining between affected individuals, groups and organizations. This pluralistic model of policy-making suggests the existence of a positive-sum game, i.e. everybody gives and takes in such a way that in the end they all register some positive gains, even if these may be less than what they had originally aimed at. This is the assumption lying at the bottom of the strategy of "disjointed incrementalism". It is also what has encouraged Lindblom to write another bock[19] praising the "intelligence" of the Western style of democracy. Wildawsky[20] has applied the same model to the study of the budgetary process in the United States. Consensus is arrived at through continuous bargaining and policies defined accordingly. Thus, once the final decision is reached, presumably all conflicts affecting the implementation of the policy have been considered and resolved. Policy execution is a straightforward matter.

The Tanzanian mode of making policies does not resemble this model. Nor does it come close to the Soviet practice of concentrating all efforts at solving ends-means conflicts within an all-powerful planning agency. There the role of planners has been to work out maximum targets and necessary links of coordination that to other public institutions serve as laws.

The Tanzanian style of policy-making differs from both these models. Its sense of urgency rules out any effective resolution of ends-means conflicts prior to the "big" decision. When this is announced, usually under dramatized circumstances and always in the name of TANU, it is expected that everybody in the affected executing agencies will abide and do his best to attain the objectives. It would be wrong to imply that these big decisions are made out of the blue. Usually they arise out of some shortcoming brought to the attention of the President or other key decision-makers in the party. Yet, these decisions are most often based on principles rather than pragmatic calculations about costs and benefits. In those cases when lengthy discussions do precede these big decisions, it is important to note that they take place within the framework of the key decision-making organs of TANU rather than in the National Assembly. The rationale for this is that frank discussions can best be held behind closed doors and that dissension in public limits the effectiveness of this mode of policy-making. At occasions when serious dissension within the party ranks has leaked to the public, as in the case of the West Lake MPs who in 1968 accused the Regional Commissioner of their region of using wrong methods in implementing the policy of ujamaa, drastic actions have been taken against those who have undermined the conception of party unity. In a policy-making situation which is guided by the notion that "we must run while others walk" there simply is no room or time for open dissension.

While TANU is monolithic, the government structure is highly fragmentary and far from the centrally controlled bureaucratic machinery that developed in the Soviet Union under Lenin and Stalin. This means that there is plenty of room for bargaining and compromise once the executing agencies get involved in trying to interpret and implement the big policy decisions. At this stage, the policy-making process takes on some resemblance with the strategy of disjointed incrementalism. Ends-means conflicts are resolved and invariably the result is a discrepancy between the original policy objectives and the practical targets that the executing agencies set themselves. In one way this is a disadvantage of the system as outcome is modest compared to the policy promises. It does also tend to give rise to the belief that the role of the politicians is primarily that of shouting slogans and wrapping their speeches in sweet words. Still, in terms of assuring party supremacy this style of policy-making has its advantage in that it always gives TANU the right to "whip" the bureaucracy. It does not have to take the responsibility for mistakes carried out. These can always be blamed on the executing agencies.

It is clear that in a society where real revolutionary conditions do not exist, Tanzania's style of policy-making does create the image of revolutionary transformation. Things happen in a way that implies distinct breaks with the past. Because policies are made before full understanding of all their implications have been obtained, this way of making policies does depend on an effective feed-back system. To ensure that policies do not end up in blind alleys or are deliberately changed in view of inadequate or unreliable information, facts about what really happens at the stage of implementation have to be fed back to the top policy-makers—by officials or by ordinary citizens. There is evidence to suggest that this does not always happen.

Plan implementation procedures and reporting systems were introduced by the McKinsey consultants with the aim of improving evaluation and control. Formalization of government structures, however, sometimes increases their bureaucratizing tendencies. Warnings against such measures have been raised by at least two observers of the Tanzanian scene—Moris[21] and Collins[22]. Mayer[23] provides some evidence to corroborate their reservations about measures aimed at formalizing the channels of communication in a situation where the policy-making style is, or ought to be, entrepreneurial and "debureaucratized". According to him, the new stystem for reporting and the new plan implementation procedures, introduced with decentralization in 1972, tend to have the effect of routinizing matters which ought to be subject to such treatment. Thus, financial and physical progress reports from individual rural health centre projects are fed into the system but at no level leading to any follow-up. This arises at least in part because of a conflict between the demands of routine administration of the government and effective management of development projects. No single person or group of officials seem to have direct responsibility for the various projects. Formally such responsibility is vested in the Development Director but he usually has little time to concern himself with individual projects. He is fully occupied with the task of running the organization and of looking after the contacts with the political authorities. Nor is, according to Mayer, the warrant-holder (who, by the way, is not always the officer in whose functional area of activity the project falls) effectively a manager. Although general conclusions cannot be drawn from his study alone, it does indicate that matters such as financial control and follow-up as well as monitoring of programmes have not been effectively solved by the procedures originally devised in 1972.

It would be wrong, however, to blame everything on the new procedures. In a situation where senior administrators and managers have to play "over-defined" roles and have to take responsibility for failures and shortcomings many will experience a sense of insecurity.[24] This often breeds reluctance to disclose information to the public and to admit mistakes in public. Under such conditions many top managers and administrators become problem-dodgers rather than problem-solvers by throwing the problem back on someone else or by blaming it on circumstances beyond their control. Inaccurate or biased reporting in mass media tend to reinforce this pattern. Again, it would be wrong to portray this as a universal problem in Tanzania. Yet, as Green[25] among others has pointed out, substitution of blame-passing for problem-solving is far too common among public institutions in Tanzania.

Particularly unfortunate is the tendency for policy executors to feed policy-makers with information that the latter wish to hear. This false sense of subservience reduces the ability of the executors to recognize on their own the ends-means conflicts arising in the process of implementing individual policies. In such situations, little thinking, if any, goes into such questions as to how implementation can be accelerated or in any other ways be made more effective and what consequences various decisions on such matters would have.

It is in view of shortcomings like these listed above that the central leadership of TANU spends a lot of its time assessing for itself the kind of progress that is made in implementing various policies. One case in point was the visit in October/November, 1974 to the regions by members of the Central Committee to evaluate the progress and problems experienced in moving people into villages. This may be a "blessing in disguise" in that it forces top policy-makers to make on-the-spot visits to various projects. Yet, in the long run, dependence on political watch-dogs will be no substitute for learning from one's own mistakes. It can be argued that the notion of the past as wholly irrelevant is gradually losing its validity as new states in Africa gain experience from development strategies and projects chosen by themselves. Van Rensburg[26] has shown how the lessons learnt in the process of initiating a development project in Botswana served as valuable sources of inspiration for future action. In a situation where full information is not insisted upon *before* policies are made, greater understanding must be accumulated *in the process* of implementation.

The strategy of we-must-run-while-others-walk, as can be seen from the account above, contradicts the notion of Western planning economists that policy-making is a sequence of steps carefully calculated in a comprehensive and long-term perspective. It is also at odds with the bureaucrat's view that policy-making for development is like a regular and steady march. Furthermore, it goes contrary to the idea that managing development is a matter of "muddling through" at a leisurely speed. Tanzania does not want to proceed at a "normal" pace. Many key policy-makers, notably political leaders in the regions and the districts but also in various other public institutions, have developed a "vested" interest in this mode of policy-making. It gives them increased autonomy of action and by being associated so closely with TANU, it gives them a sense of identity, i.e. of being different from the more gradual and cautious approach to development issues that characterizes some of Tanzania's neighbours. To fully understand both its attractiveness and its way of operation it is necessary to analyse more carefully the role of power in the policy-making process in Tanzania.

THE ROLE OF POWER IN POLICY-MAKING IN TANZANIA

Almost all literature on policy-making in Africa gives prominence to "economy" and "planning", implying that the most important thing is always to find the optimal choice on economic grounds. To suggest that we need to better understand the role of power in policy-making may appear heretic. Yet, in order to grasp fully the potentialities and limitations of the style of policy-making that Tanzania has developed, attention to the role of power is necessary.

To be sure, planning and power coexist in any complex society. Political power, as the possibility of imposing one's will continuously over a territory on the basis of a monopoly over coercive instruments, cannot be established without some medium of planning. This is recognized today even in those countries in the West where some time ago society-wide planning was considered the antithesis of the capitalist mode of production. At the other end, socialist schools of thought about planning are based on the notion of the plan as directive, as legal command, implying political power as the basis of its validity and the condition for its implementation. According to this view, the foundation of power is the specific characteristic which distinguishes "real" planning from the probabilistic prognoses of indicative economic forecasts, binding none and committing only the professional reputations of the authors of such forecasts or "plans".

The relative role of power and planning is shaped by man's relation to the forces of production and more specifically to his ability to tame these for purposes of pre-empting uncertainties in his physical and social environment. It would be wrong not to treat the case of China in this context. In many respects the productive forces in China are less developed than those of the countries in the West and the Soviet Union. Yet, the Chinese have attained more of the qualities associated with a society where planning as opposed to power serves the purpose of controlling and integrating society. The protracted revolutionary struggle by which the Chinese Communists came to power is at least one factor of importance. The struggle itself, conducted to a large extent under guerilla warfare conditions, enforced new attitudes on people affected. Participation, self-discipline and also self-criticism became the products of these revolutionary activities. The stress on power over nature (illustrated, e.g. in the parable of the old man who wanted to move the mountain) and power over oneself (manifested in puritanical behaviour) do facilitate a constructive exercise of power also in relation to other men. The Chinese example proves that it is possible to reduce the importance of power as possession of authority over others in favour of a system where rational planning provides the main impetus for integration of society.

By and large, this is also the kind of society towards which Tanzania aspires. The low level of development of the productive forces, in combination with the absence of a past revolutionary struggle and the specific conditions imposed by colonial rule, has forced it to go about this task in a manner very different from that of China. The tensions and frustration caused by the "power society" created under colonial rule have resulted in a definite nostalgia for the paradise lost—the simple society of ujamaa. Colonial society was, particularly in its human relationships, a step backwards as compared to the lost human climate of the pre-colonial society with its simple democracy, egalitarianism and solidarity. These sentiments are no better caught than in the now well-known phrase that *Ubepari ni Unyama, Ujamaa ni Utu*. Thus, Tanzania, in the interest of ujamaa, wants to do away with capitalism, but can it also reduce its dependence on power to control and integrate society?

As Uchendu[27], among others, has pointed out, in African societies control over people has always been considered much more important than control over things. And although this situation may be gradually changing, the social conceptions derived from the past still linger on. In fact, they may be deliberately revived. Thus, the old East African proverb that "the chief rules over people and not over land" is not totally invalid today. When President Nyerere, for instance, claims that development means development of people and not of things, he is echoing similar views. In all simple societies, as we have shown above, the nature of human relationships is very important. Consensus is the aim of all decision-making and in order to secure this a strong central authority to enforce and legitimize various decisions is considered necessary. It is not a coincidence that in the case of Tanzania, TANU has decided to use the concept of ujamaa to legitimize its exercise of power. The concept revives the very same principles that have always been used to regulate the affairs within the extended family. And what is politics, if not at least in part the regulation of social activities outside of the realm of the individual family?

In a society where the attainment of consensus is considered a precondition for the proper conduct of politics, the political leader must build up a network of personal followers on whom he can depend to achieve such consensus. By being personal appointees of the leader, the latter can build up a claim against his followers and thereby increase the chances that they will support his policies. Given Tanzania's ambition to achieve a major transformation of its society, it is not surprising that the number of senior appointments in the public sector, controlled personally by the President or the Prime Minister's Office, has increased in recent years.

To gain credibility as a socialist leader, the President and TANU must show concern for the welfare of the ordinary people. To build up his authority, therefore, he also needs to provide services to the people. Those dependent on him for their power, must do the same. They have to prove their loyalty to the central authority. Political success is usually counted in terms of number of followers and in order to achieve as wide support as possible no limitation is applied on the use of material resources. What Uchendu writes with reference to the past does not seem totally invalid as a description of politics also today:

> . . . the manipulation of social relations, all of which involved a high turnover of goods and services, for a net gain in political support, was the ideal of many African societies[28].

In a polity where these considerations prevail, socialist accumulation does not become easy but it may be necessary for creating the political foundation for socialism. It is in this light that the frequent calls by President Nyerere and other party leaders for self-sacrifice and discipline must be seen. Despite the inclinations to use the economy to boost the polity, Tanzania is also committed to socialist economic development, implying greater equality in distribution of resources and self-reliance. These calls, therefore, are necessary to counteract the impressions that tend to flourish in this kind of polities, that the welfare of the society is the responsibility of the political leadership alone.

Because Tanzania has been unable to build its socialism from a revolutionary base, its concern with building up a socialist polity based on a wide network of followers loyal to the centre has been a major issue since 1967. The leadership code and subsequent measures have been aimed at stipulating the preconditions for a political career in this country. As long as political leaders in the regions and the districts had an independent base of power, however, either in the district councils, cooperatives or any such institution, it was difficult to effectively enforce this socialist code of behaviour. Bienen,[29] writing about TANU in the mid-60s, was not wrong when he suggested that TANU was too weak to spearhead development in the country. He was wrong, however, in asserting that as long as Tanzania remained poor, this was bound to be the case. He did not anticipate the effects of TANU gaining stronger control of the whole range of public institutions. Not only have party branches been established in these institutions. In the course of 1975 they also got party-appointed officials—political commissars—to check on the management of these bodies. Nor did Bienen anticipate the growing strength that TANU gained from gradually eliminating the independent power base of regional and district leaders and make them more dependent on the centre or—in some cases—replace them with officials appointed by central decision-making organs. It is as difficult for these leaders today as it was ten years ago. Thus also the view advanced by Shivji[30] that TANU leaders have little leverage over the "bureaucratic bourgeoisie" may not be wholly valid. To be sure, as TANU in the last five years has continued to lay a socialist foundation in the country, the powers of the "bureaucratic bourgeoisie" have been circumscribed.

The fact that the new decentralisation officers are also dependent on recognition by the centre means that they are likely to be more interested in realizing centrally defined goals today than they were before. Although the extent to which the development directorates are able to do so differs from one place to another, there is no doubt the central sphere of control is extending. As illustrated in a number of issues, e.g. villagization and the "take-over" of the Karume Stadium these officers have not felt a need to consult or compromise with local interests.

This does not mean that there are no latent conflicts among political and government officials in the regions and districts. The "operations" have been the means by which the party leadership in the regions have acquired more effective control over the development activities. These "operations" however, have often undermined efforts to put into practice the management procedures introduced by McKinsey. The more youthful style of the "operation" has been preferred to the less glamorous task of institutionalizing new procedures. While the generalist administrators owe their allegiance to the political centre, the professional staff—now referred to as functional managers—no longer have direct ties with their respective ministries in the capital. They report directly to the development directors. This means also that professional or expert considerations are likely to be effectively circumscribed by political views in the decision-making organs in the regions and the districts. This is a matter which deserves further examination, but preliminary data suggest that rather than seeking a "confrontation" with development directors on issues affecting their professional fields, the professional staff subordinate their views to political considerations. The reason for this appears to be that in the regional and district headquarters the group of decision-makers is very small; everyone knows everyone else. Rather than causing strains in the social atmosphere by insisting on their professional viewpoints, they show a low profile. As we have suggested above, it follows from the mode of policy-making adopted that raising "inconvenient" questions may easily be interpreted as disloyalty.

Thus, in summary it appears that the elimination of capitalist structures in society does not mean a reduction in the dependence on power, and particularly power centrally controlled. On the contrary, in order to lay the foundation of socialism in a non-combat context, power becomes a much more important factor than planning. The prevailing mode of policy-making, with its reliance on power, lends itself particularly well to mobilization of efforts and initiating projects but less so to the more intricate questions of managing these projects. "We-must-run-while-others-walk" implies a preference for an outlook towards the future. Because of its strong emphasis on initiation and "getting things off the ground", it is often in conflict with the rational considerations of the economic planners and specialist administrators. As we have suggested above, the strains caused by this conflict may have positive as well as negative consequences. As a developing country, Tanzania needs to be united, energetic and full of initiative, but the effects of insisting on such qualities will be limited as long as effective organization to implement policies remains only a secondary issue.

POLICY-MAKING AND THE SOCIAL SCIENTIST IN TANZANIA

By way of concluding this paper it may be worth pondering the question why there is so much talk of planning in spite of its relatively modest role in policy-making in Tanzania, as demonstrated above. Is it because people are by and large dissatisfied with the present mode of making policies? While we are not prepared to rule this out, it is not likely to be the main reason for the strong interest in planning. After all, virtually all key decision-makers in the Tanzanian polity have something to gain from the strategy of we-must-run-while-others-walk. Thus, in the case of the policy-makers themselves the main reason may well be that whereas power is a work with ambiguous connotations, planning has almost exclusively positive connotations. Power always has to be camouflaged, made socially less transparent, less personal and less blatant. This is a universal experience. While power always is associated with domination and oppression of the small man, planning, as Pusic puts it, is "the reasonable alternative, the rational quest for a social optimum; reducing, by conscious action, the entropy originally inherent in human affairs; substituting, in the last analysis, the management of things for the government of man"[31]. It is not difficult to understand why socialist policy-makers wish to be associated with planning rather than power.

It is less easy to understand why social scientists, whether in the position of commentator or advisor to policy-makers, have by and large ignored the analysis of "power" and the "polity". At least one explanation is that while we have been very anxious to examine the social roots of behaviour of others, be they politicians, civil servants or soldiers, we have often been ignorant or naive about the social origin of our own theories and models. Is it not true that our choice of models reflect our own social background and present position?

Let us first look again at the planning models used by the planners with the orthodox Western economic outlook. These models are usually considered objective and reliable tools of analysis because their criteria of assessing performance are derived from the goals of the society under study. These models, however, are not as objective as it first seems. They are based on a number of assumptions which are not necessarily valid in countries like Tanzania. Parameters are separated from variables often on the basis of what is appropriate for advanced industrial nations. As Streeten[32] has noted, these models treat social institutions, psychological attitudes and orientations, etc. as given. Furthermore, they assume that an efficient civil service carries out government orders, that people cooperate with discipline, appear on duty on time and carry out orders, that money is spent according to conventional notions of efficiency, and that policy alternatives are considered largely on their financial merits.

In criticizing these models Killick[33] has added that they also presuppose clear and stable goals on the part of governments. They do ignore the fact that resolution or avoidance of conflicts and the maintenance of government authority, with a consequential demotion of the economic development goals, may be the main preoccupation of the political leadership.

By ignoring all these factors, it is not surprising that social scientists with this bias have concluded that governments in developing countries are ineffective in realizing their goals. What else could be expected? Measured against the Olympic heights of public goals, governments everywhere score the same: very low effectiveness. Thus, the notion of ineffectiveness develops as a result of applying the kind of model that assesses performance in relation to official goals and at the same time ignores or treats as given key environmental variables. This bias is inherent in all the "optimizing" models, whether they refer to policy choice or to the behaviour of the policy-makers.

Marxist social scientists fall victim to a similar bias. The goals of socialism are given. Therefore, Nyerere's and TANU's policies are always measured against these "objective" goals. In the same way as the conventional planning economists are optimalists, the Marxists are maximalists, being concerned exclusively with the question of how a general set of social values can be maximized. They usually ignore the distinction between "ultimate" and "proximate" goals and do not accept that governments have to select priorities and make compromises in the short-run. Yet, this is self-evident, particularly in a country like Tanzania where resources are so scarce. Furthermore, they do not necessarily agree that resources have to be used for other functions than that of realizing the "objective" socialist goals. Yet, in a situation like that in Tanzania, where the revolutionary basis was not laid through a protracted struggle but has to be laid by political means through organizations, notably TANU, recruitment of resources to strengthen the polity itself may be highly instrumental. A case in point is the villagization policy, against which virtually all Marxist observers have expressed deep reservations on the assumption that it is not socialist, i.e. not clearly aimed at maximizing the objective socialist goals. But what is there to say against the interpretation that the villagization is a necessary investment in strengthening the polity so that in the long-run the transition to socialism can be accelerated?

It is not an exaggeration to say that when social scientists, Marxists and non-Marxists alike, have assessed Tanzania's efforts at planning for development they have usually arrived at the conclusion that the outcome is at best a "poor imitation" of their respective ideal, the Western efficiency model or the Chinese socialist model (usually portrayed as that coming closest to the objective ideal). Their own models have taken them to such conclusions. But why have the social scientists almost universally accepted such models when assessing Tanzania's development efforts? The answer is that academics, and particularly social scientists, want to assume the position of social critic and reformer. In fact, they need the goal model to legitimize their own position and career in society. This is true both for local and expatriate social scientists, but particularly the latter. A Western social scientist has come all the way to Tanzania to assess or comment upon its policy-making efforts. The combination of being a foreigner and a professional advisor makes him strongly inclined to accept a model using the public goals as a yardstick for assessment of these efforts. He is not an insider and may consider it wrong to make assumptions about the way by which policies are arrived at. The goal model offers him the comfortable position of critic and reformer and the opportunity to present his criticism in what appears to him as a non-political context. The situation of the Marxist social scientist is not very different. He is in Tanzania to promote the global ideals of socialism. His preference for the goal model is dictated by his ambition to make the world more socialist. Thus, particularly in the case of the expatriate, the model brings him the satisfaction of always being in the forefront, of being in possession of ideas that in his views are even more legitimate than those of TANU.

This tendency among social scientists in relation to the policy-making process in Tanzania reveals two methodological errors. The first is that the social scientists transfer their own values to the leaders of public organizations by simple projection. They decide *a priori* that the party, government or parastatal under study is striving to achieve and to realize goals that they as observers would like these leaders to pursue. The public goals of these organizations are, therefore, often only those subjectively projected on to the units concerned by the social scientists. Usually no evidence is provided to show that these goals are really the ones pursued.

The second methodological error is related to the first. It is the disregard by the social scientists for other activities than the pursuit of public goals. The present state of a certain entity is compared with a goal—its ideal state—as if the goal were also a real state. These, however, are not comparable entities[34]. Goals depict targets and being abstract constructions they are bound to be more logically consistent than reality. Societies, like organizations, are systems of coordinated activities of many actors. As such they are bound to be less perfect than the ideal and also concerned with other activities, e.g. introducing improvements in the way the society or the organization conducts itself, settling conflicts between divergent interests, etc., tasks which are necessary but which may divert resources from the efforts to realize public goals. As Streeten and Killick have argued, most conventional planners consider such other activities beyond the realm of planning—a product of their simplistic model of politics. For Marxists any deviation from the target state is attributed to the class interests of those in charge of implementing the goals.

While it would be naive not to recognize the importance of such interests, it is equally naive to attribute the discrepancy between goal and reality to class interest alone. It ignores the simple and fundamental point that the structural position of politicians and managers, unlike that of the social scientists, compels them to compromise between differents views and interests expressed within their respective organizations. To the Marxist social scientist, the politician and the manager are compromisers, pragmatic, etc. To those who run political and administrative organizations, the Marxists are unrealistic and adopting the position of "holier than thou".

The very fact that Marxists explicitly challenge the position of policy-makers, while conventional planners ignore the structural power realities surrounding the same policy-makers, has created an interesting situation as regards the role of socialist experts in Tanzania. Many in Tanzania have called for the need to employ socialists as experts and advisors in the policy-making organs in Tanzania. Yet, expatriate social scientists recruited to the ministries, regions and the para-statals are overwhelmingly from Western countries and only exceptionally real socialists. Even expatriates from the Eastern countries are usually "technical" in their orientation. In a situation where power rather than planning is the crux of the matter it is easy to see that those expatriates who by adhering to a particular kind of model confine themselves to their "technical" problems and ignore the power realities are preferable to those who believe that the public goals can only be achieved through their own active intervention in the power structure of the country. The non-Marxist expatriate only gets into trouble if he is outright inimical to the socialist policies of the country. But as long as he is not, he can hide behind his model and continue his "expert" job. The Marxist who takes his ideology seriously is *a priori* in conflict with the policy-making process in Tanzania. He has no model to hide behind and can only effectively enter the policy-making stage by derobing himself of his Marxist attire.

Such seem to be the realities in the Tanzania-type of polities, where the transition to socialism has to be induced by political means and in this case notably through the strategy of we-must-run-while-others-walk. Social scientists still have to learn both for themselves and for others what are the implications of putting "power" rather than "planning" in command of the process of policy-making for socialist development.

NOTES

1. H. Bienen, *Tanzania: Party Transformation and Economic Development*, Princeton: Princeton University Press, 1967.
2. L. Cliffe, "Tanzania—Socialist Transformation and Party Development", *The African Review*, Vol. 1, 1971.
3. Uchumi Editorial Board, *Towards Socialist Planning*, Dar es Salaam: Tanzania Publishing House, 1972.
4. C. Thomas, "The Transition to Socialism: Issues of Economic Strategy in Tanzania-Type Economics," University of Dar es Salaam (mimeo), 1972.
5. A. O. Hirschman, *Journeys towards Progress*, New York: Doubleday and Co., 1965.
6. Y. Dror, *Public Policy-Making Re-examined*, Scranton, Penn.: Chandler Publishing House, 1969.
7. P. Blau, *The Dynamics of Bureaucracy*, Chicago: Chicago University Press, 1955.
8. A. Gunder Frank, "Administrative Role Definition and Social Change", *Human Organization*, 22,4, 1964.
9. R. H. Green, "Relevance, Efficiency, Romanticism and Confusion in Tanzania Planning and Management," paper presented to the Seminar on Improvement of Management in Tanzania, 1974.
10. F. Kunz, "Notes on Some Aspects of Tanzania's Contribution to Comparative Politics," unpublished manuscript, Dar es Salaam, 1973.
11. G. Tschannerl, "Rural Water Supply in Tanzania: Is Politics or Techniques in Command?", Annual Social Science Conference of the East African Universities, Paper No. 52, Dar es Salaam, 1973.
12. A. O. Hirschman, *op. cit.*, 1965.
13. M. Landau, "Redundancy, Rationality and the Problem of Duplication and Overlap," *Public Administration Review*, 29, 4, 1969.
14. R. Chambers, *Settlement Schemes in Tropical Africa*, London: Routledge & Kegan Paul, 1969.
15. M. Chege, "Systems Management and the Plan Implementation Process in Kenya," Nairobi, IDS, *Discussion Paper*, 1972.
16. A. Adedeji, "Formulating Administrative Reform Strategies in Africa," *Quarterly Journal of Administration* (Ife), VI, 3, 1972.
17. P. Streeten, *The Frontiers of Development Studies*, London: Macmillan, 1972.
18. A. Gunder Frank, *op. cit.*, 1964.
19. C. E. Lindblom, *The Intelligence of Democracy*, New York: The Free Press, 1965.
20. A. Wildawsky, *The Politics of the Budgetary Process*, Boston: Little Brown, 1964.
21. J. R. Moris, "Managerial Structures and Plan Implementation in Colonial and Modern Agricultural Extension: A Comparison of Cotton and Tea Programmes in Central Kenya," in D. K. Leonard, ed., *Rural Administration in Kenya*, Nairobi: East African Literature Bureau, 1973.
22. P. Collins, "The Working of Tanzania's Rural Development Fund; A Problem in Decentralisation," in Rweyemamu and Mwansasu, eds., *Planning in Tanzania: Background to Decentralisation*, Nairobi: East African Literature Bureau, 1974.
23. W. Mayer, "Implementation and Control under Decentralisation: Tanzania's Rural Health Centre Programme," unpublished manuscript, Department of Political Science, University of Dar es Salaam, 1974.
24. A. H. Rweyemamu, "The Predicament of Managers of Public Enterprises in Tanzania's Emerging Political Economy," paper presented at the Conference on the Development of African Bureaucracies, Belmont, Maryland, 1974.
25. R. H. Green, *op. cit.*, 1974.
26. P. Van Rensburg, *Report from Swaneng Hill*, Uppsala: Dag Hammarskjold Foundation, 1974.
27. V. Uchendu, "Polity Primacy and African Economic Development," Annual Social Science Conference of the East African Universities, Nairobi, 1969.
28. *Ibid*.
29. H. Bienen, *op. cit.*, 1967.
30. I. Shivji, *The Class Struggle in Tanzania*, Dar es Salaam: Tanzania Publishing House, 1975.
31. E. Pusic, "Power, Planning, Development," *Development and Change*, 1, 1, 1969.
32. P. Streeten, *op. cit.*, 1972.
33. T. Killick, "The Possibilities of Development Planning," Institute for Development Studies, Nairobi, Working Paper No. 165, 1974.
34. A. Etzioni, "Two Approaches to Organizational Analysis: A Critique and a Suggestion," *Administrative Science Quarterly*, 5 September, 1960.

Cooperation and the Production Environment in Tanzania: Social and Economic Factors Affecting Agricultural Cooperation.

DAVID AND RAYAH FELDMAN

Introduction

"... the course of cooperative collectivisation is the sole course possible in our condition to introduce into peasant farming the elements of large scale farm industrialization and the state plan."[1]

This statement was written with reference to the early attempts at cooperative farming in the Soviet Union in the 1920's. Its underlying assumptions and aspirations are, however, pertinent to many situations in the developing economies of today. In this paper we shall not attempt to deal with the aspects of agricultural cooperation that have received most attention in recent years: the role of values and ideology, and patterns of leadership and administration. Our more narrow concern is to explore certain functional relationships between the economic demands of agricultural systems, the social and demographic features of particular rural societies, and the possibility of successful co-operation in agricultural production.

Sociological discussions of the conditions facilitating the success of cooperative organisations have centred on the social structure of the community in very specific ways. They have been chiefly concerned with the structure of authority relations in the community and with the degree of cohesion or factionalism which binds or divides its members. This paper attempts to broaden the structural framework which is considered relevant in a discussion of cooperative organisation, by relating sociological and economic attributes of the cooperating community to the farming systems in which its members are involved. Thus the foremost factor to be investigated must be the needs of the crops cultivated, and the ways in which these limit the kind of organisational forms which can be used for production. Once this is established we can examine the extent to which the characteristics of the community, demographically and sociologically, allow these organisational forms to be developed. These characteristics are the other structural factors to be considered here. They include, first, the age/sex distribution of farmers and the way in which this is related to household size and composition. Secondly, we consider the types of relationships which bind the members of the community to one another, for example, kinship relations, and the kinds of demands and expectations which these entail. Third, we discuss the problem of land tenure, and other economic interests which farmers have in agricultural cooperation. Finally, we consider factors which do not necessarily arise from the social situation itself, but which are the results of the individual's previous life history and work experience.

The exploratory nature of this paper needs emphasis. What we present is in effect some very untested hypotheses that have been suggested from our own research and that of our colleagues. The illustrations used are therefore drawn almost entirely from Tanzania, and we are aware of the insularity that this gives to our analysis. The aim is not, however, to present proven generalisations, but rather to suggest possible functional linkages between factors, which should account for successful agricultural cooperation between producers, and it is in this respect that we hope this paper may be of some use.

It is particularly apposite that most of our illustrations should be drawn from Tanzania. Of all African countries, its leaders, particularly Julius Nyerere, are most committed to searching for a non-capitalist approach to rural development. In his paper. "Socialism and Rural Development", Nyerere outlines how Tanzania's economic progress can be developed through cooperative institutions. It is hoped, therefore, that our analysis could have implications for future policies.

The illustrations are drawn from agricultural developmental situations. They thus consider cooperation as it is related to commercial and technical progress and not to "traditional" communal subsistence systems. Two situations are where cooperative production institutions have been set up in response to ideological aspirations. In these cases we are concerned to show what particular features of such situations might encourage or discourage cooperation to continue. One situation is where farmers starting innovatory systems have chosen spontaneously to cooperate. We are concerned here to explain both the changes in patterns of cooperation that were observed, and how different kinds of cooperation existed in groups of individuals with different kinds of interrelationships. This will show how it is in the farmers' interests to cooperate, and how changes in those interests affect the form of cooperation. The next part of the paper will briefly describe these situations, before the main economic and sociological analysis.

PATTERNS OF COOPERATION: TWO CASE STUDIES

The two cooperative schemes which are used as illustrations are Mbambara and Kwamangugu Ujamaa Villages in the Tanga Region in the north of Tanzania. The data on Mbambara and Kwamangugu Villages have been collected from survey material used by a team from the Bureau of Resource Assessment and Land Use Planning of University College, Dar es Salaam, in 1968, in the course of a comparison of twelve rural settlements in

---

*ERB Paper 69.12

Tanzania. The data on the tobacco farmers at Nduli in the Iringa District was collected by the authors in the course of field research in the area during 1966 and 1967.[2]

Mbambara Village was established in 1963 under the impetus of members of Tanu Youth League, by 240 people who were mostly ex-labourers on the big neighbouring sisal estates. Since that time until the survey in 1968, the membership of the community dropped to 162 settlers in 80 households. Of these 50 were children. The main crop at Mbambara is sisal, and a number of food crops are also grown. In 1967, 139 acres were under sisal, and 193 under food crops. Work is carried out both individually and communally, the main cash crop, sisal, being cultivated entirely collectively. Other communal work is scheme-housebuilding, general maintenance of the village, the running of a cooperative shop owned by the community, a selfhelp scheme for improved water, as well as an experimental food farm (expanded since the survey), and a fishpond. Most food crops are grown on individual plots. The management of the scheme is by an elected manager, secretary, and treasurer. A work supervisor appointed by the manager is responsible for the work allocation. These officials cooperate with an elected executive council, which is divided into further committees for the purpose of work, education, etc. According to the survey, communal work is carried out in the mornings for four hours, while in the afternoons people work individually on their food farms. While all the marketing of the sisal is done on a cooperative basis, individual food crop surpluses are sold individually outside the settlement.

Kwamangugu Village was begun in a similar way to Mbambara in response to a political appeal from 24 Tanu Youth league members. They attempted to recruit more members, and a few people voluntarily agreed to join the scheme. A majority of the thousand people who originally came to Kwamangugu in January 1963 were unemployed men and women who had been rounded up from the nearby towns. Others were sisal workers in current employment. Within 6 months, the majority of the settlers were expelled from the scheme for failing to comply with the rules that had been established, not allowing people to hold outside jobs. Subsequently many others left, owing to difficult conditions prevailing at Kwamangugu, with the result that in 1968 there were only 123 settlers in 73 households. Of these, 22 were children under 15. The village is both commercially less successful than Mbambara, and also is less developed in terms of the number of cooperative activities. Like Mbambara, sisal is the main cash crop; there are 126 acres under sisal, and it is grown collectively, although all good crops are grown individually. There is no cooperative shop, and the survey mentions that members are building their houses separately from one another, rather than in a village. The management of the scheme is very similar to that of Mbambara.

It should be stressed that these villages are both in an embryonic stage, meeting a considerable number of difficulties. They were selected not because they are in any way ideal or typical but because a certain amount of data was available about them relevant to the hypotheses put forward in this paper, and they can legitimately be described as cooperative village settlements practising to a considerable degree communal agriculture.

The third situation is of a different order altogether. It is concerned with a group of tobacco smallholdings in Nduli, Iringa. It differs from the above two in that it was not conceived of in an ideological framework. It was in no way a planned settlement; rather farmers initially cooperated together spontaneously, with varying patterns of cooperation emerging over time. The original farmers in this group were 20 people who in 1962 began to cooperate together for the purpose of growing tobacco. After one year they split into smaller groups, while at the same time attracting new members. Within a few years the size of the groups declined further so that by the end of 1967 there were about 100 farms in the area, many of which were no longer run by groups but instead, by the members of the one nuclear family, or by a few close kin of affines. Table 1 shows the distribution of the main cooperative types among the sample of farmers studied at Nduli in July 1967. In this, cooperating groups are divided into those tobacco enterprises where a crop is cultivated, processed and sold as a single unit, and those where the cultivation is done on separate plots, where cooperation extends only to common land titles, and the collective use of fixed assets such as a curing barn, grading sheds and baling presses. Groups of kin refer to those farms where several wider kin than the nuclear family cultivate together. Individual farms refer to those one "owner" in which he works either alone or with his wife.

TABLE 1: DISTRIBUTION OF MAIN CO-OPERATIVE TYPES AMONG NDULI FARMERS

Type	*No.*	*% of Total*
Cooperating group—cultivation and process	5	14
Cooperating group—process only	6	16
Group of kin or affines	6	16
Individual farms	20	54
Total	34	100

Unlike the two Ujamaa villages described above, we were fortunate in having detailed data about the changes in composition of these tobacco farms over time. Table 2 shows the changes in composition of the groups in the sample over a period from 1966 to 1967. It can be seen from the table that there was a distinctive trend towards the individualisation of the farms following initial cooperation.

TABLE 2: CHANGES IN FARM ORGANISATION 1966-1967

Type	No. 1966	No. 1967	% 1966	% 1967
Cooperative farms—4				
Members	6	0	16	0
Cooperative farms—3				
Members	6	6	16	16
Cooperative farms—2				
Members	5	5	14	14
Cooperative farms—total	17	11	46	30
Groups of kin or affines	10	6	27	16
Individual farms	10	20	27	54
Total	37	37	100	100

ANALYSIS OF COOPERATIVE ACTIVITIES

There are a number of factors related to the particular needs of the production processes of different crops, which can account for different forms of production cooperation, and different degrees of success in achieving and maintaining designed cooperative institutions. A large number of these factors are related to the existence of economies of scale in agriculture. More particularly they are related to non-synchronisation, or discontinuities, in the extent of these scale economies for different operations contributing to a complete agricultural process. Agricultural production is a complex process involving many activities which may include investment and the first stages of manufacturing, as well as actual cultivation. For this reason, agricultural organisations have to be multifunctional. Economies of scale, or decreasing inputs per unit of output as output increases, can exist over given ranges for each of these activities. It is unlikely that such ranges will coincide however, and it is this lack of synchronisation which forms a powerful incentive to cooperation. Thus it is difficult for one organisation to operate at a scale that is optimal for all the activities of the agricultural process. Cooperation allows a flexibility to accommodate this, so that separate organisations can merge for those activities where the opportunities for scale economies are greatest, and separate where such opportunities are more limited.

This argument could be extended to cover all aspects of agricultural cooperation—marketing as well as production. It is clear that agricultural marketing is best operated on a scale larger than most individual production units. At the same time producers may wish to gain the advantages of vertical integration. The only means of achieving this, and at the same time operating a viable marketing organisation is through cooperation. Similar motives lie behind more traditional forms of cooperation which have been analysed by anthropologists in Africa. Reciprocal work groups, often based on beer parties have been used for investment activities such as land clearing or housebuilding, while most cultivation activities are continued on an individual family basis.

With respect to economies of scale, there is, therefore, a testable hypothesis relating the technical processes of the agricultural system to the individual farmer's own interests in cooperation. It can be used to help explain spontaneous patterns of cooperation in situations of commercial agricultural development, and reasons for success or failure at more planned attempts at collective farm-settlements.

The main illustration for this point is taken from our study of tobacco farming at Nduli in Iringa. The changing patterns of cooperation there have already been briefly described. They can be partly explained by the lack of synchronisation of scale economies. Three main influences can be identified: 1) technical, managerial and financial difficulties that limit the amount of tobacco that can be managed by a single farmer, particularly during the early years of the development of his tobacco enterprise; 2) the reduction in the current input needs per unit of output, particularly labour, as the tobacco acreage is extended over a limited range; and 3) the increased efficiency of larger processing units, curing barns and grading sheds, both in terms of construction costs per acre of tobacco capacity, and in terms of fuel costs in operation.

Most farmers are unable to operate more than one to one and a half acres of tobacco in their first year of production. By the third year they may be planting four acres. The farmer generally experiences difficulties in gaining access to resources, particularly cash, labour and expertise. The first two of these are interrelated in so far as labour can be hired. Considerable amounts of cash have to be used for the development costs of the farm, in the form of land clearing, building curing barns and grading sheds, and building houses. As access to cash is very restricted, the farmer is forced to depend on his own labour supplies. The acreage he can plant will then be limited to the amount he can handle with the family labour that is available, and the additional labour he can hire with his cash resources which are probably very low.

Lack of expertise is a further major factor limiting acreage. Flue-cured tobacco is a very difficult crop to grow, process and prepare for the market. International standards are very stringent. New farmers experience considerable difficulties in learning the skills that are needed. The first three or four years of tobacco production are a process of "learning by doing" for the new farmers. During this period the amount of tobacco they can handle is restricted.

The other major factor that restricts the acreage operated by a tobacco farmer during his first years is risk. Most farmers continue to maintain other economic interests, particularly other farms where food crops are grown, because of the uncertainty associated with a new enterprise. This means that substantial resources, particularly family labour supplies, farm implements and managerial inputs are not available for tobacco production. The farmers are willing to commit these resources to tobacco production only when the risks have been reduced by increasing experience.

The restrictions on the acreage grown by each farmer that have been described are paralleled by significant economies of scale, i.e. reduced inputs per unit of output, as planned output (measured in acres grown) is increased. These economies of scale arise from the increasing division of labour that can be applied to a number of separate processes that are involved in tobacco production. They also occur in larger capacity investment inputs: curing barns and grading sheds are needed to process the tobacco before sales. These economies occur over defined ranges. For the purpose of analysis three scale levels were determined: 0–5 acres planted, 5–10 acres planted, and over 10 acres planted. There were no significant changes in average input-output relations after 10 acres was being produced. Table 3 sets out the per acre labour requirements for the different production processes for flue cured tobacco at Nduli. Table 4 sets out the cash and labour inputs per acre capacity needed for different capacity capital units.

TABLE 3: LABOUR REQUIREMENTS PER ACRE FOR MID-PLANTED FLUE CURED TOBACCO PRODUCTION IN NDULI

Operation	Man-days per acre 0–5 acres	5-10 acres	10–100 acres
Prepare nursery	16	10	8
Cut grass and plant seeds	1.5	1.25	1.0
Weed and cultivate Nursery	12.5	10	8
Fertilize and fumigate nursery	0.25	0.25	0.25
Plough and ridge fields	1.0	1.0	1.0
Transplant seedlings	9	8	6
Fertilize fields	6	6	6
Weeding	24	24	24
Pluck and cure	150	135	115
Grade and bale	120	72	61

TABLE 4: CASH AND LABOUR REQUIREMENTS-CURING BARNS AND GRADING SHEDS

	Curing Barn 0–5 acres	5–10 acres	10+ acres	Grading Shed 0–5 acres	5+ acres
Cash (Shs)	120	90	78	64	49
Labour (man-days)	32	28	26	10	6.8

These data were used to define an optimal growth path of output and capital accumulation based on an assumed objective of income maximisation, subject to a number of constraints related to the maintenance of minimum food stocks and cash availabilities. This output path is shown in Table 5.

TABLE 5: OPTIMAL TOBACCO PLANTING AND INVESTMENT DECISIONS. FIVE YEAR PERIOD.

Years	Tobacco planted acres	Capacity in acres Barn Building	Capacity in acres Shed Building
Year 1	3.42	10.24	10.24
Year 2	10.01		
Year 3	18.57	9.43	9.43
Year 4	19.67		
Year 5	15.83[a]		

The most significant implication for our analysis of this is that the optimum acreage in years 1–3 is considerably greater than the limit set by the restricting factor discussed above. This apparent contradiction can only be resolved by having a number of farmers cooperate together in order to obtain the cost economies of larger acreages, and at the same time accommodate the restrictions on acreage per farmer. The data predict that three or four farmers would work together fot this purpose.

The restrictions on acreage that have been described, mainly arose from the factors with a temporary impact. Thus the limitations on access to resources will get less as the farmers accumulate experience and access to cash and other inputs. This means that the most efficient scale of operation will now become syncronised with the acreage that the individual farmer can handle. This in turn means that the need to cooperate which arises from these factors will also disappear. Thus it would be expected that such cooperation would be of a temporary nature—mainly restricted to inexperienced farmers cultivating small acreages.

This corresponds to the pattern of cooperation observed at Nduli. There tended to be a continual fissiparous process among these farmers who cooperated together. This has already been shown in Table 2. In Table 6 it can be seen that the acreage of tobacco grown by individual farmers in the sample was 2.8 times the per farmer acreage of those growing in groups. The total per farm acreage of the individual farms is only 1.1 times the acreage of the group farms.

TABLE 6: TOBACCO GROWN BY INDIVIDUAL FARMERS AND COOPERATING GROUPS

Farm Type	Mean Acreage Planted Per Farm	Per Farmer
Individual	9.9	9.9
Group	8.9	3.5

These figures also support the hypothesis relating economies of scale to cooperation. Thus those farmers whose acreage is insufficient to gain the economies of scale, cooperate so that the total acreage of their farms is not significantly different from the acreage of the more experienced farmers who individually can operate the larger acreage.

The figures of Table 5 which set out optimum paths for output and capital accumulation indicate a further discontinuity of scale economies: that between output levels and asset capacity. This arises because it pays a farmer to build larger capacity curing barns and grading sheds even if this involves temporary excess capacity. This discontinuity between capital capacity and acreage planted gives rise to further opportunities for cooperation. Three individual farmers or groups of farmers, each growing three to four acres of tobacco, could cooperate by using the same curing barn and grading shed, utilising the optimum scale of processing capacity which is related to 10 acres of tobacco. Other 'lumpier' capital inputs require even larger scale cooperation if a maximum level of technical efficiency is to be achieved. Thus the farmers at present use tractors for land preparation. A cooperative organisation has been set up to include some six hundred tobacco farmers working both as individuals and as cooperating groups, which owns two tractors, and operates even more by hiring from neighbouring cooperatives. In this way cooperation for different operations can be based on different levels of organisation, and all are functionally related to the technical needs of those operations.

The relationship between cooperation and particular crop needs can be extended beyond a consideration of economies of scale. There are particular crops and activities which are more suited to cooperative work effort than others. Woods has shown in his analysis of changing patterns of cooperation in a new settlement area in Rhodesia how farmers formed cooperative work groups for certain investment activities such as house-building and land clearing.[5] Other operations such as planting, where the timing and the method of work application are more critical, are done more efficiently by smaller groups. Woods lists four reasons why cooperative groups can be effective.

1. A large labour force allows greater division of labour, and therefore specialisation.
2. The element of reciprocity in cooperative work groups means that every member is encouraged to devote his full effort to the work group in the expectation that the other members will do the same for him.
3. There is also a competitive element within cooperative work groups by which individuals try to gain status by doing allotted tasks quicker and more efficiently.
4. A larger labour force allows a more systematic approach to work. This may be very important for such operations as weeding.

For these reasons, Woods records a labour input for land clearing of 55 man/days per acre when done by a cooperative group of 24 to 30 adults, while the same work done by an individual requires 75 man/days per acre.

These advantages are counteracted by the difficulties associated with the timing of operations where a large number of individual farmers are cooperating together. The work groups observed by Woods were formed by approximately three adult members from each of twelve farms. They met for three days each week. At that rate each farm would be worked collectively only once each month. This could be critical at harvest time where a delay of one month could cause great losses.

The large work groups created for developmental work thus broke down into smaller groups as a result of the different timing needs of cultivation operations. Even the smaller groups had a seasonal variation. They ceased to operate with the onset of the rains when planting had to be done, and resumed again for weeding which was best done collectively.

A crop which requires critical timing for each operation, and considerable care and attention as to the way any operation is carried out, is not easily grown on a cooperative basis. Tobacco would fall into such a class of crops. This is a major reason why the largest number of farmers cooperating to grow tobacco at Iringa was four. There is a further problem discouraging more extensive cooperation in tobacco production, and which may be important for other crops too. This arises from the uneven distribution of labour needs for the crop through the year.

If a collective group were to meet these peak demands from their own resources, it would mean that only a small amount of tobacco could be grown per member, and that a large amount of the labour force would not be used on the group during the slack season. The organisational difficulties arising from this would be considerable. Such crops as tobacco are most efficiently grown by seasonally increasing the size of the labour force to meet the peak demands whilst relying on the farmers' labour to cover the slacker periods. This is best organised by hiring a temporary labour force. If a cooperative labour force was maintained adequate to meet peak labour demands, it would mean that the returns from the crop are being used to support a seasonally unemployed labour force. The system becomes both inefficient and inflexible. All the tobacco farmers at Nduli, whether they farmed in groups or individually, hired substantial numbers of labourers for harvesting, curing, grading and packing tobacco.

Any procedure which evens out the labour demands through the year might thus encourage a cooperative approach to production. For this reason mechanization may be an important factor to consider. In addition to relieving peak labour constraints, mechanization also provides a standardised method of carrying out individual farm operations. This means that the individual can become less critical. An example in Tanzania, where mechanization has assisted in producing a cash crop on a collective basis has been in the Upper Kitete settlement scheme. This is based on the mechanized production of wheat. In this case, however, the number of cooperating families is too large for the amount of production and methods used. This means that a large number are not employed directly on production and the scheme is not a financial success.

It is likely that other crops are more amenable to cooperative effort, particularly those that are continuously harvested. These have often been cultivated as estate crops, relying on large permanent labour forces. The Mbambara Ujamaa village is an example of successful production cooperation based on sisal. Sisal requires a constant labour input, and in addition, most operations are amenable to economies of scale. Thus the advantages of large numbers of people working together is fairly clear. The major difficulty found in collective operations for such crops as sisal is the work discipline needed. Work norms for cutting and weeding, etc. have to be set and enforced. This is considerably easier for a hired labour force than a group of cooperating farmers. In Mbambara, however, these difficulties appear to have been overcome. This point is discussed more fully below.

We now need to turn to a number of demographic factors affecting cooperation. The literature on peasant farming systems indicates the importance of the size of the farming household and its stage in the domestic cycle for the size and organisation of the farm.[6]

This is because both the productive capacity and the consumption needs of the household vary with its size and composition. As long as the scale of farming activities are proportionate to the size of the consumption needs of the household (not a fixed quantum, but fixed to a certain extent over a time period, especially with regard to food), and are carried out mainly with labour from the household itself, we can expect to find variations in farm size according to the ages and number of its members. When new farming systems are devised, particularly for the production of a cash crop, and if they use relatively more non-household labour, we may expect that, for a time at least, food farming will be maintained. This is due to various factors such as the uncertainty of the new crop's success, fluctuations in price of the cash crop, need to maintain rights to the land on which the food crop is grown, etc. If food production is not maintained on the same level as before, then the returns from the cash crop will have at least to provide for the consumption needs of the family or household. This means that apart from the size of food crop production varying with the size and composition of the household, these factors may also affect the required size of cash crop production. In view of this it is useful to examine the structure of households and the ages of the members of cooperating production units in relation to the farming systems in which they are involved, as factors contributing to success or failure in cooperation.

The data available on this topic both from the Nduli tobacco farmers and the Ujamaa villages, Mbambara and Kwamangugu, are scant, but they nevertheless give some idea of the effect of the above factors on cooperative organisation. At Mbambara, although the members now grow a food crop as well as the cash crop sisal, communally, it is not clear from the data how much of the food crop is grown in this way. It appears that an experimental plot of 30 acres for maize and other food crops which was grown communally was successful, and this encouraged farmers to attempt communal food crop production in the 1968/69 season. Unfortunately, no data are available on the system of distribution of this crop. However, if we examine the structure of households for both Mbambara and Kwamangugu, we find that the demographic characteristics of the population may favour communal food production at the present time. It must be borne in mind, though, that these characteristics will change over time, leading to a less favourable relationship between the demographic structure and production cooperation, unless institutions develop to overcome any ensuing difficulties.

At Mbambara, when the village was established, there were originally 60 settlers of whom only 16 were married (i.e. 8 couples). Thus almost 75% of the population were unmarried. At present (1968) the proportion of single people has decreased, there being now 21 couples (42 people) out of a total community membership of 123. This is about 33% of the total. Only 20 households (25%) in Mbambara have children, and between them these households account for 50 children, all under 10. Kwamangugu has a smaller proportion of households with children—only 11 out of 73 (15%), accounting for 22 children, of whom 12 are under 10 and 10 under 15.

Because of the fact that there are so few dependants, the important point from the viewpoint of cooperation is the homogeneity of household composition in these villages. There are likely to be few problems even in the allocation of a communally grown food crop, since, in the majority of cases, households are able to contribute labour proportionate to their consumption needs. This becomes more difficult as the family size increases, as well as the consumption needs of older children who are unable to contribute much labour, especially if, as is planned on such settlements, primary education become universal. Moreover, the high average age of the farmers in these villages, associated with the small number of dependants recorded in the survey, suggests that in fact many farmers have wives and children elsewhere, who have not been included. If such people were to be brought to the settlements, new problems of the allocation of profits and food are likely to arise.

The small number of women in these villages, 27 and 23 respectively, is also likely to make cooperation easier between men. This is because rights in cooperative settlements are often allocated to the householder, usually a man. As a result women are often unwilling to cooperate with others in an enterprise in which they feel they have no stake. At Nduli, for example, many women refused to work with their husbands on the tobacco farms when their husbands were cooperating with other men because they felt the farm was not theirs. If their husbands farmed individually, though, they frequently took an active part both in work and decision making.

Another relationship between the demographic structure of the population, and problems of cooperation, can also be seen from the situation at Nduli. As in Mbambara and Kwamangugu it affects the linkages between food and cash farming, but it also affects the particular form of cooperation which occurs. At Nduli, for a number of reasons, farmers continue to maintain food farms off the tobacco land, although they are recommended by extension workers to combine two crops. They can do this by using fallow tobacco land the year following its cultivation under tobacco, when the fertilizer left in the soil will support a good crop of their staple food, maize. Because of the limits on the land available for this purpose, since only the previous year's tobacco land is suitable, there is insufficient acreage for all the members of a cooperating group to provide enough food crops to meet the varying subsistence requirements of each cooperating partner's household. Thus to share the land equally between cooperation partners, as can be done with the cash crop, would not be possible with the food crop, since what is sufficient to satisfy one family's needs, might fall far short of those of another. While food production does not put a stop to cooperative cultivation of the cash crop, it means that while cooperation is taking place, resources such as labour and land, may not be utilized as much as is possible.

The age of farmers may have an effect on cooperation in another way, apart from its relationship to household structure. Different forms of cooperation are more or less likely according to the ages of the farmers concerned. This is especially the case in a situation like that at Nduli where cooperating groups are formed spontaneously and it is up to the individual members to find partners with whom to work. An individual's age affects his ability to call on cooperation from others. Some farmers are in a better position than others not to cooperate at all, since they may be able to call on the help of a large number of kin to help them at various times. This is something that a young man cannot do so easily. At the same time it is not so easy for him to draw on older kinsmen with whom to cooperate, unless the latter take the initiative. A young man therefore must either cooperate with unrelated individuals or start by himself, unless he is able to join with older kinsmen or affines as a subordinate member of their group. This particular form of cooperation with kin will be discussed below. The data from Nduli show that in fact, more men under 40 cooperate in groups than those over 40, 68% of men under 40 as opposed by 43% over 40. At the same time, of 7 farmers in the sample who are related by kinship or affinity to the chairman of the group, and therefore likely to be in a subordinate (see below), 5 are under 40.

We have seen how the varying ages and household composition of those cooperating together may affect the success of their venture because of the different interests which stem simply from the demographic differences. Because of the sociological correlates of demographic characteristics, such as the greater linkages to others gained with age, we have also suggested that the types of cooperation between people of different ages may vary. We shall now attempt to show how other relationships which bind the members of a cooperating community or group, affect the possible ensuing forms of cooperation. This topic has been much discussed in the literature, especially with reference to the significance which such relationships had for people before the new situation. Our discussion of this subject will centre not so much on this aspect but rather on the interests which they represent for the individuals concerned in the new situation. Traditional relationships of respect and authority between individuals of various statuses represented not only obligations between the parties, but also rights, i.e. interests which they gained by adhering to them. In new situations some of these interests remain relevant. At the same time, new interests arise. It is therefore in terms of both of these that the relationships operate, and affect the pattern of cooperation, or the success with which modern agricultural cooperation can take place.

Among the Nduli tobacco farmers a difference was observed between the pattern of cooperation in groups which consisted of kinsmen or affines, and those which were formed by unrelated individuals. In the latter, cooperation was largely egalitarian; decisions on agricultural practice were taken jointly, profits and costs were shared. Outside labour was jointly recruited and used for the farm as a single entity. The quality of the members was exemplified by the fact that each year a single chairman was elected to be the representative of the group, and this post circulated among the members. There were some groups with unrelated members where there was not the same degree of collective organisation. In these there was a division of fields, with a concomitant separation of the use of labour, and consequently, final profit. In these too, however, it was not possible for a single individual to take decisions on behalf of the other members. Where common activities were involved these had to be discussed jointly. If one member did try to control the others, this was a major reason for dispute and the final fission of the group.

In groups of kin, on the other hand, this is precisely the organisational pattern that prevailed, and that was accepted as proper by the group members. Just as there was a circulation of chairman in the groups of non-kinsman, there was none in the groups of kin, the senior kinsman or affine assuming the position. On the other hand, the cultivation practice in such groups was always collective, i.e. there were no cases of division of fields and profits. We shall argue that it was not only because the senior kinsman had to be respected and his wishes complied with, that this kind of organisation was able to exist, but also that by compliance with them the other kinsmen were gaining certain advantages which they would not have if they cooperated with others. Such advantages include the certainty of inheriting the enterprise on the death or retirement from work of the older kinsman. Thus a father who is quite old and not capable of long hours of physical work may control the farm which he shares with his sons, because his experience in farming makes it in his family's interest to allow him to supervise the farm organisation in order to enable a successful farm to be passed on to the younger kinsmen. Alternatively a kinsman who is more skilled and richer than the others may farm collectively with his kin, he being the controlling partner. The younger kin accept this seemingly inequitable relationship because they know they are benefitting from their brother's skill, but it is not like a capitalistic relationship because their ties with their brother prevent it from being an exploitative one.

We suggest that because of the multiplexity of the ties linking kin who also cooperate in modern agricultural enterprises, it is unlikely that the ensuing organisational forms will correspond to the equalitarian ideals behind modern cooperatives. On the other hand, the very existence of these links may enable a form of cooperation to occur where otherwise the necessary trust and goodwill for cooperation are lacking.

It would be hard to find cooperative groupings in agriculture where no links bind the members other than their membership of that group, yet it is true that many communities are formed by people with few or no formal ties. This is particularly the case in Africa where not only urban but also rural migration is widespread. Thus at Mbambara settlement, of the heads of 80 households, 20 tribes are represented, and at Kwamangugu settlement, with 73 households, there are 21 tribes represented. At Nduli, 12 tribes are represented among a sample of 49 farmers. Such multitribal communities, like their counterparts in towns, are the result of migrations from areas with little economic opportunity, to cash earning areas. The main link which often binds such migrants is their common quest for a cash income, and also for accompanying stability. In the Nandeni and Tanga Districts of Tanzania, where the two Ujamaa villages are situated, there has been no tradition of the establishment of farms by migrants. In those areas most migrants have been workers on the now declining sisal estates, and there is now a common interest in the establishment of self-managed farms. The similar life experiences of such migrants, together with the absence of any vested interest in land in the area, makes cooperative farming a possibly advantageous solution. The objective class situation of such workers makes them not only have a common interest in establishing their own farms which will generate a cash income, but also very receptive to the ideology of cooperation which opposes the exploitation of labour.

It is misleading though, to suppose that the class situation of all migrant workers is entirely similar. The functioning of extended kin groups, and the availability of land in many areas, have enabled migrants to develop interests in more than one cash generating activity. The variety of these interests, and their relative importance to the migrant, obviously affects the "similarity" of one migrant to another, and hence also the extent of their common interest in cooperation. The Nduli farmers provide examples of workers who, far from feeling that they were an oppressed labour force, continued to work as paid labourers either in agriculture or some other activity, even after beginning independent cash farming. The same applied to some farmers at the Kwamangugu Village, who were reluctant to give up their work on the nearby sisal estates. In the latter case, those farmers were expelled from the settlement because its large scale and formal organisation could not accommodate such conflicting interests. (The sisal workers who did not give up their jobs had contributed to communal work only on Saturday afternoons and Sundays). Among the Nduli farmers, the cooperating groups being smaller and more flexible were better able to cope with the difficulties caused by the multiple interests of some farmers. However, the solution has usually been at the expense of the ideal of equal cooperation. Either the cooperating groups split into individual units, or the form of cooperation was with kin, in the manner described earlier in the paper. This suggests that where there are no links with other members of the community other than that of common membership, multiple objectives and conflicts of interest cannot be so positively incoporated into the social structure.

A farmer's attitude to his existing economic opportunities are determined not only by the immediate demands of these opportunities but also by the interests and habits he has accumulated through the course of operating in previous situations. We also need to consider such factors arising from his previous work history and social origins if we are to understand current behaviour in the new cooperative farming situation, for the latter does not form the totality of the farmer's social environment. He will tend to maintain links through his interest, both economic and social, outside the cooperative institutions. He is thus caught up in a web of rights and obligations which are related to previous activities but which at the same time affect his choices within the cooperative community. We shall first consider the interests which a farmer has outside the cooperative scheme, the ways in which these are maintained, and their effect on cooperation. Secondly, we shall examine his work experience and the effect of this on cooperative farming.

Since cooperative production organisation in agriculture is usually accompanied by resettlement, or at least a new location for the cooperative activity, then a farmer's interest in his previous land holding will be an important determinant of his involvement in the cooperative farming system. Such interests in other land holdings are mainly concerned with security, particularly against loss of income, but also in the way in which it represents membership of a community. We have already seen how at Kwamangugu Ujamaa Village some (700 out of 1,030) members were expelled because they were not willing to give up their outside wage work. Expulsion is a characteristic of planned communities. On the whole you are not expelled from your native village, although you may feel obliged to leave following a scandal or witchcraft accusations. There are thus significant uncertainties associated with landholding in cooperative agricultural enterprises. At the Ujamaa villages, the final sanction for laziness, i.e. failing to contribute to the common good is expulsion. It is inevitable that members should take precautions against them. It is not only men who wish to insure themselves against failure, either economic or social. Women have a very strong interest in land which has been traditionally allocated since it represents either dependence on or independence from their husbands. Their responses to new agricultural organisations may be partly a function of these rights.

We shall attempt to view the effects of the priority given to previously held land on forms of agricultural cooperation. The maintenance of farms off the cooperative scheme means that some resources, particularly labour and capital, are not being used for it. This is not necessarily so where wider kin maintain the previous farm, who would not have accompanied the householder to the new scheme. The effect is also mitigated where private farms are close by and are used in conjunction with the cooperative cash farm. This was common at Nduli where food farms provided rations for labourers. At Nduli, because farmers' separate holdings met needs other than those directly related to the tobacco farming system and because there was not enough room on the tobacco land for all those needs to be met by several cooperating patners, the desire to maintain them is a factor encouraging the breakdown of cooperative groups. Not all people are in an equally favourable position as far as land is concerned. Women especially have been known to respond to incentives offered by farming schemes which provide land, for some women may lack the very security in land which keeps others in an ambivalent position regarding involvement in new farming schemes. Both divorced women and concubines, i.e. not legally married women, figured prominently in tobacco farming groups in the Iringa district. Young men too, from areas of land hunger, may also be in the position of having no alternative security in land. At Kwamangugu, of 18 households studied in the sample survey, only 3 farmers had land elsewhere; at Mbambara in a similar survey, only 2 farmers out of 21 had such land. These farms were being maintained by relatives. However, the data which show that many farmers "left their farms" on coming to the scheme are not clear about the meaning of this statement. Many farmers in fact probably have links at home which safeguard their interests in land. These may exist even in land hungry districts. Rachel Yeld, writing about land hunger in the Kigezi district of Uganda: and the effect of resettlement policy, says "The incentives offered in the resettlement scheme were not sufficient to induce whole extended families, (usually only 10% to 20% of extended families moved), let alone whole communities to abandon their land in the home area and move elsewhere. In the early years of the scheme land was left by departing settlers explicitly in the care of fathers or brothers on the understanding that if the settler family had to return, their land would still be available to them."[7]

Thus ties with land and what these confer are an important differentiating factor between agricultural migrants in Africa, who become members of, or from, cooperative communities, and such migrants say to Israel, who in most cases have been unable, or at least very unwilling to return to their countries of origin.

One further factor affecting cooperative production is the skills and experience which the farmers bring with them when they begin farming collectively. Cooperative organisation makes certain demands of discipline and coordination which are not required by individual farmers on their own. In cooperatives, farmers have to work in groups at allotted hours, and complete tasks within a certain time in order to synchronise with other activities. This is something that is more analogous to patterns of wage-labour than of individual farming. Non-conformity to the required pattern not only affects the individual but the whole productive process. It is for this reason that cooperative schemes have to develop sanctions against those who fail to comply with the agreed scheme of work. At both Mbambara and Kwamangugu, most farmers had considerable experience as workers on sisal estates previous to beginning cooperative farming. Although cooperation may largely be a reaction against the exploitation of labour and the fact that discipline was imposed by an external authority for ends which did not benefit the worker, nevertheless, the ability to accommodate to such discipline is acquired through the wage labour experience.

Organisational skills are needed too for the effective running of the cooperative community, and work processes. Indeed the more democratic the community, the more widespread they must be. Many wage workers developed these by being in charge of groups of workers in their previous jobs. It is striking that attempts to recruit unemployed urbanites to both cooperative and non-cooperative settlements have generally met with failure.

CONCLUDING REMARKS

It would be a trite exercise to attempt to draw significant prescriptive conclusions from our discussions so far. It would be tempting to believe that we have identified the essential ingredients necessary for successful cooperation in agriculture, and that all that is necessary for successful policy implementation is the correct mixture of each. Our experiences are far too narrow to be able to make such an exercise. Our concern has been to show that the problems of agricultural cooperation are amenable to economic and sociological analysis. We have tried to explain systematic functional relationships between observable variables. Our only conclusion of analytical concern is that it is not necessary to take refuge in unexplainable residual factors in order to account for different patterns of cooperation and their succcess or failure. We have tried to show that it is possible to make such explanations using empirically testable hypotheses. Agricultural cooperation is enmeshed in a structure of economic and social variables.

Variations in this structure will be related to different forms of cooperation. We hope that further discussions of these relationships will be provoked.

NOTES

1. A. V. Chayanov, *The Theory of the Peasant Economy*, ed. D. Thorner, B. Kerblay, R. Smith A.E.R. Translation series R. Irwin. 1966, p. 267.
2. More complete descriptions and analysis will be found in:
   a) D. Feldman, "The Economies of Ideology," in ed. C. Leys, *Politics and Change in Developing Countries*," (Cambridge U.P. 1969 forthcoming).
   b) R. Feldman, "Social Factors in Peasant Farming" (Unpublished dissertation for Diploma in Advanced Studies in Sociology and Social Anthropology, Manchester University 1968).
   c) R. W. Kates, J. Mckay, L. Berry: "Twelve new Settlements. A Comparative Study of Success," Mimeo paper for U.S.S.C. Conference, Kampala, 1969.
3. The method used for this—separable linear programming—is described in detail in D. Feldman—"Decreasing costs in Peasant Agricultural Production," E.R.B. Paper 68.20 Economic Research Bureau, Dar es Salaam 1968 Mimeo.
4. The fall in output suggested for Year 5 arises from the limiting assumption of a five year planning period. This is fully explained in D. Feldman, *Ibid.*
5. R. Woods, "Individual, Kinsman, Cooperator," Mimeo Paper, Sociology Department, University College, Dar es Salaam, 1968.
6. See A. V. Chayanov, *op. cit.*, and ed. J. Good, *The Development Cycle in Domestic Groups*, Cambridge, U.P., 1959.
7. R. Yeld, "Land Hunger in Kigezi South-West Uganda," R. Apthorpe, "*Land Settlement and Rural Development in Eastern Africa*, Nkanga Editions, Transition Books, Kampala, 1968.

Section II

Planning for Development

INTRODUCTION

A comprehensive analysis of the planning system in Tanzania remains to be written, but it is apparent that the planning procedures already have undergone several distinct phases since Independence. The First Five-Year Plan, 1964/69, was based on the assumption that private foreign investment, operating relatively freely, would constitute a significant part of total capital formation. The results were disappointing, however, and the expected levels of investment did not materialize. As a consequence Tanzania began to formulate its own unique path to development. The Second Five-Year Plan, 1970/74, represented a sharp break from an overreliance on the private sector.

Since the Arusha Declaration the means available to the government to direct and control the economy have undergone considerable change. Thus the preparatory discussions for the Third Five-Year Plan, 1975/80, assumed as given government participation or control in all major areas of investment and the continuation of the system of wage and price controls throughout the economy. Moreover, the nature and variety of planning documents also have increased. They now include an annual and a five-year plan as well as a foreign exchange and a credit plan. These plans are partly a response to the changing economic climate and to a range of economic problems which previous plans had not anticipated.

Planners as well as economists who have considered specific aspects of planning in Tanzania could not have foreseen these developments ten years ago. The need and the challenge, then is to work out an over view of the planning process, particularly in light of the interest that has been shown in the Tanzanian approach to development and planning.

The papers in this section attempt to analyze the basic issues involved in the planning process in Tanzania. In the first paper Livingstone takes as his starting point Tanzania's vast and diverse agricultural economy and against this background he considers the issues involved in establishing crop priorities. He reviews the various recommendations on crop priorities since 1966, especially as set forth in the Second Five-Year Plan, and critically evaluates the reasoning implicit in them. The allocation of crops among different regions requires coordination of pricing policies and transport and marketing facilities. The author does not minimize the problems involved, but stresses the need of integrating farm-level research with national planning decisions.

Some of the issues that arise in the choice of technology are discussed by Williams in the context of the present planning system. The author reports on a case study of the textile industry, in which state corporations have undertaken recent investments, and establishes that the industry employs a range of techniques in the production process. He then formulates several hypotheses about the method of selecting the actual techniques embodied in a particular plant. These hypotheses point to the particular circumstances under which parastatal managers operate, e.g. controlled wages and prices, noncompetitive markets and reliance on external financing. These hypotheses might usefully provide the basis for research in other industries.

Professor Belshaw's paper on regional planning is particularly relevant to the current discussion, in Tanzania and elsewhere, on integrated rural development and decentralization in decision making. He briefly reviews the history of regional planning in Tanzania, the different regional structures, and the procedures involved in the formulation and implementation of regional plans. The methodology and implementation of integrated rural development planning are discussed from the perspective of a cyclical management systems approach that is adapted to incorporate the unique features and problems of Tanzania's planning process.

Some Requirements for Agricultural Planning in Tanzania*

IAN LIVINGSTONE

Introduction

Tanzania is a vast country, and a largely agricultural one at present. The country has 17 (shortly 18) administrative regions, divided into 60 districts. The geographical diversity of the country in terms of topography, soils, and climate, particularly rainfall, is such however that even within districts marked contrasts occur in ecological conditions. The present plan for the country asserts that the basis of and foundation for development will be expansion of this huge and diverse agricultural sector. To plan for this sector is clearly an immense task.

The Second Five Year Plan makes a start on this task, particularly by listing crop and livestock priorities for each district. We should not, perhaps, hasten to criticise those lists, it being acknowledged that the exercise which was carried out was necessarily rough, given the time and knowledge available. Various hedging statements are made to the effect that these lists are "no more than a guide", that "the order of listing is not of fundamental importance", and so on. We could also add that since the Ministry of Agriculture in Dar es Salaam has not been "pushing" these priorities since publication of the Plan, inaccuracy or inappropriateness is not important anyway (though it is not impossible that some zealous agricultural officers in the field have been pushing them, as the act of publication implies they should).

The question of district crop and livestock priorities will inevitably be raised again in the preparation of the Third Five-Year Plan, however, which should start around the middle of 1972, in about a year's time, and it may be worth firing the first shots now. But this paper is presented rather in the belief that planning, including crop priorities for districts, or areas, must be given more meaning during this Plan period, and that planned action, certainly, is required at once.

CROP PRIORITIES IN TANZANIA

It is worth reviewing in some detail the discussion of crop priorities which has gone on in Tanzania over the past few years. It is hoped in this way to bring out the different aims with which the setting of crop priorities can be made, and to show that the emphasis on and basis of interest in them has changed. At a later point this will be useful in making our own suggestions for the use of crop priorities in agricultural planning.

THE COMMITTEE OF ENQUIRY

The discussion of crop priorities originally came out of an investigation into the state of the cooperative movement and the functioning of the marketing boards, by the Presidential Special Committee of Enquiry into Cooperative Movement and Marketing Boards, 1966. Only 2 or 3 pages of the report (paragraphs 306–14) relate in any way to this subject. And the discussion of the need for crop priorities did not emerge from a concern for regional planning or for agricultural planning as a whole; there is only one brief reference (paragraph 308) to intercrop priorities, for example. It emerged first from concern for the efficient investment of union and board funds, particularly in processing plants, storage and similar capital projects (paragraph 307), that is, out of cost-benefit considerations; and secondly from a concern for a more rational system of deductions and subsidies on different crops or portions of a crop (paragraph 313). In this respect there appears to have been more interest in the equity aspects than in the production and supply aspects of agricultural pricing and tax policy.

GOVERNMENT WHITE PAPER NO. 3 OF 1966

The White Paper which followed the Committee Report[1] was much more explicit in identifying crop priorities as the foundation for price policy, in addition to mentioning their use in relation to the provision of extension, credit and other forms of assistance. It stated (p. 19):

> "Government strongly supports the suggestions in paras. 306–14 that procedures be established to draw up crop priorities. The resulting crop priorities will determine price policy, and the related issue of whether the crop is to receive a subsidy, and also will affect the degree to which the Ministry of Agriculture provides extension and advisory services, and the financial institutions assist with capital.
>
> .... The problem is not merely confined to the agricultural aspects, but should embrace any processing that the produce undergoes. Once crop priorities have been established, a price and tax policy can be drawn up. The Government recognizes the "bewildering variety" of deductions to which most crops are subject, and supports the argument that they should be co-ordinated.
>
> .... The actual tax to be levied on each crop will depend on the speed with which production is required to expand, the sensitivity of farmer's production plans to the expected price, whether the crop is enjoying a high or low world market price, and the farmers' ability to bear the tax. ..."

The comments are made under the sub-head, "Taxation", and are primarily concerned with price/tax policy. The White Paper did not offer any detailed view as to how such crop priorities would be drawn up or used, the criteria to be adopted for them, the extent to which crop priorities would be broken down regionally and by district, how they would be applied, or what

*ERB Paper 71·15

problems would arise in working them out and in their application.

INTERMINISTERIAL WORKING PARTY OF 1966–7

Right at the end of 1966, at the instigation of the Ministry of Economic Affairs and Development Planning, an Interministerial Working Party was set up with the object of establishing procedures for drawing up crop priorities. The work was to consist of two parts:

(a) the "establishment of general criteria for assessing the relative importance of various crops and for allocating resources for expansion;"

(b) study of the crops themselves, through a series of individual crop studies.

Not surprisingly the Working Party, composed of full-time civil servants, found this second task impossible, and eventually did not produce a report. This is worth noting, its significance being in underlining the dangers of underestimating the research work and analysis required in successfully bridging the gap between asserting the need for certain planning procedures and the achievement of substantive planning.[2] Subsequent discussion within Ministries, and particularly the Guidelines for the Second Five-Year Plan adopted at the end of 1967, show more awareness of the practical limitations imposed by the lack of farm-level data and the impossibility of establishing at an early stage detailed crop priorities for the whole country.

E.R.B. PAPER 68.14

In a paper[3] surveying the organisation of marketing in Tanzania, Helleiner devotes one section to arguing the case for establishing crop priorities. Helleiner takes an essentially macro-economic viewpoint. Starting with an analysis of the market prospects for different (major) commodities, he finds actual or prospective international agreements restricting potential increases in export volume for export crops accounting for a large proportion (60 per cent) of total agricultural exports; the prospect of self-sufficiency and thus an end to foreign exchange saving through import substitution, in respect of major foodstuffs such as maize and possibly wheat (he could have added rice); and urban markets for foodstuffs limited. In order to maintain the growth of the agricultural sector as a whole over a long period, therefore, it is necessary to de-emphasize crops for which long-term market prospects are poor and correspondingly to emphasize and increase the effort made in respect of crops, including livestock, not so constrained.

Helleiner was thus looking at crop priorities in the first instance from a national viewpoint, in relation to the agricultural sector as a whole, even if this had to be translated into separate efforts at the local level. Secondly he saw agricultural price and tax policy as a major instrument for guiding the efforts of peasant smallholders towards priority crops and out of those which required de-emphasis. He states (p. 19);

"The relative tax burden should on the face of it be greatest (or the grower price relative to the world price less actual marketing costs should be lowest) for those crops which are de-emphasized in the overall crop priority policy, and it should be lowest for those which are to receive emphasis."

The actual position was in sharp contrast:

"There is . . . no overall system or set of criteria to guide the pricing decisions; each case is handled on an *ad hoc* basis. There has been little opportunity as yet to see the pricing picture as a whole or . . . the priorities and principles which might guide it. As a result the pricing systems are something of a hodge podge (p. 18). He goes on (pp. 18–22) to indicate a large number of possible anomalies in pricing and price structure.[4]

This is not to say that Helleiner was not aware of other instruments or of the operation of crop priorities at the local level. He states elsewhere (p. 16):

"It is obviously essential that the infrastructure of marketing, both physical and human at the very least, be developed *pari passu* with the growth of agricultural production. Planning for access and feeder roads, storage facilities, transport capacity, processing facilities, and so forth must be co-ordinated with planning for other aspects of agriculture on a quite detailed level by region and by crop. At present, this is undertaken on a completely decentralized basis without reference to any overall priorities".

The main emphasis of this section of his paper is nevertheless as indicated above: it is on first-stage analysis of price policy in relation to overall market prospects, rather than on second-stage analysis to determine the most suitable areas within Tanzania for particular crops, that is, the allocation of output. Not much of the necessary analysis of pricing and price structures had, however, been done a year later, when the Plan was published, and its absence does indicate a major weakness of planning in a mainly agricultural economy with a limited number of major export crops.

U.S.A.I.D. STUDY OF MARKETING

To its credit, however, the Tanzanian government had at this stage commissioned a comprehensive study of agricultural marketing to be carried out by a U.S.A.I.D. team recruited from Michigan State University. Their report[5] had very comprehensive terms of reference, though the group had only twelve months in which to complete the study. These were:

"To conduct a comprehensive study of the marketing and pricing system, and the organisation and management of the marketing boards and co-operatives and prepare a detailed time-phased agricultural marketing and pricing program and an implementation plan for improving the efficiency of the cooperatives and of the marketing system".

These terms of reference cannot honestly be said to have been fulfilled in relation at least to pricing policy. The report devotes the largest part of its 100-odd pages to a useful description of the structure of the Boards, and to recommendations regarding a new organisational structure. Not much space is developed to price and tax policy in respect of different crops, and the detailed analysis called for in our earlier references is not there. Discussion of pricing concentrates mostly on maize, and the treatment here is very much less full than in a recent Economic Research Bureau paper on the subject.[6] There remains therefore much urgent analysis which needs to be done within the terms of reference, not surprisingly, in order to relate pricing policy to planning and to national and district crop priorities.

FIVE-YEAR PLAN WORKING PARTY ON AGRICULTURE

Prior to this, of course, preparatory work on the Five-Year Plan had been under way. During the year 1967–8 a number of government working parties had been established for discussion of plans for the various sectors and aspects of the economy. The Agriculture Working Party had completed most of its work by the middle of 1968, when a draft report was available. Its terms of reference had given it a strong brief to produce specific and detailed priorities. These included directions:

(a) "to formulate crop and livestock priorities on a national and regional basis in the light of production and market potentials"; and (b) "to propose appropriate institutional arrangements to co-ordinate the implementation of crop priority policy and for its revision in light of changing circumstances". The report accordingly included a lengthy appendix on this subject (Appendix IV; An Examination of Proposals for Crop Priorities in Agricultural Planning).

This provided an extremely useful detailed review of discussions up to that time, but concluded, basically, that it could not fulfil its terms of reference. It stated that: ... "the establishment of crop priorities presupposes a measure of detailed technical and agro-economic information which, as yet, is not available in Tanzania in relation to many crops and areas of the country ... in view of the lack of statistical and agro-economic data, the opportunities for centralised decision-making on crop priorities are strictly limited".

Its conclusions were therefore that more staff were needed in the Planning Unit of the Ministry; a greater number of simple agro-economic surveys should be carried out in the districts; and in the meanwhile crop priorities should be offered by the Ministry only as guidelines with full scope for interpretation and discretion on the part of Regional and District Agricultural officers in the light of their own knowledge of the locality.

The report makes some effort to indicate the criteria that should be applied in formulating priorities. The text suggests concentration on five "practical" criteria: the existing familiarity of farmers with the crop; their attitude towards it; the average cash income of the area; the need for diversification of the crop base; and the natural environment, including distance from markets. Appendix X, however, provides a list of 16 factors or criteria to be taken into account (reproduced as Appendix I of this paper).

CROP PRIORITIES IN THE FIVE-YEAR PLAN

The importance attached by the Plan to crop priorities can be gauged from the fact that these are made one of the three main principles in respect of the rural sector. Chapter 3 of the Plan starts as follows:

"The fundamental principles guiding the Plan in relation to the rural sector are:-

(i) that rural development receives top priority....
(ii) ... progress will be made towards the goal of socialist organisation of rural economic activity....; and
(iii) that the desired social change will be achieved in the context of a *programme of planned output expansion, based upon a system of crop priorities*".... (my emphasis)

The crop priorities in Volume I of the Plan are presented in two forms. Paragraph 104, (p. 43) separates "national production aims" into three categories:

(i) crops for which accelerated or rapid increases are aimed at;
(ii) crops for which present or medium growth rate is required; and
(iii) declining or limited market.

Secondly, paragraph 107 lists commodities on which the major national agricultural programmes of the Plan will concentrate some 9 or 10 items.

In assessing this section of the Plan we may note again that the work of rationalizing and clarifying the system of prices and taxes in relation to various crops, discussed earlier, still remained undone. On the other hand judgement of market prospects are implied in the announced target rates of growth for different crops. Thus expansion of cotton production is to provide the major impetus, while other crops with favourable export markets, such as tobacco, are given much higher target rates of growth; coffee, pyrethrum and similar commodities with the opposite prospects are correspondingly de-emphasized in expected physical output terms. In addition to tax-price policy not being clearly related to these, however, the detailed priorities given for individual districts appear quite independently determined.

As well as the national list of crop priorities given in Volume I of the Plan and including 14 crops under the head of "accelerated increase", Volume 3 of the Plan, which came out later, includes first a full chapter, (Chapter 3) on crop and livestock priorities and identifies general priorities for broad zones and geographical areas. Secondly it gives separate lists of crop and livestock priorities for each district of mainland Tanzania in subsequent chapters.

There are perhaps two separate reasons for formulating crop priorities at the detailed local level. The first reason is that macro or national level priorities cannot stand on their own, but must, for implementation, be translated into local district priorities: different districts naturally cannot respond identically to the same set of general priorities. The latter must in other words reflect both the demand and supply situations, so that if a particular crop is first identified as having good potential the second step is necessarily to decide which regions or districts can best supply the crop. Similarly, as discussed below, if requirements of a particular crop are strictly limited, it is necessary to allocate these requirements between alternative possible supply regions within the country.

The second reason occurs when planning is organised on a regional rather than national basis, when *regional* plans are envisaged. Without specific priorities based on local possibilities (but consistent with other regional plans and external constraints) such plans would have no content.

In summing up, we can hazard the proposition that since 1966 there have been two developments affecting the way in which crop priorities are regarded. Starting with an emphasis on national pricing and tax policy with respect to major crops, there has been first increasing awareness of the problems of translating macro-priorities into local district priorities for purposes of implementation; and secondly there has been a new emphasis—even as between the publication of Volume 1 and 3 of the Plan—on regional planning as such.

CRITICISM OF THE PLAN PRIORITY LISTS

If we look in detail at the way in which priorities are presented in these volumes, however, we can see that this has not produced wholly favourable results. In the latter, 10 crop priorities were selected for most districts. A list as long as this is practically a list of everything that can grow. It does not provide a guide as to the rough proportions of development effort to be allocated to each crop, the only use such priorities can have beyond simple description of the region. Similarly 45 districts have four or more livestock priorities, and one has as many as seven; which must include almost every possibility. The length of these lists itself indicates the absence of any basis for the priorities such as relative rates of return of the different crop and livestock activities.

The reason for this result appears to be quite simple: the lists are derived basically from responses to a questionnaire sent out to agricultural officers in the regions by the Ministry. The weakness of the results reflects the unsatisfactory design of the questionnaire. The questionnaire requested agricultural officers in all regions to list crop priorities from 1 to 10 in order of importance, and this was dutifully done.

Chapter 3 of Volume III does go on to say (p. 40):

> "The exact order of listing of particular crops . . . should not be a matter for detailed discussion. In most districts conditions vary from one part of the district to another. Cotton may be the main crop in one area and tobacco in another. Both are important and the district priority list should reflect this without seeming to choose one in preference to the other".

Clearly we should not wish to push tobacco in a cotton area, or vice versa. But this factor cannot in itself explain the length of the lists. And if a district does have distinct sub-areas, crop priorities, if they are to be meaningful, must distinguish between them, recommending, say, tobacco in Area 1 and cotton in Area 2. The priorities are after all only of use if they provide a guide to the extension service and other agencies, who must know what to push in each area.

This first point is related to another major weakness of both the general priority list of Volume I and the district lists, that they do not distinguish between major and minor crops. This renders the classification in Volume I less useful, such items as grape vines, soya beans, and kenaf appearing in the top category ("accelerated increase") while maize and coffee appear in lower categories. It would have been more useful to offer separately priorities for major and minor crops. The classification would then bear a more direct relation to the amount of development effort, in terms of extension advice and investment, which needs to be put in. There is some awareness of this point, since it is stated (p. 40):

> "A problem does arise in the priority lists with regard to the ranking of crops which have a stagnating or declining market. While in one sense these can be given a low priority, the crop may need considerable attention at district level to deal with such problems as increasing yield and quality while reducing acreage, problems of replanting and diversification, etc. These types of crop programme will need particular planning at regional and district levels".

We might ask, if these do require and warrant a lot of planning (extension effort), in what sense are they low priority crops? The criticism applies with even more force to the district lists.

These lists are further suspect, since they can be said to amalgamate non-comparable criteria. Thus in one district beans, pulses and peas were placed first, with this explanation:

> "This crop is a very important source of protein and as such we have given it priority No. 1 for expansion".

A less nutritionally-minded officer next door might not rate beans at all. Likewise maize was listed fourth in Lushoto and first in Handeni, in both cases the reason for inclusion being "staple diet". The place of maize here depends entirely on the weighting the agricultural officer decides to give this factor, one which is not in any case related to growth potential or desirable extension effort.

Another weakness, again stemming from the questionnaire used, is that crop and livestock priorities are listed separately for each district. There is no particular sense in this: all are agricultural activities, and while there *may* be some complementarity, they will in general be competing for the same scarce agricultural inputs from the farmer (land, where this is scarce, and labour) and by the State (extension assistance, credit, investment in marketing, processing and transport facilities).

This separation considerably adds to the full list of agricultural activities given as priorities for particular districts, which might thus add up to as many as 17.

Another fundamental weakness—discussed more fully below—is that there is no selection *as between* districts and regions. This lack of selection exists despite this being a major aim of establishing crop priorities and of regional planning in general. Thus it is stated very explicitly in Volume III (p. 3) that:

"Regional planning is important at two distinct levels. These are:
(a) Planning development activities *for*, and *within*, each region.
(b) Making a rational allocation of development activities *between* and among various regions".

We might first give an extreme example of this. Onions are listed among the priorities in as many as 37 districts. Clearly, unless Tanzania is to export onions on a vast scale, and there is no indication of any such optimism, this is not on. The available urban markets, as indicated by Helleiner,[7] are quite small in relation to total agricultural population.

While this is not an important example, it is also the case that 56 different districts specify poultry—keeping within their livestock priorities; and 43 include dairying (for which only 15 specify that the dairying activity is to be engaged in on a local or limited basis.) Clearly the limited internal urban markets cannot sustain this simultaneous expansion, though export markets have not been identified: thus district plans based on these priorities would be mutually inconsistent.

Again, Chapter 3 of Volume II gives general priorities for major crop and livestock zones, the last of which is given simply as "Highland Areas". This is sub-divided further into these areas: Meru, Kilimanjaro, and Pare; West Lake; Usambaras, Ulugurus; Southern Highlands; North Mara; and Mbulu/Hanang. Of these all but the last have dairying as a general priority, virtually all the highland areas. Obviously, however, if a Tanzanian dairying industry is to be developed, there will need to be a concentration of effort in a few places, apart from some supply to limited local markets.

Fruit and vegetable production is given general priority in almost the same areas, North Mara being the exception, though for some reason only vegetables are specified in respect of the Southern Highlands. This case of fruit and vegetables is considered again below in greater detail.

The production of pigs is given priority in as many as 14 Districts: Arusha, Kilimanjaro, Mbulu/Hanang, Handeni, Lushoto, Tabora, Kasulu, Iringa, Mufundi, Njombe, Mbozi, Sumbawanga, Songea and Tunduru. While this is in the Plan document, the actual current policy of the Ministry of Agriculture is, sensibly, to concentrate its efforts at developing a pig industry in the Tabora region.

These last observations in turn suggest some further points. The crop priorities largely reflect areas of potential supply: a very large number of areas *could* produce these commodities, as the agricultural officers have been able to observe. These crop priorities have obviously come up from the districts. But this should only be the first stage of the analysis; the second stage must be to sort out competing claims centrally *where present market outlets are limited.*

This obvious lack of concern for marketing outlets indicates also that those suggesting the priorities had in mind in part production for self-consumption (subsistence) as well as commercial sale. This would, for instance, be the reason for pushing poultry so widely. In this case, however, there would be no reason to omit poultry in a few of the districts, or to list vegetables in 45 districts but not in the remaining 15. There is, moreover, a danger in combining subsistence and commercial crops into a single priority list: farmers, and agricultural assistants may be given the impression that there will be a market for the former crops where there is in fact none. This can only reduce the credibility of extension advice.

The promotion of specific commodities for subsistence production would in any case require a somewhat different approach, perhaps by way of specific campaigns. The selection of commodities to be promoted will be differently based than for commercial crops: onions, for instance, which have comparatively low nutritional value, would *not* figure so prominently.

Finally, where crops are produced for both subsistence and commercial purposes these two aspects must be kept completely separate in making crop priority recommendations, just as if two separate commodities were concerned. Thus there is no reason for listing maize in all but four districts. Generally speaking there is no case for giving subsistence maize production priority anywhere, this not requiring any particular assistance. On the other hand, there is a need to select among the large number of alternative supply areas for commercial maize, those areas which should be given the opportunity to produce maize as a cash crop, whether they be the most efficient producers or those most needing an additional crop.

THE ALLOCATION PROBLEM

This section expands on some of the foregoing discussion to make a general point which we wish particularly to stress. This is that for a good number of major and minor agricultural products in Tanzania the market is limited or finite,[8] while the number of potential supply areas is large. This is true of the major foodcrops like maize and rice; and it is true of assorted commodities such as different types of fruit and vegetables, pigs, poultry and dairy products. What the district crop priority lists *do* show is that, *given markets*, such commodities can be widely produced throughout the country. This indicates two essential stages of planning. The first need is for analysis to determine the size of the overall demand and its potential growth; the second stage is to allocate this limited demand among the competing regions.

This first stage analysis has not, it would seem, been carried out for many (perhaps any) of the commodities for which it is appropriate: we need Tanzanian market surveys (and of neighbouring African countries) of commercial demand,[9] quantities which could be absorbed monthly, for pigs, poultry, dairy produce, vegetables, fruits and so on. In a further paper,[10] summarized in another section, we suggest that it still needs to be done for major crops like maize and paddy.

It thus becomes difficult to carry out the second stage analysis of allocating this potential output among competing regions. In this situation such regions are likely to make mutually inconsistent plans: crop priorities on which to base district plans cannot in fact be determined. To take the example considered more fully below, there is a danger of districts in Tanga and Morogoro Regions each basing their plans on the expectation of being allocated the same Dar es Salaam market for fruit and vegetables. And with or without coherent district plans, extension officers, credit agencies, co-operative unions, and others cannot offer firm or sound advice,[11] or make reliable investments, since rates of return associated with particular crops cannot be known in the presence of a potential but quite unassured market. This therefore requires a second level of analysis, leading up to deliberate choices among competing regions on the basis of sound and sensible criteria.

Apart from finite market demand, there is a second major reason for making these deliberate choices: the need to concentrate inputs. In the first place extension campaigns are likely to be more effective when concentrated in particular areas (not particular farmers) and on particular objectives. Secondly, the funds for improving communications and thus access to markets are limited and may be best concentrated at one strategic point. Thirdly, the tapping of potential supply may depend on a prior decision to locate a processing plant in the district which can absorb output. And fourthly, marketing being a major constraint in most cases, there may be a need for concentrated efforts at improving marketing organisation in one or a few places.

These four kinds of *indivisibilities*, infrastructural overhead costs, do require deliberate planning choices. This second aspect applies generally to all crops, including export crops with buoyant markets, but strongly reinforces the argument in the case of crops for which the market is strictly limited. The absence of such choices is perhaps the most important defect of agricultural planning as contained in the Second Plan. While some further preparatory research is desirable to improve the basis of such choices, we should argue that any long delay would do more harm than good.

In the case of fruit and vegetables, the Ministry of Agriculture did have, for a period of time, a specialist group working within its Planning Unit. The group carried out a series of useful regional surveys of fruit and vegetable production and marketing, which provides some foundation for analysis. The surveys covered Morogoro, Tanga, Mbeya, Kilimanjaro, Tabora and Dodoma Regions.

The surveys of the first four regions suggest that in broad terms (not excluding possible variations in detailed comparative advantage) the potential supply position is much the same. Everywhere the first problem is lack of market outlets and second, of marketing organisation.

For example:

"There is a lack of an organised marketing system, which leads to general unease on the part of farmers at the low prices they receive and uncertainty as to whether they will be able to sell their crops at all." (Morogoro Region)

"Vegetables often cannot be sold and are left to rot in the harvest period . . . Fruits in particular are left unharvested." (Tanga Region—Usambaras)

"One case was reported of a whole field of carrots left unharvested in the Usangu Plains area of Mbeya because of lack of a market." (Mbeya Region)

"As was shown in other regions' surveys, the lack of organisation of any marketing systems is precluding any expansion of fruit and vegetable growing."

"Extensive market research would be needed before any development, for example, as part of a coffee diversification programme."

"However they (the Kahe Irrigation Scheme) have difficulty in selling even their present production and much is left in the fields unharvested." (Kilimanjaro Region).

In this situation supply is not the basic constraint. The existence of a positive rate of return for a particular crop depends entirely on whether a market becomes available. Without this, a rate of return is not even work calculating.

The four types of indivisibility mentioned above apply with some force to fruit and vegetable production. As the surveys reveal, production in regions is largely in the hands of large numbers of peasant smallholders, with plots of only one or two acres. There is little specialisation and horticultural practices are poor, with inadequate use of insecticides, fertilisers, and other inputs. The resulting quality of the produce is thus extremely variable. This is a serious obstacle in fruit and vegetable marketing, particularly in respect of potential export markets, the existence of which will depend very much on regular supplies of good and uniform quality being forthcoming. Against this, however, lack of markets at present is made worse by poor marketing organisation. Poor returns thus often render fruit and vegetable production a marginal activity to the farmer, who then has little incentive to adopt improved practices. For individual farmers then to use insecticides, for example, becomes less profitable, partly because of the difficulty of keeping down insects on his own and partly because of the general absence of quality control and grading.[12] There is thus particular need for concentration of extension advice, for instance on an (ujamaa) village basis, alongside other measures, to break through this barrier.

Marketing organisation creates problems at both ends, at the leading consuming centre of Dar es Salaam and at the local level. Dar es Salaam being supplied from many sources generally through small-scale independent traders and even farmers themselves, arrivals are haphazard and unpredictable, with corresponding uncertainty of prices.[13] The lower average prices resulting are transmitted back to the farmer. Thus in mid-1969 the Ministry of Agriculture reported that shops in Dar es Salaam were complaining of their inability generally to obtain a regular supply and were resorting to airfreight deliveries from Kenya.

Similar uncertainty in marketing exists at the local level. In Tanga Region, for example,

> "A frequent comment was made on the uncertainty of selling. Traders may promise to collect produce on a certain day and then not turn up".

Often hired lorries do not arrive or come late. Many farmers come down themselves from the Usambaras to Tanga, on Sundays especially, in an attempt to market their produce, some farmers agreeing to carry the produce of others.

Co-operative marketing of fruit and vegetables would appear the obvious solution. Here it will be said that previous attempts (in most areas) have been notoriously unsuccessful, because of the difficulty of handling perishables, and existing co-operative societies and unions are generally very reluctant to become involved in this trade. Against this, given the unsatisfactory nature of the present unorganized system, it is difficult to visualize improvement except through co-operative means.

There is a case for concentrating assistance here. While there is a generally acknowledged case against 'pressurised' co-operation, the problem of perishables is so acute that in this case at least it appears justified. The Marketing Section of the Planning Division of the Ministry of Agriculture has already decided on and been playing on active role in relation to the Chenzema Vegetable Farmers' Co-operative Society in the Ulugurus.[14] This could be expanded into a concerted effort on all fronts if it were decided that the Ulugurus should be developed as the primary "vegetable basket" of Dar es Salaam.

Transport is however another crucial factor, access routes into the mountainous supply areas in the Ulugurus and Usambaras being short but extremely hazardous, particularly during rain. Table 1 compares prices in Soni market, only 10 miles into the mountains off a tarmac road and less than forty miles from Korogwe, with prices in the latter. On average Soni prices are just 30 per cent of those in Korogwe and are frequently much less. In Table 2 prices in Mgeta, in the Ulugurus, are compared with those in Morogoro town, just 25 miles away; they vary between 15 and 33 per cent of the latter, the average being 22 per cent. Thus the report makes the unfavourable price comparison for peas, cabbages, and lettuce of 5 cents in Mgeta, 50 cents in Morogoro, and Shs. 1.50 in Dar es Salaam. If it is uneconomic to tarmac the mountain access road into both the Ulugurus and the Usambaras there would seem to be a strong case for selecting one of the two for the privilege, together with other complementary action. The Ulugurus, only 120 miles from Dar es Salaam, would seem to have a strong claim, but this is a matter where some crude and simple cost-benefit analysis needs to be applied.

Improved road communication should improve prices to growers, and this itself should assist efforts and co-operative organization. Both of these in turn should increase incentives to farmers to improve output and to apply grading and quality control. Improved supplies should improve prospects for establishing viable processing facilities. The indivisibilities are self-reinforcing.

The same applies in relation to processing. Unions or private businessmen are generally reluctant to establish factories in advance of an assured and regular supply at low prices. Farmers are, however, not induced to organize themselves on commercial lines or to concentrate on particular crops in advance of the market provided by the factory. In different parts of the country there have been tentative attempts at different times to establish canning factories, fruit juice manufacture, or tomato puree production, and even more proposals for such establishment. The potential seems clearly there, however, and what appears to be needed is quite deliberate planning and planned action, with a willingness to take a long term developmental view.

TABLE 1: PRICES OF VEGETABLES IN SONI AND KOROGWE, 1968, Shs/Kg.

	(a) Soni Market September 1968	(b) Korogwe Market October 1968	% of (a)/(b)
Carrots	0.30	1.50	20
Peas	0.20	1.50	13
Cauliflower	0.70	1.50	47
Leeks	0.50	1.00	50
Lettuce	0.30	1.00	30
Beans	0.20	1.00	20
Onions	0.20	1.50	13
Cabbage	0.30	0.70	43
Spinach	0.30	1.00	30
Cucumber	0.30	1.00	30
Tomatoes	0.40	1.00	40
		Average	30

SOURCE: Ministry of Agriculture, Food and Cooperatives, "Fruit and Vegetable Production and Marketing in Tanga Region", Dar es Salaam, November, 1968, Tables XI and XII.

TABLE 2: PRICES OF VEGETABLES IN MGETA AND MOROGORO TOWNS, 1967, CENTS/KG.

	Cabbages		Peas		Beans		Carrots		Onions		Tomatoes		Potatoes	
	(a)	(b)	(a)	(b)	(a)	(b)	(a)	(b)	(a)	(b)	(a)	(b)	(a)	(b)
January	6	26	30	70	21	64	7	26	35	72	38	64	28	63
February	7	39	42	113	30	100	11	30	45	79	36	101	28	58
March	5	50	40	147	19	97	6	50	17	118	13	102	20	59
April	13	75	14	99	5	44	17	91	19	222	9	112	44	77
May	5	87	15	107	5	29	5	126	—	—	—	—	5	85
June	5	70	16	112	6	33	14	147	—	—	—	—	14	72
July														
August														
September	10	24	12	63	—	59	20	46	—	—	—	—	20	59
October	10	27	14	59	—	48	10	33	—	—	—	—	17	60
November	5	26	9	50	—	53	9	31	—	—	—	—	27	48
December														
Monthly average	7	50	21	95	16	59	11	69	29	148	24	92	26	66
(b)	14		20		27		15		20		26		33	

Note: (a) = monthly average prices of vegetables sold in Mgeta through the Tchenzema Farmers Cooperative Society, cents per kg.
(b) = monthly average prices at Morogoro Market Auction, cents per kg, derived from Town Council records. Prices for July, August and December not available.

SOURCE: Ministry of Agriculture and Cooperatives, "Fruit and Vegetable Production and Marketing in Morogoro Region", Dar es Salaam, July, 1968, Tables 5.4 and 5.9.

The Ministry surveys are useful and deserved more follow-up than they got. They are however only preliminary. Their main weakness is that they do not make a final selection of optimum areas for each crop, or crop for each area, and do not consider different supply regions as alternatives. This stems from the fact that the surveys were carried out separately in each area rather than as part of a single exercise with deliberate aims in mind.[15] Similarly an alternative approach in relation to the possible development of processing facilities for different crops would be a systematic comparison of different areas in respect of each crop concerned, with a view to determining the optimum location or locations. A major programming exercise is needed, involving the kind of cost-benefit calculations mentioned, to be followed by concrete action.

From what has been said already, where the market for a commodity is limited or finite, the first step is to find out just what the size of the market is: how much of the commodity can be produced. The paper referred to earlier reviews the production and price policies for two major crops in Tanzania, maize and paddy. It concludes rather seriously, that "it has never been clear exactly how much Tanzania should be aiming to produce of each commodity, how much it should be putting into storage, against what contingency, and what possibilities might exist, if any, for export."[16]

In respect of maize, much the more important crop, and indeed Tanzania's most important, the position is taken that Tanzania *should* be able to be self-sufficient, given its agricultural resources, and thus avoid expensive maize imports. Some rough analysis is offered to support this assumption. The export market is also analysed, and the conclusion is that the market is not likely to be more than "opportunistic" except at very low and uneconomic prices, offering the possibility of profitable exports only in occasional years, when the maize crop in neighbouring countries happens to fail. Generally, therefore, policy should be geared to providing for the domestic market. The most important instrument of policy is price, and maize pricing policy is reviewed.

Examination of the actual operations of the National Agricultural Products Board (N.A.P.B.) show that expensive losses have been made through imports and exports, sometimes in the same year, losses which could in part have been avoided. The reasons seem to have been, first, that there was very inadequate information on the general maize position and on its requirements, and what information might have been available was not properly presented or reviewed, partly because of inadequate review procedures, at least before the Agricultural price Policy Co-ordinating Committee was established in 1967.

Secondly, price policy was inappropriate, and may have served actually to destabilise the situation rather than the opposite. Price should have been fixed at around the level necessary to call forth the necessary supplies, taking one year with another, including a sufficient maize reserve to cover against contingencies. It is suggested that the actual price paid to growers depended on the amount deducted to cover export losses. Thus, in the year immediately following serious losses, deductions were greatest and price to grower lowest; subsequent avoidance of losses meant smaller deductions and an increase in price to the grower, in both cases with effects on supply.

Thirdly, the best decisions might not have been taken because the maize position was obscured by the need to have maize stocks in addition to regular supply. Examination of actual N.A.P.B. operations suggest that there has been no consistent policy in respect of maize reserve requirements. It is suggested in the paper that the kind of contingency against which Tanzania should have been guarding was a disastrous drought of the type occurring every 7 to 10 years or so, and involving a strategic reserve rather than the operation of a simple buffer stock to even out regular variations. This is required knowledge if production is to be planned according to national requirements.

Parallel analysis is carried out in respect of paddy. The paper does not go on to examine the further question of how national production of these major crops might be allocated as between different regions in Tanzania, but urges that this question be considered in a systematic way.

CONCLUSIONS AND RECOMMENDATIONS

This paper is not based on detailed research and its intention is to suggest ideas for consideration and further investigation rather than firm conclusions.

1. Thus the purpose of criticizing the treatment of crop priorities in the second Plan is not made for the sake of bringing critical retribution: the exercise was acknowledged from the start to be a very crude and preliminary one. The purpose of detailed scrutiny was rather to provide the opportunity for demonstrating something of what needs to be done in the future. The following is a list of points which might be considered.

Crop priority lists should be reasonably short, should be separated into major and minor crops; and relating simply to agricultural activities rather than separately to crops and livestock. Also proposals for subsistence and for commercial production should be given separately while priorities should be related to the desirable allocation of extension and other development efforts.

Secondly, district priorities must be based on a two-stage analysis incorporating both the local supply position and macro planning considerations. A choice between alternative supply regions may have to be made where the overall market is limited or where indivisibilities indicate better returns from a concentration of resources. There may also be (not discussed in this paper) opportunities for profitable specialization of production between regions.

2. While fuller knowledge gained from more farm-level research will always improve the formation of local crop priorities, all decisions should not await this. Deliberate and bold planning decisions regarding the regional allocation of output should and could be made at an early stage. While these will take into account comparative advantages as between regions, it is also the case that these planning decisions will themselves affect and partly determine crop priorities subsequently.

3. Lack of detailed agro-economic data at the farm level must remain a major handicap in formulating district crop priorities. However one can distinguish two levels of analysis: the preparation of detailed priorities for particular regions, and secondly the identification of *key commodities* in broad and macro terms. This is actually done in the Five-Year Plan, for which reason the present paper may have given an unnecessarily gloomy picture: meat and dairy products, fish, rice, wheat, tea, flue-cured tobacco, cotton, and pulse foods, oilseeds, vegetables and fruits are given in Paragraph 107 of Volume I as targets for the major national agricultural programmes. These key commodities are fairly easy to pick out by considering a combination of the national resources position for such things as livestock, forests and fisheries, and market prospects.

This list of key commodities can be varied and needs to be varied fairly quickly. Rice already needs no further expansion. Pyrethrum, which was right out of consideration, has made a comeback. The opportunity for rapid expansion of tobacco production arose particularly in consequence of the Rhodesian boycott following U.D.I. The prospects for Tanzanian cashewnuts will depend on the progress of the war in Mozambique, one of the three leading producers, with Tanzania and India. Sugar is not an important Tanzanian export, or Britain's entry into the E.E.C. could affect that. To deal with this there is need for an efficient intelligence system in respect of major export crops (also for the purpose of estimating national financial implications).

4. The fact that crop priorities at the national and local level may change, and change quickly, also has implications in terms of action required as, for instance, the allocation of personnel. It is important to be able to switch staff between regions (to where the returns are highest); and also to be able to concentrate staff, if necessary, on particular tasks within a region. This is not unrecognised in the Plan. For instance on page 3, in respect of Dodoma District it is stated that

> ". . . . In grape production it would be necessary to co-ordinate investment in such areas as seedling distribution, insecticides, technical advice, and processing . . . . The available staff probably should concentrate on these developments, even if this means leaving as second priority the wide variety of other but less important activities going on in the district".

Secondly, the kind of extension staff required will be affected, and so will the appropriate form of training programme for them. This also is recognised. The Five-Year Plan Working Party on Agriculture, for example, commented that

> ". . . instead of examining training and extension in terms of aggregates, for example projections or targets for the provision of one extension worker for so many farmers, the initial exercise should be to establish the basic extension units which are required in headquarters to give them adequate support".

The recommendation was thus for commodity demonstrators, such as tobacco specialists, and auxiliary field staff with training in limited fields. What progress has been made in this direction is not certain, but this is clearly the right move to make.

5. The recommendation of the Five-Year Plan Working Party on Agriculture that "much more manpower must be applied to agro-economic investigations" remains true, and just as urgent.

This urgency is underlined firstly by the fact that Volume III of the Plan commits Tanzania to carry out regional studies amounting to "embryonic regional plans" (p.6) in six selected regions up to the time of the mid-Plan review. Without a great deal of farm level research in these regions to determine appropriate crop priorities, as well as other aspects of regional planning, these studies will be less than fully satisfactory.

A second factor is that promotion of the ujamaa village programme would obviously benefit significantly from (and be handicapped without) the availability of well worked out farm plans focussed on appropriate crop priorities. A practical argument for ujamaa villages is in fact the facilitating of extension advice; and, like other forms of settlements and farm reorganisation schemes, the economic viability of the scheme will be a crucial determinant of successful transformation.

6. Given these needs for agro-economic research in Tanzania it would be nice to think that a full-scale programme was under way, based perhaps on the network of agricultural research stations. Recent examination of the Annual Reports of the various government agricultural research stations in Tanzania "shows almost complete concentration on purely scientific research. Virtually no work is being done on crucial aspects such as farming systems, crop economics, rates of return on different crops; marketing bottlenecks and problems; geographical possibilities for particular crops within regions and economic zones; and agricultural projects are not researched into as integrated development schemes, research in the stations simply not being organized in such a way as to make this possible".[17]

The Annual Reports show clearly, on the other hand, that where there has been at least one agricultural economist attached to the station the balance of work has been quite different. It is stated Ministry policy to have agricultural economists at each station, but serious staffing problems during the past year or two have probably significantly *reduced* the amount of agricultural economics research being carried out. Correction of this situation should be a top priority.

The paper just quoted suggests that agricultural economists attached to the research stations could also serve as link-men between the scientific researchers and regional agricultural teams, thus helping to integrate the work of the stations into the regional planning effort on a continuing basis (pp. 81–82).

Our earlier discussion above refers to the need for local crop priorities to be determined through two-stage analysis, the first relating to overall demand and allocation of output at the national level, and the second relating to the local supply possibilities. The paper just referred to also proposes (pp. 81–82) a more articulated national system of agricultural research with more co-ordination, central direction, and provision for feed-back flows of information, nationally and regionally, in both directions, from and to the research stations. Implementation of these two proposals, or similar ones, may provide the best solution in the long run.

7. Immediately, however, there is need for an agricultural economics "task force" attached to the Ministry of Agriculture Planning Unit or working from the associated University research institutes to work in a more rough and ready way and to pave the way for the planning decisions that are required, including those related to the allocation of output between competing regions. This task force should consist of senior people who could pull together existing knowledge in the regions, working with the agricultural officers and others already there, to produce coherent programmes for each region covered. Such a group would have the advantage of being able to view together several alternative areas, as well as having knowledge of the overall national and international situation in respect of different crops. This group (or groups) should of course be additional to

the existing staff of the Planning Unit and have the freedom of movement which their "tasks" would require.

The returns from this form of organisation are indicated by, for example, the reports made on fruit and vegetable production discussed earlier. However preliminary these are, the reports—prepared largely by two young British volunteers—provide much more coherent information than was previously available. Related to this is perhaps the need for more small sample agricultural surveys, more closely directed however to specific problems and questions, in contrast with the more general form of agricultural census, such as the present world census of agriculture, which do not necessarily pick out the most urgently required information.

8. Our review of the discussion of crop priorities revealed a change of emphasis over time away from the national level and away from the analysis of agricultural price and tax policy in relation to national crop priorities and towards the discussion of crop priorities in the context of regional and district planning. The analysis of price structure and tax incidence originally called for does not, however, appear to have been satisfactorily carried out and is just as urgently required. The best means of doing this would probably be to expand the current university research programmes in the field of agricultural marketing.

APPENDIX I: FIVE YEAR PLAN: PREPARATORY WORKING PARTY ON AGRICULTURE: APPENDIX X: REVISED CRITERIA FOR CROP PRIORITIES.

List of possible criteria in establishing local crop priorities:

1. value added and market prospects;
2. foreign exchange earnings (savings);
3. marginal input requirements for expansion;
   - (i) technical complexity of crop
   - (ii) alternative uses for land
   - (iii) credit needs
   - (iv) farm labour requirements
   - (v) skilled supervisory personnel requirements
   - (vi) storage, transport, and other investments required;
4. national or regional self-sufficiency required;
5. need for diversification of cash crop base;
6. nutritional value of food crops;
7. reduction of seasonal underemployment and high peaks in labour demand;
8. suitability for smallholder or communal effort;
9. likely responsiveness to extension;
10. degree of instability;
11. steadiness of market surplus over the year (to permit spreading of costs of transport and marketing);
12. potential as an input in other activities;
13. production of useful bi-products or use of available bi-products;
14. contribution to favourable crop rotation;
15. degree of flexibility and supply elasticity (how easily can farmers shift away from crop if necessary);
16. potential educational effects (for example, use of simple machinery facilitated).

NOTES

1. Government Paper No. 3 of 1966, Proposals of the Tanzania Government on The Recommendation of the Special Presidential Committee of Enquiry into the Co-operative Movement and Marketing Boards.
2. This is discussed more fully in I. Livingstone, "The Relationship between Research and Planning in Development," *Uganda Economic Journal*, Vol. 1, No. 1, December 1971, pp. 71–93.
3. G. K. Helleiner, "Agricultural Marketing in Tanzania-policies and Problems," E.R.B. Paper 68.14, Economic Research Bureau, University of Dar es Salaam, 1968.
4. For further examples in Tanzania, P. Westergaard, "Primary Societies" Marketing Cost—A Case Study and some General Remarks, mostly on Efficiency," E.R.B. Paper 69.6, Economic Research Bureau, University of Dar es Salaam, 1969.
5. H. C. Kriesel, C. K. Laurent, C. Helparn, H. E. Larzelere, "Agricultural Marketing in Tanzania: Background Research and Policy Proposals," Michigan State University, June, 1970.
6. This is an immodest reference to I. Livingstone, "Production, Price and Marketing Policy for Staple Foodstuffs in Tanzania," E.R.B. Paper 71.16, University of Dar es Salaam, 1971.
7. G. K. Helleiner, *op. cit.*
8. The existence of small or slowlv growing external markets eases the constraint but not sufficiently to change the basic problem.
9. As just mentioned, a clear distinction between commercial and subsistence demand must be made.
10. I. Livingstone, "Production, Price and Marketing Policy . . ."
11. Though, for instance, a Ministry survey of fruit and vegetable production in Mbeya Region found that market outlets for the output were generally non-existent, it was reported that "the agricultural staff were actively encouraging increased production".
12. Some indication of the combined effects on quality of cultivation and marketing methods is given in a paper by E. G. Martens, "The Establishment of Tchenzema Vegetable Farmers Co-operative Society—Morogoro: Present Situation and Future Development," Ministry of Agriculture, Food and Co-operatives, Dar es Salaam, October, 1970. Martens took two samples of cauliflower and tomatoes arriving in Dar es Salaam from Morogoro Region in order to determine the amount of wastage. The results were:

	Wastage in %	Below grade in %	Total in %
Cauliflower	35	15	50
Tomatoes	10	30	40

Irrespective of the appropriateness or otherwise of the criteria applied, these results have serious implications.

13. This has been described in some detail in respect of two commodities supplied to Dar es Salaam, cooking bananas and oranges. See S. M. Mbilinyi and A. C. Mascarenhas, "The Sources and Marketing of Cooking

Bananas in Tanzania," E.R.B. Paper 69.14; A. Mascarenhas and S. Mbilinyi, "Rationalising the Orange Trade of Dar es Salaam," E.R.B. Paper 69.15, Economic Research Bureau, University of Dar es Salaam, 1969.

14. See E. G. Martens, *op. cit.*
15. On the other hand, looking at the surveys together, it is possible to get some impression of general prospects. Supply to Dar es Salaam appears to be something for division between the Usambaras and Ulugurus, plus the more immediate Dar es Salaam 'hinterland'; Kilimanjaro region has no obvious outlets except for the special crop of cooking bananas and the possibility of airfreight overseas once the new international airport is completed; and the development of fruit and vegetable production in the Mbeya region will depend very much on the establishment of marketing outlets in Zambia. The Tabora survey reveals Tabora as providing a useful market for fruit and vegetables from Kigoma, its main supplier. It is clearly important to keep this market for Kigoma (badly needing new economic activities) and if possible to develop it. Similarly Singida appears in this report as a steady supplier of onions, and should perhaps have priority for this crop.
16. I. Livingstone, "Production, Price and Marketing Policy . . .," p. 1.
17. I. Livingstone, "The Relationship between Research and Planning in Development," p. 78.

National Planning and the Choice of Technology: The Case of Textiles in Tanzania*

DAVID WILLIAMS

Introduction

This paper is about research into the choice of technology in the Tanzanian textile industry. The apparent range of technology in use in the industry is quite wide. Moreover, the more recent additions to cotton spinning and weaving capacity appeared to have widened, rather than narrowed, the range of technologies in use. Scope for expansion of the industry is considerable with productive capacity likely to double over the next ten years. The industry is almost totally under the control of a parastatal holding corporation (TEXCO); the five major mills are its subsidiaries.[1]

The purpose of the research is to explain the variation in techniques observed in the industry. A superficial examination of the financial statements and employment statistics of the mills, reveals a relatively wide range of factor proportions. For example, one mill employs about 170 workers and Sh. 1.6 million of fixed assets per million metres of finished cloth, while another employs about 80 workers and Sh. 2.8 million. Thus the basic research questions underlying the study are: are these techniques as different as they appear; and, irrespective of the reality of differences, why and how were they chosen?

HYPOTHESES, METHODOLOGY AND SOME FINDINGS

Two major groups of working hypotheses were used in exploring the research problem. The first group was composed of hypotheses about the range of technologies and the variation between them. The second group was composed of hypotheses about the objective function underlying the process which resulted in the technologies being chosen and installed.

The general hypothesis underlying the first group was: that the apparent differences in the technologies in use in cotton spinning and weaving were not, in fact, real differences. Perhaps the mills operated at different levels of efficiency, using machines, labour, materials and other inputs in differing combinations so that, if these differences were eliminated, the differences in capital-output and capital-labour ratios would also disappear. It was also possible that the mills were designed for different products or product mixes. In this case, either the mills were, in fact, producing different products or, if the same products were being produced, some of the techniques were being used inappropriately. Again, it was possible that the various technologies appeared to differ when viewed in terms of market prices but that the use of shadow prices would show that in national (social) terms, the differences could be explained.

It was evident that while numerous hypotheses could be set up at the equipment-product level, they all required the same basic approach to testing. The mills and their equipment had to be subjected to a detailed engineering-economic analysis in order to measure the differences in technique. Data were collected from all five integrated mills. The purpose of the study was discussed with mill-managers and a questionnaire, together with an explanation of the method to be used in filling it, was left with each mill. After collection of completed questionnaires, further discussions were held with the managers to rectify any omissions or inadequate information. In general, the objective was to bring selected costs of production to a standard basis for comparison, using a standard product and output. The machine hours required to process sufficient input material to arrive at, say, 1,000 kgs. of spun yarn was calculated for each process at expected (optimal) efficiency. Process waste was added at each stage so that the number of operating hours included machine-time lost through waste.[2]

The results of the standardized cost analysis showed that the mills were indeed using different factor proportions on the same product. A strong relationship between labour-intensive/capital-intensive characteristics and total cost of production was found, the more labour-intensive, less capital-intensive combinations having lower commercial costs of production. The lowest cost combination of processes from the observed techniques was closest in its factor proportions to the most labour-intensive mill.

The application of shadow prices to the actual capital, labour and foreign exchange costs of spinning reinforced the conclusions drawn from the analysis of actual costs. The correlation between labour-intensivity and low cost was strengthened, while the difference in factor proportions between techniques was confirmed for a specified product.

To explore the possibility that product differences could explain and confirm the differences in the observed ranges of technology, a further survey of production units was carried out. Since it was not possible to cover all mills only the major mills were visited. A two-part questionnaire was designed. The first part treated product attributes. For example, yarn was characterized by the following set of attributes:

Strength	(for a given count)
Regularity	(consistency of count over length)
Hairiness	(the degree of filamentation due to broken or displaced fibres)
Elongation	(the elasticity of the twisted yarn within desirable limits)
Foreign Matter	(neps, slubs, dirt, etc.)

*Edited version of ERB paper 75.12.

The survey sought to establish, by scoring on an ordinal scale, the importance of these qualities to the performance and appearance of the end use product (i.e. apparel). The second portion of the questionnaire sought to establish the factors on which these attributes depend. The following factors were identified:

Quality of raw material
Type of equipment used
Operator skills—setting
Other factors.

Within the range of technology currently in operation in Tanzania, the research showed that, in the opinion of production managers, the product has very little influence on the type of equipment across a range of yarn construction. In effect, the mills could produce the same products at comparable quality. There were no grounds for assuming that any particular type of technology in the observed range was dictated by product characteristics.

The analysis of weaving and weaving preparation data is incomplete. The range of vintages in use in weaving is somewhat wider than in spinning. Some looms in use in Tanzania were manufactured about 1900. Capital costs for these units are extremely difficult to estimate as, over a 75 year period, the machines have taken on the characteristics of "grandfather's axe". Indications from the analysis carried out are that on certain fabrics the older less automated looms are more efficient but may lack the versatility required for other products. In general, however, it is not expected that there will be a reversal of the reality of negative technique differences and correlation between cost and capital intensity found in spinning.

Hypotheses in the second group, relating to the objective function underlying the choice process, are somewhat dependent on the results of the engineering cost analysis. If the apparent differences in technology had been explained by the analysis, then we might expect to be able to identify a set of choice criteria related to the economics of the industry, the technical characteristics of the equipment and the product. In effect, we would have been searching for some form of neo-classical economic objective function; and one subtle enough to penetrate the veil of prices, efficiencies and product differences. But the differences in technologies were not explained. Moreover, because they were not explained, the neo-classical efficiency criterion is also virtually eliminated as an explanation of the process of choice. Given the findings on factor proportions and cost, it is necessary to hypothesize an objective function which incorporates factors outside the economic model.

Several writers have sought to explain the impact of non-economic factors in the choice of technology. In particular, the work of Wells is of special relevance.[3] Wells conducted a survey of six Indonesian industries in which a range of technologies was being used. The conclusion drawn was that although relative factor costs had a role in selection of technology, other influences were of critical importance. Several hypotheses were developed from the notion that choice of technology may be made by engineering man. Generally, it is suggested that the objective function of "engineering man" leads towards more sophisticated, automated technology. This is held to be especially important where price competition does not occur and the firm has a monopolistic advantage. Capital intensive plants are seen as providing some degree of insurance against risk and uncertainty. In some cases more automated technology is believed to provide greater flexibility in accommodating to shifts in demand and more automated technology is also seen as being more "familiar" and therefore less prone to failure than older or "intermediate" methods. Furthermore the borrowing ability of the firm is likely to be affected by the nature of its equipment. While some managers and entrepreneurs simply prefer modern machines, it is also believed that machines are easier to administer than people. Many other interesting possibilities along these lines are raised by recent work in the field.

At first glance, the prospects for explaining the variation in techniques in the Tanzanian textile industry on the basis of the engineering man hypotheses are not bright. This is because of the following reasons:— The textile industry is controlled by the state and the only investments made in the last ten years were made by the state. The two most recently (1968) commissioned mills are at opposite ends of the local range of technologies. The industry is non-competitive but it is uniformly so. Input and output prices are controlled, are uniform throughout (with some special quality-related exceptions) and are adjusted so that the costs of the least efficient mill are more than covered. The industry is being expanded, but its growth is lagging behind the growth of demand. All mills are assured of full-capacity operation. The engineering man hypotheses would not predict that a single investor, facing these conditions, would set up both capital-intensive and labour-intensive plants at the same time.

There are, however, some hypotheses in the engineering man concept which may be useful in the Tanzanian context. Insurance against risk and uncertainty could have had some influence in creating the limits to the present range of technologies. There are both more labour-intensive and more capital-intensive techniques available than either of the limiting cases. The borrowing ability of textile firms in Tanzania is a function of the finance-raising ability of the holding corporation (TEXCO). While there is no evidence to suggest that TEXCO itself would quibble about technology when lending its own resources, the willingness of other institutions (e.g. TBRD, Tanzania Investment Bank, National Bank of Commerce) to finance TEXCO projects, may well be affected and may, in turn, place some constraints on technology choice. A preference for automation may be encouraged by such influences in the future.

Obviously, introspective examination of "engineering man" hypotheses is an inadequate and inconclusive test. Equally obviously, however, the engineering man hypotheses are not likely to provide complete explanation of the process which led to the adoption of varying technologies, some additional hypotheses are required, and will be discussed below.

THE BUREAUCRATIC CHOICE OF TECHNIQUES

In order to begin to establish a theory to explain the behaviour of the Textile Corporation (and the Development Corporation earlier) the researcher has turned to two areas which appear to offer some prospect for a general explanation in the Tanzanian context. The first area is the Planning System in Tanzania and the associated parastatal structure. The second area is related to the first, and is the structure and origin of project finance.

The objective of the planning system is to allocate resources across the board, control prices and wages, and generally control business activity in any other manner necessary. The current basic method of planning is to stimulate government and parastatal institution to make "proposals" for expenditures on both the recurrent and capital expenditures to which they are variously entitled. The proposals are gathered together and slashed in order to both adjust for intersectoral balance, and to fit overall resource availability. This budgeting exercise is carried out once every planning period, although some within-period adjustments are possible. Thus all proposals for investment by parastatals (whether using self-generated funds or new government equity financing) are competing with all others for the nod of the planners. There is a lack of clear and universally accepted criteria for the presentation and assessment of projects. This is related to the ability of planners to perform adequate careful examination and application of analysis techniques to all proposals. Consequently, it is often the practice to decide on government investment on the basis of the proposer's contribution to eking out scarce government resources and his degree of commitment to aid donors, foreign investors and other parties interested in the project, rather than a comprehensive appraisal of both long and short-run cost/benefit factors.

In the industrial sector a long-term strategy for industrialisation has been formulated and ratified by the planning commission. This strategy provides a basic set of priority industries for current and future development; rules for reviewing and assessing the desirability of sub-sectoral development; and a comprehensive set of criteria for screening projects in industry and mining. Theoretically the planners are expected to work within the limits of this strategy. However, the strategy is not fully accepted as an operational guide by all decision makers in government and, in any case, will not have any significant effect on industrial structure until the 1980's.

Even with full acceptance of the project analysis criteria set out in the strategy, it is not clear that a consistent, technology-related criterion for project choice would emerge. The reason lies in the environment in which parastatals operate, and their evolution as organisations in that environment. For instance, both product and factor markets in Tanzania are only nominally under the control of planners. In both areas several aspects of the competitive model have been replaced with devices which operate in quite different directions from market forces. The price-control system, for example, is in many cases based on a cost-plus formulation which both shelters the inefficient and gives only a weak incentive to become more efficient. The labour market is circumscribed by both central control of wage rates and a highly protective set of employment conditions. The incentive-structure to which the parastatal manager responds offers little in the way of personal financial rewards and, in any case, may focus on surpluses which are more related to windfall gains from the pricing system than to productive efficiency. The aspirations of the country's leadership are often expressed in such objectives as "a rapid increase in the proportion of local raw materials which are processed locally".

Given that the assessment of his performance is not made on productivity related factors, a parastatal manager begins to focus on "Development" or "growth". The way to survive and prosper in the present environment appears to be to focus on starting projects. Under the circumstance the "appropriate" project is the one which can be started most easily, given the nature of the planning system. The holding corporations are attracted to those projects which, in addition to being startable, also provide economies of scale in terms of headquarters management activities. Hence larger-scale turnkey operations may be selected—but this does not mean that they are necessarily more capital-intensive, simply more comprehensively packaged.

In the environment sketched above, sources of finance may become a dominant explanatory factor in technique choice. With tight local resources, the planners are usually more receptive to a proposal which "brings its own foreign exchange". The parastatals, relatively unimpeded by profitability criteria, respond to this attitude by shopping for aid-related projects. The projects which can be secured, presented, moved past the planners, delivered and staffed fastest and at the least effort to the parastatal is the one which is chosen. As the technology embodied in a project (i.e. a textile plant) is often closely related to the technology in the country of the consultants, donors or co-investors, so the "choice of techniques" in any particular project is often merely a fallout from the chosen source of finance and related project inputs.

It might be suggested that "bureaucratic man" be added to the list of characteristics of objective functions related to technology choice. Clearly, the process of technology choice described above is related to the kinds of factors observed during the generation of the "engineering man" hypothesis; but there are distinct differences. Both the "engineering" and "bureaucratic" hypotheses are attempts to explain the objective function of decision-makers under conditions in which both product and factor markets are distorted and some degree of monopolization exists. Under these conditions, factors not captured in the simple economic models appear to become decisive in investment decisions. Given relative freedom of choice and a high level of sensitivity to risk and uncertainty, "engineering man" develops a bias for more capital-intensive equipment than would be dictated by the economic model. On the other hand, perceiving himself as part of a system which insulates him from commercial competitive pressures and also from operational problems, the bureaucratic decision-maker attempts to achieve objectives which eliminate the choice of technology from the decision process.

PROPOSED METHODOLOGY

Four lines of approach to confirming the hypotheses implied in the foregoing description of the bureaucratic choice of technique, are being attempted. First, an effort will be made to reconstruct the steps leading to the investment decisions. Second, plans for expansion of the textile industry will be analyzed. Third, an examination of the process of choosing technology in the small private section of the industry will be made. Fourth, a brief study of variations in technology in other industries will be made.

Reconstruction and description of the investment decision process will be based on examination of documentary evidence and on interviews. Board minutes, Annual Reports, submissions by parastatals to ministries, feasibility studies or any other documents to which access can be gained, will be used in an attempt to identify the major characteristics of the process. In particular, a measure of the relative importance of technology choice as a decision factor will be sought.

Whenever possible, decision-makers will be interviewed. The purpose of the interviews will be (a) to establish the background and training of the individual; (b) to describe the role played by the individual in the decision process; (c) to attempt to classify the concept of "technology" held by the individual and, especially, his view of the importance of technology choice; and (d) to identify the source and nature of advice relied upon by the individual, especially with regard to the technological aspects of the decision.

The rationale for this structure is derived from the following hypotheses:

(a) "Technology", in the form of alternative methods of combining productive resources, is not a decisive factor in investment decisions in Tanzania.
(b) Actual investment decisions are made by persons who are not, by experience and training, in possession of special competence in the technological aspects of the industry in question.
(c) Investment decision-makers are sometimes ignorant of the possibility of alternative technologies.
(d) Investment decision-makers do not seek or use advice on the technological choice aspects of investments.

Some rough indications of the likely results of the interview approach have been gathered in casual discussions with some decision-makers. For example, one senior decision-maker indicated that he felt the most labour-intensive mill had equipment which was "very old fashioned". He was, however, primarily responsible for the acquisition of the mill and was contemplating replication of the project. Another senior official, a director of the holding corporation, volunteered the opinion that the technology of textile projects had been and probably would continue to be a matter of "pure chance, because too many other matters of importance had to be considered in investment decisions".

Analysis of the future plans for the expansion of textile capacity will be carried out simultaneously with the documentary search and interviews on past decisions. Superficial examination of current expansion proposals provides some rough evidence which points in various directions. Over the past two years, TEXCO has put forward extensive plans for adding both spinning and weaving capacity. Included in these plans were replications of both the most labour-intensive and the most capital-intensive mills. The issue of differences in technology did not appear to have been raised by either the holding corporation staff or the consultants who carried out the feasibility studies on which the proposals were based. Part of these plans is being implemented. The two most capital-intensive mills are being expanded; in one case capacity is being doubled. These mills are, on the basis of the researcher's analysis, the two highest cost units. The most labour-intensive mill is being "balanced" (i.e. weaving capacity is being expanded to match spinning), but the proposal to build another similar mill of the same size on a different site has been temporarily shelved.

It might be suggested that the actual decision made in the present plan indicates that a "technology choice" has been made. But the evidence available concerning the reason for shelving the labour-intensive expansion suggests otherwise. The potential suppliers of the new labour-intensive mill were unable to promise delivery in the time required and were in any case more interested in another project in Tanzania.

Although the private sector of the textile industry is relatively small, it may be possible to derive some useful control data in the area. We may expect to find that the private weavers are making investment decisions on the basis of a mixture of "economic" and "engineering" objective functions. Whatever the actual nature of their objectives, the expectation is that they would be consciously considering alternative techniques as a central activity in making investment decisions.

Other industries in Tanzania have an apparent range of technologies. These will be examined in an attempt to explain the variations. The main objective will be to test the proposition that the variations can be explained only by the bureaucratic choice of technique, and cannot be explained in terms of technology-related objective functions.

In several industries there are existing or planned production units with apparently different technologies. In sugar refining there are two large-scale vacuum pan refineries with contrasting capital-output and capital-labour ratios. Future plans for the industry include both more vacuum refineries and open-pan refineries, the latter being of intermediate technology. Plans for expansion of the cement industry include projects, proposed by bilateral aid donors, for both "wet" and "dry" process plants. In the garment industry both larger-scale state factories and smaller-scale private plants are planned. A large-scale automatic bakery has been recently commissioned by the National Milling Corporation to compete with several small-scale private bakers.

POLICY IMPLICATIONS

If it can be demonstrated that choice of technology in Tanzania tends to be random, due to the system within which investment decisions are made, then a number of policy questions may be raised. First, we may ask: what difference does it make? In terms of the objectives the Tanzanian Government has set, is the bureaucratic choice of technique an impediment? Some measure of the implications for employment and capital consumption was made in the study of cotton-spinning. But, given that the process is random, what is the likely total effect of continuing to choose techniques in this way?

A second set of policy issues surrounds the question of how to change the system. What are the costs and benefits of alternative ways of removing one set of incentives and replacing them with a more desirable set? Clearly, complete answers to such questions will lie beyond the scope of the present research. However, some analysis of the organisational structure of parastatals has been carried out and it may be possible to define the major alternatives and their implications.

APPENDIX

TANZANIA'S ECONOMIC SYSTEM

To understand the environment in which Tanzania's manufacturing sector operates it is necessary to know the key parameters of the country's economic system as it has evolved in recent years. The Arusha Declaration of 1967 was the first major step since Independence to bring important economic activities, including banking, insurance, wholesale trading and manufacturing in large units under direct public sector control. Since that time public sector involvement in practically all segments of the economy has steadily increased. A significant shift took place from reliance upon private initiative and indirect controls to central planning and direct controls as instruments to guide the direction and level of investment as well as the distribution of income between the various segments of the community.

Tanzania's political leadership firmly believes that the system of a private enterprise economy is incompatible with the country's desire for genuine political independence and social equality. It bases this belief on the conviction that a private enterprise system—because of Tanzania's poverty and shortage of entrepreneurial skills—would inevitably lead to dependence on private foreign investors and multinational corporations which would entail an increase in foreign political and economic influence, the consolidation or creation of elitist social structures and a pattern of development that is contrary to the interest of the majority of the people in Tanzania.

Tanzania's economic system is still evolving and the present situation cannot be described in terms of a particular theoretical conception or historical model. It contains elements of various economic systems including a centrally planned command economy, a private enterprise market economy, market socialism, and probably still others. Inevitably, some of those elements are conflicting. As fully realized by the Government, one of the toughest problems in the transition towards socialist, centrally planned economy, is to find workable substitutes for the traditional reward and penalty framework of a private enterprise economy and to find meaningful yardsticks for the measurement of economic performance.

These problems have not yet been resolved. An illustration of this is the fact that it is still quite common in Tanzania to measure the performance of public sector (parastatal) enterprises in terms of their financial profitability. Many of these enterprises, however, have little or no control over the prices at which they buy and sell and depend for their marketing, transport, import licences, senior personnel and management recruitment, wage and salary policy, etc., almost entirely on other parastatal organisations or government agencies. The rewards for efficiency and penalities for inefficiency are generally very weak which may be one of the principal reasons for the relatively low level of productivity in many parastatal enterprises. The Government and the party place strong emphasis on the need for greater discipline and in some cases fear for dismissal has become a potent check on laziness or inefficiency. Much reliance is placed on political education in and outside the places of work as an instrument to instill in workers and managers a stronger sense of purpose and a greater awareness of the need for discipline.

Fundamental choices will have to be made with regard to the future degree of consumer autonomy in determining the nature, quality and quantity of production. Increasing reliance is placed on direct Government control over the selection, supply and domestic distribution of consumer goods, especially imports. This means that the rationing of supplies by means other than the price mechanism has become a fairly common feature of Tanzania's economic system. The degree of consumer autonomy is not only basic to the nature and intensity of the links between demand, production and imports but also to the distribution of income between savings and consumption. The Tanzanian Government now has instruments to exercise direct control over the allocation of a significant portion of national income and savings. Inadequate information flows, a serious shortage of experienced administrators, leaky borders and other factors, however, still impose severe limitations on the effectiveness of those instruments.

The system of central planning and direct controls has gradually become more comprehensive and also more complex and difficult to operate. It now comprises a national Five-Year Plan, and Annual Plans within the Five Year Plan, annual budgets of the central Government and all Regional and District Governments, capital expenditure programs of all parastatal companies including the public utilities, the creation of credit and its sectoral distribution, direct controls over all foreign borrowing and all other foreign exchange transactions including dividend transfers, all important domestic prices including agricultural producer prices, the allocation of most senior manpower and all university graduates, comprehensive import licensing, the confinement of all exports to parastatal organisations, wholesale distribution, a substantial part of domestic transport, as well as the trade in and processing of the principal staple and export crops. In view of the scarcity of well trained economic planners, the paucity of data to work with and the slowness of information flows, the task of making this system work in the interest of development is an awesome one indeed while the danger of becoming trapped in bureaucratic red tape is ever present. There is no doubt, however, that the Government is sincere in its endeavours to make the system work. Implementation is the collective responsibility of all public sector organizations but the principal nerve centres are the Treasury, the Central Bank, the Ministry of Economic Affairs and Development Planning, the Prime Minister's Office, and State House.

Nearly all important industrial projects since 1967 were undertaken by the public sector and private foreign investment was limited to minority participation in some of these.[5] Usually such private foreign investment is linked to the sale of equipment and a management agency agreement. In addition, the Government has acquired a majority interest in several companies that it apparently did not originally—according to the Arusha Declaration—intend to become involved in. Another serious brake on domestic private investment is the TANU leadership code which is a code of conduct for all TANU members.[6] The code precludes TANU members from holding shares or a directorship in any privately owned company. Because there is pressure on all citizens to remain or become TANU members this effectively means that no (would be) Tanzanian enterpreneur could own or run a private company other than a small farm or a small shop.

NOTES

1. For background information on the development of textile industry see appendix I of the original E.R.B. Paper 75.12 pp. 15–17.
2. A detailed report on the analysis of the five processes used in each mill for cotton spinning can be found at Appendix II of the original paper.
3. Wells, L. T. Jr. "Economic-Man and Engineering-Man: Choice of Technology in a Low Wage Country." SEADAG Papers 75–1.
4. Abstract from "Tanzania: Industrial and Mining Sector Survey". IBRD, February 1975, to which the researcher was a contributor.
5. A notable exception to this is the recent establishment of a car battery manufacturing plant in Dar es Salaam by a private Japanese-Tanzanian combination.
6. TANU (Tanganyika African National Union) is the only political party on the mainland of Tanzania. Until November 1974, the leadership code only applied to senior party members and public sector planners earning more than Shs. 1,000 per month. (*CCM as of 5/2/77).

Decentralised Planning and Poverty-Focused Rural Development: Intra-Regional Planning in Tanzania*

D. G. R. BELSHAW

Introduction

The subject matter of this paper is limited to one segment of the range of issues connected with the application of regional planning to development policy and decision-making in Tanzania. It has often been found useful to distinguish between, on the one hand, inter-regional planning (where inter-regional resource allocation and regional-sectoral planning interactions are the central issues) and intra-regional planning (with multi-sectoral and inter-spatial integration as major features) on the other. [1]The main issues in inter-regional planning in Tanzania have been discussed in an earlier paper (Belshaw, 1977a). The object of the present one is to examine alternative methodologies for formulating a medium-term development plan for a single region (the *initial* formulation, one should say, as a process of higher-level revision—or preferably of iterative modification—inevitably occurs as plans for individual regions are co-ordinated and then combined with sectoral ministry plans into an overall national plan).

The paper proceeds from an examination in section 2 of the regional economies of Tanzania—with an attempt to analyse their major dynamic features—to a brief review in section 3 of the experience already gained in Tanzania from different approaches to regional plan formulation. In the final two sections, the case is presented and illustrated for a two-stage or dual methodology of planning for the rural regions; this incorporates integrated rural development planning into regional planning.

The emphasis throughout the paper is on identifying a planning methodology which is capable of both widespread application—in the light of realistic estimates of probable data and manpower availability—and facilitating significant progress in terms of the multiple objectives of current development policy in Tanzania. The latter has been described as being concerned with the earlier stages of a gradual and voluntary transition to socialism. In this paper, it is not the intention to enter the academic debate about the meaning of the concept of 'region' and the criteria for delineating a set of ideal regions for planning purposes, chosen in terms of predetermined objectives and the planning techniques to be deployed upon them. Rather, the emphasis is upon the identification and selection of a methodology which can be effectively used in the present administratively-defined system of regions, i.e. (i) the nineteen rural regions of the mainland, to be joined later by the rural island regions of Zanzibar and Pemba; and (ii) the urban region of Dar es Salaam and the 'impact region' of the new capital city of Dodoma (which is superimposed on parts of five predominantly rural regions).[2]

It is necessary to define the use of the terms 'methodology' and 'procedure' in the regional planning context. Planning methodology is a more complex concept than methods or techniques of analysis and decision-making (for purposes of problem identification, problem-solving, resource allocation, etc.). Methodology includes not only these analytical and planning techniques but also (i) the range, structure and behaviour of the institutions which employ these techniques or which participate in their use, and (ii) the components of one or more value systems which provide the criteria used to identify problems and reach decisions. At its widest, therefore, the term embraces the structure and behaviour of public-sector decision making and its interaction with groups and individuals, i.e. the political system. However, discussion here is focused primarily on the narrower area of formal planning methodology, in the normative sense of what is supposed to happen, i.e. the outcomes intended from the choice of planning institutions, techniques, etc. Intention and practice can diverge, of course, and the final design of an improved methodology will depend considerably on additional analysis of deficiencies observed in the planning system as it operates.

The term "procedure", on the other hand, is used to refer to a systematic working method employed within the formal planning system.[3] Both the inputs and the outputs in a planning system consist of information; planning procedures are working rules which lay down the sequential collection, analysis, transformation, routing and use in decision-making of information in both qualitative and quantitative forms. Some procedures may specify the use of a particular technique of data analysis or synthesis. Needless to say, the set of procedures should provide for flexibility and concentration of planning effort on priority areas and guard against their mechanistic application in trivial or erroneous ways. The need for a range of procedures for planning rural areas is discussed in the next section. The main focus, however, is on the formal planning methodology within which distinct procedural components can be effectively linked together.

The concern here with the "technocratic" component of regional planning in Tanzania should not be taken to imply that other components, such as village-level participation or the role of the political leadership, are viewed as less important. The view is held, however, that the effective deployment of the professional manpower and capital resources in the public sector is a

*ERB Paper 77.5

critical activity without which many welfare problems in the regions will not be ameliorated and much development potential will not be exploited. Empirical grounds for this view are presented later in the paper. Furthermore, the view is taken that the effective deployment of resources requires a new methodology for regional planning which is appropriate to the predominantly rural character of the Tanzanian regions. While recent experience in Tanzania does not provide a complete blueprint for the methodology which is required, analyses of rural development problems and of that planning experience itself suggest a promising approach which should receive further attention.

INTER-REGIONAL DIFFERENCES IN PERFORMANCE AND PLANNING TASKS

Of the twenty mainland regions only Dar es Salaam can be regarded as an urban region. It is true that the Capital Development Authority (CDA) at Dodoma is assuming some of the functions of an urban planning authority not only for the capital city district (6,400 sq. kms) but also for the much larger 'impact region' (148,400 sq. kms) (Capital Development Authority, 1976). However, the city district is embedded within one autonomous rural region while the impact region overlaps parts of four other rural regions. The CDA's formal planning powers are in effect restricted to the small city-district area. In the nineteen rural regions agriculture—crop production and livestock-keeping—is the dominant source of income in kind and cash, supplemented locally by employment in fishing, honey collection and forestry.

If the sectoral nature of the economies of the nineteen regions are all similar in that agriculture is dominant, cannot one regional planning procedure be applied to them all without the need to ascertain detailed variations within them? The operative question is whether all regions are facing the same major problem or constraint, such as low agricultural productivity arising from similar causes and requiring, therefore, similar solutions. One way to assess the value of a differentiated planning approach, it may be thought, would be to analyse the mean level of income—and its distribution in kind and in cash—which is attained in each region (or, better, in each type of farming or land-use activity within each agro-ecological zone) and analyse the causes of the observed variance. This would indicate the extent to which higher incomes were associated with certain activities, inputs, modes of production, levels of capital, spatial location, etc. Assuming that the observed associations were also causal in nature, this analysis would indicate how far it was necessary to employ different planning procedures in order to determine how to achieve a desired improvement in productivity and income in any region.

There are two problems with this approach, the first practical and the second theoretical. On the practical side, the rural household budget surveys of 1967 and 1975 (and 1977 in process) estimated rural incomes in a highly aggregated form, for groups of two to four regions, and they did not gather the farm management data required to explain the observed differences in agricultural incomes. On the other hand, existing farm management and land-use data do not provide contemporaneous nationwide coverage (nor non-contemporaneous coverage either). Furthermore, data which could be collected in a rapid national survey permit only the simplest kind of analysis. For example, a recent farm sample survey based on 40–100 farms per selected area (twenty areas representing what were thought to be relatively homogeneous agro-economic zones) has been analysed by Friedrich (1976) using production function analysis. However, the explanatory power of the analysis was poor in many instances, due in part to intrinsic weaknesses of the production function model (Upton; 1974) and in part to large variations found in the survey data.

On the theoretical side, there are two issues. First, this kind of analysis is essentially static in nature; relationships, even if accurately observed, will not continue to apply if major exogenous variables are causing changes in the system. Exogenous factors which are strongly operative in Tanzanian agriculture—and hence in the regional economies—include relative prices (in small-scale agriculture product prices are more important than factor prices), production technology and the availability of public sector resources. More flexible dynamic programming or simulation models constructed from a much fuller array of data, are required to analyse the probable effects over time of changes in these variables. Such models are currently being developed by a World Bank team working in Mwanza and Shinyanga Regions but their general application in regional planning awaits both the demonstration of their utility and considerable further investment in farm data collection and analytical capacity. Second, even if farm management data of the required quality and coverage were available, unexplained farm income variation would be encountered between farm families in similar ecological conditions and farming systems due to differences in supporting infrastructure especially transport, product processing and marketing and input supply facilities. Analysis at the village level, therefore, as well as at the farm level is required. While the creation of such comprehensive data systems is a desirable long-run goal, and high priority should be accorded to improving the present rural data base, clearly for some time regional planning will have to use much less comprehensive data supplemented by more qualitative evidence.

At the present time, some crude dynamic analysis can be carried out using the time series of mean regional income per capita maintained by the Bureau of Statistics. This series extends from 1966 to 1974. The reliability of these estimates is no better than the basic statistics underlying them—and these are certainly weak for subsistence activities and for most marketed food crops. However, as the required analysis is dynamic, interest focussed on changes in per capita income rather than in the absolute magnitudes at one point in time, i.e.

errors which are consistent between regions over time will not cause the inferred pattern of change to depart too greatly from reality. There are some grounds for thinking that causes of error in agricultural income estimates will tend to operate in similar fashion in all regions.

What independent variables are likely to cause differences in regional growth rates? The more obvious factors include new production activities, new production technology, changed product prices and improved communications. For these to be effective in raising agricultural incomes, access to production resources—adequate land areas per family with sufficient rainfall for reliable crop or grass growth—is typically essential. On the other hand, the rural population of Tanzania is growing rapidly and is unevenly distributed with respect to the quantity and quality of land resources. Wide differences in the man: land ratio, therefore, may explain differences in growth rates between regions. Also, given the current policy emphasis on the reduction in rural poverty, an indication of whether or not there are regions with a strong probability that rural poverty is caused by inadequate land resources, as distinct from other possible causes, would be relevant to the choice of an appropriate planning methodology.

Table 1 applies a neo-Malthusian two-stage hypothesis to available regional data in Tanzania. This states that natural resource availability is: (i) a significant cause of inter-regional differences in income growth in the period 1966–1974; (ii) in those regions where (i) is false, future rates of income growth will be increasingly affected over time by the per capita natural resource availability. Table 1 compares changes in mean regional income per capita and changes in the rank order of

TABLE 1: DYNAMIC ANALYSIS OF REGIONAL GROWTH PERFORMANCE IN TANZANIA: PER CAPITA INCOME AND RESOURCE SCARCITY INDICES

		Growth Performance Indices			Natural Resource Scarcity Indices[4]			
		(i)	(ii)	(iii)	(iv)	(v)	(vi)	(vii)
Category	Region	Income p.c. Rank Order 1966/67	Income p.c. Rank Order 1972/74	Income p.c. Growth 1966/67–1972/74 (%)	Land Capability Grades 5 and 6 per Standard Family 1974 (ha.)	Land with Adequate Rainfall per Standard Family 1974 (ha.)	Land: Cattle Ratio 1972 (ha/beast)	Adequate Rainfall Cattle Ratio 1972 (ha/beast)
A1: *Developing Regions:*	(i) Coast	11	5=	108.2	8.0+	3.0	241.4+	30.0+
	(ii) Mbeya[1]	12	8=	118.3	18.5+	8.5+	19.4+	4.7+
	(iii) Iringa	9=	10	97.2	16.5+	18.0+	23.8+	12.9+
	(iv) Kigoma	16	12	102.3	11.3+	14.5+	46.3+	18.1+
A2: *Development Potential Regions*	(v) Tanga	1	1=	42.7	6.5	4.4+	12.8+	2.9
	(vi) Tabora[2]	4	1=	67.5	19.4+	?[3]	14.0+	?[3]
	(vii) Morogoro	5=	7	49.2	24.9+	28.4+	64.1+	40.6+
	(viii) West Lake	9=	8+	78.9	10.6+	8.4+	12.6+	5.6+
	(ix) Mtwara/Lindi	14	15=	54.0	11.1+	1.5–	919.4+	46.2+
	(x) Ruvuma	15	17	47.5	20.4+	42.6+	235.6+	142.0+
B1: *Problem Regions*	(i) Kilimanjaro	3	5=	24.9	2.4–	1.9–	5.3	1.3
	(ii) Mara	7	13	28.9	0.6–	3.0	2.8–	0.5–
B2: *Emergent Problem Regions*	(iii) Arusha	2	1=	48.2	8.8+	1.6–	3.5–	0.1–
	(iv) Shinyanga	5=	4	47.4	2.0–	0–	3.7–	0–
	(v) Mwanza	8	11	47.0	1.8–	1.2–	2.2–	0.3–
	(vi) Dodoma	13	14	53.8	6.3–	0.5–	5.3	0.1–
	(vii) Singida	17	15=	66.6	9.5+	0–	2.8–	0–

SOURCE: (a) Performance Indices: Calculated from regional income statistics, Bureau of Statistics, Dar es Salaam.
(b) Natural Resources Indices: (iv) and (v): Calculated from World Bank (1974), *Tanzania: Agricultural and Rural Development Sector Study.*
(vi) and (vii): Calculated from Agricultural Census 1971/72: Livestock Sample Census.

Notes: 1 For 1974, Mbeya includes the new region of Rukwa; this comprises Sumbawanga District which was part of Mbeya Region, and Mpanda District, formerly part of Tabora Region.
2 In 1974, Tabora was a smaller region having lost Mpanda District to Rukwa Region.
3 Map 12308R in World Bank (1977a), *Tanzania: Appraisal of the Tabora Rural Development Project* indicates approximately 80 per cent of the Region with annual rainfall in excess of 750mm, whereas World Bank (1974) *op. cit.* gives only 3 per cent of the area receiving this amount in 9 years out of 10.
4 Natural Resource Indices:

	(iv)	(v)	(vi)	(vii)
Growth potential:	>8.0ha.	>4.0ha.	>10.0ha.	>2.0ha.
Growth Constraint:	<4.0ha.	<2.0ha.	<5.0ha.	<1.0ha.

regions, on the one hand, with levels of natural resource endowment on the other. The former criteria were grouped into three classes—high, moderate and low. Four indices of natural resource endowment per family were calculated for each region. Each set of resource values has been divided into three classes on the basis of farm systems criteria, the highest class being designated by a positive sign and the lowest by a negative sign. Without deliberately intending it, when analysed in this way the regional pattern of relationships takes a strongly dichotomous form. High growth regions have good resource endowments and vice versa; moderate growth regions fall sharply into two groups, with no region having more than one natural resource sign (+ or −) opposite to the preponderant sign.[4]

TABLE 2: CLASSIFICATION OF REGIONAL GROWTH PERFORMANCE, TANZANIA

		Natural Resource Endowment		
		Poor	Moderate	Good
Economic Growth (Regional Mean Income p.c.)	Low	2.2[a] B1 27[b]		
	Moderate	1.7 B2 53		76.1 A2 57
	High			32.6 A1 107

Notes: [a]Mean class score: adequate resources (ha. per family); the mean rank order scores are as follows:
B1 : 12.0 A2 : 5.6
B2 : 13.0 A1 : 5.5
[b]Mean class score: growth rate (%); the mean rank order scores are as follows:
B1 : 16.5 B2 : 10.6
A2 : 9.5 A1 : 2.5

The differences in total income growth are very striking. The income means are expressed in terms of current prices; unfortunately deflators are not available for the rural areas. However, from 1970 to 1975 the consumer price index of all urban dwellers rose by 88 per cent (Economic Commission for Africa, 1977). The inference can safely be drawn that the two regions whose total growth over the period 1966–74 was around 25 per cent have suffered a major decline in mean real income. It could be argued that the slower rate of growth in a relatively high-income region like Kilimanjaro has led to an overall improvement in relative income distribution across the rural sector. Two comments should be made on this proposition. First, before such a conclusion can be safely drawn, the possibility must be eliminated that the relative decline in the rich region's real income has been caused predominantly by a decline in the incomes of poorer people in that region or an increase in the numbers of poorer people, i.e. people who would also be included in the lowest income groups on a national basis. Unfortunately, recent data on *intra*-regional income distribution which are reliable enough for single region analysis are not available. Nevertheless, given (i) the agricultural sector's dominance of the economies of the rural regions, (ii) the high rates of rural population growth and (iii) low adoption rates of land-intensive technology in Tanzanian agriculture, the inference can be drawn that in those regions where the mean resource availability per capita is absolutely low, a significant part of a sustained decline in mean regional income would take place through an increasing proportion of the population being in receipt of incomes markedly below the regional average, i.e. by widening income inequality, rather than by a generally shared decline in incomes. Such a rapidly growing low-income class would consist mainly of new entrants to the labour force who either inherit land areas and livestock herds of below average size or who are forced to cultivate or graze poorer quality land.[5] Conversely, it would be safe to conclude that a relative decline in mean income in a high income region has improved the national pattern of income distribution only in those cases where continued access to adequate land resources is possible. No region with these characteristics was observed over the period 1966/67–1972/74 (see Table 1). Second, planning priorities within an individual region (the main concern of this paper) should be strongly sensitive to a significant increase in the numbers of households falling below a minimum income threshold, whether a reduction in the income of wealthier groups in the region reduces the national coefficient of concentration or not. On both grounds, therefore, these absolutely low rates of growth in high income regions should be treated as a cause for concern.

Returning to the data in Table 1, although the first part of the hypothesis appears to be non-falsifiable for the regions in groups A1 and B1, the larger number of regions in groups A2 and B2, where there is no clear correlation between income growth and resource availability, would lead to its rejection at acceptable levels of significance. However, the data seem to support the common-sense view that if population growth continues, land resource availability will become a constraint in an increasing number of regions, i.e. those grouped in the B2 class are likely to join those in the B1 class. The rejection of a simple hypothesis consisting of statement (i) above on its own, would therefore be dangerously complacent with regard to the future, although statistically correct with respect to the period 1966–1974. As befits its dynamic character, the two-stage hypothesis can be verified only over time. In the meantime, the classification in Table 1 is suggestive only; it has not been statistically demonstrated. Other hypotheses need to be tested; especially the possibility that marked changes in total revenue earned from specific cash crops, with which the fortunes of many individual regions are strongly associated, account more powerfully for the observed differences in growth rates.

TABLE 3: ILLUSTRATIVE DIFFERENTIATION OF PLAN OBJECTIVES, STRATEGIES: AND PROCEDURES FOLLOWING REGIONAL CLASSIFICATION BASED ON NATURAL RESOURCE AVAILABILITY

Category	Regional Plan Objectives	Major Strategy Components	Key Planning Procedures Required
A1 Developing Regions	Maintain rate of growth; direct larger shares of the benefits to remaining poorer groups or villages	Expand present viable improvement projects. Provide additional supporting infrastructure including new settlements	Development administration (project implementation). Population absorption planning. Infrastructure planning
A2 Development Potential Regions	Raise rate of growth to potential level	Initiate new viable improvement projects in settled areas; expand settled areas on better land	Production project identification/design/appraisal. Land resource assessment. Population resettlement project design and appraisal. Tsetse clearance and control
B2 Emergent Problem Regions	Prevent worsening income distribution by assisting poorer villages/new entrants	Relocate new entrants within the region and/or assist movement to low cost resettlement projects; introduce land-intensive technology projects in settled areas	Village viability surveys, Land-intensive farm systems planning. Soil erosion protection planning. Small-scale irrigation planning. Development administration (resettlement assistance)
B1 Problem Regions	Prevent further deterioration of real incomes in general and create new employment opportunities for new entrants	Introduce viable conservation measures; provide large-scale land-intensive projects; accelerate migration outside region	Soil erosion/protection planning. Large-scale irrigation project planning. Development administration (resettlement assistance)

For analytical and planning purposes, additional data at a district or zonal level both on income distribution and on access to resources are highly desirable. These data should be gathered by the Bureau of Statistics or the Prime Minister's Office as a matter of priority. For the present, however, the regional classification in Table 1 has important implications for the kind of regional planning methodology required if it correctly identifies a serious set of problems which require attention, even if they are not the dominant ones in every region.

> "Overall, the identification of distinctive types of development zones allows government planners to deal with regional development problems as classes of problems, thereby avoiding the need to confornt each small region as a unique event" (Abler, Adams and Gould, 1971).

Regional classifications of this type are potentially useful in identifying both the range of planning tasks, with their associated procedures, which need to be carried out by regional planners and the location of development experience which may possibly be relevant to the main planning problems.

Of course, the situation in individual regions (and a *fortiori* in districts and sub-district areas) will change for a variety of reasons over time, so that even those development strategies which are currently successful will require periodic review and reformulation. Nevertheless, the classification in Table 1 suggests that certain strategy components and planning procedures should receive priority attention. Table 3 suggests a correlation between the development problems and potentials identified in Table 1 and the major component procedures of a regional planning methodology which are required to handle them.

Table 3 is illustrative rather than operational, because when planning an individual region the enlargement of scale obviously enables a more detailed identification of problems and potentials; usually a wider range of procedures should be employed in one region than is indicated in Table 3. Nevertheless, for purposes of our present discussion, Table 3 does indicate an urgent set of planning issues not usually recognised in the literature on regional planning.[6] That being the case, how far, alternatively, does regional planning experience in Tanzania itself provide an appropriate and tested methodology which will ensure that the planning procedures and skills required to deal with these issues will be available and effectively applied in practice? This question will be addressed in the next two sections of the paper.

EXPERIENCE WITH ALTERNATIVE REGIONAL PLANNING METHODOLOGIES IN TANZANIA

Regional Planning Before the Arusha Declaration

The last part of the colonial era in Tanzania was marked by an increased (albeit insufficient) emphasis on economic development, especially in the rural reas. This period may be defined as lasting from the passing in the U.K. Parliament of the Colonial Development and Welfare Act in 1944 until Independence in 1961. However, the development policies of the colonial era were carried over into the post-independence era until 1967 when the Arusha Declaration and the policy paper *Socialism and Rural Development* (Nyerere, 1967) introduced a marked change of approach. A central issue in the rural regions, of course, is the nature of the agricultural development strategy. The growth, institutional and distributional consequences of this strategy will strongly affect nearly all other characteristics of the regional economy. Agricultural planners in Tanzania were sharply divided, even before the World Bank Mission of 1960 (World Bank, 1961) supplied the conceptual labels, between the "transformation approach" and the "improvement approach" to agricultural development. The groundnuts scheme, the settlement schemes on the same sites run by the Tanganyika Agricultural Corporation (which attempted to salvage some tangible benefits from the preceding fiasco) and, in the same mould but with a Moshav flavour, the subsequent Village Settlement Agency projects were examples of the former approach. Small-holder cash crop production programmes, (with credit and farmers training), veterinary disease control (with compulsory destocking and rotational grazing elements) and soil conservation campaigns, afforestation, famine reserve plots, etc. were elements in the latter approach. From the output and efficiency standpoints much of this experience was negative, but significant lessons were obtained about important issues which are still in the forefront of agricultural and regional planning thinking and which should not have to be relearned.[7] These lessons include unresolved difficulties facing programmes for compulsory destocking, labour-intensive conservation works and the tractorised production of annual food crops in variable physical environments. On the positive side they also include the very significant growth rates obtained up to 1970 or 1971 in smallholder cash crop output and farm income in six or seven regions which, because of this growth, are now amongst the most wealthy.

Output and then efficiency were the dominant concerns of agricultural planning in the period before 1967. But turning to the equity aspect, it seems probable that in those regions where small-holder cash cropping was promoted successfully, the intra-regional income distribution has been improved. Some speculative radical analyses have argued that the initial socio-economic differentiation between farmers associated with the improvement approach would inevitably lead (or in some areas had already led) to the emergence of an exploitative 'kulak' class of wealthy farmers (e.g. Saul and Woods, 1971). The validity of this analysis appears dubious in the absence in Tanzania of a land-owning class, of a landless labouring class, of a market in land, of rural indebtedness, etc. and in the presence of appropriate divisible technology, high price elasticities of demand for increased output and open frontiers of settlement in a land-surplus economy. The fact that inequalities in farm incomes (and to a lesser degree, total income per capita, can be observed in a rural area at one point in time is an insufficient basis for drawing the conclusion that class exploitation is the main, or even an operative, cause of poverty in this situation (See Sender, 1974). Nor do these radical analyses provide any useful guidance (without much further analysis in a dynamic framework) about effective ways of tackling the causes of poverty. In any case, more severe problems of unequal distribution of incomes are raised by (i) the alternative transformation approach, where much sharper class lines are drawn between workers and management than in the self-managed small-holder system, and (ii) the gap between formal sector incomes and rural self-employed incomes as a whole (see World Bank, 1977b). In contrast, the improvement approach to agricultural development in Tanzania has had the characteristic of fulfilling both the output and equity objectives at the same time.

Three embryonic approaches to something akin to regional planning should also be noted from this period. The first was the use of Provincial and District "Teams", comprised of civil servants in the field departments, to compile capital investment programmes for their respective administrative areas. Procedures for project appraisal and selection were weak, so that the tendency was to produce mere shopping lists of desirable physical facilities. The largely negative lessons of this administrative methodology have been capably analysed by Chambers (1973). This procedure, with its heavy administrative and technical biases and its sectoral planning and output emphases, was quite different from the *intended* practice in the present decentralised regional planning structure. Nevertheless, in practice similar features tend to recur as long as an appropriate regional planning methodology has not been introduced. For example, the way in which the 1975–80 regional development plans were formulated demonstrated a large number of features in common with the earlier experience. The second relevant approach in this period was the Ten-year Sukumaland Development Scheme which ran from 1947/8 to 1957/58 (de Wilde, 1967). This was essentially an area-based natural resource development project which incorporated bush and tsetse clearance and water supply points in order to open up new land for settlement. In de Wilde's view:

> ". . . the Government was conspicuously successful in opening up new land for settlement. It has been estimated that the area occupied by the Sukuma increased from about 4,000 square miles at the beginning of World War I to some 13,000 square miles in 1957/58. Although Government-sponsored bush clearance and water development have for the most part been discontinued since the late fifties, it is noteworthy that the Sukuma have continued to push forward into new land, clearing it with their own efforts. Since 1958, for example the huge Biharamulo District to the West is being settled in this way, although admittedly the colonization is being handicapped by a rather high incidence of sleeping sickness and a dearth of water" (1967, p. 420).

The Sukumaland Development Scheme achieved population resettlement at low cost; as the quotation above indicates, when it was suspended, spontaneous migration continued but under severe handicaps.

The scheme also has negative lessons: it was suspended in the face of political opposition to its land-use regulations, prescribed livestock: land ratios and soil conservation measures. These were inflexibly designed without taking economic or social factors, or even all the relevant technical aspects, into account. Worse, these were then enforced in a punitive manner by Native Authorities without benefit of demonstration or education programmes and certainly without any popular participation in decision-making. Similar problems and solutions are in the forefront of current policy-making in at least five regions at the present time.

Thirdly, an attempt was made to disaggregate the First Five-year Plan (1964–69) to the regional level, with the objective of setting regional investment schedules which would sum to the sectoral investment targets already decided at the national level on the basis of sectoral gross incremental capital: output coefficients (United Republic of Tanzania, 1964). The exercise is strongly oriented to a top-down initiative, of course, but the crude nature of the procedures adopted made this approach more unrealistic than is usually the case. The key elements of the procedure are described in the following quotation:

> "As a first approximation to the minimum contribution to the national target increase in GDP of the various regions during the plan period it is proposed to set them the same sectoral growth rates as for the nation as a whole. This is considered feasible because on the supply side the factors of production are generally under-employed and there is considerable unutilized productive capacity in industry. Moreover in most regions the availability of suitable land does not constitute a limitation to output growth in the medium term. The regional gross product estimates for a recent year are extrapolated forward by applying to the regional sectoral aggregates the target growth rates taken from the national plan. . . .
>
> Estimates of investment needed to sustain this target expansion of regional output are calculated next. For this purpose use is made of capital co-efficients implicit in the national plan. Gross incremental capital-output ratios for each sector of activity, explicitly or implicitly stated in the national plan, are applied to the target increases in regional sectoral output that have previously been calculated, to give annual levels of investment that regions can aim at.
>
> The levels of sectoral investment calculated in this manner must necessarily be viewed as orders of magnitude since they in no way reflect actual regional productive relations or their particular factor endowments. However, it is submitted that even crude approximations are useful in providing a basis for discussion or points of departure for Regional Development Committees (or their working parties) charged with drawing up regional plans.
>
> The difficulties that will be encountered within regions in collecting data on prospective gross investment are certainly not inconsiderable. But such data can and should become available to regional planning authorities" (Karmiloff, 1965).

The first two paragraphs contain the three dubious and totally unsupported assumptions. At least the title of Karmiloff's journal article contains the word "experiment", so in Popperian mood one might conclude that the negative results of this exercise would ensure that a similar lesson need not be learned again. However, in 1975 regional food crop production "guidelines" for the period 1975–80 were laid down by the Prime Minister's Office, again on the basis of centrally determined growth rates (United Republic of Tanzania, 1974c). The regional targets for the seven categories of food were calculated so as to achieve national self-sufficiency by 1980, each region's target being directly proportional to its share of production in the single-year baseline (1975). The base-year estimates of production were even less reliable than usual (a large part of each estimate relates to unmeasured subsistence output) because the black market for food grains over much of Tanzania in the first half of the year reduced the reliability of the official estimates of the marketed surplus.[8] Even if the latter point had not applied, the exercise would have been as totally without empirical validity as the regional breakdown of sectoral target growth-rates carried out in 1964/65.

Regional Planning Since the Arusha Declaration

The policy reviews of the Arusha Declaration period placed the overt policy emphasis upon the development of the rural sector. A concomitant policy has been the gradual introduction of a decentralised approach to development planning and implementation. By "decentralisation" is meant the devolution of decision-making power from the centre to lower levels, in the political and administrative hierarchy (in effect to the rural reas), as distinct from the "disaggregation" of central plans into smaller component areas (as was attempted in 1964–65). Initially decentralisation was intended to be accomplished through (i) the transfer of powers of decision over the allocation of development expenditure and (ii) the upgrading and creation of additional senior civil service posts at the regional and district levels. In 1967 a new post of Regional Economic Secretary was created; these posts were filled initially by a small number of expatriate economists (for an assessment of their role, see Saylor and Livingstone, 1969). Much of their time between 1970 and 1974 was taken up with the administration of the Rural Development Fund which was increasingly used to provide the new ujamaa villages or groups with subsidised or free production inputs (Collins 1971, 1974). These two measures, however, represented only a minor transfer of capital and manpower from the centre to the regional level. At the same time a degree of centralisation occurred through the progressive reduction in the powers of District Councils between 1969 and 1972 and their transfer to sectoral ministries (see Jones, 1974).

The original intention when preparing the Second Five-year Plan had been to finalise the regional volume at the same time as the other three volumes. This would have enabled both the national and sectoral strategies to be framed in part from the insights and project proposals generated at the regional planning level. In the event the regional volume fell considerably behind schedule, due in part to problems in staffing a United Nations technical assistance team, and the work suffered a further major setback when the senior expatriate planner who was in charge of the regional work died. The regional volume contained (when it was published a year after the other three) the following components:

(i) a brief description of the economic structure of each region together with an outline of its development strategy (these had been compiled by *ad hoc* regional planning teams partly staffed by University of Dar es Salaam economists who assisted the Regional Economic Secretaries; see Raikes *et al.*, 1968);
(ii) crop and livestock production priorities listed for each district of each region[9]; and
(iii) a disaggregated list of national projects which were to be located in each region.

It seems that the lack of impact of regional development proposals on the national plan in 1969 is about to be repeated in the case of the Third Five-year Plan in 1977, as virtually no use has been made at the centre of the Five-year Regional Development Plans which were submitted in 1974 for the period 1975–80, and resubmitted in 1975 for the period 1976–81.

The second plan's national strategy centred on two components of relevance for regional planning (United Republic of Tanzania, 1969):

(i) a "broad development front" for rural development, based on a rapid expansion of the ujamaa villages and work groups which were to receive priority in allocation of credit, subsidised inputs and other public sector resources;
(ii) the dispersion of industrial location to nine "growth poles"—administrative and commercial centres in nine regions outside Dar es Salaam.

How adequate was this dual policy as a basis for regional development planning? Appendix I indicates that something of a plateau had been reached by 1973–74 in the creation of ujamaa villages or groups—even with the assistance of compulsory villagisation operations in the first group of regions listed in the Table. By 1974, 12 or 13 regions had fewer villages or groups than at an earlier stage.[10] This position was radically altered by the national "Operation Sogeza"—the movement of people into pre-selected villages. This was carried out largely in the first half of the financial year 1974/75. The 1974 plateau reflected in part no doubt, a standstill whilst awaiting this national exercise. Nevertheless, the financial and management problems of many registered groups had caused them to become dormant or to disappear altogether by 1974, whilst the limited planning and capital resources in the public sector meant that not all groups could receive support immediately. Some of the financial problems arose from the use of a capital-intensive agricultural production technology on ujamaa plots to produce crops such as maize which were in competition for labour with similar crops grown on the members' individual plots (see UNDP/FAO, 1976). Perhaps these problems could have been solved given time. Two other problems remain. Firstly a limitation of the ujamaa approach in isolation (which was recognised at the policy level) was that the villages' economic performance could be adversely affected by the lack of adequate supporting infrastructive (such as feeder roads and marketing facilities) in the service sectors of the rural economic system. This realisation probably reinforced the decision to decentralise the planning process. A second limitation which is less well recognised concerns the effectiveness of ujamaa in relation to the equity objective in Tanzania's rural development policy. No matter how equitably is income distributed *within* individual villages, widening economic differentiation can occur *between* villages, and between larger areal units up to districts and regions. Tackling this problem requires both the creation of opportunities for the absolutely poorer villages and an appropriate set of development policies and projects which are brought to bear at levels above the village in the rural economic system (Belshaw, 1974). On these two grounds, therefore, village-level planning is not sufficient (even if the capacity were there to plan and assist all villages) to remove poverty or to even out income distribution in the rural sector.

The other leg of the Second Five-year Plan's regional policy was decentralised industrial location. Growth pole theory itself has problems at the planning stage; in particular the fact that the criteria for the selection of industries for inclusion in growth poles are not related to specific policy objectives (Hansen, 1967). Further, the Tanzania planners do not appear to have estimated the probable scale of external economies at the selected sites with alternative ones. Indeed, with the primate city pattern in Tanzania, where the whole country serves as the hinterland of Dar es Salaam, it can be argued that for a considerable time to come only that city has the accepted characteristics of a growth pole.[11] One is left to surmise that Livingstone's statement (1969) that "the glib use of the concept of poles of growth serves only to draw attention away from a close identification of actual linkages between industries" is a reasonably accurate assessment of the planning activity in this area.[12]

The main features of the decentralisation policy (Nyerere, 1972) are well known. These were the creation of new senior posts of Development Director and Planning Officer in the regions and districts; the severance of the direct links between the executive ministries and their regional field staffs, who now came under the newly-established Prime Minister's Office;

TABLE 4: PROGRESS, MULTI-YEAR REGIONAL PLAN FORMULATION AND IMPLEMENTATION: TANZANIA END - 1977

(i) Stage	(ii) Outline Regional Plan Proposals			(iii) Partially-integrated Regional Project Proposals			(iv) Regional Integrated Plan Proposals		
A: PLAN FORMULATION									
1. Work not yet started							Mbeya	FAO[4]	
2. Work in progress				Lindi	UK	1976[3]		University of Dar es Salaam (BRALUP)	
				Mtwara	UK	1976[3]			
				Mara	IBRD[2]		Rukwa		1975
3. Proposals received	Lindi	Finnplanco for Finland Govt.	1975						
	Mtwara	Finnconsult for Finland Govt.	1975						
	Arusha	SIDA	1975[1]				Shinyanga	DHV/ILACO for Netherlands Govt	1976[7]
	Coast	CIDA	1975	Kigoma	IBRD	1974			
	Dodoma	CIDA	1975				Morogoro	Netherlands Govt.	1975[8]
	Dar es Salaam	CIDA	1975	Tabora	Brokonsult		Tanga	FRG	1976
	Singida	Indian Govt.	1975		SIDA	1975	Mwanza	SIDA for IBRD	1976[7]
	Dodoma	CIDA PPAL for CIDA	1976		for IBRD	1977	Iringa	FAO/ODG for UNDP	1976
	Ruvuma	Yugoslav Govt.	1976				Kilimanjaro	Japan Govt.	1977[6]
	W. Lake	Project team for DANIDA	1975[1]						
	Mbeya	NORAD	1976[1]						
B: PLAN IMPLEMENTATION									
1. Aid agreement negotiated				Tabora	IDA, CIDA, UK	Shs. 146m 1978–83			
2. Project execution in progress				Kigoma	IDA, UNCDF	Shs. 95m 1974–79	Tanga	FRG Shs. 180 m	1973–81
				Iringa	EEC	Shs 64m. 1977–81			

Notes: [1] Report not adopted by Regional Authorities; USAID has agreed to take over responsibility for Arusha Region.
[2] The World Bank team commenced work in October, 1977.
[3] The intention is to work up regional integrated plan proposals by 1980, derived in part from experience with implementation of individual projects in 1978 and 1979.
[4] FAO was requested to take on responsibility for Mbeya Region in 1976; funds were being sought during 1977.
[5] A long-term regional development strategy for the productive sectors was submitted in 1976.
[6] A detailed interim report was submitted in 1977.
[7] Revised proposals for a rural development project to be implemented in Mwanza and Shinyanga Regions were received from IBRD Nairobi in 1977. These were subject to the report of a Project Appraisal Mission from IBRD Washington which was being awaited at the end of 1977.
[8] Netherlands Government capital and technical assistance to Morogoro Region was being negotiated at the end of 1977.
Regions underlined are those where assistance for the integrated planning stage had yet to be secured.

and the intended transfer to the regions of the initial powers of decision-making over the allocation of up to 40 per cent of the Development Budget. The regional planning machinery embarked on the formulation of Annual Regional Plans (on a two-year rolling plan basis) from 1972/73 onwards (for the abortive 1971/72 attempt, see Jones, 1974 and Waide, 1974).

A major new task was the formulation of regional plans for the Third Five-year Plan, 1975–80; it was intended that each region would have the assistance of a technical assistance team (five expatriate planners were suggested by the Prime Minister's Office as adequate for this task). Guidelines were issued to the technical assistance agencies (United Republic of Tanzania, 1974a) and to the regional planning officials (United Republic of Tanzania, 1974c). The terms of reference for the technical assistance teams is reproduced as Appendix II of this paper. These instructions correctly emphasised that a rural-oriented planning approach should be followed, but the stages specifically mentioned consisted essentially of project identification within a sectoral planning framework, formulated at the regional level; (a set of district plans were to have been drawn up prior to this by the district planning officials, but these would also use a sectoral framework). Guidance was lacking on the procedures to be followed for integrating the sectoral plans into a multi-sectoral regional plan and for spatially-differentiated development strategies adjusted to local conditions in different parts of the region. The earliest regional proposals formulated for donor finance were prepared by a World Bank team for Kigoma Region. This had originated, in fact, in support of an earlier villagisation exercise—Operation Kigoma. It consisted of an agricultural production-cum-physical infrastructure project for new development villages, embracing 50 per cent of the regional population. The Prime Minister's Office initially advocated this as a model for other regions to follow, but this project approach was replaced elsewhere by attempts to plan the entire region, using either the recommended sectoral planning approach or procedures which would lead to a more fully integrated set of proposals.

The state of preparation of regional plan proposals by technical assistance teams at mid-1977 is shown in Table 4. Only a few of these have led to capital and technical assistance follow-up, as was the original hope when technical assistance teams were asked to assist with plan formulation. In the majority of cases, however, the proposals have been made use of, to a greater or lesser extent, in the regional five-year plan submissions. The majority of these are now deemed to be outline or interim proposals, and further donor assistance is being sought to work up more detailed Regional Integrated Development Plans (RIDEPs).

The regions are now, as it were, strung out along a track with three or four years work separating the most advanced from the least. However, the situation is less inequitable than appears at first sight. In terms of plan quality several donor teams' proposals were not acceptable to the regional planning authorities, and several that were accepted added little or nothing to existing knowledge. On the question of inter-regional capital allocation, the usual issue of "additionality" intervenes to narrow the gap between the assisted and the non-assisted regions.[13] In any case, with the recent small inflows into the regional development budgets, a major factor has been the proportion of expenditure on "national projects' (these are run directly by the central executive Ministries and capture much the greater share of foreign aid) which have been located within each region.[14]

A TWO-STAGE INTEGRATED REGIONAL PLANNING METHODOLOGY

Tanzania's regions typically show marked internal variation in their geographical characteristics—especially in altitude, rainfall, soils and vegetation. This variation in the natural environment inevitably causes heterogeneity in the land-using production activities, such as crop and animal production, which dominate the regions' economies. Similarly, areas which are similar in that they have not yet been settled and developed will possess markedly different potentials for alternative forms of development. For this reason alone, economic development plans which have been drawn up for an administrative region or district are likely to be unsatisfactory in both content and implementation. An approach which will reduce the heterogeneity within a region or district is thought likely to have considerable value in these circumstances.

This is not to suggest that circumstances planning at the regional and district levels can be superseded. At these levels, the sectoral expertise and resources of the public sector are concentrated. Horizontal coordination between these agencies may be a key prerequisite for the solution of specific rural development problems. They also represent important stages in assembling proposals and feedback information for transmission upwards to the national level; in receiving and interpreting the local significance of, policy guidelines financial and other resource allocations; and in coordinating activities within the region with national projects and programmes initiated by the central sectoral ministries.

Nevertheless, the array of sectorally-specialised agencies in the public sector leaves without a "parent" body two other areas which are of major significance for regional planning in Tanzania. The first of these, given the strong equity emphasis within rural development policy, is the identification of priority targets for the achievement of reduced inequality in the rural areas and the alteration of rural poverty generally. Real incomes reflect both levels of private consumption and access to public goods and services. No one ministry is charged with responsibility for the array of activities which together determine rural income levels. A separate trans-sectoral planning approach is required to identify target groups—most probably at the village level of aggregation initially—and to monitor and evaluate the effectiveness of the policies and projects undertaken in response to the identified problems.

The second major gap in the current government system is the absence of analysis and appropriate action which relates the functions performed by the geographical hierarchy of towns and service centres, and their connecting transport networks, to the changing needs of the local rural population. Such attention as is devoted to this area tends either to stress the interests of the urban communities or to assume that urban located initiatives are the most important. The effective delegation of development activities between the two sectors requires explicit attention within the regional planning methodology.

One integrated regional planning procedure which has been used in the formulation stage of one regional plan in Tanzania (UNDP/FAO, 1976) addresses the problem of local environmental and agricultural diversity within the administrative area framework. With over 8,500 registered villages in Tanzania, planning capability is currently inadequate to plan each individual village in detail. As an interim stage, a system of multi-village rural development areas (RDAs) is proposed. Each district would be divided into between four and eight RDAs. Within each of these RDAs a similar development strategy (usually defined in terms of the leading crop and/or livestock activities for which viable projects can be mounted) will be implemented. These RDAs will often have similar boundaries to those of agro-ecological zones, or some other method of classifying the physical environment, but the clustering of villages in this way may change over time as the development strategy itself alters. Each RDA in effect is an area-based multi-village rural development project. The sum of such area-based projects equals the exploited land area of the region. Each RDA project can be monitored and evaluated in the same way as the more traditional type of development project.

It is also proposed that the same framework is used to specify the set of poverty-focused measures; the delineation of the RDAs would itself be based on survey data indicating relative village prosperity and the crucial problems which require attention in the relevant development strategy. Finally, the integration of the services provided by the lower levels of the urban hierarchy and the associated communications network can be achieved once the major features of the rural population strategy for each RDA has been determined. Cost-saving complementarities between adjacent RDAs can be identified and secured as the proposals are assembled at the district and regional levels of planning.

In essence, this dual methodology is intended to secure the maximum advantages of both coordinated multi-sectoral planning at the regional level, and of integrated rural development planning at the local, area-based project level. If the former operates without the latter, local problems are not identified or are not accurately diagnosed and dealt with. If rural development planning operates without the vertical access to higher levels of decision-making and the comprehensive sector and a real coverage provided by the regional planning framework, a set of isolated project enclaves tends to result. These often exacerbate the problem of rural inequality rather than help alleviate it.

A REGIONAL PLANNING METHODOLOGY INCORPORATING INTEGRATED RURAL DEVELOPMENT PROCEDURES

The remainder of this paper presents an outline of a regional planning methodology (proposed for adoption in Tanzania) which incorporates integrated rural development planning as the key sub-routine.

This planning methodology is shown operating over time as a cyclical management system in Fig. 1. The central planning focus is on the rural development area. Enlarging the scale, this is shown as an interative process in Fig. 2. The full system appears complex; in practice the components can be spread out across several years with the annual plan being used to update the medium-term plan. The principle of doing first what is most urgent takes priority over attempting to plan in detail across the entire spectrum of activities.

It is essential that the planners find out what is most urgently in need of attention. Villagers or leaders will tell them their perceived priorities but these need to be checked against each other and against unperceived constraints or overlooked potentials revealed by the application of the relevant professional planning skills. These insights can in turn enter into an iterative dialogue with the regional political process (which includes the villages). The component parts of the planning methodology at the regional level are indicated in Figs. 1 and 2 by letters. Each of these is briefly described below; the accompanying procedures are not discussed partly for reasons of space, but also because the final choice of procedures will be affected by data, manpower and time constraints.

(a) *Evaluation of the Regional Development Strategy:* This is a fundamental component. The region is not an empty stage; the public sector is currently implementing a development strategy and the villages also have their own objectives and plans. Is the overall impact of these activities sufficient to remove the major problems at a reasonably satisfactory rate? If not, why is that? This analysis will probably suggest ideas to be pursued in greater detail in part B below; it should also identify unsatisfactory aspects of national policy or project selection which the region will need to discuss at the central planning level.

(b) *Resource Inventories, Sectoral Performance Audits and Project Evaluation:* These terms are self-explanatory; professional skills to carry them out will be in scarce supply, so that only the most important tasks, in terms of the probable consequences of measurement or analysis, can be tackled in the early stages. The choice of technique for resource inventories and land classification systems for regional planning is a complex issue which is discussed in detail

Fig. 1: A NETWORK DIAGRAM OF A MANAGEMENT SYSTEMS APPROACH TO NATION-WIDE REGIONAL PLANNING

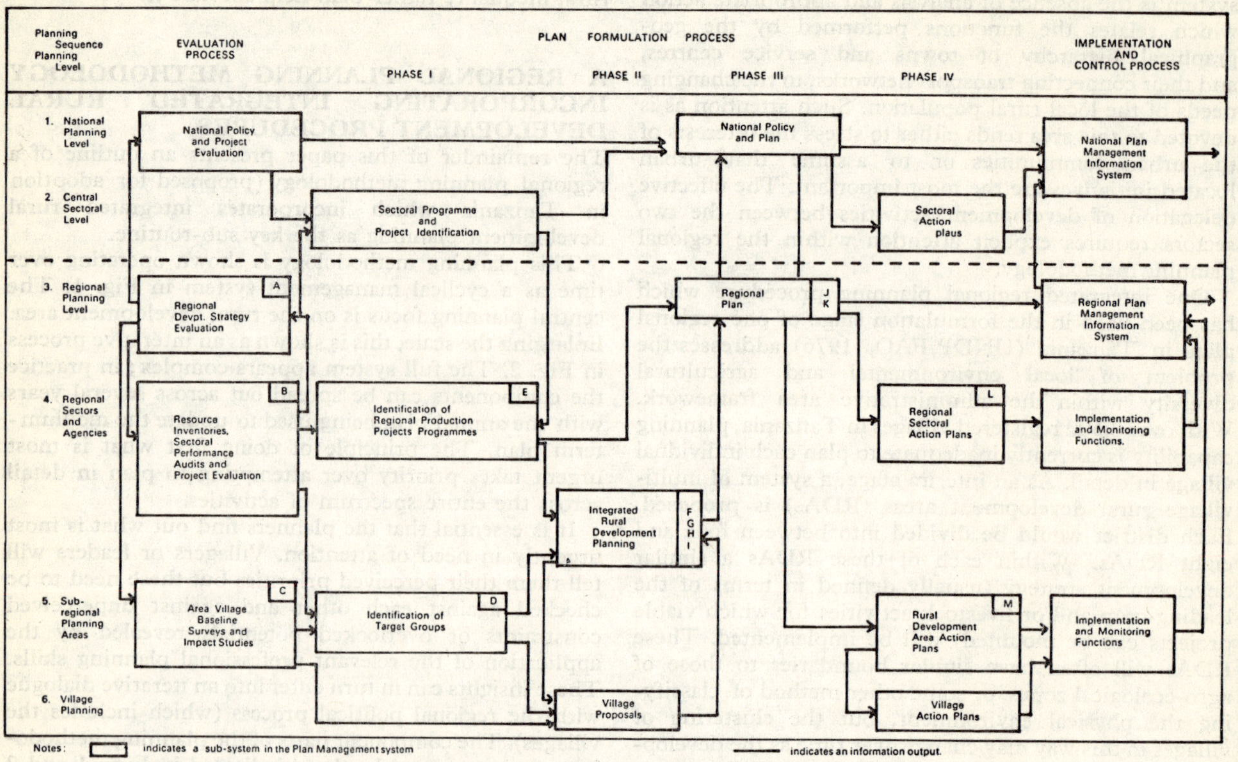

Fig. 2: AN ITERATIVE SYSTEMS MODEL OF THE REGIONAL PLAN FORMULATION PROCESS: PHASE II.

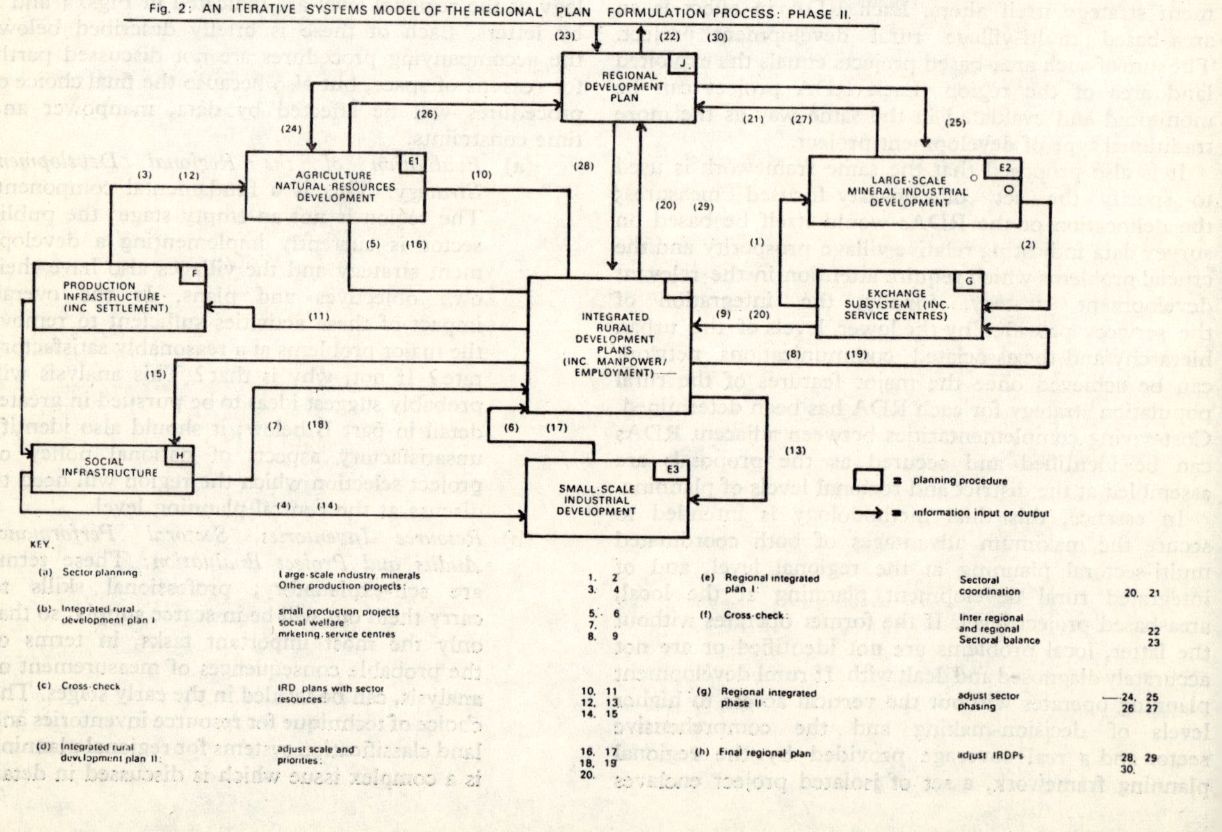

elsewhere (Belshaw and King, 1978). The critical issues, however, are to provide planners rapidly with information relating environmental potential to the choice of alternative land use systems and to avoid the acquisition of large quantities of static, descriptive information unrelated to the decision process. Some development projects worth evaluating may have been implemented at some time in the past (as was suggested in a previous section). Of the present projects, it may be that some have been wrongly selected, but equally the difficulty may either be a design fault or a management aspect which could be rectified). cheaply. Alternatively, lack of capacity in another sector, or at a higher-level in the same sector, may be limiting the effectiveness of the project under scrutiny.

(c) *Area/Village Baseline Surveys and Impact Studies:* Ideally, all villages should receive trained manpower inputs which will institute self-recording systems of economic performance. In the interim, sample surveys drawn from villages with similar development problems may be necessary. In any case, some constraints on village performance can best be studied over a wider area than the village itself (road transport efficiency, for example). A major use of this survey data is to assist in dividing each district into a small number of rural development areas (RDAs), as described above.

(d) *Identification of Target Groups:* Criteria may include family cash income levels, evidence of malnutrition, poor access to specified public facilities, etc. The focus is again upon multi-village communities or areas for which a common strategy can be designed.

(e) *Identification of Production Projects and Programmes:* The initial focus is on identifying additional income-generating activities where profitability is sufficiently attractive that the commitment of private and cooperative sector resources will be secured without difficulty. Divergencies between market and accounting prices leading to the selection of projects which are not socially profitable must be handled through decisions on pricing and other policies at levels above that of the individual region. Agricultural and natural resources projects will be the major sectors where acceptable projects can be identified, but some industrial projects may also be found which meet the planning objectives.

The next four elements are components of an integrated planning procedure which combines sectoral and spatial analyses to achieve the desired impact on the target groups in the most efficient manner. An illustrative list of sub-areas to be analysed and planned is given for each of the four sub-systems. In the proposed system this integrated planning would be carried out for each rural development area; in the interim, district planning has been a partial substitute for this.

(f) *The Production Infrastructure Sub-system:* This sub-system examines the current support infrastructure available for the identified production activities and identifies additional resources and institutional modifications or innovations which are required to relieve existing or anticipated bottlenecks. The following sub-areas are those thought most likely to be relevant in Tanzania:
- (i) Agricultural production research and development;
- (ii) Agricultural extension;
- (iii) Agricultural mechanization;
- (iv) Population settlement planning;
- (v) Irrigation works;
- (vi) Animal disease control programmes;
- (vii) Soil/water protection and erosion control;
- (viii) Industrial "site and service" schemes;
- (ix) Rural power sources;
- (x) Fisheries research and development;

(g) *The Exchange Sub-system:* The performance of the exchange system can provide a powerful explanation of poor performance on the production side of a rural economy. The most relevant sub-areas are likely to be:
- (i) Rural transport services;
- (ii) Rural network and feeder roads;
- (iii) Crop storage facilities;
- (iv) Processing and marketing facilities;
- (v) Rural service centres;
- (vi) Wholesale and retail trade facilities;
- (vii) Production input supply systems;
- (viii) Production credit and banking facilities;
- (ix) Postal services and telecommunications.

(h) *The Social Welfare Sub-system:* This sub-system has the crucial task of translating the development projects and public sector inputs into improvements in the "quality of life" especially for the poorer or more hazard-prone villages, families and individuals. These procedures amplify and differentiate many components which are not easily measurable in income or employment terms. The main sub-areas are:
- (i) Domestic water supplies;
- (ii) Health facilities and education;
- (iii) Nutritional surveillance and improvement;
- (iv) Family spacing;
- (v) Rural housing;
- (vi) Home economics education;
- (vii) Law and order maintenance;
- (viii) Social security (formal and informal);
- (ix) Cultural and religious activities.

(i) *Employment, Manpower and Training Sub-system:* This sub-system provides a summary cross-check of the adequacy of the initial set of projects and programmes to meet the demand for improved incomes and employment. It then assesses the adequacy of the educational and training programmes to meet the new opportunities. This focus would be on education systems to meet the self-reliance and rural development objectives. The initial analysis would be at the RDA level, but the major activities would probably be handled best within the regional sectoral programmes. The main areas of analysis are likely to include:

(i) Demographic projections;
(ii) Employment/income demand and supply projections;
(iii) Manpower and education planning;
(iv) Formal educational programmes;
(v) Adult education;
(vi) Informal education—farmers/fishermen, youth, etc.

The RDA proposals would be summarised both as a set of area-based projects (RDA plans) and as a cross-cutting set of regional sectoral programmes. These summaries would indicate both financial and additional high-level manpower resources required from the public sector and the self-help contributions committed by local communities.

The next two stages are concerned with obtaining consistency between the resource requirements of the RDA projects and the regional sectoral programmes on the one hand and the national sectoral programmes on the other. Regional and community financing may be available for high-priority projects not funded by central government. Element J represents the process of finally adjusting regional plan requirements against public sector resources which are allocated higher up the planning hierarchy. Element K concerns final adjustments at regional and sub-regional levels to resource allocation between projects in the light of the higher level decisions. This should be based as far as possible on participatory discussion with the leaders of the villages within each RDA.

In the final planning phase the approved regional plan should be broken down into action plans and work schedules relating to: (a) sectoral programmes affecting all or a large part of the region (element L); (b) integrated multi-sectoral projects for each RDA (element M). These programmes in turn may need to be integrated with individual village action plans as far as some components are concerned.

These action plans and work schedules should be designed to provide the management information required for the subsequent monitoring, control, evaluation and plan revision elements in the subsequent cycle of the regional plan management system (Fig. 1). The integration of specialist management functions should occur at two levels; at the regional level for inter-sectoral and inter-district coordination, and at the district for ensuring the necessary coordination within and between each RDA.

Integrated rural development planning is proposed as the central methodological component of regional planning for the nineteen rural regions. As we have seen, this incorporates procedures for planning the rural service centre network. The positioning of urban planning is assymetrical to that of rural planning in a country with Tanzania's economic structure. Urban planning needs to be developed at the national-to-regional level, rather than to be placed within the planning methodology for each region.

The point remains to be emphasised that the planning system within each rural region needs to be related to the higher-level system for inter-regional planning. This higher-level methodology should include:

(i) A procedure for determing the inter-regional allocation of scarce public sector resources, including the question of balance between regionally-executed and sectoral Ministry-executed projects;

APPENDIX I: UJAMAA VILLAGE/GROUP NUMBERS (1969-74) AND DEVELOPMENT VILLAGES (1975)

Region	Number of Ujamaa Villages or Ujamaa Groups						Number of Development Villages
	1969	1970	1971	1972	1973	1974	1975
Mtwara	264	465	748	1088	1103	1052*	773
Lindi	148	285	592	626	589*	339*	315
Iringa	60	350	651	630*	659	619*	464
Dodoma	40	75	246	299	336	354	388
Kigoma	14	34	132	129*	132	123*	193
Mara	19	174	376	376	271*	111*	303
Coast	46	56	121	185	188	238	238
Singida	12	16	201	263	263	317	258
Ruvuma	26	120	205	205	242	180*	315
Mbeya	22	91	493	713	715	534*	933
Rukwa	—	—	—	—	—	121	385
Tabora	41	52	81	148	174	156*	324
Morogoro	16	19	113	116	118	96*	397
Tanga	37	37	132	245	245	255	302
Kilimanjaro	7	9	11	24	24	14*	16
Arusha	20	25	59	92	95	110	180
Shinyanga	6	98	150	123*	108*	134*	369
Mwanza	10	28	127	211	284	153*	106
W. Lake	21	22	46	83	85	77*	72
Dar es Salaam	0	0	0	0	0	25	53
Total No. Villages/Groups	809	1956	4464	5556	5628	5008*	6944
Average Membership of Village/Group	n.a.	272	345	356	360	511	1260

SOURCE: United Republic of Tanzania (1975).
Note: *signifies a decline in the number of ujamaa villages/groups compared with any previous year.

(ii) A national land use planning/population settlement outline plan operating with a time-horizon of 15–20 years;
(iii) A national urban/marketing/communications planning system.

Any new regional planning methodology requires testing under operational conditions and subsequent modification. Those regions which have not yet received adequate donor agency planning assistance suggest themselves for this task; Mbeya Region seems especially suitable with its highly diversified conditions both within the agricultural sector (associated with an altitude range from 1500 - 10,000 ft. a.s.l.) and across the sectoral spectrum (which is broadened by the existence of sizeable coal and iron fields). The tested methodology and component procedures then require working-up into in-service training materials for the cadre of regional and district planning officers, who have yet to be equipped with relevant planning skills (Belshaw, 1976). Whatever the details of the planning methodology which is finally adopted, it is clear that the planner working at the regional level and below must have a specific amalgam of skills relevant to Tanzania's economic, social and environmental circumstances and to its chosen development goals. This practical polymath planner who is needed in Tanzania will certainly require a different training from the specialist regional planners who are currently being produced elsewhere in the world.

PROPOSED TERMS OF REFERENCE FOR PREPARING REGIONAL INTEGRATED DEVELOPMENT PLANS, UNITED REPUBLIC OF TANZANIA, 1974.

Regional integrated development planning teams will be established to study the existing rural sector position in each rural sub-sector including supporting rural institutions, the constraints currently impeding sectoral development, and the potential for each Region and to recommend appropriate development strategies and investment programmes by which this potential can be realized. The following specific aspects are required for inclusion in the plans:

1.1 To review the factor position of the Region with a view to determining development and investment opportunities in appropriate sectors.

1.2 To review the present role of each rural sub-sector: agriculture including crops, livestock, fisheries, forestry, marketing, agro-industries, small scale industries and non-agricultural commercial ventures.

1.3 To analyze the current facilities and use of modern inputs and techniques, e.g. use of improved crop seed varieties, livestock strains, fertilizers, insecticides, improved farm tools, farm mechanization, irrigation, research and extension services, fish receiving stations, boat building capacity, electricity supply, etc.

1.4 To appraise development strategy for each rural sub-sector.

1.5 To propose requirements for achieving a more productive rural sector including but not limited to the following considerations:
(i) To appropriate combination of goods and services to be produced—by whom, when, where, etc.;
(ii) An analysis of the requirements for preparing such projects e.g. feasibility studies, market surveys, etc.;
(iii) an analysis of improvements needed in the national supporting services—training, extension, resources and communication.

1.6 The plan should finally, outline a set of priorities in terms of specific investments in the Region within projected available resources. The following points would be relevant; (i) a tentative identification of key projects, (ii) an analysis of requirements for the Region with respect to planning further sectoral programmes—e.g. increase in Regional planning capacity improvements in the Regional statistical base, projected supporting staff for project preparation and implementation.

NOTES

1. An earlier version of this paper was read at the Economic Research Bureau Seminar held on Friday 19th August 1977 in the Council Room of the University of Dar es Salaam. The author is grateful for the comments of participants to the discussion at that meeting.
2. For an application of this distinction to regional planning in Tanzania, see United Republic of Tanzania, 1970. The distinction reflects the obvious differences in the policy instruments which apply at the two levels. The precise nature of these differences will be affected by the extent to which authority has been devolved from the centre to the regions.
3. In practice one unique set of regions cannot consistently fit the requirements of a multiple set of development objectives. Each different objective requires a specific set of planning criteria. Planning with one selected set of regions, therefore, amounts to much the same thing as planning with another at the plan formulation stage, i.e. the regional scheme will be efficient for some purposes but not for others. However, an administratively-defined regional system is likely to be superior to others at the plan implementation stage when the public sector's role is an important one, as public resources, information and institutional jurisdictions will be largely consistent with that system.
4. The use of the word 'system' here implies the value of conceptualising the planning process in systems analysis terms. For applications of the systems approach to regional planning, see McLoughlin (1969) and Chadwick (1971); application to rural development and agricultural planning have been made by Kulp (1970), and by Belshaw and Chambers (1975) and Belshaw *et al.* (1975) in East African situations.
5. A possible exception to this is Tabora Region, but the area with poor rainfall appears to be overestimated. The region falls into the favourably endowed class A^2, rather taking an ambivalent middle position, if allowance is made for an overestimation.

6. It is relevant to consider the effect that the dramatically higher producer prices for coffee since 1975 have had on income distribution in the coffee-growing high income regions—Kilimanjaro, Arusha and West Lake in particular. In the first two regions in mid-1977 there was a Shs. 6.00 per Kg. parchment differential between producer prices in Tanzania and Kenya (due to differences in export taxes). This coupled with the lower prices and better availability of consumer goods in Kenya, has probably created hidden employment in smuggling which has mitigated the otherwise strong tendency for the intra-regional income distribution to become more strongly concentrated. The employment benefits accruing to Tanzanians through coffee smuggling from Uganda into the third region were probably much less significant.
7. It is also clear that the problems of certain regions cannot be solved, or can be solved only at unacceptably high cost, by these regions acting alone. For example, it does not seem sensible to try to absorb the regional population growth through settlement in hazard-prone and environmentally fragile areas within Kilimanjaro Region, when in other regions it is not possible to exploit high return development projects because of a shortage of people to carry them out. Similarly, it seems irrational that the public sector should attempt to prevent the movement of people and cattle to empty areas in the south from over-populated northern regions where compulsory destocking is being applied (i.e. a diminution in the capital base in the face of rising population growth). The need for an inter-regional cooperation on these and other issues has been examined in an earlier paper (Belshaw, 1977a).
8. Popper's view that the experience of a failed development project should be carefully analysed and added to the body of knowledge in a way similar to those scientific experiments where the hypothesis is rejected appears to have much to commend it (see McGee, 1974). The acceptance of this view by government would lead to an increased awareness of the value of carefully applied analyses of rural development experience.
9. The same kind of criticism can be made of many of the key indicators proposed by the McKinsey Corporation team in 1974 (United Republic of Tanzania, 1974b). These proposals were clearly in ignorance of the reliability or existence of information at the regional level; e.g. tonnage harvested per capita of starchy roots; child mortality rates; percentage total population malnourished; cases of disease per 1000 population—malaria, bilharzia; m^3 of finished building wood produced, etc.
10. These crop priorities can be criticised on various grounds; e.g. no indication is given of the basis for their ranking; changing exogenous factors will make the ordering rapidly obsolete and the activities are not grouped by farm systems or crop sequences (for other criticisms, see Livingstone, 1973). It seems that work on the economic aspects of the crop priorities was never completed (UNDP/FAO, 1970, p. 8). Nevertheless, the crop priorities did represent a state of knowledge, unsatisfactory though it was, about agricultural possibilities which some donor agencies regional planning teams five years later would have done well to consult or, better, to have revised and improved.
11. The decline in Tabora Region might be accounted for by the loss of Mpanda District to the newly formed Rukwa Region; the declines in Mtwara, Lindi and Kigoma Regions, where together with Dodoma compulsory villagisation operations were mounted prior to the national villagisation exercise in 1974–76, could be accounted for by the deliberate creation of a smaller number of larger villages. In the other nine cases the falling off in numbers seems to represent a loss of momentum.
12. On the same issue of the need for a sense of proportion in the literal meaning, Boudeville (1963) has stated that Denmark just fulfils the minimum requirements with respect to area, population and income in order to qualify as an 'independent' region (quoted in Hansen, 1967). Yet Gapper (who also appears to be the originator of the application of Friedmann's 'corridor of development' term to the entire tract lying between Dar es Salaam and the Zambian Copper Belt) has strongly advocated the development of Mbeya as an autonomous region (1970. p. 16).
13. A confirmatory hint is contained in Waide's dismissive reference to the UNDP regional planning team which was responsible for work on industrial location, *inter alia* (1974, p. 49). Grundmann (1970) had proposed an industrial allocation procedure which took the choice of growth centres as already given, rather than relegating that fundamental set of decisions to empirical analysis.
14. That is, the tendency for funds controlled by the recipient government to be reallocated away from the region or sector where relatively high levels of donor support have been obtained.
15. The proportion of the development budget allocated to the regions rose from 7 per cent in 1972/73 to 14 per cent in 1975/76 but fell back again to 10 per cent in the 1976/77 estimates. This major short-fall from the 40 per cent target represents the combined effects of a number of factors. These include: (i) bottlenecks in regional project implementation capacity; (ii) inadequate project identification and/or design at the regional level; (iii) donor preference for large-scale national projects; and (iv) continued sectoral ministry dominance of the budgetary process.

REFERENCES

R. Abler, J. S. Adams and P. Gould, (1971), *Spatial Organisation: The Geographers' View of the World.* Englewood Cliffs/London: Prentice Hall.

D. G. R. Belshaw, (1974), Dynamic and Operational Aspects of the Equity Objective in Rural Development Planning in East Africa, in V. F. Amann (ed.), *Employment and Labour Migration in East Africa*, Kampala: Makerere University.

D. G. R. Belshaw, (1976), Training Regional and Rural Development Planners in Tanzania, Dar es Salaam, UNDP/FAO (mimeo.).

D. G. R. Belshaw, (1977a), The National and Inter-regional Policy Context of Regional—Level Planning in Tanzania, *Bureau of Resource Assessment and Land Use Planning, Joint Working Party on Regional Planning Methodologies, Working Paper* No. 4 (mimeo.).

D. G. R. Belshaw, (1977b), Rural Development Planning: Concepts and Techniques, *J. Agric. Econ.*, *25*, 3, 279–294.

D. G. R. Belshaw, (1977c), Regional Plans in Tanzania: The Planning Methodology Employed by the UNDP/FAO Planning Team in Iringa Region, 1974–75, *Bureau of Resource Assessment and Land Use Planning, Joint Working Party on Regional Planning Methodologies, Working Paper* No. 19 (mimeo.).

D. G. R. Belshaw, (1978a), Regional Plans in Tanzania: An Overview of Regional Planning Methodology and Procedures employed by Technical Assistance Teams in Tanzania, 1973–77, *Bureau of Resource Assessment and Land Use Planning, Joint Working Party on Regional Planning Methodologies, Working Paper* No. 20. (in preparation).

D. G. R. Belshaw, (1978b), Models of Regional Development and Planning: The Relevance of the International Literature to Regional Planning in Agraman LDCs,

Bureau of Resource Assessment and Land Use Planning, Joint Working Party on Regional Planning Methodologies, Working Paper No. 15 (in preparation).

D. G. R. Belshaw and R. Chambers, (1973), A Management Systems Approach to Rural Development Planning, *Institute for Development Studies, University of Nairobi, Discussion Paper* No. 161.

D. G. R. Belshaw, T. J. Bjorlo and M. M. Shah, (1975), A Hierarchical Systems Formulation of the Rural Development Process, *Automatica*, 11, 401–408.

D. G. R. Belshaw and R. B. King, (1978), Improved Environmental Data Systems for Regional Planning in Tanzania, *Bureau of Resource Assessment and Land Use Planning, Joint Working Party on Regional Planning Methodologies, Working Paper* No. 12 (mimeo).

J. R. Boudeville, (1963), *Les Programmes Économiques*, Paris.

Capital Development Authority, (1976), *National Capital Master Plan, Dodoma, Tanzania: Vol. 6, Regional Impact Plan*, Toronto: PPAL.

Robert Chambers, (1973), Planning for Rural Areas in East Africa: Experience and Prescriptions, in D. K. Leonard (ed.) *Rural Administration in Kenya*, Nairobi, East African Literature Bureau.

G. Chadwick, (1971), *A Systems View of Planning: Towards a Theory of the Urban and Regional Planning Process*, Oxford, Pergamon.

H. Chenery, J. Duloy and R. Jolly (eds.), (1974), *Redistribution with Growth*. London: Oxford University Press.

P. D. Collins, (1971), Politics, Policies and Local Administration for Development in Tanzania: The Case of the Rural Development Fund, (D. Phil. Thesis), Brighton, University of Sussex.

P. Collins, (1974), The Working of Tanzania's Rural Development Fund: A Problem in Decentralisation, in A. H. Rweyemamu and B. U. Mwansasu (eds.), *Planning in Tanzania: Background to Decentralisation*, Nairobi, East African Literature Bureau.

Economic Commission for Africa, (1977), Economic Survey and Biennial Review and Appraisal of Tanzania, 1976. Addis Ababa (mimeo.).

FAO, (1977), Expert Consultants on Policies and Institutions for Integrated Rural Developments, 2 Vols. (Ed. by M. A. Zaman).

K. H. Friedrich, (1976), FAO/IBRD Cooperative Research Project: Raising the Productivity of Small Farms in Tanzania Case Study: Interim Report, Rome, FAO.

G. Gappert, (1970), Regional Development, Economic Planning and Agro-urban Balance, Seminar on Changes in Tanzanian Rural Society and their Relevance for Development Planning. Leiden: Afrika Studiecentrum, University of Leiden.

H. E. Grundmann, (1970), A Framework for Regional Allocation of Industries, *Economic Research Bureau, University of Dar es Salaam, Paper* 70.17. (mimeo.).

N. M. Hansen, (1967), Development Pole Theory in a Regional Context, *Kyklos*, 20; reproduced in H. W. Richardson (ed.) (1970) *Regional Economics, A Reader*. London, MacMillan.

International Labour Office, (1976), *Employment, Growth and Basic Needs: A One World Problem*, Geneva, World Employment Programme.

D. B. Jones, (1974), Rural and Regional Planning in Tanzania, in A. H. Rweyemamu and B. U. Mwansasu (eds.), *Planning in Tanzania: Background to Decentralisation*. Nairobi: East African Literature Bureau.

G. Karmiloff, (1965), Regional Plan Implementation: Tanzania's Experiment, *E. Afr. Econ. Rev.*, 1, 2, 85–93.

E. M. Kulp, (1970), *Rural Development Planning: Systems Analysis and Working Method*, New York, Praeger.

I. Livingstone, (1969), Socialist Planning in Tanzania: The Second Five Year Plan, *Economic Research Bureau, University of Dar es Salaam, Paper* 69.13.

I. Livingstone, (1973), Some Requirements for Agricultural Planning in Tanzania, in V. F. Amann (ed.), *Agricultural Policy Issues in East Africa*, Kampala, Makerere University.

B. M. McGee, (1974), *Popper*, London, Fontana (Modern Masters Series).

J. B. McLoughlin, (1969), *Urban and Regional Planning: A Systems Approach*, London, Faber.

J. K. Nyerere, (1967), *Socialism and Rural Development*, Dar es Salaam, Government Printer.

J. K. Nyerere, (1972), *Decentralisation*, Dar es Salaam, Government Printer.

P. Raikes, P. Lawrence, D. Warner and G. Saylor, (1968), Regional Planning in Tanzania: An Economic View from the Field, *Economic Research Bureau, University of Dar es Salaam, Paper* 68.29.

J. S. Saul and R. Woods, (1971), African Peasantries, in T. Shanin (ed.), *Peasants and Peasant Societies*, Harmondsworth, Penguin.

G. Saylor and I. Livingstone, (1969), Regional Planning in Tanzania, *Economic Research Bureau, University of Dar es Salaam, Paper* 69.25 (mimeo.).

J. Sender, (1974), Some Preliminary Notes on the Political Economy of Rural Development in Tanzania based on a Case-study in the Western Usambaras, *Economic Research Bureau, University of Dar es Salaam, Paper* 74.5.

UNDP/FAO, (1970), *Regional Economic Planning: Report to the Government of Tanzania*, (No. TA 2877), Rome.

UNDP/FAO, (1976), *Iringa Region, Tanzania: Integrated Rural Development Proposals for the Third Five-year Development Plan 1976/77–1980/81*, 2 Vols. Norwich, Overseas Development Group, (ed., D. G. R. Belshaw).

W. Scott with H. Argalias and D. V. McGranahan, (1973), *The Measurement of Real Progress at the Local Level: Examples from the Literature and a Pilot Study*, Geneva, United Nations Research Institute for Social Development.

United Republic of Tanzania, (1964), Guide for the Preparation of Five-year Plans. Dar es Salaam, Ministry of Development Planning (mimeo.).

United Republic of Tanzania, (1969), *Tanzania Second Five-year Plan for Economic and Social Development 1st July, 1969–30th June, 1974, Vol. I: General Analysis*, Dar es Salaam, Government Printer.

United Republic of Tanzania, (1970), *Tanzania Second Five-year Plan for Economic and Social Development 1st July 1969–30th June, 1974. Vol. III: Regional Perspectives*, Dar es Salaam, Government Printer.

United Republic of Tanzania, (1972), *1969 Household Budget Survey, Vol. I, Income and Consumption*, Dar es Salaam, Bureau of Statistics.

United Republic of Tanzania, (1974a), Guidelines on Technical Assistance for Increasing Planning and Control Capacity of Regions, Dar es Salaam, Prime Minister's Office (mimeo.).

United Republic of Tanzania, (1974b), Provisional Key Indicator Reports on Five Year Plan Development Levels: Revised Version, Dar es Salaam, Prime Ministers Office (mimeo.).

United Republic of Tanzania, (1974c), Guidelines for Third Five-Year Development Plan, (1975/76–1979/80), and Annual Plan for 1975/76, Dodoma, Prime Minister's Office (mimeo.).

United Republic of Tanzania, (1975), *Maendeleo ya Vijiji*, Dodoma, Prime Minister's Office.

United Republic of Tanzania, (1977), Report on the Listing Exercise 1975/76 for the National Household Budget Survey 1976/77, Dar es Salaam, Bureau of Statistics (mimeo.), (in preparation).

M. Upton, (1974), *Farm Management in Africa*, London, Oxford University Press.

E. B. Waide, (1974), Planning and Annual Planning as an Administrative Process, in A. H. Rweyemamu and B. U.

Mwansasu (eds.), *Planning in Tanzania: Background to Decentralisation*, Nairobi, East African Literature Bureau.
J. de Wilde, (1967), *Experiments with Agricultural Development in Tropical Africa, Vol. II: The Case Studies*, Baltimore, Johns Hopkins for the World Bank.
World Bank, (1961), *The Economic Development of Tanganyika*, Baltimore, Johns Hopkins for the World Bank.
World Bank, (1974), *Tanzania: Agricultural and Rural Development Sector Study*, 3 Vols., Washington D.C.
World Bank, (1977a), *Tanzania: Appraisal of the Tabora Rural Development Project*, Washington D.C.
World Bank, (1977b), *Tanzania: Basic Economic Report. Annex III: Labour Market Allocation and Income Distribution*, Washington D.C. (Confidential), (prepared by P. Collier).
World Bank, (1977c), *Tanzania Basic Economic Report. Annex III: Appropriate Technologies in Tanzanian Agriculture: Some Empirical and Policy Considerations*, Washington, D.C. (Confidential), (prepared by I. Singh).

Section III

Industrial Development

INTRODUCTION

The postcolonial structure of the Tanzanian economy is largely characterised by dependency and underdevelopment in the sense that the economy is not capable of generating a self-sustaining development process without an excessive reliance on foreign imports and technologies. Neither is it able to achieve a reasonable balance in the structure and patterns of production and consumption. Thus, the post-Arusha development strategy must be viewed as directed toward the expansion of the economy's productive capabilities as well as the transformation of the entire economic structure.

In the first reading, Rweyemamu traces the historical process of industrialization in Tanzania and examines the structural characteristics of Tanzania's industries inherited from colonisation. As such, Rweyemamu's paper is of great instructive value to understanding the background and logic of Tanzania's basic industrial strategy in the post-Arusha period. Among other things this strategy calls for the establishment and expansion of basic need-oriented, capital and intermediate goods industries. It is evident that Tanzania requires heavy industries and substantial capital investments to achieve this goal.

At the same time, rural based small scale industries that use local resources and the minimum of capital must also be stimulated and encouraged. Such local industries, provided they are efficient and productive in the sense that they generate a surplus, are consistent with the philosophy of *Ujamaa* and self-reliance. In this context, David Phillips analyses the critical role of small-scale industries in Tanzania, and outlines some of the possibilities and prospects for developing such industries.

The remaining Readings relate to two important industrial policy issues that are particularly relevant to the present Tanzanian situation. First, price control is recognized to be a most potent and important policy tool in a planned economy. Rice's article is concerned with the equity and efficiency aspects of the price-setting policies in Tanzania. The paper critically evaluates current procedures for price control and suggests alternatives for a revision of the price-setting mechanism. In the final selection, Wangwe addresses the problem of capacity underutilization in Tanzanian industry. Using his own survey data, the author looks into various factors responsible for underutilization from the standpoint of both supply and demand. The problem of idle capacity is related to the structural weakness inherent in the Tanzanian type of a "dependent" economy. This problem has received special attention in the Third Five-Year Plan.

The Historical and Institutional Setting of Tanzanian Industry*

J. F. RWEYEMAMU

Introduction

This article presents a descriptive examination of the pattern and course of industrial development in Tanzania in a historical perspective. In particular, the causes of slow industrial development in the period before Independence, and the circumstances which have contributed to more rapid industrialization thereafter, are explored. The final section uses cross-section data to provide general information on certain aspects of Tanzanian industry—cost structure, inter-industry and sectoral linkages, efficiency and factor productivity—and concludes with a brief examination of industrial location.

THE HISTORICAL SETTING

Industrial development on any significant scale is of very recent origin in Tanzania. As indicated in an earlier paper, there existed during the precolonial period such "cottage" industries as weaving, blacksmithing, pottery and woodworking.[1] Many of these crafts, however, did not survive the competition of imports and colonial regulation. Manufacturing establishments were few before 1946, for a variety of reasons. The urban population was very small, most needs were met by imports from Kenya and export processing—because of the change in colonial administration—was still embryonic. This picture, however, altered significantly between 1946 and 1965. Of the 569 manufacturing establishments employing 10 or more persons in 1965, only 18 per cent were established before 1946. Almost half of the total establishments (48 per cent) were set up between 1946 and 1960, and over one-third of the total appeared during the four years after Independence.[2] This indicates an acceleration of industrial development in the post-war period generally, with a higher rate of growth in the number of manufacturing establishments in the post-Independence period. Part of this inquiry will endeavour to unravel the causes and "sources" of this growth.

It should also be noted that prior to 1946 about 50 per cent of the manufacturing establishments were involved in sisal decortication and cotton ginning and cleaning. This means that at least half of the industrial activities in this period were export-oriented. Of the remainder, 30 per cent of the manufacturing establishments were concentrated in food processing, beverages and repairs of transport equipment. In the post-war period, on the other hand, there has been a proliferation of new industrial activities such as paper, printing and publishing, rubber products, chemicals and chemical products, clothing and footwear; the two-digit ISIC classification conceals the diversity of new products that have recently been introduced.[3] A noticeable feature of this post-war industrial development is the emergence of import substitution activities not only for final consumption goods but also for certain intermediate products.

Unfortunately, no value added data exist for manufacturing establishments by industrial activity over the period. There is reason to believe, however, that the relatively large establishments were set up in the post-war period, and especially in the post-Independence period. This observation is indirectly supported by the importance of foreign interests in the newer establishments,[4] since foreign owned plants tend to be relatively large-scale. The predominance of foreign ownership in most of the newer activities noted above is, of course, not surprising as many of these industries are generally capital-intensive. It is also interesting to note that foreign ownership is dominant in some of those industries with relatively high growth elasticities as compared to average manufacturing.[5]

Despite the growth in the number and size of manufacturing establishments in the post-war period, industrial output in Tanzania was relatively low at Independence. The share of industrial output in total production was significantly below the expected "normal pattern", given Tanzania's population and national income levels.[6] In 1966, the actual share of industrial output in total production was 6.6 per cent compared to an "expected" share of 10 per cent. It is appropriate therefore to examine the causes of the deviation from this "norm", although it should be emphasised that Chenery's "norm" is merely descriptive and implies no normative interpretation.[7]

As is now well-documented, industrialization in underdeveloped economies may emerge from (1) any lasting external disequilibrium that disrupts the balance between demand and production (wars, depressions, chronic balance of payments deficits, etc.), (2) export growth leading to an expansion of the domestic market, (3) deliberate official development policy, and (4) the gradual processing of traditional exports into "higher forms".[8]

In the Tanzanian context, wars, depressions and balance of payments deficit have played a minor role in inducing industrial development. It is true, of course, that the First World War brought a short burst to activity when the attempt was made to make the country economically self-sufficient. The produc-

*Excerpted from ERB Paper 71.6. For a discussion of the sources of data, see the Appendices of the original paper. The original paper is also incorporated in J. F. Rweyemamu, *Underdevelopment and Industrialisation in Tanzania: A Study of Perverse Capitalist Industrial Development*, (Nairobi: Oxford University Press, 1973); see especially Chapter 4.

tion of articles which had become scarce owing to the allied blockade was improvised and considerable ingenuity was shown in producing manufactured goods and medical supplies normally imported from Europe. However, these activities were abandoned after the war, domestic production being replaced by imports.[9] There was industrial development during the interwar period, even during the depression This was due to several interrelated factors. Foreign investments tended to flow to Kenya rather than Tanzania. The British settlers in Kenya were a well-established pressure group in London while Tanzania's settlers were of mixed nationalities, without a cohesive force. Tanzania was merely a conquered territory with less value to Britain since her economy had been partly moulded to suit the needs of the German market. Thus, because of the uncertainty of the status of the country (especially after Hitler came to power and threatened to reconquer Germany's lost colonies), the colonial administration's pessimism about the viability of investment opportunities and the centripetal pressures converging on Kenya (to which the common market arrangements gave full play), industries tended to be established in Kenya.

The adoption of a common external tariff with the other East African territories (a tariff structure which was conceived in the interests of Kenyan industrialists) and the elimination of all trade barriers among the partner states not only deprived Tanzania of a significant amount of customs revenue but also, by protecting Kenya's industries, forestalled for a considerable period their establishment in Tanzania. These factors explain the relative industrial stagnation of Tanzania during the depression and the Second World War when considerable industrialisation was taking place in Kenya, Rhodesia, South Africa and various Latin American countries.[10] Frank's hypothesis that "satellites experience their greatest economic development and especially their most classically capitalist industrial development if and when their ties to their metropolis are weakest",[11] must be qualified when there is a neighbouring "periphery-centre". The "spread effects" of an industrialising Kenya to her less developed neighbours tended to strengthen the "satellite-periphery-centre" relationship. Kenya's industrial growth was strengthened by her free access to Tanzania's primary produce and to the Tanzanian market for her manufactured goods—a fact that is revealed in the structure of their inter-country trade. Some of these problems were pointed out at the time the common market arrangements were being set up. In 1924, for example, the Treasurer and Comptroller of Customs in Tanganyika officially, "advised against a customs union on the ground that it would make this country a commercial satellite of Kenya, and subordinate Tanganyika to Kenyan influence."[12] However, because of the strong political power of the Kenyan interests in the United Kingdom, the British Secretary of State for the Colonies directed that the institution of a customs union should no longer be delayed, and in 1927 the articles were brought into force. There has been a continuing debate on the detrimental effects of the *colonial-based* common market arrangements on Tanzania's industrialisation.[13] It is sufficient, here, to note that regardless of whatever other benefits the common market arrangements may have generated to Tanzania, they contributed relatively little to her industrial development in the colonial period.

After the Second World War, there was an upsurge of export earnings caused by post-war shortages of raw materials, the devaluation of the pound sterling and materials shortages resulting from the Korean War. The earlier post-war industries to be established in Tanzania were supply-based and were prompted by shortages of certain products in the sterling block. There followed a number of demand-based industries. However, this increase in industrial activity in the early 1950s began to subside towards the end of the decade because of worsening terms of trade.

Data on inter-East African trade in 1954, 1960 and 1966 display significant changes, which inevitably reflect shifts in industrial structure (and protectionist policies) over the period.[14] 1954 is the base for the comparison because it was the first year in which the SITC classification system was adopted by the East African Customs and Excise. The "satellite" status of Tanzania is shown by the fact that in 1954 food, crude materials and animal vegetable oils (SITC 0, 2 and 4) accounted for 80 per cent of her exports to Kenya and Uganda, while beverages, tobacco and manufactures (SITC 1, 6–8) accounted for 60 per cent of her imports from the rest of the region. By 1960, this pattern had not changed substantially; the decline in the share of beverages and tobacco imports was offset by the increased share of manufactured imports (SITC 6–8) from 12 per cent in 1954 to nearly 36 per cent in 1960, reflecting the diversification of the industrial base in Kenya and Uganda. Tanzania's manufactured exports, on the other hand, grew from 3 per cent to 9 per cent of total exports to the rest of the region in the same period—a rapid growth rate but on a very slender base.

By 1964, the imbalance in trade and industrial structure in the region had reached a point where Tanzania's deficit, especially with Kenya, was rising to significant proportions.[15] Tanzania initiated negotiations with her East African neighbours (after Kenya became independent at the end of 1963) with a view to redressing the trade imbalances. These difficult negotiations culminated in the Kampala Agreement, which urged, among other things, (a) a shifting of the productive facilities or capacities in certain industries (cigarettes, footwear, beer, cement) in such a way as to increase production capacity in deficit countries, thereby reducing their imports from the surplus countries and (b) intra-regional allocation of major new industries including aluminium, bicycle manufacture, electric light bulbs, radio assembly, nitrogenous fertilizers and motor vehicle tyres. It was agreed that these would be distributed under the Territorial Industrial Licensing Ordinance on the basis of an exclusive license to a firm basing operations throughout the region. Tanzania was allocated the manufacture of aluminium sheets and foil, tyres and tubes, and radio assembly and parts production. Although the Kampala Agreement was not ratified by Kenya, it was effective in inducing the setting up of certain industries in Tanzania.

Partly because of the Kampala Agreement, partly because of other government measures taken to quicken the industrial tempo, and partly because of foreign investors' motivations to invest (which received a new impetus after Independence), Tanzania's industrial growth accelerated between 1961 and 1966. This, again, can be seen in the changes in inter-East African trade patterns between 1960 and 1966. By 1966, manufactured goods accounted for 47 per cent of Tanzania's exports and 48 per cent of imports, a situation which compares very favourably with the developments in the 1950s noted above.[16]

From the above analysis, an important conclusion emerges. The low industrial level of the economy in relation to the expected "normal pattern" may be largely explained by the "satellite" status of Tanzania vis-a-vis Kenya's "peripheral-center" position, although the lack of an indigenous capitalist class to champion industrialization also played an important role. It is possible to argue that the high rates of industrial growth experienced in the post-Independence period[17] may be interpreted as an adjustment to the disequilibrium in Tanzania's productive structure caused by her relationship with Kenya and Britain. If this is so, then Tanzania's industrial growth may be expected to slow down considerably after approaching her "normal pattern", unless the new opportunities of investment planning acquired after nationalization enable her to sustain the present tempo. These conclusions, however, fail to take full account of the part played by foreign companies' motivations to invest, especially after Independence—a consideration to which the analysis now turns.

THE INVESTMENT PATTERN IN THE POST-INDEPENDENCE PERIOD

It is often said that investment decisions are largely influenced by the extent of the market. However, in the case of Tanzania, there is evidence to indicate that, in a number of industries, there has been a considerable lag between the attainment of technological thresholds—indicated by the volume of imports[18]—and the establishment of import substituting industries.[19] For example, although textile imports had accounted for a substantial proportion of total imports since the early days of colonial rule, (textile and clothing accounted for 52 per cent in 1897), the first textile mill was established only after Independence; between 1961 and 1968 five textile plants were established. The textile market attained the technological threshold well before the 1940's; the first textile mill's capacity was 8 million square yards, whilst imports of cotton piece goods amounted to nearly 38 million square yards in 1942 and 52.6 million square yards by 1959.[20] The data also suggest that when "delayed" investments have finally been made, they have been followed by a cluster of investments in the industry.[21]

It appears that the major part of the industrialization that has taken place, though influenced by the size of the market,[22] has been induced by the change in government that took place when political power was transferred from Britain to the people of Tanzania. Certainly the import substitution that has taken place during the post-Independence period has been largely carried out by the former foreign suppliers and has been brought about by both deliberate government policy and the suppliers' eagerness to protect their stake in their former export market. These factors were largely complementary. Unlike the colonial government, which hoped that industry would seek the country "naturally when it sees, through the growth of purchasing power of our people, an expanding market which will assure it a reasonable prospect of profitable operation,"[23] the newly independent government went out of its way to attract new industrial investments by designing a tariff and tax incentive structure, publicizing existing investment opportunities, guaranteeing foreign investors against nationalization, establishing industrial estates, etc. As noted above, the country's trade deficits with Kenya and Uganda were instrumental in the government's efforts to shift industry to Tanzania. On the supply side, the former suppliers' fears of losing their market as a result of expected changes in the pattern of trading partners after Independence, rises in protective duties and competitors' moves into the market, provides the major motivation for moving into domestic production and largely explains the increase in industrial activity in this period.[24] However, there have also been some cases in which gaining a foothold in a new market, or moving into manufacture at the source of supply of the raw materials (thus "protecting" the supply and averting possible competitors' moves), have been the significant motivations of international firms.

The available information on the sequence of Tanzanian industrialization indicates (though it does not prove) the significance of these factors. The textile industry was long delayed—as noted above—because of the absence of any threat to the existing suppliers. After Independence, however, the traditional suppliers feared the invasion of their markets from new sources (USA, China etc.). As a result, Tasini Textiles was set up in 1961 and a cluster of investments in the industry followed in the period after Independence—Mwanza Textile Mill and the Chinese-built Friendship Textile Mill in 1966, and Kilimanjaro Textiles in 1967.[25] A number of smaller manufacturing establishments were set up by local Indian entrepreneurs who were former textile importers. The case of radio assembly also provides some empirical evidence for the "threat to the market" hypothesis.[26] The Netherlands had maintained a fairly stable, major share of wireless sets imports between 1958 and 1962. (Phillips Industries account for over 90 per cent of Dutch sales). However, Japan overtook the Netherlands by a substantial margin in 1963 and increased her lead in the following year, due probably to the relatively low prices of her imports and the aggressive marketing strategies of the Matsushita Electric Company. Between 1958 and 1964, Japan's share in the Tanzanian market rose from 1.4 per cent to 60 per cent. The Netherland's share fell from its peak level in 1962 (58 per cent) to only 21 per cent in 1964.[27] Although the Kampala Agreement allocated "wireless receiving sets and components thereof" to Tanzania, there is—given the short time interval between the government's initiative to set up the plant and its establishment—a *prima facie* case for believing that Phillips Industries had already decided to build the plant in order to avert the loss of the market to the Japanese. Phillips formed Phillips Electronics (EA) Ltd. which, with a 50 per cent tariff protection, was able to break down Japanese competition. The Matsushita Electric Company, having lost its radio market, immediately set up a battery factory in Dar es Salaam.

Supply based industrialization has taken place in meat and meat preparations, pyrethrum extract, wattle extract, meerschaum pipes, cashewnut processing, cordage, rope and twine, coffee, tea and diamonds. The case of cordage, rope and twine is particularly instructive. Fearing competition from a local manufacturer and wishing to be closer to the supply source, British Ropes Limited (which controlled 80 per cent of the British sisal twine market and was previously a buyer of more than 35 per cent of Tanzania's sisal output) established Craven & Speeding in 1964 just before Noorani (an Indian sisal plantation owner) was able to install his plant. Immediately, the Tanganyika Sisal Spinning Company (owned by a consortium of predominantly West German interests) joined production and, in 1966, the largest and youngest rope factory—one of three ventures of the Tanganyika Industrial Corporation—began operating in Tanga.[28] It is interesting to note that in 1930s the Tanganyika Cordage Company was formed at Tanga but, when it began exporting its products to the United Kingdom, a strong representation to the British government was made by the British Rope, Twine and Net Makers Federation to the effect that "their home market (was) being menaced by the sale here by the Tanganyika Cordage Company of binder twine produced by the low-paid African labour in Tanganyika." A 100 per cent *ad valorem* duty was imposed on binder twine imported from Tanganyika and the factory was closed down in the following year. When British Ropes Ltd. came to Tanzania to establish a subsidiary in 1964, it enjoyed tariff protection of 15 per cent.

An example of an international firm wishing to gain a foothold in a new market is provided by the case of the Italian government firm, ENI, which has built several oil refineries in various parts of Africa, thus effectively breaking the monopolistic position of the big British and American companies. Consolidated Petroleum Company, a consortium of Shell, British Petroleum, Caltex and another American company, had built a two million ton capacity refinery at Mombasa in 1964, which may have satisfied a greater part of East African needs for some time. However, by building a refinery (TIPER) at Dar es Salaam, ENI gained a foothold in Tanzania which also gave it the opportunity to build a pipeline to Zambia, with plans to build a refinery there.

Before concluding this section, an additional factor which has played a role in inducing industrial investment should be noted. This is the desire, on the part of some foreign investors, to dispose of machinery and equipment. An example of this motivation, in the case of an import-substitution industry, is provided by the Amenital Holding Registered Trust's participation in the Mwanza Textile Mill. It is likely that the motive for Amenital's participation (which probably explains its meagre share capital participation) was to dispose of Société-Alsacienne des Constructions Mecaniques de Mulhause's machinery. The terms of the machinery's provision suggest that profits may have accrued through overpricing.[29] In the export-processing field, a similar motivation is illustrated in the case of Tanita, a cashewnut processing plant, although in this case machinery was new and Tanita was the first large-scale mechanized plant for cashewnut processing in the world. The developers of the new plant, the Italian firm Ottremare, took a 31 per cent participation, over half of which was know-how.[30]

As is evident from the above discussion of investment motivations, tariff protection played an important role in the realization of industrial investment opportunities in Tanzania. This historical review will conclude with a discussion of the nature, mode and effects of tariff protection in the post-Independence period.

INCENTIVE STRUCTURE AND PERFORMANCE

It has already been noted that foreign suppliers' motivations to invest in import-replacing industries indicate a fear of being pushed out of their export market by competing exporters, external restrictions, or competitors moving in to create a monopolistic or oligopolistic situation by local manufacturing behind tariff barriers. In this case, as in the case of firms wishing to gain a foothold in the market for the first time, the competition-restricting effect of a tariff is a factor of central importance. For the price of an industrial investment, including the risk of its possible failure, a seller can transform the competitive market he currently faces into a monopolistic (or at least oligopolistic) market. In consequence of the restriction of competition, a firm will be able to expand its total sales, and increase net earnings by an even greater amount as a result of a tariff-enhanced anti-profit margin. Not only does the tariff secure the industrialist against the competition of similar products, but it also shields him, to a substantial degree, from more technically advanced products which, in the absence of fiscal discrimination, might pre-empt the market.

There is little doubt that the import-substitution industrialisation which has taken place in Tanzania has been conditional on the establishment of an "adequate" protective tariff structure. The available information shows several obvious cases of the simultaneous establishment of industrial projects with the granting of tariff protection.[31] This suggests that protective tariffs have not been set by the government on its own initiative but rather by a process of negotiation between government and investors. Indeed, from accounts given by the officials of the Ministry of Commerce and Industry who deal with these issues, the initiative has come from the investors who submitted requests for tariff protection (and in some cases for duty relief on imported raw materials, component parts or machinery), supported by accompanying investment proposals and sets of cost estimates. Because of the officials' lack of knowledge, investors have invariably managed to obtain "sufficient" (sometimes more than sufficient) protection.

The important problem here is to try to assess the gains to the economy as a result of granting such protection. To discuss this issue meaningfully, it is necessary to examine briefly the concept of "effective protection". It will then be possible to discuss the significance of the levels of protection afforded to different industries. Recent studies on tariff protection have concluded that nominal tariff rates on the prices of imported final products are inadequate and often misleading indicators of the protection afforded to domestic producers.[32] Firstly, tariffs on imported inputs used in an industry should also be taken into account, as a tariff on an industry's input will raise the costs of production and therefore reduce the protection received by the domestic producer. Secondly, it is argued that protection should be measured in relation to value added in an industry and not in relation to the total value of production. This is because from the point of view of (static) efficient resource allocation, it is the scarce factors (skilled labour and capital) which should be offered protection, particularly if it is assumed that the supply of other inputs (raw materials, etc.) is highly elastic. Under certain assumptions (which are not too unreasonable in the Tanzanian context) it is shown that the "effective rate of protection" is the percentage increase in value added made possible by the tariff structure, relative to the situation where tariffs are absent, but the same exchange rate obtains. An industry's rate of "effective protection" will be high if its own rate of tariff protection is high, if the rates of tariff protection of its supplying industries are low, and/or, if its share of value added in total output is small.

Kessel, using Kenyan input-output data taken from the 1963 census of industrial production and Tanzania's tariff structure in 1966, computed the "effective protection" rates of a significant proportion of Tanzania's industries in 1966.[33] His use of Kenyan input-output data was due to the unavailability of sufficiently detailed data on Tanzania. As these data are still unavailable, Kessel's results will be outlined here. The use of his results may be justified for the following reasons: (a) the computed value added in those Tanzanian industries for which data has been collected are close to those used by Kessel; and (b) the connectedness of the industrial structures of Kenya and Tanzania makes it possible to assume (in using Kenyan value-added and input-output structures) that production functions and earnings of primary factors for different industries are similar for the two countries.

It is apparent from Kessel's study that "effective rates of protection" give a somewhat different picture of the structure of protection of industry in Tanzania from that given by nominal tariff rates.[34] Some industries show a lower "effective protection rate" than the nominal rates, but in most industries (and in virtually all import-substitution industries), the "effective protection rates" are considerably greater than the nominal tariff rates. This is because import duties on most raw materials and other inputs are either zero or very low and because the share of value added in gross output is relatively small. Thus, the level of protection of capital and labour in Tanzania is much higher than is indicated by nominal tariff rates on final products (which themselves exceed 50 per cent for eight industrial sectors and 100 per cent for three sectors). The data also show that "effective protection" is generally highest for import-substitution industries producing non-durable consumer goods. This observation corresponds to that made by Soligo and Stern in the Pakistan case.[35] There seems to be a tendency for consumer goods industries, and, in particular the less durable and luxurious types, to be heavily protected.

For seventeen of the thirty-five industries examined, the "effective protection rates" are 95 per cent or higher. This implies, under static conditions, in these industries, that capital and/or labour is receiving at least twice the remuneration it would have received under "free trade" conditions.[36] This may lead us to expect that firms in these industries will be earning substantial profits (unless they are operating inefficiently or at well below full capacity). In order to test the validity of this view, the profitability of protected firms has been calculated for 1966, using the rate of return on turnover as the measure of profitability.[37] In the cases of beer, paints, matches, tobacco and sugar refining, high effective protection rates would seem to be cushioning high profit rates. The losses observed in the dairy produce firm, one of the clothing firms and the glass products firm (with rates of effective protection of 216 per cent, 144 per cent and 51 per cent, respectively) are explained by special factors. (The dairy plant suffers from inadequacy of the locally available raw material and works considerably below capacity, the clothing firm and the glass products firm had only recently been established and were still suffering from teething troubles). If these firms with negative rates of return on turnover are eliminated and the firms' rates of return are averaged for cash industry, it is found that the rate of return on turnover varies directly with the rate of effective protection. These results, subject to qualifications with respect to the nature of the data, would seem to suggest that the tariff structure, in general has tended to allow the realization of high profits. This is consistent with firms' expectations as discussed, in the context of the motivation to invest, above and in an earlier paper.[38]

STATIC CHARACTERISTICS OF TANZANIAN INDUSTRY

It is important to examine the static cross-section aspects of the industrial structure in order to understand the inter-relationships which constitute that structure at a particular point in time. This is attempted in the final section of this paper, so as to provide some general information about Tanzanian industry. The discussion will be largely confined to two areas: cost structure and inter-industry relations, and efficiency and factor productivity. Finally, a note is added on industrial location.

Cost Structure and Inter-Industry Relations

In classical and neoclassical theory, the cost of production determines the commodity's supply price, and also the total of distributive payments to the factors utilized in the production process. The cost structure indicates the relative significance of the inputs used in the production process, and hence the extent to which a given productive activity depends on other activities in the economic system as well as the primary factors of production. The cost structure of manufacturing activities can therefore be used to look at various aspects of intersectoral relations. A primary concern here is the degree of dependence on various material and service-supplying sectors in particular, the extent of the industrial base and the extent to which manufacturing industry depends on imports.

An examination of cost structure along these lines faces the problem of availability and accuracy of data. The information that is available—under the two-digit Standard Industrial Classification (SIC)—does not fully satisfy the requirement of the analysis. Apart from cost aggregation problems, there are many ambiguities because of the lack of uniform accounting methods in the various enterprises. Moreover, the survey that has been used does not always separate categories of cost that are pertinent to the analysis. For example, administration, transport, rental and repair and maintenance costs are all included in one catch-all category, "other costs." In spite of these difficulties an attempt has been made to look at the structure of unit costs for each industry, in order to gain some insight into the issues mentioned above. The problems underlying the data do not necessarily invalidate the analysis but they do qualify the acceptance and interpretation of the results.

From the available data, the value of output for each industrial classification has been broken down into materials costs (including packing materials and chemicals), depreciation charges, energy costs (electricity, fuels, lubricants and water), costs of services from other activities (work given out), wage costs, salary costs, "other costs", and surplus. The cost components have then been apportioned between "variable" and "fixed" costs, although the allocation is, necessarily, somewhat arbitrary in some cases. In the "variable costs" category have been included materials, energy, wages, and services from other activities. All these costs are assumed to vary with the level of output. "Fixed costs" are made up of depreciation, salaries and "other costs" as defined above. The surplus is obtained by subtracting total variable and fixed costs from the value of output.[39]

This analysis shows that, on an average for all manufacturing industries, variable costs account for over 70 per cent of total costs. However, the distribution of the proportion of variable costs in total costs around this average could be taken to indicate that the industrial structure is dualistic.[40] On the one hand, there are some industries with a very high variable cost component, whose degree of capitalization can be taken as low. Many of these industries are likely to be dominated by small firms with a significant element of local ownership. On the other hand, there are some industries with relatively low variable cost and relatively high capitalization. These industries are likely to be foreign-owned. These observations are offered in a tentative manner since, as pointed out above, the allocation of costs between fixed and variable is far from being perfect.

There is also considerable variation between industrial groups in the composition of variable costs. For industry as a whole, materials account for about 65 per cent of total costs. An examination of the variation around this average indicates, among other things, the industries which are supply-based. These considerations have considerable significance when, for example, the interest is in designing incentives for changing location. The data on energy costs indicate that Tanzania has not yet developed an energy-intensive manufacturing sector. The energy component constitutes, on average, 1.8 per cent of total costs. The relatively low energy cost per unit of output reflects the fact that most industries are close to final demand. Amann has pointed out that activities which add "final touches" only, are generally not energy-intensive.[41] The low energy cost components in industries such as chemicals, metal products, and electrical machinery (relative to other countries, as shown by Amann) also reflect the level of product development in these fields. For example, in more developed economies, simple metal products constitute 6 per cent of the output of the metal products industry, whereas in Tanzania they constitute 100 per cent of the industry's output.[42] The same can be said of other industries.

The wage bill component is relatively low: 6.6 per cent of total costs, on average, as compared, for example, to 11.9 per cent in Greece and 21 per cent in the United States.[43] It is clear that the cost of wages is not a decisive factor in the total cost of production. This may be due to a low employment coefficient, that is, the existence of capital intensity, or to low remuneration per labour unit employed, because of the unskilled character of the labour force, or both. The identification of the cause of low labour cost will be discussed below. The cost of "work given out" indicates that inter-industry cooperation is weak. This may be because of the lack of facilities to process by-products. The number of zero entries in the services column denotes rather meagre economies of agglomeration. It is probable that Tanzanian firms send their by-products either to Kenya or overseas for further processing.[44]

Salary costs account for a low proportion of total costs in comparison with other countries, although their share relative to wage costs is very high when compared with the industrialized economies. This indicates the high cost of management, which in turn reflects the use of expatriate personnel who receive the same level of salaries that they would receive elsewhere.

The results of this examination of the structure of costs have important implications for policy which will be discussed in a subsequent paper. Before turning to factor productivity, the extent of the industrial base and the origin of industrial inputs will be briefly considered.

A relatively high ratio of value added would imply relatively low material content in the value of output and hence a greater demand for primary factors. Conversely, the high material cost component noted above means that the share of value added in gross output in Tanzanian manufacturing is fairly small. This observation is consistent with the point made earlier, that industry is for the most part limited to the final stages ("last touches") of the manufacturing process. A comparison with corresponding data for other countries shows that the share of value in manufacturing industry's gross output is indeed relatively small.[45]

An attempt has been made to estimate the structure of manufacturing inputs by sectoral origin. What has been done, essentially, is to isolate the inputs, both primary and secondary, used to produce domestic output. The contributions of the primary sector (agriculture and mining), services (commerce and public utilities), other domestic manufacturing activities, imports, labour, and capital, have been computed.[46] There is a wide disparity in the dependence of different industrial classifications on the various sources of inputs. For example, industries that are dependent upon domestic primary sectors include food and soft drinks, cordage, rope and twine, leather and rubber products, non-metal mineral products and processed export crops. Obviously, processed export products must depend to a large measure upon the domestic primary sectors. However, it is the contribution of inputs from other domestic manufacturing enterprises which shows the extent of the industrial base. The data indicate, as would be expected, that the industrial base is very narrow. It is supplemented by the foreign sector and a considerable dependence of manufacturing industry on imports can be discerned. In fact, the import components should be taken as the lower limits, since the estimates have included only those categories of inputs which were clearly identifiable as imports. It should also be noted that the import dependence that has been identified here does not take into account capital dependence. The policy implications of the various aspects of import dependence will also be taken up in a later paper.

Efficiency and Factor Productivity

An examination of factor productivity is not an easy task, given the limited information that is available on the structure of Tanzanian manufacturing industry. The observations made below are approximate only, but still provide useful comparisons between industries and sectors, and with other countries.

Manufacturing output per man (that is, in terms of value added) in 1966 amounted to Shs. 9,460. This was over three times greater than labour productivity in estates agriculture, but only about one-sixth of labour productivity in mining and about one-quarter of that in commerce.[47] In general, average labour productivity in manufacturing appears relatively low, given its capitalization, in relation to other sectors. An inter-country comparison reveals that average labour productivity in Tanzanian manufacturing is also very low in comparison with other countries.[48] Value added per person employed in Tanzanian manufacturing (1966) amounted, for example, to about 55% of that in Zambia (1965), 35% of that in Yugoslavia (1963), and less than 10% of that in the United States (1966).

These comparisons are presented with the qualification that, despite attempts to standardize methods of measurement, the individual country data are still based on different accounting procedures. Moreover, comparisons of this type normally assume that firms operate on the same neoclassical production function, so that differences in labour productivity reflect differences in the supply of complementary factors per worker.[49] This is a particularly relevant consideration when comparison is on an international basis. With these reservations in mind, comparative data on labour productivity by industrial sector have been collected for Tanzania, India, Japan, U.K. and U.S.A.[50]

Significant inter-industry differences in average labour productivity are evident in Tanzania and in the other countries. In virtually all sectors, Tanzania's labour productivity is significantly lower than that of Japan, the United Kingdom and the United States, although in several sectors, it is higher than that of India. These differentials with respect to India may be accounted for by the difference in classification, since Tanzania's figures relate only to firms employing 10 or more persons, while data for India (and the other countries) cover all establishments irrespective of size. The low labour productivity compared with the more industrialized countries must be explained largely by differences in capital utilization.

With respect to the measurement of capital productivity in Tanzanian manufacturing industry, the task is even more difficult. Data on capital employed are fragmentary and for the greater part of industry non-existent. The results of the author's survey of 36 firms, arranged in the appropriate industrial categories, provide the only information available on capital productivity. An international comparison on capital productivity has therefore not been attempted. From the survey results, it can be seen that footwear and apparel, wood products and chemicals are the industries with the highest capital productivity, and that average capital productivity, as measured, tends to vary inversely with the capital labour-ratio.[51]

Industrial Location

From the *Survey of Industries 1966* the spatial distribution of industrial establishments and employment, and the relative shares of various economic zones in the country's manufacturing activity have been computed. The data show the percentages of all manufacturing establishments (employing 10 persons or more) and total industrial employment in Dar es Salaam, three other towns (Tanga, Arusha and Moshi) and the rest of mainland Tanzania, in 1966.[52] The data are also broken down by industrial sector. The results show that 37 per cent of establishments and 41 per cent of total employment are concentrated in the Dar es Salaam area, and that 69 per cent of the establishments and 65 per cent of total employment are located in the country's four major urban centres; Dar es Salaam, Tanga, Moshi and Arusha. The results also indicate the degree of concentration of establishments and employment in these areas for each industrial sector.[53]

The available information on small-scale and cottage industries (that is, establishments employing less than ten persons) show that 50 per cent of the employment and 61 per cent of the establishments are concentrated in the same four urban areas whose combined population accounts for 19.3 per cent of the country's total.[54]

NOTES

1. J. F. Rweyemamu, "The Structure of Tanzanian Industry," ERB Paper 71.2, 1971.
2. See original paper: J. F. Rweyemamu, "The Historical and Institutional Setting of Tanzanian Industry," ERB Paper 71.6, Table 1.1, p. 2. *Source:* United Republic of Tanzania, *Survey of Industries 1965*, Dar es Salaam, Central Statistical Bureau, 1967, Table 5.
3. *Ibid.*, Table 1.1, p. 2. For a fuller picture of the diversity of new manufacturing industries, see also Appendix II, Table 1.3, pp. 80–86.
4. *Ibid.*, Table 1.2, p. 6. *Source:* United Republic of Tanzania, *Survey of Industries 1965* Dar es Salaam Central Statistical Bureau, 1967.
5. Growth elasticities for industrial sectors are taken from H. B. Chenery's study, "Patterns of Industrial Growth," *American Economic Review*, September 1960.
6. *Ibid.*, for an explanation of Chenery's concept of the "normal pattern".
7. For a discussion of Chenery's "norm" along these lines, see J. F. Rweyemamu, "The Historical and Institutional Setting of Tanzanian Industry," footnote 3, p. 7; also G. C. Archibald, *Industrialisation and Capital Requirements in Greece*, Athens, Centre of Economic Research, 1969.
8. A. O. Hirschman, "The Political Economy of Import-Substituting Industrialisation in Latin America," *Quarterly Journal of Economics*, February 1968.
9. M. J. H. Yaffey, *Balance of Payments Problems of a Developing Country: Tanzania*, Munich: Weltforum Publishing House, 1970, p. 46.
10. G. Arrighi, *The Political Economy of Rhodesia*, Mouton, The Hague, 1967; A. G. Frank, *Capitalism and Underdevelopment in Latin America*, New York: Monthly Review Press, 1969, 2nd ed. rev.
11. A. G. Frank, "Development of Underdevelopment," *Monthly Review*, September 1966, reprinted in his *Latin America: Underdevelopment or Revolution*, New York, and London: Monthly Review Press, 1969.
12. M. J. H. Yaffey, *op. cit.*, p. 231.
13. For a review of the debate on this question see D. Ghai, "Territorial Distribution of the Benefits and Costs of the East African Common Market," *East African Economic Review*, June 1964; A. Hazlewood, "The East African Common Market: Importance and Effects," *Bulletin of the Oxford Institute of Economics and Statistics*, February 1966; and A. R. Roe, "Terms of Trade and Transfer Tax Effects in an East African Common Market: An Empirical Study," University of Dar es Salaam, ERB Paper 68.10, 1968.
14. J. F. Rweyemamu, "The Historical and Institutional Setting of Tanzanian Industry," Table 1.4, p. 12. *Source:* East African Customs and Excise, *Annual Trade Report*, 1954, 1960 and 1966.
15. *Ibid.*, Table 1.5, p. 13. *Source:* East African Customs and Excise, *Annual Trade Report*, 1962, 1963 and 1964.
16. *Ibid.*, Table 1.4, p. 12. *Source:* East African Customs and Excise *Annual Trade Report*, 1954, 1960 and 1966.
17. *Ibid.*, Table 1.6, p. 16. *Source: Background to the Budget*, 1968–69, 1969–70.
18. See A. O. Hirschman, *The Strategy of Economic Development*: New Haven, Yale University Press, 1957, pp. 61–90, for a discussion of the role of imports in indicating the extent of the market and the point at which it will support domestic production.
19. Similar information on Nigeria is provided in P. Kilby, *Industrialisation in an Open Economy: Nigeria 1945–66* London, Cambridge University Press, 1969.
20. J. F. Rweyemamu, "The Historical and Institutional Setting of Tanzanian Industry", Table 1.7, p. 18. *Sources:* HMSO, *Colonial Report* (1942); East African Customs and Excise, *Annual Trade Report*, 1949, 1959 and 1965.
21. *Ibid.*, Table 1.6, p. 16. *Source: Background to the Budget*, 1968–69, 1969–70.
22. A. O. Hirschman, *The Strategy of Economic Development*, p. 125, points out that the extent of the market, as indicated by imports, provides a necessary, but not sufficient, condition for inducing investment in domestic production.
23. Budget Speech by the Finance Minister, 1960.
24. For similar conclusions in the case of Nigeria, see A. N. Hakam, "The Motivation to Invest and the Locational Pattern of Foreign Private Industrial Investment in Nigeria," *Nigerian Journal of Economic and Social Studies*, March 1966.
25. See J. F. Rweyemamu, "The Historical and Institutional Setting of Tanzanian Industry," pp. 20–21, for a summary of the composition of investments.
26. This hypothesis was originally advanced, in the Tanzanian context, in J. F. Rweyemamu, "The Structure of Tanzanian Industry."
27. J. F. Rweyemamu, "The Historical and Institutional Setting of Tanzanian Industry," Table 1.8, pp. 23–25. *Source:* East African Customs and Excise, *Annual Trade Report*, 1958–66.

28. K. Schadler, *Manufacturing and Processing Industries in Tanzania*, Munich: IFO Institute, 1969, p. 15.
29. See J. F. Rweyemamu, "The Historical and Institutional Setting of Tanzanian Industry," p. 20. This venture also consolidated the position of Sodefra (one of the managing agents of Mwanza Textile Mill and representative of Amenital) in Tanzania.
30. *Ibid.*, p. 28. See also Z. Dobraska, "Criteria for Public Investment in Manufacturing: Five Tanzanian Case Studies," ERB Paper 68.28, 1968, pp. 71–72.
31. J. F. Rweyemamu, "The Historical and Institutional Setting of Tanzanian Industry", Table 1.9, p. 31. *Sources: Directory of Industries* 1967, Finance Ministers' Budget Speeches, 1961-66.
32. W. M. Gorden, "The Structure of a Tariff System and the Effective Protection Rate," *Journal of Political Economy*, June 1966, pp. 221–237; H. G. Johnson, "Tariffs and Economic Development," *Journal of Development Studies*, October 1965; G. Basevi, "The United States Tariff Structure: Estimates of Effective Rates of Protection of United States Industries and Industrial Labour," *Review of Economics and Statistics*, May 1966, pp. 147–160.
33. D. Kessel, "Effective Protection of Industry in Tanzania", ERB Paper 67.8, 1967, published with minor revisions, in the *East African Economic Review*, June 1968.
34. See J. F. Rweyemamu, "The Historical and Institutional Setting of Tanzanian Industry," Table 1.10 and the accompanying notes to the Table, pp. 35–39; the data are taken from D. Kessel, "Effective Protection of Industry in Tanzania", *Sources:* Kenya, *Census of Industrial Production*, 1963, Nairobi, Ministry of Economic Planning and Development, 1965; East African Customs and Excise, *Customs and Excise Tariff Handbook* 1966 and *Annual Trade Report*, 1966.
35. R. Soligo and J. J. Stern, "Tariff Protection, Import Substitution and Investment Efficiency," *Pakistan Development Review*, Summer, 1965.
36. B. Balassa, "Integration and Resource Allocation in Latin America," Cornell University, paper presented at the Conference on the Next Decade of Latin American Development, April 1966.
37. J. F. Rweyemamu, "The Historical and Institutional Setting of Tanzanian Industry," Table 1.11, pp. 42–43; *Source:* Survey by the author.
38. J. F. Rweyemamu, "The Structure of Tanzanian Industry."
39. J. F. Rweyemamu, "The Historical and Institutional Setting of Tanzanian Industry," Table 1.12, pp. 47–49. *Source:* United Republic of Tanzania, Survey of Industries, 1966, Dar es Salaam, Central Statistical Bureau, 1969, See also p. 50 for a discussion of the treatment of fringe benefits and the allocation of "other costs."
40. See also *Ibid.*, Table 1.21, p. 52. *Source:* United Republic of Tanzania, *Survey of Industries*, 1966, Dar es Salaam, Central Statistical Bureau, 1969.
41. H. Amann, *Energy Supply and Economic Development in East Africa*, Munich: Weltforum Publishing House, 1969, p. 75.
42. C. Cukor, "The Growth of Engineering Industries in the Developing Countries," *Acta Oeconomica*, 3, 1968, p. 189.
43. G. Contsoumaris, *The Morphology of Greek Industry*, Athens, Centre for Economic Research, 1963.
44. For example, at an Arusha sugar refining plant, the manager informed the author that as there were no facilities to process molasses, he was obliged to ship the by-product abroad.
45. J. F. Rweyemamu, "The Historical and Institutional Setting of Tanzanian Industry," Table 1.13, p. 56. *Sources:* United Republic of Tanzania, *Survey of Industries*, 1966, Dar es Salaam, Central Statistical Bureau, 1969; United Nations, *Studies in Inter-Industry Relations*, New York, 1967.
46. *Ibid.*, Table 1.17, pp. 59–60. See also pp. 55–57, and Appendix III, pp. 87–104.
47. *Ibid.*, Table 1.18, p. 63. *Source:* United Republic of Tanzania, *Background to the Budget; an Economic Survey*, 1968–69, Dar es Salaam, 1968.
48. *Ibid.*, Table 1.19, p. 64. *Sources:* United Republic of Tanzania, *Background to the Budget; an Economic Survey*, 1968–69, Dar es Salaam, 1968; United Nations, *The Growth of World Industry; Volume I. General Industrial Statistics 1953–66*, New York, 1969.
49. R. R. Nelson, "A Diffusion Model of International Productivity Differences in Manufacturing Industry," *American Economic Review*, May 1968.
50. J. F. Rweyemamu, "The Historical and Institutional Setting of Tanzanian Industry," Table 1.20, pp. 67–68. *Source:* H. B. Larry, *Imports of Manufactures from Less Developed Countries*, New York, 1968.
51. *Ibid.*, Table 1.21, pp. 70–71. *Source:* Survey by the author.
52. *Ibid.*, Table 1.22, pp. 72–73. *Source:* United Republic of Tanzania, *Survey of Industries 1966*, Dar es Salaam, Central Statistical Bureau, 1969.
53. *Ibid.*, see also p. 69.
54. K. Schadler, *Crafts, Small-scale Industries and Industrial Education in Tanzania*, Munich: Weltforum Publishing House, 1969, Table 7 and Appendix I.

Industrialisation in Tanzania—The Case of Small Scale Production*

DAVID PHILLIPS

INDUSTRIALISATION STRATEGY AND THE REQUIREMENTS FOR TRANSFORMATION

The strategy for transformation of industrial structures in underdeveloped economies typically involves the eradication of the system in which the country is preoccupied—either the processing of agricultural products and imported intermediate manufactures (mixing, refining, packaging, rerolling, assembly, etc.), or the simple import-substitution and manufacture for a lopsided urban-based consumer market (beer, cigarettes, spirits, soda, synthetic fibre fabrics and garments, radios, etc.). The transformation thus implies the development of a system whereby the country relies primarily on its own needs, a system which bases industrial expansion on the basic processing of local minerals and primary products for the local market, the development of local technical capability, an indigenous science and technology, and capital goods manufacturing capacity.

It is not the intention here to survey the field of development theory, but rather to isolate that which seems to correspond best with the syndrome of underdevelopment outlined above. As our starting point therefore we take the position of Clive Thomas in "The Transition to Socialism: Issues of Economic Strategy in Tanzanian-Type Economies."[1] Thomas defines two "laws" of economic transformation, arising from his analysis of dependency as (i) the reliance on foreign technology: (ii) the critical role of foreign decision-making in the major employment: output and income earning sectors, and (iii) reliance on foreign finance; materials and equipment and resulting persistent income and capital drains overseas. The laws derive from the critical impediment to development, namely "the lack of an organic link, rooted in an indigenous science and technology, between the pattern and growth of domestic resource use, and the pattern and growth of domestic demand." The first "law" therefore concerns the need for convergence of resource use and demand. The second "law" of transformation concerns the need for convergence of needs with demand. These are the *sine qua non* of development in an ex-colonial primary producing country.

In taking this global strategy as the starting point, the first task of industrialisation is to select deliberately those industrial sectors which will make the link between resources and needs. These industries will be of two types:

a) those producing essential consumer or wage goods mainly within the food, clothing, and housing fields;
(b) those producing basic capital and intermediate goods most essential as inputs into domestic agriculture and manufacturing, using local materials.

In such a strategy, foreign trade takes a subsidiary position, and export earnings become a criterion of minor importance in evaluating the feasibility of projects. The domestic market is of primary, but not total concern.

In the second category of basic industries, selection is made on the basis of (a) extent of backwards and forwards linkages within the domestic economy,[2] and (b) income or growth elasticity of the industry. In either case high values are required.

Industries which figure most clearly in these categories are textiles, leather, iron and steel and non-ferrous metals, petroleum products, paper, industrial chemicals, rubber, timber, glass, cement, machinery and electrical equipment.

The above strategy, involving the selection of a core of industries central to the technological development process, conflicts with strategies based on notions of comparative advantage supported by neo-classical economic theory, which normally favours the establishment of processing industries based on primary production (for export). Such strategies usually cite the alleged uneconomic size of the local market as a barrier to setting up local basic industries, and also the difficulty of exporting capital goods to extend the market. Hence industrial strategy is based on export earnings from primary processing providing the funds for expansion of further (light) industrial capacity while capital goods are generally imported. Needless to say, this strategy is not capable of transforming industry as it does not attack the roots of underdevelopment but tries to build upon the system of underdevelopment itself. For various reasons discussed this is unlikely to be successful except possibly in the case of major oil exporters and countries with some resources with which they can earn long-term superprofits and which have high income elasticity of demand. This, however, is not by any means proven and depends on the manner in which the surplus is reinvested.

Effective basic industry strategy automatically implies certain things about the economic and political organisation of the country. As the strategy calls for simultaneous and co-ordinated development of a number of basic industries, it is therefore quite distinct from the piecemeal approach based on seemingly random selection of supposedly profitable projects, e.g. the well-known "shopping list" which is presented each year for the

*Edited version of ERB Paper 76.5.

annual plan. It is also distinct from a "leading sector" approach whereby one sector (e.g. textiles or, as in the above-mentioned case, primary processing) is relied upon to induce further investment via the creation of profitable industrial and consumer markets. Finally, it is distinct from the general approach of private enterprise which almost by definition cannot support such a broadly based internally oriented strategy in the Tanzanian or similar context. In fact, extensive public sector involvement would be required at least within the initial basic industries. The system of control and ownership already set up in Tanzania could provide the institutional and political base for such a strategy.

The gulf between this type of strategy and reality so far may be illustrated by analysing the existing resource base and existing industrial capacity.

In the case of mineral resources, it is symptomatic of the lack of co-ordination characterising an economy oriented towards manufactured goods imports that the mineral resource map of the country has not been completed, and that over time piecemeal surveys often duplicated and triplicated have been carried out by numerous agencies, mostly foreign. Nevertheless, substantial reserves of coal, lime, gypsum, iron ore, kaolin and clays, phosphates, potassium salts, natural gas (and possibly off-shore oil), soda ash, silica sand, and other important industrial minerals are known to exist in various parts of the country which remain unexploited on any scale. The two major local mineral based industries are glass containers and cement, set up in 1966. Nevertheless, the glass factory still imports soda ash and other minerals. Extensive local soda ash reserves are currently planned to be processed for sale to Japan. The cement factory uses imported petroleum. Building, especially in urban areas, is based mostly on cement and metal sheets, while burnt clay bricks, though traditionally established in a few areas, has been generally ignored. Lime for mortar is hardly known, despite extensive limestone deposits, and in some places the production of lime has died out (Kondoa). Roofing tiles of clay are hardly known except in a few missions; tiles have been imported from India. Coal reserves appear to be almost untapped. The largest mine, Ilima, produces only about 3,000 tons per annum, from one seam reported to contain 500,000 tons. The importation and local manufacture of corrugated sheeting has preempted the establishment of local capacity for tiles. The fertilizer factory imports nearly all raw materials while local deposits of potash and phosphate remain so far unexploited. Six thousand tons of imported ceramics (worth about 15 million shillings) are needed, though local deposits of kaolin and felspar exist; proposals for investment in ceramics have been under consideration for over 10 years. Importation of aluminium and plastic ware combined with minimal efforts at production of ceramics or upgraded traditional earthenware have again preempted the local market and oriented it towards imports.

The plastics and chemical products industries have undergone preliminary development, but quite independently of the domestic resource base (natural gas, naphtha, petroleum byproducts, etc.). Pyrethrum-based insecticide manufacture is established but the pyrethrum mostly goes overseas for processing and is reimported for mixing and packaging. The metal industry is entirely dependent on imported materials and equipment.

The above list could be duplicated in the agricultural and other sectors. In the case of agricultural products exploitation for the export market has been extensive, whereas in the case of minerals, exploitation has been relatively insignificant either for local or export markets, with the exception of diamonds and gold. Some major examples are cotton of which 15% is locally processed into fabric up to 1975, while both cotton and synthetic fibre fabric garments are imported. Approximately 14% of hides and skins are processed locally into shoes, the rest exported as semi-finished or dried hides; while in 1974 over 300,000 pairs of leather shoes valued at over 10 million shillings were imported. Sisal and especially coil fibre have not been fully exploited for ropes, mats, sacks, etc. Coil is exported while a local brush company imports coil fibre.

In the case of wood, the vast majority is used as fuel, matches have until recently used imported splints and paper is not produced (imports amount to 30,000 tons per annum worth about Shs. 100 million).

Lack of integration within the industrial sector also promotes a situation whereby waste products are not used in any planned way—for example, molasses, rice and maize bran, cashew nut shell liquid, fruit wastes, wood chips, cotton rags, coconut husks and scrap metal (from rolling and fabrication plants).

Many of the above problems are currently scheduled for solution during the next few years. For example, leather and cotton textile production are to be rapidly expanded, a cement factory based on coal is under evaluation; a paper mill and ceramics factory are scheduled; utilisation of local phosphates for the fertilizer plant is under investigation. Sisal processing is to be expanded and clay brick production promoted.

However, the problem is not to be solved by piecemeal changes, but by a fundamental change in strategy. The Third Five-year Plan remains heavily weighted towards primary processing and light manufacturing though basic industries are to be expanded (paper, cement, etc.). Simultaneously, the absence of fundamental change is reflected in the lack of emphasis on capital goods manufacture (machinery, transport, equipment, etc.), not because of the lack of ability to see the necessity, but because of the existing structure of the economy and the commitments towards primary products export.

THE ROLE OF SMALL-SCALE PRODUCTION IN INDUSTRIAL TRANSFORMATION

The previous section has outlined a transformational strategy for industry. It is a global strategy and leaves many detailed questions unanswered. They are taken here as the starting point.

One of the immediate questions is the one about the economic scale of production. The answer in this case was to select those techniques of production which allow the earliest possible economic introduction of basic industries. In the case of steel, for example, this is regarded as meaning the selection of "minimum economic scale" (the point where the long run average cost curve supposedly begins to level out) which is about 250,000 tons per annum, and in the case of paper 200 tons per day.[3]

However, for a country such as Tanzania, these are still very large-scale plants. In the first case, probable set-up cost would be in excess of Shs. 4,000 million, taking into account infrastructural requirements, and in the second (65,000 tons paper per annum), the cost at current prices would exceed Shs. 800 million. Export markets would be required, especially for steel. The guideline about "minimum economic scale" does not in practice seem to help Tanzania to develop basic industries in the foreseeable future.

Furthermore, the global strategy does not directly consider the problem of industrial location or alternative productive techniques in the sense of avoiding the use of highly capital-intensive, organisation and skill-intensive technology in a country where such resources are relatively scarce and underemployment apparently prevalent. In fact, the strategy assumes that techniques are more or less standardised according to scale of production and materials used. The large capital outlays required to finance such a programme, vast in proportion to the current level of national economic surplus would have to depend on "comradely generosity" from socialist countries, providing long term soft loans, grants, etc.

The strategy avoids explicit reference to employment and manpower development and the development of a "labour aristocracy" of industrial workers which would be certain to occur due to the fact that the limited funds available would be spent on capital and skill-intensive plants.

Finally, it is difficult to see how the problems of financial and technological dependence would be solved, and the goals of balanced regional development and popular control over the means of production achieved.

Our aim in this study will be to demonstrate that fundamental difficulties in this transformational strategy for Tanzania could be partially circumvented by a multi-technology approach based essentially on small-scale labour-intensive units, and that small-scale techniques are essential to industrial transformation and a balanced egalitarian economy.

In 1973 a special Party directive on small scale industries was issued. It called for a technological revolution in the rural areas based on control of industry by the people, using existing skills and materials and avoiding heavy capital expenditure. There is at least in some quarters of the country a realisation that an alternative industrial strategy could mobilise resources for development in a manner more consistent with the stated national objectives, particularly as regards local control over the means of production and utilisation of existing skills and material resources.

To begin with, some relevant definitional problems must be cleared up. Normally, small scale production is defined in terms of input and output levels.[4] The party directive on small-scale industries in the case of Tanzania avoids any formal definition: "A small scale unit is any unit whose control is within the capability of our people individually or collectively in terms of capital required and know how." This is a concept related to political economy rather than to technology. It avoids any formal technical measurement of scale and concentrates on the local resource mobilisation aspect of small-scale production. This concept is consistent with the transformational strategy for Tanzania and will be used as the definition of small-scale unit in this paper. Thus, the principal objective of any special programme for the development of the small-scale sector is to mobilise local resources which would otherwise be wasted. A large-scale advanced technology programme may fail to mobilise the extensive reserves of local manpower, materials and skills and may instead generate its benefits to a small section of the population.

We may now define the meaning of the special resources in the context of small-scale production.

Manpower

Small-scale labour-intensive techniques of production have a higher employment potential relative to capital invested and output, and can therefore avoid or reduce the problem of the development of a narrow employment base associated with large-scale production in developing countries. Artisan skills can be upgraded and utilised instead of being eradicated by mass production, and extensive spread of skills and organisational know how is more likely to occur. Existing or potentially unemployed (underemployed) rural and urban labour can be effectively mobilised, and entrepreneurial ability fostered at local level.

Raw Material Resources

Scattered deposits of agricultural and mineral resources in relatively small quantities or in inaccessible locations, which would not permit establishment of feasible large-scale plants and would be too costly to transport to centralised plants or to markets, may be exploited for local markets with small-scale techniques of production. This would apply, for example, to isolated deposits of coal, limestone, clay, phosphates, grasses (for pulp), sugar cane, seasonal gluts of fruit, etc., and also to scrap (scrap metal, waste paper, etc.) which is too costly to transport for central reprocessing.

Capital

Small-scale production may be expected to induce local savings and investment. Establishment of profitable local projects for processing farm produce or providing important agricultural inputs (such as gunny sacks, fertilizer, and implements,) at competitive prices, will induce expansion of crop production and savings for investment.

Anticipation of rising incomes from a successful local industry may also be expected to induce non-monetary capital formation (e.g. self-help construction programs for godowns, sheds), thereby reducing the monetary capital intensity of production.

Both of these may be regarded as elements of "disguised savings potential" which would otherwise be wasted or expended on consumer goods.

Capacity Utilisation
Nearness to resources of raw materials and small-scale operation are likely to ensure fuller utilisation of productive capacity than is the case in Tanzania at the moment in medium to large-scale industries of the primary processing group (fruit canning, sawmilling, etc.). This would lower effective capital/output ratios. Underutilised craft skills may be stimulated and expanded by a special small industry support program.

Land
Small-scale primary processing plants tend to substitute land for capital, e.g. small sugar or canning factories would be better able to rely on non-irrigated smallholder production of cane, fruit, etc., involving lower capital cost per unit of output.

Gestation Periods
Small-scale plants tend to have shorter gestation periods than large-scale, allowing programs to be got under way at relative speed, and more rapid mobilisation of resources.

The above advantages may be regarded as applying not only to industries in rural or semi-urban areas, but also to some extent for urban small factories and feeder plants set up to supply components, sub-assemblies, and packaging, etc. to larger plants. Sub-contracting of component parts, manufacture or repair and maintenance works, may gain advantages of lower capital-intensity of production and organisational simplicity in smaller units, and probably higher employment potential. Industry can thereby be more closely integrated with local resources. A special ancillary development program may also be able to concentrate on providing the internal linkages essential for an integrated industrial sector. However, this category of industry does not necessarily have special advantages from the point of view of spatial (rural) development.

A small-scale industry's program may be expected to save relatively scarce resources.

Capital and Skills
Decentralised small-scale production is likely to be less capital-intensive and to use a lower average level of skills. In-plant training for control of the production process is more likely to be practicable, avoiding specialist training facilities outside. At this stage in Tanzania's development lesser reliance on capital implies lesser reliance on foreign exchange for replacement and spares, foreign personnel, and, as experience to date appears to show, reduced reliance on imported fuels and raw materials. This is largely because large-scale plants are mostly set up as joint ventures with foreign partners whereas small plants are set up with local capital.

Economic Infrastructure
Expenditure on utilities such as electricity and water may be reduced per unit of output in small enterprises, or in the case of water could be supplied through self-help programs. Transportation systems will be reduced as raw material transport will be reduced if small units are located close to supplies. If local markets are supplied from local resources, transportation cost of finished products per unit of output will also fall. In assessing the capital intensity of production in large-scale plants, the capital cost of associated transportation systems should be included.

Technical Infrastructure
As is the case with the transportation system, small labour-intensive plants will need reduced repairs and maintenance capacity, and reduced expenditure per unit of outputs on setting up repair capacity and training technicians to operate it. Improvisation of replacement parts will allow further reductions of expenditure on spares.

Inventories
Small processing and manufacturing plants may require lower levels of stocks in relation to output if they are based on nearby supplies, reducing working capital requirements. Co-operative labour receiving payment from sales proceeds may be more likely in small units, further reducing working capital requirements for wages.

Social Infrastructure
The need to provide housing and facilities associated with concentrations of population may be lower per unit of output. The social benefits of industrial decentralisation are otherwise fundamental to the whole argument for small-scale industries.

Finance
Central capital expenditure and associated financial requirements may be reduced not only through reduced capital-intensity of output (including working capital), but also through inducements to local savings (monetary and non-monetary), thereby reducing the required monetary budget from central sources.

The above points relate to the resource mobilisation potential of small-scale labour-intensive production. This mobilisation potential is by definition transitional and over the course of time small-scale production expands or is replaced by larger units corresponding to accumulated capital and infrastructural development. These points are to be viewed, therefore, in a dynamic context. Small-scale industry is a nursery or training ground for the long-term future and a method of redistributing income and markets. The object is not merely to alter resource utilisation patterns in the short-run, e.g. by simply providing more jobs. But in the short to medium term, the ability to exploit existing resources is essential to the global transformation strategy and the long-term manpower, capital and technology development. The possibility of setting up industries with lower import-dependence in manpower, machinery, and finance with better prospects for absorption of technical know how is clearly integral to the transformational strategy, and an essential, possibly critical, part of it. In the following section, some general findings concerning the problems facing large-scale plants in Tanzania are outlined to provide some evidence for the above points.

ECONOMIES AND DISECONOMIES OF LARGE-SCALE PRODUCTION

The transformation strategy proposed by Thomas in his cited work assumes that standardised types of technology are adopted and that "minimum economic scale" of production should be aimed for in the set-up of basic industries. Investment scheduling in industry would, therefore, depend on the rate at which available markets could be expanded to allow minimum economic capacity to be installed. At the same time Thomas pointed out that economies of scale are location-specific and factor-price specific. In other words economies of scale are dependent on the pattern of available resources (e.g. capital availability) and specific location of plants, since in, for example, inaccessible locations factors such as transport costs are important and may affect scale economies.

It is the contention here that factor prices (or relative factor endowments) and location are, in fact, critical in determining economies of scale; and that in situations of varying factor endowments —e.g. an underdeveloped as opposed to a developed economy—economies of scale may not be attainable.

The existence of economies of scale is very important to the evaluation of small-scale production as a component of industrial transformation, for obvious reasons. It is a commonly, if vaguely, used argument in favour of centralisation by parastatals both on technical and administrative grounds.

It is also, as pointed out previously, the argument used to justify the continued absence of basic capital and intermediate goods industries in primary producing underdeveloped economies, on the grounds of supposed comparative advantage, and underdeveloped local markets.

Economies of scale have evolved steadily from the long-run process of capital accumulation in now industrialised countries, and from the continuing concentration of capital leading recently to the emergence of multinational corporations.

According to Paul Bairoch,[5] the first innovations of the 19th century British Industrial Revolution at cottage level cost in terms of investment per worker the equivalent of 4 months wages (about Shs. 1,600 per worker in Tanzania in 1975). In the U.S.A. by 1953 this had risen to 29 months, and in a typical developing country in 1963 was about 350 months wages (about 140,000/- per person employed at 1975 wages in Tanzania). The notorious Dar es Salaam automatic bakery cost about 800 months wages per person employed (based on Shs. 400 a month). The proposed Sao Hill paper plant will cost about 2,000 months wages at 1975 levels, sugar refineries about 800 months, and cement plants about 1,600 months wages per person employed.

Another study by Francis Stewart[6] estimated that on the basis of current levels of investment per person employed in the U.K. (in industry, agriculture, etc.) only 40% of the Argentinian labour force could be employed, 30% in Brazil and Jamaica, 12% in Sri Lanka and 5% in India.

It is difficult to see how a developing country can find the resources to finance the employment of more than a small minority of potential industrial job seekers at these rates. Secondly, without the parallel development of equally expensive infrastructure, electricity, water systems, roads, transport equipment, repair, maintenance and training capacity the economies expected to be derived from large-scale capital-intensive plants may not arise because of inability to utilise capacity, shortages, breakdowns, etc.

The clear inability of underdeveloped economies to generate the surplus to finance these huge investments, and the equal inability to finance, organise or even plan the required supporting infrastructure and skill development for such discontinuous leaps in technology, means that the few large-scale plants will either operate inefficiently and at great cost to society or will require special concentrations of resources to establish support facilities, in industrial enclaves, at the cost of reducing the possibilities for development of other industries. Even in the case of the oil states, such as Nigeria, which has drawn up massive investment plans financed through oil earnings, the other problems such as skill development and organisational requirements will probably prove insurmountable in the short-run, and the industrial employment potential may be severely restricted because capacity may hit the ceiling of the local or West African market well before anything like full employment of industrial job seekers can be achieved, while at the same time an acute shortage of skilled workers will occur.

The problem of technology and scale is aggravated for developing countries by their inability to influence the factor composition of technologies developed abroad in supplier countries with different factor availability. In some cases (e.g. Tanga Fertilizer Factory) the worst compromise seems to have been achieved, involving a modern capital-intensive plant which is at the same time not on a sufficient scale to be able to compete at international market prices, and too sophisticated to allow switchover to use local materials, or allow local control at this stage.

It appears that economies of scale may be attainable in "enclaves" or resource concentration. Even if this is so however, it is precisely such enclave development which has not been able to lead to dynamic growth of the economy as a whole, because it cannot mobilise existing local resources and because it tends to be import and export-dependent. Historically, the attempt to reap economies of scale and concentration by locating industries in Dar es Salaam or Tanga may therefore have been self-frustrating because it may have caused far more structural problems and waste of the country's resources in the long run than the short run advantages of scale, or external economies of concentration. In fact even within these enclaves it is doubtful whether economies of scale can always be exploited. Here we may try to classify the various factors involved alongside some examples from Tanzanian industry.

Transport and Distribution Systems

Within and outside of urban areas these may not be adequate and marketing and supply bottlenecks often develop leading to excess capacity or high transport markups on production cost. Examples of this have been numerous. Partial stoppages in the fertilizer factory necessitating changes of product mix in 1973 were as follows: 75 days stoppage on phosphate production due to lack of phosphate (imported from Jordan); 30 days lost due to delays in import of potassium sulphate; 55 days stoppage due to water shortages.[7] Fertilizer production has reached 65,000 tons by 1975 out of capacity 85,000 tons (original rated capacity of the manufacturers was 105,000 tons p.a.). In the case of the Dar es Salaam fruit cannery and a tomato cannery in Dodoma considerable excess capacity appears to exist. Dodoma, in fact closed down, while Dar es Salaam operates at an annual average of well under 50% at 1 shift. There is a tendency to set up food processing capacity in relation to estimated supplies but without any idea about the costs of collection. Dar es Salaam cannery runs a transport fleet up to 100 miles around the city. Another problem is the processing delays due to the irregular or inadequate supplies. This leads to an estimated 30% wastage of mangoes before they enter the production line. The same problems are almost certain to apply to the Korogwe cannery. Dar es Salaam capacity is 20 tons a shift, while Korogwe is 12 tons. Either capacity was installed without regard for cost of obtaining the supplies which theoretically exist; the problem is aggravated by the need for standardised fruit sizes and qualities with mechanised plants.

The same types of problems apply to the meat cannery, which has faced declining supplies and is most vulnerable to this problem because of its scale and location and transport costs of cattle. The tannery has faced similar difficulties, and intended monopolisation of all hides and skins processing into 3 tanneries is certain to increase significantly transportation and collection costs.

East African Kenaf (gunny bags) was established with intended supply from a 10,000 acre plantation. Failure to achieve adequate levels of supply resulted in the importation of kenaf in order to keep the plant operating. The cement factory has faced problems in limestone supply, of which it currently consumes about 1,400 tons per day, due to the shortage of spares needed to run a fleet of sophisticated heavy vehicles. In this case the supply source is only 1 km. distant; nevertheless the problem of expensive transportation infrastructure still applies in principle. Stoppages are more costly, the higher the plant overheads. Large-scale plants incur relatively heavy depreciation and maintenance charges per unit of output.

Sawmills have been established at medium scale with greater regard for ease of central control and social infrastructure, than for operating economies and transport requirements. Yet in Tabora forests it is estimated that vehicles are written off in one year and operating costs of transporting logs are high. Again, the failure to maintain the transportation system will lead to inefficient plant operation and high production costs, preventing the attainment of scale economies.

Economic and Technical Infrastructure

Similar points may be made about the need to set up facilities such as electricity, water supplies and handling facilities. The fertilizer factory investment cost was increased by 25% due to the need to build a special deep water jetty for material import handling; problems were also faced with water supply as mentioned. The need to establish electricity generators specific to individual plants results in increased maintenance and operating bottlenecks and high cost electricity.

In many cases this is unavoidable, but it also aggravates problems of utilising large-scale capacity. Repairs and maintenance facilities have to be adequate to support complex plants. Breakdowns and stoppages which occur through inadequate repair facilities affect operating economics. One fibreboard company and a mechanised cashewnut processing factory within the last 3 years were forced to have the entire plant replaced by the foreign suppliers due to operational problems, in the first case wrong specifications.

It may be argued that these problems in principle are of a static character, and that in the long run the object should be to aim at efficient operation and overcome bottlenecks. It is necessary therefore to consider the dynamic aspects of the problems as well.

Data do not currently exist which specifically evaluate resource wastage or production cost increases resulting from the above problems, nor from longer run problems. It is necessary then to depend upon rather abstract reasoning, without gaining any definite perspective on the problem.

The main points are as follows:

(a) Established (large-scale) industry has tended in developing countries to be biased against capital goods production and to favour consumer goods of relatively high input and export dependence. This has resulted in a lack of internal linkages reinforced by the complexity of the technology and technological dependence. The import-dependence of industries obliges a country to seek export markets, thereby reinforcing external trade dependence.

(b) The new industries use relatively capital-intensive techniques and are in monopolistic positions behind tariff walls, often operating inefficiently and investing in excess capacity.

(c) The economic and technological dependence may result in problems of surplus drain via transfer pricing or super normal profits expatriated via management agreements or other means.

(d) The industries are capital-intensive and established in urban enclaves, incapable of adequately mobilising existing resources of manpower or distributing income to create extensive markets for their products. They are forced to concentrate on a narrow (urban) market which they themselves have created.

(e) Employment potential is limited but demand for highly skilled people is proportionately high. There is little scope for upgrading or absorbing the existing craft sector because complex plant operations tend to be divided into either technically relatively sophisticated tasks or routine standardised production line tasks. Skill development is discontinuous and special skills have to be created for specific plants. Where technology is supplied by several different countries manpower development is made more difficult.

To these factors should be added the previously discussed points about failure to induce local savings, long gestation periods, and failure to utilise local deposits of mineral and agricultural resources.

The problem of manpower development may be singled out as of special importance. A study quoted above (Barker, Bhagavan, Wield, Collande) claims that skill transfer in 30 relatively large-scale plants in Tanzania has been almost entirely restricted to the training of maintenance technicians and lower level technical personnel, and that the large plants have not been able to train local engineers for positions of top responsibility capable of design, installation or improvisation in these plants. On the other hand, the establishment of training grounds via small less sophisticated plants could be expected to encourage and oblige local people to take control of the process in both management and technical fields.

One case may be cited as of special relevance to the above general arguments this is the Dar es Salaam automatic bakery project, which has by now become a classic. This is a foreign aid venture (Canadian) tied to Canadian machinery. It is highly capital intensive using approximately 20 times as much capital per job as existing bakeries and approximately twice as much capital per unit of output. Total capital cost is about Shs. 18 million. The foreign exchange component is higher than that of capital used in small bakeries. Originally it was calculated that bread prices per kg. from this bakery would be about 30% lower than from existing small-scale bakeries. Cost overruns on equipment, high depreciation and maintenance, changes, etc. have now raised the estimated price to an unofficially calculated 2/50 per loaf, at least 25% higher than competitive bakeries and the controlled price, thus requires a government subsidy.[8] The plant is import-dependent not only for spare parts but also for wheat, because the process is normally based on Canadian hard wheat. A mixture will be required at best, so that local wheat may be partly used. Special training for 6 Tanzanian graduates in bakery technicianship was required abroad in order to provide maintenance staff for the plant. Startup delay of about one year has induced a proportion of these to resign. The delays were due to equipment deficiencies. The capacity of the bakery at 3 shifts is expected to cater for 40% of the entire Dar es Salaam market by 1977, though a single oven threatens serious supply shortages if breakdowns should occur. The entry of these new products on the market will, if competitive, cause stagnation and possibly production and employment cuts in existing small bakeries for the next 3 years or more, whereas total demand is expected to increase 25% per annum according to the original feasibility study. If it is not competitive, the plant will operate with excess capacity and at high cost, requiring increased subsidy. The chances are that target output will not be achieved and operating stoppages will occur due to the material import-dependence of the plant and the need to obtain spare parts from abroad. The choices before the controllers of the plant are filled with ambiguity. If it succeeds in producing competitively it will reduce employment growth and partially eradicate existing local craft skills. It will centralise control of the industry, at least in Dar es Salaam, and increase foreign exchange cost of production, while no real potential exists for product improvement. If it fails it will not be able to cause this damage to the social fabric of the city, but it will imply wasted years, wasted training investment and wasted expenditure on fixed assets equivalent to the annual savings and tax payments of about 18,000 city workers (about 6% of the urban wage labour force for the whole country).

The problems of large-scale production are related to those of the existing underdeveloped industrial structure, and with the whole complex of factors affecting the operation of import and export-dependent plants, lack of internal linkages, surplus drain alongside inefficient operation, etc. In these circumstances the concept of economies of scale is meaningless, except in isolated cases; the long run necessity for planned resource mobilisation is of overriding importance, and implies an approach based on phased and logical progress in and development of manpower and capital, and the phased build up of the industrial base, infrastructure, and markets, via widely distributed labour-intensive plants.

THE CHOICE OF TECHNOLOGY AND ITS IMPLICATIONS

Considerable debate has occurred on the subject of technological choice for developing countries, and this debate is highly relevant for any analysis of industrial strategy. The need for technological alternatives has been implied throughout this paper, but here we may consider the subject more explicitly, if relatively briefly.

The neoclassical position, and the one most frequently (if unknowingly) adopted in papers on choice of techniques, asserts that choice of technology is based on relative factor prices and that if factor inputs (capital, labour, etc.) are selected in such a way that their relative productivity is proportional to their relative prices, optimum productive efficiency is achieved, or maximum short run output per unit of input. Various assumptions are made in order to make this assertion; they are not relevant here. Policy implications are that a country should maximise its comparative advantage in certain factors of production (e.g. land and unskilled labour in Tanzania) by adjusting the prices of these factors—e.g. putting tariffs on imports of capital goods, and subsidising the use of unskilled labour (e.g. through payroll subsidy). This adjustment of prices is said to alter techniques of production (e.g. substituting labour for capital) to promote productive efficiency. This position also regards factor prices and the choice of technology as a central policy issue for developing countries, arguing that it determines the distribution of income and hence the rate of profit and investment. The objective of optimum allocation of productive resources is based on a static analysis.

A second position argues that neoclassical technique choice is in practice non-existent in a developing country because the country is dependent on the machinery supplied from industrial countries which design their plants according to their own factor availability (i.e. relative price of labour and capital) for their own home market. Meaningful technique choice is therefore preempted by the historical monopolisation of technological development in a few high income capital-intensive economies.

A further position holds that choice of technique is not determined by factor prices at all; but is directly determined by the rate of accumulation of capital and rate of growth of output which is under control of the class owning the means of production. The rate of growth of capital is an independent variable with regard to factor prices, and factor prices and choice of technique are determined by capital accumulation rather than the other way round.[9]

Policy implications of this last position are that tariff and tax changes will not affect the technology of a developing country and are therefore futile. The solution lies in structural changes, income spread, and control of industry by national or local representatives of the people of the country whose interest is in channelling investible surpluses towards essential consumer goods and wealth-creating basic industries. Reorientation of strategy will change the resource-use and output characteristics of the economy; appropriate technology will automatically flow from appropriate production and appropriate materials. This is therefore calling for political and economic transformation rather than technical solutions to the problem of technology.

This last position is clearly relevant to the transformational strategy outlined, which assumes that technology will follow automatically from decisions about long-term production, raw material usage, manpower development, etc.

Another variation in approach which is current appears to have features of both static neoclassical factor price solutions and dynamic structural solutions. Leading exponents of this approach are the numerous "intermediate" or "appropriate" technology groups currently offering their services to developing countries. These include Intermediate Technology Development Group (U.K.), Brace Research Institute (Canada), Volunteers in Technical Assistance (U.S.A.), various offshoots of these (in Ghana, Nigeria), appropriate technology units attached to the Indian Government, etc.

Basically the general approach looks upon technology per se as a critical element in development policy. It further argues that it is important to alter the factor utilisation pattern of investments to be more consistent with resource availability of an underdeveloped economy. So far it has a neoclassical ring. However, instead of recommending static factor price adjustments by tariffs, etc., the approach recommends the adoption of alternative techniques of production directly. In doing so it avoids the assumption that choice of techniques is determined by factor prices; it also recognises the point made above that most underdeveloped countries have no meaningful choice in the types of plant they instal due to the fact that the foreign suppliers build them according to their own factor availabilities at home. The answer is seen to be the development of a "self-help technology" consistent with local factor availabilities (e.g. scarcity of capital and skilled manpower), which can be built and maintained locally.

This approach does not however go as far as to suggest that the primary requirement for the successful adoption of "appropriate" techniques is the restructuring of the economy, and it does not link technology directly with capital accummulation and growth. As a result there is a tendency to rely on isolated model projects (for example, simple tool production for local village use) for "demonstration effect", and a tendency to assume that factor substitution (e.g. job creation) is an end in itself. This is often a reaction to previously general beliefs that development is measured in terms purely of GDP growth per capita. This reaction is however prone to being associated with the static neoclassical position of so-called optimum allocation of resources, and represents a purely technical solution, divorced from the real processes of change at work. In a dynamic context however, based on a definition of the motive force of economic development (small-scale local capitalist co-operatives, state corporations, etc.), the approach has relevance to the problems of economic transformation.

The appropriate technology "movement" is therefore subject to a number of interpretations, and encompasses an assortment of interests and viewpoints which are not altogether consistent.

The most realistic solution for developing countries seems to be to make the link between technology and growth and form technical collaboration agreements with supplier countries whose own socio-economic structure and techniques of production are more akin to that of the recipient underdeveloped country, and which are at the same time viable and dynamic techniques offering long-term growth prospects rather than isolated and piecemeal improvements requiring special protective measures. For Tanzania, as will be discussed, the appropriate techniques may be absorbed from countries such as India or China; few other developing countries are in a position to supply technology. But these two countries represent quite different development paths, and the ultimate choice will depend upon the emerging socio-economic structure of Tanzania.

The adoption of appropriate small-scale labour-intensive techniques from abroad may be expected to permit more rapid skill transfer, early establishment of machinery productive capacity locally, low expenditure on economic infrastructure and wider dispersion of production. It may therefore also be expected to permit absorption and development of existing craft and industrial skills and techniques within the country to arrive at some hybrid technology integrated to local resources.

The potential pitfalls of devising an industrial policy on the basis of neoclassical notions about appropriate technology may be seen in the long study by the I.L.O. in 1972 ("Employment, Incomes, and Equality—A Strategy for Increasing Productive Employment in Kenya"). The following industrial development criteria were proposed: (a) industries using domestic raw materials (e.g. agro-processing), (b) industries having potential for development of a comparative advantage in export markets, (c) labour-intensive plants, (d) plants suitable for rural location, (e) industries having high backward linkages to employment. The resultant strategy–based on labour-intensive local resource-based small-scale plants, export markets and foreign investment, with the apparent emphasis on factor substitution rather than growth–was to develop a sector of industries as follows: meat preparations, vegetable and fruit processing, cotton fabrics, wool, clothing, leather tanning and footwear, vegetable oils, sawmilling, plywood and furniture. Certain basic intermediate goods industries (e.g. cement and paper) were also recommended on the grounds that they could feed the above extractive industries. These industries were also to face suitable tariffs such as on capital goods imports.

This list of industries conforms to the structure of Tanzania's industry in 1949, recommended for continuation in a 1961 I.B.R.D. report. In terms of our analysis, it is the opposite of a transformational approach and its employment-creating potential would therefore be short term, even if such a strategy could practicably be adopted.

If it is accepted that capital accumulation and growth and its controllers are the determinants of income spread, rates and pattern of investment, and that technology derives from the decision about goods to be produced and materials to be used, this still does not however say much about precisely what techniques are to be used and by whom.

The assumption of the transformational strategy outlined that technology is determined by input and output plans and that "minimum economic scale" of production for basic industries should be employed, implies in the Tanzania context state-level control and ownership. If, however, the "minimum economic scale" constraint is relaxed (as the previous section argued should be the case) so that a variety of techniques at various scales of production are possible, the choice of input, output and technique becomes indeterminate, because none of the three variables is independent of the others, each being able to affect the rest. In this case technology choice is a significant influence on the resource and production characteristics of the economy instead of being merely dependent upon planners' choices about output. It affects the scale, concentration, location and resource use of production.

The determining variable is presumably the decision maker and controller. The structure of production as regards scale and location will depend on the degree of centralisation of decision-making, ownership and control, over productive resources. Small-scale capitalism implies decentralised control; rural cooperatives likewise. Monopoly capital or state capital implies centralised control. Hence the pattern of investment input and output is determined by the "locus" of control over the means of production. Technology will similarly be dependent on this control structure, and the degree to which small-scale labour-intensive techniques are possible depends on the degree of decentralisation of control and ownership. The Tanzanian economy is characterised by centralised control, strongly influenced by external trade and foreign technology and capital dependence. It follows that Tanzania's objective of relocation of industry and small scale-industrial development will not be achieved, and technological alternatives will not be adopted, unless a far-reaching redistribution of control occurs in industry, involving local enterprises, cooperatives, district development corporations and other organisations able to control appropriation and distribution of investible surpluses, bank credit, savings, employment policy, raw material supplies and markets.

Experience to date does not suggest that decentralisation has been effective in terms of industrial strategy, as will be discussed with reference to the 3rd 5 year plan. It may also be considered that without the withdrawal, at least, partial of large-scale foreign capital, it will not be effective, because control will continue to be concentrated for major sectors of industry and often import-export oriented. Technology choice is therefore rooted in the political economy of the country and technology policy is dependent on political and economic processes.

Industrial planning in Tanzania must recognise the need to decentralise control if technological alternatives and small-scale production are to be successfully implemented. India and China, the two countries which have made the most intensive efforts in this respect, are good examples of the close link existing between the pattern of ownership and control of productive resources and the pattern of technologies adopted in industry.

The need for decentralised control must be recognised by adopting three levels of control—national level, region/district level, and village or urban craft, or primary cooperative level. The pattern of productive techniques needs to be planned in relation to the pattern of control.

SMALL-SCALE INDUSTRIES: TANZANIAN EXPERIENCE

Small-scale production makes a significant contribution to the industrial sector of all countries including industrialised countries. Despite the fact that economic development has led historically to increasing concentration of industry, small-scale production has survived particularly in specialised markets not susceptible to mass production, or industries in which technological progress has been relatively unimportant. In an underdeveloped economy, as the case of Tanzania in 1961, small-scale production may be the rule rather than the exception, although recent years have seen the superimposition of larger-scale plants on to the small-scale structure backed by national and international capital.

At the time of Independence the industrial structure consisted mostly of small-scale agro-processing and extractive industry, crafts, and some light manufacturing industry. Organised small units (employing 10-100) have stagnated over the past few years in Tanzania and their share of employment and gross output has dropped. In 1966, 346 small units (78% of the total) accounted for 36% of gross output. In 1971, 348 recorded small units (74% of the total) accounted for 29% of gross output. In the largest units (employing over 500) a steady increase of output share has occurred, and in 1971 the 15 largest enterprises (3% of the total) accounted for 25% of recorded gross output. Since 1971 this category has further increased its share, and the small-scale share has declined further.

The stagnation of small enterprises is caused by two complementary trends: firstly, the emergence of the parastatal sector at national level controlling all the largest enterprises; and secondly, the relative decline of the private sector previously engaged in relatively small-scale production.

Sectors in which larger-scale units have not been established are characterised still by private ownership; this includes furniture, wearing apparel (including knitwear), printing, paper products (except for one state owned packaging enterprise), rubber and plastics (one state enterprise). Subsectors in which the private sector predominates include oil milling, soft drinks, soap, glue, insecticides, bricks and concrete products. These have also remained at fairly small-scale. Medium and large-scale capital (including private capital) has mainly entered industries which were not previously represented at small-scale—textiles, cigarettes, fertilizer, cement glass, petroleum, steel and aluminium rolling, metal containers, sugar, cashewnuts, meat. However, it has also taken over in areas which were previously and still are represented at small-scale—tobacco, grain milling, vegetable oil (planned), bakery, fruit canning, sawmilling, leather tanneries, shoes.

This tends to imply that the major factor involved in establishment of large-scale units has not been one of technical necessity or alleged economies of scale, etc., but one of wanting to control market supplies and production at national level (parastatals) or international (foreign capital), a latter example being the shoe factory set up by BATA.

This deduction is reinforced when one considers that two sectors of major importance—chemicals and engineering–account for relatively low share of output and are fairly fragmented (except for the fertilizer factory) in small-scale units. Neither of these sectors is under the control of a specific national parastatal, and international capital has not moved into these areas on any large scale. Yet these are the areas which would normally interest a national level manufacturer because of their relatively high import requirements, skilled labour requirements and technological sophistication.

The statistics available from the 1971 survey of industries reveal that the small-scale share in total industrial output showed sharpest declines over 1969–71 (see Table 1).

The available data are not, however, very helpful, and the small sample size involved in each industry means that even if accurate, they do not provide a good guide to future planning of industrial concentration levels. The overall trends, however, seem to be fairly clear.

For the craft and cottage industry sector, fairly comprehensive information is available from the Ministry of Labour files although they exclude small family enterprises and rural units. It also appears that the files have not been kept to date. The tabulation of data compiled from the files showed a total of 12,900 people employed in industrial units of less than 10 employees in 1975, and 18,000 in enterprises employing 10–50 (see Table 2).

The 1971 survey of industry showed only about 6,500 people employed in enterprises of 10–50, excluding vehicle repairs, sisal decortication, and government

TABLE 1: SMALL-SCALE GROSS OUTPUT SHARE BY INDUSTRIAL GROUP

	1969	1971
Beverages	37%	18%
Tanneries	100%	16%
Shoes	13%	8%
Petroleum and Other Chemicals	62%	35%
Rubber Products	100%	77%
Non-metallic Mineral Products	20%	6%
Machinery	100%	56%
Electrical Equipment	100%	4%
Transport Equipment	100%	45%
For the following categories, small-scale contribution was negligible in both years.		
Sugar (Jaggery)	2%	2.6%
Tobacco	1%	—
Textiles and Textiles Goods	8%	6%
Breweries	5%	5%
Cordage, Rope and Twine	3%	8%

workshops which at this scale probably employed about 4,000 people in total. The discrepancy of 7,500 people between the two surveys suggests that either or both of these statistical sources may not be reliable. Nevertheless, we are forced to use the available data to examine the structure of craft and mini-scale enterprises.

Of the total number of units reported in Table 2, about 80% are known to be using power (diesel engines, electricity, etc.). Those not using power are mainly bakeries, footwear, tailoring, and leather tanning. As can be seen, a large proportion of employed is recorded in grain milling (35%), wearing apparel (tailoring), carpentry (furniture), and vehicle and bicycle repairs (all over 10% of total employment). The negligible contribution of industries such as brick manufacture, oil milling, metal products, knitwear and soap, suggests that the records are incomplete. Small-scale brewing is also vastly underestimated, not surprisingly, and crafts such as mat and basket weaving, pottery, boat building, often seasonal or part time cottage activities, are not reported at all.

In order to assess the contribution of craft industry to the economy, some estimates of its contribution to output and employment will be useful. Unfortunately as mentioned already, available data are not very reliable. Thus, the contribution of this extensive labour force can only be approximated.

Table 3 presents estimates for total value-added in organised industries (over 101 employees) which are based on Devplan's estimate,[10] adjusted for the inclusion of certain sectors such as sisal processing, vehicle repairs and government workshops. Employment is based on calculations from the Ministry of Labour files, which include these sectors. The estimated contribution of the craft sector to output (30%) in rural and urban areas is approximate; however, it does conform with an estimate quoted for China in 1954 (25%), and it also appears to conform with what is known about India.[11] The expansion of factory industry is likely to erode this share rapidly over the next few years. Nevertheless, it suggests that an extensive and unorganised capacity exists for production of simple manufactured goods. Selective promotion of these trades is a promising possibility for the development of low-cost light manufacturing.

TABLE 2: SMALL-SCALE AND CRAFT ENTERPRISES 1974–5

	No. of Units Employing less than 10	*Employment*	*Employment Share*
Meat, Dairy Products	17	55	
Grain Milling	3,020	4,916	35%
Bakeries	86	415	3%
Jaggery Mills	40	222	
Confectionery	7	40	
Edible Oil	9	68	
Coffee Curing, Roasting	137	646	5%
Miscellaneous Foods	35	182	
Brewery	2	9	
Soft Drinks	27	116	
Tobacco Processing	27	42	
Cotton Ginning	5	14	
Cordage, Rope, Twine	17	42	
Kapok, Coir	5	24	
Footwear	109	327	2.5%
Wearing Apparel	623	1,526	11.5%
Sawmilling and Wood Products	38	174	
Furniture, Fixtures	324	1,306	10%
Printing, Publishing	28	96	
Leather Tanning	33	128	
Rubber Products	3	22	
Basic Chemicals and Non-edible Oil	18	38	
Pharmaceuticals and Insecticides	18	44	
Soap, Cosmetics	20	141	
Bricks, Tiles	5	23	
Concrete Products	19	102	
Metal Products	17	111	1%
Vehicle, Bicycle & Machinery Repairs	476	1,817	14%
Other	74	268	
Total	5,242	12,916	
Average size of Unit		2.6	

SOURCE: Ministry of Labour.

TABLE 3: ESTIMATES OF VALUE-ADDED IN CRAFT AND MINI-SCALE PRODUCTION

	Total Employ-ment	Value added per Head Shs. per annum	Total Value Shs. million
Urban	13,000	4,500	58.5
Rural (full-time)	100,000	2,500	250
Rural (part-time)	300,000	1,000 (average)	300
Total Organised Industries (1974) (above 10 employees)	83,000	17,000 (rounded)	1,400
Total	496,000	—	2,008.5
All Crafts % of Total Industrial Value-added	—	—	30%

SMALL-SCALE INDUSTRIAL STRATEGY IN TANZANIA

Small-scale industries in industrialised countries are peripheral to the principal motive force—large-scale capital, though fill in important gaps for specialised products, tailor-made equipment, and products or markets generally not feasible for mass production.

Small-scale production in most underdeveloped countries, however, is the central, not the peripheral, type of industrial organisation because of the existence of an extensive rural population and urban fringe population (80% rural in India, 92% rural in Tanzania).

Large-scale capital is often the most dynamic force, but in many regions (including India, Latin America, etc.) it is narrowly-based and apparently incapable of spreading incomes to, or mobilising resources of, the country and population as a whole.

As a general rule in all countries, with notable exceptions, small-scale production is mainly concentrated in primary processing and light consumer manufactures; these are food processing, textiles and garments, leather and shoes, ceramics, bricks, tiles, wood products, furniture, printing and light fabricated metal products. The large-scale sector is concentrated in industries such as cement, industrial chemicals, fertilizers, basic metals, petroleum, petro-chemicals, heavy engineering and transport equipment. In addition sugar manufacture and pulp and paper are predominantly large-scale.

It is not possible here to go into the precise reasons why specific industries have been established on a large-scale; in general, however, they are the ones which have been established later in the industrialisation process when the capital-intensity of industry as a whole has been relatively high. They are both capital and technology-intensive, requiring relatively high proportions of high level technical manpower. They are also usually those with the highest growth elasticities, and long run growth potential.

Rweyemamu[12] provides some calculations of growth or income-elasticities of demand in higher growth-elasticity industries, as follows:

TABLE 4: GROWTH ELASTICITIES BY INDUSTRY

Machinery	2.80
Paper	2.69
Petroleum	2.22
Basic Metals	2.14
Rubber	2.00
Wood Products	1.77
Clothing	1.69
Chemicals	1.66
Leather	1.64
Non-Metallic Minerals (cement, glass, ceramics, etc.)	1.62
Textiles	1.44

The above figures show, with an inconsistency in the case of chemicals, that the highest growth elasticities occur in the industries that as a general rule have been set up on larger scales.

International comparisons of capital-intensity in industry (capital employment) based on Japan, the U.S.A., and Tanzanian statistics (survey of industry estimates based on depreciation/employment calculations) show general correspondence in identification of most highly capital-intensive industry. These are petroleum and coal products, chemicals, iron, steel and non-ferrous basic metals, and non-metallic minerals. Generally therefore, although with apparent exceptions (e.g. non-metallic mineral products and machinery) it appears that high growth elasticities and high capital-intensity coincide. Machinery is an important exception, but it can be argued in this case that the "technology-intensity" of production (embodied in skilled manpower and high training capital expenditure) is particularly high, and therefore increases the effective capital-intensity. Paper production in the U.S.A. is highly capital-intensive, though relatively less in Japan. Textiles, which are of relatively low capital-intensity in U.S.A. and Japan, are particularly high in Tanzania due to the especially intensive large-scale investment in this sector. Industries with normally the lowest capital inputs are leather, printing, wood industries, textiles, wearing apparel and rubber. Consequently, underdeveloped capital-scarce economies with an extensive small industries base tend to concentrate in the latter industries, and also food processing.

In determining what types of industries should be developed on a small scale in Tanzania, there is, therefore, no doubt about the fact that light industries are generally suitable from the lessons of industrial experience in all other countries. This means that Tanzania should aim firstly at small-scale food processing, textiles and garments, leather, wood products, furniture, printing, pottery and ceramics, bricks, tiles, some fabricated metal products, and machinery and equipment repair work. These industries in general are unambiguously suited to small-scale production for two reasons:

(a) small-scale and craft production already exists in most of these areas, which can be used as a base;
(b) they tend to have the lowest growth elasticities and/or capital-intensity of production in highly industrialised countries, and therefore do not justify especially high concentration of investment funds in the long term in an industrial development programme.

More difficult to decide is the role of small-scale production in the basic heavy industry sector. We may assume that certain heavy industries are definitely ruled out for small-scale sector production in Tanzania on grounds of especially high capital requirement; these are tyres, petroleum refining, and basic metals (steel and aluminium, etc.) and heavy engineering. However, other basic industries—chemicals, fertilizer, cement and paper—are not necessarily to be ruled out. Japanese and U.S. statistics conflict where the capital-intensity of paper production is concerned, and small-scale paper manufacture for certain segments of the market is carried out in India and China. In the case of fertilizer and cement, small-scale production is widespread in China despite the apparent existence of internal economies of scale.[13]

One of the most important differences between Chinese and Indian industry seems to be reflected in the existence of these basic industries on a small-scale in China and not in India. This derives from China's objective of decentralised industry and local integration, with each locality supplying as far as possible its own basic capital and intermediate goods for local agriculture, manufacturing, and construction. India's system is based on surplus extraction from and not integration within rural areas. If Tanzania is also aiming at rural development and regional or sub-regional economic integration, it follows that attention must be paid to these small-scale basic industries, and not merely to the extractive industry and light manufacturing sectors for small-scale production. It also follows that decentralisation of ownership and control in Tanzania must be reinforced.

Industries such as sugar and textiles, which come within the light industry sector but are normally set up on a relatively large-scale, may require special investigation, but the experience of India and elsewhere suggests that small-scale decentralisation is feasible and a promising possibility.

A large number of other manufacturing industries such as paper products, rubber products, basic and other chemicals (soap, detergent, plastic, adhesives, paint, insecticides) pharmaceuticals, concrete and clay products, and light engineering (machinery, equipment, and component manufacture and repair, and precision instruments) are appropriate for small-scale production, and are already produced in many cases in Tanzania (some of these are discussed in another section). Small-scale glass manufacture is a possibility, though highly skill-intensive. Although steel production is apparently based, even in China, on units of not less than 50,000 tons, pig iron production is at a smaller scale, and may be regarded as a possibility for certain rural locations with small concentrations of iron ore, coal, etc., in the future.

If decentralised planned development is to succeed in Tanzania then rural small-scale industry must be planned on similar lines to national large-scale industry strategy. A transformational strategy at national level, involving the convergence and domestic resources and domestic demand must be paralleled at regional and sub-regional levels by a similar transformational strategy aimed at the development of both heavy (capital and intermediate goods) industry and light industry. Regional industry must adopt techniques of production appropriate to the size of the local market and to the types of raw materials available.

Urban small industry on the other hand should concentrate on light manufacturing (foods, textiles, shoes, furniture, paper, printing and paper products, chemical products excluding fertilizer, rubber and plastic products, some fabricated metal products, and light engineering (components, equipment and machinery and vehicle repairs). This is because urban markets, urban manpower availability, and infrastructural facilities may justify localised large-scale production, and therefore in the heavy capital-intensive industry area, small-scale production may not be able to compete with large-scale production.

A demarcation of output between small and large-scale production must be made. No industry (with the possible exception of light manufactures such as some foods, garments, shoes, furniture) would justify 100% small-scale production because there are market and resource concentrations which do justify larger-scale production (e.g. urban and export markets). (In Tanzania "urban" applies to Dar es Salaam and seven smaller towns of over 30,000 inhabitants). No industry except, for example, steel, petroleum, tyres and heavy engineering justifies 100% large-scale production, for reasons previously discussed relating to the need for local integration and resource mobilisation.

The degree of decentralisation must be carefully worked out for each industry, taking into account firstly the existing industrial base and secondly the long-term potential for development at different scales of production and with different technologies.

Small-scale basic industries may be set up to manufacture substitute products or use substitute materials, as follows:

Material	*Substitute*
Cement and Cement Products	Lime, Clay, Bricks, Tiles and Pipes
Steel, Aluminium, Plastic for containers, equipment, (roofing, building fittings, etc.)	Wood, Clay (ceramics), Glass
Synthetic Fibre (nylon, polyester, etc.)	Cotton, Wool, Sisal, Coir, etc.
Petroleum Fuel	Coal, Charcoal, Hydro-electricity

By substituting materials and products, it may be possible to avoid the need for capital-intensive investment, or investment in skilled manpower in basic industries.

Although more detailed investigation is essential, from the above analysis certain conclusions may immediately be drawn.

(a) Central government investment should be oriented towards basic industry, while light industry and primary processing of essential consumer goods should become increasingly the concern of regional and sub-regional authorities.

(b) Selected small-scale basic industries should be also set up at regional and sub-regional level where appropriate materials are available, aiming at covering regional markets.

(c) The following industries (among others) should be decentralised and largely restricted to small-scale production for the foreseeable future foods (fruit and vegetable canning, grain milling, vegetable oils), wearing apparel (including knitwear) and shoes (leather), tanneries, sawmilling, furniture, printing, bricks, tiles, pottery and ceramics.

(d) Partial decentralisation moves should be made for sugar, cashewnuts, textiles, sisal and coir fibre and products, paper manufacture, and metal products (containers, aluminium utensils).

(e) Partial decentralisation should be investigated and implemented for cement, fertilizer, chemicals and glass.

(f) Other areas which are already characterised by relatively small-scale production—paper products, chemicals, pharmaceuticals, and chemical products (plastics, paint, insecticide, adhesives, etc.), rubber products (excluding tyres), bricks, tiles, concrete products, light engineering and machinery and equipment repairs—should serve as a base for further expansion at small-scale, while the establishment of larger-scale projects in these industries should be carefully evaluated to determine their necessity and their social cost-benefit characteristics.

The above proposals generally conflict with Tanzania's current policy. Particularly, in case (c), many existing projects and plans seem to conflict with this proposal. There seems to be no doubt that if Tanzania is to embark upon a transformational strategy for industry she must concentrate central investment funds on basic industries and manufactured goods which do not already have a relatively healthy productive base, and/or which do require relatively high investment in fixed assets and skilled manpower. The industries of group (c) in terms of this analysis must be confined to the small-scale sector, bearing in mind certain provisions made in the following section of the paper.

A FRAMEWORK FOR DECENTRALISED INTEGRATED INDUSTRIAL STRATEGY

A proportion of industrial output is to be demarcated for (a) local control, (b) smaller-scale labour-intensive plants using relatively simple equipment.

Smaller plants will be set up in rural areas, small towns, and cities. In the first two cases, as discussed, they will principally be concerned with laying the foundation for an integrated regional or sub-regional economy. In the third case they will be principally concerned with light industry and ancillary production feeding larger-scale urban industry (components, semi-finished materials, packaging, etc.). Light industry in cities should be concerned with consumer goods as well as ancillary products, as described in the previous section.

Rural and small town industries will generally cater primarily for the local market (a small town may be classified as having in 1975 less than 20,000 inhabitants), concentrating on the use of local materials and manpower.

Locations in which resources of minerals, crops or livestock are highly concentrated, and surplus to local requirements (including plantations) will establish projects of larger-scale and either under national control (where national or export markets are aimed for) or regional district control (where regional markets are attainable), or else under dual control of the locality and regional or national authorities. Examples of this could be:

Product	*Market*	*Level of Control and Scale of Enterprise*
Cut Diamonds	Export	Large-scale national
Processed Cashewnuts	Export	National/local dual authority, various scales of production
Grain Milling	Regional and Sub-regional	Regional, district or village control, small-scale production
Tanned Leather	Regional/National Export	Local/regional dual authority small to medium scale production
Iron, Steel	National/Export	National/large-scale

Dual authority in the case of cashewnuts could be split into (a) hand processing under primary co-operative, (b) mechanised processing and all export handling and packaging under national parastatal control (C.A.T.A.). Dual authority in the case of tanneries for national markets would be in the hands of (a) local co-operatives, D.D.C.s, etc. for procuring of hides and production of leather, (b) under national control for marketing nationally or export.

Similarly, in cases of local plants using a large proportion of imported (ex-region or ex-country) inputs, central co-ordination of supplies will be required. For example, local engineering enterprises which require outside supplies of materials and machinery could come under "national engineering corporation" control in conjunction with local enterprise managers. Co-ordinations of supply facilitates co-ordination of investment and production. Large-scale petroleum and fertilizer based on imported materials would logically justify national level control.

A definition of a regional, district or village-level project is one which has over 50% local production value-added, and sells over 50% of its products locally, or combinations of these two. Regional, district and village level policy will be to find ways of increasing local production value-added and local market share, given the need to establish efficient plants, and taking into account the use of substitute materials available.

Medium to large-scale production will cater mainly for urban and export markets, and also rural markets where it is established that a particular production cannot be feasibly carried out on a small-scale (tyres, petroleum, steel, complex equipment (diesel engines, tractors), heavy electricals, etc. However, the possibilities for decentralisation will increase as capital and skills are accumulated throughout the economy.

In drawing up a decentralised industrial strategy, the following steps should be taken:

(a) definition of the national pattern of ownership and control, and establishment of general principles regarding what types of products should be produced at what levels of control;
(b) estimation of long-term demand and production targets, industry by industry, taking into account future structural change;
(c) definition of resources available, region by region, capable of potential exploitation by local industry;
(d) output demarcations for a range of basic industries and essential consumer goods according to level of ownership and control, and scale of production;
(e) definition of appropriate techniques of production available at each scale of production, based in available materials and manpower.

The above procedure is merely phase one of the process; phase two and beyond, which concern identification of projects within the plan guidelines, decision to go ahead, implementation, start up and operation are of course the actual substance of development. Tanzania has an established public sector local development institutional structure which could be invigorated and reinforced as the basis of rural and small town industry. Food processing plants (fruit, oil extraction, grain, starch, cashewnuts, meat, fish processing, jaggery) and other extractive industries (ginning, sawmilling, tanneries, etc.) could logically come under control of the co-operative system (primary village societies up to district and regional unions) because the rural co-operative system is already handling many of these materials in the course of crop and livestock marketing.

Mineral extraction (salt, lime, coal, etc.) may be handled by the same organisations at village level (primary societies) or by district development corporations. Local light and heavy manufacturing plants would be under the control of district development corporations and, if they were established, regional development corporations.

Village organisations should also handle a range of light manufacturing activities—garments, shoes, furniture, matches, and other wood products, handloom textiles, sacks and rope, soap, metal products, agricultural implements and bicycle repair, bricks, tiles and pottery ware.

Near-city villages may handle manufacture of components and ancillary products (e.g. hoe handles, cotton bobbins, cardboard, shoe lasts) for urban industry, as well as local consumption.

POLICY CONCLUSIONS: THE PROMOTION OF SMALL-SCALE INDUSTRIES

The main objective of this study has been to provide a background for formulation of small-scale industrial strategy.

Tanzania, like many underdeveloped economies, has not developed a private enterpreneurial class capable of adequate mobilisation of resources for extensive development, and is unlikely to do so.

In order to mobilise what resources are available and expand the currently weak and dependent industrial base, Tanzania has embarked upon socialisation of industry via public ownership and control of the means of production. It follows from this that an effective and powerful public and cooperative control system is necessary. The following are some conclusions of this relating to development of small-scale industries.

(1) If a small-scale and rural industrialisation programme is to be effective it is important that resources (capital, manpower, and skills) be directed into regional, district and village organisations to a far greater extent than is currently planned for 1975–80. Without such structural change the small industries programme will fail to mobilise rural resources, and rural industrialisation will not develop in the face of domination by urban large-scale capital.

(2) Demarcation of organisational jurisdiction for control of industry should be undertaken; i.e. what share of industrial investment and output and which industries are to be controlled by which organisations—national, regional and district organisations, primary societies and village organisations. This would require the development of a powerful central planning authority capable of (a) analysing industrial development possibilities with regard to scale of production, technology and location of industry; (b) formulating a multi-technology stratified plan; (c) initiating investigations of required industries; (d) evaluating proposals; (e) issuing binding directives, where necessary, to development corporations concerning development plans and required characteristics of the industries they are setting up,

especially with regard to scale, technology and location.

What this also implies is the need for a national technology policy.

(3) Light industries should be steadily decentralised to regional, district and village control in phase with the development of local capabilities. Certain heavy industries should also be introduced at regional and district level, as proposed in the previous section.

Such industries as shoes, garments, sawmilling, furniture, bakeries, oil milling, drinks, fruit canning, and grain milling should be considered for an immediate regional control. In particular, the possibility of rapid decentralisation for sugar, leather and cashewnuts industries should be investigated.

(4) The strengthening of regional capability has to be undertaken. The trained manpower should be drafted into the district development corporations and other local organisations. The D.D.C.s must be linked directly to a national planning and advisory body (e.g. S.I.D.O., I.F.M., National Consultancy Service, Central Planning Authority). Regional and district planning units may also be linked directly to the Central Planning Authority.

(5) Some incentive system may be required such as "collective productivity bonus" to be based perhaps on assessment by local government or party authorities, and payable to the personnel of the organisation running local industries.

(6) Training of business and technical personnel has to be rapidly developed at regional and district level. Part-time and "sandwich-course" training for specific skills must be started especially in the areas of finance sales and purchasing management, investment appraisal, product identification and technology policy. Regional and district business training centres may be set up to cover areas under their control. Training for village industry may be organised through an invigorated version of the current R.T.C. network.

(7) For the start of the 4th plan, a regional and a co-operative/village sector industries' plan should be worked out together with industrial sector plans involving demarcation of output within each industry. Separate promotional programmes may allow a different approach to be made for each, under different authority. The initial regional industries' plan could be drawn up by regions in conjunction with national planning and advisory services (S.I.D.O., I.F.M., National Consultancy Service, Central Planning Authority). The village and cooperative industry plan could be drawn up by villages in conjunction with regional or district planning and advisory service. This may permit localisation of decision making combined with access to central technical capability. Direct central control of a village industries' plan does not seem practicable and is not desirable if appropriate types of technology are to be introduced, relevant to local resources and needs.

(8) Given the existing scarcity of technical manpower and entrepreneurial strata, a special technology development programme for regional and district industry may be started at natinoal level, using initially foreign personnel and technology. This may be in the form of a pilot project programme introducing new technologies to the country. Each pilot project would be evaluated during this time in order to determine potential for expansion. Pilot projects could be set up in all light and heavy industries considered appropriate for regional industrial development. These projects should include the following small-scale units excluding those which are already well represented within the country (e.g. garments, shoemaking, furniture, soap); sugar, fruit canning, cassava and maize starch, hand cashewnut processing, alternative oil milling technologies, alternative textile spinning and weaving technologies, integrated sisal and coir fibre processing and product manufacture, tannery, mobile saw mill, paper manufacture, small chemical plants (sodium silicate, alcohol, caustic soda, sulphuric acid, etc.), chemical fertilizer (phosphate or nitrogen based), insecticide, pottery and ceramics manufacture, lime, small-scale cement, mechanised and hand made roofing tiles manufacture, farm equipment, implement manufacture and repair plant, transport and industrial equipment repair plant.

Each pilot plant should be set up on a commeicial basis and should act as a training centre for apprentices to be redeployed to similar projects elsewhere after training is completed. The plants should be based as much as possible on local manpower and materials and should cater for local markets and aim at commercial profitability. Local personnel should be involved in plant design machinery selection, implementation, and installation.

On successful completion of the initial introduction period the pilot plants should be integrated into regional or local organisations and control should pass from the national to local level. Most of these projects can also be scaled down to village level.

At village level a craft development programme involving mobilisation of existing technology may act as the counterpart of the pilot plants using imported technology. Craft development may be handled through various promotional schemes as discussed below.

(9) Experience in other countries, including China, suggests that rural industrial wage rates are generally lower than urban rates. This is due to the lower general levels of labour productivity in industries of low capital intensity. It is also justified by the lower general price levels that prevail in rural areas consuming locally processed products.

It is necessary to come to a decision about whether rural industrial workers should receive rural rates (about 60% of urban) or industrial rates (urban rates). It seems desirable that a minimum wage differential should prevail if rural industry is to be competitive with urban industry in some cases. The wage differentials should correspond to productivity differentials.

(10) The above suggestions have not considered existing promotional methods employed in other developing countries.

The list typically includes credit facilities, raw material hirepurchase funds, government purchase programmes, marketing, industrial estates, ancillary development programmes, "intensive campaigns" designed to mobilise entrepreneurial ability, prototype development and training centres or consultancy services.

The priority in Tanzania is to decide on the allocation of investment and output to different levels of control, to introduce a technology policy, and to redirect resources for rural industrial development. These, as in any country, are the preconditions for a successful rural industrial programme. This study has been concerned with preconditions and implementation mechanisms (e.g. pilot projects). The detailed and elaborate promotional programmes may be grafted on to the proposed base. It is clear, however, that credit facilities or special investment incentives, are relevant more to a private enterprise-based programme as in India. The allocation of output and financial and manpower resources in a centrally controlled economy renders the question of investment incentives less important.

NOTES

1. C. Thomas, ERB Seminar Paper, November 1972. Also see his book, *Transformation and Dependency*, New York: Monthly Review Press, 1976.
2. Tanzanian industry is currently characterised by a low level of internal linkages; see J. F. Rweyemamu, *Underdevelopment and Industrialisation in Tanzania*, Nairobi: Oxford University Press, 1973.
3. See C. Thomas, *op. cit.*
4. E.g. India under R's 0.75 million worth of machinery; Japan under 100 employees, etc.
5. Quoted in J. F. Rweyemamu, *op. cit.*
6. Francis Stewart, "Technology and Employment in Less Developed Countries", *World Development*, March 1974.
7. *Source:* forthcoming study by Barker, Bhagavan, Wield and Collande, University of Dar es Salaam.
8. *Source:* National Milling Corporation.
9. See, for example, M. Wuyts, "The Choice of Techniques: Some Critical Questions," ERB Paper 74.3.
10. 1961 Census of Industrial Production.
11. See ERB Paper 76.5, pp. 53–54.
12. J. R. Rweyemamu, *op. cit.*
13. For details of intercountry comparison, see the original ERB Paper 76.5, pp. 57–71.

The Tanzanian Price Control System: Theory, Practice and Some Possible Improvements*

ROBERT C. RICE

Introduction

Tanzania has a long history of using price controls, going back to the colonial period. However, with the passage of the Price Control Act in 1974 and the formation of the National Price Commission, the number of products and services controlled has been extended. The purpose of this paper is to analyse the theory of the present price control system under the jurisdiction of the National Price Commission (NPC) and its successes and shortcomings.

In general terms the functions of NPC are: (a) to determine reasonable price structures on a national basis and provide for their orderly variation when necessary; (b) to ensure that prices of goods and services in Tanganyika are compatible with and conform to the principles of socialism and the political, economic and social aspirations of the people of the United Republic; (c) to perform such other functions as are conferred on it by this Act or as the President may from time to time confer upon it.[1] This statement of functions gives only a general picture of what the goals of the price controls should be.

A more detailed picture about the goals of controlling prices is obtained when the factors to be taken into account in determining the price structure are examined. According to the Regulation of Prices Act, 1973,

> The Price Commission shall, in determining the price structure of any goods or services, have to regard:
>
> (a) the commodities and services essential to the community;
>
> (b) the need to avoid unduly rapid or frequent variations in prices;
>
> (c) the need to preserve and promote the competitive position of local products in the domestic market as well as in foreign markets;
>
> (d) the need to prevent the income of peasants and workers in the United Republic from being affected adversely by unnecessary and unjustified price increases;
>
> (e) the need to maintain fair relationships among the incomes of different sectors of the community;
>
> (f) the need to ensure the continued ability of the Government to finance development programmes and recurrent expenditure;
>
> (g) the need to provide circumstances under which local manufacturing, processing and service industries are able to maintain efficiency and expand their business;
>
> (h) the need to provide circumstances conducive to a healthy and orderly development of trade and commerce in rural as well as urban areas;
>
> (i) such guidelines as to margins or otherwise as the Minister may from time to time issue.[2]

It is not implied that price controls alone can achieve these goals but that they will contribute towards their fulfilment. For example, fiscal and wage policies are normally the primary instruments used to achieve goal (e). Implicit in goal (d) would probably be the prevention of monopolistic or oligopolistic pricing both at ex-factory, wholesale and retail levels. Goal (f) implies that prices should be set high enough so parastatal enterprises realise surpluses which can be used for financing further investment. Revenues for financing investment can also be raised through taxation rather than price controls. Goal (g) states that maintaining efficiency at the firm level is important but does not place an emphasis on using the price system to promote efficiency and increases in productivity.

Another part of the Act lists other factors that need to be considered in determining the price structure. These cannot be considered as goals but are only factors such as the cost of production of the product, rate of turnover, etc.

For some goals the more one is achieved, the less another one can be achieved. For example, goals (f) and (g) are both inconsistent with goal (d). Generally the more the NPC is able to put pressure on productive enterprises to keep their prices low so they remain competitive and prevent price increases, the lower their profits will be, and therefore the lower will be their capability to generate resources to expand their businesses and to pay taxes so the government can finance its programmes. In practice this inconsistency seems to have been resolved by the NPC attempting to keep the prices charged by producers as low as possible, subject to the constraint that they are permitted to make up to a certain maximum margin on their production and sales. Thus the firms are allowed to generate surpluses for expansion, the second part of goal (g). Still, however, resources to fund industrial expansion and government programmes would be greater with no price controls than with the present system.

DETERMINATION OF PRICES

Who Sets Price Ceilings?

Under the terms of the Act a National Price Commission was established with the power to fix maximum prices for the sale of goods, maximum service charges, maximum hire charges and maximum commissions except when these powers had already been delegated to other government bodies. It has no power to regulate wage rates. The chairman and chief executive officer of the

*ERB Paper 76.4.

Price Commission is the Price Commissioner. The Regional Development Directors and District Development Directors are normally the Assistant Price Commissioners in their respective regions and districts. The Assistant Price Commissioners together with the Regional Price Control Advisory Committees have the power to set maximum prices of goods and services in their regions for the areas where these maximum prices have not been established by the National Price Commission.

Goods Controlled by NPC

The National Price Commission has the power to set maximum prices of all goods, service charges, hire charges and commissions which are not controlled by other government bodies. Producer prices for most agricultural commodities and retail prices for the most important basic foods are set by the Economic Committee of the Cabinet, after considering the recommendations made by the Ministry of Agriculture and other Ministries. Electricity, railway, rental, postal, telephone, telegraph, water, bus, ocean shipping, foreign exchange and wage rates are set by other agencies without requiring the approval of NPC. There is a large number of goods whose prices are still not controlled, especially both imported and domestically produced ingredient inputs (except for textiles) and capital goods.

The prices of the majority of consumer goods domestically manufactured in medium or large-scale factories, and some imported manufactured consumer goods are controlled by the Commission. Maximums are set for ex-factory, importers, wholesale, sub-wholesale and retail prices. However, the regions and districts in which the price ceilings set by the Commission apply vary with the product. For some the pan-territorial price ceilings set by the Commission, apply in all areas of Tanzania; for others they only apply in some or all regional centres and towns where the manufacturer or wholesaler has sales agents. For others they only apply in the city where the factory or importer is located.[3]

Because the NPC in determining the price structure should have regard to the commodities and services essential to the community, goal (a), the implication is that there should be more emphasis on controlling the prices of essential than luxury goods. Before 1973 only a few items were brought under price control, such as matches, khanga, grey sheeting, white and dyed sheeting, jute and sisal bags, etc. In early 1973 the Government formed a price Control Task Force (the predecessor to NPC) which fixed the ceiling prices of about 400 commonly consumed items. The Household Budget Survey was used to find out which items were most important in the consumers' budget. By March 1974, 602 groups of domestically produced items and 464 groups of imported items were controlled.[4] Included in this list were items such as imported cheese, liquor, terylene/worsted suiting, sarees, tape recorders, refrigerators, deep freezers, records, electric typewriters, etc., which cannot be considered to be essential goods for the majority of Tanzanians.

There are some medium or large-scale manufacturers producing consumer goods whose prices have not yet been controlled, such as Tanzanian Shoe Co., Sunflag Ltd., National Garments Manufacture Ltd., Tanganyika African General Engineering Co., Tanganyika Enamelware Co. Ltd., Wire Drawing and Allied Industries Ltd., Daikin Air Conditioning Ltd., African Metals Industries, Mabati Ltd., and A.G. Abdulhussein and Co. Ltd.

The NPC does not distinguish between goods sold by private firms, DDCs and cooperatives and whether it is a private firm or a parastatal producing the goods, as the price controls apply to all of them. The power to impose price ceilings on used goods has not been exercised except for motor vehicles. There is no provision made for a buyer to pay a price above the ceiling price if he needs the goods immediately.

The NPC also has the power to prescribe the type of packing, weight, size, quality and the processing and ingredients of any goods manufactured in Tanganyika. The Commission has exercised these powers somewhat with respect to packing, weight, size and ingredients.

Factors in the Determination of Price Ceilings

In setting price ceilings the Commission is required to consider the factors and the effect of the ceilings on the achievement of the goals stated earlier. However, these do not provide very specific guidelines. Section 12 (2) of the Price Control Act deals with this matter. Essentially it states that in setting maximum prices of domestically produced goods the commission should also take into account all the costs of producing and supplying the goods, i.e. the direct costs of production, general overhead expenses, the normal wear and tear of capital assets, the cost of holding stocks of goods and materials, a margin in relation to the turnover and the capital employed, the level of various indirect taxes paid, and transportation costs. For imported goods they should take into account the cost of importing and clearing the goods, the indirect taxes paid on them and allowances to cover inventory carrying and storage costs and a margin in relation to the turnover and capital employed.

Soon after the Price Control Task Force was established, it was subjected to strong pressure to prevent price increases. Because they had to produce a list of maximum prices of manufactured goods in a short time, many of the ex-factory ceiling prices in their list of May 15, 1973 were the prices in effect at that time, but the margins permitted to wholesalers and retailers were reduced in many cases. During the next ten months they were able to examine the costs of production of many firms and received many requests for price increases that resulted in a new price list with many changes that was issued on March 28, 1974. The Commission continually receives applications for price changes and since then many additional changes in ceiling prices have been made.

Let us now look at the process followed by NPC in evaluating applications for price changes. Applications are made when there are changes in the cost of importing or producing an item.

IMPORTED ITEMS

The process is straight forward in that when submitting the applications, the documents that go along to support various costs and charges are easily available and are not prepared by the importer. This can be elaborated more clearly in following up the application for the review of prices on Phoenix bicycles model SPL 65 (Commission Paper 76c). Documents attached to the application were:

(a) Invoices showing the CIF cost of the item, i.e. one invoice for the old CIF and another for the new CIF cost;
(b) Customs duty documents;
(c) Sales tax document;
(d) Clearing and forwarding documents;
(e) Bank charges documents; and
(f) Wharfage and handling documents.

(b) – (f) are calculated as a per cent of the CIF cost. (a) – (f) comprise the landed costs to the importer. From this a margin of five per cent was calculated for the pan-territorial equalisation fund. The total of all this is the basis for calculating the various margins that will be awarded to the importer (8%), the wholesaler (5%) and retailer (10%) in order to set the maximum prices at each level.

This system gives the importer an incentive to (a) buy the product from a higher cost supplier or overvalue the CIF price of the product if the number of units permitted to be imported is unchanged and he can still sell the goods at the higher price, as his gross profits from importing the goods will then be greater; and (b) import goods with higher import duties. If the quantitative restriction on imports is according to the foreign exchange value instead of the number of units, there is still a slight incentive to buy from a higher cost supplier and overvalue the CIF price as the number of units imported will then be less and the overhead costs (which are not directly included in the formula determining the ceiling price) will therefore be lower resulting in the same gross profit but a larger net profit.

De facto the margins have for the most part been historically determined and are supposed to cover costs other than those mentioned above, i.e. administration expenses, rent of buildings, salaries, etc. Thus importers have an incentive to cut these costs which are only indirectly included in the margin. *De jure* the margins are based on the rate of turnover and capital employed. The latter implies an incentive for importers to increase their capital employed. Capital employed in this case is capital used to import the goods, for warehouses, and for vehicles for transportation to the wholesaler.

LOCALLY MANUFACTURED GOODS

Because the process is not very straightforward, it is difficult to say exactly in what form the submissions usually are. The method used varies somewhat with the officer evaluating the application. In general, information is sought on direct material costs, direct labour costs, manufacturing overheads and administrative and selling expenses, which are presented in a broken down form. The variations that occur in these cost items depend on the product or product line that is being presented in the application. In short, all costs associated by the manufacturers in the production of an item plus the cost of obtaining and handling raw materials are considered in determining the total cost for producing that item, provided that they are checked and verified by NPC. The manufacturer's margin (or factory mark-up) and all other margins to distributors are calculated as percentages of these costs. Ideally the margin is set at a level which enables the manufacturer to earn a "normal" rate of return on capital employed.[5] The NPC usually is not able to go to the extent of ascertaining whether certain costs, especially operating costs, were really warranted or not or whether the manufacturers had in fact tried alternative methods of reducing these costs before resorting to cover them through applying for price increases.

This system results in (a) there being little or no incentive to manufacturers to cut costs; in fact they can even report non-existent costs that cannot be easily traced by the limited staff of NPC; (b) there being initially an incentive to lower efficiency, because if the manufacturing costs are high because efficiency is low, and a price increase is granted, firms can increase their profits later by lowering their costs of production through increased efficiency without the controls.

There are other factors affecting the profit margin permitted to be added to the cost of producing or importing goods, for example, the expected rate of turnover. If the turnover is rapid the margin permitted is small, and vice versa. The rate of turnover is more important for importers, wholesalers and retailers than for manufacturers. Another factor which has affected the margin allowed in some cases is how rapidly it is expected the cost of manufacturing or importing the goods will increase. In this case the faster the cost of production is expected to increase, the larger the margin allowed, so the frequency of price increases will be less.

A final factor considered for products in demand in Kenya is the Tanzanian ceiling price in relation to the price in Kenya. If the ratio of the Kenyan price to the Tanzanian price is too high, there is a danger of the product being smuggled into Kenya. Khangas, cooking oils, and ghee are products where this possibility is taken into consideration. The price in Kenya is also a factor in setting the ceiling price on detergents and GI sheets.

A fully cost-plus system in setting retail ceiling prices is not used in that the margin applied on the wholesale price is the same for all retailers. Other costs such as rent of the building, cost of air-conditioning and higher costs of maintaining larger inventories of goods are not permitted to be passed on to the consumers.

If a cost-plus system of price ceilings is followed under conditions of a seller's market and restricted imports as is usually the case in Tanzania, then increases in the cost of production from increasing inefficiency and decreasing productivity can be passed on to consumers, as they also could be without price controls within certain limits. There is no independent control over efficiency as is usually provided by competition among domestic producers (because there are usually very few domestic producers of a product in Tanzania) and by competition with imports when there are no quantitative import restrictions.

The cost-plus system of setting ex-factory price ceilings could be changed so that no increases in costs caused by decreases in productivity are allowed to be passed on in the form of higher prices and so that all benefits from decreases in costs due to increases in productivity are permitted to accrue to the firm. This would give producers a strong incentive to increase their productivity.

Increases in the costs of production beyond the control of producers would be allowed to be passed on to the consumer. In order to separate out changes in cost due to changes in productivity from changes in cost beyond the control of the producers, the cost of production of each product assuming no change in productivity must be calculated. The formula for this for each product i is

$$(1/Q_{io})\left[(1+\frac{a}{100})\left(\sum_{j=1}^{n} W_{jt}L_{jo} + \sum_{k=1}^{r} P_{kt}X_{ko} + K_t + \sum_{m=1}^{s} I_{mt}K^*_{mo} + \sum_{q=1}^{u} E_{qt}\right)\right]$$

where a is the maximum percentage of direct production costs allowed to cover overhead costs (excluding capital costs),

Q_{io} is the full capacity output of product i,

W_{jt} is the wage rate in period t for performing job j to produce product i,

L_{jo} is the number of hours worked on job j in the base period to produce product i,

n is the number of jobs performed to produce product i,

P_{kt} is the price in period t of intermediate input k used to produce product i,

X_{ko} is the quantity of intermediate input k used to produce product i in the base period,

r is the number of kinds of intermediate inputs used to produce product i,

K_t is the amortisation cost of fixed capital invested to produce product i at a certain annual interest rate in period t,

I_{mt} is the interest rate for period t paid on working capital type 1 used to produce and market product i,

$K_m{}^*{}_o$ is the amount of working capital type 1 used in the base period to produce and market product i,

s is the number of types of working capital used to produce and market product i,

E_{qt} is the cost of service q performed by other firms in period t, used to produce product i and

u is the number of different services performed by other firms in period t used to produce product i.

This real cost of production per unit of output of each product, assuming the same productivity as in the base period, is then calculated for the period under consideration. If the W's, P's, K's, I's or E's increase resulting in an increase in the average cost of production in the period under consideration, these cost increases can be passed on to consumers with the approval of the Commission. On the other hand, if costs go up because of changes in the Q's, L_j's, X_k's or K^*_m's they are not permitted to be passed on, and if the costs go down because of these changes, all of the benefits are permitted to accrue to the firm in the form of higher profits.

One difficulty with the above method will be that for some products it is impossible to calculate the cost of production for each individual product. When this is not possible, then the formula can be applied to each product group, with the increase in the cost of production of the product group being permitted to be applied proportionately to increase the ceiling prices of each product in the group.

A primary disadvantage of applying the above formula is that it gives an incentive to firms to use more capital intensive methods. This is so because if they decrease the amount of labour used and increase K, the cost of production in the index will increase and they can increase their selling prices. The difficulty lies in that it is impossible to measure the amount of capital used, other than by its value. To overcome this difficulty the amounts of labour and capital used by the firm and any possible substitution of capital for labour and vice versa should be investigated, and the ceiling prices adjusted accordingly. For example, if the firm decides not to replace a particular machine and therefore employ more labour to do the job formerly done by the machine, L should be permitted to increase in the formula, and K be correspondingly decreased.

A second disadvantage with using the formula is that it gives firms an incentive to (a) underestimate Q_o as this will make the base period cost of production higher and, (b) to produce inefficiently when they first start up a new production line, as this will make the L_j' sX_k's and K^*_m's higher in the formula. Therefore whenever a new production line is started up, the NPC could independently evaluate or have some other competent agency, such as the task force to be formed to do efficiency audits when considering wage increase in the textile industry, evaluate the line's productivity and Q_o and adjust the L_j's, X_k's, K^*_m's and Q_o in the base period accordingly. UNIDO might be able to provide some assistance in this area.

A third disadvantage with using the formula is that it gives firms an incentive to over-report costs of production and gives them no incentive to hold down unit costs as these can be passed on to consumers in the form of higher prices. In the case of private manufacturers and to a lesser extent parastatals this disadvantage is particularly serious as some managers will very likely purchase inputs at inflated prices from friendly firms in exchange for the payment of kickbacks, resulting in higher costs and prices. A comparison of the prices paid for inputs with their prices if purchases from alternative sources can partially solve this problem, but the only way to solve it completely is to base ceiling prices on the prices of imported substitutes instead of the average cost of production.

FACTORS NOT CONSIDERED IN SETTING CEILING PRICES

One could ask what are the factors which are not considered in setting ceiling prices. No cost is charged to the recovery of equity capital invested over the lifetime of the investment. This results in two types of distortions: (a) even though the amount of capital invested is the same for two identical production processes producing identical products, the firm borrowing a higher percentage of the capital invested will be permitted a higher ceiling price because the interest payments can be included in the cost of production and there are no interest payments on equity capital. Therefore the price control system gives an incentive to manufacturers to increase the ratio of their loan to equity capital as the rate of return on capital invested in firms with lower equity/loan capital ratios will be higher. There is no logical reason why the system should give an incentive in this direction. (b) All labour costs can be included in the cost of production but not all capital costs, since only the interest cost component of capital cost can be included. This gives an incentive to firms to use more labour-intensive methods of production than would otherwise be the case.

As stated above a margin is applied to the manufacturer's cost of production to arrive at his ceiling price. When submitting their applications for price increases the manufacturers include a margin. The tendency has been for the NPC to accept the margins submitted as long as they are not too out of line with what they have been historically.

The following method of determining the capital costs of production which takes into account inflation could be used to eliminate these two types of distortions.

First determine what the capital investment has been and how long it will be before that capital is economically obsolete or physically depreciated, whichever is sooner. It can then be easily calculated using the social discount rate, estimated to be 15% per year in Tanzania in real terms, and the gross profit that must be earned each year and per unit of output to completely amortise the capital investment within the depreciation period. A higher discount rate must be used if there is inflation. It is this per unit capital cost which should be included in the average cost of production with there being no separate provision for the inclusion of interest costs (except on working capital) and the effects of wear and tear of capital assets. The main difficulty with this method is that it is difficult to calculate.

For domestically produced goods the most important factor not considered in setting ceiling prices is the cost of importing the good, i.e. the cost of producing and exporting other goods to earn the foreign exchange necessary to import it.

In somewhat simplified terms, the social cost of an additional unit of a good is either (a) the cost of resources used to produce it domestically, or (b) the cost of resources used to produce export goods sufficient to import it, whichever is lower. The cost-plus system of setting price ceilings takes into account only the first cost in determining the price of a good whereas for some goods the cost of domestic resources required to supply the goods through international trade is lower.

Therefore in some cases Tanzanian ceiling prices and domestic costs of production are higher than the social cost of producing the good through international trade, i.e. the cost of importing the good. If this is true, then the social value of output of the economy using a given amount of resources can be increased through a reallocation of the resources already being used. In fact, nowhere in the price control legislation is economic efficiency stated as a goal of price controls.

Domestic producers can be given a strong incentive to cut costs and increase productivity by tying in some way their ex-factory ceiling prices to the prices of imported substitutes. In this way the costs of producing products through international trade will also be taken into account. I call this the imported substitute system of setting price ceilings on domestically manufactured goods. If it were adopted in Tanzania it would have to be adopted gradually in order to allow a reasonable amount of time for domestic producers to adapt to it. It should be applied first to a few firms where the danger of transfer pricing is the greatest, namely foreign companies purchasing a lot of their imported inputs from their parent companies abroad. Priority in implementation should also be given to industries where there is little or no competition among domestic enterprises, imports of substitutes are quantitatively restricted and the cost in terms of time and resources of comparing the prices and quality of the domestically produced and imported products is not excessive.

THE IMPORTED SUBSTITUTE SYSTEM OF SETTING PRICE CEILINGS ON DOMESTICALLY MANUFACTURED GOODS

In the imported substitute system of setting price ceilings, the ceiling prices of domestically produced products are set equal to or are directly tied in some other way to the costs of importing the same types of goods of the same quality from the lowest cost sources of supply abroad, assuming that these products are not being dumped in Tanzania, and also assuming that the official foreign exchange rate is equal to the social cost of foreign exchange. The ceiling price can either be tied to the C.I.F. cost plus clearing charges or to the landed cost—the C.I.F. cost plus clearing charges plus sales, excise and import taxes—with the C.I.F. cost in both cases being converted into shillings at the official exchange rate or some other rate. It seems preferable to use the landed cost of the imported substitute to determine the ceiling price as the ceiling price will then reflect the amount of protection the government wishes to grant the industry. If the landed cost is used, tariff rates directly affect ceiling prices, and therefore must be set at desirable levels before the imported substitute system can be effected.

If immediately the ex-factory ceiling prices were set equal to the landed costs of the imported substitutes a lot of domestic high cost producers would soon close down, without being given time to cut costs. It is probably desirable to adopt a system which gives domestic firms a definite transition period during which they are expected and required to decrease their costs of production. Perhaps an attractive way of doing this would be immediately to set the ceiling prices equal to the landed cost of the imported substitute if the cost of production of the domestically produced good is less than the landed cost of the imported substitute; but if the domestic cost of production is higher, then after a certain grace period during which the present system would be used, set the ceiling price equal to the average of the landed cost of the imported substitute and the cost of production, with there being a definite time frame for gradually lowering the ceiling price until it is equal to the landed cost of the imported substitute.

Under this system the average cost of production only becomes a criterion for setting ex-factory prices if the average cost is greater than the landed cost of the imported substitute, and then only for as long as the average of the cost of production and cost of the imported substitute is used.

If the domestic manufacturer changes the quality of its product, the imported substitute would change and therefore also its price. Changes in the quality of the domestically produced good in practice will probably be difficult for the Commission to detect. Unfortunately, there will be an unintentional incentive for domestic firms to lower the quality of their goods in order to lower the costs of production, as long as it is not detected by the Commission.

Only if the official exchange rate accurately reflects the social cost of foreign exchange is it correct to relate the ceiling prices to the landed cost of imported substitutes converted into shillings at the *official* exchange rate and to compare average costs of production with the cost of imported substitutes. Some adjustments in the calculations must be made if the official foreign exchange rate is unequal to the social cost of foreign exchange. These are discussed in the Appendix.

There are three problems with using the landed cost system to set ceiling ex-factory prices. One is that it is difficult to know what the landed cost of a perfect substitute for the domestically produced product from the lowest cost source of supply is. However, organisations such as General Superintendence Co. Ltd. could probably be hired to supply close estimates, but there is a foreign exchange cost in obtaining this information.

The second problem is that for some domestic industries the average variable cost of production is higher than the landed cost of a perfect substitute, and unless they were subsidised, they would close down. If their average variable cost of production using shadow prices of inputs is higher than the social cost of the imported substitute, assuming that foreign suppliers are not dumping the substitutes, and it is not possible for them to further lower their average variable cost, then the income of society would increase by their closing down. This cannot be considered to be a loss. However, the government may have other than economic reasons for wanting them to continue production, in which case the government can subsidise them. If their average social cost is higher but their average social variable cost lower than the social cost of the imported substitutes, then on economic grounds it is desirable that the existing plants continue to produce but that investment not be made in new plants whose average social cost of production is greater than the social cost of the imported substitutes.

There will be some cases where the average variable social cost of production is less than the social cost of the imported substitute but where the average variable monetary cost is higher, for example as may be caused by the social cost of labour being less than the wage rate. In these cases the firm should continue producing even though to do so they must be subsidised.

There will be a third problem if the costs of production of domestic firms increase rapidly, perhaps because they are heavily dependent on imported inputs or for some other reason. If a cost plus system is used they can easily and quickly calculate their increases in costs and apply for a price increase to the Commission; or if there are no controls on retail and wholesale prices and costs of production increase rapidly due to increases in the prices of imported inputs, the Commission may even permit them to automatically increase their ex-factory prices according to a certain formula. If the ceiling price is tied to the price of the imported substitute, it will be more difficult to show that the price of the imported substitute has increased. A partial solution to this problem would be to temporarily permit them to pass on any increases in ingredient input costs in the form of higher prices but not permit them to pass on other increases in costs until it can be shown that the cost of the imported substitute has also increased. A better solution would be to improve the contingency fund concept and use other instruments so that increases in ceiling prices do not have to be granted every time the cost of production or cost of imported substitutes increase.

Adoption of the import substitute system would result in a better allocation of resources and improved productivity, and in this way have a positive effect on the resources available for financing development and recurrent expenditure. The competitive position of local firms in domestic and foreign markets, goal (c), would be better achieved, although some high cost domestic producers would eventually be forced to close down.

The attractiveness of the landed cost system clearly depends on whether present tariff rates result in a level of effective protection of domestic industries that is the most socially desirable. The present tariff and sales tax structure would need to be examined to see what changes could be made to make the levels of effective protection more socially desirable.

PERFORMANCE OF THE PRICE CONTROL SYSTEM

Objectives (b), (d) and (i), the provision for the orderly variation of price, the prevention of unduly rapid or frequent variations in price and unnecessary and unjustified price increases are partially achieved by the price control system, especially in the short run. If there are inflationary pressures and sellers desire to increase prices, the fact that they must apply for these price increases and that it takes time to approve them has a one time effect of slowing them down. However, as will be discussed below, price controls on imported products have been much less effective than on domestically manufactured products.

Price controls are most useful in preventing monopoly pricing. Monopoly pricing at all levels is certainly incompatible with Tanzanian socialism and therefore the prevention of monopoly pricing must be a very important part of function (a) of the Price Commission. Closely related to this are goals (b) and (d).

For goods whose elasticity of demand confronting the firm is less than infinity, as is especially the case of oligopolies and monopolies, if firms are profit maximisers, up to a certain point a decrease in the price ceiling placed on the firm's products below what it desires, *ceteris paribus*, will result in an increase in the quantity supplied (Qs) with Qs still being equal to the quantity demanded (Qd) and there being no possibility of a black market, if initially the firms are producing less than their engineering capacity of production. This will be true as long as the ceiling price is not below the marginal cost of the firms when they are producing the quantities demanded. In Tanzania apparently in most cases the price ceilings have prevented factories from maximising their profits by setting higher prices but the ceilings have not been set so low that output has decreased. The net result has probably been lower prices and increased domestic production in the short run.[6]

These price controls in another way have to a certain extent prevented unnecessary and unjustified price increases. Especially in recent months with some cutting back of imports of consumer goods, if the market were left to determine prices, only a rapid increase in prices could bring supply and demand back into equilibrium. Instead as the costs of importing these consumer goods have been little positively affected by the curbing of imports of close substitutes, and the price ceilings for imported consumer goods are based on their landed cost, their prices have not been permitted to increase as rapidly as otherwise would have been the case. Instead the quantity demanded is greater than the quantity supplied for many of these goods and we find shortages in the market. Consumers pay lower prices but spend more time seeking out the same quantity of goods. The time and resources used in seeking out the goods are real, whereas if the quantity demanded is brought into equilibrium with the quantity supplied through price increases the real resource cost is smaller. Opportunity for private gain are created for trading company and store employees who may inform their friends or partners in advance when the goods are going to be available so they can buy them up immediately at the ceiling price. I do not know how common this practice is at the present time.

Unless price controls are combined with rationing or production is subsidised, they can have practically no effect on slowing down the rate of inflation aside from their once-for-all effect of reducing the profit margins of manufacturers, importers and merchants, except when monopoly profits are increasing. We can distinguish two cases. If the costs of production and importation are increasing and if production and importation are not to decrease, then the costs must be passed on to consumers unless supplies are subsidised. If they are not passed on supply will decrease and beyond a certain point black markets will develop. If there is no increase in the cost of supply but an increase in demand or a decrease in supply because of other reasons, then also unless the price is increased with the increase in demand black markets will probably develop.

There is a certain range within which the quantity demanded can be greater than the quantity supplied without there being sufficient disequilibrium to support a black market, but with the firstcomers to the stores-getting the goods. There will probably be a lower percentage of the poor than the rich who are the first-comers because the rich can hire others to queue for them, a higher percentage of the rich live in urban areas, the rich are more flexible in their working hours, have better access to information, etc. Still, however, the price controls especially when combined with rationing can be used to ensure that essential goods in short supply are distributed more evenly among the population. But the costs of rationing must be weighed against its benefits.

There are some cases where the price controls might cause a more rapid increase in some prices in the short run. If the costs of production of firm A supplying an ingredient input to another firm B increase rapidly above his cost of production, but he cannot soon get the increase in his price approved, he might cut his production and supply of goods in the meantime to firm B, with the result that firm B's production would fall, his average costs of production rise as these include his overhead costs, with the end result being an increase in the prices of firm B's products. However, as there are few price controls on intermediate goods in Tanzania this does not seem to be a problem now. This possibility suggests caution in using price controls on truck tires, tin cans, paint, cement, fertilizers, fabric, leather, various metal products and other ingredient inputs, if the ceiling prices do not automatically increase with increases in the costs of production and the users of these inputs cannot import them. Prices of the first six products are now controlled.

Another example of this case is where the margins between the retail and wholesale, and wholesale and ex-factory and import prices of *ingredient inputs* and *spare parts* are so low that it is not profitable for wholesalers and retailers in some areas to stock any or a sufficient quantity of the goods. The inadequate quantities of these goods then cause a decrease in production in these regions and a corresponding increase in costs of production and prices or perhaps a decrease in the quality of the goods. In some regions there may have been temporary shortages of GI sheets, flour and hand farm implements caused by price controls that have adversely affected production but this has not been proved. The adverse effects on production have been small because there have been few price controls on ingredient inputs, and where there have been, the margins permitted seem to be sufficiently large. There are no price controls on spare parts.

Ceilings on the prices of *consumer goods* can also theoretically cause an increase in the *de facto* prices paid by some consumers. Other consumers will pay lower prices because of the controls. For example, *if* the imposition of a price ceiling causes a decrease in output or imports, as sometimes is the case when the selling price is fixed while costs of production or importation increase, or supply then decreases because of other reasons, a black market for the good may develop. Because of the smaller quantity of goods and because selling in a black market is risky, the black market price will be above the price that would have prevailed with no controls. This seems to have happened for Voil cooking oil, some textiles and eggs. However, black markets in other goods whose prices are controlled so far have been uncommon, but this may be much less true during the coming year unless policy changes are made.

There is another way that retail price ceilings might cause higher prices, at least for some consumers. With uncontrolled prices it is easier for a consumer to argue that the retailer's price is too high, he can buy the good somewhere else for a lower price, etc. and request a discount. With price ceilings the retailer can justify the price by stating it is "the government price" and he cannot lower it, even though the controlled price is a ceiling price, not a fixed price. Therefore in some cases, especially when there is a lot of competition among retailers retail prices might be lower, or at least some retailers might offer lower prices for some goods with no controls than with controls.[7]

The effect of price controls on the level of investment in the production of a certain product must also be considered. A likely chain of events is that the imposition of price controls results in more risk and a decrease in the expected rate of return from investment for potential investors, which in turn results in less investment in the production of a certain product, which in turn results in less supply and potentially a higher price in the long run. It also might result in larger investment in the production of uncontrolled goods. A critical factor affecting this possible chain of events is who makes investment decisions and what is the basis on which they are made. Price ceilings very likely have a significant adverse effect on the level of private investment. Consequently in those sectors in which private investment is important, including joint ventures between private investors and the Government, probably price ceilings have caused less investment and less output in the long run, even though as discussed above they will probably affect output positively in the short run as they decrease producers' monopoly power. Therefore the price controls may have had an adverse effect on investment in cooking oils and margarine, ghee, coconut oil, some textiles, blankets, knitwear, socks, radios, beds and mattresses, plastic ware, leather products, stoves, soap, detergents, chipboards and plywood, iron products such as nails, welded mesh and fencing wire, bread, retailing, wholesaling and transportation. Empirical work is required to determine the extent and importance of these hypothesised adverse effects.

The price controls have been somewhat effective in avoiding unduly rapid or frequent variations in prices (goal b), especially ex-factory prices and prices in regional centres. The Act provides that the prices of locally manufactured items shall be reviewed once in a year and the prices of imported items once in three months unless the Price Commission is satisfied that special circumstances exist to warrant the review of controlled prices. Because of frequent changes in world market prices of both imported consumer goods and inputs to domestic industries, often the prices of locally manufactured items have had to be reviewed more than once a year. In order to decrease the frequency of changes, the Commission has used a system of contingency reserves. When a price increase is approved the increase is purposely made larger so initially surpluses will be larger permitting the firm to build up a contingency reserve. When the costs of production have increased to the point where the firm's surpluses are less than the permitted amount, the firm draws on the contingency reserve. Only after the contingency reserve is exhausted is the firm then permitted another price increase. There have been serious operational difficulties with the system, but the Commission is taking measures to improve it.

When the costs of production increase and ex-factory and ex-importer ceiling prices must be increased, these increased costs are passed on to consumers only as a last resort after exhausting several other methods of covering increased costs without increasing prices

to consumers. The most commonly used methods are:
1. Manipulating margins at various levels of handling goods, i.e. margins at the wholesale, sub-wholesale and retail levels. An example is how the Commission handled a request for an increase in the price of imported table salt. Given that table salt was an essential good, the Commission resolved to maintain the same price to consumers but at the same time grant the request for an increase in the importer's price by reducing the margins given to packers, wholesalers and retailers in the following manner: the importer's margin was left unchanged at nine per cent, the packers' margin was reduced from 20 to 17 per cent, the wholesalers' margin from 11 per cent to 10 per cent and the retailers' margin from 25 per cent to 18 per cent.
2. Reducing the chain of agents handling the item. In the case of cement BHESCO was removed from the chain of those handling cement, so that sub-wholesalers and regional trading companies could then buy directly from the factory. This has also been true of other building materials and fertilizers. In the cases of Kenya Co-operative Creameries butter and NMC canned and bottled products sub-wholesalers were omitted from the chain.
3. Considering the nature of the item itself. If an item is in great demand and is available sporadically, margins tend to be adjusted downward because storage and handling costs will be low. Examples are cooking oils, detergents, etc.

The principal limitation in using these methods to decrease the frequency of price fluctuations is that they can only be used once. However, they do result in permanently lower prices to consumers, but can result in stores stocking fewer goods.

Price controls on manufactured goods seem to have had little effect on achieving objective (c) preserving and promoting the competitive position of local products in domestic and foreign markets. In any case, this would not ordinarily be an important objective of controls, as it can be more easily achieved by using other policy instruments, such as varying the foreign exchange rate, export subsidies, import duties, quantitative import controls, sales taxes, and certain labour regulations.

The effect of these price controls on maintaining "fair" relationships among the incomes of the different sectors of the community, objective (f), is unclear as there have been both positive and negative effects. Presumably a "fair", relationship means that either the real income distribution will become more even or it will not become more uneven because of the price controls. Because the percentage of essential goods which are subject to price controls is greater than other goods, the controls have created a greater downward pressure on the prices of society.

In some cases when the costs of production of products have increased, the Commission has permitted the prices of the less essential goods to increase more than the more essential goods, thus theoretically favouring the consumers of the more essential goods. However, there are limits to the extent this policy can be followed, because if the price increases permitted for the essential items are too small, the firm may decrease production of those products and increase the production of the less essential goods, if these are being produced by the same firm.

As discussed below, the controls have been more enforced in large retail shops than small stores and stalls.[8] If the hypothesis that people with lower incomes buy a higher percentage of goods from small shops is valid, this factor operates to make the distribution of real income more uneven.

In evaluating the effect of the controls on income distribution one must also compare what would have happened to the ratio of prices of luxury to essential consumer goods with and without the price controls. Under the present price control system a lower percentage of luxury goods are controlled than essential goods. If there were no controls, and a policy of cutting back imports of luxury goods more than essential goods and promoting the production of essential goods more than luxury consumer goods were followed, as has been and will probably continue to be the case during the coming year, then with no price controls the prices of the luxury goods would increase much more than the prices of the essential consumer goods. Very likely the ratio of the average prices of luxury goods to essential goods would have been higher without the controls than with, even though average prices of most manufactured consumer goods were probably lower because of the controls. Other policy instruments such as income, sales, excise and import taxes would be more effective than price controls in evening out the income distribution.

Goal (h) can be broken down into two parts, providing circumstances under which these industries can (a) expand their business and (b) maintain efficiency. The price control system permits them to make surpluses which can be used to expand their businesses, but does not permit them to maximise their surpluses and therefore maximise the resources available for the expansion of their enterprises.

What has been the effect of price controls on the efficiency of production? Here we mean the efficiency of production of the plant rather than the efficiency of allocation of resources in the whole economy.[9] Specifically, have the price controls caused the cost of production in terms of real resources used to manufacture a given output to be less than otherwise would be the case? Has the use of labour, capital, the use of ingredient inputs, the use of electricity, the average level of inventories, etc. been less for a given level of output because of the price controls?

One would expect the greater the pressure on and the greater the incentive to the management to cut costs, the more efficient the firm would be. Under the present price control system if costs are high because the efficiency is low, these costs can be passed on for the most part to consumers and there is little pressure or incentive to keep them low. However, there is more pressure than there would be without the controls, assuming there were still the same quantitative import restrictions. How much more is dependent on the extent to which the firms can successfully create out of thin air costs which are then used to justify the price increases without being detected by the Commission. In spite of the diligent effort of the Commission's staff to prevent this, very likely much of it is going on because of the limited material and human resources the Commission has at its disposal and the large number of products it is controlling. On the other hand the incentive to management to cut costs is less because cutting costs will not yield higher profits, as the selling price will normally be correspondingly lowered as the average costs of production are decreased.

To throw some light on the question of price control and efficiency I have made some estimates of the prices of the products produced compared with the costs of imported substitutes. I have compared ex-factory prices including sales taxes with the landed costs including import taxes, sales taxes and a ten per cent profit margin, of similar type imported goods. I have also compared ex-factory prices excluding sales taxes with the cost and freight prices, including a ten per cent profit margin, of similar type imported goods. A summary of the comparisons for selected goods is reported in tables 1 and 2.[10] For goods whose prices are presently being controlled the ex-factory prices are ceiling prices.

TABLE 1: THE EX-FACTORY PRICES AND LANDED COSTS OF SELECTED GOODS**

*Ex-factory Price within ± 4% of Landed Cost****	*Ex-factory Price 5% or more higher than the Landed Cost*	*Ex-factory Price 5% or more lower than the Landed Cost*
radios	gents socks	
dry cell batteries	axes	orange and pineapple squash
mild steel flats*	R/E majembe (hoes)	baby blankets
men's leather shoes*	galvanised welded mesh	poplin, plywood
	mild steel round bars*	wire nails
	mild steel angles*	barbed wire
	high tensile deformed bars*	ladies' leather shose*
	children's canvas shoes*	Pride cooking fat
	men's canvas shoes*	GI sheets

*Good whose price is not controlled at the present time.
**The ex-factory price here includes sales tax. The landed cost includes the C & F price, sales and import taxes and a 10% profit margin.
***It is assumed within a ± 4% range we do not know whether the ex-factory price is higher or lower than the landed cost because of measurement error.

TABLE 2: THE EX-FACTORY PRICES AND COST & FREIGHT PRICES OF SELECTED GOODS**

Ex-factory Price within ± 4% of C & F Price	*Ex-factory Price is 5% or more higher than the C & F Price of the Imported Substitute*	*Ex-factory Price is 5% or more lower than the C & F Price of Imported Substitute*
Pride cooking fat		
GI sheets	gents socks	
Baby blankets	axes	Orange and pineapple squash
	R/E majembe (hoes)	plywood
	galvanised welded mesh	barbed wire
	radios	
	mild steel round bars*	
	mild steel angles*	wire nails
	high tensile deformed bars*	
	men's leather shoes*	ladies' leather shoes*
	men's canvas shoes*	
	Children's canvas shoes*	
	poplin	
	mild steel flats*	
	dry cell batteries	

*Good whose price is not controlled at the present time.
**The ex-factory price here does not include sales tax-
The cost and freight and figure used here includes a 10% profit margin.

Quantitative restrictions have been placed on the importation of all the goods included in this sample. The question I will attempt to throw some light on is given these quantitative restrictions, how have the price controls affected ex-factory prices and levels of output? Quantitative import restrictions cause an increase in demand for domestically produced products and when there is much competition among domestic producers usually cause an increase in the domestic output and price of the product. However, if there is a small number of producers of a product and its close substitutes, then quantitative restrictions at the same time increase the monopolistic power of the domestic producers. This is the case for all the products included in our sample and indeed for the majority of manufactured goods in Tanzania. This gives them an incentive to increase prices and will result in an increase in domestic output if the domestic producer is a sufficiently low cost producer compared to foreign suppliers and is a profit maximiser.

Depending on the observed relationship between the ex-factory and C & F prices and landed costs, we can draw the following conclusions, if we assume that the quality of the domestically produced goods is lower than or the same as the quality of the imported substitute. This assumption is probably valid for all products in our sample except radios. They are derived from price theory which is not discussed in this paper.

1. If the ex-factory price including sales tax is greater than the landed costs, then the price controls have not kept the domestic price to a level it would be at if there were unlimited imports. However, it still could have kept it lower than what it would have been without the controls. These are the goods listed in column 2 of Table 1. The prices of five of these were not controlled.

2. If the ex-factory price is less than the landed cost, then the price controls have been more effective in keeping prices down than in case 1. These are the goods in column 3 of Table 1. If the domestically produced and imported goods are recognised by consumers to be the same quality, then the price controls have kept the domestic prices down to the level they would have been had there been free imports. This is probably the case with Pride Cooking fat which is only a slightly lower quality than imported Kimbo cooking fat, according to two grocery store managers. If the quality of the domestic product is considered by consumers to be lower than the imported product, then we cannot say for certain whether the domestically controlled price is as low as it would be if there were free imports. However, it is likely that the controlled prices of orange and pineapple squash, baby blankets, poplin, plywood, and barbed wire are close to what they would be with free imports and perhaps even lower in some cases, as we will see below. In other words, in these cases the price controls have been effective in keeping ex-factory prices significantly below what they would be without the controls with the same quantitative import restrictions. If the import duties are relatively low and sub-

sidies to these industries are small, they are in most cases relatively efficient producers.

3. If the ex-factory price minus sales tax is less than the C. & F. price (including a 10% margin), then the price controls are very effective and the domestic industry is generally efficient depending on the differences in quality between the imported and domestically produced goods and the extent of subsidies to the domestic producers. This is especially true if the exchange rate is overvalued. These are the goods listed in column 3 of Table 2.

If they are of the same quality and no subsidies are extended to the domestic industry, the domestic industry is in most cases very efficient. All of the goods in our sample in this category are lower quality than the imported substitutes. In any case the price controls on ex-factory prices have been effective and they are relatively efficient producers. An anomaly is ladies' leather shoes, the prices of which are not presently controlled.

To summarise, the ex-factory prices of 83 per cent of the uncontrolled items but only 33 per cent of the controlled items in this sample are five per cent or more higher than the landed cost of the imported substitute. This is an indication that for most items the price controls, given the quantitative import restrictions, have depressed ex-factory prices and have probably resulted in an increase in the efficiency of production. More research is needed to prove it.

A second question that can be asked is how the price controls have affected the level of output. If there are no price controls and there are quantitative restrictions on imports, producers of differentiated products who are profit maximisers will set their price higher than they would be if there were free imports but at a level such that Qs will still equal Qd. This corresponds to point A in figure 1 below. DD is the demand for the domestically produced product with quantitative import restrictions. However, at A, when marginal revenue equals marginal cost, their output is less than at full capacity. If price controls are imposed and the ceiling is lowered from OA' to OB', or the ratio of P to average costs is decreased, the firm will maximise its profits by increasing output from OA" to OB" although at any price between OA' and OB' the quantity demanded will be equal to the quantity supplied. Assume that OC' is the price at which this firm would maximise its profits under conditions of free imports. In this case the ceiling price at which domestic output will be maximised, assuming the firm is a profit maximiser, will be higher with quantitative import controls than with free imports. However, if the price ceiling is set at OB' the firm will be making windfall profits from the quantitative import restrictions and it will be possible for it to make profits even if it is a high cost producer compared to foreign producers.

If the price ceiling is set below OB' then the quantity demanded will be greater than the quantity supplied and wholesalers and retailers will be queuing up to buy the factory's products. As part of the MC curve between C and B may be vertical, it does not necessarily

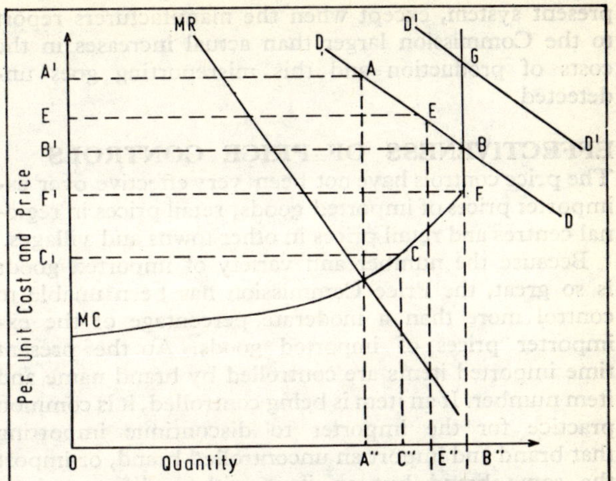

Fig. 1: SUPPLY AND DEMAND UNDER CONDITIONS OF MONOPOLY AND QUANTITATIVE IMPORT RESTRICTIONS

follow that a decrease in price below B' will result in a decrease in output, but eventually as the ceiling price is lowered output will fall.

Until the present time for most products the price controls on domestically produced manufactured goods have operated either to increase or not change the quantity produced and quantity demanded along the demand curve for domestically produced goods from A to B. As long as there are not shortages of the domestically produced good in the market this must be the case. However, the existence of shortages with the imposition of price controls may or may not be an indication that output has decreased because of the controls. There have been reported shortages of the following domestically produced products that are subject to price control: cooking oil, lantern globes, bread, khanga, kitenge, detergent, wheat flour and barbed wire. Price controls on khanga and kitenge have resulted in illegal exports causing shortages in the domestic market. The short run effect of price control on output also needs to be further researched.

During the coming year the foreign exchange allocated for the importation of manufactured consumer goods will be substantially less than during the last year. In terms of figure 1 this will mean that demand for many domestically produced consumer goods will increase, as represented by a shift outwards in the demand to D'D'. At the new levels of demand it is likely that shortages of a lot more goods will appear than is presently the case. If the present cost-plus price control system is followed, the gains from the controls will accrue either to the black marketeers who are more likely to be the traders than the manufacturers, misusers of position or to the consumers who buy the goods at the controlled prices. The basic point is that these windfall profits will not accrue to either the manufacturers or the Government under the present system, except when the manufacturers report to the Commission larger than actual increases in the costs of production and this misreporting goes undetected.

EFFECTIVENESS OF PRICE CONTROLS

The price controls have not been very effective over ex-importer prices of imported goods, retail prices in regional centres and retail prices in other towns and villages.

Because the number and variety of imported goods is so great, the Price Commission has been unable to control more than a moderate percentage of the ex-importer prices of imported goods. At the present time imported items are controlled by brand name and item number. If an item is being controlled, it is common practice for the importer to discontinue importing that brand and import an uncontrolled brand, or import the same brand but an item with a different item number, and therefore is not controlled. One example is Chinese baby blankets. The price controls unintentionally give an incentive to import goods whose prices are not yet controlled. Domestic producers also introduce new brand names to avoid the controls, but can do it to a much lesser extent. If a price is not controlled at the ex-factory or ex-importer level, it is practically impossible to control it at the retail level.

Manufacturers and importers who evade the controls by supplying different brand names can be prevented from doing this in the following manner: when a ceiling price is set on a product, ceiling prices must at the same time be set on all brand names, sizes and types of the product. Control can still be by brand name, but whenever a new brand name is imported or produced it is automatically subject to price control too. When there is an insignificant variation in the quality of different brands of a product, control can be by genetic name instead of brand name.

Importers are normally not required to report to the NPC when they import an uncontrolled item. If NPC tried to set a new ceiling on every new item imported at all levels in the distribution chain it would greatly overtax its resources. Because the present foreign exchange crisis has required a drastic cutback in imports of luxury and semi-luxury goods, importers are able to greatly increase their margins on uncontrolled items and still sell all they are permitted to import.

For many products retail price ceilings are set by the NPC only for Dar es Salaam, the city where the good is produced, or for regional centres. When price ceilings for a regional centre, other towns or villages have not been set by the commission, the Assistant Price Commissioner for the region or district together with the Regional Price Control Advisory Committee has the authority to set ceiling prices at those levels. Even when a retail ceiling price has been announced for a regional centre or for the whole country (a Pan-territorial price) in most cases in fact it is the ceiling price only in regional centres as the transport costs only to the regional centres are included. The Assistant Price Commissioner responsible must calculate the cost of transporting the good to the place of sale outside the regional centres, and add this to the announced ceiling retail price. For any area where the retail price ceiling is not set by the Commission, in setting prices at the local level the Assistant Price Commissioner must calculate transportation and other costs to arrive at the ceiling price in his area for each item. This involves much computational and investigative work, especially because of the large number of items and frequent changes in the price ceilings set by the Commission under the present conditions of worldwide inflation.

The greatest deficiency in the price control system has probably been the failure in many cases to establish and enforce price controls at the retail level in towns that are not regional centres and villages, where the vast majority of Tanzanians do their shopping. There are two aspects to this problem: (1) ineffective enforcement of the controls at the retail level and (2) a lack of controls over many goods at the retail level in towns and villages that are controlled at the ex-factory and ex-importer levels.

ENFORCEMENT OF PRICE CONTROLS

The price regulation easiest to enforce is the requirement that all prices must be marked in retail stores. This regulation is supposed to apply countrywide. Even in Dar es Salaam a substantial number of stores do not mark the prices of all their goods and it is not difficult to find stores marking few of their goods, such as MAHEN and some other chemists, many hardware stores and stalls in Kariokoo and other markets. Commonly small shops in the densely populated areas of Dar es Salaam mark prices on only part of their products. The posting of correct ceiling prices in most medium-sized and large retail stores in Dar es Salaam very likely has had a downward effect on the prices of small retailers because of the competition between them and the larger stores.

In order to obtain additional information about the extent of enforcement of price controls around the country a comparison was made between the ceiling prices set by NPC and retail prices reported by the Bureau of Statistics gathered for their Survey of Retail Prices in Towns series. The data available for the 3rd and 4th quarters of 1974 and 1st quarter of 1975 for regional centres was used. There were incomplete reports from 11 regional centres composed of 340 prices of controlled items.

The most surprising results apparent from the data were that the percentage of prices exceeding ceiling prices was higher in Dar es Salaam (34%) than for the other ten regional centres (22%); but both were high, and 25% for the eleven centres together (see Table 3). Most of the goods listed could be considered as essential. The P's for aspro, durable household articles and good and drinks were very high and for cigarettes no prices were above the ceiling price. From the data the tentative conclusion can be drawn that the percentage of prices above the ceiling prices set by the NPC is quite high but also varies from regional centre to regional centre and from product group to product group.[11] The variation among product groups is greater than among regional centres.[12] There appears to be no significant correlation between P and the distance of the regional centre from Dar es Salaam.

TABLE 3: THE PERCENTAGE OF PRICES IN REGIONAL CENTRES EXCEEDING CEILING PRICES

	Dar es Salaam	*Ten Other Regional Centres*[a]	*Total for 11 Regional Centres*
Textiles[b]			
N	28	83	111
N*	6	14	20
P	21	17	18
Foods & Drinks[c]			
N	12	0	12
N*	6	0	6
P	50	0	50
Aspro			
N	1	8	9
N*	1	5	6
P	100	62	67
Durable Household Articles[d]			
N	27	16	43
N*	17	8	25
P	63	50	58
Non-durable Household Articles[e]			
N	12	33	45
N*	1	6	7
P	8	18	16
Radio & Drycell Batteries[f]			
N	10	89	99
N*	0	19	19
P	0	21	19
Agricultural Implements[g]			
N	0	10	10
N*	0	2	2
P	0	20	20
Cigarettes			
N	1	10	11
N*	0	0	0
P	0	0	0
Total			
N	91	249	340
N*	31	54	85
P	34	22	25

N.B.
[a]The other regional centres are Tanga, Moshi, Singida, Lindi, Musoma, Mwanza, Songea, Mbeya, Tabora and Kigoma.
[b]The textile items included are Tanzanian made poplin/cotton and tetoron/cotton shirts, and Tanzanian made khaki drill, cotton linen, cotton poplin, cotton kitenge and cotton khanga. Poplin/cotton shirts were frequently overpriced.
[c]The foods and drinks items included are maize and wheat flour, local rice, white bread, cottonseed oil and flower brand ghee substitute.
[d]The durable household articles included are Kioo Ltd. non-coloured glasses, 14 cm.; enamel kettles, kerosene cookers, hurricane lamps and bicycles. Enamel kettles were frequently overpriced.
[e]The non-durable household articles included are detergent washing powder or laundry soap, toothpaste and toilet soap.
[f]Four types of both National and Philips radios and one type of National and Eveready 1.5 volt batteries are included. Eveready batteries were frequently overpriced.
[g]The agricultural implements included are one iron hoe, one iron panga and one axe.
[h]N is the number of prices of controlled items reported. N*is the number of prices of controlled items reported that exceed the ceiling prices. P=(N*/N)x100 or the percentage of prices of controlled items exceeding the ceiling prices. The extent of coverage of the reporting varied greatly from region to region. The periods covered were the 3rd and 4th quarters of 1974 and the 1st quarter of 1975.

Probably most consumers in the regions are little aware that ceiling prices have been set by the Assistant Price Commissioner and his advisory committee. One way of partially alleviating this problem would be to have *Uhuru* and or the *Daily News* publish special supplements announcing these price ceilings for distribution only in the respective region whenever they are set.

There is a lower limit below which ceiling prices cannot be set without black markets developing even though tremendous resources are committed to enforcement. If imports normally account for a substantial portion of domestic demand and they are cut sharply, then even if ex-factory ceiling prices are set at just those levels such that domestic factories are operating at full capacity, the quantities demanded will exceed the quantities supplied to such an extent that black markets will proliferate and there will be little benefit to consumers from the controls. Such would be the case if in Figure 1 the ceiling price were set at OF' and demand were DD'. In order to eliminate the black market a sales or excise tax on the good equal to GF would need to be set. Rationing, if administratively possible and not too costly, would also lessen the problem. The sales tax has the advantage that it would have little effect on actual retail prices and would result in a transfer of funds from black marketeers to the Treasury.

A similar situation exists when price controls are used to try to keep retail prices of imported goods from increasing when imports are sharply cut back through quantitative restrictions.

RETAIL PRICE CEILINGS IN TOWN AND VILLAGES

The Regional Price Control Advisory Committee Files in the Ministry of Communication open registry were examined to obtain some information on the extent to which Committees are setting price ceilings in their regions on items which the National Price Commission only sets ceiling prices for Dar es Salaam, selected cities or regional centres. The Regional Commmittees send in reports on some of their decisions on price ceilings to the Ministry, with the reports being contained in these files. The files for 19 regions were examined, as there was no file for the 20th. For each region the number of product groups on which the Regional Committees had set ceiling prices in 1974 and 1975 was noted. The results are summarised in Table 4 below.

TABLE 4: PRICE CEILINGS ON PRODUCT GROUPS SET BY REGIONAL PRICE CONTROL ADVISORY COMMITTEES[a]

The number of Product Groups with Price Ceilings set by the Regional Committees	*Regions*
None	Iringa, Dodoma, Tabora, Kilimanjaro, Lindi, Mbeya, Ruvuma and Mtwara
One through five	Arusha, Bukoba, Shinyanga, Tanga, Mara, Morogoro,
Six through ten	Coast
More than ten	Mwanza, Dar es Salaam, Singida, Kigoma

The results shown in Table 4 are an indication that there are only a few regions where the Regional Committees set retail ceiling prices on more than ten product groups where ceiling retail prices have not been set for the region by NPC but where the NPC has set ex-factory and ex-importer prices.[13] This is in comparison with 1,066 groups controlled by NPC in March 1974. Apparently the prices of most of the products controlled by NPC down to the regional centre level but not to the town and village levels are also not controlled at these levels by the regional administration. Therefore most of these products are not controlled at the retail outlets in towns and villages where most consumers purchase them, remembering that approximately 94% of Tanzanians live outside regional centres.

Very few of the items controlled by the Regional Committees were imported. Therefore the effect of setting ex-importer price ceilings on retail prices is less than the setting of ex-factory price ceilings on domestically produced goods in towns and villages, and even most regional centres.

Goal (d), the need to prevent the income of peasants and workers from being affected adversely by unnecessary and unjustified price increases, is therefore not being adequately achieved. The controlling of prices at the ex-factory and ex-importer levels but not at the retail level results in a shifting of profits from producers and importers to wholesalers and retailers with there being only a small downward effect on prices to consumers.[14] In many cases the controls are shifting profits from primarily parastatal producers and importers to wholesalers and primarily *private* retailers.

Price controls to prevent retail monopoly pricing are needed the most in areas where there are a small number of retailers competing with each other, such as in district centres and villages, and are needed the least in the larger cities. The controls now are least effective in the areas where they are needed the most.

One of the principal objectives of price controls is lower prices to consumers. If controls are only placed on ex-factory, ex-importer and wholesale prices then this objective will not be achieved as now appears to be the case. This suggests that a greater emphasis should be placed on ensuring that once price ceilings have been set at one level in the distribution chain, they should be set at all levels. The exception to this is luxury and semi-luxury goods where the objective of the Government in setting ex-factory ceiling prices is probably more to increase efficiency and output and prevent them from realising monopoly profits and surplus profits from shortages than to obtain lower prices for consumers. Also many luxury and semi-luxury goods will be sold only in cities where there is little spatial monopoly. If regional trading companies are given a monopoly in wholesaling these goods and there is no control of wholesale prices then any surplus profits caused by shortages will accrue to them rather than to private traders.

CONCLUSION

In this section we will review the principal conclusions reached in the study.

Price controls have been partially successful in keeping prices paid to domestic manufacturers lower than they would be without the controls and have probably had a positive effect on domestic output, at least in the short run, and the efficiency of price changes.

In setting ex-importer ceiling prices a certain percentage margin is applied to the cost of importing the goods—a cost-plus system. This gives importers an unintended incentive to import goods with higher import duties and to purchase from higher cost suppliers and over-value the CIF prices of goods imported when quantitative import controls are according to the number of units rather than value. Ex-importer price controls have been less effective than ex-factory price controls because it is easier for importers to evade them.

A cost-plus system is also used to set ex-factory prices of domestically produced products. It gives little or no incentive to producers to decrease their costs of production. However, it makes it more difficult for producers to increase prices as the increases must be justified in their applications for increases in ceiling prices. It gives producers an incentive to initially lower their efficiency of production at the time they apply for a price increase, so their average cost of production, on which the price ceilings are based, will be higher. A method for preventing producers

N.B.
[a]From the reports sent in to the Ministry we only know the *minimum* number of product groups controlled by the Regional Committees because most of them probably have not reported every product group they control.

from passing on increases in costs from decreases in efficiency and to give producers incentives to cut costs is discussed.

The present method used to estimate the capital component of the cost of production is inadequate because it does not include the cost of equity capital. This can be corrected by changing the method of calculating capital cost in the manner discussed.

A serious deficiency of the cost-plus system of setting price ceilings on domestically produced products is that a firm can be a high cost inefficient producer and still show a profit. It results in an inefficient allocation of resources in the economy. The system does not take into account the cost of producing goods indirectly through the production of other goods for export and using the foreign exchange earned to import the first goods. An improvement would be to tie ex-factory ceiling prices in some way to the cost of imported substitutes.

Perhaps the greatest deficiency in the price control system is that the prices of most products that are controlled only at the ex-importer, ex-factory and wholesale levels by the NPC are not controlled at the retail level in most towns and villages by the Regional Price Control Advisory Committees. Therefore the controls have resulted in a shifting of profits from primarily parastatal importers and manufacturers to primarily private town and village retailers, although there has still been some downward effect on retail prices of domestically produced goods but little or no downward effect on imported goods at the retail level when the retail price is uncontrolled. Enforcement of the controls also is incomplete. A greater emphasis on setting controls at the retail level in towns and villages is needed.

NOTES

1. The United Republic of Tanzania Acts Supplement, No. 1, 9th March, 1973, p. 284.
2. *Ibid.*, p. 287.
3. When the same ceiling prices are set for all regional centres or everywhere in the country, a transport equalisation payment is normally paid to the manufacturer/wholesaler based on his costs of transporting goods to the particular area.
4. The number of controlled prices is several times this as there are several different sizes and types for many of the groups of items that are counted as one item in this list.
5. The "normal" rate of return varies from industry to industry. For beer it is 17 per cent per year.
6. See the later part of this section for an elaboration of this.
7. This point is made by Helen Kimble, *Price Control in Tanzania*, Dar es Salaam, East African Publishing House, 1970, p. 35,
8. In Ghana price controls were to all intents ignored in rural areas and urban markets. See Tony Killick, *Price Controls, Inflation and Income Distribution: The Ghanian Experience*, Economic Development Report No. 223, Centre for International Affairs, Harvard University, 1972, p. 15.
9. For a discussion of the effects of import-substitution industrialization on economic efficiency and technical efficiency or the efficiency of production in the plant, see John H. Power, "Import Substitution as an Industrialisation Strategy," *Philippine Economic Journal*, Vol. V, No. 2, 1966.
10. For details of the calculations, see Tables 1 and 2 on pages 26–30 of ERB Paper 76.4.
11. The null hypothesis that the percentage of prices exceeding the ceiling prices is independent of the regional centre and the product group is rejected at the one per cent level, using a chi square test.
12. The coefficient of variation of the percentages of prices exceeding ceiling prices among product groups was 0.72, and among regional centres 0.65.
13. These results are only an indication because it is very likely that not all ceiling prices set by the regional committees have been reported to the Ministry. According to the National Price Commission the number of ceiling prices set by the regional committees is substantially greater than is indicated in Table 4.
14. The size of the downward effect on prices depends on supply conditions. The downward effect on retail prices of domestically produced goods will be greater if the quantity of goods supplied by factories increases with the imposition of price ceilings on ex-factory prices. If the quantity of goods imported is fixed by foreign exchange control, the downward effect on retail prices of ex-importer ceiling prices will be practically nil.

APPENDIX: METHOD OF CALCULATING THE CEILING PRICES OF DOMESTICALLY MANUFACTURED PRODUCTS USING THE IMPORTED SUBSTITUTE METHOD WHEN THE OFFICIAL FOREIGN EXCHANGE RATE IS UNEQUAL TO THE SOCIAL COST OF FOREIGN EXCHANGE

If the official exchange rate is unequal to the social cost of foreign exchange, then a different method must be used to calculate the ceiling prices of domestically manufactured products. This method is described below.

If the exchange rate is overvalued, then the social cost of foreign exchange, or the shadow exchange rate, will be higher than the official exchange rate. If the shadow exchange rate were used in calculating the landed cost of the imported substitute and the costs of tradable goods,[a] the landed cost of the imported substitute would increase relative to the average domestic cost of production. If the landed cost of an imported substitute converted into shillings using the official rate were used to determine the ceiling price, it would be too low in relation to the domestic cost of production, compared with the case where the shadow price of foreign exchange were used in making the conversion.

Therefore the average cost of production and landed cost of the imported substitute must both be calculated in a different manner. An overvalued exchange rate affects both the cost of production of domestically manufactured products through its effect on the costs of tradable inputs and the landed cost of imported substitutes. A devaluation of x per cent would result in an increase in the landed cost of imported substitutes to

$\left(\frac{1}{1-x/100}\right)C^*$ where C^* is by definition the landed cost per unit of the imported substitute converted at the official rate from the lowest cost source of supply, including the normal importer's margin, and assuming there is no dumping of the product. The new average cost of production after devaluation would be

$$\frac{\dfrac{1}{1-\dfrac{x}{100}}\,C+C}{Y} \qquad (1)$$

where by definition

C is the total cost of tradable inputs required to produce output Y converted at the official rate,

Y is the full capacity level of output, and

$\bar{C}$ is the total cost of production of output Y before devaluation minus C.

Before devaluation the average cost of production would be

$$\frac{C+\bar{C}}{Y} \qquad (2)$$

The following sequence should be followed in determining the ceiling price. First inform the firm that if he has no objection, the ceiling price of each product will be set equal to

$$\left(\frac{1}{1-\dfrac{x}{100}}\right)C^* - \frac{C(x/100)}{\left(1-\dfrac{x}{100}\right)Y} \qquad (3)$$

If he complains that using this method he cannot make a profit, then request him to submit data on his average cost of production. The NPC will then calculate his average cost of production in the manner described in the text. If C^* is greater than his average cost, set the ceiling price equal to formula (3) as at this price he will still make a profit.[b] If C^* is smaller than the average cost, then compare the landed cost of the imported substitute after the hypothetical devaluation with the average cost of production after the hypothetical devaluation. If the former is larger than the latter, still set the ceiling price equal to (3). If the former is smaller than the latter[c] then after a certain grace period set the ceiling price equal to the average of the landed cost of the imported substitute (after the hypothetical devaluation) minus the increase in the average cost of production (after the hypothetical devaluation) and the average cost of production, or equal to (2) + (3),

$$2$$

but gradually reduce the ceiling price to the level shown by (3), thus giving enterprises a certain transition period during which they are expected to become efficient producers and after the point at which $\frac{\bar{C}+C}{Y}$ is decreased through increased productivity, until it is equal to expression (3). All benefits from further increases in productivity will accrue to the firm.

---

[a]A tradable good is one which is normally imported or exported, or would be if there were no restrictions on international trade and the foreign exchange rate were equal to the social cost of foreign exchange.

[b]$\frac{C(x/100)}{(1-x/100)Y}$ is the increase in the average cost of production that would result from a hypothetical devaluation of x per cent.

[c]Formula (1) expresses the average cost of production after the hypothetical devaluation. If $\frac{1}{(1-x/100)}C^*$ is less than (1) then clearly (3) will be less than (2).

Excess Capacity in Manufacturing Industry: A Case Study of Selected Firms in Tanzania*

S.M. WANGWE

Introduction

The existence of a substantial degree of idle industrial capacity has been an increasingly prevalent phenomenon in developing countries. Most developing countries are characterised by a shortage of capital and foreign exchange, while investments in development ventures in these countries remain highly dependent on imports. The high import content of investments compounds the already acute scarcity of foreign exchange. In these circumstances it would be reasonable to expect that the productive capacity in industry would be substantially utilised. The machinery and other capital equipment, obtained by means of scarce capital and often in spite of foreign exchange crises, have been paradoxically underutilised in many developing countries as various studies have shown.[1] The degree of underutilisation of capacity is surprisingly greater in developing countries than in developed countries.[2] When the scarcity of capital is compounded by that of foreign exchange the waste of resources resulting from an underutilised productive capacity becomes even greater.

Not only does a fuller utilisation of capacity reduce waste of such scarce resources, but it is also capable of providing additional employment[3]. To the extent that employment depends on the rate of capital accumulation, fuller utilisation of capital equipment will generate more employment with the same amount of capital resources.

Furthermore, underutilised capacity means that less output is generated from a unit of capital equipment than if capacity were fully utilised. In other words, the actual capital-output ratio becomes higher than the full capacity capital-output ratio. In an economy like Tanzania the performance of the economy is largely determined by its capacity to supply output to meet domestic requirements. This is evident from continuing inflationary pressures and the unhealthy balance of payments position in Tanzania. Underutilisation of productive capacity is an unfavourable phenomenon in that it deprives society of the output of goods. This is undesirable in the welfare sense as well as in the implications it has for inflation and the balance of payments problems.

Finally, underutilised industrial capacity increases the cost of manufactured products. High costs of manufactured goods decrease the profitability of industry, unless industry is in a position to raise prices of goods and to maintain its profit margin. From the point of view of an industrial firm, price increases may appear a way out of the problem, but the fact is that this merely transfers the losses to the economy. Such transfer of losses is manifested in rising living-costs to consumers and in decreased local demands for these commodities. When domestic demand declines the problem of underutilisation becomes even more serious unless an export market can fill in the gap. The existence of idle capacity in the light of the above discussion represents clear losses to the economy, yet such idle capacity is substantial in the manufacturing industry in Tanzania. This paper is an attempt to examine the causes of excess capacity in the manufacturing industry of Tanzania. The analysis is based mainly on the results of a survey of the manufacturing firms for the period 1973 to 1975.

CONCEPTUAL AND METHODOLOGICAL ISSUES

The theoretical and empirical studies on capacity utilisation reveal that the concept is a nebulous one. There is no consensus as to what full capacity utilisation actually means. In analysing the issue of excess capacity the definitional problem is not the most important one, but given the controversial nature of the concept it is necessary to specify the definition that will be employed in this paper.

The Concept of Capacity Utilisation

Four main variants of the concept of capacity utilisation can be distinguished in the literature:

(a) In terms of a single firm, full capacity technically defined as the output rate at which the average cost curve is vertical.[4] This implies that all factors of production are engaged at their maximum speed and none remain idle during the 24 hours in a day and during the 168 hours in a week. This is a strict engineering definition where the objective is to achieve the maximum physical output that can be generated regardless of costs.

This definition is theoretically precise, but in practice such maximum output can be sustained only in special cases where the production process is strictly continuous.

In practice it is not possible to produce at this maximum because the production processes generally involve down time for repair and maintenance of machines. Even on a theoretical level, the average cost curve asymptotically approaches the hypothetical maximum output so that at any output level it is possible to produce slightly more if sufficiently high costs are incurred, e.g. the CES production function.

(b) The second variant of the concept of capacity utilisation relates to the efficiency of resource allocation in the Paretian sense of economic welfare. Here full capacity utilisation refers to the output rate at which the average

*ERB Paper 76.2

cost curve is minimum.[5] The definition calls for the estimation of cost functions, a problem which is well known. The inadequacy of available data, however, is a main constraint to giving empirical content to this definition and to specifying the form of the cost functions. As L. R. Klein has noted, "In statistical analysis, practitioners have usually been less dogmatic and simultaneously fit both linear and non-linear functions to the same sample data, many times being unable to choose clearly among them.[6]

Even if estimation of cost functions were actually made, the optimum rate of capacity utilisation is likely to be associated with a range of output rates such that a single full capacity utilisation rate could not be identified. In this case, it is impossible to identify a unique capacity output.

(c) Full capacity utilisation is alternatively conceived as an output rate representing a point where marginal revenue equals marginal cost.[7]

This definition implies that attempts to maximise profits would solve the problem of excess capacity. The practical difficulties involved are similar to those discussed for the case of the preceding definition.

(d) The fourth variant of the concept of full capacity utilisation relates to the output rate that can be maintained for a reasonable period of time with given plant and machinery under normal working conditions.[8] Due allowance is given for such factors as necessary repairs and maintenance, normal number of shifts, normal speed and so on. This definition loses some degree of precision as subjective elements are bound to be introduced. Nevertheless, since this version of definition is readily amenable to an empirical study, it will be adopted in this paper.

Measurement of Capacity Utilization

In the literature at least five methods of measuring capacity utilization have been employed.

(a) Comparing actual output with a linear interpolation between two peak outputs or with a linear extrapolation of previous peak outputs.[9]
(b) Comparing a bench mark capital-output ratio assumed to represent full capacity with the current capital output ratio.[10]
(c) Utilisation of econometrically estimated production functions where capacity output is calculated as a function of the actual stock of capital and full employment labour.[11]
(d) Use of direct engineering estimates of maximum production.
(e) Ascertaining capacity and its utilisation rates by survey methods.

Detailed discussion of these alternative methods appears elsewhere, so such a discussion need not detain us here.[12]

The first two methods assume that demand fluctuations are the main causes of excess capacity. In our study of Tanzanian manufacturing firms however, fluctuations in product demand were a significant cause of excess capacity in no more than 10% of the sample firms. Thus, these two methods were discarded.

The next two methods require extensive data to estimate the production functions and the quality of the data has to be quite high. Since neither condition is satisfied in the Tanzanian situation, these methods also were discarded. However, when engineering capacities are specified by the machine manufacturers, it may be possible to utilize such information.

The survey method was selected in this study, because of the advantages it has over other methods of estimating the rates of capacity utilisation. This method has the particular advantage in that it can identify the causes of excess capacity more easily by interviewing the knowledgeable individuals about the performance of the firm in question. With this method it is possible to identify phenomena which might be specific or limited either to certain types of industrial activities or to particular social and political conditions.

The concept of capacity utilisation assumes fixed capital stock, and the researcher must impose the limits on the use of the other factors that influence production. In the process of defining these limits, due allowance for certain phenomena will have to be made in the light of conditions pertaining to a particular type of industrial activity or to the particular social and political conditions in which the firm is operating. Empirical identification of both the optimal level of capacity utilisation and the full capacity point is difficult because of the various margins on which the utilisation of capacity must be optimised. The optimisation of such margins varies from one industrial activity to another; and the survey method is more flexible than other methods in establishing these margins.

To identify the optimal level of capacity utilisation, two different margins were considered:

(i) The first margin arises from the number of shifts worked per day. The issue is whether a firm that operates only one 8 hour shift per day should be regarded as utilising only one third of its capacity or otherwise. In this case the full capacity number of shifts was the "norm" of the industry such that due allowance was made for time required to maintain and repair machines and for any other activity necessary for the type of industrial activity in question. If from the technical point of view working three shifts a day would overstrain the machines, then the optimal number of shifts per day was taken to be less than three, the exact number being determined by what is technologically necessary for the particular industry. In some cases, product quality considerations were so important that the firms would never operate night shifts, which might jeopardise the quality of the product. In such situations there was no convincing reason to assume anything contrary to what the knowledgeable persons clearly indicated.

(ii) The issue of product-mix posed problems, to the extent that a change in the composition of output required changes in the rate of capacity utilisation, even if all other things remained unchanged. This problem is more or less serious, depending on how deeply involved the firm is in producing a wide range of products. It was deemed best to assume a normal product-mix derived from the experience of the firm in the year under investigation. Capacity estimates were thus based on such "normal" product-mix.

In many firms it was not possible to quantify the impact of any single cause of excess capacity independent of other causes because of the problems of aggregation. Several factors often appeared to contribute simultaneously to particular cases of underutilisation. Any attempt to force the causal structure of underutilisation into an additive or other cumulatively aggregative expression would result in an incorrect and meaningless interpretation of the data. It was therefore necessary to identify the main causes of capacity underutilisation without attempting to qualify precisely the effect of each factor. Moreover such attempts at precise quantification were not possible because many firms did not keep accurate records of which factors were responsible for what proportion of total idle time. Despite this difficulty in most cases the main or at least the significant causes were identified.

THE EVIDENCE AND CAUSES OF CAPACITY UNDERUTILISATION

The Evidence of Capacity Under Utilisation

(a) Rates of capacity utilisation estimated in the survey of 40 firms and the results are summarised as follows:

Rate of capacity utilisation	*Cumulative frequency*
Not more than 20%	4%
Not more than 30%	8%
Not more than 40%	16%
Not more than 50%	27%
Not more than 60%	38%
Not more than 70%	58%
Not more than 80%	69%
Not more than 90%	100%

(b) For some of the NDC companies the rates of capacity utilisation haxe been given as follows:

Name of firm	*Rate of capacity utilisation*
1. Tanzania Tanneries Co. Ltd.	80
2. Tanzania Shoe Co. Ltd.	65
3. Tanzania Breweries Ltd.	68
4. B.A.T. Tanzania Ltd.	90
5. Tanzania Distilleries Ltd.	57
6. Tanganyika Instant Coffee Co. Ltd.	63
7. Tanzania Fertiliser Co. Ltd.	45
8. General Tyre E.A. Ltd.	46
9. Metal Box Co. of Tanzania Ltd.	54
10. Alluminium Africa Ltd.	60
11. Steel Rolling Mill Ltd.	100

SOURCE: N.D.C. *Annual Report 1975*, p. 11.
N.B. These rates of capacity utilisation refer to the year 1975.

CAUSES OF CAPACITY UNDERUTILISATION

The factors responsible for capacity underutilisation can be broadly categorised into supply and demand factors. Other factors might appropriately be categorised as institutional, but to the extent that their impact on capacity utilisation is ultimately felt on either the demand or supply side of industrial output, their impact is included in the categorisation adopted here.

Supply Factors of Capacity Underutilisation

This category includes those factors which impose a constraint on the supply side of industrial output. Typical of this category are shortage of raw materials and other inputs and complementary factors.

Shortage of Raw Materials

Shortage of raw materials was a factor affecting the smooth operation of 80% of the firms. 70% of the firms stated that the principal reason for the shortage of raw materials was lack of foreign exchange and that they were unable to obtain enough foreign exchange to operate according to their output targets. It is therefore not surprising that firms which required inputs with a high import content were more severely affected by the shortage of foreign exchange.

Shortages of foreign exchange were more severe constraints for those firms which either could not modify their product-mix in order to produce the domestic-resource-using products or did not have other operative constraints on capacity utilisation.

For 18% of the firms, shortage of raw materials was a result of inadequate transport facilities. However, only 2 firms provided clear evidence that inadequate transport facilities actually affected the quantity produced. These two firms were located some distance from the source of raw materials, which were so bulky that it was impossible to provide uninterrupted and regular transport.

In the rest of the firms transport only caused occasional delays and the depletion of existing stocks of raw materials, but did not necessarily affect capacity utilisation. These firms were able to compensate for lost output once the raw materials arrived, because other constraints were more binding on capacity utilisation.

Working capital was reported to be inadequate in 25% of the sample firms. It was generally true that most of the firms which faced problems in obtaining credit facilities were the small ones. The larger firms obtained credit more easily and subsidiaries of either large parastatal organisations or of large foreign corporations did not encounter the problem of working capital constraints.

Shortage of Other Inputs and Complementary Factors

Machine breakdowns and maintenance problems compounded by the unavailability of spare parts affected 80–90% of the firms, but capacity utilisation was affected in 25% of the firms which reported these problems.

One of these was the Mara Dairy Industry where, between November 1973 and November 1974, an estimated 50,200 kg. of raw milk and 23,800 kg. of skimmed milk were wasted due to transport problems between the collection centres and the milk processing plants. Most of the spoilage was caused by interruptions at the Kirumi Ferry which connects South Mara to North Mara. In addition, milk collecting vehicles frequently break down or get stuck during the rainy seasons and the milk goes bad before it reaches the plants.

A more serious impact of the poor transportation facilities is that an undetermined but large quantity of milk is never collected. In areas where roads are impassable during the rainy seasons, milk collection centres are closed.

Machine breakdowns affect capacity utilisation only if it is not possible for the production unit to compensate for the output lost due to machine breakdowns. This can happen in two ways. First, the level at which the firm is operating can be so near to capacity that when output is lost due to such interruptions the firm cannot compensate for the lost output. This usually is the case for firms which work on a three shift day. Second, the demand for the product may be nearly instantaneous and the lag between production and sale of output is consequently short.

Lack of foreign exchange, inadequate working capital and the difficulty of procuring spares from suppliers whose capacity to produce had been adversely affected by the world wide shortage of steel are some of the factors which induced a shortage of spare parts. As regards procurement of spares from suppliers it appears that firms whose source was tied to one supplier of spares experienced greater difficulties than those whose sources were more diversified. It is in the former type of firms that some machines were found to have been lying idle for the past two, three or even four years.

Shortage of technicians and engineers might have contributed to frequent machine breakdowns because of inadequate service and maintenance. In one firm at least the situation improved a great deal after the arrival of two expatriates from Pakistan who were working with the firm as technicians. In the other firms where problems of machine breakdowns were very rare, either the machines were new or they were being regularly and thoroughly serviced and maintained.

Lack of experience on the part of the machine operators in some cases was mentioned as a reason for frequent breakdowns of machines. Although this is difficult to verify, it is not unexpected in a developing country.

A number of firms had their own workshops and the range of spares made in the workshops varied from one firm to another. In general, however, workshop manufactures were limited to the simpler spares whose specifications did not require very sophisticated technology. Those firms which had their own workshops making a wide range of spares experienced fewer problems involving machines lying idle for lack of spare parts.

Inadequate supply of power and water emerged as an important factor of capacity underutilisation. About 70% of all firms reported that power interruptions were a problem, but capacity utilisation was attached in only 55% of these firms. Out of the firms affected, 75–80% were working three shifts, 20–25% were producing final products whose demand could not be postponed until power supply was restored and another 20–25% were involved in production processes in which the product was spoiled by such interruption.

The relationship between those firms which operated at lower capacity because of power interruptions and the level of capacity utilisation can be shown as follows:

Rate of capacity utilisation	*Relative frequency of affected firms:*
Less than 20%	8%
21–40%	0%
41–60%	16%
61–80%	24%
81–100%	52%
	100%

The firms which were affected by power interruptions without affecting their capacity utilisation were usually faced by other demand or supply constraints such that the power interruption constraint was secondary. The ratio of the cases was six to ten in favour of other supply constraints as opposed to demand constraints. Although capacity utilisation was not affected in cases of this kind, for planning purposes it is also useful to identify the constraints which are likely to emerge after the currently binding constraints are relaxed.

The observation of power interruptions was based mainly on the 1974 situation where both power interruptions and loadshedding posed serious problems for firms in Dar es Salaam, Tanga and Mwanza up to May, 1975. Following the coming into operation of the Kidatu power station in May 1975, there has been an improvement of power supply to Dar es Salaam and Tanga.

Water shortage was experienced by 33–40%, of all the firms. About a half of these were situated in Dar es Salaam, although Dar as Salaam firms accounted for only ¼ of the sample of firms. Those firms which suffered most from water shortage were the intensive users of water, e.g. breweries, and those whose capacity was nearly fully utilised. Capacity utilisation was affected because of the following reasons:

Reason	% of affected firms
1. Intensive users of water	35%
2. Working at near full capacity	75%
3. Demand is not postponable	25%

The fact that the percentage figures add up to more than 100% only confirms the operational simultaneity of the various factors rather than some kind of an absurdity.

Of the firms which experienced shortages of water, there was evidence of decreased capacity utilisation in 60% of the firms. The other 40% had their rates of capacity unaffected because other supply and demand factors were more constraining or because they were capable of changing their output-mix by concentrating on activities which were non-users of water.

Demand Factors of Capacity Underutilisation

The deficiency of demand for industrial output occurred in 45% of the firms. Demand may not match the productive capacity of industry for at least one of the following reasons:

(i) The advantages accruing from economies of scale may exceed the disadvantages of underutilisation of capacity. This is the case when the short-run cost curve corresponding to a particular size of plant compares unfavourably with the long-run or envelope cost curve of an individual firm. The relationship between output and cost per unit at a given point in time therefore depends on the size of plant that is selected.[13] At the level of output equal to expected domestic demand, the Marshallian long-run cost curve which represents average cost for each level of output when the most efficient single plant for each output level is used, may give rise to relatively higher efficiency than that which a cost curve of many plants of the same capacity may depict.

The larger size of plant with a capacity in excess of the domestic market may be established purely on technological grounds. This may occur when it is impossible to obtain capital equipment designed exactly to produce a level of output equal to domestic demand. In fact, domestic demand may be much less than the capacity output of the minimum plant size available. This possibility is more real in an economy which is highly dependent on foreign technology such that whatever capital equipment is imported has been designed to suit the conditions of the manufacturer's country, usually the developed economies. In developing countries, therefore, the discrepancy between the size of the market and the production possibilities of imported capital equipment is compounded by their need to employ foreign technology which has been developed to serve the large markets of the United States and Western Europe.[14]

(ii) Excess capacity can exist at a point in time if a larger plant is deliberately selected to serve current demand and to retain some capacity to meet future growth of demand. Economies of scale are also relevant here as output grows over time and as additions are made to the capital stock. These economies may offset the optimisation undertaken in a static sense. The faster domestic or export demand is expected to grow, the more these economies of scale are likely to be important. A situation in which foreign exchange is the operative constraint will make the economies of scale appear more attractive by imposing a premium on the cost of imports.[15]

(iii) The deficiency of domestic demand can be aggravated or even created by inadequacies in the distribution system and by errors in the estimation of the relationship between supply and demand. About 10% of the firms were in a situation where annual demand was insufficient to match supply yet shortages were experienced in some regions of the country. Some firms experienced a shortfall of demand, because too much of the product they produced was imported into the country.

This problem faced Ubungo Farm Implements in 1972 and Kibo Match in 1974. In both cases the extent of capacity utilisation was adversely affected by deficiency of demand created by imports of the commodities they produce. The relationship between quantity of local production and domestic demand was wrongly estimated because of lack of coordination between the producers and the importers. At present in the case of UFI this problem is not likely to occur again, since UFI is responsible for both the production and the importation of farm implements.

(iv) Demand deficiency can also occur when the product-mix projections turn out to diverge from actual requirements. Since the import licence is given in value terms, allocation of foreign exchange allowances with respect to various production lines is left to the discretion of the firms themselves. For the multiproduct producing firms, this involves projections of the expected demand structure for at least a year ahead in order to plan an output-mix which will satisfy the demand structure. The actual demand structure may therefore turn out to diverge from the projected demand structure. In cases of this kind excess demand for some products co-exists with deficient demand for other products. Between 10 and 15% of the firms whose capacity utilisation was constrained by demand fell in this category.

(v) Fluctuations in demand also may be responsible for excess capacity at times. If demand is likely to fluctuate, the firm will probably wish to be able to meet at least a reasonable proportion of the peak orders without unduly long delays in delivery. This factor was significant only in the clothing firms and does not seem to be a general determinant of industrial capacity underutilisation. In fact most firms enjoyed quite a stable demand.

(vi) Deficiency of demand hit some firms which had been established to meet the entire East African Market following the Kampala Agreement, e.g. General Tyre Co. at Arusha.

(vii) Slightly more than 10% of the firms experienced the demand constraint because of the oligopolistic structure of the industry. The characteristic of such industries was such that a few firms controlled most of the output and none of them was fully utilised because their total productive capacity exceeded demand. If their number was reduced the likelihood is that capacity utilisation of the remaining firms would increase.

(viii) Even if domestic demand is insufficient to allow full capacity utilisation, the firms in question have the option to utilise their idle capacity for the export market. The export market however has not been significantly tapped, because of the uncompetitive nature of the world market and also because of deficiencies in export promotion services. Uncompetitiveness resulting from higher domestic prices can be explained by the high cost of imported (as well as local) materials and excessive protection. Observations of the unfavourable results of excessive protection have also been made elsewhere.[16] In some cases excessive protection proved to be a disincentive either to adopting efficient production methods or to making efforts to cut down on unnecessary costs.

Even for some firms whose products could penetrate the export market, the export promotion effort was not sufficient to enable them to do so because of financial and manpower constraints. Export promotion can be an expensive exercise although it involves significant economies of scale in reducing the costs of carrying it out. When these high costs of export promotion are compounded with the lack of the incentive to export, the export market appears to be rather unattractive.

Although from the point of view of the economy foreign exchange is badly needed, it is difficult for some individual firms to see the advantage of earning foreign exchange if their export receipts are not in terms of foreign exchange. One firm was particularly unhappy when the application for an import licence was not fully accepted despite the fact that this firm had earned more foreign exchange in the previous year than the amount it was presently requesting. The firm claimed that it was not possible to expand the exports of the product unless all foreign exchange requirements for imported inputs were actually met.

Services of the Bank of Tanzania were held responsible for some failure in entering the export markets. One firm reported that it was possible to penetrate foreign markets provided that the product could be delivered to the export market before the harvest season in the purchasing country and payment was accepted after the harvest season. This requirement contradicted the regulation which the Bank of Tanzania had imposed that payment must be received within 60 days. Since the purchasers of the product could buy from elsewhere, there was a general reluctance by purchasers to accept to pay within 60 days. During the year 1975 the firm had to reduce its capacity utilisation because of the failure to penetrate the export market.

Policy Implications

1. Underutilisation of capacity has in several instances coexisted with investments for capacity expansion in the same industry. Whether the real incentive to expand capacity has been to increase output as such is questionable, at least in the face of existing underutilisation of capacity. In some cases where capacity utilisation could be raised but an import licence for purchasing new machines was being requested, the response from firms was varied. One set of firms was interested in modernising the plant in order to increase the quality of the product. This applied for firms which sought to penetrate export markets. Another firm concerned with labour troubles, stated that the management thought it was not to the interest of the firm to increase the number of people employed because this was likely to increase labour troubles.

Studies in other developing countries have shown that as a consequence of tight exchange control, export of capital has been done through excessive importation of machinery and other capital equipment.[17] The incentive to undertake such practice is enhanced by the overvaluation of the domestic currency. Although it was not possible in this study to quantify the magnitude of this kind of malpractice, there is no convincing reason to assume it away. Tighter control on capacity creation in preference to capacity utilisation could be an area of interest for the Bank of Tanzania. Scrutiny of the necessity to expand productive capacity by importing additional machinery not only will relax the imported inputs constraint to other firms but it also might reduce the chances of "export" of foreign currency that way. Every firm should therefore justify all the significant expansions before an import licence is given to purchase additional capital equipment.

2. If individual firms do not have the incentive to penetrate the export market or if some firms lack the incentive to increase efficiency, then the internal taxation policies could be used to create such incentives.

As regards the incentive to export, some kind of an export subsidy may play an important role to increase exports.

On the question of efficiency there may be a need to enhance the activities of the National Institute of Productivity, which could intervene more on the productive efficiency of industry. Meanwhile areas of excessive protection leading to undesirable monopoly positions need to be identified. Along these lines some kind of limit to an infant industry in each case might be required. An industry cannot continue to be treated as infant indefinitely. At least after some period to be determined more specifically in each concrete situation, serious concern should arise as to why the firm in question is still at the infancy stage. The protection of an infant industry should be a temporary phenomenon instead of assuming a permanency that often hinders further attempts to increase efficiency.

3. This study has found that those industries which depend on imported inputs experienced a more severe foreign exchange constraint on the degree of their

capacity utilisation. Of the firms which experienced shortages of inputs, about 70% of them had shortages of imported inputs. For 60% of this group, imported inputs constituted more than 80% of their inputs. If industrial capacity utilisation is so sensitive to the foreign exchange position, it is because of the high degree of dependence on imported inputs including, both raw materials and spare parts. To the extent that industries continue to use what other industries do not produce, and produce what other industries do not use, this dependency relationship is bound to be increasingly sharpened as industry grows. Although some established industries may not have much freedom to choose between domestic and foreign raw materials, often because their raw materials are not locally produced, some industries may be able to move towards the greater use of local raw materials.

Where the same type of raw materials can be obtained locally, reluctance to use such local material often is based on quality and cost arguments. Local material is either of lower quality or more expensive than imported material. These claims are usually made from the individual and micro-level points of view.

Regardless of how severe the foreign exchange crisis may be, a number of firms seem to put little if any premium on the cost of foreign exchange. Consequently, slight quality and cost differences arrived at by market prices are not tolerated. However, shadow price consideration for foreign exchange can be meaningfully carried out, only by a central body. If the central body deems quality and cost differences too small to warrant a preference for imported raw materials, then the firm in question can be obliged to make use of domestic raw material. The magnitude of cost differences to be tolerated should depend on the foreign exchange shadow price deemed best by the central body along with any other considerations which might be peculiar in each concrete situation. The import licence controller will therefore accept applications for imported raw materials only after satisfactory scrutiny of the available alternatives.

However, in the long run the structure of industry needs to change in favour of a more integrated type with respect to sources and uses of raw materials and other inputs. It should be a deliberate policy to produce raw materials for industry and to set up industries which make use of local raw materials. If this is not done, then, on the one hand industrial performance will continue to be dependent on the balance of payments situation, and on the other hand, industrial growth will contribute to a deterioration of the balance of payments situation.

The problem of spare parts has become rampant following the unfavourable balance of payments position and the world wide shortage of steel. In fact firms which had their own workshop or could obtain spares from local sources were in a relatively better position on the problem of lack of spares. However, the main constraint on the range of spares that could be made locally is technological. What is lacking is the technological base.

With a weak technological base even simple modifications of imported capital equipment can hardly be made, even if the local conditions require such modifications. A large quantity of maintenance inputs have to be imported following every move to create additional productive capacity. It is at this juncture that the basic industry strategy is required to strengthen the technological base, and in the long term to reduce the dependence on inputs of both capacity expansions and maintenance inputs.

NTOES

1. UNIDO, "Industrial Excess Capacity and its Utilisation for Export," *Industrialization and Productivity*. Bulletin No. 15. New York: United Nations, 1970; also UNIDO, *Utilisation of Excess Capacity for Export*, New York: United Nations, 1969.
2. G. C. Winston, "Capital Utilisation in Economic Development," *The Economic Journal*, March 1971.
3. S. M. Wangwe, "The Problem of Excess Capacity in the Mara Dairy Industry," ERB Paper 75.4.
4. R. Noyes, "Certain Problems in The Empirical Study of Costs," *American Economic Review*, 1941, p. 482.
5. J. M. Clark, *Studies in the Economics of Overhead Costs*, (Chicago, 1923), p. 91.
6. L. R. Klein, "Measurement of Capacity," *Econometrica*, 1960, p. 277.
7. A. D. Knox, "The Principle of Acceleration and the Theory of Investment: A Survey," *Economica*, August, 1952, pp. 269–297.
8. E. G. Nourse et al., *America's Capacity to Produce*, (Washington, D.C. 1934), p. 23.
9. L. R. Klein and R. S. Preston, "Some Results in the Measurement of Capacity Utilisation." *American Economic Review*, March, 1967, pp. 34–58; and L. R. Klein and R. Summers, *The Wharton Index of Capacity Utilization (Studies in Quantitative Economics No. 1)*, Wharton School of Economics Research Unit, Department of Economics, Wharton School of Finance and Commerce, University of Pennsylvania, 1966.
10. D. Creamer, "Capital Expansion and Capacity in Post War Manufacturing," *Studies in Business Economics*, No. 72, New York: National Industrial Conference Board, 1961.
11. L. R. Klein and R. S Preston, *op. cit.*
12. A. Phillips, "Measuring Industrial Capacity and Capacity Utilization in Less Developed Countries," *Industrialization and Productivity, Bullettin No. 15.* UNIDO, 1970: A. Phillips, "An Appraisal of Measures of Capacity," *American Economic Review*, May 1973; S. M. Wangwe, *op. cit.*
13. A. S. Manne, *Investments for Capacity Expansion: Size, Location and Time Phasing*, London: George Allen and Unwin Ltd., 1967; R. B. Sutcliffe, *Industry and Underdevelopment*, London: Addison Wesley Publishing Company, 1971.
14. M. Merhow, "Excess Capacity Measurement, Causes and Uses: A Case Study of Industry in Israel," *Industrialization and Productivity* Bulletin No. 15, UNIDO, 1970; J. Haldi and D. Whitcomb, "Economies of Scale in Industrial Plants," *Journal of Political Economy*, August," 1967.
15. A. S. Monne, *op. cit.*; and R. B. Sutcliffe, *op. cit.*
16. M. A. Bailey, *Capital Utilization in Kenya Manufacturing Industry*, Ph.D. dissertation, MIT, 1973; J. F. Rweyemamu, *Underdevelopment and Industrialization in Tanzania*, Nairobi: Oxford University Press, 1973.
17. See G. C. Winston, "Overinvoicing. Underutilization and Distorted Industrial Growth," *The Pakistan Development Review*, Winter 1970.

Section IV

Money and Banking

INTRODUCTION

Following the Arusha Declaration the Tanzanian Government nationalized the banking system, established the Central Bank of Tanzania and gave it the power to play an active role in directing the nation's monetary economy. The institutional changes that have affected every sector of the national economy in the past decade also have continued to shape the present banking system in Tanzania.

The readings in this section consider the changing nature of the monetary and fiscal institutions in Tanzania and the role they exercise in the nation's transition to socialism. In the first reading Loxley examines the paramount position of the Central Bank in the socialised banking system and how the banking institutions control financially the public sector. A number of mechanisms have been developed or extended to implement government policies in this area: provision of credit and credit security to both public and private sectors, creation of long term finance facilities, control of the interest rate on loans and credit, and the establishment of the national insurance corporation.

In a second paper Loxley goes on to examine the behaviour of the money supply since the founding of the Central Bank in 1970. As part of this analysis he describes the main monetary indicators, i.e. the money supply itself, foreign reserve holdings, and the volume of credit outstanding. The paper recommends financial and credit planning by means of integrated budgetary, foreign exchange and flow of funds forecasting accounts.

A low income dependent economy such as Tanzania is particularly vulnerable to fluctuations and crises in the international market economy. Rwegasira presents a monetary analysis of the Tanzanian economy for the period 1966–73 and attempts to explain the causes and impact of the inflationary pressures that characterized the economy during the Second Five-Year Plan, 1969/74. In the final reading of this section, Huang analyzes the distribution of the tax burden and its impact on different income groups across the economy. These two seminal papers are important for both methodology and content and should provide the basis for further study into factors that monitor, in some sense, Tanzania's progress toward a socialist and self-reliant economy.

The Monetary System of Tanzania Since 1967: Progress, Problems and Proposals*

J. LOXLEY

Introduction

While the 1967 nationalization measures were accompanied by legislation establishing new public enterprises and the broad principles on which they should operate, no basic guidelines were laid down at that time as to how the activities of public sector enterprises were to be conducted in detail or the actions and policies of different public sector enterprises were to be inter-related. Neither was any mention made as to the terms on which the newly created public sector was to deal with the still sizeable private sector. Any problems which might arise in these areas were left to be resolved on an "ad hoc" basic as and when they arose and, given the haste with which nationalisation was effected, this was only to be expected. Yet what is more interesting and important than the mere change of ownership that nationalisation entails is, in fact, precisely how enterprises behave once they join the public sector; what their goals are, how far they reflect national goals and how far their day to day business reflects or departs from stated enterprise and/or national goals; how far the activities of different enterprises are mutually consistent and what happens if they clash; and to what extent, if at all, should the continued existence of a relatively large private sector modify public sector policies and actions. These are the questions that need to be answered unless public enterprises are to behave exactly as their private enterprise predecessors behaved, i.e. unless nationalisation is to mean nothing more than mere change of ownership.

Such questions are particularly pertinent to the financial sector where the 1967 legislation merely enjoined the new public institutions "to provide in accordance with the conditions appropriate in the normal proper conduct of (banking and insurance) business, adequate and proper (banking and insurance) services and facilities throughout the United Republic."[1] We immediately ask, "what is normal and proper conduct?" While the legislation gives no answer we can be sure that what was normal and proper under the pre-1967 private enterprise system might not be considered so after that date. But since the immediate pre-occupations were with such "mundane" matters as ensuring the day to day survival of the new institutions, it took some months before any significant amount of consideration could be given to the point. And, of course, the legislation in no way prescribed how the National Bank of Commerce (NBC) and National Insurance Corporation (NIC) should deal with the other public sector financial institutions which had existed prior to 1967. Neither were the rules and regulations of these other institutions, the Bank of Tanzania, the National Co-operative Bank, the Post Office Savings Bank, etc., in any way altered to allow for the fact that two very important and closely allied financial institutions had also joined the public sector. Each institution was therefore left to fend for itself and adapt its behaviour as it saw fit, subject to broad policy directives being issued from the Ministries.[2]

The aim of this paper is to examine in general terms some of the major issues that have been raised since 1967 concerning the role of the larger financial institutions, their operating principles and practices, their relationships with each other, with the public production and service sectors and with the private sector in general. The paper further seeks to assess the monetary institutions from the point of view of their influence on the real performance of the economy—in particular their effect on savings and investment with special emphasis on the direction of and control over investment resources. It will be a basic argument that the cost to the economy of providing financial services should be minimized in terms of real resources consumed, and that the growth of financial bureaucracies which perform few if any *real functions* as far as savings and investment are concerned, should be discouraged.

THE ROLE OF THE CENTRAL BANK

This question is commonly asked by visitors to Tanzania who seem surprised that the Bank of Tanzania continued to exist side by side with a monopoly commercial bank. They point to the fact that in almost all socialist countries nationalisation of the banking system was quickly followed by the creation of a single, large, "Mono-bank" performing the functions of the commercial banks and absorbing the former central banks. With the advent of fully centralised physical planning and the development of financial planning which exactly spelled out in money terms the detailed implications of the physical plan, the need for a separate institution having as its main function the formulation and implementation of macro-monetary policy as we know it in western capitalist economies totally disappeared. This being so, the purely banking functions of the Central Bank—currency issue control of government accounts and management of foreign assets, all of which are provided for in detail in the financial plan—become routine functions requiring the exercise of little or no bank discretion and are easily absorbed by the commercial bank. These functions, together with commercial bank lending, become virtually automatic functions where detailed physical and financial plans are centrally administered in Government departments. "In an economic system where money was divested of all its economic functions, except that of serving as an accounting unit, the banks could at best

*Edited version of ERB paper 69.30.

aspire to the function of an auditor of state owned enterprises, but more often were reduced to the function of a ledger clerk."[3]

What is more relevant from Tanzania's point of view is that as decentralisation of decision taking has developed in eastern Europe the banking system has gradually been given a more important role to play. This is particularly so for the commercial banks but in at least two countries with relatively advanced socialist-market economies, e.g. Czechoslovakia (until the Russian invasion, and Yugoslavia, central banking functions have once again been isolated from those of commercial banking. The reason behind this is that the more discretion is given to enterprises, the greater is the prospect of divergence between macro physical and financial plans and hence the greater the need for an independent body to follow real and financial developments in the economy and to exercise control over bank lending when this becomes excessive in any particular direction or in total.

In Tanzania the activities of the public sector are governed by loose indicative planning while those of the private and co-operative sector are virtually unplanned. There is no overall detailed physical plan and certainly no comprehensive financial plan. The NBC does not have a banking monopoly and there is a proliferation of public and private financial institutions. Until this situation changes the need for an institution performing central banking functions is just as great as under any capitalist system and since the Bank of Tanzania is a well established and relatively efficient organisation there seems to be little or nothing to be gained by amalgamating this with the NBC at this stage. There is a fair degree of specialisation in its functions and little duplication between its work and that of the NBC.

The Arusha Declaration and the nationalisation of commercial banking do, however, have implications for the Bank of Tanzania. The whole of the banking system is now in public hands and this makes the formulation and implementation of monetary policy much easier than it is in a system in which a central bank faces private institutions which in general cannot be relied upon to co-operate fully with policy guidelines if these involve adverse effects on profit performance. Co-operation within the banking sphere should therefore be enhanced and the use of formal directives and orthodox monetary tools should give way to close co-operation and regular informal contact between the two institutions. Tanzania should in fact be a central banker's paradise from this point of view. But perhaps the principal functions of the Bank of Tanzania will in future be not so much monetary policy formulation in any given situation, but more likely the forward planning of domestic and foreign financial resource availabilities in terms of overall targets and sectoral distribution. This crucial aspect of planning is currently neglected in Tanzania and of all the institutions presently existing, the Bank of Tanzania is certainly the best equipped (in terms of manpower) and the best placed (in terms of legal powers and of its present relationships with ministries and parastatals) to carry out such exercises. Forward planning of foreign exchange availabilities will be the most urgent requirement in the short run and indeed some work has already begun on this, but in the medium and longer run Tanzania should be building up comprehensive flow-of-funds accounts with detailed sectoral breakdowns and the overall plan should then be fitted into this framework. The recent decision of the Bank to schedule certain financial institutions is potentially a first step in this direction, but if comprehensive financial planning is to be the goal the Bank will have to broaden its interests to seek information from producing and servicing industries as well as from financial institutions. The absence of any reliable information on sources and uses of funds by industry and trade is one of the major gaps in available financial statistics. The immediate need is to obtain detailed and accurate data on "ex-post" flows; the ultimate aim must be for the Central Bank to provide Development plan with reliable annual or longer term financial *forecasts* and consistency checks on the basis of declared plan targets. The appropriate monetary policy for any plan period or section of a period might then be known in advance in general terms, enabling the Central Bank to play a more positive role in monetary planning rather than adopting "ad hoc" monetary policies as circumstances change or more accurately, usually only after they have changed, as it does at the moment. The Central Bank must therefore adapt itself to become an integral part of the planning machinery in Tanzania rather than confining itself to the rather negative role of watchdog over the commercial banking system. This implies that special emphasis must be placed on building up the Research Department of the bank as a planning and forecasting unit.

The Bank will of course continue to exercise its control functions over credit institutions and to play its important role in assisting the creation of new financial institutions (as it has done in the past with TAFCO, NBC and Karadha), both of which will continue to be essential; but in the future these functions should be performed in the framework of a comprehensive financial plan, and the creation of such a plan would seem to be a task fully befitting a Central Bank in an economic system in transition towards socialism.

It will be argued below that the Central Bank should re-assess the role of each local financial institution with a view to rationalising the whole institutional structure. Proliferation of financial organisations makes financial planning and control more difficult than it need be, may lead to misallocation of investment resources and is extremely costly to the economy in terms of skilled manpower and other resources. The Bank of Tanzania is again ideally placed to view and advise upon the present institutional arrangements, but it will be shown later that there is a real need for the Bank to re-think some of its present policies regarding competition and specialisation in the financial sector.

THE BANKING SYSTEM AND THE PUBLIC SECTOR

Perhaps the most fundamental principle that the NBC has had to vigorously assert in its dealings with other public sector bodies, is its right to critically examine their requests for credit and its prerogative to refuse credit unless and until satisfied with the production and financial details of new or continuing projects. Initially there was a feeling in some quarters that the Bank had no right to refuse to assist a project which had been approved by the board of the public sector enterprise in question and cleared by the relevant operating ministry. It was argued that bank credit and other ancillary facilities should be automatically forthcoming without further scrutiny of the project and that the Bank should passively comply with requests for finance. Had the NBC acceded to this argument then, with respect to public sector credits, it would almost certainly have developed into no more than a "bureaucratic appendix of the planning and fiscal machinery"[4] as indeed were the State banks in Stalinist Russia and other Eastern European countries until the economic reforms of the 1950's. The Bank's functions would have been reduced to those of an elementary book-keeper or accountant and it would have become a mere credit channel having no discretion and requiring no banking expertise in the field of lending. All questions relating to the finance of public projects would have been left entirely in the hands of the public sector enterprises concerned and in those of the physical planners. Even ignoring the relatively high level of expertise in the banking sector which would have been under-utilised as a result of such a development and, even ignoring the relatively weak manpower situation of the planning ministry and most public enterprises, the senior personnel of which tend, in any case, to be grossly overworked, experience has shown that this control is desperately needed and that almost all public sector projects presented to the Bank benefit from close financial assessment. This is not surprising since experience elsewhere has shown that the banking system is an indispensable complement to the control tools available to physical planners and indeed in all Eastern European countries, without exception, the trend over the last twenty years has been to give greater and not less discretion to the banks over the financial plans of enterprises.[5]

The NBC has therefore successfully argued that it will not be a mere rubber stamp and cheque clearing institution, but will utilise its abundant supply of relatively highly skilled senior personnel to critically examine credit requests, assess the consistency of physical and financial targets and scrutinise the short and long term foreign and domestic financial provisions. This control will be exercised not just on new applications but will be continuing throughout the lifetime of the project with special emphasis on annual review of the enterprise's performance. The banking system has therefore in effect become integrated into the planning machinery with its own positive discretionary role to play in the financing of public sector projects. It will be appreciated that the present emphasis on encouraging co-operatives, local councils, NUTA and other "socialist" organisations to enter fields of production and trade currently dominated by private enterprise renders financial control by the Bank much more critical (given their personnel problems) than if the NBC and the Bank of Tanzania were merely dealing with the larger parastatals; but even in the case of the latter the need for control is still indisputably there.

It will be appreciated that this discretion is even more important where many public sector investment projects involve participation by foreign investors and where the foreign partner participation increasingly takes the form of contractor finance credits for plant purchase. Here the banking system can rightly claim to be consulted well in advance of contracts being signed, for two additional reasons: (a) in order to safeguard his investment the foreign partner will normally require that his principal and interest repayments be covered by letters of credit and guarantees underwritten by a reputable bank in his own country. Such facilities may need to be established on an "ad hoc" basis and will have to be negotiated by the NBC; and (b) contractor finance agreements need careful scrutiny as to the true rate of interest being charged, the ability of the project itself to generate sufficient foreign exchange earnings to cover interest and capital repayments in foreign exchange, the true purchase price of the capital goods including cash discount losses, and the general foreign exchange impact of the project on the reserve position of the country as a whole. This latter function is clearly one to be performed by the Bank of Tanzania which is charged by law to manage the foreign exchange reserves of Tanzania in a manner "conducive to the rapid growth of the national economy."[6] Just as the NBC has successfully established the principle that it will not be committed by public enterprises either to giving credit or to arranging foreign payments and guarantees without first having full opportunity to scrutinize the details of investment projects, so the Bank of Tanzania has had to impress upon the rest of the public sector that any commitment of existing or anticipated foreign exchange resources requires its prior approval, which will only be given after careful appraisal of projects and of the prevailing and expected foreign exchange reserve position of the country as a whole.

NBC LOANS TO THE PUBLIC SECTOR

The necessity for the commercial banking system to insist on the right to undertake financial appraisals of public sector projects before granting credit stems partly from the belief that requesting the public sector to provide conventional forms of commercial banking security is a meaningless exercise in an economy in which the major means of production are under the control and ownership of the peasants and the workers themselves through their government and their cooperatives. Taking a legal mortgage on a debenture over the fixed assets of an enterprise in a socialist economy adds nothing to the security of the resources of the economy, nor does it in any way safeguard the interests of the bank's depositors and "shareholders", who are the people of the country. Certainly a public sector enterprise should not be allowed to conduct its financial affairs as it pleases simply because it can offer traditional security to the banking system in sufficient amounts to cover all credits utilised. Orthodox security has little value in the changed circumstances although some institutions find this difficult to accept. In a socialist economic system it is also clearly inappropriate that credits for either working capital or longer term requirements should be restricted by notions of the forced sale value of fixed assets, the risk margins on stocks, debtors and fixed assets, the avoidance of geographical concentration of securities lest they all suffer from a general depreciation due to localised trade depressions, the avoidance of concentrating large credits in individual enterprises, and other such security considerations which constitute the essence of "sound" banking in free enterprise capitalist countries.[7] Socialist credit must be strictly related to the current value of the real goods and services it is intended to finance and to other financial availabilities in an enterprise, and should not be restricted by estimates as to what the assets of an enterprise would be worth if for some reason the venture was unsuccessful. If a project fails in a socialist economy then it must be appreciated that the loss is a *national* loss and that the loss of financial resources by the bank represents only part of the overall loss of resources by the nation as a whole. There seems to be no "a priori" reason why the bank in particular should try to cover its own losses by sale of remaining assets although it is *not* inconceivable that this may be the best administrative way of ensuring that the remaining physical assets are not wasted but are put to their best alternative use (which must again be consistent with overall plan objectives). Thus when both the banking system and the means of production are entirely in the hands of the public sector, security for bank advances takes on an entirely different character from that which it assumes in a system where either or them, or both of them, are in capitalist hands. The only meaningful security for public sector projects is the viability of projects and their efficient management.

SECURITY FOR CREDITS TO THE PUBLIC SECTOR

The situation in Tanzania is, however, complicated by the continued existence of a large private sector, operating side by side with, and in some cases jointly with, the public sector. The question of the disposal of residual physical assets of a defaulting enterprise could, in this case, have more than merely administrative implications. While the private sector could not under any circumstances buy its way back into majority share ownership of industries designated by the Arusha Declaration to form part of "the major means of production,"[8] it will always offer an attractive market for the smaller productive activities not covered by the Declaration, e.g. medium and small scale producing and trading activities which are increasingly being taken over by co-operatives, unions and local councils. Indeed as the public sector consolidates its entry into the manufacturing, processing and large scale trading industries and as the existing short term speculative outlets for private capital (such as luxury housing, office building and transport) exhaust themselves, the private sector will be increasingly on the look-out for ways of profitably employing its surpluses. In the absence of an abundance of new investment outlets, and assuming the maintenance of strict exchange controls, the surpluses from existing private investments will be increasingly invested in Government paper or in Government savings institutions. In this situation the NBC could, by calling up its security when public sector credits are unpaid, be a vehicle for the net transfer of fixed investments from the public to the private sector.[9] To-date this has not been a problem but it could become one in future and some guidance may have to be given to the Bank to discourage such transfers. And yet the existence of a large private sector does make it imperative for the NBC to request public sector enterprises to furnish orthodox security against credit advanced, in at least two situations: (a) where the public sector enterprises operate on the basis of extensive credit from the private sector in the form of credits for the supply of raw materials purchased from the private sector or of credits for services rendered; and (b) where public sector enterprises have borrowed from the private sector for investment purposes. While the latter is quite rare in Tanzania, the former is not, and in both cases it is important that the NBC secures its credits in such a way that in the event of failure of the public sector company the Bank's claims are met before those of the private sector, and the disposal of residual real assets remains in the hands of the public sector rather than the private.

GOVERNMENT GUARANTEES AND SUBSIDIES

There may be an argument for a national bank to seek government guarantees for credit to extremely marginal public sector companies for while the payment by government on such a guarantee does not in any way reduce national resource availabilities (while the failure of the enterprise does), by charging the development budget for such bad debt write-offs it does place the responsibility clearly where it belongs and ensures the independence of the banking system as a controlling institution. Similarly, for banking control purposes long term subsidisation of enterprises should always be explicitly achieved through payments from the development budget rather than through extended bank credit, even though the effect on overall financial resources is the same, and notwithstanding the need for additional bank credit facilities in the event of *short run* departures from planned performance.

We conclude therefore that if orthodox banking securities have any place at all in a socialist system it will be as an administrative tool for fixed assets transfer in the event of enterprise failure, but they can be important where a national bank and a large publicly owned producing sector operate side by side with a large private producing sector. Thus although the NBC may still seek traditional security from public sector enterprises, its main security lies in close scrutiny of planned real and financial targets and in close surveillance of enterprise performance.

LONG-TERM FINANCE

The NBC has already begun acting as an investment bank by undertaking initially medium and now long term finance of investment projects. The aim of the Bank is to provide term finance facilities which did not exist on any scale before nationalisation and secondly, with the specific approval of the Bank of Tanzania in each case, to provide an alternative to foreign contractor finance which at times can be extremely expensive once the true costs are reckoned. But the Bank also sees its entry into term lending as being a natural extension of the role it plays in the short term lending field as financial controller of public sector credits. In particular it foresees the possibility of some development budget financing being channelled through the banking system.[10] There may also be a strong argument for tighter control over *reinvestment* of surpluses by parastatals, marketing boards and even co-operatives, to ensure that all long term public sector investments receive adequate scrutiny and to enable much more comprehensive physical and financial planning, and the banking system may have a role to play here. Certainly there has been a pronounced shift in favour of Bank loan as opposed to Central Government grant finance of investment projects in Eastern European countries.[11] This is partly in order to make the interest cost of capital more explicit, thereby discouraging misuse of resources (as evidenced by the fact that even where grants are still given, interest is now payable), but also to bring this kind of finance within the sphere of banking control. This move coincides with giving enterprises more discretion over physical investment decisions, reducing the power and workload of the planning ministries and pushing more responsibility onto the branch banking system, thus achieving a greater degree of decentralisation of decision-taking in the investment field without loss of efficiency. It is interesting to note that while Tanzania's Second Five-Year Plan discusses the difficulties of controlling parastatal investment and operating plans and performances, it nowhere suggests that the banking system might have an important role to play in this area—indeed the banking system seems to be regarded almost entirely as a channel for savings and a source of finance.[12] There is no doubt however that both the Bank of Tanzania (with regard to the use of foreign reserves) and the National Bank of Commerce see themselves as having important roles to play in the field of control of parastatal activities; and in practice both the Ministries and parastatals seem to have accepted this in principle—it now remains to be extended in practice, particularly in the field of long term finance.

There is a view that once the volume of long term projects (rather than the value) has reached a certain level, a separate investment bank should be established which might also act as a channel for official foreign loans and grants to the productive sectors.[13] If Central Government finance of the public producing sectors is to be increasingly channelled through the banking system in future, then there may well be a sufficient volume of business to justify this, since 30% of parastatal expenditures in the plan period will be financed by the Central Government.[14] In the meantime while the NBC handles term lending, any limits placed on the total amount to be loaned by the Bank should ideally be fixed strictly in accordance with the "financial plan" and not fixed arbitrarily by the National Bank of Commerce. However, since no such plan exists at the present time[15] the imposition of upper limits on term finance, provided these are regarded as flexible guidelines and not immutable directives, may constitute necessary caution.

LOANS TO THE PRIVATE SECTOR

Periodically during the last three years the view has been expressed that the national banking system should cease lending to the private sector as this runs contrary to declared national policies of socialism. This view is somewhat short sighted in that it ignores the fact that considerable efforts are already being made to reduce the size of the private sector and that these efforts face real constraints in the form of trained manpower available for running ventures which are currently in the hands of private businessmen. As long as these constraints are important, credit restrictions on private businessmen will merely tend to disrupt the economy. However, since the sale of goods produced in the public sector relies heavily on the privately owned distributive outlets, restricting bank credit to the latter may well result in the public sector companies providing a substitute in the form of extended credit repayment terms—so that the public sector would borrow more from the banking system to substitute for reduced private sector borrowing and the net effect would be one of little change. Finally it is not true to say that government policy discourages private investment—on the contrary, outside the scheduled industries private investment "will be welcomed and . . . will receive full co-operation from the Government and people . . ."[16] and few can say that the protection and inducements given to the private investor are not generous. The NBC should not therefore adopt credit policies which might disrupt the economy and which run contrary to Government policy. On the other hand, it does have an obligation to give every possible assistance to socialist organizations attempting to break the monopoly of private enterprise in certain sectors of the economy and such assistance will need to be as much advisory as financial. While it is not the function of the banking system to attempt to spearhead structural changes in the economy in the direction of socialism, it does carry the responsibility of actively encouraging such change and of seeing that its own policies do not impede that change.

The NBC's Act states that the Bank should "conduct its business without discrimination except on such grounds as are appropriate in the normal and proper conduct of banking business.[17] Again no guidance is given as to what constitutes "normal and proper conduct" and while economic conditions in Tanzania have so far not necessitated any restrictions on credit advanced by the banking system, thus enabling "even non-socialist institutions to have what they need",[18] there can be no doubt that if ever credit is to be contracted the private sector should as far as possible be the first to feel the impact.

THE EFFECT OF INTEREST RATE ON CREDIT

Does the rate of interest have any use or justification other than that it allows banks to cover their costs and to make profits? In theory this latter is surely not the justification for the rate of interest even though this might be one practical outcome of interest rates being determined by some more objective criterion. What is required of the rate of interest in theory is that it relates future income and consumption to present income and consumption—it is a discount factor which indicates the price society is to pay for foregoing income and consumption now in order to have income and consumption in the future. If we assume that the "sacrifice" of society in terms of savings (i.e. consumption foregone) over the planning period is more or less pre-determined by the authorities fixing the planned level of investment —a not too unrealistic assumption—we may determine the rate of interest as being that discount factor which when applied to the net future contributions to national product of all investment projects competing for funds, would maximise the present value of those projects the sum of whose initial costs would be just equal to the sum of investment resources available. Or in other words all available projects could be ranked according to the social yield they offer and the rate of interest is determined by the yield on the project which just exhausts available investment resources—all other projects accepted offering a return which equals or exceeds this rate of interest. It must be emphasized that this method of approach is concerned with social marginal productivity, the returns to the economy as a whole, and not with the internal rate of return or the capitalist yield of a project.[19]

The rate of interest on credit should therefore be equal to the rate of discount so determined. There may be arguments for the banking system charging more than this rate, e.g. on loans for private consumption and hire purchase, if these are to continue in future, on the grounds that these "projects" generally have indirect adverse effects on the economy. If, however, we accept the principle outlined above that all longterm subsidies should be explicit and not hidden in bank credit figures, then to be consistent, no projects should receive credit at rates less than that determined in the above manner. Instead all projects should pay at least that rate and again if subsidisation is needed this should be made directly from the development budget. Only by charging one uniform rate, determined in accordance with social marginal productivity of capital principles, can we ensure that the present value of future additions to national product will be maximised and subsidies to public sector projects clearly isolated and minimised.

The determination of the rate of interest by reference to real returns to investment projects with the investment budget clearly leaves no room for alterations in that rate being made by the banking system on account of any increases or decreases in its operating expenses—these are irrelevant to the determination of the national rate and hence profits of the banking system are also equally irrelevant except to the extent that the costs of providing banking facilities should be minimized. In other words, if manipulation of interests rates on lending is used in an attempt to improve banking efficiency there may be a heavy price in misallocation of resources in the rest of the economy.

We conclude, therefore, that the rate of interest should be strictly related to the social discount rates on investments in the manner described and that deviations from this rate should be few and in an upward direction only. Under no circumstances should interest rates be related to the management expenses or profits of banks and the rate charged by one publicly owned bank on credit to a particular project should be exactly the same as that charged by all other banks.

THE NATIONAL INSURANCE CORPORATION

Structure of the NIC

The direct financial gains from nationalising the insurance sector undoubtedly outweigh those from nationalising any other sector. This is partly because this was effected essentially through the transfer of trading rights to the National Insurance Corporation, compensation being limited to the purchase of shares from minority shareholders in the old NIC which was a very small institution in terms of paid-up capital (Shs. 2,000,000), and its share of the market. More important than this though (particularly since this also had costly implications in terms of administrative efficiency as discussed below), was the fact that the insurance sector had persistently been a net exporter of funds both from Tanzania to Kenya and from East Africa in general to other parts of the world. These remittances are over and above the very large totals of net reinsurance outflows and would seem to constitute unrecorded flows, the income and principle of which will never return to East Africa.[20]

It appears as if these unrecorded flows may have been in the region of Shs. 350 million between the years 1960 and 1966, while during the same period net reinsurance outflows totalled no less than Shs. 140 million, both figures relating to East Africa as a whole.[21] The limited figures available also indicate that between 1964 and 1966 approximately Shs. 44 million left Tanzania in the form of unrecorded outflows while net reinsurance outflows during this period amounted to a further Shs. 15 million. Nationalisation of insurance business and the formulation of a domestic investment policy for surplus funds could in itself, therefore, be expected to lead to positive national resource gains without any departure from accepted private enterprise insurance principles. It will be argued later that departures from these principles might also lead to further gains on the reinsurance side.

An important negative effect of the NIC not taking over the buildings and staff of former private operators was that it has faced, from its inception, staffing and administration, problems of a size many times greater than those faced by other newly created or expanded parastatals. It has had to rely on a large number of mainly private agents for handling a great part of its administration, and its Head Office was created by expanding the old Dar es Salaam Headquarters of the pre-1967 NIC—an office originally designed to handle a much smaller volume of business. These inadequate administrative arrangements at the hastily expanded Head Office and the acute shortage of skilled or semi-skilled personnel suitable to man Head Office posts resulted in a large backlog of work building up in Dar es Salaam. This was exacerbated early in the life of the new NIC by the decision of private dealers to cease issuing policies for general business well in advance of the legal deadlines of 1 January 1968. Since then branches have been opened in other towns and the backlog of work has been reduced.[22]

Indeed NIC's progress has been spectacular. Nevertheless the signs are that the NIC will take many more years before it has a full complement of trained staff, and this is in an industry which typically throughout the world carries high administrative expenses. In East Africa as a whole, expenses of management amounted to between 25 and 30% of gross premiums in the years 1964 to 1966.[23]

In the first eight months of business in 1967, management expenses (including commissions paid) of the NIC amounted to over 54% of gross premiums, and while this had fallen to 38% in 1968, there is still considerable scope for increasing efficiency. But even if this figure could be brought down to that for East Africa as a whole in preceding years the question still arises as to whether or not it is necessary to devote as many real resources to the provision of this financial service in a socialist economy and leads one to question the necessity of insurance for parastatals.

Insurance of Parastatals

While individual and even privately owned firms take out insurance policies in order to safeguard against the risk of loss of wealth and future profits, it is essential to recognise that a claim on NIC by a parastatal does nothing to safeguard the wealth or future income of the public sector as a whole but merely redistributes these from one public sector institution to another since, in replacing the destroyed assets, public sector investment is reduced elsewhere—investment which would have been financed directly or indirectly by the NIC. The net result is merely a redistribution of resources within the public sector but no overall compensation to that sector as a whole. Once the physical asset is destroyed, it is destroyed and insurance does not alter this fact. But the provision of insurance services is costly in terms of a real resources such as skilled staff, building and equipment. By simply making their own provision for an insurance reserve (invested in Government paper) and by adding to this annually to offset losses or to allow for a growth in the stock of physical assets, parastatals would be saved most of the huge volume of administrative work involved in taking out insurance coverage for their multitudinous risks and in making claims for losses. NIC's work load would be reduced and this would reduce the demand for skilled staff at Head Office and allow the Corporation to devote more attention to the replacement of private commission agents by salaried employees of the Corporation.

It can be argued that the risk of destruction of assets represents a real cost which will differ among different investment projects and which should therefore be accurately assessed, through the formal insurance mechanism (NIC), for comparative project evaluation purposes. There are the following counter arguments to this: (a) The insurance market in Tanzania is very small and "imperfect"; past statistics on which to base premiums are almost totally non-existent and even if they were available, as in all small markets past experience may be no guide to the determination of correct future prices. For the insurance of new projects and risks reliance is often placed on premium assessments from London. These assessments are based on claims experience elsewhere in the world and, of course, there is absolutely no way of gauging their relevance to Tanzania. Also London profit margins are included (as well as NIC's) and these inflate the rates. Indeed the local quotations from NIC also reflect to some extent the efficiency or otherwise of different NIC departments and for project evaluation purposes this also entails a distortion of relative premium rates. (b) The risk of destruction of assets will always be a highly marginal consideration anyway and, since accurate risk assessment is extremely difficult, the returns from attempting to improve estimates are probably not worth the bother. It would appear to be much simpler to make fairly rough and ready provisions in the budgets of parastatals for small risks and perhaps a lump sum provision in the development budget for large fixed asset replacement.

Bearing in mind that the Government sector is almost entirely not covered by formal insurance one might well ask why should the parastatal sector be treated differently. From an investment point of view they both compete for limited resources and risk considerations are as relevant or irrelevant to one as they are to the other. Since our argument here rests on the desirability of reducing the real resources consumed by the insurance sector, we would argue that it would be preferable for parastatals to adjust by ceasing to insure, as opposed to achieving consistency by requesting ministries to begin formal insurance through the NIC.

Parastatals would be allowed with the approval of their respective Boards to automatically replace relatively small assets and stocks, but would not be allowed to automatically replace large physical assets which had been destroyed. Their replacement would be considered along side all other current investment projects competing for available resources, and the ultimate decision would lie with the planning authorities. Indeed at least one Eastern European country exempts the capital equipment of the public sector from the insurance system purely on these grounds. In Poland, as Fedorowicz has explained, "the reason for this exemption is that the reconstruction of reduced economic capacities should not be decided automatically, as the reconstruction of just the same plant in just the same place because in many cases a more efficient way of recovering damaged capacities is either the construction of a new plant elsewhere or supplementary investments in the existing plants.[24] He goes on to explain that reserves are held centrally in the state budget to meet claims for repair or reconstruction of "reduced capacities."

In short it can be said that the interest of the NIC as a limited liability, profit maximising, growth-seeking company and those of the nation as a whole may not coincide on the question of the insurance of parastatal properties. The view of the writer is that parastatals, like Government, should not insure through NIC as this is likely to save real resources and also to prevent destroyed assets being automatically replaced without fully investigation by the planning authorities as to the overall benefits to be derived from this replacement relative to those obtainable from other investment projects competing for scarce resources.

Reinsurance

Another area in which the NIC, acting as a profit maximising limited liability company may find its policies running contrary to national interest, is in the field of reinsurance. One would expect, of course, that even if NIC used orthodox reinsurance principles the volume of annual reinsurance outflows would be reduced below pre-1967 annual average levels simply because these principles would be applied to the whole of Tanzania insurance business, whereas previously each private company applied them to a fraction of the national business, i.e. the risk of overall loss declines as the number of similar size risks covered increases, so that as the volume of business rises the need for reinsurance rises less than proportionately. This is the familiar argument for concentration of insurance. But even then the NIC would still insure with the specific aim of minimizing losses, and it has been suggested that this may be inappropriate from a national point of view.[25]

What is more important than whether or not NIC makes an annual surplus or deficit is the extent to which in the course of reinsurance business it utilises scarce foreign exchange resources. It must be realized that while in the short run it is conceivable that reinsurance claims may exceed reinsurance premiums paid by Tanzania, it is just as likely that they will not, and in the long run reinsurance has a definite net cost and this cost is entirely in foreign exchange. Since there is a positive cost of reinsurance there is little sense in attempting to cover purely local risks (those having no foreign exchange content) by reinsuring abroad since replacement of these assets or risks has to be met from local resources anyway. There are however sound reasons for reinsuring large risks which have a high foreign exchange content—either large individual risks or collective risks since, although in the long run Tanzania will pay more than she receives, in the short run the replacement of these assets would make embarrassingly large calls upon Tanzania's foreign exchange reserves in any one year. Examples of the kind of assets in mind here are the Oil Refinery and East African Airways' fleet of aircraft. Insurance of these assets would of course constitute an exception to the general rule that parastatals should not insure with National Insurance Corporation. *The ultimate aim must be zero reinsurance of risks abroad*, but while the level of reserves is such that repacement of one or two large assets (or a large group of small assets) could have a significant effect on the total national foreign reserve figure, reinsurance is justifiable.

By using the foreign exchange content approach to reinsurance it has been calculated that the NIC could reduce reinsurance premium outflows but there is one major implication of this criterion which the NIC, in its present legal form, cannot accept. This is that there would always be the possibility that the NIC would experience an operating deficit on account of its carrying its own purely domestic risks, and that it would need subsidising by government. To the extent that Government would never see the NIC collapse there would be no doubt that the subsidy would be forthcoming, but this would mean a radical departure from the "normal and proper conduct of insurance business" to which the Insurance (Vesting of Interests and Regulation) Act of 1967 enjoins it to adhere.

Lending Policy

Finally, the investment policy of the NIC calls for comment. At least 50% of Life Insurance Funds are to be invested in Government securities, the remainder will be invested in mortgages and loans for building flats and commercial premises, in physical building themselves, in loans against life policies, and in shares and debentures of first class companies. At least 10% of the General Fund will be invested in Government securities, a large portion will be held in liquid form and the remainder in mortgages, properties, shares and debentures. In the case of its loans, preference will be given to parastatals and co-operatives and the objects of the investment policy may be summarised as being: (a) to maintain security of the reserve funds, (b) to earn maximum possible yield, and (c) to enable prompt payment of claims.[26]

So far the investment portfolio has been dominated by liquid assets and Government paper although some loan applications have been approved. The following arguments may be advanced for restriction of NIC's assets to these two types in future: (a) ease of administration of the investment portfolio and avoidance of the necessity to build up yet another project evaluation unit in the public sector; (b) maximising yields may well lead to holdings of Government paper and investment in other public sector projects being minimised since investments in private sector luxury flats and offices will normally offer a more attractive rate of return.

The interest on bonds purchased by NIC could be fixed at a level sufficiently high to enable bonus and profit payments to life policy holders if it is felt that the average bond rate is too low for this. Alternatively, the NIC could channel its funds through an investment bank.[27] Certainly in more centrally planned socialist economies, insurance companies neither have nor need any discretion in their asset portfolio except as far as liquid balances are concerned. The Polish insurance system is typical: "the surplus of payments above expenditures is divided into two equal parts, a part being paid to the state budget as its participation in the benefit, and the second part is added to the reserve funds of the company. The reserve fund is lent to the state budget as a termless and interestless loan.[28]

In short a departure from the current operating principles in the state insurance sector might lead eventually to a situation in which:

(a) the parastatal sector undertook no formal insurance through the NIC except of risks with high import content—reserve funds could be held in parastatals or allowed for in the Central Government budget, whichever is administratively easier;

(b) the NIC ceased all reinsurance abroad except for covering large collective or individual risks which have a high foreign exchange content;

(c) the NIC held an asset portfolio consisting entirely of liquid assets and Government paper or loans to the National Bank of Commerce Development Bank; and of course

(d) the NIC handled all the business currently being canvassed and serviced by private agents.

CONCLUSION

There is need for continuing assessment of the role to be played by financial institutions in Tanzania's progress towards socialism. The efficiency of these institutions has to be guaranteed by the building of audit and work performance controls into their daily operations and the broader policies of each institution should be subject to greater discipline in the form of consistency with a national financial plan—the drawing up of which should be the major responsibility of the Central Bank. The role and determination of the interest rate in a socialist Tanzania requires more consideration.

The foremost task of the banking system under socialism will be that of controlling the activities of the public producing and service sectors. To facilitate this an increasingly larger proportion of enterprise short and long term funds should be channelled through the banking system. Within the context of the financial plan consideration should also be given to greater control being exercised over the ploughing back of internally generated, profits of parastatals, marketing boards, and co-operatives. Until such time as the efficiency of these is undoubted a strong case could be made for *all* their investments requiring bank scrutiny.

NOTES

1. The National Bank of Commerce (Establishment and Vesting of Assets and Liabilities) Act, 1967, section 4(1)(a).
2. For a discussion of how the NBC has tackled its own internal problems and how its relationships with the Bank of Tanzania and the Ministry of Finance have developed, see K. E. Svendsen, "Problems of Decision-Making in the Financial Structure of Tanzania—the NBC as One Case", ERB Paper 67.11, September, 1967.
3. Adolf Herman, "Czechoslovak Banking in the Wind of Change", *The Banker*, June, 1968.
4. *Ibid*., p. 507.
5. See G. Garvey, "Money, Banking and Credit in Eastern Europe", *Federal Reserve Bank of New York*, 1966.
6. The Bank of Tanzania Act, 1965, Section 5(2).
7. H. P. Sheldon and S. B. Drover, *The Practice and Law of Banking*, MacDonald & Evans, 1962, p. 336.
8. For a clear statement to this effect see President Nyerere's "Public Ownership in Tanzania", reprinted in *The Arusha Declaration*, pp. 21–25, especially p. 24.
9. Private sector surpluses might alternatively be diverted from investment in the joint public sector/private sector projects allowed for under the Arusha Declaration in which the public sector always has a majority holding and therefore ultimate control. This diversion would also constitute a loss of control over private sector surpluses.
10. *NBC Annual Report, 1969*, "Chairman's Statement", p. 10.
11. See Garvey, *op. cit*., pp. 113–116.
12. See Tanzania's *Second Five-Year Plan*, pp. 122–213, 223–224.
13. This was effected at the end of 1970 with the establishment of the Tanzania Investment Bank.
14. *Second Five-Year Plan*, p. 213.
15. The Finance and Credit and Foreign Exchange Plans were initiated in the fiscal year 1971/72 as part of the Annual Plan.
16. President Nyerere, "Public Ownership in Tanzania", p. 24, in *The Arusha Declaration*, Government Printer, 1967.
17. National Bank of Commerce Act, Section 4(1)(b).
18. The Governor of the Central Bank, "The Bank of Tanzania" in supplement to *Sunday News*, July 27, 1969, p. 12.
19. In calculating these returns true opportunity costs of factors should be used and attempts should be made to measure the more important indirect benefits and costs of each project. The main point here is merely to stress the basic *principle* on which the rate of interest on loans should be based.
20. J. Loxley, "Financial Intermediaries and their Role in East Africa", University of East Africa Social Science

Conference, Kampala, December 1968.

21. These figures have been calculated in the same manner as that in the above paper but have been updated to take account of more recent basic data.
22. *National Insurance Corporation Annual Report, 1967*, pp. 2–10.
23. *East African Insurance Statistics 1966*, E.A. Statistical Department, September, 1968, p. 32.
24. Fedorowicz, "Financial Mechanisms of a Socialist Economy on Poland's Example", United Arab Republic, Institute of National Planning, Memo No. 502, October, 1964.
25. The main proponent of the foreign exchange criterion for reinsurance of NIC business has been Lars Osberg who for a short time worked with the author in a joint Economics and Statistics Department of NBC and NIC. What follows draws heavily on arguments he advanced for this view.
26. *NIC Annual Report, 1968*.
27. I am grateful to Dr. R. H. Green for these two points.
28. Fedorowicz, *op. cit.*

The Behaviour of the Tanzania Money Supply 1966-70 and the use of Monetary Indicators*

J. LOXLEY

Introduction

The main aim of this paper is not to present a detailed analytical explanation of the behaviour of the Tanzania money supply during this period but rather to seek to throw some light on what that behaviour actually was. What emerges is an investigation of three monetary indicators which, potentially, might be useful to the monetary and planning authorities. These are the money supply itself, the holdings of foreign reserves and the volume of credit extended by the monetary system. The final section of the paper discusses briefly (1) the need for Tanzania to build up integrated budgetary, foreign exchange and flow of funds forecasting accounts, and (2) the way in which monetary data can be used to check on the accuracy of these forecasts and how they might be adjusted in the light of unforeseen developments.

THE MONEY SUPPLY AND ITS BEHAVIOUR 1966-1970

Of all the economic statistics published in Tanzania those relating to money supply are prepared with the greatest regularity and speed. The money supply total for any end of month date is known two weeks afterwards; bank deposit figures are collected even more frequently on a weekly basis for internal use by the banking system. For these reasons it might be thought that the compilation of money supply figures is a straightforward task. Indeed the very regularity of publication, usually without any detailed qualifying or explanatory notes, lends an air of accuracy and authority to them. Our study, however, shows that many adjustments must be made before the Tanzania data are meaningful for any purpose.

According to figures published by the Bank of Tanzania, money supply grew at an average compound rate of growth of 22.9% per annum between 1965 and 1969. These growth rates were uneven, being 10% in 1967-68 and reaching 33% in 1965-66, and they seemed high enough to warrant the assumption of an inflationary situation. For this reason, and not because the author believes in the *general* applicability of the monetarist approach, it seemed reasonable to fit the money supply data into the following simple quantity theory equation:[1]

$$M_t - M_{t-1} = (Y_{rt} - Y_{rt-1})\left(\frac{M_{t-1}}{Y_{mt-1}}\right) + [(Y_{mt} - Y_{mt-1}) - (Y_{rt} - Y_{rt-1})]\left(\frac{M_t - 1}{Y_{mt-1}}\right) + Y_{mt}\left(\frac{M_t}{Y_{mt}} - \frac{M_{t-1}}{Y_{mt-1}}\right)$$

Where M = money supply,
Y_r = the level of income at constant prices in the monetary sector,
and Y_m = the level of income at current prices in the monetary sector.

This states that with a constant income velocity of circulation (the inverse of the ratio of money to income) an increase in the quantity of money in circulation will be absorbed either by an increase in real income or by a rise in the general price level or by a combination of both. If the velocity of circulation itself changes (some possible reasons are discussed below) then a greater or lesser quantity of money will be demanded to conduct operations at a given level of real income and a given general level of prices.

During this same period the growth of monetary (non-subsistence) sector income at current prices was very much below that of money supply. Since the general price level rose in these years, the rate of growth of GDP at constant prices was even lower than that at current prices. Hence neither real income growth nor price increases were sufficiently large to absorb the expanded money supply.

This can be seen more clearly in Table 1 where the relative importance of the three "absorptive" factors is applied to the actual changes in money supply as indicated by the published figures. Price changes are seen to be negligible and real income changes of importance only in 1965-1966. On the whole these two factors do not account for the bulk of the increase in money supply. On the basis of the quantity theory equation velocity changes are therefore the dominant factors explaining the increased demand for money, accounting for 65%, 88% and 68% respectively in the years 1966 to 1968 while price increases accounted for only 5%, 4% and 8%.

What is surprising about the figures in Table 1 is that despite the rapid expansion of the money supply, price changes were rather slight. The apparent significant increase in the ratio of money to GDP—a significant fall in the velocity of circulation—is equally surprising. During the previous ten years period there was a consistent and even more significant increase in the velocity of circulation, taking East Africa as a whole and measured on the basis of five accepted velocity criteria. This increase was most pronounced in the year 1954 to 1960, but the tendency also persisted in the years 1960 to 1964. The principal reasons for that increase appear to have been the very rapid growth of a

* Edited version of ERB paper 71.3.

wide range of financial intermediaries in East Africa, the growth of money subtitutes, a tremendous expansion of banking facilities and the spread of the banking habit.

How can we explain this sudden, marked reversal of the pronounced trend of increasing velocity? As a first approach we observe from the quantity equation that the magnitude of money absorbed by velocity changes is in fact derived as a residual item and is therefore only as accurate as the figures for GDP and money supply themselves. Before discussing possible institutional reasons for the velocity change, therefore, it would seem advisable to check the accuracy and consistency of the money supply and GDP data.

DERIVATION OF MONEY SUPPLY DATA

Allowance for the Transition from the Currency Board to the Central Bank

TABLE 1: ABSORPTION OF CHANGES IN MONEY SUPPLY, 1965–1966 (UNIT: MILLION SHILLINGS)

	1965–66	1966–67	1967–68
(a) Money absorbed by real income change: —constant velocity $(Y_{rt}-Y_{rt-1}).\dfrac{M_{t-1}}{Y_{mt-1}}$	75.18	19.97	29.88
(b) Change in income due to prices: $(Y_{mt}-Y_{mt-1}) - (Y_{rt}-Y_{rt-1})$	+61	+40	+32
(c) Money absorbed by price changes: $\dfrac{M_{t-1}}{Y_{mt-1}}.[(Y_{mt}-Y_{mt-1}) - (Y_{rt}-Y_{rt-1})]$	12.95	10.11	9.76
(d) Change in velocity $\dfrac{M_t}{Y_{mt}} - \dfrac{M_{t-1}}{Y_{mt-1}}$	+0.0404	+0.0521	+0.0201
(e) Money absorbed by velocity change: $\left(\dfrac{M_t}{Y_{mt}} - \dfrac{M_{t-1}}{Y_{mt-1}}\right).Y_{mt}$	160.27	212.23	84.35
(f) Total change in money supply = a + c + e	248.4	242.3	124.0

Prior to June 1966 it was impossible to tell exactly how much currency circulated in Tanzania because the country shared a common currency with the rest of East Africa. The East African Currency Board which managed the currency supply could not ascertain the distribution of its currency between countries. However, the two currency conversions that took place in October 1964 and June 1966, respectively, shed some light on this problem. In estimating total currency supply for December 1966, the Central Bank made two errors: First it over-estimated EACB currency still in circulation in Tanzania as of December 1966 by Shs. 65 million.[2] Second, cash held by banks was given as being only Shs. 15 million in the first Bank of Tanzania Report whereas in actual fact this figure should have been Shs. 32.5 million.[3] The total currency error in the 1966 figure was therefore Shs. 82.5 million.

The major currency error in subsequent years has been the exclusion of residual EACB currency from the Bank of Tanzania money supply series. By subtracting actual cumulated redemptions at the date in question from the final figure of total currency redeemed, plus Shs. 20 million estimated lost, one arrived at an estimated figure of Shs. 32.3 million outstanding by December 1967 and Shs. 26.0 million by December 1968. The problem in making estimates in this way is that it ignores any inter-territorial flows of currency that may have taken place between the date in question and the date at which redemptions ceased (we assume December 1969 for our purpose; since almost all notes have been redeemed while unredeemed coins have been written off, this is not an unreasonable assumption).[4] The resultant figures will therefore be too high if currency flowed into Tanzania from Kenya or Uganda post-December 1966 and will be too low if there was an outflow after that date. There are grounds for believing that the total of East African currency circulating in Tanzania in December 1966 was in fact higher than Shs. 60 million, because with the introduction of exchange control between Tanzania and the rest of East Africa following the Arusha Declaration the only uncontrolled way in which funds could leave Tanzania was in the form of notes and coins convertible in the rest of East Africa—and this meant East African Currency Board notes and coins.

Currency Estimates

The second potential problem with the money supply data is that the currency figure for December 1965 was a pure estimate. As far as one can judge it appears to be somewhat on the high side. In October 1964 the Currency Board began converting the old Queen's Head notes into "Lake notes." The total recovered in Tanzania reached Shs. 372 million, which would indicate the total notes outstanding in October 1964 subject to any subsequent inter-territorial flows. Such flows amounted to an estimated Shs. 60 million to Kenya 1965/66,[5] and if one assumes that most of this outflow took place during the crop season, i.e. between October and December (as apparently do most currency flows)[6], then a large part of this amount has to be deducted from the estimated October 1964 figure. Onto the resulting figure, arrived at after subtracting an estimate of such flows, must be added an estimate of coin in circulation (say about Shs. 40 million) and an estimate of trend plus seasonal expansion of currency between October 1964 and December 1965. During this period bank demand deposits rose by approximately Shs. 30 million, and hence, on the basis of past observations it would not seem too unreasonable to assume that currency supply expanded by between Shs. 10 and 15 million. From this total of about Shs. 380–390 million must be deducted Shs. 33 million for cash held in bank vaults. The Bank of Tanzania figure of Shs. 382 million seems then to be too high when cross checked by this rough method, which has, at least, some advantage of hindsight over the Bank of Tanzania estimate. A better estimate would put currency supply in the region of Shs. 355 million. This is, however, still very much an estimate.

Demand Deposits

A third problem with the money supply figures is that the definition of demand deposit figures used is not consistent from one year to the next. For December 1965 and 1966 the demand deposits figures were arrived at by deducting from total demand deposits those deposits which were held by the Central Government, the East African Common Services Organisation, the Regional Governments, Local Government, other non-commercial bodies and public enterprises. In subsequent years only deposits held by the Central Government at the Bank of Tanzania are excluded. Since in 1966 the Central Government ceased holding deposits with the commercial banking system and in 1967 the public sector took over the major means of production, the present breakdown of demand deposits seems to be operationally superior to that used for 1965 and 1966.

Time Deposits

A further point of consistency concerns the breakdown of deposits between demand and time deposits. The first statistical returns introduced by the Bank of Tanzania suffered from several defects. The most serious one was that it was impossible to tell whether public sector deposits were held in the form of demand or time deposits. The explanatory notes accompanying the returns were also inadequate with the result that not only was it impossible to know the form in which the public sector held its deposits but, in addition, some public sector holdings of deposits were classified under "others" in accordance with the breakdown of deposit by type. Many such errors were discovered by the NBC, necessitating constant revision of figures. The same applies to returns from at least one of the other commercial banks operating in Tanzania. For this reason the more careful reader of the various editions of the Bank of Tanzania annual and half yearly reports will notice many changes in the figures for particular dates from one edition to the next.

Co-operative Bank Deposits

The co-operative Bank deposits also present problems. When a customer borrowed from the Co-operative Bank he was simultaneously credited with a demand deposit, whereas in the other banks where the overdraft system is in operation, deposits are only affected when the overdraft is drawn upon, i.e. unused over drafts have no impact on balance sheet deposit or credit totals. The Co-operative Bank deposits are, therefore, not comparable with those of the other banks unless the unused portion of loans outstanding is deducted from the total of deposits outstanding. This difference in the treatment of credit and deposits was mentioned by the Bank of Tanzania in its first report, December 1966, but no adjustments were made to deposits figures at that time. In 1969 when several large accounts were transferred from the NBC to the NCB, total deposits and credit outstanding inexplicably rose by large amounts.

The Treatment of Zanzibar

A major complication not easily apparent in the published data of money supply and Gross Domestic Product is that the former include Zanzibar while the latter do not. This would not cause any major distortions in velocity calculations if income growth in Zanzibar was relatively stable and arising at approximately the same rate as that of the mainland, if the payments mechanism was likewise stable and similar to that of mainland. Unfortunately, neither of these conditions is fulfilled. With the 280% rise in the price of cloves and a 150% increase in the value of clove exports in 1969, Zanzibar's GDP and foreign exchange totals rose dramatically to record heights. With the complete reorganisation of internal production, trade and the banking system in the years following the Revolution, it is also obvious that the payments mechanism has been undergoing radical change in Zanzibar. For these reasons it is important that the figures for money supply or GDP be adjusted either to include Zanzibar in both or to exclude it altogether. Since it is impossible to determine the GDP of Zanzibar, an attempt has been made to exclude Zanzibar from the money supply figures.

Transit Items

Published data on money supply are not adjusted to allow for items in the process of clearing (float) and hence current accounts are over or underestimated by the net value of these transit items. In the USA and UK it is the standard practice to adjust demand deposits by the net value of float. This is somewhat arbitrary since net indebtedness to banks or by banks to customers could conceptually be paid off either by adjusting demand deposits (current account credits) or by adjusting overdrafts (current account debits). Unless every single item of float is separately considered, one cannot tell precisely which of these would adjust and by how much. This does not matter too much in advanced economics with mechanised data processing systems since float is, as a result, relatively insignificant. But this is not the case in Tanzania and so far in our exercise, by ignoring float we have tacitly assumed that all float adjustments would affect overdrafts. We now must adjust demand deposits for float. We can thereby derive a range of estimates for money supply within which the "true" money supply total will lie.

The derivation of monthly figures of float is a tedious task that involves both removing Zanzibar totals from figures for deposits, lending and foreign reserves and subtracting the resultant mainland figures for domestic lending and foreign reserves from those of demand and time and saving deposits. Our approach to float is therefore to define it as the balancing item in the "sources of change in money supply" exercise. Table 2 below illustrates this more clearly for December figures as an example.

It can be seen that in all December months float was a relatively large positive asset item for the banking system. This implies either that credit extended is underestimated in these months or that money supply has been overestimated. The first alternative is the situation assumed under *Co-operative Bank Deposits* above; the second one is assumed here by adjusting money supply for float. This has the effect not only of reducing money supply at all end-of-year dates but also of considerably increasing the growth rate of money in 1966/67 and 1968/69 compared to the seasonally unadjusted growth rate derived above.[7]

TABLE 2: DERIVATION OF MONEY SUPPLY ADJUSTED FOR FLOAT—TANZANIA MAINLAND (UNIT: MILLION SHILLINGS)

December	1966	1967	1968	1969
Currency with public	468	544	555	625
Demand deposits	574	655	728	888
Total money	1,042	1,199	1,283	1,513
Growth rate %	15.1	7.0	17.9	
Near money	313	287	437	464
Total money and near	1,355	1,486	1,721	1,977
Growth rate %	9.7	15.8	14.9	
Net foreign assets	477	552	624	601
Net govt. borrowing	−36	78	26	197
Other domestic lending	776	799	876	1,071
Balancing item (float)	+138	+58	+195	+109
Total sources	1,355	1,486	1,721	1,977
Total money supply plus float	904	1,141	1,089	1,404
Growth rate %	26.6	−4.8	28.9	

We thus have four separate money supply series containing the following data:[8]

(a) current accounts and cash outside bank (Y_1)
(b) current accounts, cash and float (Y_2)
(c) current accounts, cash and near money (Y_3)
(d) current accounts, cash, float and near money (Y_4).

Near Money

The definition of money employed above approximates that used by the IMF and excludes time and savings deposits of commercial banks. There are, however, strong grounds, both theoretical and practical, for arguing that these deposits should be included. It might be the case, for instance, that our rapid increase in money supply of Table 1 was nothing else but a change in the form in which money was held, i.e. movement out of time and savings deposits into current accounts and cash. For this reason it was felt desirable to derive a money supply series with these "near money" elements. This was done by removing Zanzibar time and savings accounts from the official published totals and adding the remainders to the two money supply series derived under *Transit Items* above.

Seasonality and Trends

Perhaps the most important drawback in using end of year figures to indicate growth in money supply is that they are completely unadjusted for seasonality in the economy. The crop season in Tanzania generally takes place in the last four months of the year and hence December money supply figures are inflated relative to those in the first two thirds of the year. Furthermore seasonality may not be of uniform importance from year to year. It is therefore necessary to deseasonalise money supply data and if end of year figures are to be used, to calculate these on a deseasonalised trend basis.

For this purpose it was necessary to draw up monthly figures for each of the above four definitions of money supply. The basis for each of these series is the Bank of Tanzania money supply figures adjusted for East African Currency Board currency outstanding (as described above) and net of the total of Zanzibar demand deposits for each month. After some consideration it was decided that it would not be advisable to deduct Zanzibar currency estimates because of their unreliability. It should be noted, however, that Bank of Tanzania figures for currency in the hands of the public excludes currency held by Zanzibar banks, so the data chosen cover demand deposits in mainland Tanzania plus currency held by the non-bank public in both mainland Tanzania and Zanzibar.

The monthly time series of money were derived on this basis for the period March 1967 to June 1970. The moving average method was employed to remove seasonality. Having obtained a twelve month moving average series for the period (covering 28 observations) the method of least squares regression was used to fit a trend line to the data. It was assumed that money supply grows at a constant trend rate rather than by equal absolute amounts in each period. The regression equation is expressed in the form $\log Y = \log a + bt$

where y = money supply,
a = a constant,
b = a constant growth rate,
and t = time.

Estimating this equation for each of the four definitions of money supply gives the following results:

TABLE 3: REGRESSION COEFFICIENTS OF FOUR DEFINITIONS OF MONEY SUPPLY DESEASONALISED BY CENTRAL MOVING AVERAGE METHOD

28 observations	y_1	y_2	y_3	y_4
log a	6.9499	6.9123	7.2038	7.1754
s.e.e.	(0.0059)	(0.0110)	(0.0016)	(0.0051)
b	0.898	1.027	1.156	1.254
s.e.e.	(0.0004)	(0.0007)	(0.0001)	(0.0003)
R^2	0.961	0.902	0.998	0.984
Durbin Watson statistics	0.0883	0.0702	0.3198	0.0939

It can be seen that the multiple correlation coefficients and standard errors of estimate are all highly significant and the results show: (i) that growth rates of money supply range between 11.4 and 16.2% per annum between 1966 and 1970. For y_1 this is significantly lower than the unadjusted growth rates; (ii) that the narrowest definitions of money yield the lowest growth rates; (iii) that the most comprehensive definitions yield the highest growth rates; and hence (iv) that taking the period as a whole, the growth in currency and demand deposits holdings cannot be explained by reductions in the demand for time and savings deposits, i.e. by a redistribution of the public assets between the narrow definitions of money (y_1 and y_2) and "near money."

However, the very low Durbin Watson statistics indicate the presence of strong serial correlation in all four series. After visual inspection of the graphs of actual and forecasted data it was decided that the most likely cause of serial correlation was a break in the money supply series and hence all four deseasonalised series were split into two parts (one of 12 observations covering September 1967 to August 1968 and the other of 16 observations covering September 1968 to December 1969) and regression equations were estimated for both parts of all four series.

The results were, on the whole, an improvement on those of Table 2. Once again the estimates of the regression coefficients are highly significant, but the Durbin Watson statistics are still very low even after splitting the data. In a bid to see whether this could be improved upon, it was decided to re-run the exercise but this time removing seasonality not by the centred moving averages technique but by the use of dummy variables.

The results showed considerable improvement over the ones in Table 2, the correlation coefficients and Durbin Watson statistics being much higher. A final refinement that involved splitting the data once again was made in order to improve the results further.

The results obtained can be seen from Table 4. The correlation coefficients and the Durbin/Watson statistics are much more significant than those for the split data on the moving average basis. On the whole our trend line estimates, with a break in 1968, give an extremely close fit to the data and the dummy variables give an accurate measurement of the seasonality in the money supply.

TABLE 4: REGRESSION COEFFICIENTS OF FOUR DEFINITIONS OF MONEY SUPPLY DESEASONALISED BY DUMMY VARIABLE METHOD

First 20 observations	Y_1	Y_2	Y_3	Y_4
b	0.614	0.016	1.136	0.682
s.e.e.	(0.0013)	(0.0017)	(0.0009)	(0.0008)
R^2	0.9999	0.9999	0.9999	0.9999
D.W.	0.9131	1.7122	1.7273	1.2685
Second 20 observations				
b	1.309	1.554	1.099	1.28
s.e.e.	(0.0011)	(0.0011)	(0.009)	(0.0009)
R^2	0.9999	0.9999	0.9999	0.9999
D.W.	2.865	2.723	2.3824	1.9186

The resulting estimates of money supply growth cover a wide range, the extremities in the first period being 0.2% and 14.6% per annum and in the second 14.1% and 20.5% per annum. But if we take only the most reasonable definitions of money supply—which are y_2 (currency and demand deposits adjusted for float) and y_4 (currency demand deposits and near money adjusted for float)—then the ranges are considerably reduced to between 0.2 and 8.5% in the first period and between 16.7% and 20.5% in the second, hus highlighting the split in the data around September 1968. Using these two definitions we can then compare

TABLE 5: ADJUSTED MONEY SUPPLY DATA AND DESEASONALISED TREND VALUES

	Adjusted Money Supply Raw Data				Trend Values			
	y_2	% Growth	y_2	% Growth	y_3	% Growth	y_4	% Growth
Dec. 1966	904	+26.2	1,217	+17.3	1,138	+0.3	1,316	+8.5
1967	1,141	−4.5	1,428	+6.9	1,141	−0.13	1,428	+9.5
1968	1,089	+29.0	1,526	+22.5	1,126	+20.6	1,563	+16.6
1969	1,405	+4.8	1,869	+5.2	1,358	+9.4	1,823	+9.4
June 1970	1,472		1,966		1,486		1,995	

deseasonalised trend estimates with raw data figures on a year to year basis as follows:

These figures clearly demonstrate that the use of raw data can be very misleading. In the period under discussion failure to deseasonalise data not only leads to a overestimation of the overall growth rate of money supply but also, and more important, it gives a false impression of the distribution of growth throughout the period. The deseasonalised data emphasize that money supply was either stagnant or grew moderately between 1967 and 1968, and that since then there has been an unbroken rapid growth in the region of 17 to 20% per annum. Contrary to the impression given in the raw data (which is itself a considerable improvement over official figures), money supply did not expand rapidly in 1967 and neither was there any appreciable slowing down in the growth rate in the first six months of 1970.

GROSS DOMESTIC PRODUCT AND PRICE DATA

GDP at factor cost at current prices is probably not the best indicator of the extent to which price changes have an absorptive effect on money supply. Conceptually, GDP at market prices would seem to be better since it seems reasonable to postulate that indirect taxation will have an impact on the transactions demand for money. The new series of GDP recently released by the Central Statistical Bureau together with market price adjustments is given in Table 6 below:

TABLE 6: NEW SERIES AT CURRENT AND CONSTANT PRICES (UNIT: MILLION SHILLINGS)

GDP Factor Cost	1966	1967	1968	1969
Current prices				
Money sector	4,530	4,771	5,174	5,557
Growth rate	5.3	8.4	7.4	
+Indirect taxes	546	627	708	854
—Subsidies	18	18	21	13
GDP at market prices	5,058	3,380	5,861	6,398
Growth rate	6.4	8.9	9.2	
GDP 1966	4,530	4,801	5,127	5,417
Growth rate	6.0	6	5.7	

TABLE 7: ABSORPTION OF CHANGES IN TREND GROWTH OF MONEY SUPPLY, 1968–69

	Definition y_2			Definition y_4		
Shs. million	1966–67	1967–68	1968–69	1966–67	1967–68	1968–69
Money absorbed by real income rise	61.0	69.1	55.7	70.5	86.5	77.3
Money absorbed by price changes (including tax effects)	11.5	32.9	47.4	13.3	41.1	65.9
Money absorbed by velocity changes	−69.5	−117.0	+128.9	28.2	7.3	116.8
Total change in Money Supply	−3.0	−15.0	+232	+112	+135	+260

Fitting these data and those of the trend growth rates of money supply into the quantity theory equation used in Table 1, we derive Table, 7 which serves to demonstrate more clearly the relationship between Table 5 and 6, i.e. the relative importance of real income and price effects in money absorption.

This shows that according to the IMF definition of money supply (y_2), velocity of circulation was rising between 1966 and 1968 but fell sharply in 1969 with the growth in money supply rapidly outpacing the growth in money income.

According to the more comprehensive definition of money supply, (y_4,) velocity was falling throughout but most markedly in 1968/69. Both series reveal that absorption through price increases steadily grew in importance over the three year period but almost 70% of this increase was directly traceable to increases in indirect taxes. However, two thirds of the direct non-tax increase in prices took place in 1968/69 during the period of the rapid money supply increase. On the whole, however, velocity is revealed to be highly variable and no simple relationship is observable between money income and prices. This result will not surprise non-monetarists who, like Keynes, believe that velocity "depends on many complex and variable factors (and) is, in itself, merely a name which explains, nothing." The author also shares this point of view.

FOREIGN EXCHANGE

Foreign exchange reserves would seem to be a much more sensitive indicator of the need for change in monetary policy than is money supply for the following reasons:

(a) In open dependent economies the importation of goods is the most important source of short run elasticity of supply. Hence, excessive monetary expansion tends to influence reserves well before it influences local prices or output.

(b) Foreign exchange levels are more or less fixed by law so that a rule-of-thumb measuring rod is available by which to assess the degree of urgency in the situation. As we have seen, the fluctuations in velocity render no such rule of thumb available in money supply analysis.

But whatever we use as an indicator, we must ensure that it is statistically sound and consistent from one period to the next. With this in mind we have adjusted the published foreign reserve figures in three ways: (a) allowance has been made for the foreign exchange counterpart of the estimate of EACB currency circulation in Tanzania until December 1969, when Shs. 20 million was paid by the Board to the Tanzania government on account of that portion of currency estimated to be irredeemable; (b) figures of Zanzibar foreign assets have been excluded; and (c) figures have been deseasonalised and trend lines fitted.

The effect of removing Zanzibar from foreign exchange figures is even more dramatic than removing it from money supply data (see Table 8).

TABLE 8: SEASONALLY UNADJUSTED MOVEMENTS IN THE FOREIGN EXCHANGE POSITIONS—INCLUDING AND EXCLUDING ZANZIBAR

Shs. million	Official figures including Zanzibar	Adjusted figures excluding Zanzibar
December 1967 to Dec. 1968	+118.2	−72.2
December 1968 to Dec. 1969	+126.0	−22.9
December 1969 to March 1970	+103.1	+40.9
March 1970 to August 1970	−176.9	−213.5
Total	+170.4	—123.3

These figures show that the bulk of the increase in reserves between December 1967 and March 1970 is explained by expanded Zanzibar clove proceeds, while the huge decline between March 1970 and August 1970 was due entirely to activities on the mainland. Over the whole period covered by the table mainland foreign reserves declined by 22.4%.

From the point of view of using foreign exchange reserves as a monetary indicator, it is the precise timing of the decline in reserves that is of interest. This can only be seen if the data are deseasonalised. Figure 1, which compares undeseasonalised published data with the deseasonalised adjusted data (published figures plus EACB estimate, minus Zanzibar), reveals that mainland reserves began declining as long ago as April 1969. This contradicts the following statement to be found in the September 1970 Economic Bulletin of the Bank of Tanzania (page 1):

> "The foreign exchange position, whether measured by Bank of Tanzania holdings, or the total holdings of banks and government, continued the decline which started in the second quarter of the year."

As the graph shows, the decline started fully twelve months previously if the holdings of the Peoples Bank of Zanzibar are excluded and if allowance is made for seasonal fluctuations. Splitting the data, and using the dummy variable technique, separate estimates were made of the trend line of March 1967 to April 1969 observations and that of April 1969 to November 1970 observations. The results were as follows:

"These indicate a trend growth rate of mainland reserves of 7.3% per annum in the first period and a decline of 26.2% per annum in the second. The question we must try to answer is: should the Bank of Tanzania have taken action to stem the foreign exchange outflow before they did so in September 1970? If their statistics had been processed in the way they have been in Figure I, what would have been the minimum time lag needed to recognise that the foreign exchange position was

Fig. 1: TANZANIA'S FOREIGN RESERVE POSITION 1967 – 1970

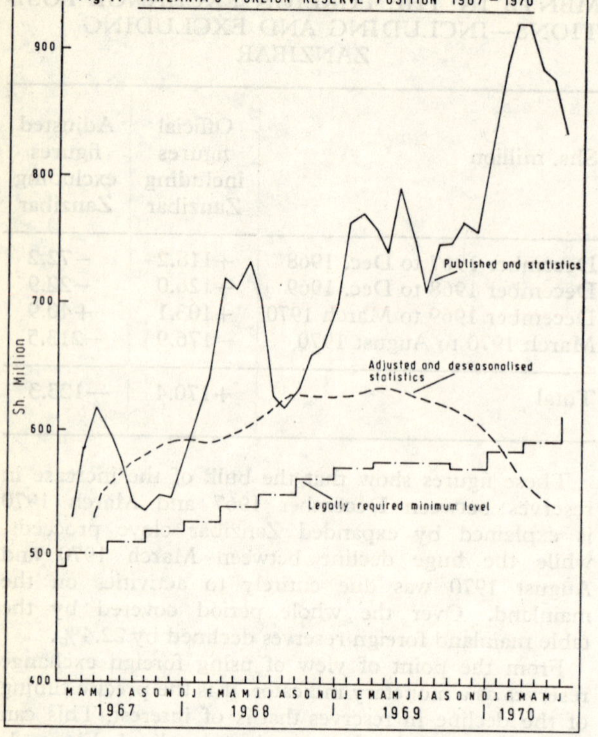

TABLE 9: REGRESSION EQUATION OF FOREIGN EXCHANGE AGAINST TIME

	March 1967 to April 1969	April 1969 to November 1970
b	0.59	—1.937
s.e.e.	0.0013	0.0023
R^2	0.9999	0.9999
D.W.	0.9001	1.0023

seriously deteriorating? If moving average techniques only were used, then there would be a six month time lag between the loss of reserves and its impact being felt on the trend. Thus to plot the adjusted and deseasonalised figure for December 1969 requires a knowledge of the January-June 1970 data. Even then it would appear from the graph that the Central Bank would have known sometime between March and June 1970 that the position was serious. Had dummy variables been used then it is highly likely that the seriousness of the situation could have been recognised between October 1969 and January 1970. In both cases it might, therefore, have been possible for the Bank to take action which would have prevented at least some of the very large loss of reserves between May and August 1970".

Deseasonalisation of data should therefore be standard procedure for the Central Bank. Had this been the case in the past and had there been an explicit recognition of the very different monetary situations prevailing on the island and the mainland, then this may have made a difference in the timing of the Central Bank's restrictive credit policy.

BANK CREDIT

Deseasonalisation of total credit figures, allowances being made for Zanzibar non-central Government borrowing, reveals a trend rate of growth of 24.2% per annum between March 1967 and June 1970. Once more, visual observation of the residuals suggested a break in the data around September 1968 and hence separate trend lines were estimated for the two halves of the data. The results of the regression exercises, including that for the whole period, are given below in Table 10.

Thus the growth rate of credit in the second half of the period, at 32.5% per annum, was over three times that of the first half (9.8% per annum) and clearly, any persistence of this rate would undoubtedly have inflationary effects on the economy. It is already known that some of the credit had an immediate 100% effect on foreign reserves, e.g. (1) expansion of lending to STC to enable cash purchases to replace foreign credit purchases of imports, (2) expansion of government borrowing to finance importation of goods for which foreign aid finance had been promised but not received, (3) NBC refinancing of projects previously receiving loan finance from abroad, (4) introduction of medium and long term lending facilities for the purchase of equipment from abroad, and (5) introduction of hire purchase finance by Karadha financed entirely by bank credit. But these would not account for all of the expansion in lending, and certainly not in the first half of the second period, i.e. between September 1968 and September 1969. Neither would they therefore explain the foreign reserve decline in 1969, although

TABLE 10: REGRESSION COEFFICIENTS OF TOTAL CREDIT DESEASONALISED USING DUMMY VARIABLES—MARCH 1967 TO JUNE 1970

	March 1967 to June 1970	March 1967 to September 1968	October 1968 to June 1970
b	1.808	0.781	2.343
s.e.e.	0.0010	0.0021	0.001
R^2	0.9999	0.9999	0.9999
D.W.	0.4848	0.8342	2.0102

they would certainly be a major explanation of the 1970 outflow. Some recognition of this is perhaps to be found in the fact that the Bank of Tanzania has imposed a general credit restraint which affects the whole of the private sector and much of the public sector apart from STC and Karadha credits. In the circumstances this seems to be the right approach. Some restriction on government borrowing may also be necessary, but insufficient published information is available to enable one to say with precision what is causing the big rise in Government borrowing from the Central Bank.

It would, of course, be extremely helpful if a more direct connection could be established between credit expansion and foreign reserve loss so that in the future, apart from being able to isolate more effectively the trend performance of the time series of both, one could have some advance idea of what the impact of a certain credit policy would be on foreign reserves. We now turn to a discussion of credit and foreign exchange budgeting.

FISCAL, FOREIGN EXCHANGE AND FLOW-OF-FUNDS FORECASTING

As a direct result of the recent foreign exchange problems, a sudden interest has arisen in the forecasting of likely future reserve levels. The arguments in favour of foreign exchange budgeting for up to at least one year ahead are strengthened in Tanzania by the fact that public sector activities constitute such an important proportion of foreign payments and receipts and are already extensively budgeted. In addition, so many of the foreign transactions of the private sector are tightly controlled or are capable of being controlled by the public sector. Several important items in the Central Government's recurrent budget, e.g. import, sales, transfer and export tax revenues, account for about 40% of total revenue and imply detailed assumptions about the foreign trade position of the country. Other recurrent budget items such as transfers (pensions, gratuities, etc.) and debt interest have a directly calculable, if small, impact on the balance of payments position. The development budget also makes explicit assumptions about foreign grants and net loan inflows.

The major problem in budgeting for the foreign exchange implications of government activities is determining the import content of Government recurrent and capital expenditure since one is not likely to obtain this direct from ministry estimates. However, customs figures for past purchases of standard consumption items provide a rough guideline for direct recurrent imports, and forecasts could also be checked against actual purchasing figures of government stores. Capital budget imports are much more important and can only be meaningfully estimated if the import content of each project is explicitly indicated by ministries or calculated by Devplan along with some idea of the timing of receipts and payments.

Much less is known about parastatal sector sources and uses of foreign exchange because this sector does not budget as regularly or extensively as the Central Government. If project feasibility studies and cash flow analysis were performed correctly it should be possible to derive from an annual project by project investment plan a sources-and-uses-of funds chart which specifically isolates the foreign exchange implications of each project.

But without some estimates of the remainder of the foreign exchange budget, one would not be in a position to accept the feasibility of public sector targets. This essentially implies forecasting total non-public sector exports, invisible flows and net capital flows. Estimates of service receipts and payments and of private transfers will have to be based on past figures adjusted for whatever information is available on changing trends, e.g. expanded tourist accommodation or rising freight charges. With regards to imports, capital and intermediate goods purchases should be calculable on the basis of applications for industrial and import licences, but the introduction of an annual questionnaire with a six months follow-up for major private producers might be a better approach. The results could be compared with the calculation of private non-consumer imports on a residual basis from total minus estimates of public sector imports. Consumer goods imports could be estimated from previous years' figures adjusted for anticipated export performance, for the introduction of any import substituting industries, and for any changes in tax or STC pricing policy.

Changes in foreign reserves will therefore emerge as a residual, and it is on the acceptability or otherwise of the movements in this residual that the overall forecast is accepted or amended. In the future it might be advisable to set five year targets and annual targets for reserve changes with the minimum holding being fixed not in terms of imports but by reference to a maximum allowable margin of error in an otherwise balanced budget forecast. Our borrowing powers at the IMF would form part of the calculations of the margin. This approach would explicitly recognise the connection between all exchange flows and the stock of reserves while the present limit of four months' imports relates the stock entirely to one type of flow.[9]

Whatever the exchange guideline is, we must then check it against our budget forecasts for consistency. If the estimates of outflows are either too low or too high relative to those of inflows then adjustments will be made. If too high, as is more likely to be the case, then a decision will have to be made about priorities. Some leeway still exists for restricting consumption imports and STC's control over this sector should in future facilitate greater flexibility here. STC could draw up a list of its consumption import commodities and classify them according to priority so that in the event of the future need for import control, a plan of action will already be on hand. But there is likely to be a distinct limit to the extent to which consumer imports can bear the brunt of an ambitious development programme. Hence, a rough priority ranking of other exchange expenditure is called for. The final form of the exchange budget will, therefore, be the outcome of a rough balancing process between alternative uses of reserves.

Ideally the budget should be estimated on a quarterly basis but this would be extremely ambitious at the present time. Certainly a six months estimate is the minimum requirement because of the significant seasonal differences in the two halves of the year. Checking on the progress of the budget can be done by referring to both the seasonalised and deseasonalised aggregates of foreign exchange reserves while more detailed examination of developments is possible, with a longer delay, by examination of the results of the ticket system payments data. There would still be a time lag involved in ascertaining when things go wrong and what is causing them to go wrong, but the use of deseasonalised data should give a much earlier indication of possible deviations from trend than otherwise, while the payments statistics could confirm the cause of developments within a two to three months period. This should give a maximum recognition lag of about six months which is a considerable improvement over the present state of affairs.

Having accepted the need for fiscal and foreign exchange budgeting as well as for the annual planning of parastatal investment programmes, the next logical step would seem to be the forecasting of the flows of funds between various sectors of the economy. All too often in the public sector there is a misconception of the role of finance and a tendency to be too optimistic about the volume of real resources available in any given period by confusing financial with real flows. The lack of direction given to the banking system by policy makers also serves to encourage these misunderstandings. Thus it was only with the introduction of the credit squeeze that the NBC had any guidelines at all about where to lend its funds, and yet for many years now the planners have complained that the Bank was not buying sufficient government securities. Some form of monetary planning seems to be required and given that all our financial institutions are publicly owned or controlled and tend to specialise in separate credit fields, such planning should not prove impossible.

CONCLUSION

The movement towards more integrated national planning on a short term, financial basis, is a logical development in a country which has placed the major productive institutions under public sector control but which has not the capacity for detailed physical planning. Many of the statistics required are already estimated and the remainder are either implicitly forecast in the former or can without too much difficulty be derived on the basis of certain key assumptions (such as export performance) underlying all forecasts. Such projections would make it possible to formulate credit policy guidelines for public sector financial institutions and would help separate the real financial bottlenecks from those that exist in the eyes of planners. Fully integrated forecasts could only be drawn up on a one year basis at present but the development of the monetary flows could be checked at quarterly or six month intervals. This would help throw light on sectoral flows and performance. Simple aggregate monetary indicators such as money supply, foreign reserves and credit extended will continue to be more or less useful as guidelines to developments, but sectoral money flows should become increasingly more important indicators of plan fulfilment. In the meantime we must ensure that the indicators we use are meaningful and this suggests refining some of our more commonly used monetary statistics along the lines suggested above.

NOTES

1. See Bhatia, Szapary and Quinn, "Stabilisation Programme in Sierra Leone," in *IMF Staff Papers*, Vol. XVI, No. 3, November 1969 for an example of the application of this equation.
2. See *Bank of Tanzania Annual Report*, June 1970, p. 49; and the *Annual Plan*, 1970/71, p. 10.
3. This mistake may have been the result of taking figures expressed in pounds to be in shillings. See *East African Economic and Statistical Review*, December, 1966, pp. 75 and 77.
4. See the *Annual Plan*, p. 10.
5. See *E.A. Currency Board Report*, 1966, p. 79.
6. See *Bank of Uganda Annual Report*, 1968/69. Table on Note flows, p. 50.
7. The two separate money supply figures—one adjusted for float and one not, but both taking into consideration all other adjustments made so far—have been calculated for all months between March 1967 and June 1970 (see ERB Paper 71.3, Appendix 3). Our calculations show that the volume of "float" varies significantly from month to month. Surprisingly, in only 17 out of the 40 observations float is an asset item on the bank's balance sheet. Generally one would expect it to be an asset since in processing cheques commercial banks credit the payee customer's account before debiting the account of the drawer of the cheques. However the predominance of negative float (bank liability) is due partly to the immediate postnationalisation problem of reconciling external and internal transactions and partly to the fact that our float figure contains many residual items.
8. The figures for each series are reported in Appendix 3 or ERB paper 71.3.
9. For a critique of this limit see Idrian Resnick, "Tanzania's Foreign Reserve Position," *East African Economic Review*, Vol. 3 (New Series), No. 1, June, 1967.

Inflation and Monetary Expansion: The 1966-73 Tanzanian Experiences*

DELPHIN RWEGASIRA

Introduction

This paper is concerned with the macroeconomic relationships among monetary expansion, income and balance of payments for the period since the founding of the Central Bank in 1966 until the end of the Second Five-Year Plan in 1973.[1] In particular, it attempts to examine the relationship between monetary expansion and inflationary pressures that were building up toward the end of the First Five-Year Plan. Although our data base in terms of both quantity and quality is admittedly weak,[2] certain interesting conclusions have emerged: before 1969 changes in income and velocity were mainly responsible for explaining changes in the price level and the balance of payments but after 1969 there were noticeable, parallel movements of money supply and the price level partly associated with increased deficit financing. Over the entire period the money supply variables remain only weakly related to inflation, thereby raising some doubts as to the inflationary role of money supply in the economy.

THE ANALYTICAL FRAMEWORK

The analytical framework employed in this paper is the monetary analysis model developed by the Organization for European Economic Cooperation (OEEC).[3] This model assumes an open economy by distinguishing two broad economic sectors: the national economy sector and the rest-of-the world. As for the former, a product account registers the origin and destination of product flows, and a financing account matches expenditures with the means of financing. For the latter, a consolidated account is presented. This consolidated account eliminates all transactions that are internal to the rest-of-the-world economy, listing only import and export transactions, various types of transfers, and lending and borrowing between the national economy and the rest of the world. The national economy is further subdivided into the money-creating-institutions subsector or banks, and the nonbank sector. In this way the banks' and the nonbanks' financing accounts are distinguished.

The main variables and relations employed in this paper are as described below:

Y	=	Gross National Product at current prices,
y	=	Gross National Product at constant prices,
X	=	Gross Domestic Expenditure,
I	=	Imports,
E	=	Exports,
ΔM	=	Increase in Money Supply,
k	=	M/Y, the money-income ratio, i.e. the reciprocal of the velocity of circulation,
Ai and Ae	=	Respectively, changes in the Banks' domestic and foreign assets,
Li and Le	=	Changes in the banks' domestic and foreign liabilities, respectively,
Fi	=	Internal Credit monetisation; i.e. the increase in banks' domestic assets less the increase in banks' domestic liabilities other than money,
Fe	=	External Credit monetisation; i.e. the increase in non-banks' net external liabilities plus net transfers from abroad,
Fm	=	Liquidity Financing; i.e. the difference between the money balances which the public would have held on the basis of the previous year's money-income ratio (k_0), the amount K_0, and the money balances actually held by the public, amounting to kY. Thus $Fm = (K_0 - k)Y$,
Ne	=	Change in net foreign assets of the banking system, i.e. increase in banks' foreign assets less the increase in foreign liabilities.

The Relations

(a) For the *national economy*, total goods and services available to the nationals, i.e. (Y + I) are partly used for consumption and investment (totalling X), and partly traded as exports (E). The national economy product account can therefore be stated as

$$Y + I = X + E \qquad (1)$$

(b) For the non-bank subsector, purchases of final goods and services (X), together with its 'purchases' of money, i.e. the increase in the public's cash balances (ΔM) must have been financed out of the factor incomes accruing to this sector, (Y), and the funds it has obtained from other sectors during the period of account. Such borrowed funds originate partly from net credits obtained from the domestic bank subsector (Fi) and partly from the external sector (Fe). The financing account for the non-banks is therefore:

$$X + \Delta M = Y + Fi + Fe \qquad (2)$$

(c) The banks' financing account

$$Ne + Fi = \Delta M \qquad (3)$$

*ERB Paper 76.8

can be derived by comparing the banking system's balance sheet at the beginning and the end of the period of account.[4]

(d) On a consolidated basis, the rest-of-the-world sector can increase its indebtedness to the bank sector of the national economy by an amount Ne. It can also obtain other funds from selling exports to the national economy. On the uses side, the rest-of-the-world sector can purchase national economy exports (E) and lend or transfer funds (Fe) to the national economy. Thus

$$E + Fe = I + Ne \qquad (4)$$

represents the rest-of-the-world consolidated account.

If we consolidate either accounts (1) and (2) or (3) and (4), an interesting relationship emerges, showing three sources of money creation:

$$(E-1) + Fi + Fe = \Delta M \ (5)$$

balance of trade surplus (defined broadly to include services), internal credit monetisation, and external credit monetisation.

Let us now derive an equation expressing sources and uses of finance in one statement. As a first step, recall that $k = M/Y$, so that

$$M - M_0 = \Delta M = kY - k_0Y_0$$
$$= k_0(Y-Y_0)-(k_0-k)Y \ (6)$$

The first term on the right hand side of (6) measures the increase in money if the public retained a constant velocity. The second term measures relative contraction in the public's money holdings which we defined as liquidity financing (F). This financing results from the fact that a rise in velocity releases extra liquidity[5] which could be used to finance a larger volume of transactions or to accommodate other changes in liquidity preference. Thus (6) can be rewritten as

$$\Delta M = k_0(Y-Y_0)F_m \qquad (7)$$

The increment in money income $(Y - Y_0)$ can be sub-divided between a real income change valued at previous year's price level P_0 and a change due to price increase $(P — P_0)$ which is evaluated on the basis of the current year's real income:

$$\Delta Y = (Y-Y_0) = (y-y_0)\,P_0 + (p-p_0)\ y \ (8)$$

Substituting (7) in (2) and noting that $k_0(Y - Y_0) = K_0\ \Delta Y = k_0(y-y_0)\ P_0 + K_0\ (P-P_0)\ y$, we obtain

$$Fi+Fe+Fm = ko(y-y_0)\ P_0 + k_0\,(P-P_0)\ y+(X-Y)\ (9)$$

Since $(X - Y)$, the excess of expenditure over domestic production, is equal to the import surplus (to be denoted by D), (9) can be written as

$$Fi+Fe+Fm = K_0\ (y-y_0)\ P_0+k_0\ (P-P_0)\ y+D \ (10)$$

which is the basic OEEC sources and uses of funds relationship. It states that total monetary financing as originating from internal credit monetisation, external credit monetisation, and liquidity financing must be absorbed by real output growth, price rises and the balance of payments deficit.

It is important to note at the outset that the above basic relation (10) is essentially an extension of the cash balance equation $(M = kPy)$ and therefore that it represents no more than true relationships among ex-post magnitudes; it does not represent causation among the relevant variables. It has, however, the advantage of explicitly dealing with an open economy by introducing the balance of payments deficit and external financing, and therefore of avoiding the over-simplified relationship which the simple quantity theory suggests between monetary expansion and increases in the price level. This is an important methodological consideration for the analysis of monetary developments in open and dependent economies. Indeed, in an open economy, price changes as well as balance of payment developments must both be examined in the analysis of inflationary pressures.

THE PATTERN OF DEVELOPMENT

Table 1 shows the decomposition of monetary financing in Tanzania for the years 1967–1973 by the sources and uses of funds, as described by equation (10). The figures for 1966 have been excluded because data on net foreign assets of the banking system and money supply are either unavailable or unreliable. We have, however, included 1966 in the general analysis where possible. Estimates of consistent time-series data were obtained by reworking through scattered, official information on national product, money supply and the balance of payments.[6] In constructing the series of money supply data, we have followed the narrow definition of money supply as used by the Bank of Tanzania, which is currency in circulation outside banks plus demand deposits excluding those held by the central government.

One striking feature about the monthly money supply totals is the conspicuous seasonal difference between the first and second half of any year. This is attributable to the predominance of agricultural activity in total monetary-sector production. For this reason, it was decided to obtain annual money supply series by averaging quarterly figures.

The figures for gross national product (GNP) must at present be estimated because Zanzibar's data are not available. The main difficulty has been that while national product data exist for Mainland, official balance of payments estimates and money supply series have always included Zanzibar. Thus for consistency, Zanzibar has to be either fully included or excluded altogether. It was decided to incorporate Zanzibar by estimating the latter's national product.[7] The resulting estimates are reported in Table 2.

Two other biases in estimating the GNP figures should be pointed out. First, due to the unavailability

TABLE 1: MONETARY DEVELOPMENTS 1967–1973* (SHS. MILLION; FIGURES IN BRACKETS SHOW THE MAGNITUDES AS PERCENTAGES OF THE PRECEDING YEAR'S MONEY SUPPLY)

	1967	1968	1969	1970	1971	1972	1973
1. Internal Credit Monetisation Fi = (a)—(b)	−13.6	15.7	19.9	282.0	314.2	−219.3	119.8
(a) Change in Gross Bank Lending	−111.3	98.7	243.2	389.3	521.9	275.7	215.5
(b) Change in Non-money Domestic Bank Liabilities (i) + (ii)	−97.7	83.0	223.3	107.3	207.7	495.0	95.7
(i) Change in Time & Savings Deposits	44.1	144.6	142.4	167.2	128.9	130.6	183.7
(ii) Change in other Bank Domestic Liabilities*	−147.8	−31.8	80.9	−59.9	78.8	264.4	−88.0
2. External Credit Monetisation (Fe)	147.7	50.1	153.6	217.4	270.3	164.0	146.0
	(15.1)	(4.7)	(13.0)	(16.0)	(17.4)	(8.4)	(6.7)
3. Total Current Monetisation (Fi + Fe)	134.1	65.8	173.5	499.4	584.5	−55.3	268.0
	(13.7)	(6.1)	(14.7)	(36.6)	(37.6)	(−2.8)	(12.2)
4. Liquidity Financing (Fm)	−33.3	−18.7	−89.0	44.2	−259.2	0.0	−126.6
	(−3.4)	(−1.7)	(−7.6)	(−3.3)	(−16.7)	(0.0)	(−5.7)
5. Total Sources (3 + 4)	100.8	47.1	84.5	455.2	325.3	−55.3	111.4
	(10.3)	(4.4)	(7.2)	(33.5)	(20.9)	(−2.8)	(6.4)
Absorbed by:							
6. Income Growth	69.0	71.9	68.6	93.2	99.7	89.6	93.6
	(7.1)	(6.7)	(5.8)	(6.9)	(6.4)	(4.6)	(4.2)
7. Price Increase	−5.2	12.7	21.1	59.6	35.7	164.9	116.0
	(−0.5)	(1.2)	(1.8)	(4.4)	(2.3)	(8.5)	(7.5)
8. Deficit	−27.6	117.0	−180.0	−37.4	92.9	−154.6	21.7
	(−2.8)	(10.9)	(−15.3)	(−2.8)	(6.0)	(−7.9)	(1.0)
9. Total Uses (6 + 7 + 8)	36.7	201.6	−90.3	115.4	228.3	99.9	281.3
	(3.7)	(18.7)	(−7.7)	(8.5)	(14.7)	(5.1)	(12.8)
10. Balance of Payments Errors and Omissions	64.4	−154.5	174.8	339.8	97.0	−155.2	−139.9
	(6.6)	(−14.4)	(14.8)	(25.0)	(6.2)	(−8.0)	(−6.3)

*Excluding Net Transfers and TAZARA Project Aid.

of a suitable GNP deflator, an implicit GDP deflator derived from the Mainland product series has been employed for obtaining real GNP figures. Second, Mainland GDP data are derived at factor costs. That is, changes in the terms of trade have not been taken into consideration. This could result in the overestimation of real income given the adverse trend in Tanzania's terms of trade. Despite these difficulties, however, we have no reason to assume that these biases will systematically affect our broad conclusions.

TABLE 2: THE MONEY-INCOME RATIOS

	Money Supply*	Monetary Sector GNP**	Money-Income Ratio (k)	Annual Percentage Change in k
1965	762.5	3931.4	0.1940	
1966	978.4	4525.5	0.2162	11.4
1967	1075.6	4820.3	0.2231	3.2
1968	1178.8	5199.4	0.2267	1.6
1969	1357.3	5595.1	0.2426	7.0
1970	1554.1	6224.8	0.2497	2.9
1971	1948.8	6767.2	0.2880	15.3
1972	2203.5	7650.9	0.2880	0.0
1973	2589.6	8552.3	0.3028	5.1

*Quarterly average for the year
**Estimated Mainland and Zanzibar GNP

In the analysis we shall also be using monetary-sector product data since that is the directly relevant variable.[8] Attempts to use total product resulted in imbalance between sources and uses of finances that could not be sufficiently accounted for by errors and omissions in the balance of payments.

Finally, it is important to note that the estimates in Table 1 have been derived using a narrow definition of external credit monetisation by excluding net transfers and the major bilateral project (TAZARA).[9] The reason for this is that the category of transfers, under which items like receipts from abroad by missionary institutions, scholarships received by Tanzanian students abroad, long term foreign technical assistance staff employed are recorded, have consisted of many elements that do not involve monetisation. Similar bilateral aids which involve essentially the flow of imports as in the case of TAZARA have not led to external monetisation.

On the sources side, the two tables indicate that external credit monetisation has been important throughout the period reflecting external loans and grants flowing to Government and Parastatal organizations. Internal credit monetisation has become increasingly important for the period as a whole so that if we exclude the year 1972 in Table 1, this source increases from a mere 6% of total current monetisation (Fi + Fe) during the period 1967–69 to the high proportion of

53% during 1970–73. This reverses the order of importance on the sources side during the two sub-periods.

An important force offsetting internal credit monetisation has been the relatively high rate of expansion in time and saving deposits of commercial banks as shown in Table 3. These deposits were about 39% of money supply in 1968, and rose to over 50% in 1973. This expansion is partly a result of banking facilities extension and other changes in monetary arrangements, as well as a result of rising per capita income.

Liquidity financing (Fm) which is actually recorded on the sources side in equation (10) has on the contrary 'absorbed' funds through the persistently rising money-income ratio, as can be seen from Table 2. Such liquidity increase neutralized about 38% of current monetisation in the period 1967–69 (on the basis of Table 2) and continued to 'absorb' over 33 percent during 1970–73.

On the uses side income growth 'absorbed' quite a high proportion of over 56 percent of the total current monetisation in the period 1967–69, but then declined in the subsequent period to only 29 percent. Accordingly, a greater proportion of monetary expansion must have resulted in financing price increases, additions to liquidity, and/or balance of payments deficits. Price increases which had absorbed only 7.7% of total credit monetisation during 1967–69 absorbed about 33 per cent of the total monetisation in the period 1970–73. Thus although the rising money income-ratio neutralized more or less the same proportion of total credit monetisation in the two subperiods an inflationary process was already developing in the later period. It is therefore important to analyze the forces behind internal credit monetisation, and the possible consequences on the price level. These issues will be examined in the next section.

The role of the balance of payment deficits is rather difficult to characterize because of the difficulties involved in identifying the items that actually entailed external monetisation. Table 1 allows no easy generalization as the situation changes from year to year. A casual observation of monetary performance during the entire period, however, indicates that the role of the balance-of-payments deficits had been less important during 1967–69 as compared with the subsequent period. This conclusion is consistent with changes in foreign exchange reserves to finance current account deficits as shown in Table 4 for Mainland Tanzania.

This table shows that although the reserves were accumulating up to 1969, they declined rather sharply in 1970, and continued to decline in 1971. Credit controls were imposed on commercial bank credit in 1970, and in 1971 import controls were extended partly to protect the balance of payments. Monetary absorption through deficits was very likely reduced during 1972/73 because of the continued control on imports and relatively encouraging performance in exports. In 1971, however, the money-income ratio rose by the highest rate of 15.3 percent, as shown in Table 3. The extension of payments controls that occurred early during that year together with a continued monetary expansion might have led to the holding of excess cash balances by the public.

TABLE 3: COMMERCIAL BANK TIME AND SAVING DEPOSITS* (SHS. MILLION)

	Time Deposits	Saving Deposits	Total	Percentage Increase
1966	163.0	140.5	303.5	—
1967	206.0	141.6	347.6	14.5
1968	308.4	154.0	462.4	33.0
1969	435.3	169.5	604.8	30.8
1970	577.7	194.3	772.0	27.6
1971	692.7	208.2	900.9	16.7
1972	882.0	249.5	1,131.5	25.6
1973	1,000.0	314.6	1,315.2	16.1

*Observations for 1967 are end of year figures, while the rest are quarterly averages·
SOURCE: Computed from the Bank of Tanzania, *Economic and Operations Report.*

INTERNAL CREDIT MONETISATION

A general impression of the forces behind internal credit monetisation[10] can be gained by looking at gross bank lending as presented in Table 5.

TABLE 4: THE FINANCING OF BALANCE OF PAYMENTS CURRENT ACCOUNT DEFICITS* (SHS. MILLION)

	1966	1967	1968	1969	1970	1971	1972	1973
Deficit on Current Account	36	21	153	–62	340	874	643	849
Financed by:								
Decrease in Reserves	–374	–72	–52	–40	114	35	–390	–214
Capital Inflow and Net Errors and Omissions	410	93	205	–22	226	839	1,033	1,063

*Refers to Mainland Tanzania only.
SOURCE: National Accounts of Tanzania 1964–72 (Bureau of Statistics, DSM, Feb. 1974) for the years up to and including 1972 and *Annual Plan* for 1974/75 for 1973 data.

TABLE 5: TOTAL BANK LENDING 1966–73* (SHS. MILLION)

	Bank of Tanzania	Central Government Commercial Banks	Total	Non Government Lending
1966	72.5	98.0	170.5	806.9
1967	61.3	34.1	95.4	770.7
1968	64.9	80.1	145.0	819.8
1968	75.6	168.3	243.9	964.1
1970	291.3	164.7	456.0	1,141.3
1971	506.4	247.4	753.8	1,365.4
1972	572.4	424.9	997.3	1,397.6
1973	484.9	558.6	1,043.5	1,566.9

*The figures are given in quarterly averages.
SOURCE: The Bank of Tanzania, *Economic and Operations Report.*

As can be seen from the table, the year 1969 was the beginning of continued rapid increase in bank borrowing both by the Government and the non-government sectors. While non-government borrowing expanded about 12.9 percent p.a. between 1969 and 1973, government borrowing expanded at a very fast rate of over 43% p.a. during the same period accounting for close to 60% of total bank credit increase.

The major force behind this rapid expansion of government borrowing from the banks was the desire to increase development finance. The available estimates show that the recurrent budget registered surpluses throughout the entire period 1964/65–1973/74, during which the First and Second Five-Year Plans were in force.[11] Government borrowing from the banking system was relatively insignificant during the first three years of the First Plan, but thereafter expanded rapidly for the fiscal years 1968/69 and to 1970/71. The following two years saw a decrease in borrowing as the Finance and Credit and the Foreign Exchange Plan went into operation to guide the economy's short term macro-monetary policies. However, borrowing from the banking system during the Second Plan increased nearly five times the amount borrowed during the First Plan. This sharp increase during the 1973/74 period must be considered rather as exceptional, having arisen from a number of exogenous internal and external developments during that year.[12]

There are at least two explanations for this rapid expansion of government borrowing beginning with the last two years of the First Plan. First, the establishment of an institutionally independent national financial system[13] that started with the founding of the Central Bank in 1966 meant that the many constraints on borrowing prevailed under the Currency Board system were overcome. At the same time, the banking sector began to assume an active role in financing development expenditure in the period following the Arusha Declaration.

Secondly, Tanzania's target rate of growth during the First Plan seems to have been mainly constrained by inadequate project preparations and implementation capacity rather than by financial resources. As evidence of this, one can compare the figures for actual development spending with those for the spending envisaged. Table 6 shows that actual expenditure remained considerably below budget estimates in the first few years of the First Plan period. After the Fiscal 1967/68 only the government's capacity to spend on planned development projects rose sharply.[14]

The shortfalls in expenditure during the early years of the First Plan appear to reflect the problem of lower capacity to spend rather than that of financing development. Also the rapid expansion of government borrowing from the banking system during the Second Plan is attributable to the fact that the manpower constraint had somewhat eased and the government was able to spend on the planned projects.

As for credit expansion to sectors other than Central Government, the bulk of non-agricultural credit had been channelled to parastatal organizations which, as public institutions, enjoyed relatively easy access to bank credit.[15] This together with the inflationary development during the later period of the Second Plan led to rapid increases in commercial bank credit. Credit during 1972 and 1973, however, expanded at the rate of only 2.4 and 12.1 percent respectively, principally due to the Finance and Credit Plan policies. Thus although non-central government credit rose quite rapidly during 1968–71, for the Plan period as a whole this must not be considered as excessive so long as such expansion was not accompanied by a much faster expansion in government borrowing. During 1973/75 however, the exogenous developments referred to earlier in relation to government borrowing caused an abnormally sharp increase in commercial bank credit to various sectors of the economy.

TABLE 6: ACTUAL AND PLANNED DEVELOPMENT EXPENDITURE, 1964/65–1970/71* (SHS. MILLION)

	1964/65	65/66	66/67	67/68	68/69	69/70	70/71
Actual (1)	203.8	230.0	294.4	344.1	461.0	611.0	829.0
Planned (2)	441.8	450.0	475.0	669.0	625.0	676.4	950.9
(1) as % of (2)	46.1	51.1	62.0	51.4	73.8	90.3	87.2

*Includes transfers to Parastatals.
SOURCE: Minister of Finance (Budget Estimate) Speeches to National Assembly for "Planned expenditure" and Table 7 in ERB Paper 76.8 for "Actual expenditure."

In order to characterize the nature of government borrowing used for development expenditure, let us comment on some aspects of the Second Plan's sources and uses of finances. First of all, the Plan envisaged a transfer of Shs. 620 million from the recurrent to the development budget over the plan period under the assumption that recurrent expenditure would be restrained.[16] At the same time, there would be a continued attempt to increase the tax system's income elasticity.[17] As a result, tax receipts as a proportion of GNP rose from 10.4% in 1964/65 to 15.1% in 1969/70, and to over 18% in 1972/73.[18] Over the entire Plan period, tax and other revenues rose 17% annually but contrary to the expectations of the Plan, recurrent expenditure also rose at a corresponding rate of 16% per annum. As a result, only about 50% of the envisaged total budgetary surplus had been transferred during the first four years of the Plan. This was a significant shortfall given the fact that during 1969–73 the general price level increased by over 6% p.a. We can conclude therefore that one important factor contributing to the rapid government credit expansion was the failure for the recurrent budget to generate budgetary surpluses as originally planned.[19] It is well to recognize that the resulting deficit financing was *unplanned* and was therefore not accompanied by appropriate compensatory policies.

The second important source for the revenue-expenditure gap during the Second Plan period was the planned transfer of Shs. 650 million from Central Government to the parastatals. Over the period, however, about twice that amount was actually transferred. Thus, borrowing from the banking sector had to be increasingly relied upon for financing the gap. The large gap between the actual and planned transfers seems to have resulted from the fact that on the one hand, parastatal investment requirements were largely underestimated given the subsequent proliferation of the parastatal institutions in Tanzania, and on the other, financial controls were generally inadequate.[20] Deficit financing clearly did not take place on any planned basis but developed as a result of unanticipated developments in the parastatal system.

Total government borrowing from the banking system during 1966–73 was roughly split in the ratio 55 to 45 between the Bank of Tanzania and the commercial banks. This is another important distinction for the understanding of the inflationary implications of a budget deficit, for although it is generally true that central bank borrowing is necessarily expansionary, commercial bank lending to government may not necessarily lead to further expansion.[21] If, for instance, the commercial banks do not have adequate reserves with the central bank, or if they are operating with an inadequate liquidity ratio, government borrowing may simply provide the necessary increase in liquidity without thereby providing any basis for credit expansion. Alternatively, government borrowing may take the specific form that does not lead to an increase in the bank's liquid assets or even if it does, the central bank may be unwilling to lend to commercial banks against government securities. Another possibility leading to the same conclusion is the case where overall credit ceilings for the commercial banks are set, or where a credit planning is operative. In the latter situation, government borrowing may increase commercial bank liquidity but then the banks remain unable to extend credit beyond the limits set by the credit plan. The consequence of this will be a rising ratio of liquid assets to deposits, and if deposits are expanding sufficiently fast, a falling loan-to-deposits ratio. Under credit planning it is important to note also that the induced effects of government borrowing from the central bank are limited as is the case with commercial bank borrowing; in both cases the commercial banks have to stay within the limits of the credit plan. However, if government borrowing extends beyond such limits it is possible that the expansionary impact of such excessive borrowing becomes sufficient to push overall credit expansion beyond the planned limits as the ensuing inflationary process can affect transactions demand for cash balances.

In the case of Tanzania, these induced effects[22] of government borrowing from the banking system may have been important before 1969 but appear to have been rather limited thereafter. The first step to limiting these effects was the encouragement of the commercial banks by the Bank of Tanzania to purchase government securities other than treasury bills. As a result, the purchase of such securities increased by three and a half times between December 1968 and the end of 1969, while treasury bill holdings declined from Shs. 104 to Shs. 41 million. Government securities have continued to dominate in the commercial bank's loan portfolio. Although the Bank of Tanzania could grant loans against such securities to the commercial banks, the terms have been relatively unattractive. Thus the result of the 1969 move must have been to depress the effective liquidity ratio and therefore to decrease the potential credit-creating capacity of the commercial banks. In September 1970, the Bank of Tanzania imposed a ceiling of Shs. 1,000 million on the National Bank of Commerce lending for activities other than harvesting and marketing of cash crops and the export business. At the beginning of fiscal year 1971/72 the Finance and Credit Plan was introduced to regulate credit expansion with similar plans to be launched annually as part of the Annual Plan.

These measures greatly reduced the induced effects of government borrowing particularly since the launching of the Finance and Credit Plan. As a result, the ratio of liquid assets to deposits began to rise and the loan-deposits ratio decreased at the same time.[23]

FURTHER CAUSES AND CONSEQUENCES OF MONETARY EXPANSON

The rising money-income ratio,[24] as shown in Table 2, reflects not only the rapid credit expansion we have been discussing but also other forces pertaining to demand for money. Let us examine these issues more closely.

To begin with, there is some evidence for East Africa as a whole that there has been a reversal in the direction of movements of the money-income ratio in the post-Currency Board period.[25] This was bound to happen with the establishment of national financial systems that were likely to reverse the policies of an inelastic colonial monetary system. Thus one important factor contributing to the rise in the money-income ratio particularly in the first few years of the Central Bank must be seen as an institutional one, the institution's increased willingness and ability to expand credit and money supply. This together with others described earlier were probably most important in explaining the rapid expansion of the stock of money from the supply side.

From the demand side, a number of plausible explanations have been advanced for the tendencies or the rising money-income ratio at early stages of development. The first explanation relates to the structural change in the composition of national product. As the share of monetised-sector output rises in the economy, the economy's money-income ratio is bound to increase.[26] This rise, however, will eventually be counteracted by other forces that tend to raise the income velocity of ccirulation. A good example of this is the spread of the banking system at early stages of development.[27] This enhances the possibilities of holding saving and time deposits which in a less developed economy tend to compete with cash holdings and even with demand deposits. The argument that increased monetisation[28] of the economy leads to a decrease in velocity can also be applied in a modified form to the monetary sector of a developing economy: if only monetary GNP is used to calculate velocity as described in Table 2, then increased monetisation will raise the money-income ratio, assuming that monetary GNP includes activities in which the degree of monetisation is relatively low and tends to rise as the country's per capita income grows. In that case the stock of money will rise faster than monetary product and therefore lead to a rising money-income ratio, if velocity and rate of income growth in the relatively more monetised sub-sector remain constant.

In the monetary economy, however, transactions demand for money may be more important in raising the money-income ratio. First, as the economy grows production is likely to become increasingly differentiated and sophisticated demanding a greater volume of cash balances to meet the increasing transactions per unit of final product. Secondly, the average size of the firm may increase rather rapidly at early stages of development; this may lead to the expansion of the transactions demand at a faster rate than that of output. In general, the amount of cash and demand deposits held by a firm will depend on the volume of transactions, the opportunity cost of holding such non-interest bearing assets, and its financial management sophistication.[29] In a less developed economy, the range of debt instruments is usually limited and sophisticated financial management techniques and personnel scarce. As a result, the volume of the firm's holdings of cash and demand deposits may be higher than optimization behaviour would require.

For households, most of their liquid assets are likely to be held in cash as such liquid assets are on the average a small proportion of their wealth. The typical household is unlikely to gain much by exploring the possible ways of investing cash.

Alternatively, the phenomenon of the rising money income ratio as per capita income increases may be viewed as a reflection of the fact that money is a luxury suggesting that the income elasticity of money demand is greater than unity.[30]

Finally changes in the rate of interest and price level may affect demand for money.[31] The near constancy of official rates and the moderate inflation rate during the period in consideration, however, make these factors unimportant. Changes in the 'unorganized' money markets could be relevant but such markets were quantitatively negligible in Tanzania.

Given all these reasons the persistent upward tendency of the money income ratio in a developing economy should not be surprising. Indeed, empirical evidence shows that at early stages of development the money income ratio tends to rise with per capita income.[32] We can therefore conclude that the forces tending to raise the money-income ratio in the economy both from the supply and demand sides have been stronger relative to those tending to reduce the economy's liquidity.

It is useful to point out the rather obvious although important implications of the secular rise in the money-income ratio as far as development finance is concerned. If money demanded grows faster than income during the early stages of a country's development, then it is possible to use deficit finance or some form of bank credit creation to accelerate capital formation without generating inflation. The scope for absorbing monetary expansion in this way, however, seems limited because structural factors leading to increased money demand are likely to change only gradually. The possibility, therefore, exists that after a certain period the price level and money-income ratio could start moving together as the rise in that ratio reflects the increased holding of unintended cash balances. In these circumstances one would expect a positive impact of monetary expansion on the price level.

As can be imagined, during the early years of establishing an independent national financial system, it was unlikely that the rise in the money-income ratio led to immediate inflationary pressure since increased monetisation of the economy and other factors were strongly at work for maintaining monetary equilibrium. This can be seen from equation (10) rewritten as:

$$\Delta p = \frac{B_0}{y}(Fi + Fe + Fm - k_0 p_0 \, \Delta y - D) \quad (11)$$

where $B_0 = \frac{1}{k_0}$.

Equation (11) tells us that a given volume of money creation (Fi + Fe) will exert a smaller impact on the price level the greater the relative importance of F_m, Δy, and balance-of-payments deficit in absorbing the liquidity created.

As shown in Table 1, liquidity increases neutralized about 38% of actual monetisation during 1967–69 and accounted for only an 8% price absorption. Table 4 and other balance-of-payments data show that during 1966–69 foreign reserves were actually increasing every year. At the same time income growth absorbed over 56% of the current monetisation. One can conclude from this that the bulk of money creation during this period went to finance income growth and desired increases in liquidity, leaving only a little excess that partly 'leaked' through the balance-of-payments deficits and partly financed the small 1.4% annual increase in the price level. The period since 1970/71, however, gives a different picture of monetary development: increases in liquidity absorbed a smaller proportion (33%) of current monetisation than the previous period, price level changes absorbed a much larger proportion (33%) while income growth took a much reduced proportion of 29%. Balance-of-payment deficits allowed a stronger 'leakage' during 1970 and 1971 although the exceptional export performance of 1972 together with the continued import controls reduced this leakage considerably for that year.

Thus, summarizing monetary development during this latter period, it is seen that the money-income ratio was absorbing proportionately less and less of total money creation just as was real income growth, with a larger proportion going to finance annual price level increases and the remainder 'leaking' through the balance-of-payments deficits.

The preceding observations seem very important for the future of monetary management; they stress the fact that the period since 1969/70, unlike the earlier one, was characterised by parallel movements of money supply and the price level. The regression equations below, although based on the entire period 1966–73, point to this conclusion.

It is well to emphasize now that because these regression-equations are based on data for two sub-periods during which we expect different impacts of monetary expansion or prices, one should not expect high 'degrees of fit' ($\bar{R}^2$). Also, the price control scheme exercised during the period may also raise some doubts as to the suitability of prices as indicators of excess demand. But this is not a serious problem since only a few specific items (22 during fiscal 1970/71 for example) had been subject to the control before the establishment of the Price Commission in 1973. It will also be seen that only the increase in money supply, among the variables appearing in equations (10) and (11), is included in the regressions; this is because it was the only variable which was statistically significant, and the inclusion of the other variables in fact reduced the $\bar{R}^2$.[33]

Another important point to keep in mind is that we have used the single-equation estimation method. This is because as described earlier, money supply in the period 1966–73 can be considered as largely exogenously determined.

$$P_i = -0.74 + 0.018\,M \qquad \bar{R}^2 = 0.25$$
$$(2.53)\quad (0.01) \qquad ;\ D.W. = 2.37$$
$$P_i = -3.22 + 0.011M + 0.22M_{-1} \qquad \bar{R}^2 = 0.50$$
$$(2.66)\quad (0.009)\quad (0.011) \qquad ;\ D.W. = 2.02$$
$$P_r = -1.96 + 0.035\,M \qquad \bar{R}^2 = 0.46$$
$$(3.41) + (0.014) \qquad ;\ D.W. = 1.42$$
$$P_r = -3.06 + 0.03\,M + 0.016M_{-1} \qquad \bar{R}^2 = 0.39$$
$$(4.73)\quad (0.0017)\quad (0.02) \qquad ;\ D.W. = 1.55$$
$$P_c = (1.02 + 0.02\,M \qquad \bar{R}^2 = 0.31$$
$$(2.15)\quad (0.009) \qquad ;\ D.W. = 1.05$$
$$P_f = -4.16 + 0.42M \qquad \bar{R}^2 = 0.65$$
$$(2.82)\quad (0.011) \qquad ;\ D.W. = 2.4$$
$$P_f = -5.84 + 0.037\,M + 0.014\,M_{-1} \qquad \bar{R}^2 = 0.62$$
$$(3.87)\quad (0.014)\quad (0.017) \qquad ;\ D.W. = 2.67$$
$$PK = (3.58 + 0.013\,M \qquad \bar{R}^2 = 0.02$$
$$(3.08)\quad (0.012) \qquad ;\ D.W. = 2.34$$

Where

P_i is the increase in the implicit GDP deflator (1966 = 100);

PK is the increase in the implicit GDP deflator for the construction industry (1966 = 100);

P_r, P_c are the increases in the Dar es Salaam based Retail (wage-earners) and Cost of living (middle-grade civil servants) indices respectively (1963–100);

P_f is the increase in the Food index component of the Retail Price Index (P_r) and

M is the increase in Money Supply.

The final point to note about these regressions is the introduction of the previous year's increase in money supply as an explanatory variable. It is reasonable to assume that past increases in money supply influence current price changes although given our sample size it would be useless to elaborate the detailed lag structure. A one-year lag, however, seems a good empirical approximation of monetary adjustments in developing economies.[34]

The regression results show that first of all, the 'goodness of fit' is generally low, which suggests a tenuous relationship between price changes and changes in money supply. This is as expected in view of the previous discussion of monetary development during the two sub-periods.

Secondly, the introduction of the lagged money supply variable M_{-1} improves the 'degree of fit' for the GDP deflator equation from $\bar{R}^2 = 0.25$ to 0.50. The t value of the M_{-1} coefficient is greater than that of the current money supply change variable M. They are both significant only slightly beyond the 10 percent level. The previous year's change in money supply appears to produce a greater impact on the current price change. This to some extent explains the upward trends in the movement of the money-income ratio and the price level: the actual money-income ratio during the later subperiod was probably growing at a rate faster than the desired proportion to which spenders reacted with a time lag.

Thirdly, the food price equation in the unlagged form shows the best fit with the M variable significant at the 2 per cent level. The lagged form equation shows almost the same 'goodness of fit' but the M_{-1} variable is statistically insignificant and can be dropped from the equation. A similar conclusion can be made for the retail price equation: M is the only significant variable. This is as expected since the food price series is closely correlated with the general retail price series.[35]

The cost-of-living index equation, on the other hand, shows much lower 'degree of fit.' The lagged form of this equation gives a better result with $\bar{R}^2 = 0.5$ but the coefficients of both money variables indicate lower significance. Also the presence of autocorrelation is noticeable in the equation. The construction price equation is the last one in the set with the poorest result.

These regression results show that on the whole the link between money and price changes was not very close during the period. A possible explanation for this is that before 1970 the economy, as we have seen, had been using the bulk of monetized credit for financing liquidity increases as well as income growth. Since 1970, however, there has been a marked reduction in the proportion of total monetisation absorbed by these sources. Thus while it is possible that monetary expansion in the latter period led to inflationary development, for the entire period to which the above regressions pertain, the link between monetary expansion and price increases is then unlikely to be very significant.

Another explanation could be that the relevant variables other than money supply are missing in the regressions. For example, the heavy dependence of the economy on imports implies the susceptibility of domestic price levels to inflation abroad. Another example is the existence of import controls and shortages which may cause prices to rise even if money supply were to increase by a given amount.

The food price regressions reveal that money supply change moves most closely with the price of wage goods, of which food is the most important, and that this inflationary impact is immediate. For a low-income country like Tanzania where the proportion of food expenditure in total consumption is close to 50 percent, monetary expansion is bound to have a sizeable and immediate effect on food demand. Although we do not have sufficient data to generalize for wage goods, demands for such goods are expected to expand rapidly with the rise in money income. Excess demand may not manifest itself through rising prices because of the existing price control scheme, but the shortages with which the economy has lived since 1970/71 is an indication of the inflationary process.

Finally, the very low fit of the construction price equation is partly a reflection of the fact that the country's construction capacity has become a constraint only in the later period of the Second Plan. Also one has to take into account the high import component in the calculation of this index.

A further attempt was made to determine whether the proportionate change in price (inflation rate) could be explained by corresponding changes in money supply. For the general and the construction price equations, the fits were very poor and the results insignificant although the signs of the coefficients were as expected. The cost-of-living and the food price equations gave some encouragement. The food equation yielded an $\bar{R}^2$ of 0.29 with the DW statistic of 1.52 with the coefficients of the variables insignificant at critical levels. The cost-of-living equation showed the corresponding parameters of 0.25 and 0.08 respectively again with insignificant coefficients. In general, the relations between prices and money supply remained tenuous during the period in consideration.

We were also tempted to look at the quarterly observations for the retail, cost-of-living and food indices. The results for the cost-of-living equation were all insignificant at acceptable levels. The rate of change in money supply lagged one quarter was the only variable significant beyond the 10 percent level for the retail price equation and at less than the 10 percent level for the food price equation.[36] The 'degrees of fit' for the two regressions were, however, poor with the corresponding low F ratios for testing the significance of the regression. Similar attempts were made using quarterly data for the later period but no better results were obtained.

These results show that the inflation rate during the period cannot be explained by the rate of monetary expansion alone.

CONCLUSION

This paper has examined the nature and impact of monetary expansion for the period 1966–1973. Among other things, monetary expansion has been shown to be partly responsible for inflation in the period since 1969. The statistical results, however, remain insufficiently explanatory, and the relationship between money supply and prices became weaker when specification was made in terms of rates of change, i.e. when the rate of inflation became the dependent variable. The use of quarterly data did not improve the results. It is well to emphasize, however, that these results can not be a basis for rejecting the monetarist hypothesis (which relates inflation primarily to monetary expansion). There is clearly the need for further analysis, perhaps the need for incorporating other variables, if the nature of inflation is to be better understood. Let us therefore conclude this paper by considering mainly the broad implications of credit expansion to the government sector in a Tanzanian-type economy.

First of all, the expansionary impact during the early years of a national financial system had been counteracted mainly by liquidity increases and income growth. The establishment of a more elastic credit system clearly helped reverse the trend in the money-income ratio that had been established during the colonial period without disrupting price stability.

Such period, however, cannot be too long, for as time passes the economy's investment-absorption capacity increases as manpower and other nonfinancial constraints ease. At the same time, the economy may have been long committed to a target rate of growth higher than the historical rate—as was the case with the First Five-Year Plan. Both the government and nongovernment sectors therefore attempted to increase development finance through various forms of borrowing. Thus in 1969, for instance, the Development Credit Department, which became the precursor of the Tanzanian Investment Bank founded in 1970, was established within the National Bank of Commerce mainly to finance development expenditure. At the same time government borrowing from the banking system began to rise sharply.

Monetary expansion, as shown by our empirical results, produces a substantial and immediate impact on the demand for wage goods—particularly for food which accounts for close to 50 percent of consumption expenditure in Tanzania. Thus even if monetary expansion remained at a reasonable, given rate, inadequate growth in food supply is bound to lead to immediate rise in the price level.[37]

Given the economy's high import-propensity, credit expansion is bound to increase demand for imports. The parastatal organisations, for example, which have been the major borrower from the banks, generally have a high import intensity estimated at around 45 percent in recent years.[38]

The effect of this heavy import-dependence of parastatal investments has been to tie credit expansion to the economy's import capacity and therefore to exports. As shown in Table 4, 1970 and 1971 witnessed considerable losses in foreign reserves as a result of the strong credit expansion that had begun a year earlier. Certainly, an analysis focusing on the supply side (dealing with export-supplies and the country's capacity to import, etc.) will shed new light on the nature of inflation given the economy's high dependence on its capacity to import. We may note in this regard, for instance, that during the 1968–71 period of credit expansion, exports increased only by over 3 percent per annum and real current capacity to import by less than 2 percent p.a.; imports over the same period rose annually by over 14 percent.

Another possible consequence of the high import dependence is an imported cost-inflation: rising prices and decreases in foreign reserves are the likely companions of a given rate of growth if imports are obtained under conditions of inflation abroad.[39] The consequence is more serious in an underdeveloped economy with high rigidities in production structure. Tanzania's main import suppliers – Western Europe, United States, Canada and Japan with the exception of Mainland China – experienced an acceleration in the average rate of inflation from 2.4 percent p.a. during 1960–65 to over 4 percent in the second half of the decade. The high averages continued in the 1970's; having risen to 6.7 percent during 1969–70 and declined slightly to 5.5 percent in 1970–71.[40] As these rates were sizeable, they were bound to have significantly affected the general price level in Tanzania.

Producer goods imports required for the government investment programme would also tie its borrowing to foreign exchange use although the accompanying imported inflation problem is likely to manifest itself in this case through an accelerated rate of foreign reserve decrease and an increasing deficit per unit of development expenditure. This is because the cost of government output is not passed on to the consumer directly.

Apart from the general impact of government expenditure on both domestically produced goods and imports, it is important to note that the direction of this expenditure has been strongly biased toward infrastructural investment, which tends to have relatively high capital and import intensities as well as longer gestation periods. This direction of expenditure has a stronger inflationary impact and would require explicit counter-inflationary policies for the maintenance of monetary stability.

The findings of this paper, on the whole, support our original statement about the relationship between money, prices and the balance of payments. Although the bulk of monetary expansion during the early period was absorbed by liquidity and income increases without a significant price rise, the latter has absorbed a greater proportion in recent years with proportionately less of credit creation going to the financing of income growth and additional liquidity. Thus, the price level and the money-income ratio have tended to move together, as shown by our regression results.

Another point that must be noted is that monetary expansion has led to the possibility of a foreign exchange constraint upon growth particularly in post-1970/71 years. These results suggest that internal and external stability could be maintained only if monetary policy were to be conducted in the light of these objectives; this realization, as alluded to earlier, was the basis of the annual Finance and Credit, and Foreign Exchange Plans.

The inadequacy of the money supply variables for explaining price movements during the period necessitates further analysis if the nature of inflation is to be better understood. An approach to this problem would be to accommodate other relevant factors in the analysis along the lines suggested previously. Once all the main factors are taken into account, it may still be necessary to divide the entire period into shorter ones and identify the most important factors during each sub-period in order to obtain a more accurate intertemporal picture of the main forces at work. This exercise could lead to a sounder basis for characterising the nature of inflation.[14]

NOTES

1. The 'crisis' year, 1974, is excluded in this discussion.

The First and Second Five-Year Plans were in force during 1964–69 and 1969–74 respectively.

2. Money supply, National Product and Balance of Payments data used in this paper are presented in two appendices of ERB Paper 76.8.
3. Organisation for European Economic Cooperation, *Statistics and Sources and Uses of Finance 1948–1958* (Paris, 1960).
4. By considering the initial and terminal moments of an accounting period, it is seen that $Ai+Ae=Li+Le$ . . . (3a), i.e. increase in assets+increase in liabilities. Increase in domestic liabilities can be divided between money and non-money as $Li=\Delta M+(Li-\Delta M)$ . . . . (3b) which is substituted in (3a) to obtain $Ne+Ai-\Delta M-(Li-\Delta M)=0$ . . . . (3c) where $Ne=Ae-Le$ as defined in the text. By noting that $Fi=Ai-(Li-\Delta M)$ from the text definition, and substituting in (3c), the banks' financing account (3) is obtained.
5. For further discussion, see, for example, E. H. Brau, "The Variability of Velocity and Credit Ceilings" in the *IMF Staff Papers*, Vol. 18, November 1971.
6. Details of estimation and related data problems can be found in two appendices of the original ERB paper 76.8.
7. See Footnote 6.
8. This was obtained by multiplying the total GNP figure by the proportion of monetary-sector GDP in total Mainland GDP.
9. For the corresponding estimates obtained on the basis of a broader definition of external monetisation, see the original ERB Paper 76.8, p. 9.
10. In calculating Internal Credit, Monetisation, we used equation (3) in the text. $Fi=\Delta M-Ne$ is the expression used to obtain the figures for Fi in Table 1. Our calculations, however, introduce an element of inconsistency since ΔM is an average for the year while Ne is calculated from the balance of payments statement compiled at the end of the year.
11. For the figures for the recurrent budgets, see ERB Paper 76.8, Table 7, p. 18.
12. For details see the Bank of Tanzania, *Economic and Operations Report*, June, 1974.
13. A brief discussion of these changes can be found in J. Loxley, "Structural Changes in the Monetary System of Tanzania", in L. Cliffe and J. Saul (eds.), *Socialism in Tanzania*, Vol. 2, Dar es Salaam: East African Publishing House, 1973; for an analysis of the Tanzanian banking system, see C. Caselli, *The Banking System of Tanzania*, Cassa di Risparmio delle Provincie Lombarde, Milan, 1975 and H. H. Binhammer, *The Development of a Financial Infrastructure in Tanzania*, Nairobi: East African Literature Bureau, 1975.
14. See United Republic of Tanzania, *The Annual Plan for 1971/72*, Government Printer, Dar es Salaam, 1971, p. 7.
15. It has been estimated that 40% of total credit from financial institutions (excluding Bank of Tanzania and National Insurance Corporation credit to Government) went to parastatal organisations in 1969, and that the proportion grew to 71% in 1972. See W. E. Clark, *Socialist Development and Public Investment in Tanzania, 1964–73* (Unpublished Ph.D. thesis, Harvard University, 1974), p. 279.
16. United Republic of Tanzania, *Tanzania Second Five-Year Plan for Economic and Social Development, 1969 1974*, Dar es Salaam: Government Printer, 1969.
17. For a summary of this discussion, see J. Loxley, "The Finance of Government Spending in Tanzania since Independence", *Rasilimali* (Tanzania Investment Bank Outlook, No. 1); and also U. Hicks, "The Revenue Implications of the Uganda and Tanzania Plans", *The Journal of Development Studies* (Vol. 2), April, 1966.
18. Evidently this is quite high given the level of Tanzania's per capita income. The limit of tax effort may have been reached for Tanzania; see, for example, J. Loxley, "The Finance of Government Spending . . ." For an international comparison, see R. J. Chelliah, H. J. Baas and M. R. Kelly, "Tax Ratios and Tax Effort in Developing Countries, 1969–1971", *IMF Staff Papers* (Vol. XXII) March, 1975.
19. Tendencies for overspending by Government Ministries is also pointed out in J. Loxley, "Financial Planning and Control in Tanzania", in Uchumi Board (eds.) *Towards Socialist Planning*, Dar es Salaam: Tanzania Publishing House, 1972.
20. *Ibid.*
21. The expansionary implications of government borrowing from the banking system are discussed in N. Ahmad, *Deficit Financing, Inflation and Capital Formation: The Ghanaian Experience*, Munchen, Weltforum Verlag, 1970; and in V. K. R. V. Rao, "Deficit Financing for Capital Formation and Price Behaviour in an Underdeveloped Economy", *Indian Economic Review* Vol. I, February, 1963.
22. By 'induced effects' we mean further credit expansion as a result of initial government borrowing.
23. The movements since 1969 of commercial bank liquidity ratio and the proportion of loans to deposits are as follows:

	1969	*1970*	*1971*	*1972*	*1973*
Liquid Assets/ Deposits (%)	24.3	22.6	30.3	35.1	31.1
Loan/Deposits (%)	69.5	75.6	69.7	63.9	61.7

Source: Computed from the Bank of Tanzania, *Economic and Operations Report*, June, 1974.

Liquid assets include cash with banks, deposits with the Bank of Tanzania, treasury bills and foreign liquid assets. The loan deposits ratio is obtained by dividing total domestic lending by total domestic deposits (assets of residents).

24. It will be recalled that GNP data in Table 2 is an estimate for Zanzibar and Mainland Tanzania. Since 1971, the Bank of Tanzania has made estimates of Mainland money supply which we have divided by Mainland GNP (which is available from *National Accounts of Tanzania 1964–1972*, to obtain a more accurate Mainland money-income ratio. The movement in this ratio is similar to that given in Table 2 as can be seen below:

1970	*1971*	*1972*	*1973*
0.1822	0.2143	0.2094	0.2193

The money supply data used here are again quarterly averages. Money supply estimates for Mainland are obtained by excluding the People's Bank of Zanzibar demand deposits.

25 During the Currency Board period, the money income ratio for East Africa moved as shown below:

1954	*1956*	*1958*	*1960*	*1962*	*1964*
0.40	0.35	0.30	0.27	0.27	0.26

Source: C. Caselli, *The Banking System of Tanzania*, Table 6, p. 56.

After the founding of the East African central banks the same ratio moved in the opposite direction:

	1967	*1968*	*1969*	*1970*	*1971*
Money Supply (Shs. Mn.)	3,316	3,975	4,678	5,305	5,882
GDP (Shs. Mn.)	21,252	22,752	24,605	27,188	29,716
Money-GDP Ratio	0.156	0.175	0.190	0.195	0.198

Source: Money Supply data from IMF *International*

Financial Statistics and GDP from the *East African Economic and Statistical Review.*

26. This is true under the assumption of a constant velocity in the monetized sector. A mathematical proof of this proposition is given in ERB Paper 76.8, p. 27.
27. A study by B. K. Short, "The Velocity of Money and Per Capita Income In Developing Economies: Malaysia and Singapore" in *The Journal of Development Studies*, Vol. 9, January 1973, yields a statistically significant positive influence of the number of bank offices on velocity.
28. A study by J. Melitz and H. Correa, "International Differences in Income Velocity" in *The Review of Economics and Statistics* Vol. III, February, 1970, finds a statistically significant relationship between monetisation and income velocity of money.
29. For a fuller discussion of these issues see J. S. Duesenberry, "The Portfolio Approach to the Demand for Money and Other Assets" in *The Review of Economics and Statistics*, Vol. XLV, February, 1963, Supplement.
30. This interpretation based on U.S. long term time series data is given by M. Friedman in "The Demand for Money: Some Theoretical and Empirical Results", *The Journal of Political Economy*, Vol. LXVII, August 1959.
31. For an empirical evidence see, for instance, O. Ojo, "The Money Market" in *The Nigerian Journal of Economic and Social Studies*, Vol. 16, July, 1974.
32. See, for example, H. Ezekiel and J. O. Adekunle, "The Secular Behaviour of Income Velocity: An International Cross-Section Study" in the *IMF Staff Papers*, Vol. XVI, July, 1969 ; J. G. Gurley, "Financial Structures in Developing Economies" in D. Krivine (ed.), *Fiscal and Monetary Problems in Developing States*, New York: Frederick A. Praeger, 1967; B. K. Short, *op. cit.*; and J. Melitz and H. Correa, *op. cit.*
33. R^2; is R^2 corrected for the degrees of freedom.
34. This is the conclusion reached by R. Porter, "Income Velocity and Pakistan's Second Plan" *Pakistan Development Review* (Summer 1961); and A. C. Harberger, "The Dynamics of Inflation in Chile" in C. F. Christ (ed.), *Measurement in Economics*, Stanford: Stanford University Press, 1963.
35. For evidence, see United Republic of Tanzania, *Statistical Abstract*, 1970 Dar es Salaam: Government Printer, 1972, p. 170.
36. The regressions were

$$PF^* = 0.58 - 0.005M^* + 0.12M^{**};\ \bar{R}^2 = 0.^{17}\ D.W. = 2.07$$
$$(0.75)\ (0.068)\ \ (0.067)\ \ F_{2,23} = {}_{1\cdot 62}$$
$$P^* = 0.88 + 0.019M^* + 0.083M^{**};\ \bar{R}^2 = 0.^{11},\ D.W. = 2.09$$
$$(0.57)\ (0.052)\ \ (0.051)\ \ F_{2,23} = {}_{1\cdot 36}$$

P_f^* and P_r^* respectively refer to the quarterly percentage changes in the Food and Retail price indices (1966 to 1973), while M^* and M^{**} represent current and lagged percentage changes in the money supply (smoothed to remove seasonality). F with numerical subscripts refers to the F ratio with the indicated degrees of freedom.
37. See (ERB Paper 76.9), "Inflation and the Structure of the Tanzanian Economy"
38. W. E. Clark, *op. cit.*, Ch. V.
39. See D. G. Rwegasira, "The Tanzanian Monetary Experience, 1974–1973", (Unpublished Ph.D. thesis, Harvard University, Cambridge, Mass., 1976) Ch. II.
40. International Monetary Fund, *Annual Report, 1972*, Washington, D.C., 1972.
41. Further analysis of these issues is given in ERB Paper 76.9.

Distribution of the Tax Burden in Tanzania*

YUKON HUANG

Introduction

There is an emerging consensus that inequality in the distribution of income in developing countries is increasing, and that in addition to the obvious moral considerations, such inequality may be detrimental to development. The importance of the tax system in effecting redistribution is usually discounted, since most studies conclude that taxes are regressive or proportional. Reliance on indirect taxes on consumption and the limited impact of income taxes (which are often only mildly progressive) are used to explain these results. Many economists also believe that government price and tax policies discriminate against the relatively poorer rural sector in favour of the richer urban sector.

This study estimates the burden of taxes in Tanzania by income class and urban-rural sectors. The evidence indicates that both indirect and direct taxes are very progressive and that the urban sector pays much more relative to its income. The study makes use of a household budget survey which is unusually detailed for a country which ranks among the poorest twenty countries in the world. This survey permits more accurate allocation of indirect taxes than previously possible since it provides data on specific commodities and also on in-kind consumption. This is the first study to investigate directly the effect of in-kind consumption. How it is treated can greatly affect tax burden estimates, and should not be ignored as it has been. The budget survey makes possible for the first time a detailed tax burden study for a sub-Saharan African country. The relatively greater poverty in Africa indicates that these results may differ from other burden studies which have concentrated on Latin America and Asia.

DATA AND INCIDENCE ASSUMPTIONS

A brief discussion of the data and methodology is presented here; for a fuller discussion, the reader is referred to the appendix. This study makes use of the *1969 Household Budget Survey* to determine the pattern of consumption and income. The survey covered a total of 3,068 households, 2,196 in rural areas and 872 in urban areas. The household was defined as an individual or group of individuals living together in a housing unit and sharing their consumption. Over 430 specific consumption items were recorded, including whether it was obtained through cash purchases or was in kind (meaning that it was home produced or obtained as a gift or for services rendered). Consumption in kind was valued at local prices for aggregation purposes.

In order to reflect the current tax structure, but still retain the implied income distribution of the survey, this study uses the calendar year 1971 to estimate the burden of taxes. Income in each class was adjusted upwards by 20% as an estimate for income in 1971 (but the limits stated for the classes remain at their 1969 levels). This does not alter the distribution of taxes, or income, but provides a more accurate base to estimate the effective tax rate (the percentage of income that is absorbed by taxes).

The allocation of taxes generally follows that of Musgrave's work with some modifications.[2] The appendix provides a fuller discussion of the method. The unique feature of this study is the explicit consideration of in-kind consumption. Since the budget survey provides an item by item breakdown of in-kind consumption, the allocation of the tax burden assumed that only cash income was subject to taxation, whether direct or indirect, but in-kind consumption was counted as part of income. The role of in-kind consumption is extremely important and partially explains why the tax system is both progressive and urban-biased. On balance, if there is error in the incidence assumptions, the bias is to make the tax system seem more regressive than it really is, which strengthens the conclusions of this study.

As much as possible, indirect taxes are broken down into individual items to permit more accurate allocations. Taxes which cannot be allocated directly are classified under a "miscellaneous" category. This category was allocated between classes in proportion to total consumption expenditure (including food) but excluding all consumption in kind.

PATTERN OF INCOME AND TAXES

Tanzania is one of the poorest developing countries, with a *per capita* GDP of approximately 700 shillings for 1971. Table 1 presents the distribution of household income, by income class and urban-rural sectors. The urban sector accounts for 5.6% of the households and 21.9% of the income, while the rural sector accounts for 94.4% of the households and 78.1% of the income.

Table 2 indicates the shilling amounts of the main taxes; also provided are urban-rural breakdowns, both in shillings and in percentages. Individual income

The *Economic Journal*, March 1976.

*This study was conducted while the author was a visiting lecturer at the University of Dar es Salaam, 1972–4, under the auspices of the Rockefeller Foundation. He would like to express his great appreciation of the invaluable help received from the *Economic Journal's* referee and from Professor Reddaway as editor.

TABLE 1: DISTRIBUTION OF HOUSEHOLDS AND INCOME 1971 (PERCENTAGE BY INCOME CLASS)

	Income class* (shillings)					
	0–999	1,000–1,999	2,000–3,999	4,000–7,999	8,000–24,999	25,000+
Households†						
Total (2,936,473)	30.4	39.8	20.4	7.3	1.8	0.4
Urban (165,464)	2.9	8.6	28.6	34.8	20.5	4.8
Rural (2,771,009)	32.0	41.7	19.9	5.7	0.7	0.1
Income*						
Total (6,564,785)	10.3	26,9	26.0	18.4	9.2	9.2
Urban (1,438,387)	0.2	1.4	10.4	24.6	27.3	36.0
Rural (5,126,398)	13,1	34.0	30.3	16.7	4.2	1.7

SOURCE: 1969 Household Budget Survey with adjustments.
*The income-classes are on a 1969 basis; in 1971 all limits would be about 20% higher.
†Data in parentheses are estimated number of households and income for that sector.

TABLE 2: ANALYSIS OF TAX REVENUES 1971 (THOUSANDS OF SHILLINGS)

		Analysis by sector			
		Urban		Rural	
Type of tax	Revenue yield	Amount	%	Amount	%
I. Individual income	300,489	236,936	79	63,553	21
II. Other taxes					
1. Excise	244,819	89,612	37	155,207	63
2. Domestic sales	131,571	43,889	33	87,682	67
3. Import	333,803	110,356	33	223,447	67
4. Corporate income	81,728	34,265	42	47,463	58
5. Foreign sales	95,037	31,362	33	63,675	67
6. Motor vehicle	39,670	18,248	46	21,422	54
7. Miscellaneous	9,237	9,151	99	86	1
8. Total other taxes	935,865	336,883	36	598,982	64
III. Total of all taxes	1,236,354	573,819	46	662,535	54

taxes account for approximately 24% of total revenues; the other taxes, most of which are indirect taxes, account for 76%. Among the other taxes is a sales tax, part of which is collected by local revenue authorities on domestically produced items and is referred to as the domestic sales tax; the other part is collected by the East African Community and is referred to as the foreign sales tax. The miscellaneous taxes consist of an entertainment tax on cinema charges and a tax on electricity use.

The incidence of the tax system is presented in Table 3, where the pattern of effective tax rates is presented. (Construction of this table is described in the Appendix.) The overall incidence of the tax system is very progressive. The top two classes pay 49.1% and 37.0% of their income in taxes while the bottom two classes pay 9.6% and 10.7%. If the same total revenue were obtained with a proportional tax it could be obtained with an effective rate of 18.8% paid by all classes.[3] The redistribution effect of the tax system can be summarised in terms of the following Gini coefficients:

A.	Income before taxes	0.431
B.	Income minus other taxes	0.411
C.	Income minus other taxes and individual income taxes	0.377

The individual income taxes are very progressive, due to progressive tax rates, and this is accentuated by the exclusion of in-kind income from taxation.

TABLE 3: INCIDENCE OF TAXES ON INCOME CLASSES* (PERCENTAGE OF INCOME ABSORBED BY TAX IN EACH CLASS)

Type of tax	0–999	1,000–1,999	2,000–3,999	4,000–7,999	8,000–24,999	25,000 +	All
I. Individual income							
Total	—	—	0.2	3.5	14.5	27.8	4.5
Urban	—	—	1.7	7.1	15.7	28.9	16.5
Rural	—	—	—	2.0	12.9	21.4	1.2
II. Other Taxes							
1. Excise							
Total	2.2	2.6	3.8	4.9	5.9	3.8	3.7
Urban	3.7	5.0	7.9	7.7	7.7	3.7	6.2
Rural	2.2	2.6	3.4	3.8	2.4	4.3	3.0
2. Domestic sales							
Total	1.4	1.6	1.9	2.5	2.9	2.3	2.0
Urban	2.1	2.6	3.3	3.4	3.6	2.3	3.1
Rural	1.4	1.5	1.8	2.1	1.5	2.5	1.7
3. Import							
Total	3.8	4.1	4.6	5.4	7.4	7.8	3.1
Urban	6.2	7.0	7.1	7.3	8.7	7.3	7.7
Rural	3.7	4.1	4.3	4.6	5.0	10.9	4.4
4. Corporate income							
Total	0.9	0.9	1.0	1.2	1.9	2.8	1.2
Urban	1.8	1.8	1.7	1.8	2.4	3.0	2.4
Rural	0.9	0.9	0.9	1.9	1.0	1.6	0.9
5. Foreign sales							
Total	1.1	1.2	1.3	1.6	2.1	2.2	1.5
Urban	2.0	2.0	2.2	2.1	2.5	2.1	2.2
Rural	1.1	1.2	1.2	1.3	1.5	3.1	1.2
Total other taxes†							
Total	9.6	10.7	13.0	16.3	22.2	21.3	14.2
Urban	16.3	18.7	23.0	23.5	27.8	20.8	23.6
Rural	9.5	10.6	12.0	13.2	12.7	26.2	11.7
III. Total all taxes							
Total	9.8	10.7	13.1	19.8	37.0	49.1	18.8
Urban	16.3	18.7	24.7	30.6	43.1	49.6	39.9
Rural	9.5	10.6	12.0	15.3	25.7	47.5	12.9

*The income classes are on a 1969 basis; in 1971 all limits would be about 20% higher.
†Including some not shown separately.

The other taxes, most of which are indirect taxes, also reduce inequalities. In general, these taxes range from proportionality to progressivity, in contrast with other studies which indicate that such taxes are quite regressive. It appears that indirect taxes do not have to be regressive. A well-chosen system can yield a progressive pattern. The reasons for this are connected with the type of items taxed and the role of in-kind consumption. Many taxed items are consumed by the rich, and indirect taxes on such items are progressive. The best examples are taxes on durables, electricity, cinema charges and motor vehicles. Furthermore, the exclusion of in-kind consumption eliminates much of the income of the poor from taxation, increasing the progressivity. Finally, since in-kind income is more common in rural areas where incomes are lower, the tax burden for both sectors combined will be more progressive.

For comparison with other studies, the Tanzanian tax system reduces the Gini coefficient by 12.5%.[4] This redistributional effect is much greater than that found in Meerman's survey of ten other developing countries, where in no case did the reduction exceed 3.6%. In general, these studies found the indirect taxes to be regressive and thus the overall effect of the tax system depended upon the importance of the progressive income taxes. Unless the income taxes were very important relative to the indirect taxes, the overall effect was generally regressive or proportional.

The differing results in this study are due to explicit consideration of in-kind income and data permitting more accurate allocation of indirect taxes. In other studies, this has not been possible. McLure's excellent study illustrates the ingenuity required with poor or non-existent data. For example, "the total of taxes on alcohol, beer, and tobacco . . . was allocated arbitrarily

TABLE 4: RURAL CONSUMPTION, CASH AND NON-CASH DISTRIBUTION (SELECTED ITEMS, BY PERCENTAGE.)

	Cash	Non-Cash
Total	60	40
Food and drink	35	65
Cereals	26	74
Sugar	91	9
Eggs	34	66
Vegetables	16	84
Oils and fats	78	22
Meats	43	57
Housing	47	53
Fuel	23	77
Furniture	92	8
Durables	100	0
Clothing	98	2
Miscellaneous	96	4
Education	100	0
Transport	100	0
Tobacco products	92	8
Non-consumptive outlays	100	0

to income brackets on a somewhat less than *per capita* basis in the lower range and on a somewhat more than *per capita* basis in the upper range . . . all import duties, and all other indirect taxes were allocated on the basis of non-food expenditures".[5] His results essentially assumed that taxes on alcoholic and tobacco products are regressive and taxes on imports and other indirect taxes are at best proportional. The detailed allocation in the present study indicates that many of these same indirect taxes are progressive.

Since the incidence assumptions made in allocating the taxes are, on the whole, biased toward more regressivity, the degree of progressivity is probably underestimated. For example, the rate of taxation is often greater for the more expensive luxury products which are consumed primarily by the rich. In many cases, the allocation of a specific indirect tax underestimates the degree of progressivity, since it is based on the assumption that all commodities of that type are taxed at the same rate. In allocating the corporate income tax it is assumed that most of it is shifted to consumers, and this probably further underestimates the progressivity.

ROLE OF CONSUMPTION IN-KIND

Table 4 indicates the distribution between cash and non-cash consumption for the rural areas for the five main survey categories with some selected sub-items included for illustrative purposes. About 40% of the total income and 65% of the food and drink is in-kind. Within food and drink, such items as vegetables are 84% in-kind, while items like oils and fats are basically cash items, since they must generally be processed. Under housing, in-kind consumption is important because locally gathered firewood is the main component of fuel. Clothing is practically all cash, while under miscellaneous, only tobacco products have a significant in-kind component.

The allocation of taxes has excluded all in-kind consumption. In some cases, even some of the cash consumption is excluded when the commodity is produced by small-scale rural households or individuals not subject to taxation. The most important items in this category are tobacco and alcoholic products. Locally produced brews sold by individuals escape taxation, unlike bottled beer produced by the national beer company. In rural areas, these local brews are very important, accounting for 95% of the alcoholic consumption, while in urban areas bottled beer is the main alcoholic drink.

The exclusion of in-kind consumption has been partly responsible for the implied progressivity of indirect taxes. The progressivity would be substantially reduced if in-kind consumption were in fact taxed. The impact is most significant in terms of taxes allocated on the basis of consumption of (1) alcoholic products, (2) tobacco products, (3) food products and (4) miscellaneous expenditures. The significance of in-kind income cannot be exactly determined since this would be a hypothetical situation.

As an estimate of the maximum effect of including in-kind consumption, assume that in-kind consumption of these four items is taxed at the same effective rates that cash consumption is presently being taxed, thus yielding greater tax revenues. This assumption depicts the economy as in-kind income becomes monetised and taxed under the present tax structure. For urban and rural areas together, Table 5 compares the effective tax rates on the four commodities when in-kind consumption is excluded from taxation, line E, and if it were included and taxed at present rates, line 1.

In the case of alcoholic products, the tax becomes very regressive compared with the present situation, where it is very progressive. For cigarettes, the tax changes from being moderately progressive to proportional (if the two richest classes are combined). The taxes based on food and miscellaneous expenditures change from being modestly progressive to very regressive.

Since tax revenues increase, these four taxes will now carry greater weight in estimating the total tax burden. Table 6, line labelled "maximum", indicates the effective tax rate for the total of "other taxes", if in-kind consumption were taxed at present rates. At present the other taxes as a whole are quite progressive (Table 3), but if in-kind consumption were taxed the total picture would become mildly regressive.

The effect of including in-kind consumption is probably over-estimated in the above calculations. If in-kind consumption is taxed, consumption of such commodities would fall and tax revenues would not be as great as estimated, so the above four taxes should not be given such large weights in the hypothetical

TABLE 5: EFFECTIVE TAX RATES FOR SPECIFIC PRODUCTS (PERCENTAGE OF INCOME ABSORBED BY TAX IN EACH CLASS)

Product*	Income class† (shillings) 0 — 999	1,000 — 1,999	2,000 — 3,999	4,000 — 7,999	8,000 — 24,999	25,000 +	All
Alcoholic products							
E	0.2	0.2	1.0	2.8	4.6	3.7	1.6
I	9.7	9.5	9.4	7.2	5.1	8.4	8.1
Tobacco products							
E	1.0	1.4	2.1	2.0	2.1	0.8	1.7
I	1.9	1.9	2.2	1.8	2.0	0.7	1.9
Food products							
E	0.5	0.5	0.5	0.6	0.7	0.5	0.5
I	1.8	1.7	1.4	1.2	0.7	0.4	1.3
Miscellaneous Expenditures							
E	3.6	3.8	4.1	4.4	4.5	4.6	4.1
I	11.2	10.8	9.5	8.3	6.3	6.3	9.2

SOURCE: Appendix and Tables 1–3.
*E, In-kind consumption exempt. I, In-kind consumption taxed at same rate as cash purchases.
†The income-classes are on a 1969 basis; in 1971 all limits would be about 20% higher.

TABLE 6: EFFECTIVE TAX RATES FOR TOTAL OTHER TAXES, INCLUDING IN-KIND CONSUMPTION (PERCENTAGE OF INCOME ABSORBED BY TAX IN EACH CLASS)

	Income class* (shillings) 0 — 999	1,000 — 1,999	2,000 — 3,999	4,000 — 7,999	8,000 — 24,999	25,000 +	All
Maximum	28.9	28.6	27.7	24.9	24.3	22.6	26.8
Minimum	13.7	13.8	13.9	13.7	16.2	16.1	14.3

SOURCE: Tables 1–3, Appendix, and own estimates.
*The income distribution is on a 1969 basis; in 1971 all limits would be about 20% higher.
Both rows assume that in-kind consumption is taxed at the same rate as cash purchases, instead of being exempt. "Maximum" assumes present rate of tax for each item, "minimum" assumes rate to be reduced, so as to yield the present revenue for the item.

calculations. For a minimum estimate of the effect of in-kind consumption, an alternative formulation assumes that in-kind consumption is taxed at the same rate as cash purchases, but that the rate is reduced so that total tax revenues are unchanged for each item. This situation greatly underestimates the role of in-kind consumption. The total impact of indirect taxes in terms of effective tax rates would then be as shown in Table 6, line labelled "minimum". Compared with the present rates (Table 3), the direction of change is of course toward less progressivity, but the magnitude of the effect is much less. The two projections may be considered as indicative of the maximum and minimum effects of including in-kind consumption.

These effects show up in terms of the Gini coefficients. Recall that the pre-tax income coefficient is 0.431 and the coefficient after deducting other taxes when in-kind income is not taxed is 0.411. Under the "maximum" hypothesis, when in-kind income is taxed, the coefficient for income minus other taxes is 0.445. Under the "minimum" hypothesis it becomes 0.427. Thus if in-kind income were subject to such taxes, it is likely that inequality would be increased rather than reduced as it is presently.

As indicative of what is likely in the future as the economy becomes more market-oriented and in-kind income decreases in importance, the first projection giving the maximum effects would seem to give a better estimate of the pattern of the incidence. This projection appears to depict what is happening in the richer developing countries, such as those in Latin America, and what has happened in the developed countries where indirect taxes are found to be regressive. Often the bulk of this regressivity is due to taxes on alcoholic and tobacco products, which in this study are progressive due to the exclusion of in-kind consumption. Unless the tax structure and rates are changed along with the monetisation of the economy, the indirect taxes will become more regressive over time. Whether the total tax burden is progressive or regressive would then depend on the relative importance of individual income taxes to indirect taxes.

In summary, the role of in-kind income can drastically change the implied distribution of the tax burden and if ignored can lead to misleading results. In many studies where in-kind consumption is not directly considered, the tax system is probably more progressive than the estimates would indicate.

URBAN-RURAL DISTRIBUTIONS

Table 2 provides rural-urban tax distributions, and Table 3 presents rural and urban effective tax rates. The urban sector accounts for 22% of total income, 47% of total tax revenues, and pays 40% of its income in taxes. The rural sector accounts for 78% of total income, 54% of total tax revenues, and pays 13% of its income in taxes. This disparity is due to several factors. The urban sector pays 79% of the individual income taxes although it accounts for only 22% of total income. Looking at the effective rates for individual income taxes, the urban middle class is taxed more heavily than the rural middle class due to lower tax rates for rural residents, coupled with the exclusion of in-kind income from taxation. For the richest class (25,000+) in-kind income is insignificant, but the urban sector still has a higher effective rate. It is more affected by the progressivity of the East African Income Tax because the average income in this class of 65,000 is much greater than that for the rural sector which is 33,500.

The other taxes present a similar but less severe disparity. The urban sector pays 36% of the other taxes. Effective tax rates are much higher for the urban sector than the rural, except for the richest class, where urban average income is so high that its consumption to income ratio is reduced enough so that the indirect taxes are relatively less of a burden. For the other classes, the higher effective urban rates are due to the exclusion of in-kind income from indirect taxation in rural areas, and the fact that many taxed commodities are basically for urban consumption. The best examples are taxes on electricity, entertainment, motor vehicles and many of the import taxes.

If in-kind consumption were taxed at the same effective rates as cash consumption and tax revenues increased, then the urban sector would be paying 29% of the taxes and the rural sector about 71%. The overall effective tax rates would become 42% and 28% respectively. Under this assumption, the urban sector would be paying about 30 million more and the rural sector about 790 million more. If in-kind consumption were included in allocating taxes, but the total tax revenue constrained to equal the present total revenues, then about 90 million shillings would be transferred from the urban to the rural sector, changing the percentage of taxes paid by the urban sector to 39% and that for the rural sector to 61%. Their overall effective tax rates would become 34% and 15% respectively.

The present tax system has an obvious urban bias. This bias, however, can be justified on equity grounds. Pricing policies that discriminate against agriculture, are ignored in this study.[6] The most significant involve the over-valued exchange rate, which does not reward export crops sufficiently, and government pricing and marketing policies, which result in arbitrarily low prices for agricultural products, in favour of government sponsored marketing organisations and ultimately urban consumers and manufacturers. A prime example is government controls on food prices to pacify urban residents. These factors in total amount to a very large transfer of resources from the rural economy to the urban, but with the limited data available no meaningful estimate can be presented. Although the tax burden may have a heavy urban bias, other pricing policies in the economy discriminate against the rural sector, and the total impact of both tax and pricing policies may be more equitable than either aspect analysed separately.

CONCLUSIONS

This study has made use of an unusually detailed budget survey to determine the distribution of the tax burden in Tanzania. This survey makes possible an item-by-item allocation of indirect taxes according to income class. In addition, the role of in-kind income is explicitly considered. The findings indicate that both direct and indirect taxes are progressive.

It appears that by choosing particular commodities consumed by the rich and excluding in-kind consumption, indirect taxes can be both progressive and urban oriented. Other studies pertaining to developing countries, which conclude that the tax systems are proportional or regressive, may or may not be accurate. Lacking such detailed data as that available for this study, allocation of indirect taxes is often done on a broad basis or by intelligent guesswork, resulting in a more regressive pattern. If in-kind income and consumption are important and not treated properly, this may accentuate the regressivity.

This study is significant in counteracting the prevailing belief that tax systems in developing countries always have little redistributional effect and are, if anything, regressive. The findings are important since the question of the role of the government in redistributing income is becoming prominent with the concern over inequality in developing countries.

The progressivity and urban bias in Tanzania, however, must be viewed cautiously since it is obvious that as in-kind income becomes monetised, and the economy more market-oriented, an unchanged tax structure with a heavy indirect tax base will become less progressive over time. To counteract this tendency, requires adjusting indirect taxes so that commodities consumed by the rich are taxed more heavily. Ultimately, however, significant redistribution in a monetised, market economy requires a comprehensive progressive income tax and/or a wealth tax as the main components, placing less importance on indirect taxes.

APPENDIX

DATA

The *1969 Household Budget Survey* is used to determine the pattern of consumption and income.[7] Its extraordinary scope and importance for this study merit a detailed description. The survey covered mainland Tanzania divided into nine zones. Zones 1–6 covered rural areas, zones 7–8 covered the capital of Dar es Salaam, and zone 9 covered nine smaller towns. Data for zones 7–9 represented the urban areas.

A random sample of households was selected based on the 1967 population census. Households were interviewed monthly (in Dar es Salaam bi-monthly) for one year. In addition, households were asked to keep records covering their consumption during the month, although some found this to be impossible because of illiteracy. Data problems were also accentuated by differences in units of measurement and in some cases items were aggregated instead of being recorded individually. Such problems were most severe in rural areas. Both cash and in-kind consumption were recorded, but there was probably some significant under-reporting of in-kind consumption in rural areas, especially of home produced food items.[8]

Unusually detailed data were recorded, including non-consumption outlays such as savings, loans, and gifts. The sum of these and consumption provides an estimate of household income. Five main categories were used: (1) food and drink, (2) housing, (3) clothing, (4) miscellaneous, and (5) non-consumption outlays. Under food and drink, there are 16 main subcategories such as cereals, vegetables, dairy products and eggs, which cover almost 150 items.

Under housing there are 58 items: fuel, for example, is broken down into charcoal, firewood, kerosene, gas, and electricity. Under miscellaneous, data are available for such items as books, toys, cameras, and cinema charges. In total, the survey covers approximately 430 items.

Although the absolute figures for particular items are in some cases unreliable, the data provide good estimates for the distribution of consumption and income which is the main concern here. For the urban areas, the data are less satisfactory, because interviews were less frequent, and because a large emigration of Asians during the period due to political difficulties in East Africa introduced complications. Since the Asians were concentrated in Dar es Salaam and in the upper income groups, this resulted in fewer households being surveyed in Dar es Salaam than planned, and in the richest income class being under-represented, but data obtained from the East African Community Income Tax Department provide a good estimate of income for the richest class. Survey data on the number of households and the aggregate income for the richest class in the urban sector were adjusted upwards to conform with the Income Tax Department figures. The consumption pattern for this class is assumed to be that of the average for the income level as indicated in the survey. The survey data for the remaining income classes in the urban sector, as well as the entire rural sector are unaffected.

As in most studies concerning developing countries, one must exercise extreme caution in the use and interpretation of data. Compared with other studies of this nature, the Tanzanian data appear to be more detailed and probably more accurate. For analysing the effect of in-kind income in a developing country, more accurate data are probably not possible, since such accuracy is unlikely under poor economic conditions.

A commonsense test for the accuracy of the data is basically whether or not they seem reasonable. The pattern of consumption depicted here agrees with the patterns in other surveys at the aggregate levels, and the in-kind data offer empirical evidence to confirm what many would have guessed.[9] It is also probable that any errors in the estimation of the income distribution and the tax distribution will ordinarily be parallel, since the allocation of taxes generally depends upon the underlying income distribution estimated.[10] If true, errors can be expected to be at least partially offsetting when effective tax rates are calculated for each income bracket; thus the estimated pattern of effective tax rates will be more accurate than either of the two estimates from which it is derived. The focus, therefore, should be on the pattern of effective rates and not the underlying income distribution.

INCIDENCE ASSUMPTIONS

The methodology used here follows that of Musgrave's work with some modifications. His approach has generally been followed by others. The typical assumptions, that there is full shifting of indirect taxes to consumers and that individual income taxes fall fully on wage earners, may be unrealistic. But the nature of price and salary determination in Tanzania's socialistic economy makes these assumptions more plausible than they are for other studies. The government controls or owns almost all the main manufacturing industries and much of the wholesale, retail, and foreign trade activities, and to a large extent it sets most of the prices for processed and imported products. These are the commodities that are generally subject to indirect taxes. When taxes are changed or imposed, it almost always causes a change in the retail price by the same amount, implying that taxes are fully shifted. If taxes are not fully shifted, then the distribution is probably more progressive than indicated here, since producers and owners would share part of the burden. Backward shifting on to labour is unlikely. Pay scales are set by the government for all public sector enterprises, which include most of the main commercial and industrial activities, and these are also closely followed by the private sector.

As far as possible, indirect taxes were broken down into individual items to permit more accurate allocations of the revenue between income-classes. Taxes which could not be allocated directly were classified under the "miscellaneous" category. These are taxes on intermediate commodities, goods which are not specifically itemised in the survey, and items which are not monetarily important enough to merit individual analysis. In allocating taxes based upon the miscellaneous category, the distribution used was based upon total consumption expenditure in each income-class but excluding all consumption in kind. This means that all non-market transactions are ignored, but all cash food and drink consumption is included.

Detailed descriptions of the methods used to allocate the revenue from each separate tax are available from the author, together with figures for the distribution between income-classes for both urban and rural areas.

Given the structure of Tanzania's economy, these assumptions concerning the incidence of indirect taxes seem reasonable. Karageorgas, in an attempt to avoid the usual shifting assumptions, estimated a price function with taxes as a variable, but his findings are not substantially different from the full shifting hypotheses. He found that some indirect taxes are shifted by 100% and the rest by over 80% in Greece. Given the structural differences in the Tanzanian economy, it is likely that the degree of shifting is even greater in Tanzania.

INDIVIDUAL INCOME TAXES

There are two types of individual income taxes.[11] The *personal tax*, which permits no deductions, applies to all income classes except those making less than 170 shillings per month in urban areas and 325 shillings per month in rural areas. The rates are slightly lower for rural areas, but in both cases are mildly progressive up to the middle income levels, then proportional, and finally regressive for incomes above 2,027 shillings per month. The *East African Income Tax* is very progressive, with rates ranging from 12½% to 77½%, but deductions are very liberal. A family of four can exclude up to 19,200 shillings per year. The two taxes yielded about 300 million shillings in 1971, with the personal tax accounting for about 120 million shillings.

In allocating the personal tax by income class, non-cash income was deducted from total income, and the resulting average cash income in each class was increased by 20% to bring it to 1971 levels and then multiplied by the legal tax rates. This provided estimates for the legal burden on each class which totalled 142 million shillings. Since the actual amount collected was 120 million, the estimated amounts were scaled down proportionately for each class so that the total was 120 million. The difference between tax collected and the estimated legal burden, which seems very small under the circumstances, is probably due to evasion, data inaccuracies, and assumptions concerning the distribution of incomes within classes.

The *East African Income Tax* was allocated to income classes based upon cross-classifications provided by the East African Community Income Tax Department. The role of in-kind income is unimportant in this case, since the high exemption levels exclude most of the households with significant in-kind income. Using data on residence and occupation, a rural-urban breakdown is estimated.

CORPORATE INCOME TAX

No conclusive empirical evidence has been presented on the burden of the corporate income tax. Many studies for developing countries have merely assumed that 50% of it is shifted forward to consumers and 50% falls on the owners. The problem in Tanzania is complicated by the fact that many companies are either government owned, or jointly owned by government and either foreigners or private individuals, and pricing policies are difficult to predit. The normal profit-maximising models or other behavioural models of the firm are not particularly relevant for enterprises which are publicly owned in a developing socialist economy like Tanzania.

The method used here assumes that a portion of the tax falls on foreign owners and is excluded from analysis. Of the rest, a portion (10%) due to profits of the state-owned electricity company is allocated according to consumption of electricity. The remaining 90% involves profits of numerous companies, but very significant are the profits of banking institutions, which are publicly owned. For financial services, the demand curve is probably very inelastic. The assumption is that 85% of the remaining corporate income tax is shifted to consumers and is allocated on the basis of the miscellaneous distribution. The other 15% is assumed to fall on the owners and is allocated to the top two classes with 80% of this portion falling on the richest class. The allocation is quite speculative as in most studies, but here the assumptions, if biased, would seem to make the tax more regressive than it really is.

NOTES

1. For example, see Adler (1952), Karageorgas (1973), Lovejoy (1963), McLure (1971, 1974) and Shoup (1950). The evidence is summarised in Bird and De Wulf (1973) and Meerman (1972.)
2. See Musgrave (1951, 1965).
3. These comparisons are hypothetical, since it is likely that in the absence of all taxes the distribution of income would not be the same as the ex.sting distribution gross of taxes.
4. The Gini coefficient has been under question recently; however, these criticisms are not directly relevant for the purpose of this study. As long as the coefficient falls, which it does, when income is transferred from a richer to a poorer person, then it indicates that inequality for a specific distribution is reduced. The significant fall in value in this study contrasts with the findings in other studies, and it is this significant *decrease* compared with other countries that is of importance. Comparison of the *absolute values* of the coefficients across countries to indicate relative degrees of inequality may not be meaningful since the coefficient is sensitive to the distribution of income and the underlying welfare function

assumed. For a summary analysis of this issue, see Sen (1973, chapter 2).
5. McLure (1971, p. 254).
6. This study has ignored export taxes on agricultural products which are impossible to allocate by income class. For 1971 they were not very significant, totalling less than 50 million shillings. In considering the urban-rural burden, these taxes should be included, but the effect is minimal.
7. The findings are summarised in three volumes but only a small portion of the data was published. This study relied on the unpublished computerised tabulations of the Department of Statistics.
8. To the extent that this is true, the tax system is more progressive than calculated, even after adjustments are made for the role of in-kind income.
9. For example, Meerman (1972) in his survey of tax burden studies speculates that if subsistence consumption were explicitly considered, then the implied regressivity might be fallacious.
10. See McLure (1972, p. 67).
11. The two taxes were combined into one income tax in 1974, with no deductions and more progressive rates for the richer classes.

REFERENCES

1. Adler, J. H., *et al*, (1952). *Public Finance and Economic Development in Guatemala*. Stanford University Press.
2. Bird, R. M. and De Wulf, L. (1973). "Taxation and Income Distribution in Latin America: A Critical Review of Empirical Studies," *I.M.F. Staff Papers*, November.
3. East African Income Tax Department (various years), *Annual Report*.
4. East African Customs and Excise Department (various years), *Annual Trade Report*.
5. Karageorgas, D. (1973). "The Distribution of Tax Burden by Income Groups in Greece," *Economic Journal*, June.
6. Lovejoy, R. M. (1963). "The Burden of Jamaican Taxation, 1958." *Social and Economic Studies*.
7. McLure, C. (1971). "The Incidence of Taxation in Colombia." In M. Gillis (ed.), *Fiscal Reform for Colombia*. Harvard University Press.
   —— (1972), "The Incidence of Taxation in West Malaysia." *Malayan Economic Review*, October.
8. Meerman, J. (1972). "Fiscal Incidence in Empirical Studies of Income Distribution in Poor Countries." A.I.D. Discussion Paper No. 25, December.
9. Musgrave, R. A., *et al*. (1951). "Distribution of Tax Payments by Income Groups: A Case Study for 1948." *National Tax Journal*, March.
   —— (1965). "Estimating the Distribution of the Tax Burden." In *Problems of Tax Administration in Latin America*. Johns Hopkins Press.
10. Sen, A. (1973). *On Economic Inequality*. Oxford University Press.
11. Shoup, C. S., *et. al*. (1959). *The Fiscal System of Venezuela: A Report*. Johns Hopkins Press.
12. United Republic of Tanzania (1972). *1969 Household Budget Survey*. Bureau of Statistics.

Section V

International Economic Relations

INTRODUCTION

The long term national goal for Tanzania is to build a socialist and self-reliant economy. Although the precise contribution that international trade and capital can make to a low income and dependent economy remains problematical, it is clear that the goal of self-reliance formulated in the Arusha Declaration does not mean that Tanzania is to seek total disengagement from the international economy.

The readings in this section examine various aspects of Tanzania's relationship to the international economy and how Tanzania might best utilize the limited options open to her. In the first selection Malima relates the essential elements of socialism and self-reliance to a concrete national trade policy. He analyses the macro-economic effects of international trade on the national economy and looks at the positive features of foreign trade and capital investment in facilitating Tanzania's transition to a self-reliant socialist economy.

In the present international economic system, developing countries occupy a vulnerable position vis-a-vis the developed countries. Their dependent economies have few of the policy tools and little of the political leverage available to developed economies. In this context, Nyirabu identifies the importance to Tanzania, as a typical Third World country, of reforms in the international financial and monetary system.

A guiding principle in Tanzania's trade policy is to expand cooperative activities and trading relations with other African nations in an endeavour to overcome their dependency on the industrialized market economies. The East African Community was a working example of this type of cooperation prior to its break-up. In the third reading, Kim places the major problems of the Community in their historical perspective, with an emphasis on the economic and institutional factors that hindered the progress of regional economic integration. As he indicates, the experience of the East African Community provides valuable lessons for future attempts to build regional institutions of economic cooperation.

Historically Tanzania's monetary economy has been geared to the production of agricultural crops and other primary products for export. Primary products account for 70 to 80 percent of total export earnings. Because of this dependency of the economy on primary product exports, particularly agricultural commodities, the formulation of a rational export pricing strategy that is consistent with national development objectives is of paramount importance. In the final reading of this section Helleiner evaluates the economic effects of alternative pricing schemes for Tanzania's agricultural exports. In his recommendations he places particular importance on the determination of an appropriate pricing or taxation policy in relation to each specific policy goal. As such the analysis points to policy conclusions of continuing relevance to Tanzania.

International Trade and The Economic Transformation of Tanzania*

KIGHOMA A. MALIMA

Introduction

The question frequently posed in development literature is whether a less developed country should adopt an 'outward looking' development strategy along comparative advantage lines or an "inward looking" development strategy in accordance with the balanced growth thesis. By no means has this issue been settled one way or the other. Moreover, it has come to be increasingly realized that the choice of a development strategy will very much be influenced by the circumstances of the economy in question. That is, while large countries, for instance, may be tempted to adopt an "inward looking" approach, small countries are more likely to follow an "outward looking" strategy.[1] Nor has the issue been examined in the recent literature in an "either-or" fashion. It is now also recognized that a country must explore unsuspected domestic interdependence, especially between agriculture and manufacturing and within manufacturing itself, that could give development an on-going character. Also, if profitable export opportunities exist, why not take advantage of such a stimulus that could take the country out of stagnation.

As to the question of international trade and the economic transformation of Tanzania, it may be of interest to examine what the theoretical issues really are or have been. As already pointed out, the problem essentially arises because there are economists who think that trade offers the stimulus for growth to a less developed country. This optimistic point of view of international trade can be traced back to the writings of Adam Smith, Ricardo, John Stuart Mill, Alfred Marshall and their successors. According to J. S. Mills, for example, "a country which produces for a larger market than its own can introduce a more extended division of labour, can make greater use of machinery, and is more likely to make inventions and improvements in the process of production."[2]

The emphasis here is on the dynamic benefits from international trade due to specialization and economies of scale that in turn would lead to rapid technical progress. A similar view on the role of international trade in a less developed country can be found in Meier, who feels that "in the future for currently poor countries as in the past for the other countries, foreign trade may operate as an engine of growth transmission—provided there are latent indigenous forces of development that can be released through trade. The gains from trade can facilitate development, but they cannot be a substitute for the developmental forces that must necessarily be created within the domestic economy".[3] Thus, the case for international trade as an engine of growth is made even stronger by emphasizing that if trade does not stimulate growth in a less developed country it must be due to the presence of the domestic forces preventing international trade from accomplishing its proper function.

Not all economists, however, have subscribed to this view of international trade as an engine of growth. There have been a number of economists who have questioned this optimistic view. Most of them do not question that international trade could stimulate growth. What they question, however, is whether this is as certain as is made to appear. That is, it cannot be taken for granted that international trade will necessarily stimulate growth in less developed countries. Nurkse, for example, believed that to "push exports of primary commodities in the face of inelastic and more or less stationary demand would not be a promising line of long-run development".[4] In other words, the contention here is that less developed countries cannot expect that given the current international economic conditions, economic growth would be induced from outside through an expansion of world demand for their exports. Since most of the less developed countries are exporters of primary commodities and most of these commodities face a demand which is income inelastic in the markets of the industrialized countries, the prospects are such that the less developed countries must look for, as a general policy, alternative means of bringing about development of their economies. This skeptical view on the role of trade in today's less developed countries has been shared by Myrdal, Seers, Prebisch, Nurkse and others.[5]

Thus, the debate is still continuing, though perhaps not as vigorously today as it was the case, say, fifteen years ago. This debate has, however, failed to produce fruitful policy recommendations or even to provide worthwhile theoretical insights into the problem of international trade for the less developed countries. Indeed, few of the proponents of growth-cum-international trade theory would make the unqualified recommendation that trade is always beneficial to a less developed country under all circumstances at anytime. For we have cases of countries where trade failed to induce economic development, and where one could not with any sincerity attribute the whole fault only to domestic factors.

On the other hand, no skeptics of an "open economy" policy would seriously contend that international trade is necessarily harmful to the growth of all less developed countries. For again, we have cases of countries that have successfully launched economic developments not just through domestic efforts but also by means of

*ERB paper 70.10.

external resources and cooperation. What the skeptics would probably point out is that the present international trading and payments arrangements have often worked to the detriment of some less developed countries. However by overplaying the case against international trade, the skeptics have probably not been of much help to those less developed countries making earnest efforts to develop their economies. These countries know only too well that they cannot consume all the sisal, coffee, cotton, diamonds, etc., which they produce. Nor can they cut the level of production of these primary products to that of domestic demand without serious social and political consequences, unless sensible alternatives are being offered simultaneously. Furthermore, their industrialization and development programmes, to get off the drawing boards and planning documents, would require the importation, at least at the initial stage, of almost all capital and intermediate goods and some technical skills. In the absence of massive foreign assistance, these items would have to be paid for by foreign exchange resources earned from exports. Rapid economic development will have to go together with expansion of exports, simply because imports will be rising too. What is needed most, therefore, is not an excessive dose of trade as the panacea for all their economic problems. Nor will the less developed countries find consolation in an exaggerated view that trade will strangulate their economies. Their main concern rather should be with the question of what kind of policy measures regarding international trade would be appropriate, given that rapid economic development is their overriding long-term goal.

TRADE AND THE ECONOMY OF TANZANIA

We have so far surveyed some theoretical issues on international trade and development. Admittedly, the survey has been so brief that it could be misleading. But in a study intended for a specific country, generalities may have to be kept to a minimum. In fact, mainly because of the difficulty of appraising such broad generalizations, one has to look at what is happening in a specific country in order to be able to come to meaningful conclusions, albeit cautious ones.

Thus, in this paper we shall analyze the role of international trade in the economic transformation and development of Tanzania. A number of specific questions are relevant for this kind of analysis. For instance, what is the magnitude of international trade in Tanzania, in relation to gross domestic product? How fast have exports and imports been growing over the relevant period? How significant are the pertinent coefficient for exports and imports? What is the balance of payments position and where has it been pointing? What are the implications of all the findings for specific policy measures in terms of export promotion, import substitution, balance of payments problems, foreign borrowing and self-help and general economic transformation? By no means are these the only relevant and leading questions, they are only some, among many, that could be asked to assist in the analysis of the problem at hand.

Let us begin by looking at the magnitude of foreign trade in Tanzania in relation to domestic production, i.e. the value of exports and imports as proportions of total gross domestic product (G.D.P.). Table 1 shows the figures for exports and imports as percentages of gross domestic product for selected years between 1954 and 1970.

TABLE 1: FOREIGN TRADE AS A PERCENTAGE OF GROSS DOMESTIC PRODUCT IN TANZANIA

	1954	1958	1962	1966	1968	1970
Exports	28	28	27	32	27	21
Imports	27	25	24	29	26	24

SOURCES: *Budget Surveys* for 1959/60–1965/66; and *Background to the Budget: An Economic Survey*, 1966/67–1969/70, Government Printer, Dar es Salaam.

TABLE 2: INTERCOUNTRY COMPARISON OF FOREIGN TRADE AS A PERCENTAGE OF GROSS NATIONAL PRODUCT IN 1966 (FOREIGN TRADE: AVERAGE EXPORTS AND IMPORTS

Country	*Percentage*
Zambia	54
Ceylon	50
Belgium-Luxembourg	36
Netherlands	35
Iraq	31
Eire (Ireland)	29
Venezuela	26
Denmark	24
Costa Rica	24
Switzerland	24
Tanzania	24
Kenya	22
Uganda	21
New Zealand	20
Sweden	20
Cuba	19
Canada	18
Egypt	14
U.K.	14
Ghana	10
India	5
U.S.A.	3
U.S.S.R.	2

SOURCES :I.M.F., *International Financial Statistics*, October, 1969 U.N., *Yearbook of National Accounts Statistics*, 1968.

The magnitude of international trade in Tanzania has been around 25 and 30 per cent of gross domestic product. In 1966, for instance, the figures for foreign trade as a proportion of gross domestic product using the computation similar to that employed by Kindleberger[6] were as given in Table 2 for different countries.

Based on these figures, Tanzania is in what we may call the medium category. That is, neither does a large proportion of her economy consist of international trade, as is the case of Zambia and Ceylon, nor can she claim to be self-sufficient in comparison with, say, India, the United States, or the Soviet Union.

How diversified are Tanzania's international trade transactions in terms of exports and imports? In the case of exports, Tanzania is mainly an exporter of primary products, the majority of which are agricultural products with cotton, coffee, sisal and diamonds as the leading commodities. However, the position of these leading export products in relation to total exports has not been stable over the years. Sisal, for instance, accounted for about 30% of total exports in 1954; this proportion had declined to 10% by 1970, as shown in Table 3.

TABLE 3: EXPORT COMMODITY-COMPOSITION IN TANZANIA: PERCENT OF TOTAL EXPORTS

	1954	1958	1962	1966	1968	1970
Cotton	9	17	14	19	17	14
Coffee	27	18	13	17	16	15
Sisal	30	25	31	13	10	10
Diamonds	9	11	11	10	8	10

SOURCES: *Statistical Abstracts*, 1959, 1961, 1962, 1963; and *Background to the Budget: An Economic Survey*, 1968/69–1969/70, Government Printer, Dar es Salaam.

It is clear from the above table that Tanzania's export earnings have not heavily depended upon one commodity. According to D.P. Ghai, Tanganyika has a more diversified export base than most underdeveloped countries.[7] The four most important exports— sisal, cotton, coffee and diamonds—account for 60% to 70% of total domestic exports.

We find, in fact, that Tanzania is nowhere near near being a one-commodity exporter, as is the case with many other less developed countries. In this respect Tanzania may be compared with other countries, again using Kindleberger's method of computation.[8]

TABLE 4: COMMODITY CONCENTRATION BY COUNTRY, 1968

Country	Principal Commodity	% of Total Exports in Single Commodity
Zambia	Copper	94
Venezuela	Petroleum	93
Mauritius (1966)	Sugar	92
Iraq	Petroleum	91
Cuba (1966)	Sugar	83
Chile (1966)	Copper	73
Liberia (1966)	Iron Ore	70
Ceylon	Tea	60
Colombia	Coffee	58
Ghana (1966)	Cocoa	58
Panama	Bananas	58
Ethiopia	Coffee	57
Haiti	Coffee	57
Sudan	Cotton	57
Egypt (1966)	Cotton	54
Uganda	Coffee	53
Burma	Rice	45
Uruguay	Wool	43
Malaysia	Rubber	31
Kenya	Coffee	25
Pakistan	Jute	52
Tanzania	Cotton	18
Taiwan	Plywood	6

SOURCE: I.M.F., *International Financial Statistics*, October 1969; U.N., *Yearbook of International Trade Statistics*, 1967.

From the above figures we can see that Tanzania does not come anywhere close to Sudan, Uganda or Burma which could be considered relatively single commodity exporters.

Unfortunately, the import statistics do not go as far back as those of exports. Tanzania's imports classified by commodity categories are tabulated in Table 5 for the selected years beginning from 1962.

TABLE 5: COMMODITY COMPOSITION IN TANZANIA'S IMPORTS: PERCENT OF TOTAL

	1962	1966	1968	1970
Consumer Goods	48	43	33	30
Intermediate Goods	14	16	16	40
Transport Equipment	9	12	13	8
Capital Goods	26	27	37	21

SOURCE: *Background to the Budget: An Economic Survey*, 1968/69—1969/70, Government Printer, Dar es Salaam.

As the figures indicate, over the eight year period there has been a noticeable decline in imports of consumer goods and an impressive increase in capital and intermediate goods as a percentage of total imports. Tanzania's imports have covered a wide range of items with intermediate goods, capital goods and transport equipment accounting for 50 to 70 per cent of total imports.

Next let us see how significant Tanzania's leading exports are, from the world market point of view? This is particularly important because when it comes to trade policy, a country which is a dominant supplier is likely to employ measures different from those used by a country which is not a dominant supplier of the particular commodity in the world market. The following figures indicate Tanzania's position in this regard:

TABLE 6: TANZANIA'S SHARE IN WORLD EXPORTS

(in thousand metric tons)	1958	1962	1966	1970
Cotton				
Total World Export	2,993	3,383	3,924	3,942
Tanzania's Exports	33	31	86	61
% of Tanzania's share	1.1	0.9	2.1	1.5
Coffee				
Total World Exports	2,194	2,865	3,085	3,267
Tanzania's Exports	26	26	51	45
% of Tanzania's share	1.2	0.9	1.6	1.3
Sisal				
Total World Exports	574	671	578	589
Tanzania's Exports	201	223	117	217
% of Tanzania's share	35.0	33.0	31.0	37.0
(in thousand metric carats)	1960	1962	1966	
Diamond				
World Production	26,100	28,000	26,000	
Tanzania's Production	548	660	828	
% of Tanzania's share	2.1	2.3	3.2	

SOURCES: U.N. Food and Agriculture Organisation, Rome, *Trade Year-books*, 1961, 1967 and 1971; Institute of Geological Sciences, Overseas Division, *Statistical Summary of the Mineral Industry, 1960–65*, H.M. Stationery Office, London, 1967.

It is clear from the scanty data available that except for sisal which accounts for about a third of world exports, the other leading export commodities of Tanzania amount to a trivial proportion of total world exports. On the whole, Tanzania is not a dominant supplier in any of her leading export products.

Now let us turn to the question of how fast Tanzania's exports and imports have been growing over the years. This is again important because it gives an indication of whether international trade has actually helped to promote or hinder economic development in Tanzania. In the words of Professor Lewis, for example, international trade "can stimulate growth if exports are tending to increase faster than imports, or be a brake on growth if imports are tending to increase faster than exports."[9] The following were the rates of growth per year for domestic production, exports and imports during the period 1954–1968:

Annual Growth Rates	1954–68
Total G.D.P.	+5.4%
Monetary G.D.P.	+7.6%
Total Exports	+5.9%
Total Imports	+4.6%

Not only has the growth rate of exports in Tanzania been a little higher than that of total gross domestic product but also exports have grown at a much higher rate than imports (by 1.5%). Thus, if we use Lewis' criterion of whether or not trade is promoting growth in Tanzania, the answer in this case must be positive at least for the period in question.

What has been done so far is to demonstrate that Tanzania's economy is relatively less dependent on international trade and more diversified in the export of commodities than many less developed countries, and also that her balance of payments position seems well under control. The analysis has still concealed one fact which deserves close attention. That is, not only has international trade been a major source of government revenue in Tanzania but also, perhaps for this reason, it has had a significant impact on the growth of gross domestic product and the effectiveness of government economic policy. Fluctuations in export earnings derived from such leading export products as sisal, cotton and coffee have affected the economy as a whole and in particular the monetary activities. In addition, more than 40% of government revenue is derived from the imposition of export and import taxes. Thus, even though exports and imports may account for not more than 30% of total G.D.P., what actually happens in the international trade sector has greatly affected the growth of the Tanzanian economy.

The next problem is thus to quantitatively assess some of the relationships between international trade and the economy of Tanzania. For this purpose use has been made of regression analysis, but first let us introduce the following notations:

Y_1 = Total G.D.P.,
Y_2 = Monetary G.D.P.,
Y_3 = Total G.D.P.–Gross Investment,
Y_4 = Monetary G.D.P.–Gross Investment,
X = Total Exports,
M = Total Imports, and
I = Gross Investment.

The results of our regressions are as follows:

Total G.D.P. on Exports:

$$\begin{array}{llll} \text{(i)} & Y_1 = 587.63 & + 2.95X; & \bar{R}^2 = 0.93. \\ & \quad (268.11) & (0.21) & \\ & \quad [2.192] & [13.688] & \end{array}$$

Monetary G.D.P. on Exports:

$$\begin{array}{llll} \text{(ii)} & Y_2 = -502.87 & + 2.68X; & \bar{R}^2 = 0.95. \\ & \quad (212.41) & = (0.17) & \\ & \quad [-2.367] & [15.721] & \end{array}$$

Imports on Total G.D.P.:

$$\begin{array}{llll} \text{(iii)} & M = 107.38 & + 0.24Y_1; & \bar{R}^2 = 0.86. \\ & \quad (113.41) & (0.17) & \\ & \quad [0.947] & [8.862] & \end{array}$$

Imports on Monetary G.D.P.:

$$\begin{array}{llll} \text{(iv)} & M = 368.15 & + 0.26Y_2; & \bar{R}^2 = 0.87. \\ & \quad (82.18) & (0.028) & \\ & \quad [4.479] & [9.178] & \end{array}$$

Imports on Total G.D.P.–Gross Investment:

$$\begin{array}{lllll} \text{(v)} & M = 90.42 & + 0.019Y_3 & + 0.54I; & \bar{R}^2 = 0.89. \\ & \quad (104.89) & (0.037) & (0.17) & \\ & \quad [0.862] & [5.084] & [3.203] & \end{array}$$

Imports on Monetary G.D.P.–Gross Investment:

$$\begin{array}{lllll} \text{(vi)} & M = 292.89 & + 0.21Y_4 & + 0.571; & \bar{R}^2 = 0.90. \\ & \quad (83.73) & (0.038) & (0.16) & \\ & \quad [3.498] & [5.439] & [3.614] & \end{array}$$

The figures in the parentheses are the standard errors for the respective coefficients, and those in the square brackets are the respective t – statistics. The first two regression results show the presence of significant, positive relations between gross domestic product and exports; also the coefficient of determination, R^2, is in both cases fairly close to one. What this implies indeed is the very important role of exports in Tanzania's economy.

The next two regression results were to show how responsive imports would be to changes in both total G.D.P. and monetary G.D.P. Again, not only are both dM/dY_1 and dM/dY_2 quite high, but the $\bar{R}^2$ for both equations are also highly significant. Thus, the marginal propensity to import for total G.D.P. is 24%, and that for monetary G.D.P. is even slightly higher. For whatever these estimates are worth, it is clear that imports in Tanzania appear to be quite sensitive not only to changes in monetary output but also to changes in total output. Finally for the last two regressions, investment expenditure has been included in the import equations to see if this changes the picture. The results show that not only is dM/dI quite high, 54%, with the rest of total G.D.P. and 57% with the rest of monetary G.D.P., but also the $\bar{R}^2$ is now higher than it was when investment expenditure was excluded. Thus, the relation between imports and domestic production is explained better when investment expenditure is included as an additional independent variable. Moreover, we find that investment expenditure is twice as import-intensive as the rest of the economy of Tanzania. And lastly it is worth pointing out that when investment expenditure is included as an additional independent variable to explain the behaviour of imports, both dM/dY_3 and dM/dY_4 are reduced by five percentage compared with the marginal propensities to import with respect to total G.D.P. and monetary G.D.P.

What the above exercise has in fact shown us is that the importance of international trade for the economic development of Tanzania cannot in any realistic way be underestimated. It has been found, for example, that not only are both total G.D.P. and monetary G.D.P. fairly responsive to changes in exports, but imports also are very sensitive to changes in total and monetary G.D.P., on the one hand, and domestic investment expenditure, on the other.

CONCLUSION

The purpose of this paper was to look at the experience in Tanzania and see what this experience tells us about international trade and economic transformation in Tanzania in the light of the theoretical debate surveyed at the beginning. Perhaps at this point, one can readily agree with Kindleberger that economists "are still a long way from knowing all that needs to be known about the connections running between trade and economic growth. . . . Trade can stimulate growth, when the demand is right abroad and the supply is right at home."[10]

In a sense, merely to put the problem in this way is nothing more than begging the issue, because this conclusion does not take us any step beyond what we in fact already know. In another sense, however, Kindleberger here provides us with a useful reminder. In the first place, for a country like Tanzania, availability of adequate and reliable data is a serious constraint. Comprehensive statistical reporting is a costly undertaking in terms of both financial and manpower resources. A less developed country like Tanzania can only afford what is reasonably within its reach as far as those resources are concerned. Consequently in using such data, either because the coverage is so short timewise, or because their reliability is at best questionable, one must settle, willy nilly, for rather tentative conclusions. Secondly, even if all the needed statistical information were available, there are still a good number of aspects to the whole question of international trade and development that are hardly quantifiable. According to Cairncross, for example, international trade "does much more than provide a market and encourage the growth or reallocation of resources necessary in order to supply it. It also transmits experiences and ideas, changes in attitudes and institutions, and blows up obstacles to further development. . . . The larger the indirect gains the less reliable is the growth of exports as a measure of economic development."[11] Clearly, there is, in fact, more in international trade than just finding markets for domestic goods in excess of demand or meeting domestic demand which is in excess of local production.

Nevertheless, tentative as our findings must be, they provide insights into a number of policy problems. On the question of export promotion, for example, it now becomes obvious that exports could not be neglected without at the same time slowing down the overall economic growth that there is at present. For not only do exports in Tanzania directly influence gross domestic product, but they also do so indirectly by providing foreign exchange needed to pay for the import requirements of the country. Thus, efforts need to be made to diversify exports, not only in terms of products, i.e. primary, semi-manufactured, and manufactured, but also in terms of markets. Trade with neighbouring African countries, for example, ought to be encouraged as much as possible. In connection with the first point of export diversification, Maizels pointed out that development planning in the less developed countries "needs to allow for structural changes in the export sector. The planners need to make careful and objective assessments of the probably future trends in world demand for both present and potential export commodities, so that a rationally based programme of diversification into relatively expanding export lines can be drawn up. To the extent that the dynamic commodities would normally consist of manufactured goods (including semi-manufactures), export diversification also implies industrialization."[12]

As regards the second point of possibilities of trade with neighbouring African countries, Maizels also observed: "Intra-trade between primary-producing countries could be more vigorously expanded; it is at the moment small in relation to their population and national incomes. There is scope for a good deal more trade in food, as well as in semi-processed and manufactured goods; for manufactured goods, this would help to provide the size of market which would make new manufactures economically viable. Finally, there is still undoubtedly scope in expanding trade with centrally planned economies, whose consumption of tropical beverages and other general primary commodities is still very low in relation to population and the level of economic activity."[13] While Maizels was referring to the less developed sterling area countries, in view of the previous analysis they would seem to be just as pertinent for Tanzania.

What also becomes obvious now is the fact that vigorous export promotion and import substitution are not necessarily mutually exclusive—they could in fact reinforce each other. At the beginning and also for sometime after, import substitution, to be viable, requires not just a market but also capital and intermediate goods. In some instances, spare parts and basic raw materials have to be imported as well. Clearly, in such cases growing exports will make it possible not only to import the requisite capital and intermediate goods but also to expand domestic income which in turn provides a market for the import substitutes. In addition, import substitution should be given preference to goods that seem to have high income elasticities so that there would be an opportunity to expand production as incomes rise and to take advantage of economies of large scale production. Thus, a policy of export promotion is clearly a sensible one in view of Tanzania's circumstances, and also a carefully planned and executed import substitution programme ought to be pursued.[14]

In emphasizing that a programme for import substitution in Tanzania ought to be "carefully planned and executed", we come to the point which has been stressed by Hirschman:

"Among the characteristics of import-substitution industrialization, the possibility of proceeding sequentially, in tightly separated stages, because of the availability of imported inputs and machinery, plays, as was shown, a particularly commanding and complex role, direct and indirect, positive and negative. Thus, the sequential or staged character of the process is responsible not only for the case with which it can be brought underway, but also for the lack of training in technological innovation and for the resistance to both backward linkage investments and to exporting that are being encountered. The most important consequence of sequentiality, however, is the fact that it has become possible for industrialization to penetrate into Latin America and elsewhere among the latecomers without requiring the fundamental social and political changes which it wrought among the pioneer industrial countries and also among the earlier group of latecomers."[15]

After pointing out the problems and prospects of proceeding with an import substituting industrialization in stages, Hirschman further notes that "the fact that import-substituting industrialization can be accommodated relatively easily in the existing social and political environment is probably responsible for the widespread disappointment with the process. Industrialization was supposed to change the social order and all it did was to supply manufacturers! Hence one is too ready to read evidence of total failure into any trouble it encounters."[16] All this of course goes to underline the point we have made that import substitution programmes must be carefully planned and executed.

Lastly, does a positive trade policy necessarily contradict the self-reliance spirit that Tanzania considers to be a vital social objective? I do not think it does. Self-reliance could not be jeopardized by a positive attempt to exchange the fruits of one country's efforts with those of another on mutually agreed terms. Nor could it be impaired by a sheer attempt to borrow capital for purposes of development, which in any case have to be paid back from domestic resources. Nor does self-reliance mean that a country ought to refuse genuine foreign assistance that could boost domestic efforts for development to a level higher than could have been realized without such assistance.

Thus we are left with the same observation made in the first section of this paper. If economic development is indeed an important objective, if at this early stage of her development effort Tanzania must rely on imported capital and technical skills and if foreign aid is neither adequate nor available at terms considered consistent with other national political and social objectives, then the role of international trade is vital in the country's development. To say that international trade is important to Tanzania is one thing; to insist that international trade theory, as represented by classical and neo-classical doctrines, is also relevant to a country like Tanzania is another. The two are not necessarily related—they do not have to be in the same package. A theory may not explain a concrete situation properly but it is equally true that an incorrect theory could not make a concrete situation it is trying to explain any less real or important.

NOTES

1. H. B. Chenery, "Comparative Advantage and Development Policy", *American Economic Review*, Vol. II, No. 1, March 1961.
2. J. S. Mill, *Principles of Political Economy*, London: Longman, Green and Sons, 1929. Edited with Introduction by Sir W. J. Ashley, Book 3 Chapter 17, Section 5.
3. G. N. Meier, *International Trade and Development*, New York: Harper and Row, 1964, p. 190.
4. R. Nurkse, *Problems of Capital Formation in Underdeveloped Countries*, Oxford: Blackwell, 1960, p. 22.
5. G. Myrdal, *An International Economy*, New York: Harper and Brothers, 1956; A. R. Nurkse, *Equilibrium and Growthi n the World Economy*, Cambridge: Harvard University Press, 1962; R. Prebisch, "Commercial Policy in Underdeveloped Countries," *American Economic Review*, Vol. 49, No. 2, May 1959; D. Seers, *A Quarterly Journal of Economics*, February 1968, p. 31.
6. C. P. Kindleberger, *Foreign Trade and the National Economy*, New Haven: Yale University Press, 1963, p. 10.
7. D. P. Ghai, "The Growth of Money Incomes in East Africa 1946–1960", *Editions Presence Africaine*, Paris.
8. C. P. Kindleberger, *op. cit.*, p. 31.
9. W. A. Lewis, *Development Planning*, New York: Harper & Row, 1966, p. 38.
10. C. P. Kindleberger, *op. cit.*, pp. 209–11.
11. A. K. Caincross, *Factors in Economic Development*, London: George Allen & Unwin, 1965, p. 203.
12. A. Maizels, *Exports and Economic Growth of Developing Countries*, Cambridge: Cambridge University Press, 1968, p. 21.
13. *Ibid.*, p. 22.
14. B. Van Arkadie, "Import Substitution and Export Promotion as an Aid to Industrialization in East Africa", *East African Economic Review*, December, 1964.
15. A. O. Hirschman, "The Political Economy of Import Substituting Industrialization in Latin America", *Quarterly Journal of Economics*, February 1968, p. 31.
16. *Ibid.*, p. 32.

The International Monetary Fund, the World Bank and the Third World with Special Reference to Tanzania*

C. M. NYIRABU

In examining the roles of the International Monetary Fund (IMF) and the World Bank in the Third World, a preliminary point to note is that because of the differences in the objectives for which each of these institutions was established the IMF'S relationships with the Third World have not been as close and direct as those of the World Bank.

The Fund was established primarily to promote international monetary cooperation and thereby to facilitate the expansion of employment and real income and the development of productive resources in all member countries. The World Bank's Articles of Agreement, on the other hand, emphasized the task of postwar reconstruction and development of territories of members by facilitating capital investment. Thus the operations of the Fund have been mainly concerned with both promotion of orderly exchange arrangements and provision of assistance to countries experiencing balance of payments difficulties.

In contrast, the World Bank's direct concern has been the problem of development. Its investment activities have been based on the following three-tier system: International Development Administration (IDA) loans on soft terms for infrastructural development; government-guaranteed loans for directly productive purposes in the territories of the members; and International Finance Corporation (IFC) loans to private sectors without governmental guarantees.

These two Bretton Woods institutions were created thirty years ago with their structures geared toward meeting the needs of the founding member countries at a time when most Third World countries had not attained political independence. Thus, the constitutions and institutional arrangements of the Bretton Woods system largely reflect the interests of the industrialized countries.

THE WEIGHTED VOTING SYSTEM

Policy-decisions in both institutions are based on a weighted voting system. Each member has to pay its quota to the Fund and its subscription to the Bank, and both of these payments are determined broadly on the basis of a member nation's economic strength. Each country is entitled to 250 votes plus one vote per each 100,000 units of Special Drawing Rights (SDRs) of its quota/subscription. This is hardly expected to affect the distribution of the voting strength in favour of the poorer countries. In both institutions the industrially advanced nations still have overwhelming voting strength. The present voting arrangement in these institutions is largely a reflection of the past economic linkages and dependency relationships between the Third World and the industrialised nations. The fact that the Third World countries comprise over 70% of the total population of all members has been given no weight in the decision-making process of the institutions. This shows, as I have already mentioned, that the policies of these institutions are guided basically by the interests of developed countries. The Third World has rightfully been demanding that this voting principle, which may be appropriate for the corporate sector but not for international institutions, be changed so as to give the developing countries a greater role in decision-making.

PROSPECTS FOR INCREASED SHARE IN DECISION MAKING

In considering the prospect for an increased share of the Third World in decision-making in these financial institutions one has to recognise two basic problems. First, any constitutional change in these two institutions is an extremely lengthy process because it involves not only an agreement on principles through multilateral discussions but also a validation of the agreement by getting the necessary legislation passed by the Parliaments of the member countries. Secondly, and this is even more important, it is not enough to have the constitutions amended. Effort has still to be made to ensure that the major industrialised nations do not circumvent these institutions when making decisions on vital issues. A glance at the monetary history of the past decade will suffice to bring home this point. Whether it was the question of creating a new form of international liquidity, of dismantling the fixed exchange rate system so carefully built throughout the postwar years, of evolving the Central Rate and a system of wider margins or of devising methods to meet the balance of payments problems caused by high prices of oil, the major industrialised nations have decided these and other important issues outside the existing international forums. What is therefore needed, more than the constitutional change, is a *modus operandi* for a fair opportunity, whereby the Third World can effectively influence decision-making in these institutions.

FACILITIES PROVIDED BY THE WORLD BANK AND THE INTERNATIONAL MONETARY FUND

The International Monetary Fund currently provides resources to its members under the following four

*Adopted from a speech given at the University of Dar es Salaam, November 20, 1975.

methods: (a) Normal Tranche Drawings; (b) Compensatory Financing; (c) Buffer Stock Financing; and (d) Extended Facility. It may also be noted that during the period, 1970–1972, the IMF created a new type of international liquid asset called Special Drawing Rights (SDRs). A total of nine billion SDRs were created, and they were distributed to the members who joined the SDR Account Scheme according to their quotas in the Fund. Of this amount the Third World member countries' allocation was SDR 2.3 billion or only 25%. Also when the steep escalation of oil prices in late 1973 caused serious balance of payments problems, the Fund instituted a new facility, called "the oil facility," under which members received loans in amounts related to their annual imports of petroleum and related products. This facility, initially made available for 1974 only, was renewed for 1975. Thereafter, in spite of the continuing need for such a facility, especially by the poorest among the non-oil producing countries, the oil facility was discontinued because of the opposition from certain rich countries. Of these four facilities mentioned above, only Compensatory Financing and Buffer Stock Financing are designed to meet the special problems affecting developing countries. The others are designed for the benefit of every member country, although as would be expected, developing countries have had more frequent occasion to use them because of their persistent balance of payments problems. In terms of total amounts, however, developed countries have been the largest users because of their large drawing rights which are based on quotas.

COMPENSATORY FINANCING

This facility is designed to assist particularly primary commodities producers who suffer shortfalls in their export receipts, provided that these shortfalls are short term in character and attributable to circumstances largely beyond the country's control. Thus failures of export crops due to unfavourable weather or declining prices for primary commodities due to a recession in the importing countries would qualify the exporting country for assistance from the Fund under this facility. The maximum assistance is 75 percent of the quota, which, in the case of Tanzania, is T.Shs. 304 million. Of this amount, the first 50% can be obtained if the IMF is satisfied that the member country will cooperate with the Fund to find appropriate solutions, where required, for its balance of payments difficulties. For a country to obtain the next 25% the Fund must be satisfied that the member has actually been cooperating with it. The advantage of this facility is not only than the criteria applied by the Fund are less stringent than those under the tranche policies but also that the drawings under it are *in addition* to the normal drawings. They are also in addition to the Extended Facility. However a drawback of the present procedure is that resources become available much later than the time the fall in incomes actually takes place. The usefulness of the facility can be improved if the formula used in working out the shortfall is so revised as to enable foreseeable falls in exports to be taken into account. Another suggestion has been to make the facility available when there has been a fall in receipts from export of services due to causes similar to those in the case of commodity exports.

BUFFER STOCK FINANCING

This facility is also intended for the benefit of exporters of primary products. Its object is to enable such members to avoid shortfalls that would result from fluctuations in the prices of their exports. Thus this facility assists members *before* the shortfalls in export receipts occur whereas the Compensatory Financing facility does it *after* they have occurred. The policy has recently been modified so that the drawings under it do not count against the member's reserve (gold tranche) position with the Fund.

PROFITS FROM GOLD SALES AND THE TRUST FUND

One other method by which the IMF has provided limited assistance to developing countries is the sale of $\frac{1}{6}$ of the Fund's gold holdings (i.e. 25 million ounces) in the free market and the use of the receipts of about SDR 2 billion for the benefit of developing countries. Another $\frac{1}{6}$ of the Fund's gold holdings is being returned (restituted) to member countries in proportion to their quotas at the price of SDR 35 to an ounce—in effect most of the benefit from this operation accrues to the rich countries. Since under the existing Articles of Agreement the Fund has no authority to sell gold at any price other than the Fund's official price of SDR 35 to an ounce, a new entity called the Trust Fund has been established to dispose of the gold in the free market and to use the profits for loans on soft terms to the developing countries. According to the Fund's calculations Tanzania is likely to receive about Shs. 77 million (SDR 8 million) from this source. The loan will be for a period of 10 years and will carry an interest rate of 0.5% per annum. In addition to profit from the sale of gold, the Trust Fund may receive finances from voluntary contributions or from loans.

THE LINK

The Third World countries have been demanding that distribution of newly created SDRs should be linked with the needs of developing countries. This is a very good example of how the dominance of the rich countries in decision making in these institutions prevails over the united voice of the Third World countries and affects them adversely. During the course of the recent discussion on international monetary reform this idea has been thoroughly examined and several practical methods of giving effect to it have been suggested. Moreover, the idea has received support from a number of developed countries also. But further progress toward an agreement to establish some kind of link has been held up because of the opposition of a few rich countries, notably, the United States and West Germany.

USE OF THE FUND'S FACILITIES BY TANZANIA

Until the middle of 1974 Tanzania did not use the Fund's resources except SDR 7.8 million out of SDR 14.3 million which had been authorised to us. This use took place over the three year period, 1970–72. During 1973 our balance of payments position improved so rapidly that we were twice included in the Fund's quarterly list of the countries designated to receive SDRs, i.e. the member countries which should sell foreign exchange to others in balance of payments deficits in exchange for SDRs from them. Tanzania also had incurred a repurchase obligation which brought us in the full gold tranche position—i.e. the position in which 25% of our quota was paid into the Fund in convertible currencies.

During 1974 the position reversed dramatically due to the combination of high oil prices, food shortages and world inflation. So far, Tanzania has used the following Fund's resources: (a) gold and first credit tranche drawing rights amounting altogether to SDR 21 million; (b) another SDR 5 million out of its SDR allocation; (c) SDR 31.5 million representing the full amount of the 1974 Oil Facility to which Tanzania was eligible; and (d) SDR 20.6 million representing 50% of the 1975 Oil Facility. That is, Tanzania has used a total of SDRs 78 million or Shs. 754 million of the Fund resources. In addition Tanzania entered into a stand-by agreement with the Fund to draw SDR 10.5 million, representing the 2nd credit tranche, at any time before the end of August 1976.

However, because a serious imbalance in the government budget necessitated borrowing by the government from the banking system far beyond the limits agreed to in the stand-by provision, the agreement became void. Meanwhile the balance of payments difficulties worsened because in addition to high oil prices and food shortages there was a substantial fall in exports caused by both price and output declines. Tanzania, therefore, in early 1976 made a drawing of SDR 21 million (Shs. 202.86 million) from the Compensatory Financing Facility. During early 1977 a drawing of SDR 4.7 Million (Shs. 45.6 million) was made out of the so-called balance of the first credit tranche, and we have also received SDR 2.2 million (Shs. 21.25 million) as the first instalment of the loan from the Trust Fund.

The so-called balance of the first credit tranche is explained as follows. From time to time the quotas of IMF members are revised so as to increase the resources of the Fund and to reflect the changes in the relative positions of the members in international economic transactions. These quota revisions also increase the amounts that can be drawn by Fund members under its various facilities. The revisions become effective only after they are accepted by a 80% voting majority in the Fund. The last such revision, called "the Sixth General Review of Quotas," was agreed in 1976 but has yet to be formally accepted. Since, however, a number of countries were in serious balance of payments difficulties and urgently in need of the Fund's resources, it was decided to increase by 45% the amounts that could be drawn under the various credit tranches before the acceptance and activation of the new quotas. For Tanzania this decision meant that the size of our credit tranches increased from SDR 10.5 million (Shs. 101.43 million) to SDR 15.2 million (Shs. 147.07 million). Since we had already used the initial credit of SDR 10.5 million, a balance of SDR 4.7 million still remains to be drawn.

The drawings in credit tranches and under the three facilities mentioned earlier are repayable within three to five years; those under the Oil Facility have a term of seven years. Also the former carry an interest rate of four to six per cent per annum, the percentage increasing with both the amount and the period for which it is outstanding. The Oil Facility drawings are at rates which average seven per cent per annum. This difference is due to the fact that the credit tranche drawings are from the Fund's normal resources, namely, members' quotas, while for the oil facility the Fund has had to borrow from the oil exporting countries at interest. However, Tanzania, as well as other developing countries in the very low income group, has benefited from an interest subsidy. The rate of interest has been at only 2.71% per annum.

THE FUND AND ORDERLY EXCHANGE RATE ARRANGEMENTS

The establishment of a system of orderly exchange rates is perhaps the single most important objective of the Fund. The examination of its record up until the middle of 1971 gives the impression that the Fund had succeeded in achieving this. The system of fixed par values was universally accepted by the Fund's members. The members departing from the system were urged to come back to it as soon as possible and the majority did so. An important aspect to note was that at the same time there had been considerable efforts to relax exchange controls and an increasing number of countries had attempted to make their currencies convertible. The fixed par value system was of considerable benefit to the Third World because so long as it operated the developing countries were spared the adverse effects of speculation in major currencies on their trade and payments. Third World countries are particularly vulnerable to such speculative practices because they lack adequate safeguarding mechanisms such as a broad based forward exchange market.

The events that have taken place since August 1971, when the US authorities decided to float the dollar, show very clearly that the success achieved by the IMF was not of an enduring character and that the major industrialised nations have the real power to modify the exchange rate system in whatever way suits their convenience. These nations have taken decisions like letting their currencies float without support from their central banks, making adjustments in their rates vis-a-vis each other and evolving arrangements for different versions of the "snake" in forums other than the Fund.

The latest example of this practice of by-passing the Fund was the Six Nation Summit at Rambouillet which reconciled the differences between France and the USA over the type of future exchange system that should be brought into being. This Franco-American compromise became the basis of the revision of one of the most important Articles of Agreement of the Fund, namely, Article IV, which deals with the question of exchange rate systems. The breakdown of the fixed par value system, painstakingly built up by the IMF during the post-war period, led to the discussions which were expected to produce a framework for an international monetary system which would feature stable, yet flexible rates, and enable adjustments to be made in a smooth manner whenever needed. It would control the supply of international liquidity, replacing in the process gold and such reserve currencies as dollars and sterling by the SDR, the supply of which could be adjusted to the requirements of the international economy. It was also expected that the reform would facilitate the transfer of real resources to the Third World countries. The IMF was to be entrusted with the responsibility of ensuring the proper functioning of the new monetary system, and for this purpose the original Articles of Agreements were to be amended accordingly. As this would be the second time the Fund's Articles were to be amended, the Amendment was to be called the Second Amendment.

As the discussions progressed it became clearer that the rich countries had sharp differences of opinion on several important issues and that the only way to get some measure of reform was to make compromises and agree to second best or worse solutions. The result is that the Second Amendment, although a very bulky one, accepts the *fait accompli* by the rich countries, or postpones action on the really important issues. The bulk of the changes are either concerned with minor matters or are of a drafting nature. The former course is adopted in regard to exchange rate systems. The new Article IV leaves it entirely to each country to determine the form of exchange rate regime and obliges each only not to manipulate the exchange rate to prevent balance of payments adjustments. In other important matters like SDRs and control of international liquidity action has been postponed. It is only in respect to the agreement to reduce the role of gold in the international monetary system that some progress has been made. The IMF will no longer have an official price for gold. Nor will the Fund or its members be obliged to use gold in their transactions with each other. The Fund's accounts are already being maintained in terms of the SDR which is valued on the basis of a weighted average of the exchange rates of 16 important currencies in international trade (including the South African rand!). The Fund has begun the process of reducing its stock of gold by selling a part in the market and returning a part to the Fund members. From the standpoint of the developing countries, these reforms provide no assurance that a stable international monetary system will emerge in the near future nor that the Fund's policies will be sufficiently responsive to the needs of the developing countries. The Third World countries are still far from having an effective voice in such vital issues.

THE WORLD BANK AND THE TRANSFER OF RESOURCES TO THE THIRD WORLD COUNTRIES

There are two major aspects about the activities of the World Bank (IBRD); namely, the actual lending operations of the Bank institutions and the Bank's involvement in preparing and presenting the case for a much higher quantum of resource transfer from the developed to the Third World countries. This latter aspect has become much more prominent in recent years, thanks to the vision of its present President, Robert McNamara. As a result of the work done by him and his colleagues we now know how bleak a future awaits the developing countries. The World Bank's Annual Report for 1975 has this to say: "Bank estimates indicate that if developing countries, as a whole, are to reach a growth rate of 6% annually by 1980—a rate necessary for them to attain a reasonable degree of economic and social development—through additional capital inflows alone the amounts required would be massive. Indeed the sums would have to go far beyond any amount likely to be forthcoming—even assuming that economic growth in the industrialised countries is rapid. Such massive additional capital flows are unlikely."

There are three main factors responsible for this pessimism. First, with the exception of Sweden no other OECD countries have been able to meet the target of 0.7% of the GNP to be given as official development assistance, although this target has been accepted in principle by a majority of its members. Secondly, what is even more serious is that the concessionary assistance expected from these countries is likely to drop to 0.24 per cent of their GNPs by 1980 whereas it should really increase to 0.81% if the 6% growth rate target for developing countries is to be achieved. Thirdly, the countries in the OPEC group which have significantly increased their financial assistance to developing countries in recent years have now decided to give high priority to domestic development as long as their per capita incomes remain lower than those of industrialised nations. This means that the non-oil producing Third World countries cannot expect any increase in assistance from this source either—it might even decrease.

OPERATIONS OF THE WORLD BANK GROUP

The lending operations of the World Bank Group have to be viewed in this context. The Group has been trying to accomplish the following objectives: (a) to increase progressively the amount of its lending to the developing countries; (b) to increase the share of the poorest countries in its lendings; and (c) to widen the purposes for which money is lent. Thus over the last 10 years the amount of loans approved has increased in the case of the Bank from $839 million in 1966 to $4,320 million in 1975; and in the case of the IDA, from $284 million to $1,576 million. The increase from 1974 to 1975 amounted to 34% in absolute terms and 25% in real terms for the Bank and 44% and 34%, respectively, for IDA. Again in 1975 agriculture loans accounted for a record 32% of all commitments (it was 22% in fiscal 1974). Lending in the Bank's "traditional" sectors—power, transportation, and telecommunication—continued to decrease as a proportion of the total (29% in fiscal 1975, as compared with 43% in the previous year).

In 1975, more than half of all Bank and IDA operations for agriculture—involving commitments of nearly one billion dollars—were related to rural development projects designed specifically to increase the productivity of the rural poor. In addition, the amount of $80 million was committed to nine educational projects whose primary objective was to increase productive skills in rural areas. An additional $130 million was earmarked to the construction of rural roads. Thus the total amount committed by the Bank and IDA together for rural development in fiscal 1975 exceeded twice the figure committed in fiscal 1974.

The Bank's management has also been considering the possibility of financing buffer stocks of primary commodities with a view to assisting the primary producing countries. Since the Bank can provide medium and long term finance and does not have the kind of limitations that the IMF has in making its resources available, any such scheme by the Bank would be of great benefit to the developing countries.

THE THIRD WINDOW

This is a new facility provided by the World Bank for one year to the very low income countries. Under this facility the interest rate on loans given by the Bank to such countries will be only 4% per annum instead of the normal 8 per cent or so. In order to subsidize the interest costs the Bank has been aided by a few industrialized countries. However, unless this becomes a permanent feature of the Bank's operations the facility is unlikely to be of much benefit to poorer countries such as Tanzania.

TANZANIA AND THE WORLD BANK

By the end of June 1977 Tanzania had been sanctioned loans amounting to $192.5 million from the Bank and credits of $246.6 million from IDA. The Bank loans have been mainly for power and such industries as cashewnut and sugar. In addition they include a programme loan of $30 million received during 1976 as general balance of payments support to import machinery, equipment and raw materials. The IDA credits covered a variety of purposes ranging from the development of infrastructure in rural areas to directly productive activities in tobacco, tea, cotton and sugar industries and a programme loan amounting to US $15 million received during 1977.

CONCLUSION

This paper has examined the experience of the IMF and the World Bank in dealing with the Third World countries on such issues as the Third World participation in decision-making in these institutions, international monetary arrangements and the transfer of real resources. It is quite clear that the Bretton Woods institutions require fundamental reforms. The decision-making structure in these institutions should provide more equitable distribution of voting power. Their membership should be expanded to include the socialist countries to make them truly international. The cries about the "tyranny of the majority" when the majority is only there to be seen (and not even to be heard) are merely a defence mechanism. Even with a revamped IMF and World Bank the question of whether they are needed by the Third World countries must be raised and the answer would depend largely on what the alternatives are. To me the alternatives are two: (a) complete disengagement by the Third World countries from the rest of the world. This can be unilateral or collective. In the case of the latter, one would expect establishment of new institutions owned and controlled by Third World countries; and (b) the dependence on bilateral contracts between developed and Third World countries. These alternatives suffer from certain serious defects, but it is beyond the scope of this discussion to examine them adequately. Therefore, one is tempted to urge a radical reformation of these institutions and greater reliance by all member countries on the World Bank/IMF forums.

Africa's economic cooperation. Finally, the main themes of the paper are summarized in the concluding section with the discussion on their policy implications.

An Appraisal of the East African Economic Integration Scheme: Critical Issues and Possibilities*

KWAN S. KIM

Introduction

From the standpoint of our perceptions of experiences in regional integration today, the approach to integration can be classified basically into two types. They are the conventional approach to integration which is predicated upon the principle of the freeing of trade within the region and the recent growing recognition of the importance to include regional planning of industrial development within the institutional framework of integration to be employed.

For brevity, the former type of strategy will be referred to in this paper as "the trade approach," and the latter referred to as "the planning approach." In reality, the integration institutions in a specific case do not lend themselves sharply to this dichotomy. The actual scheme may stand in between, based on a mixture of the two approaches. For instance, a customs union could include schemes for the development of territorial industries involving some form of planning at supranational levels.[1]

Broadly viewed, the current integration scheme in East Africa can be considered as largely reflecting the features of "the trade approach." It is true that the East African system includes a few features resembling "the planning approach" to integration. By and large, these are an exception to the rule and have not proved very significant in importance.[2] Political conditions in East Africa have not been of the kind that could sustain integration based on a planning scheme for industrial development at the regional level.

The main thesis of this paper is this: given the unique, historically-conditioned, structural imbalance existing in the East African economies, integration through "the trade approach" would not be viable. The implication emerging from this is the need for emphasis on "the planning approach" to integration if the present system is to remain capable of surviving on its own.

The paper begins with a brief examination of the characteristics of economic structure in the East African region as a whole. Then follows a section which relates the East African conditions to the trade-creating and the diverting effects of integration and another that examines the efficacy of the transfer tax system in bringing about regional industrial balance the last part is concerned with the empirical relevance of the analysis in light of the historical evolution of East

STRUCTURAL CHARACTERISTICS IN EAST AFRICA

Much of the present industrial structure of the three East African countries—Kenya, Uganda and Tanzania—has its origin in the colonial policy of the past. There are two distinct, colonially-inherited, structural characteristics common to the three East African economies.

The first characteristic of the region's economy is the general lack of complementaries in the production and industrial structure between the neighbouring countries. Economic policies under colonial administrations had been geared to develop an industrial structure of the region in a manner that strengthened complementaries with the overseas metropolis, and not with the neighbouring countries—a fact that has been revealed by the region's trade pattern. Despite the long existing common market arrangement among the three countries, both the volume and range of the products for intra-regional trade have historically been insignificant in relation to the region's trade with the rest of the world.

Secondly, the economic structure of the East African region is characterized by the disparity in the level of industrialization between the member countries. In addition to the colonial effort for establishing a vertical linkage between the metropolis and the periphery areas, industrial development tended to be concentrated in Kenya during the interwar period, gradually establishing Kenya as a periphery center in relation to its satellite areas of Uganda and Tanzania.[3] Thus, investments tended to flow into Kenya rather than into Uganda and Tanzania. At the time of the independence of the three countries, their economic structure had become increasingly similar rather than complimentary, and at the same time within the framework of the similarly-structured region's economy a marked disparity in the level of industrialization had developed between Kenya and the other two countries.

AN IMPACT ANALYSIS OF INTEGRATION

In these circumstances, it is then expected that the freeing of trade within the territory leads to the deepening of trade imbalance between the more industrialized and the less industrialized partner states. The economically stronger partner will have an edge over the weaker partner in securing the market for competitive export products, and the fact that there are no complementaries in industrial structure between the partners implies denial of the opportunities to the weaker partners of exporting the products that would be complementary with their importables.

The theoretical implications of a lop-sided trade on the trade-creating and trade-diverting effects of the

* ERB Paper 76.7

TRADE-DIVERTING AND-CREATING EFFECTS OF A CUSTOMS UNION

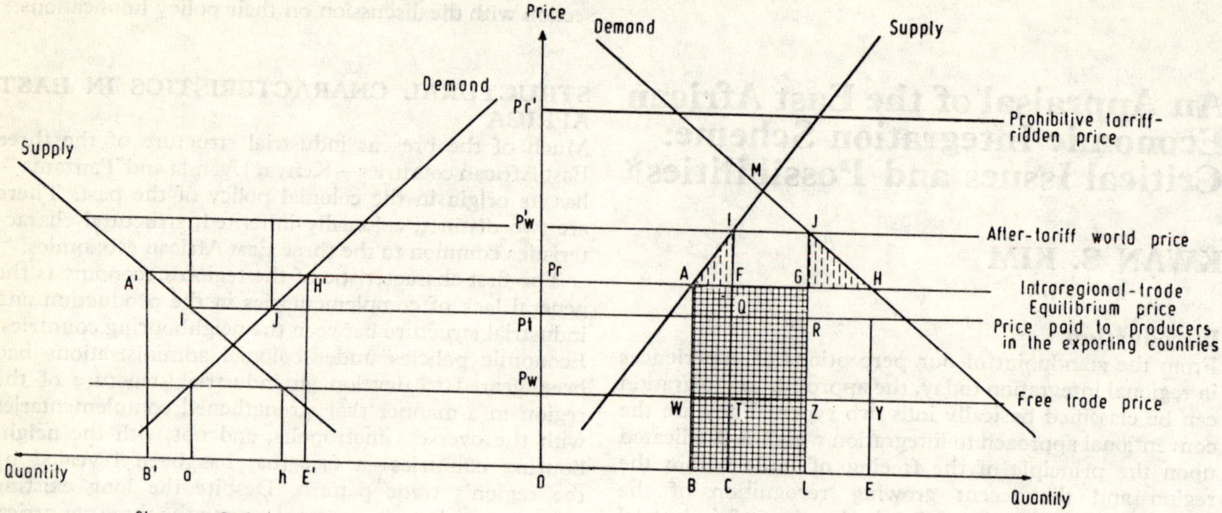

Stronger Portner stote
Fig I(A)

Weoker Portner stote
Fig I(B)

participating countries are illustrated in Figure 1. For illustration, we shall assume that the integration community consists of two countries; the economically stronger partner shown as the exporting country in Figure 1 (A) and the weaker partner as the importing country in Figure 1 (B). Each country by itself is assumed very small in the world market so that the world supply schedule is infinitely elastic at the given price P_w. However, it is reasonable to assume that the price of traded goods between the member countries is affected by the reciprocal demand of each. The autarkic price in the weaker member country is greater than that prevailing in the stronger member, which in turn is assumed to exceed the free trade world price P_w.

Let P_w' be the domestic price prevailing in the importing country after imposition of a tariff on imports from the rest of the world. In Figure 1 (B) the tariff rate on imports from the other member state is shown to be prohibitive prior to formation of a customs union. With the formation of a union between the two countries, the equilibrium price will be set at P_r, determined by the usual market equilibrium condition that the excess supply A'H' from the exporting country is equal to the excess demand AH in the importing country.

As shown elsewhere,[4] the movement to a position of freer trade than prevailed prior to the formation of the customs union gives rise to the expansion of trade, referred to as the trade creating effect, and to the shift of trade from the world's most efficient producer to the most efficient within the union, referred to as the trade-diverting effect. The welfare gain to the importing country through the trade-creating effect is usually represented by two triangle areas AIF and GJH. The former represents the difference between the domestic resource cost of producing quantity BC and the foreign payment for importing the same quantity. It shows a net saving in the use of real resources to the importing country. The latter reveals net increase in the consumer surplus as the difference of the area JLEH, which reflects the marginal gain in the surplus as a result of an increased consumption of LE, and the area GLEH representing the payment for the corresponding consumption of LE. The net welfare effect then depends on the relative magnitude of the trade-creating and trade-diverting effects.[5] The trade-diverting effect is shown by area FTZG Figure 1 (B).

In addition, the liberalization of intra-regional trade in East Africa gives rise to another important macro-economic effect on the importing country. The elimination of internal trade barriers leads to the contraction of import-competing industries in the weaker member. There would be no loss to the importing country if the variable factors such as labour, released from the import-competing industries were to be re-employed in other productive sectors of the economy. Several reasons may be given, however, for believing that such released factors are likely to remain idle in the economically weaker partner states.

First, as previously seen, less industrialized partner states are likely to incur a deficit in the trade with more industrialized states. The expansion of some export industries in the deficit country following the formation of a union will not be sufficient to absorb completely the variable factors released from its import-competing industries. Secondly, as is the case with many developing countries, effective demand in each national market of the East African countries is limited in scope to begin with. Possibilities of an expansion of other productive sectors in the face of increased imports are small. Thirdly, the resources in developing countries are relatively immobile between uses, and adjustments through structural shifts to changed demands are generally sluggish and costly.

Thus, the welfare effects of integration in the context of East Africa, among other things, should include as an additional element the unemployment effect in the economically weaker member state. In Figure 1 (B) this can be shown to be the area FABC when measured in value terms. From the point of view of static analysis, the relevant comparison for evaluating the effect of integration is between the shaded area JGH and the cross-hatched area ABCTZG Figure 1 (B). The net loss incurred on the less industrialized partner following the formation of a customs union is far more than the sheer difference between the trade-diverting and the trade-creating effects, as shown in the traditional analysis.

That there will unequivocally be a loss to the weaker member becomes apparent if we take the case of a common price level and compare at this price level the alternative situations of joining and not joining in the customs union. We may suppose that the external tariff rate has been reduced so that the free-trade world price after a tariff becomes competitive with the regional free trade equilibrium price indicated at P_r in Figure 1 (B). Given these alternatives, the importing country would clearly be better off by staying away from the customs union. For the less industrialized partner state, importables in the quantity of AH could be obtained at price P_w rather than at price P_r in this case. There would then be a net saving of real resources to the importing country by the amount indicated by the area AWYH.

Turning to the economically stronger partner state, it is patently obvious that under the assumption of the existence of unemployment in the less developed country, the principal gain from integration accrues in the form of expanded employment and income. In Figure 1 (A) the expanded income is shown by the area A'B'E'H'. Of course, the gain would be the larger if initially the more developed partner had been a net importer from the rest of the world prior to the formation of a union. In Figure 1 (A) the initial level of imports in a free trade situation is shown by distance ah. Comparison of variations in the consumer and producer surpluses is not attempted here. The income effect of integration overrides other welfare considerations for the exporting member.

THE TRANSFER TAX SYSTEM

Mention must be made as regards the efficacy of the so-called transfer tax scheme envisaged in the 1967 Treaty for Economic Cooperation as a device to safeguard the widening of trade imbalance for less industrialized partner states. The transfer tax is an intra-union tariff that can be imposed by a partner country on imports from other partner states with which it has an overall trade deficit.

According to the Treaty, a transfer tax may be imposed

1. only on imports of manufactures from the partner states with which the importing country has a deficit,
2. only on those goods for which the importing country has a productive capacity sufficient to meet at least 15 per cent of domestic demand, and
3. at the rate not exceeding 50 per cent of the external tariff rate for the same product.

Finally, the transfer tax scheme itself was envisaged for a limited period of eight years with the eventual discontinuation of the system after fifteen years.

In theory, the transfer tax could make the exports of manufactures produced within the union competitive with the overseas imports in the importing country. It can be shown, however, that the effect of the tax is only to alleviate the extent of income losses sustained by the weaker members as a result of the stronger members' seizing the opportunity to supply the wider market following integration.

This can be seen by referring to Figure 1 (B) once again. This time, we may assume that the transfer tax rate is set so that importables from the union's most efficient producer are made competitive with the overseas imports in the importing country. That is, we let the transfer tax rate to be determined so that $P_r(1+t) = P_w'$, the after-tariff overseas import price.

As already shown previously except in the reverse order this time, the movement from initial position P_r to P_w' through imposition of the transfer tax rate t entails benefits to the importing country in the form of expanded employment and income by area ABCI. The same protective effect can be had if the importing country opts to stay away from the union and continues to import from the rest of the world. An important difference, however, is that with the option for the latter there will result in a net saving of real resources equal to area QTZR in the importing country. Alternatively viewed, if imports are to be obtained from the union's most efficient producer, the price paid to the foreign producer remains at P_t, which is higher than P_w—the price charged by the world's most efficient producer. The aforementioned area then represents the trade-diverting effect resulting from a movement from the world's most efficient producer to the union's most efficient producer.

The main objective of the discussion in the preceding section was to prove that the economically weaker partner state would be made worse off by participating in an integration scheme stressing trade-liberalization. It is now clear that incorporation of the transfer tax device into the scheme does not affect the validity of the above proposition.

From a longer run perspective, the transfer tax scheme is not an effective method for achieving significant expansion in intra-regional trade. The tax is designed merely to protect domestic import-competing industries, and will not in itself foster development of new industries along complementary lines within the framework of the region's economy. It would seem more economically justifiable for promoting trade cooperation in the future to encourage complementary industrial development in the less industrialized partner countries.

Furthermore, since the transfer tax is to be removed in the future, possibilities exist that competition from more efficient producers in the partner countries eliminate the hitherto protected industries. Either substantial capital investment will have been wasted, or further attempts to restrict trade will likely follow. In these respects, the transfer tax scheme could lead to serious distortions in conditions of production within the integration region.

THE EAST AFRICAN EXPERIENCE IN INTEGRATION

Much of the discussion, so far, has been concerned with the explanation of structural characteristics of the region's economy and the implications of an exclusive reliance on the 'trade approach" for effecting integration. At this point, a summary review of the historical evolution of integration in East Africa will be appropriate.

Historically under the British rule, the markets of the three states had long been well integrated and linked with each other. The East African Common Market institutions, however, lacked the formulation of concrete planning for regional industrial development. In this sense, the colonial scheme for regional integration is conceived as largely reflecting "the trade approach" to integration.

The experience of the East African Common Market provides a vivid illustration of the difficulty of adopting the "trade approach" in effecting integration. Since the inception of the common market, the better industrialized Kenya has been able to continue to maintain surpluses in its trade with the less industrialized Uganda and Tanzania. A distinct trend towards trade imbalance has been established in the intraregional trade. During the early sixties Kenya's exports of manufactures to Uganda and Tanzania were on the average four to five times as large as its imports from them.

In this connection, it is interesting to note the particular pattern of trade that emerged. All the three countries had deficits in their trade with the rest of the world, but the freeing of intra-regional trade enabled Kenya to increase its exports of manufactures intra-regionally without a comparable impact on its imports from Uganda and Tanzania. Kenya's imports of non-manufactures from Uganda and Tanzania were relatively small to begin with. The trade in agricultural products had been severely restricted by Kenya's farm price support policy and its use of quantitative controls on imports. Thus, for Kenya the overall deficit in its trade outside has been partly offset by a surplus in its intra-regional trade.

Within the framework of the common market institutions, there had been a succession of measures aimed at alleviating the problem of trade imbalance. For instance, under the industrial licensing system, the allocation of new industries to each member country, as conceived in the original scheme, was to be determined by agreement with the granting of an exclusive license to an enterprise in a member country for operation in

TABLE 1: INTER-STATE TRADE IN TRANSFER-TAXED GOODS

A. Tanzania's Imports From Kenya and Uganda

(Shs. 1,000)

	1969	1970	1971	1972	1973
Total Imports of Transfer-taxed Goods from Kenya	49,769	56,596	42,235	43,753	42,213
Total Imports of Transfer-taxed Goods from Uganda	3,719	3,292	1,609	236	—
Total of (1) and (2)	53,488	59,888	43,844	43,989	42,213
Total Imports from Kenya	256,957	295,042	294,860	352,721	337,076
Total Imports from Uganda	34,261	39,893	16,329	5,826	2,246
Total of (5) and (6)	291,218	334,935	311,189	358,547	339,322
Transfer-taxed Goods as per cent of Total Imports	18.36	17.88	14.08	12.25	12.44

B. Uganda's imports from Kenya

(Shs. 1,000)

Total Imports of Transfer-Taxed Goods from Kenya	20,352	42,184	44,461	24,651	58,717
Total Imports from Kenya	318,985	333,954	382,998	330,146	437,953
Transfer-taxed Goods as per cent of Total Imports	6.38	12.63	11.6	7.48	13.4

SOURCE: Economic and Statistical Review, September, 1974.

the entire region. The decision on the location of new industries, however, has been left to the investor, and in practice Kenya has ended up with the major share of new industries under this arrangement. The financial compensation scheme instituted on the recommendation of the Raisman Committee in 1961 provided for the creation of a common distributable fund made up of each country's income and profit tax revenue and of

TABLE 2: TRANSFER TAX COLLECTION (Shs. 1,000)

	1970/1971	1971/1972	1972/1973
Tanzania	10,625	8,920	8,656
Uganda	7,626	7128,	6,962

SOURCE: Ibid.

customs revenue. A half of the fund was to be used of the operation of the common services, and the other half to be redistributed to the member countries The scheme had a limited success in alleviating financial burdens of the less developed partners, and had apparently little to do with the basic issue of trade imbalance.

The growing disparity in the intra-regional share of integration benefits has become a major source of friction among the partner states in the post-independence period.[6] The 1967 Treaty for Economic Cooperation was a new attempt to revitalize the regional integration institutions. The three governments agreed to establish the Economic Community of East Africa, which would aim at continuing a common market, and in addition would provide a framework for the coordination of economic policies and programmes. The Treaty also included provisions for the continuation of the common services (airlines, harbours, communications and research and development) to be administered by the newly established transnational corporations.

The novel features of the Treaty, however, were the creation of the transfer tax scheme and the establishment of a jointly-financed East African Development Bank. The limited effectiveness of the transfer tax system as a protective device for less industrialized partner states has already been pointed out. Analysis of the recent data for intra-regional trade flows largely confirms this conclusion. During the 1969–73 period, volumes of transfer-taxed goods as percentage of total imports on the average accounted for not more than 15 per cent for Tanzania and about 10 per cent for Uganda (see Table 1).

The Development Bank was established to deal with the channeling of jointly financed investment loans for development projects. With a view to redress the existing structural imbalance, priorities would be given to investment in less developed partner states. The financial resources of the Bank, so far, appear to have been too limited in size to be of any significance. Moreover, the Bank is only to partially finance viable projects. Although in principle the Bank's investible funds are to be allocated more favourably to less developed partners, there has been no clear evidence that this has happened. As shown in Table 4, the proportion of the Bank's investment funds actually disbursed to Kenya has for the selected years 1971–73 been far greater than that of total funds stipulated for

TABLE 3: KENYA'S EXTERNAL AND EAST AFRICAN TRADE

Unit: K '000

	Visible Trade Balance in Trade with			Volume of Trade in Relation to		Per cent of East Africa in Total Volume
	East Africa (Tanzania)	(Uganda)	External World	East Africa	External World	(%)
1964	9,189	5,337	−23,046	37,234	130,144	22
1965	9,517	8,204	−36,995	41,131	141,079	22
1966	9,475	8,302	−50,088	40,024	174,704	18
1967	8,094	4,631	−47,007	39,631	166,185	19
1968	9,377	4,615	−51,829	38,676	177,699	17
1969	8,830	8,146	−48,440	40,618	185,160	17
1970	8,814	6,650	−64,575	47,436	219,477	16
1971	6,811	11,124	−105,763	49,850	262,447	15
1972	10,399	8,924	−82,166	46,264	273,075	14
1973	9,226	17,229	−76,864	51,047	334,723	13

SOUSCE: East African Customs & Excise Department, *Annual Trade Reports.*
Note 1. Negative figures imply a deficit in the trade balance.
2. The figures for exports include Domestic Exports and Re-exports.

TABLE 4: EAST AFRICAN DEVELOPMENT BANK: DISTRIBUTION OF APPROVED AND DISBURSED INVESTMENT FUNDS (IN PERCENTAGE)

As of	December 31, 70		December 31, 71		February 28, 73	
	Approved	Disbursed	Approved	Disbursed	Approved	Disbursed
Kenya	40	53	39	41	22	36
Tanzania	42	12	44	35	38	44
Uganda	18	35	17	24	40	20
Total (million sh.)	76	21.2	90.4	58.1	210.3	90.2

SOURCE: East African Development Bank, *Annual Report*.

allocation to Kenya.[7] Most importantly, the Development Bank itself has been incapacitated in its role to stimulate the growth of the Community's industrial sector by the sheer lack of coordination and implementation of the plans for regional industrialization. Implementation of major projects would require a joint financing and an integrated regional market of the three States. The present integration scheme includes no provisions for cooperative planning for industrialization. Thus, the East African Community institutions do not basically differ from the previous Common Market system in that the *primium mobile* of integration is liberalization of intra-regional trade.

Casual observations on the region's trade pattern reveal an evidence that the present integration scheme has led to an unbalanced distribution of the benefits from an integrated market. As indicated in Table 3, the process of a polarization in trade balance between Kenya and its partners has continued for the entire period 1964–1973. The historical pattern of Kenya's deficit in trade with the rest of the world remains unchanged. In terms of the volume of trade, we observe a trend towards the diminution of the importance of intra-regional trade relative to external trade. The share of the intra-regional trade has been gradually diminishing from 22 per cent high in 1964–1965 to 13 per cent low in 1973.

It seems that the present scheme is not designed to directly confront the basic issue of the less developed partners' inability to meet each other's import requirements for diversified capital and manufactured goods. The weakening of the intra-regional trade link can be perhaps best explained in this context.

After 1970, erosion of the intra-regional trade has taken the form of a series of trade restrictive measures adopted first by the less industrialized partners and to a less degree later by Kenya itself.[8] Although the restrictions on imports arose in the particular circumstances of balance-of-payments difficulties of the East African countries in connection with the global inflation and oil crisis in the early 1970s, it is nevertheless significant to note that the restrictions were equally applied to imports from other partner states.

CO-ORDINATED PLANS FOR INDUSTRIALIZATION

If the main objective of regional integration is to mutually assist in industrialization of each member country, it is essential that appropriate measures for securing a balanced distribution of the integration benefits be incorporated into the framework of the institutions to be employed. The choice of the mode of such framework should, of course, hinge upon the socio-economic context of the particular region. Given the prevalence of the colonially-instituted structural characteristics of the East African economies, it has been maintained on both theoretical and empirical grounds that the approach based on the cooperation through trade would not be effective in bringing about an equitable distribution of benefits from an integrated market.

In this connection, it is well to note that at the root of disunity in economic cooperation are also the differences in ideologies and approaches to development between the partner states. Since the inception of the East African Community, the predominant scenario of East African cooperation has been nationalistic conflicts and the overriding Community interests. In particular, the ideological difference in the economic system appears to have profound implications for regional integration. In Kenya, and to a less extent in Uganda, decisions for investment are largely left in the hands of private investors with foreign firms still accounting for a significant portion of investments. There are many problems to be overcome, particularly in relation to the dominant position of foreign capital. Policies regarding restrictions and control of foreign corporates still have to be worked out for agreement among the partner states. So long as the operation of foreign corporates is to be viewed as being guided by motives other than overcoming the underdevelopment of the host countries, Tanzania would be in a difficult position to welcome trade liberalization policies. For instance, investments in Kenya for the most part have tended to be concentrated in consumer goods industries frequently oriented toward higher income classes. Clearly, such a pattern of trade that emerges from the dictates of market forces runs contrary to the avowed Tanzanian policy to prohibit luxury goods imports. Much of the decrease in the share of Tanzania's imports from her partner states after 1967 can be explained in this light.

Rejecting the trade-based approach to integration as a viable strategy, the alternative left open to East African countries then is the planning approach to integration.[9] That is, if an integration scheme is to remain viable in the region, it must aim at forcefully attaining the objective of complementary and reasonably balanced industrial development for the region as a whole. A suggested line of strategy to achieve this goal is the adoption of cooperative planning for industrialization at a regional level with a view to promote export diversification and to redress industrial imbalances existing between the member states. Co-ordinated plans for industrialization would also call for the restructuring of the entire pattern of regional trade to support expanding regional industries. It would be important that such regional industries be given benefits of a region-wide market by a specific form of guarantee from each Government. Only in this way would future cooperation in strengthening the trade link in East Africa be possible.

The issue of the benefits-distribution aside, mention must also be made of the economies-of-scale argument for regional industrialization. The argument is that for certain categories of industries in developing countries, economies of scale and greater efficiency can be achieved only through a coordinated planning for industrial development at a regional level. In view of the limited size of each national market, unco-ordinated efforts for industrialization would lead to a proliferation of facilities in production with the resulting excess capacities in industries.[10]

A study by A. Seidman[11] exhibits a list of industries in East Africa which are considered as falling within the category of industries for which the minimum-sized market for an optimum sized project would require heavy capital outlay and an integrated regional market for their products. These industries are steel and iron, chemicals, phosphate and nitrogenous fertilizers, coal and tar, pharmaceuticals, cement, machinery, glass plates, engineering and other manufactures, etc. The allocation of some of these industries to each partner state had already been provided in the abortive 1964 Kampala Agreement.

The correction of the structural distortions to effectively exploit economies of large scale integration is not, of course, all that there is to support the argument for regional industrialization. Like in any other economic issues, the concept of integration should be understood in as much qualitative status as quantitative. The political and social dimensions existing within a member state as well as between the member states must be carefully explored before a plan is considered for implementation. It is beyond the scope of this paper to get into the details of a new blueprint. The modest aim of this paper was to demonstrate the critical limitations of the orthodox theory of integration-cum-trade in the context of the formerly colonized Third World countries where the structural contradictions inherited from Western colonialism have been manifest in the form of structural imbalances within a regional community.

NOTES

1. An example of this is Central American integration (CACM). In addition to provisions for liberalization of trade, the Agreement on the Regime for Central American Integration Industries provides that the plants which are accorded the status of "integration industry" would receive the *exclusive* privilege of free access to the entire regional market (consisting of five countries) for their products.
2. For instance, the operation of the East African Development Bank and the East African Community corporations dealing with various common services for the region is certainly based on an effective coordination at a supranational level. Much will be said later about the limited role of the Development Bank. It suffices to observe here that the purposes of establishing the Community Corporations had little to do with the aim for an industrial development at the regional level. Moreover, the sharing of the regional corporations' activities has been considered to be uneven between the member states. Despite the decentralization measures that led to relocation of the headquarters of some corporations from Nairobi, major activities have still been concentrated in Kenya. For the data on the locational pattern of expenditures by the Community corporations, see *Common Market & Economic Affairs*, 1972/73.
3. One of the major factors explaining the heavy concentration on Kenya for industrial development during the interwar period was the decisive role played by a well-established pressure group in England. A similar pattern of "periphery-center industrialization" can be found in the case of Rhodesia and South Africa. See Giovanni Arrighi, *The Political Economy of Rhodesia*, Mouton, The Hague, 1967.
4. See H. G. Johnson, "The Economic Theory of Customs Union," in *Money Trade and Economic Growth*, Harvard Press, 1962; Leamer and Stern, *Quantitative International Economics*, Allyn & Bacon, 1970, 184–196.
5. As may be well-known, various criticisms may be directed against use of this kind of apparatus. For lack of an alternative apparatus, the framework would nevertheless be useful as a first approximation of the welfare effect.
6. The question of benefits incidence has been discussed in this paper on a national level. It must be noted that in order to analyse the incidence of benefits internal to an economy one needs to distinguish between domestic product and national income measures. This distinction is crucial to the analysis of Kenyan data in view of the dominance of foreign capital in the Kenyan economy. For details of influences of foreign capital in Kenya, see A Working Party, Department of Christian Education, *Who Controls Industry in Kenya*, Nairobi, E. African Publishing House, 1969.
7. This may simply be attributable to the fact that more viable projects have been undertaken in Kenya with a better investment climate.
8. The restrictive measures largely included various devices of exchange controls for restricting imports. In Uganda, importers were required to maintain deposits with the Bank of Uganda for six months for imports from outside and for three months for imports from its partner states. Importers were prohibited for the

products found available locally. In Tanzania, different categories of imports were subject to different national ceiling levels following an import plan designed to be consistent with the national planning objectives. The import licensing scheme was to be enforced by the Bank of Tanzania with the restrictions equally applied to imports from the East African partner states. Restrictive measures adopted by Kenya were less severe. Imports from the partner states in general were not subject to requirements for import-licensing. The State Trading agencies of the three countries were known as having given preferences to domestic suppliers over rival suppliers in the partner states in their purchasing decisions Administrative delay and inefficiency of state enterprises experienced by importers also generally discouraged imports from abroad.

9. It has frequently been argued that an integration scheme would be viable only when all the member states subscribe to a common ideology. Given the underlying political reality in East Africa, however, the best that can be hoped for would be an attempt to agree upon the need to restructure the community institutions along the lines of planned industrialization at a regional level.

10. At the moment, each partner state draws up plans for industrialization separately with little or no consultation with each other. Such potentially regional industries as cement, fertilizers, steel, tires have been developed separately in each state, in many instances operating below an optimum capacity.

11. A. Seidman, "Comparative Industrial Strategies in East Africa," ERB Paper No. 69.21.

Agricultural Export Pricing Strategy for Tanzania*

G. K. HELLEINER

Introduction

It is a commonplace that the East African economy is based primarily upon agriculture. About 60% of gross domestic product is earned in the agricultural sector, and so we find 80% of total employment and 80% of total export earnings originating there. Though the development plans seek to move the economies away from this extreme degree of dependence upon agriculture, even so, substantial proportions of their capital programmes are earmarked for agriculture. Again, a large proportion of the revenues drawn from the economy for the use of the government originates in the agricultural sector making it essential for governments, in these circumstances, to have a clear, consistent overview of their policies in the agricultural sector.

In an attempt to arrive at an agricultural development plan the greatest emphasis has conventionally been placed upon the problem of allocating government efforts and expenditure between various approaches, various crops and various regions. This is an important aspect of governmental efforts in the field of agriculture—one of which we still know too little and in which our techniques are still sadly deficient. But the planning and execution of government agricultural development schemes and services is not the whole picture. Regardless of whether it is a planned, free, or mixed economy the outcome in the rural sector is also bound to be greatly affected by the level and structure of agricultural prices. In most underdeveloped areas, and East Africa is no exception, the government exerts considerable influence upon these prices.

At the very least, agricultural price policy must be consistent with the rest of the agricultural programme of the government. Stated more positively, pricing policy can be a useful instrument in the pursuit of agricultural policy targets. Evidence continues to accumulate to the effect that peasant producers in Asia and Africa are, contrary to the earlier views, normally price-responsive. In certain circumstances, the responses are muted as a result of socio-cultural forces, middlemen's operations, transport difficulties, etc. but the responses are there. One cannot ignore them in the formulation and implementation of agricultural plans; indeed, one should seek to employ them.

This paper addresses itself to the problems of agricultural pricing and taxation in Tanzania. The discussion will be confined to the pricing of agricultural exportables, since the problems of domestic foodstuff (particularly maize and rice) price policy involve a variety of extra issues which I would prefer to avoid. Since the establishment of domestic producer prices for exports is essentially a matter of deciding as to the amount by which they should differ from world prices, this discussion might equally be described as one of agricultural taxation policy.[1]

ASPECTS OF AGRICULTURAL TAX-PRICE STRUCTURE

Taxes upon the sales of cash crops have generally not found favour with the economist's profession because of their tendency to encourage movement into leisure, untaxed agricultural (primary subsistence) production, urban unemployment, services, petty trade, etc. and their frequent inequity. Still, because of the difficulty of collecting direct taxes from the rural sector, and the fear that there are limits to the increases in import duties which are possible without setting off urban wage pressures and price inflation, levies on agricultural exports will continue to be an important source of government revenues.

Given this fact, it becomes the task of the economist to devise a tax-price system which minimizes the economic costs of tax-induced resource misallocation. More positively, his task is to ensure that the incentives in the *structure*, as opposed to the level, of these taxes are working in the appropriate direction. Since elasticities are undoubtedly greater as between alternative crops than they are between agricultural cash crop production and the other pursuits mentioned above, the *structure* of taxes and prices may well be more important than their levels.

The most important considerations in such policies are:[2]

a) effects upon national income,
b) effects upon foreign exchange earnings,
c) effects upon export processing possibilities, and
d) equity or neutrality.

AN ILLUSTRATIVE DIGRESSION

It may be worth illustrating the fact that differing objectives may give the policy maker very different pricing policy conclusions with a simple example drawn from the recent literature on commodity schemes. In Harry Johnson's recent study of commodity issues he criticises the *simplistic* approach to commodity policy which seeks as its objective the maximization of foreign exchange earnings and neglects the resource costs of the commodity's production.[3] He offers recommendations based instead upon the objective of income maximization. It is possible, however, despite its strictures, for

*Edited version of ERB Paper 66.6.

a government quite consciously to pursue the objective of foreign exchange earnings maximization. I have elsewhere suggested the possibility of a third commodity policy objective—that of the maximization of government revenues.[4] One can easily think of others. But let us, for the sake of illustration, stick to only these three.

In Figure 1, AR is the world demand curve facing the country which is to make the commodity (domestic) pricing decision. The marginal revenue curve based on this world demand is shown as MR. The supply curve which is also the economy's marginal cost curve, is labelled S (= MC). In order to maximize foreign exchange earnings one would want to produce to that level at which marginal revenue falls to zero. Clearly, the producer price should be set at OA (= CD). This involves a subsidy to the producer; he is paid a price higher than that which his output will earn on the world market, OB (= CE), because of the high value imputed by the government to the foreign exchange which his produce earns.

If, however, income maximization is the objective, the marginal revenue must be equated with the marginal cost to the economy, as shown by the supply curve. The domestic producer price should then be set at a lower level, OF (= HJ). The world price earned per unit when this price is paid is OG (= KH). This is higher as a result of the reduced output coupled with the country's market power.

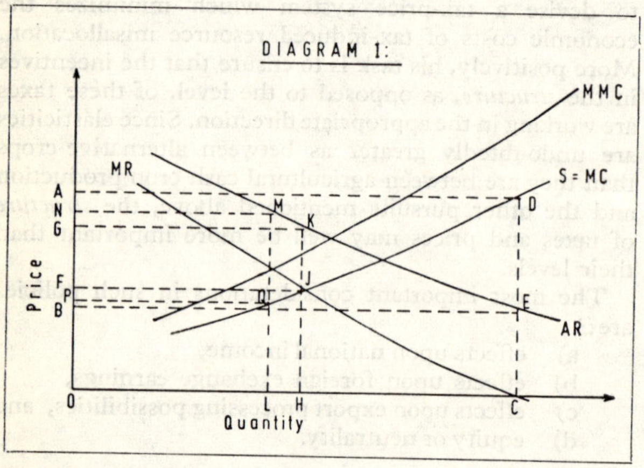

Now suppose that the policy objective is to maximize government revenues; then the marginal revenue to the government (= MR) must be equated with the marginal cost to the government which now acts as a monopsonist as well as a monopolist. The curve labelled MMC is a curve marginal to the supply curve which shows the marginal cost to the government at each price and output. Tax revenues will be maximized, through the exertion of maximum monopsony power by paying a still lower price, OP (=LQ), to the producer. At this producer price, the nation will earn a still. higher price, ON (= LM), on the world market.

Thus the pursuit of three different policy objectives, based on the needs of foreign exchange, income, and tax revenues, clearly results in three quite different pricing policies. In our cases, the need for tax revenues is assumed to have already determined the aggregate tax burden to be borne by agriculture. Thus it is foreign exchange and income effects upon which we should focus in determining tax-price structure. And Johnson's case for using the latter rather than the former seems to be correct for East Africa today.

THE SPECIAL CASE OF COFFEE

The world demand schedule facing an individual coffee producer like Tanzania today is a discontinuous one, a sharp break occurring once sales volume (or production) reaches the country's ICO quota. The marginal revenue curve, shown in Figure 2, is also discontinuous. The domestic producer price, shown by line pp, is unaffected by this discontinuity. So, of course, is the economy's supply curves.

The Tanzanian situation is represented by the point A, at which output is OB although the quota is only OC[5]. Domestic producers are paid OD. Sales on quota markets earn the world price OE, on nonquota markets OF. Clearly, marginal costs to the society are not equated with marginal revenue at the ICO quota output; if national income maximization is the objective it is not being attained. Also, if foreign exchange earnings are the objective, higher than quota sales are called for.

Can this policy be rationalised? If the land at present

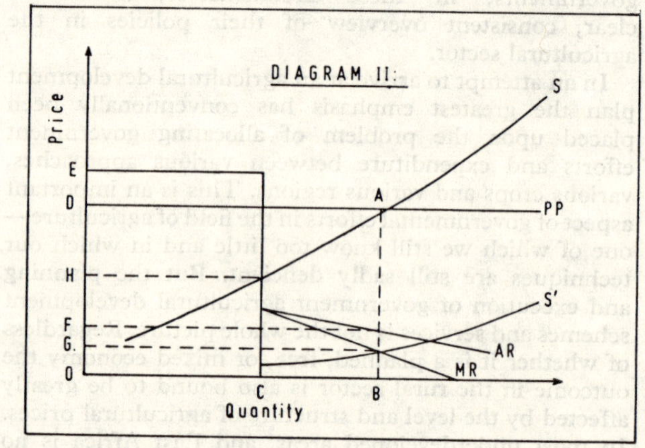

under coffee has no or limited alternative uses the society's marginal cost curve (the supply curve) will be much lower than the one shown—say S'. If the true supply curve is S' OB is the appropriate level of production. But then, of course, the producer price should only be OG, much less than the actual producer price. Only if the marginal cost to society shown by S' is lower than the private supply curve of the producer, S, can the present producer price policy achieve the postulated income maximization. There is no reason of which I am aware for believing this to be the case.

Subsidies to encourage total sales volume greater than the ICO quota might be justified by the desire to raise (even maximize) foreign exchange earnings. But this does not seem to be consistent with the taxes which are everywhere else incurred on export production. Nor can one easily find alternative rationalizations of the present pricing policy. The producer price ought to be set at that level, OH, which results in the quota output. This has the added advantage of producing healthy government revenues, perhaps even of maximizing them.

INPUT PRICES AND PROCESSING POSSIBILITIES

The effects of agricultural tax and pricing policies upon processing possibilities may not be so obvious. Policies which result in lower domestic prices for agricultural inputs to processing establishments than would be paid upon world markets for these inputs constitute subsidies to domestic processing. Taxes on raw material exports can therefore be industrial subsidies.[6]

The effective protection offered to processing is the amount of the subsidy divided by the value added in the process.[7] These implicit subsidies may partially offset the heavy effective protection offered to processing industries in the industrial nations through the "escalation" in their tariffs (i.e. the increase in rates with higher stages of processing and production).

TABLE 1: EXPORT DUTIES AND EFFECTIVE PROTECTION FOR PROCESSING ACTIVITIES

	Value Added in Processing Per Unit Value of Final Output	Effective Protection in		Export Duty Required to offset effective protection in	
		U.K. %	EEC %	U.K. %	EEC %
Rope, cordage, twine	.40	22.5	32	15	21
Processed coffee	.40	3	45	2	30
Ground-nut oil	.12	65–80	140	9–11	19
Castor oil	.10	32	80	4	9
Soyabean oil	.06	88	160	6	10
Cotton-seed oil	.30	34	34	15	15

SOURCE: Value added data from different sources. Processed coffee and castor oil are outright guesses. The remainder are derived from Harry G. Johnson, *U.S. Economic Policy Towards the Less Developed Countries: A Survey of Major Issues* (Brookings, 1966). Rope, cordage, twine is cited directly therein. The remainder are implicit in the tariff rates and Johnson's effective protection figures.

NOTES:

(1) The difference between c.i.f. European and f.o.q. East African prices has been ignored. These figures are therefore slightly understated. The possibility that the exchange rate of the East African currency is overvalued is also ignored.

(2) U.K. and EEC tariffs were applied to the value added data to obtain effective protection, as follows:

$$f = \frac{t - m(1 - v)}{v}$$

where f is the European effective protection on processing, v is the value added in processing per unit value of final output, t is the European tariff on the processed product, and m is the European tariff on the raw material input.

(3) The figures of "*Export Duty Required*" were obtained from the U.K. and EEC effective protection and the value added data, as follows:

$$x = \frac{fv}{1 - v},$$ where x is the necessary offsetting export duty.

Table 1 roughly estimates the effective protection offered the developed country processors of some of Tanzania's exports, and those levels of export tax upon the primary products which would be required to provide incentives for Tanzanian processing sufficient to offset the European protection of processors. These estimates can be improved. It is clear that fairly modest taxes on some materials can overcome substantial protective barriers in the developed nations. For example, British protection of 80 per cent for its groundnut crushers can be offset by an export tax on groundnuts of 11 per cent. The same factor which tends to produce higher effective protection rates in the developed countries, a high material input component in the total value of output also increases the ease with which raw material exporters can offset them. It is worth noting that as the prices of exports rise, in those cases in which progressive export duties are applied to agricultural products, the effective protection rate for domestic processing also rises. When taxes are specific, however, this percentage effective protection *falls* with price increases.

EQUITY OR NEUTRALITY

If the desire is to raise government revenues with a minimum distortion of the incentives which would result in the absence of such taxes and a minimum discrimination (inequity), an attempt should be made to achieve equi-proportionate taxes on each crop. What is a neutral tax system in this sense? This is by no means self-evident. It is best defined, I believe, as one in which equal proportions of *value added* by the agricultural sector are deducted in taxes from each. "Value added" as employed in this context is the value of output less the value of all intermediate (non-factor) inputs; this is the same as total factor earnings in production—whether they are wages, interest, rent or profit.

NOTES

1. The excerpted discussion is mainly concerned with the structures of agricultural prices (or taxes) and their economic effects as opposed to the problems of tax burden.

2. I have consciously omitted stabilisation as an objective of pricing policy in this discussion.
3. Harry Johnson *U.S. Economic Policy Towards the Less Developed Countries: A Survey of Major Issues*, Washington, D.C.: Brookings Institute, 1966.
4. G. K. Helleiner, "The Fiscal Role of Marketing Boards in Nigerian Economic Development, 1946–7," *Economic Journal*, Vol. LXXIV, No. 295, September 1964, pp. 604–605.
5. This assumes a situation of the excess supply of coffee in the world market.
6. Taxes on imported or non-exportable inputs to industry, of course, are disincentives to industry.
7. See for example, W. M. Corden. "The Structure of a Tariff System and the Effective Protection Rate," *Journal of Political Economy*, Vol. LXXIV, No. 3, June 1966, pp. 221–237.

Section VI

Rural Development

INTRODUCTION

The Arusha Declaration has given the general direction of Tanzania's transformation to a society based on socialism and self-reliance. President Nyerere in the major policy statement, "Socialism and Rural Development," spelt out in some detail how the general approach was to be translated into action by means of Ujamaa villages.

Already in the period following Independence, village settlements had been designated as the organisational form through which Tanzania's rural development was to be achieved. By the end of the First Five-Year Plan, however, most of these settlements were in difficulty or had collapsed. The Second Five-Year Plan, based on the Arusha Declaration, incorporated the Ujamaa village as a new form of organization that was to spearhead rural development. Unlike the earlier settlement programme, this was to be a frontal approach based on local initiative. The central government's role was to be restricted to that of supporting and encouraging the people.

Although the Ujamaa villages are still in their infancy, they have effected far reaching changes in the lives of the majority of rural Tanzanians. Many of these changes are too recent to be chronicled or analyzed in detail. At the same time the progress of the Ujamaa villages in itself has given rise to a variety of new problems that require immediate attention. The first four papers in this section touch on some of these changes and point to some of the problems. The first paper by Peter Temu examines the principles upon which the strategy of Ujamaa villages is based and evaluates the achievements up to 1973.

In the second paper Sumra traces the development of Ujamaa villages in Handeni District. Although some villages have succeeded better than others in their efforts to build Ujamaa, most face similar problems. Sumra mentions one of these problems, the low rate of attendance in the cultivation of communal plots and the consequent adverse effect on village agricultural production. Msambichaka and Mabele consider the role of credit programmes in assisting Ujamaa villages to improve productivity. They evaluate the initial steps taken by the Tanzanian Rural Development Bank to promote the socialist transformation process and make several specific recommendations on how the TRDB might play a more active role in this process. The brief summary of Mohele's longer study indicates that credit programmes hastily planned and carelessly implemented can adversely affect villages by imposing a burden of debt and uncertainty that impedes their future development.

To increase production, however, it is not sufficient to provide peasant farmers with credit and a range of modern inputs. Suitable marketing and transportation arrangements as well as a pricing strategy which will induce farmers to increase their marketed output must be worked out. Malima analyszes the price responsiveness of peasant cotton farmers. The refinements that he introduces in his study not only are methodologically illuminating but also lead to important implications for pricing policy.

Mascarenhas and Mbilinyi in the concluding paper of this section analyze the supply and demand factors that are operative in the Dar es Salaam banana market. As they indicate, the problems of marketing and pricing policy are even more acute in the case of food crops.

The Ujamaa Experiment*

PETER TEMU

Introduction

On all traditional criteria the agricultural economy of mainland Tanzania exhibits the usual characteristics of dependent, underdeveloped economies. Of the country's estimated population of 13 million, 95 per cent work and live on the soil, but their average productivity is so low that their share of GDP is only 40 per cent. A lot of the agricultural activity is still carried out outside the monetary sector: out of an estimated agricultural GDP of 3,044 million shillings* in 1969, about 1,581 million shillings was produced in the subsistence sector. (Then a shilling was valued at 14 US cents).

The agricultural monetary sector is itself largely export-oriented, with cotton, coffee, sisal and cashew nuts providing the bulk of the 1,793 million shillings worth of exports in 1969. Conversely, production for local consumption is relatively small in the absence of an integrated local market to sustain the growth of internal trade. As in other ex-colonial countries, Tanzania's trade and communication routes seem designed less with a view to creating an integrated local economy than to serving external markets and the handful of local urban centres which dot the trade routes.

The geographical and ecological environment is also, unfortunately, somewhat harsh. True, Tanzania is an enormous country, approaching the size of Nigeria. Yet, the amount of good arable land is severely limited. Much of the territory including large parts of the interior consists of tsetse-infested grassland, bushland, or swamps. Most of the good arable land is to be found in a few geographical area on thes country's perimeter — the northern highlands of Kilimanjaro and Arusha, the Usambaras, the Lake Victoria region, Tanga, and the southern highland region comprising Iringa, Mbeya and parts of Ruvuma. It is in these same scattered areas that the country's rural population is clustered.

Until independence in 1961, the great majority of the people of Tanzania lived in isolated rural homesteads, on individual smallholdings where they grew food crops and sometimes cash crops too. In some parts of Tanzania, notably the drier areas, cattle rearing was common and communal grazing was often practised. However, the standard of animal husbandry, like that of crop husbandry, was generally very poor. Overgrazing tended to cause serious soil erosion on land occupied by the principal cattle tribes, notably the Maasai, the Wasukuma and the Wagogo. Attempts by the colonial administration to introduce conservation measures, such as compulsory destocking, tie-ridging, cattle dipping, etc., failed miserably and make sad reading.

Even today, except in a few isolated areas, the introduction of high-grade cattle has nowhere made much impact, any more than has the introduction of high-yielding seed varieties of maize, wheat, sorghum and millet. Custom continues to place a higher utility on the size of the livestock herd than on its quality; the payment of bride wealth, for one, is still reckoned as so *many* head of cattle, not as so *much* worth.

Taken together, these facts have a certain logic to them, which compels the attention of the economic development planner, and conditions his approach to the rural sector. For the TANU[1] Government the overriding question has been how to bring about rapid agricultural change in a large and underdeveloped country whose population of barely 13 million is thinly sprinkled across its length and breadth, and how to do this in the face of severe resource limitations.

From the outset, one thing has always been clear. The TANU Government, under President Nyerere, became convinced that *ujamaa*[2] was the only policy which would improve the well-being of the peasants, who were the backbone of the Tanzanian economy, and which would pave the way both to rapid economic development and to social and political emancipation. Today, *ujamaa* is no longer viewed as one possible path of development among many; rightly or wrongly, it is seen as the only logical path. And as far as rural development goes, the *ujamaa* village has become the focal point of the current approach to integrated rural development.

AN OLD TRADITION

It is worth recalling that neither the decision to build *ujamaa* villages in rural Tanzania nor to adopt socialism in Tanzania at large began with the Arusha Declaration.[3] The first clear philosophical articulation came in 1962, with the publication of Nyerere's *Ujamaa—The Basis of African Socialism.* According to Nyerere, Africans, by tradition, have always been socialists. Their socialism, or *ujamaa*, was governed by three fundamental principles: first, people lived together and worked together; second, all the basic goods were held in common—no one could go hungry while others hoarded food, or be denied shelter if others had some to spare; third, everyone (even guests) had an obligation to work.

The first principle can tell us what *ujamaa* villages are all about: the second, what lies behind the nationalizations and the whole gamut of measures against private capital accumulation; the third explains the emphasis on hard work and self-reliance. It also, incidentally, refutes those Western observers who are never tired of

**ceres*, July–August 1973, pp. 71-75.

TABLE 1: TOTAL NUMBER OF UJAMAA VILLAGES AND THEIR ESTIMATED POPULATION ACCORDING TO REGION ON 31 MAY, 1973

Region	Number	Population	Average population per village	Per cent of total population
Arusha	95	20,112	211	3
Coast	188	115,382	613	21
Dodoma	336	378,915	1,127	47
Iringa	659	243,527	369	29
Kigoma	129	114,391	886	22
Kilimanjaro	24	4,934	205	1
Mara	271	108,068	398	16
Mbeya	715	103,677	145	9
Morogoro	118	19,732	167	3
Lindi	589	169,093	287	36
Mtwara	1,103	466,098	422	64
Mwanza	284	49,846	175	4
Ruvuma	242	42,385	175	9
Shinyanga	108	12,052	111	1
Singida	263	59,420	225	12
Tabora	174	29,295	168	5
Tanga	245	77,957	318	7
West Lake	85	13,280	156	2
Total	5,628	2,028,164	360	15

SOURCE: Ujamaa Village Division of the Prime Minister's Office, Dar es Salaam.

preaching that the African extended family fosters parasitism and is inimical to development. For, what is often forgotten is that the member of the extended family has an obligation to *contribute to production*, as much as he has a right to a share of the product. The fact that he may not always live up to his obligation is an aberration, which surely cannot be blamed on the system itself. Against this background, we may now proceed to analyse these principles of its policy of integrated rural development.

I do not object to those who refer to our efforts as the Tanzanian "experiment." In reality that is all it is. For one thing, the rural *ujamaa* policy is still relatively new—five years old at most—having been preceded by other approaches which proved fruitless and had to be abandoned. The policy has therefore not had sufficient time to bear fruit; indeed the very statistics are only

TABLE 2: UJAMAA VILLAGES REGISTERED AS MULTI-PURPOSE COOPERATIVES

Region	1969	1970	1971	1972	31 March 1973
Arusha	1	1	1	8	8
Coast		1	26	48	55
Dodoma	1	2	2	66	66
Iringa		1	24	80	80
Kigoma				1	1
Kilimanjaro				1	3
Mara			10	38	34
Mbeya	2	2	6	6	7
Morogoro	1	1	1	1	1
Lindi				2	2
Mtwara				2	9
Mwanza				14	14
Ruvuma				3	3
Shinyanga				8	9
Singida				5	5
Tabora				14	14
Tanga	1	1	1	13	13
West Lake			8	18	18
Total	6	9	79	328	342

SOURCE: Ujamaa Village Division of the Prime Minister's Office, Dar es Salaam.

just beginning to be gathered. For another thing, the Tanzanian experiment, like all experiments, may succeed or fail, for any number of different reasons, including the opposition of vested interests and other factors which cannot at present be foreseen.

Therefore, it behooves those who will perform the postmortem—if their time comes—to be as objective as possible, since the resulting lessons will certainly be of interest not only to Tanzania but to other countries of Africa and indeed the Third World.

Many observers already acknowledge that the Tanzanian *ujamaa* policy is unique, and we in Tanzania know full well that there are as many enemies who would like to see it fail as there are friends who would like to see it succeed. This awareness of course only adds to our sense of mission—a feeling that we owe it to ourselves and to posterity to demonstrate that modern development is possible without the sacrifice in equality and humanity which has everywhere accompanied the "development" of the present industrialized states.

Given Tanzania's population distribution, the idea that agricultural mobilization can only be brought about effectively by concentrating people in villages comes as no surprise. Capitalist economists acclaim it because of economies of scale—the reduction in the cost of providing infrastructure and of supplying communal services. Socialism adds to this the most important dimension of all: that by living together people will not only be able to improve productive or distributive efficiency, but will be able to learn a new style of life—working together, sharing their produce communally, marketing cooperatively, and living democratically at the village level. The apparent consensus among capitalists and socialists on the system of "villagization," however, is quite spurious, at least below the surface. This becomes obvious as soon as we examine the agricultural policies that have actually been advocated in Tanzania over the past decade and are followed today in neighbouring countries.

HIGHEST-RETURN POLICY

Until 1961, the agreed way to develop the traditional rural sector was what was called the "progressive farmer approach." This policy aimed at concentrating the use of resources on those areas, crops and people promising the highest returns. A visiting World Bank mission endorsed this policy on the eve of independence. Armed with the conventional wisdom of the time, its report blamed the problem of agricultural stagnation on poor extension services and asserted that "one major reason why the extension services have made such a limited progress is undoubtedly the extreme conservatism of the farmers . . . and their traditions of group and tribal life . . . which militate strongly against the development of individual initiative."[4] These ideas have of course long been discredited. Lionel Cliffe, for one, has written, "peasant 'conservatism' is often a healthy scepticism of bad plans."[5]

Side by side with the progressive farmer approach went the so-called "transformation approach." This was aimed at settling people, on a planned basis, in fertile, empty areas on the naive assumption that people are more likely to accept innovations when moved out of their familiar surroundings. The result was the creation of "settlement schemes," in which the Government invested a lot of capital and manpower resources but which failed to take root. The reasons for their failure have been well documented; they boil down to bad planning, over-capitalization, lack of voluntary participation and a general failure by the settlers to view the schemes as their own.

A USEFUL FAILURE

The point of this brief historical excursion is not simply to show that the policy of concentrating on the progressive farmer failed but equally to underline that if it had succeeded, as it is doing in some countries, the result would simply have been the creation of a privileged class of rural capitalists in the midst of a vast sea of poor and often landless peasants. Indeed there is evidence to suggest that this is exactly what the framers of the policy had wanted to happen. The aim seems to have been to enhance the political ability of a few relatively wealthy individuals to impose their will on the poverty-stricken masses and thereby create "stability." They apparently preferred to "spearhead" development, rather than seek a genuine way of uplifting the lot of the peasantry. A policy of this type, of course, tends to have a strong sectional appeal to the already privileged segment of the population, and it would be idle to pretend that it lacks adherents even today.

That such a policy was not altogether unsuccessful in its aims in Tanzania can indeed be seen today in the existence of isolated pockets of rural capitalist development—maize farmers in Iringa, tobacco growers in Tabora, coffee farmers in Moshi and Bukoba, and wheat growers in Mbulu districts. By and large these are the same areas where progress toward *ujamaa* has been slowest, and where the use of force to break the back of the capitalists is sometimes openly advocated.

Tanzania is still far from its professed socialist goal. One current study of the development of rural capitalism in the Ismani area of Iringa district, based on a stratified sample of 9 out of 28 *ujamaa* villages, reveals that 9 per cent of the households own 47 per cent of the cattle, 51 per cent of the sheep and goats, 53 per cent of the cultivated land, 88 per cent of the purchased land, and 96 per cent of existing capital equipment.

To complete the picture, a word must be said about the agricultural export sector. The export-oriented policy, particularly that based on plantation agriculture under the ownership of foreign capitalists, was exalted even by scholars because export production was supposedly the dynamic sector, the "engine of growth."

INTEGRATION NEEDED

One study of agricultural change in Tanzania concluded with the words: "Plantations and estate agriculture have been invaluable in providing rapid development of large areas of previously unproductive land; in demonstrating the value of modern methods of production; in earning large sums of foreign currency from massive exports; in meeting the increasing demand for foodstuffs; and in providing large sums of government revenues through taxation." But on the smallholder sector, it was not quite so complimentary: "The use of fertilizers is almost negligible; methods of land preparation and crop husbandry remain largely primitive; true livestock husbandry is nonexistent and land use methods largely destructive"; and, once again, the remedy was thought to lie in a "vastly expanded extension service, staffed by well-trained men, but, above all, a revolution in the outlook of the farmer himself and in the organization of smallholder production."[6]

The one thing which receives no mention at all in these studies is the obvious need to integrate the plantation economy with the "primitive" smallholder sector, in which, after all, 95 per cent of the African population live and die; to break away from an export-oriented sector, which is controlled and exploited by foreign capital; to eliminate the small but influential class of rural capitalists whose interests are tied up with those of the industrialized countries, and not at all with the rural Tanzanians who produce the very wealth which sustains that class.

A CLASSIC CASE

In short, until the policy of socialism and self-reliance was launched in earnest, Tanzania's "development path" was a classic case of a neo-colonial, export-oriented, "dual economy" that every schoolboy knows by heart. The Arusha Declaration, however, changed all that.

Since then it appears that the number of Tanzanians who have voluntarily chosen to live in *ujamaa* villages has risen from virtually zero to more than two million, or over 15 per cent of the population. There is every indication that the tempo is picking up, judging especially by the considerable momentum it gathered in 1972, and the tremendous educational campaigns, including radio propaganda, that continue unabated. Though there are still marked regional differences in response, the wind of *ujamaa* continues to sweep over the entire land.

It cannot be repeated too often that socialism in Tanzania is an attempt to build a different *quality* of life for its people, not merely to raise their material well-being, important as that may be. The purpose of development is man, not things, and his dignity, his freedom, his democratic right and duty to participate in production and consumption decisions are basic, and cannot be "traded off" against a little extra income here, or a few extra jobs there.

The interpretation of data on *ujamaa* villages therefore calls for greater caution and insight than are customary by economic statisticians. But even in purely quantitative terms there is a great deal more to be known about the *ujamaa* rural development programme before any meaningful evaluation is possible, e.g. the size and setting of the villages, demographic structure, system of government, and the nature and range of their economic activities. There is also a lot to be learned on the motivation to join, or not to join *ujamaa* villages; on the extent to which life in *ujamaa* villages is, on some chosen criterion, better or worse than life outside, and how far one *ujamaa* village differs from another. Research on these and related questions is proceeding apace but with so much more still unknown it is probably better to withhold judgement.

One point to remember about the present *ujamaa* villages, however, is their heterogeneity, that is how far along the road each village can be said to be fully *ujamaa*. Typically, it passes through three phases. The first is when a group of persons, say 50 or 100, decides to form a village, where they want to locate it, what they hope to grow, what initial feeder roads, water or other facilities they think will be needed, and so forth. In other words, this is the embryonic stage when the nascent villagers are still feeling their way, shaping their organization, picking their leaders and beginning to plan their economic and social life. The second stage begins with the implementation of the village life plan in a more settled, organized and systematic pattern: the construction of buildings and the provision of food, water, transport, etc. During these two early stages the villagers rely heavily on self-help, usually in the form of their own voluntary labour; they are also entitled to technical advice and limited financial and material help from the Government. But the initiative remains squarely theirs and outside help is clearly minimal.

In the final stage, the *ujamaa* village will have grown into a fully viable economic unit, carrying out all its activities (from production to marketing) cooperatively, and distributing the proceeds according to work contributed by each member. At this stage, the village becomes registered as a multi-purpose cooperative and is eligible to receive credit on commercial terms from public institutions such as the National Bank of Commerce, and the Tanzania Rural Development Bank established for this purpose.

From Table 2 we note that the number of villages in stage 3 was only 342 on 31 March 1973 compared with a total of 5,628 at all stages reported to be in existence on that date (see Table 1). Second, we observe that the pace of village formation has accelerated rapidly since 1971; third, by comparing the total number of *ujamaa* villages reported with those known to be in the most advanced stage in each region, we get an idea of the regions in the country where the newest villages are located and that in many regions most remain in the nascent stage.

Moreover, there is still no direct integration between the large farm sector and the smallholder sector, except that the former, the one time foreign "enclave," has at last been nationalized and socialized. Freehold land has been abolished, and land is now subject to a right of occupancy which can be revoked. The sisal estates are presently owned and run by the Tanzania Sisal

Corporation; some of the large tea, coffee, and tobacco plantations have been taken over by the State, others by cooperatives and a few are still in private hands. The idea is to have all these converted to state farms or cooperatives, but the cooperative leadership at present still leaves something to be desired. To the extent that these pangs of transition are tolerated, they tend to be viewed as a necessary price for our philosophy of *ujamaa* which emphasizes education and persuasion and shuns the use of force to exact compliance.

Here is President Nyerere's reply to a journalist's blunt question:[7]

Q: *You are trying to bring about your socialism by voluntary means. In other countries it has been through force, very considerable force. What makes you believe that in the case of Tanzania it can be different?*

A: The theoretical answer is very simple . . . socialism is a society of free people . . equal in every sense, politically, socially and economically. Then who is this god who will stand above everyone else and say, "I'm going to build equality for you but in the meantime you are not my equal"?

NOTES:

1. Tanganyika African National Union, formed in 1954, the ruling and only party under President Julius K. Nyerere.
2. Swahili for "socialism" or, translated literally, "familyhood."
3. The Arusha Declaration was proclaimed by TANU in February, 1967. It enunciates TANU's policy of socialism and self-reliance and is probably the most important turning point in Tanzania's contemporary history.
4. IBRD, *The Economic Development of Tanganyika*, Baltimore: Johns Hopkins University Press, 1961, p. 60.
5. Lionel Cliffe and John S. Saul (eds.), *Socialism in Tanzania*, Dar es Salaam: East African Publishing House, 1972, Vol. 1. p. 23.
6. N. R. Fuggles-Couchman, *Agricultural Change in Tanganyika: 1945–1960*, Food Research Institute, Stanford, 1964, p. 97.
7. David Martin, *New Internationalist*, May 1973, pp. 6–10.

Problems of Agricultural Production in Ujamaa Villages in Handeni District*

SULEMAN SUMRA

Introduction

The publication of "Socialism and Rural Development" in 1967 committed Tanzania to revolutionize its rural areas through the voluntary and gradual formation of Socialist Ujamaa Villages.[1] Since then, ujamaa villages have been formed in various parts of the country.

During the colonial and pre-1967 period, the policies and practices aimed at creating yeomen type of progressive farmers.[2] The kind of development that was taking place was creating individual peasant producers who were gradually "adopting the incentives and the ethics of the capitalist system."[3] Policy of Ujamaa vijijini is an attempt at subverting the kind of capitalist development that was taking place, by bringing changes in the modes of agricultural production. Ujamaa villages were to be formed as "economic and social communities where people live together and work together for the good of all."[4]

This envisaged changes in the settlement pattern, land tenure and work habits. It meant that instead of peasants living in scattered dwellings, they would move into villages. It also meant that not only land or at least part of it would be in the joint ownership of all the members, but cultivation too would be done communally.

This paper analyzes the progress of these villages in Handeni District. Data from 32 villages in Handeni District were collected from January to March 1973. Since this period many changes have been taking place in the district, but it is hoped that this paper will provide information for the better understanding of these recent changes.

FORMATION OF AN UJAMAA VILLAGE

In practice it is difficult to say what factors are considered to qualify a village as an ujamaa village. It appears that there are two basic determinants, residence and communal work. An ideal village will be, as Nyerere puts it. where "people live together and work together for the good of all."[5] In practice you can find various combinations of these factors. Some ujamaa villages have been built where there was no settlement before, while for others old villages provided the nucleus for ujamaa villages. Based on residence and communal work, mainly communal cultivation, several kinds of ujamaa villages were seen:

(a) villagers from several adjacent villages having a common communal farm which they cultivate together;

(b) most members of a village living together but others from adjacent villages joining in for communal activities;

(c) Most of the villagers living in a particular village are members but some are not, and thus do not participate in communal activities.

Ujamaa villages in Handeni District have been established in two phases. The first phase was the period immediately following the publication of Mwalimu's policy document. 1967/68 food shortages in the district appear to be the main reason for this concerted effort at forming ujamaa villages in the district at the time. Although it was stated in the document and over the radio that the move to ujamaa was going to be completely voluntary,[6] the local government leaders in their over zealousness often resorted to the use of force to make people move into ujamaa villages.[7] These early ujamaa villages were established in the poorer eastern part of the district. This initial attempt at ujamaa faced several problems. Apart from the unwillingness of the people to move into these villages and the resultant force used by the authorities, serious organisational problems came to the forefront. Most of these villages were sited in previously uninhabited areas, without due consideration about their suitability for agricultural purposes and the availability of other necessities like water. In some cases the villagers were moved during the months of March and April when they already had prepared their fields in the old villages. Building of huts after the move and preparation of fresh fields meant that fields were planted late and this inevitably resulted in crop failure.[8] This phase ended with the intervention of the Central Government, and the transfer of the Area Commissioner.

Not all villages were started through the use of force some were established voluntarily. Villagers saw the movement into concentrated villages as a way of getting aid from the government. By 30th April, 1971 there were 25 officially recognized ujamaa villages in Handeni District.[9]

1971 was a year of serious food shortages within the district. This was the beginning of the second phase. Provision of famine relief was conditional on one being a member of an ujamaa village. As a result of this policy, ujamaa villages were formed all over the district. In 1974, there were 82 ujamaa villages in the district with 40,635 people, nearly 27.0 per cent of the population.[10]

Formation of ujamaa villages was meant to bring people together in order to create centres of services and to raise the standard of living of the rural population. So far ujamaa movement in the district has been successful on the first front. A substantial proportion of the district's population lives in ujamaa villages.

*ERB Paper 75.3

Sizes of these villages vary a great deal. Of the 33 ujamaa villages visited, Mkata, the largest, had 713 adult members while Komsara, the smallest, had 60 adults as registered members.

Some of the larger ujamaa villages have become centres for services. Schools, dispensaries, piped water and grain stores have been built in many villages. An elaborate plan is at hand to bring water, the most serious problem in the district, to nearly all the ujamaa villages on the eastern side of the district.[11] The provision of services to the villages is seen as the reason and not as the result of the moving into villages. So there is a danger, due to the limited resources of the government, that some villages may disappear if the services are not provided.

In almost all the villages visited, membership was open to all those willing to participate in some kind of communal activity. There were no elaborate procedures for joining or opting out of the village. This kind of open membership has created several problems. There are people who belong to a particular village but do not reside in the village. This problem may die out as more and more people move into the villages. Many hours are now wasted, however, in moving to and from their villages to the communal farm. Some villages have individuals who live in houses built communally but who do not participate in communal activities.[12]

Fluctuation in attendance lead to the problem of organizing agricultural operations properly. The number swells up when there is a food shortage in the area and famine relief is available. Data collected during the 1972 growing season in various ujamaa villages in Handeni District indicate that attendance also fluctuates with the kind of operations to be carried on. Attendance is highest during the clearing period. People attend the clearing work on the communal plots after clearing their own farms. Data collected from Mwaki Ujamaa Village[13] illustrate this. As soon as the rain falls the numbers attending decreases considerably as work on their individual plots increase. There is always a conflict between work on communal farm and on individual plots. Unless famine relief is provided, work on the individual plot is given preference. This attitude is mainly as a result of peasants being still unsure of obtaining sufficient production on the communal farms. As a result important operations like weeding and guarding against vermin are not done properly. The overall result is that yields on communal plots are much lower than on the individual plots.

Crops that suffer most are those for which labour requirements are higher. For example sorghum needs constant guarding against birds after tasseling, and cotton needs spraying and regular picking once the balls start opening. It is these crops that show very poor yields on the communal plots. Table 1 compares the yields of various crops on communal plots with those from individual plots.

Fluctuations in attendance make it difficult to calculate the number of acres of communal plots cultivated per member. Taking the number of registered members at the time of the visit, in Handeni District the number of acres per person of communally cultivated land in various ujamaa villages varied from as low as 0.08 acres per member to as high as 2.16 acres per person. The average for the district was 0.3 acres per person. On the whole it appears that the villages with low membership seem to have a higher acreage cultivated per person and those with high membership have a lower acreage cultivated per person.

The above discussion clearly points out the need for limiting membership to those seriously committed to ujamaa way of life. In most villages there is a core of people who are committed. It would be better if the membership was restricted to these few. Ujamaa villages would be more successful if the emphasis was on the quality of work done rather than on sheer numbers of members as appears to be the case at present.

The greater portion of communal land is under maize, although most of the areas in the district are not suitable for maize.[14] It is striking that the types of crops grown and the proportion of land under these crops is identical to that grown on their own plots.[15] This indicates that although there are changes that have occurred in settlement patterns, work habits, and land ownership little if anything has changed overall. They still produce the same crops.

As was seen earlier there is a conflict between the labour requirements on the communal and on the individual plots. The bottleneck of labour arises mainly because the crops grown are the same and in most cases labour demand coincide. The conflict will necessarily continue under the present set up of crop allocations. One answer would be to make attendance on the communal plots compulsory. Another would be to develop communal activities and grow crops on the communal plots which do not require labour at the same time as is required on individual plots. Things that immediately come to mind are tree crops, livestock and poultry. If the communal plots were planted with tree crops like oranges, mangoes or even coffee and cardamon then the labour demand would not be heavy when it is required on individual plots. It is surprising that no village had communally owned cattle and goats. In view of low and unreliable rainfall, keeping of cattle and goats is less risky than growing of crops. At present all the livestock found in ujamaa villages belongs to individuals who are then the sole beneficiaries of the dips provided for the villages.

One reason why the ujamaa villages have not proved successful so far in attracting large numbers of people to move into them and to increase the area under communal ownership, is their failure to produce a reasonable amount of monetary income. Income calculations made on all the crops produced on the communal plots were sold at the prevalent prices and the income divided equally among all the registered members. The most striking aspect of the table is the generally low levels of possible incomes. The income per person varies from 77.88 shillings per year to as low

TABLE 1: COMPARISON OF AVERAGE YIELDS OF SOME CROPS ON COMMUNAL PLOTS AND ON INDIVIDUAL PLOTS IN THE THREE ZONES OF HANDENI DISTRICT

	HANDENI WESTERN		HANDENI CENTRAL		HANDENI EASTERN	
	Yields Kg/Ac		Yields Kg/Ac		Yields Kg/Ac	
CROPS	Communal Plots	Individual Plots	Communal Plots	Individual Plots	Communal Plots	Individual Plots
Maize	220	385	180	268	130	310
Beans	090	318	110	280	—	
Sorghum		—	060	150	120	456
Simsim	—	—	030	200	100	367
Kunde		—	130	246	200	381

as 1.03 shillings.[16] Not all the crops are sold and not all the income derived from the sales of the crops is distributed or distributed equally. Part is kept as a village fund, which may be in the form of cash with the Chairman or in the Bank.

The amount of money kept as the village fund varies from village to village. Suwa in Eastern Handeni had a village fund of Shs. 8,095. Generally, the older the village is the greater the possibility that more funds are saved. The way in which this is used leaves a lot to be desired. In most cases the fund is used for consumptive purposes. As 1972 was a year with food shortages in the district, travelling allowances for members to go to Handeni Town to inform the authorities that food for famine relief was finished, consumed a substantial amount of the communal fund. These expenses may have been unavoidable but money spent for entertaining guests or on feasts could have been put to better use. The only productive activity into which money has been put is the village shop. Most ujamaa villages either had a communally owned shop or were intending to open one, in 1972. The experiences with these village shops have been varied. Recent reports from the area suggest that some have already closed down after less than a year's operation. Closures have mostly resulted from the inefficient and sometimes dishonest activities of the people who are appointed to manage them. Private shops which are allowed to operate in villages may have contributed to the downfall of the communally owned shops.

Not all shops have done badly. Some successful examples were seen but these were rare. For example, the shop at Suwa was started in October 1969 with a capital of Shs. 450; by October 1972 the shop was worth Shs. 4,000. This increase was solely from the profits made.

No example was seen where the money was ploughed back into agricultural activities. For agricultural inputs the villagers were dependent on Government help. Provision of this help was seen as the duty of the Government.[17] Government help in most cases has been confined to providing basic inputs and social amenities. The help was limited in most cases to seeds. Some villages were provided with fertilizers. Recently due to the very real problem of vermin, most villages were supplied with nets, traps and in some cases guns. A person selected by the villagers was trained in the use of the gun. As the villagers were responsible for the purchase of the ammunition, most guns were lying idle.[18]

In some instances where the villagers appeared to be performing satisfactorily, Government helped them by either clearing the communal farm by the use of a bulldozer or ploughing their land with small tractors. This policy of limited mechanization does not seem to have been a success. It becomes beyond members' abilities to carry on other activities like planting, weeding and harvesting manually. Thus only a part of the cleared or ploughed area is ever used. Limited mechanization does not appear to be the solution to increasing production.

These communal plots are different from individual plots only insofar as they are cultivated communally. The tools used, crops grown and the techniques used are the same. Attempts have been made at the use of fertilizers, but as these have been done without the proper understanding of the soils, they have not succeeded. It then becomes doubtful if there are going to be any changes in the income and welfare of the people, let alone skills, knowledge and attitudes unless some changes are brought about in the technology used and in farm management.

In practice there seems to be no clear thinking at the village level as to the purpose of the communal farm in these villages. They are not viable commercial ventures as the incomes have shown and they have failed to improve the diets of the people. Most people in the district suffer from poor diet. Emphasis should be on crops and activities that not only would improve the diets of the people but also would find ready markets. Keeping of cattle, goats and poultry, growing of vegetables and fruits tree appear to be practicable. Fruit trees like pawpaws, guavas, oranges, mangoes and jack fruits are grown successfully by many individuals in most parts of the district. Ujamaa must be seen as a way for people to achieve better living standards.

An increase in production has to be accompanied by an efficient marketing system. At present the marketing is unsatisfactory in two ways. First, it is inefficient. Marketing of most agricultural crops is in the hands of the three primary co-operative societies in the district.

Chanika-Mgambo Co-operative Society is responsible for buying agricultural produce in Central Handeni, Kwasunga-Kwamsisi Co-operative Society in Eastern Handeni and the Nguu Co-operative Society in Western Handeni. In most villages markets are held twice a year by the societies. Transport is a problem as these co-operatives have to hire lorries from private individuals. Often the unavailability of these lorries, as well as bad roads make it difficult for the co-operatives to fix these market days. Frequently peasants find themselves unable to attend on the day fixed, and then they wait in vain to sell their crops which they might have brought from miles around on their heads. If anything is harvested after the last market day, then it has to wait for a year or be taken to Handeni by buses or lorries.

Second the marketing is geared towards export crops. Cotton, castor, beans, maize, cashewnuts, cardamon, coffee and simsim are the major crops bought by the co-operatives. This means that even if changes were made at the village level to grow crops other than these export oriented crops, it would be difficult to find markets for them. For example, if the villagers decided to grow tomatoes to improve their diet, any surplus would have no market.

Recently attempts have been made at diversifying the crops grown in the villages by providing seedlings of fruit trees. In 1971 nurseries were set up in various parts of the district where orange seeds were planted. Seedlings were then distributed to various ujamaa villages. Within weeks most of these had died as the seedlings were distributed in June, after the rains were over. One may hope that they might have better success with pineapples which have been planted in these nurseries.

The role of extension workers, especially the agricultural officers, has changed since 1968. Instead of providing advisory service to all the peasants, agricultural officers are to concentrate on ujamaa villages. This narrowing down of their area of operation seems to have had a limited effect as is evident from the production on these communal plots. One reason may be that they do not see themselves as part of these villages. Regular guaranteed salaries ensure that their personal welfare is not dependent on production in the village farm. If on the other hand, their income was tied to what the communal plots produced, they would feel more committed.

CONCLUSION

There are several things which stand out from the above discussion.

(a) The policy has succeeded in creating villages with sizable numbers of people. In Handeni peasants live in scattered hamlets. A traditional village contains 10–15 or even fewer huts of related people. Ujamaa villages thus have created viable units for provision of some basic services. On the other hand this may raise more problems. In traditional villages, due to the poverty of the soil, peasants cultivate a plot of land for 2 or 3 years and then abandon it for another piece of land. This kind of rotation ensured fertility of the soil. In ujamaa villages where large tracts of land have been cleared, sometimes with tractors, abandoning these plots after every two or three years will be uneconomical; yet the continuous use of soils without additional nutrients reduces the yields. Despite a number of people having cattle in the area, cattle yard manure is seldom used. This can be one activity planned during off seasons.

(b) Having a communal farm has brought some degree of co-operation among members. This is important in Handeni where this kind of co-operation is lacking at the homestead level. In Handeni most of the farming operations are done by women and usually each woman has her own shamba. So a person with more than one wife, generally has more than one plot of land. A wife and her children are both the consuming and producing unit.

(c) Growing of annual crops means that labour is utilized for only a part of the year on communal activities. This may be at the most for 3 or 4 months; for the rest of the year there are no communal activities. There is need to introduce activities that would take care of this off season underutilization of labour. Keeping of cattle and growing of tree-crops would not only use labour more evenly but also increase the output of these villages.

(d) The move to the villages does not seem to have solved the basic problems faced by the peasants in the area, i.e. that of frequent food shortages and poor living conditions. This is partly due to the fact that production in these villages is always geared to the market. Peasants grow crops that have ready markets, and not what they need to improve their diets. This I think is the direct result of the emphasis being placed by the government officials. For example during my visit to the area in 1973, villages in Eastern Handeni were instructed that every member should have at least one acre of cotton. This kind of directive not only robs the peasants of the right to decide but has helped in some cases in reducing the amount of communal operations. For example after these instructions were given, some villages decided to do away with cultivating communally by giving an acre of land from the former communal plots to be cultivated individually. This breaking of former communal plots into blocks was a widespread phenomena during 1973.

It is time that operations on communal plots are geared to satisfy the needs of the peasants. The first priority is to reduce the frequent food shortages—cassava could be one crop that can eliminate food shortages from the district. Cassava has become unpopular due to the time it requires in guarding it against vermin. It has to be guarded by day against baboons and at night against pigs. This 24 hour guarding to my mind is the main reason for the unpopularity of the crop. Provision of guns does not seem to have solved the problem. One way to overcome this problem would be to change the planning of these villages. At present most villages are linear with huts built along the roads. The communal plots is some distance away. If instead the huts were built around the cassava plot, the amount of guarding could be reduced to a great extent.

Attempts should be made to produce crops on the plots that would improve the diets of the peasants. Things like vegetables and fruits should be grown for the consumption of the villagers. The surplus could then be put for sale. This would require changes in the marketing arrangements.

There is need to establish exchange relations among various ujamaa villages. For example, villagers from Nguu Mountain could sell or exchange their beans and maize for meat and milk from villages on the plains.

Careful planning can create healthy exchange relations among villages even at the district level and they would increase production and raise the standard of living.

These suggestions have probably all been made before. The difficulty of implementing them, to my mind, is not organizational alone, but is rather the portrayal of the existing conditions in the country.

1. Julius K. Nyerere, "Socialism and Rural Development," Dar es Salaam: Government Printer, 1967.
2. For discussion on the colonial government's agricultural policies in Handeni District see Suleman Sumra, "A History of Agriculture in Handeni District up to 1961." A paper presented to History Department Seminar on 14th November, 1974.
3. Julius K. Nyerere, *op. cit.*, p. 31.
4. *Ibid.*, p. 12.
5. *Loc. cit.*,
6. *Ibid.*, p. 21.
7. See for example Michaela von Freyhold, "The Government Staff and Ujamaa Villages. The Tanga Experience." A paper presented to the Annual Social science Conference of the East African Universities, Dar es Salaam 1973, and Lionel Cliffe, "The Policy of *Ujamaa Nijijini* and the Class Struggle in Tanzania," in Lionel Cliffe and John Saul (eds.). *Socialism in Tanzania: Volume 2, Policies* Dar es Salaam: East African Publishing House, 1973, pp. 131–140.
8. In Handeni District the rainy season is short and the rainfall is not only low but very unreliable. Unless the crops are planted at the onset of the rainy season, plants feel water stress after the rainy season is over and this results in greatly reduced yields.
9. Michaela von Freyhold, "Rural Development Through Ujamaa Vijijini: Some Considerations Based on Experiences in Tanga," University of Dar es Salaam (mimeo), p. 1.
10. See *Ratiba ya Sherehe Miaka 20 ya TANU Mkoani Tanga*, Dar es Salaam: Tanganyika African National Union, 1974, p. 39.
11. See for example Gerhard Tschannerl, *et al*, "Handeni Water Supply: Preliminary Report on Design Criteria," BRALUP Research Paper No. 22, University of Dar es Salaam, January, 1971.
12. This seems to be as a result of traditional practices. Traditionally when a person wanted to build a house, he had to cut the poles from the forest and pile them near the house site. All other activities were done communally. The hut became the property of the individual. Huts in the ujamaa villages were built in the same way and the villagers see the individuals as the owners of the huts. There are then individuals who benefit from all the services provided for the "wajamaa" but do not participate in communal activities.
13. See S. Sumra, original ERB Paper, pp. 6 and 7 for these data.
14. See Suleman Sumra, "An Analysis of Environmental and Social Problems Affecting Agricultural Development in Handeni District," University of Dar es Salaam, M.A. Thesis, 1975, Chapter 2.
15. See S. Sumra, original ERB. Paper, p. 11, for these data.
16. *Ibid.*, p. 13, for these calculations.
17. For example one village, Nkama, despite having 5,000/- in the village fund, waited a whole year for the Government to build a store for them. As a result 200 bags of maize went bad as they were left outside in the open during the rainy period. What is more surprising is that no attempts were made to save the maize. This kind of attitude to neglect the communally held goods was also visible by the way maize seeding machines were handled. They were left outside to be washed in the rains; after 6 months these machines had become rusted.
18. The nearest place where they could buy ammunition is Tanga, which is more than 100 miles from most villages in the district. If these journeys were to be made frequently, it could consume a lot of money.

Agricultural Credit and the Development of Ujamaa Villages in Tanzania

L. A. MSAMBICHAKA AND ROBERT B. MABELE*

Introduction

Credit to the agricultural sector in Tanzania has been of two types. The first type of credit was issued to middlemen and later to cooperatives to enable them to purchase agricultural commodities from farmers. This is what is known as credit for crop financing. Crop financing has always been the responsibility of the commercial banks: initially, the British banks (Barclays, National and Grindlays and the Standard Bank): and after the Arusha Declaration, the National Bank of Commerce (NBC).[1] The second type of credit is given to producers to purchase inputs and machinery and to invest in any other projects designed to raise the productivity of their farming operations. This is termed production credit.

This paper deals with production credit. It traces the general development of agricultural credit institutions in Tanzania from the British colonial period to the present day. In particular it focuses both on the evolution of production credit programmes designed to help smallholders, and on the present programmes in their relationship to the building of socialism in rural Tanzania. The present situation will be evaluated from a historical perspective, for it is our contention that agricultural credit programmes in independent Tanzania largely continued the programmes started in the colonial era. As such they therefore were inconsistent with the socialist policies of the country.

This argument will be developed in the following section in two parts. In the first, we look at the colonial programmes, their objectives, their achievements and the problems they encountered. In the second, we look at the changes introduced during the early years after independence and examine the failure of these programmes to bring about any radical transformation in the orientation of rural credit programmes. We then consider the Tanzania Rural Development Bank (TRDB), the agency charged with the mobilization of financial resources for the economic transformation of rural Tanzania, and assess its attempts to provide agricultural production credit in accordance with Tanzania's socialist policies.

We then discuss the economic aspects of providing credit to ujamaa villages. The credit criteria used in capitalist countries are evaluated and compared with the criteria used in socialist economies. A final section considers some of the problems of devising an appropriate credit system for the Ujamaa Villages.

THE HISTORICAL BACKGROUND TO CREDIT INSTITUTIONS IN TANZANIA

For the most part the African peasant in earlier colonial times had no access to credit. Banks were few and he could not borrow from them since he lacked security. Neither could he borrow from private traders since under the Credit to Natives (Restriction) Ordinance of 1923 no debt was legally enforceable against an African other than the one holding a licence. On the other hand, non-African farmers, mostly European, could borrow from commercial banks. In addition, the Land Bank was started in 1947 to provide credit for them. In 1957, the minimum bank loan per borrower was raised from £10,000 to £15,000.[2]

The institution of the Land Bank was consistent with the colonial policy of exploiting a colony's resources. In the words of a British Governor, "The first object of the government is to induce the native to become a producer directly or indirectly, that is to produce or to assist in producing something more than the crop of local foodstuffs that he requires for the sustenance of himself and his family."[3] So, along with coercing Africans to work on foreign-owned export-oriented plantations, the colonial Government ensured that settlers received credit to expand their production. African peasants could participate in the direct production of export crops provided that this neither interfered with the supply of labour to the estates nor posed any other economic threat to settler grant interests.

Given the limited resources of the African peasants, their response to this economic opportunity was phenomenal. Thus in Bukoba Region, peasant exports of coffee rose from 1,138 tons in 1918 to 10,881 tons in 1935. In Kilimanjaro, coffee produced by smallholders increased from 32 tons in 1923 to 2,141 tons in 1939. Cotton production, introduced by the Germans in Sukumaland and the Musoma area, increased from 3,714 bales of lint in 1913 to an average of 34,681 bales a year between 1935 and 1939.[4] In some isolated areas in the south coffee and tobacco were introduced. For the most part, however, the population in the south and many other parts of the country did not enter into cash crop production and continued either to supply labour to the export enclaves or to stagnate in a subsistence mode of production. Later, credit programmes for African producers were initiated, but they were geared towards those farmers who were producing for the export market. To this extent, credit to African peasants helped to increase the regional differentiation process that had started with the introduction of the export crops in suitable areas. Credit institutions continued to be preoccupied with export crops until after Independence.

Let us discuss in more detail the early credit programmes as a prelude to a later analysis of whether or

*ERB Paper 74.10.

CREDIT AGENCIES AFTER INDEPENDENCE

The Agricultural Credit Agency (ACA)

As a result of the World Bank Report, the newly independent Government of Tanganyika established the Agricultural Credit Agency (ACA), which opened for business in early 1962. The ACA took over the assets and liabilities of the Land Bank and the Funds, thus ending, in principle at least the provision of agricultural credit along racial lines. The ACA was to issue three types of loans: (a) short-term loans, not exceeding 12 calendar months; (b) medium-term loans, over 12 months but not exceeding five years; and (c) long-term loans, more than five years but not exceeding 25 years. No loan below £5 was to be issued and single loans to individuals were not to exceed £10,000. Cooperatives, local government authorities, agricultural associations and limited liability companies could obtain single loans of up to £25,000.[12]

District Loan Committees were appointed by the Minister of Agriculture and could approve loans of up to £200 to individual farmers. The ACA Executive Committee with headquarters in Dar es Salaam approved larger loans. District Agricultural officers were to be Executive officers of the Loan Committees.[13]

Table 1 gives the number and amount of loans disbursed for 1962, the first year of operation of the ACA. As the figures clearly show, the provision of credit to the African population was basically solved in much the same way as it had been prior to independence. Very few individual African peasants could qualify for these loans. In the words of the Deputy General Manager, "With a capital of £2,500,000 of which some £1,500,000 was committed at the start to Land Bank Loans to non-African farmers, one can see that the agency can only scratch the surface at trying to get credit to the farmers."[14]

It was evident that the ordinary African peasant benefitted little from this credit innovation. At the local level the same officials continued to allocate limited loan funds to a few select individuals in the export-oriented regions. One could argue that a local "Committee" advised the Agricultural officer. In most instances this committee consisted of representatives of the local elite. Only those with access to the committee or those who in the opinion of the District Agricultural Officer were "progressive farmers" could hope to get loans. The concept of the "progressive farmers" is itself a capitalist one. We are of the opinion that developing countries, especially those who have chosen the socialist path to development, cannot formulate successful developmental programmes on the basis of such an approach.

The National Development Credit Agency (NDCA)

By 1964, it had become clear that the ACA was not performing satisfactorily. It was therefore reorganized into the National Development Credit Agency. However, its objectives remained about the same. The emphasis on export-oriented crops was still there.

TABLE 1: ACA LOANS IN 1962

A. Executive Type Loans

Purpose of Loan	*Number*	*Amount (£)*
Purchase of Land	2	11,197
Permanent Improvements:		
Buildings	8	9,256
Water Supply	7	3,100
Crops	91	30,463
Purchases: Machinery	71	45,353
Fishing Equipment	16	9,849
Cattle and Oxen	24	13,334
Poultry and Equipment	4	1,620
Annual Crop Production	133	136,986
Total	356	261,158

B. District Type Loan

Purpose of Loan	*Number*	*Amount (£)*
Permanent Improvements:		
Water Supply	1	10
Crops	655	37,570
Forestry	4	21,265
Purchase: Machinery	279	15,129
Fishing Equipment	148	33,025
Cattle and Oxen	520	3,782
Poultry and Equipment	—	—
Annual Crop Production	—	—
Total	1,607	110,791

SOURCE: V. S. Makame, *op. cit.*

In addition, the World Bank provided funds for loans to smallholder farmers in the tea and cotton growing areas. As a consequence the World Bank was to be consulted on almost everything about the NDCA, including the appointment of the manager and the structure and functions of the organization.

The main innovation introduced by NDCA was that money was to be lent to peasant farmers through the cooperatives. In principle this practice was consistent with the socialist policies of the country; in practice the NDCA was lending to individuals through the cooperative movement. As President Nyerere himself has said: "Although marketing cooperatives are socialist in the sense that they represent the joint activities of the producers, they could be socialist institutions serving capitalism if the basic organisation of agricultural production is capitalist."[15]

NDCA therefore differed little from its predecessors. Indeed by the time of its dissolution in 1971, it had given credit to only one ujamaa village, although the policy of ujamaa villages was clearly expressed in 1967.

not the post-Independence programmes differ from their colonial predecessors.

THE LOAN FUNDS FOR AFRICAN PRODUCERS

By the 1950s some Native Authorities and marketing cooperatives provided agricultural credit to African producers. The authorities, already burdened with the provision of social services such as primary schools and dispensaries, operated only small scale and limited revolving loan funds. Lending by cooperatives was also very limited.

In 1947, the Local Development Loan Fund (LDLF) was established on funds drawn from the Colonial Agricultural Development Reserve. Later in the decade the African Productivity Loan Fund (APLF) was established with funds provided by the United States Foreign Operations Administration.[5]

At the end of 1959 the LDLF had given or had committed to give 252 loans valued at £56,831, for agricultural and other agrarian activities.[6] APLF had given or committed to give 308 loans totalling £92,456, of which £71,000 were for agrarian activities and the rest for small-scale industry. Of the agricultural loans, half were for small maize mills and over a third were for agricultural tractors. In actual fact, by the end of December 1956, the LDLF had disbursed only £29,032 out of the committed funds and the APLF had disbursed only £43,562. Almost £51,000 remained uncommitted. The LDLF loans averaged nearly £228 per loan and the APLF loans were about £300.

The above figures bring out the salient characteristics of the early colonial credit schemes. The amount involved was very little, and the number of people involved were very few. Nevertheless, given the low monetary incomes in rural Tanzania at that time, these loans were quite an economic shot in the arm for those few that managed to get them. In this respect the loans contributed to the differentiation of African producers and promoted the economic development of the more advanced regions.

Raikes and Meynen's assessment of the colonial credit schemes is to the point:

> Such small amounts of rural credit as were distributed accrued entirely to the larger farmers. Apart from the Native Authority revolving funds, which were under the control of powerful local figures, the first country-wide credit schemes for Africans, the Local Development Loan Fund, was set up in 1947 with £50,000 . . . Small as it was, this fund was not distributed so as to aid the largest number of farmers. Nearly all the loans made were for sums over Shs. 1,000 and were mostly for structural transformations of farming systems, particularly mechanization. In the first two years of operation, out of 12 loans, 7 were made for the operation of tractor ploughing schemes.[7]

The situation with regard to the equitable distribution of funds, did not improve with the creation of the APLF, as Raikes and Meynen state:

> Even later . . . when the Fund had been brought up to £100,000 and supplemented with the African Productivity Loan Fund, with a similar sum, the number of loans made annually by both funds was around Shs. 150 a year and the average amount over Shs. 2,000. Since this constituted the total government credit to all African farmers and businessmen, and the amount lent outside the schemes must have been very small, the degree of concentration was considerable. Few Districts, for example, would have had more than 10 farmers receiving loans at any one time.[8]

The very use to which most of these loans were put helped to promote differentiation among individuals in the same area. Thus there arose a group of people who had tractors, hired labour to work on their farms, hired their tractors to other peasants, milled maize for others, etc. In short there arose a class of petty rural capitalists.

The World Bank Report discussed some of the problems of the loan funds. First, there was the problem of repayment. Repayments six months and more overdue amounted to 44 per cent of total LDLF repayments due and 53 per cent of APLF repayments due. This high rate of "defaults" was attributed to two fundamental causes: (a) some projects were technically or economically unsound; and (b) borrowers failed to accept responsibility for repayments.[9]

With regard to loans for the planting of permanent crops the Report found that the decision by the Loan Fund Committee to discontinue the repayment "moratorium" until the farmer had started to market the crop was too harsh. The Committee had decided that only those who had successfully grown and marketed their own crop would be provided with loans to expand their production. The Report spoke of the limits "to which the risk of defaults can be met by progressively tightening up of repayment terms. Beyond a certain limit, loans would cease to be worthwhile."[10] The Committee's decision was another indication of the capitalistic orientation of these programmes.

The Report also dealt with the administrative problems besetting the Fund.

> At present the African Loan Funds are virtually run by one man in Dar es Salaam, under the general direction of the African Loan Funds Committee, an interdepartmental body augmented by several unofficial members. Planning of loan applications —in fact often their preparation—and the supervision of loans is left to local, administrative, agricultural, veterinary and other officers. To these officers, often hard pressed with other work, the applications said to 'flood into District offices' are frequently a nuisance, taking valuable time needed for other work.[11]

The Tanzania Rural Development Bank (TRDB)

In late 1971, the Tanzania Government created the Tanzania Rural Development Bank to replace NDCA. Its mission, as summarized in its first Annual Report, was to provide "a comprehensive credit system for transforming the subsistence living into a modern cash economy with its attendant increased employment opportunities and income distribution."[16]

To what extent has TRDB translated these aspirations into actions? For TRDB to accomplish the mission of setting up a comprehensive credit system capable of transforming rural Tanzania into a modern agricultural economy would call for programmes qualitatively different from those of its predecessors.

A comparison of the types of loans issued by NDCA in its last year of operation (Table 2) and those offered by TRDB in its first two years of operation (Table 3) may illustrate some of the qualitative differences between the two.

NDCA gave loans to purchase agro-chemicals and farm machinery in the production of export-oriented agricultural commodities. In contrast, TRDB attempted to launch a more comprehensive credit programme that included loans for crop production, fisheries, livestock, off-farm processing, storage and rural transportation, although relatively little money was allocated to some of these activities.

TRDB also provided loans to ujamaa villages for production of food crops, mainly maize and wheat. The funds allocated to these essential food crops accounted for 3.5 per cent of total loans in 1971/72 and 7.6 per cent in 1972/73.

TRDB gave loans to 29 ujamaa villages in 1971/72 and 54 ujamaa villages in 1972/73. These loans accounted for 13.7 per cent and 19 per cent of all loans disbursed by TRDB in 1971/72 and 1972/73 respectively. In contrast NDCA had given only one loan to an ujamaa village in 1970/71. Indeed TRDB seems to have been aware of its responsibility to ujamaa villages. It devoted a few paragraphs of its first annual report to a brief exposition of the ujamaa village policy in the country and stated that the crucial development issue was the growth of these villages. In passing judgement on TRDB as to whether or not it was discharging its responsibility fully one has to bear in mind the following:

(i) Government policy restricts TRDB loans to those ujamaa villages that are registered as Multi-Purpose Cooperative Societies and classified as Stage III villages. In 1972 there were 160 ujamaa villages of this type (an additional 4,386 villages had not yet registered).[17]

(ii) Because Government policy encourages TRDB to lend to the traditional marketing coops as a socialist exercise, then the share given to these coops will remain large although in fact this may retard the socialistic mobilization of the rural masses, since individuals continue to receive help from these coops.[18]

What is needed is a complete reorganization of the cooperative movement. As the mobilization of the people into ujamaa villages gathers momentum, the present cooperative societies should be abolished. Ujamaa villages, as producer-cooperative units, should take over the marketing and other functions and form unions among themselves. The unions would form a national organization to replace the present Co-operative Union of Tanganyika (CUT) which basically represents individualistic and capitalist-oriented farmers. In addition to promoting the exchange of ideas among ujamaa villages at the district, regional and national level, an exchange that is lacking today, these unions would also ensure that they really have people who represent them in TRDB and other national organs.

To sum up, while we are of the opinion that TRDB needs to provide more credit to ujamaa villages, it should be understood that at present there are factors beyond TRDB's control that the Government needs to look into in order to enable TRDB to discharge its responsibility. The first is that ujamaa living should be promoted in all regions more vigorously. Moreover the provision of credit to ujamaa villages should not be limited to Stage III Villages only. Finally, the Ujamaa Village Movement should replace the existing capitalist-oriented marketing coops.

TABLE 2: N.D.C.A. LOANS (1970/71)

A. Loans by Type	Shs.	%
Fertilizers, insecticides and sprayers for cotton	9,488,362	26.8
Coffee sprays	8,746,302	24.7
Tobacco, tea, castoroil and pyrethrum plant and machinery	3,596,309	10.1
Farm Equipment	2,939,400	8.3
Coffee pulperies	1,607,889	4.5
Tea Stumps and Fertilizers	9,085,690	25.6
Total	35,463,962	100.0

B. Loans by Recipients	Number	Shs.	%
Coop. Unions & Societies	58	44,020,389	91.7
Individuals	44	3,210,364	6.7
Ujamaa Villages	1	7,500	0.02
Others[a]	7	774,700	1.6
Total		48,012,953[b]	100.0

SOURCE: The National Cooperative Bank Group (The National Cooperative Bank, The National Development Credit Agency): Final Report and Accounts 1969/70 and 1970/71.

[a] Includes capitalist agricultural associations and companies.
[b] The difference between the two totals may be due to the fact that the total in (B) represents committed funds while the total in (A) represents funds actually disbursed.

TABLE 3: TANZANIA RURAL DEVELOPMENT BANK LOANS[a]

	1971/72			1972/73		
A. Loans by Type	No.	Amount	%	No.	Amount	%
Seasonal Inputs	56	20,983,564	58.7	71	61,961,939	57.6
Crop establishment	3	949,420	2.6	5	24,482,600	22.7
Rural transportation	12	6,565,184	18.4	7	8,590,000	8.0
Farm machinery	13	1,016,861	2.8	6	2,012,304	1.9
Storage	1	5,317,916	14.8	2	1,900,000	1.8
Commercial ventures	5	465,121	1.3	1	36,000	0.0(0.03)
Fisheries project	—	—	—	3	862,300	0.8
Livestock	1	486,000	1.4	7	7,759,525	7.2
Off-Farm processing	—	—	—	1	18,000	0.0(0.02)
Total	91	35,784,066	100.0	103	107,622,068	100.0
B. By Borrowers						
Coop Unions	71	12,163,271	34.0	29	32,324,352	30.0
Coop Societies	9	11,282,063	31.5	7	30,283,670	28.1
Ujamaa coop Societies	29	4,914,786	13.7	54	20,423,096	19.0
Individuals	26	2,418,895	6.8	1	10,000	0.0
Companies	1	2,316,654	6.4	5	7,168,300	6.7
District Develop. Corps.	5	1,593,900	4.4	5	4,485,525	4.2
Partners	2	267,500	0.8	—		
Associations	2	826,997	2.3	2	12,929,125	12.0
Total	91	35,784,066	100.0	103	107,622,068	100.0
C. Programmes						
Tobacco		18,317,752	51.2		45,580,514	42.4
Coffee		497,550	1.4		7,488,734	7.0
Cotton		924,712	2.6		727,425	0.6
Wheat & Maize		1,243,550	3.5		8,165,266	7.6
Tea Development		949,420	2.6		24,484,000	22.7
Farm Machinery		1,016,861	2.8		2,012,304	1.9
Rural Transport		6,565,184	18.3		8,590,000	8.0
Off-farm Processing		—			18,000	0.0
Livestock		486,000	1.4		7,759,525	7.2
Storage		5,317,916	14.9		1,900,000	1.8
Fisheries		—			862,300	0.8
Commercial Ventures		465,121	1.3		36,000	0.0
Total		35,784,066	100.0		107,622,068	100.0

SOURCE: TRDB Annual Reports. Loans include about Shs. 28 million approved during 1972/73 but for 1973/74 inputs.

ECONOMIC ASPECTS OF PROVIDING CREDIT TO UJAMAA VILLAGES

Credit and Ujamaa

According to Nyerere, the traditional African societies lived according to a philosophy of togetherness which is now known in Tanzania as "Ujamaa".[19] This philosophy was based on three principles—mutual involvement and respect for one another, communal ownership of property, and the obligation to work by all members in the community. The inadequacies of traditional society were that there was inequality among men and women, i.e. women were subservient to men, and that because of the low level of technology available at that time, the standard of living was generally low. The aim of Tanzanian socialism therefore is to re-establish this kind of society with the *proviso* that the inequality of the sexes is abolished and that modern technology is used to raise the standard of living of everyone. This, simply stated, is the basic socialist policy that is to guide the development of rural Tanzania. Credit institutions, along with other institutions, have the responsibility of ensuring that their programmes are in line with and effectively promote this policy.

Western economists advising on the provision of credit in rural areas of the Third World view the problem as one of trying to reconcile three conflicting objectives of agricultural credit programmes, viz. equity, efficiency and institutional viability.[20] A programme preoccupied with efficiency and institutional viability will attempt to eliminate all loan defaulters even if that means the programme will reach only a few farmers. Equity is seen as opposed to efficiency, though it might be consistent with institutional viability. Although we do not consider these objectives to be irrelevant, we disagree with their analysis of the purpose of credit in a developing society.

What are the merits of these opposing views and can the objectives be reconciled?

First, in a situation where "small farmers" exist along side "big farmers" it is a contradiction to speak in terms of equity. As one expert has pointed out credit programmes in developing countries invariably benefit big farmers rather than small farmers, even though they might have been launched with small farmers in mind![21] The reality behind this statement is that the pursuit of equity cannot take place in a socio-political vacuum. An Indian economist has noted that unequal distribution is also caused by the concentration of political and economic power in the hands of large farmers who thereby have special access to credit institutions, which ration credit in their favour.[22] In a capitalist or feudal situation, however good one's intentions may be, it is all but impossible to establish an equitable system for anything including housing and credit. Hence the establishment of co-operative–production units becomes the *sine qua non* condition for an equitable credit programme in any country. Conversely, for a country like Tanzania, refusing to give credit to ujamaa villages, or continuing to aid non-Wajamaa directly, or indirectly through cooperatives, is to defeat or slow down, at least, the building of a socialist rural economy.

Secondly, with regards to efficiency, our view is that giving credit to those who can afford it, to wit the big farmers, does not *per se* ensure efficiency. Indeed evidence abounds that better off farmers are also bigger defaulters. Lele cites studies from both India and Ethiopia. In a survey of 34 small and 33 large cooperative credit societies in India the percentage of overdue payments on loans outstanding was significantly higher among large farmers than among small farmers. Studies in Ethiopia indicate that as high as 97 per cent of small farmers have repaid credit in the first years of establishing package programmes. The performance of the large farmers is relatively much poorer.[23] Evidence from Tanzania points to the same conclusion. Raikes and Meynen note that "in Mbulu (in Northern Tanzania) a special effort was made in 1955 to produce a group of large farmers by giving credit to a few individuals to enable them to expand their holdings from about 40 to 300 acres. The results, as a cautious banker would have probably predicted, were large-scale failures to repay."[24] The premise that preoccupation with equity will, of necessity, endanger efficiency is therefore a false one. We shall show below how efficiency can be pursued in the most equitable system, i.e. under socialism.

Third, institutional viability to us means service to the masses of the people. It means providing the kind of assistance the people themselves need, which implies that the people themselves must participate in the decision making. That is why the direct representation of the Wajamaa in decision making is a crucial issue. Our review has shown that past programmes and decisions were dominated by the national and local bureaucrats and political elites.

The scattered nature of the peasant households provided another constraint. Given the skilled manpower limitation in most LDCs, even if a government were genuinely committed to providing credit to the masses of its rural population, it would not be possible from an administrative point of view to carry out such a policy because of the widely dispersed population. Thus after Independence, there was considerable effort to extend Government credit programmes to small farmers, but as one observer notes, "only one fourth of one per cent of the nation's farmers could be reached in 1962. As the burden began to tell on the implementation machinery, and recovery problems became apparent, coverage fell even from this modest level. . . . Funds were channelled to already commercial operators."[25] Grouping the rural population into collective production units would facilitate the launching of a credit programme designed to reach the majority of the peasants. In this regard Ujamaa Villages can provide the basis for an equitable, efficient and viable credit programme.

The overall responsibility of the financial institutions can be summarized as follows:

(i) to enable the ujamaa villages to develop to the point where they can be independent in acquiring their own means of production for their agricultural activities;
(ii) to prepare and identify sources of funds for credit programmes and to specify how these funds can be disbursed to producer co-operatives and other customers so that production plans can be implemented effectively;
(iii) to teach the Wajamaa the importance of saving their money; and
(iv) to clearly explain to the Wajamaa the advantages achieved from insuring their lives, household possessions and the crops grown in the ujamaa village.

Given the initial successes of ujamaa villages, what remains is to establish and follow the most suitable credit techniques. Again we start by showing the unsuitability of capitalist techniques in the Tanzanian context and go on to discuss techniques used in socialist countries and how they can be applied to ujamaa villages.

THE CREDIT WORTHINESS CRITERION IN CAPITALIST CREDIT PROGRAMMES

The principle of "credit-worthiness" is purely and predominantly for capitalist and pro-capitalist developing countries. It is not for Tanzania. The principle states that credit should be issued only with a *guarantee* of fixed assets such as land. In India, for example, credit worthiness is associated with land ownership, and the size of landholdings determines the amount of credit a farmer can obtain on medium and long-term loans from cooperatives and land banks.[26] Consequently, credit funds go mainly to large farmers, notwithstanding the fact that in some cases the negative relationship between productive assets and size of holding has been empirically determined before issuing the loan.[27]

In the absence of individual landholding rights, the little credit given to the African peasant during the colonial era went to export crop producers. This is one example of how the colonial economies became externally oriented. To a great extent this trend continues to this day. Ujamaa villages seek to establish integrated, self-sustaining economic units which will be the basis of an integrated agricultural national economy. To emphasise the provision of credit to individual farmers who grow industrial crops as is being done now is to perpetuate, probably unwittingly, the external economic dependence inherited from colonialism.

In other developing countries, particularly India, bourgeois economists have attempted to recommend the issue of credit by using the following variants of the "credit-worthiness" criterion:

(i) Credit is given to a member of a Cooperative Society in proportion to the total shares he holds in the cooperative. Thus a member of a cooperative society is entitled to several times the amount of his total shares in the cooperative, in credit. The concept of an ujamaa village is radically different from this kind of "a cooperative", which works in such a way as to favour the richer farmers who have the most shares in the cooperative.

(ii) Credit is given in proportion to the rent a farmer pays to a landowner. The method also favours the big capitalist farmers and leaves the desperate small peasants to their own resources.

(iii) A third technique is to provide credit up to 50% of the market value of the land. The land in turn serves to guarantee the loan to the credit institution.

(iv) Yet another variant of credit-worthiness often used is down payment. This effectively prohibits small farmers from making use of public loans offered in this way.

(v) The last and the most popular method used is the system of hypothecs (mortgages or other securities). This is a mere extension of the above methods to include private assets other than land. Thus a peasant with more cattle, a bigger and more modern house, larger bank deposits, etc. is considered more credit worthy.

Advocates of the "credit-worthiness" criterion argue that an institution should not issue credit to borrowers who do not have sufficient assets either to guarantee repayment or to minimise the risk of default. Furthermore they argue that communally or publicly-owned land must be transferred to private hands before it can be considered as such an asset. However, we shall demonstrate later that a credit system is possible on other grounds than this principle of "credit worthiness". We maintain that this principle is inconsistent with the policy of ujamaa villages and can actually annihilate ujamaa villages in Tanzania if it is followed. A credit system which gives rise to an inequitable distribution of income does not fit into the strategy of the socialist transformation of the economy. The Arusha Declaration era will not accept this as the acceleration of rural economic differentiation intensifies anti-socialist activities. Institutions in Tanzania should aim at eliminating rural differentiation, and this can be done by gradually but effectively introducing a socialist credit system along the lines proposed below.

The Principle of Production Credit in a Socialist System

A socialist agricultural credit system is imperative for a progressive and consistent economic transformation of Tanzania's agriculture. Successful implementation of the socialist credit system demands a complete rejection of the "Principle of Credit-Worthiness". Two socialist methods of issuing credit are quite relevant to ujamaa villages.

The Simple Credit

This form of credit applies mainly to crop growing and livestock rearing areas. The credit allows the *crop grown or livestock reared in the village to act as a guarantee.* It is mainly a short-term credit of 12 calendar months. The calculation of a credit limit is based on the expected yields per hectare in the case of crops, or any other value in the case of livestock. After having assessed the expected yields, a village should then be allowed to receive up to 50% of the expected yields as credit, and in kind. Such short-term credit is specifically for issuing circulation assets such as seeds, fertilizers, pesticides, seed cakes and other concentrates which can act as feed stuffs for animals. For an effective operation, the credit institution should take into consideration the type of the crop grown, the type of livestock reared, the reason and the location of the village. In Burma and many other non-capitalist developing countries which have tried to introduce the system, it has worked satisfactorily. The method offers a high guarantee of repayment, when compared with the purposeless cash credit, and a relatively simple control over the utilization of credit which otherwise is often used for purposes other than the increase of production and income.

Intensification Credit

The issuing of this type of credit is based on the Farm Production Plans. This method demands that ujamaa villages which submit an application to the bank must show a production plan that clearly indicates how the required seeds, agro-chemicals, farm equipment, etc. will be used.

In addition, the ujamaa village must show its economic activities for the previous year. The record of the previous year should specify: (a) credit received if any; (b) the amount of repayment; (c) total hectarage in each crop; (d) total output by volume and value of each crop; (e) total sales of each crop; and (f) the net income of the village.

The credit and production record should be easy to read and understand. This important and meaningful economic advice is to be given to the ujamaa village. In addition, the evaluation of the application will largely depend on what is recorded. The accuracy of the application will have to be certified by an economic adviser as well as by the Board, which deals with the issuing of credit. If the Board is convinced that what has been tabulated is real rather than wishful thinking and if the Wajamaa agree that the targets they have set are realistic, then the fulfilment of the plan should acquire a *legal status*.

Several questions must be asked before credit is issued to an ujamaa village. For example, will this loan increase production in this ujamaa village? Will this credit cause a financial burden for the ujamaa village? If the use of credit is not likely to result in higher income for the village, the village will not be in a position to make the repayment and interest on schedule. Or if a village incurred a loss on a previous loan, the credit agency concerned must find out the reason. If the loss was due to unavoidable circumstances such as adverse weather conditions, the credit agency might postpone repayment to the next production period. But if it found that members of the village misused the credit extended to them, they must be held legally responsible for the repayment of the loan despite the loss incurred. The issuing of credit in socialist countries is not based on the principle of charity. All peasants are entitled to credit facilities but they must work for them. The financial institutions have to abide by economic laws. Issuing credits to the ujamaa villages even when the credit institution is more than 50% sure that the village will default does the Wajamaa more harm than good. Villages in particularly handicapped areas, e.g. villages that historically are more backward or that suffer disasters such as floods, can receive grants from the Government or from the credit institution itself, provided that it is understood from the very beginning that what is involved is a grant rather than a loan. As a general rule, however, *credit funds should not be converted into grants.*

STRUCTURING A SUITABLE FINANCIAL SYSTEM FOR UJAMAA VILLAGES

Tanzania, like all other low income countries, has a problem of capital accumulation. Prior to 1967 most of the dominant positions in the economy were controlled by foreign capital. One consequence was a continuous outflow of resources from the country. Since the Arusha Declaration this drain has been reduced somewhat, but the problem of inadequate capital accumulation has not been resolved.

Agriculture is the major source of accumulation in Tanzania, yet the rate of agricultural development has been slow in recent years. As a consequence and in an attempt to deepen its productive forces and accelerate capital accumulation, Tanzania remains dependent on external sources of capital, in the form of bilateral and multilateral aid. This aid normally is accompanied by restrictions imposed by the donor country or agency. One such restriction is that the credit principles of the donor country be followed, even though they may conflict with the goal of transformation of rural Tanzania to socialism.

Agricultural development requires an expansion of the physical infrastructure in the form of improved transportation systems, investment in irrigation works, etc. In addition rural Tanzania lacks adequate financial institutions to provide working capital for small holder and village productive activities and to mobilize savings in the rural areas. The villagization programme already has facilitated the establishment of such institutions in many areas, but much remains to be done in educating the Wajamaa in the role that credit can play in increasing production and improving the village structures.

The creation of a financial system to meet the needs of the ujamaa villages must overcome specific problems. Practically all credit institutions are characterized by insufficient credit funds and fundamental economic weaknesses. There is a general lack of understanding of the proper use of production credit and an inability to review the totality of agricultural activities as a system. This means that if credit for production is issued, arrangements for the supply of improved inputs and for the purchase of the produce should be included in the formulation of the credit programmes.

The ujamaa villages and their continued development would seem to contain the potential for the transformation of the rural areas in Tanzania. The Tanzania Rural Development Bank and the Regional Development Fund have been charged with the responsibility of providing credit to the ujamaa villages and to other public institutions. These institutions must transform the credit system itself in a manner consistent with the national policy of socialist transformation and educate the people in the advantages to be gained from a proper use of credit. A careful evaluation of credit utilization and repayment practices and the flexible adaptation of successful institutional forms are essential if the credit facilities are to be productive.

CONCLUSION

Credit is indispensable to the development of ujamaa villages, not only because it bridges the time elements involved in the production process, but also and more importantly because it is an economic instrument for hastening the transformation of the underdeveloped rural areas of Tanzania into a productive and dynamic sector of the national economy. Tanzania's conditions are unique in some respects, and successful accomplishments in other socialist countries cannot be duplicated in all respects here; yet, Tanzania has much to learn from a careful study and systematic evaluation of the experiences and achievements of other countries.

The task of transforming rural Tanzania is the responsibility of all Tanzanians. Failure to do so will place increasingly heavy burdens on future generations. An important element in this transformation is the development of suitable financial institutions to meet the credit needs of the ujamaa villages.

NOTES

1. The Arusha Declaration which was promulgated by the Tanganyika African National Union (TANU), the ruling and only political party in mainland Tanzania, provided *inter alia* for the complete nationalization of all banking and insurance activities in the country. NBC then became the only commercial bank in the country and took over the assets and liabilities of the nationalized foreign banks, i.e. the former Tanganyika. In this paper Tanzania refers to Mainland Tanzania.
2. International Bank for Reconstruction and Development (IBRD), *The Economic Development of Tanganyika*, Baltimore: John Hopkins University Press, 1961, pp. 115–21.
3. Sir Donald Cameron, "Agriculture and Labours". The 5 August 1926, Tanzania National Archives 215/121/48. Quoted by John Iliffe, *Agricultural Change in Modern Tanganyika*, Nairobi: East African Publishing House, 1971, p. 6.
4. J. Iliffe, *Ibid.*, p. 19.
5. Food and Agricultural Organization (FAO), "Agricultural Credit in Three Village Areas in North-Eastern Tanzania," in *Agricultural Credit Case Studies: Working Paper No. 2*, 1953.
6. IBRD, *op. cit.*, pp. 117–121.
7. P. L. Raikes and W. L. Meynen, "Differentiation, Dependence and Diffusion: A Critique of Extension Theory and Practice." Paper read at 8th Annual Social Science Conference of the East African Universities, Nairobi, 19–23 December, 1972.
8. *Ibid.*
9. IBRD, *op. cit.*, p. 119. We shall point out later that the decision to favour the bigger farmers does not, and in this case, did not ensure repayment.
10. *Ibid.*, p. 119.
11. *Ibid.*, p. 120.
12. V. S. Makame, in *Agricultural Development in Tanzania*, ed. H. E. Smith, Dar es Salaam: Institute of Public Administration, 1965, pp. 70–75.
13. *Ibid.*
14. *Ibid.*
15. J. K. Nyerere, "Socialism and Rural Development," in *Ujamaa: Essays on Socialism*, J. K. Nyerere, Dar es Salaam: Oxford University Press, 1968, p. 116.
16. Tanzania Rural Development Bank, *Annual Report and Accounts for the Year Ended 30th June, 1971–30th June 1972*, Dar es Salaam, January 1973, p. 7.
17. S. Mbilinyi, R. Mabele and M. Kyomo, "Economic Struggle of TANU," in *Towards Uhuru—Twenty Years of TANU Leadership*, ed. G. Ruhumbika, Nairobi: East African Literature Bureau, 1974, p. 83.
18. The breakdown of recipients in Table 2 and 3 is therefore misleading since coops have a big element of loans destined to individuals. It may appear from Table 3 that individuals now receive a very small proportion of TRDB funds.
19. See Nyerere, *op. cit.*, pp. 106–44.
20. Judith Tendler, "The Trouble with Goals of Small Farmer Credit Programmes," in A.I.D. *Spring Review of Small Farmer Credit*, Volume XIX, June 1973, No. SR 119, Agency for International Development, Department of State, Washington, D.C., 1973.
21. H. Blair, "The Distribution of Agricultural Credit and Benefits: Political Economy and Small Farmers," A.I.D. *Spring Review*, June 1973.
22. U. Lele, "The Role of Credit and Marketing Functions in Agricultural Development," *Rural Banking*, eds. V. Pandiker and V. C. Mehta, Bombay: Institute of Bank Management, 1974, p. 10.
23. *Ibid.*
24. Raikes and Meynen, *op. cit.*
25. M. P. Collinson, "Tanzania's Cooperative Movement and Farmer's Credit in the 1960s," unpublished paper quoted in Lele, *op. cit.*
26. Lele, *op. cit.*
27. *Ibid.*, p. 16.

The Ismani Maize Credit Programme*

A. T. MOHELE

Introduction

The Tanzania Rural Development Bank came into being by the 1971 Act as the chief means of transforming the rural economy. Ujamaa villages, as the nation's basic economic units, need sustained support if they are to develop management capabilities, adopt improved technologies and husbandry practices and increase productivity.

The rapid growth of ujamaa villages called for a parallel expansion of TRDB credit facilities to support ujamaa villages as multi-purpose cooperative societies. The usual approach of TRDB and its predecessor, NDCA, had been to select villages for support based on their individual creditworthiness. However, in 1972/73, a new approach was necessitated by the launching of the Ismani Operation in Iringa Region. Ismani was an area famous for maize production by petty and capitalist farmers, although there was insufficient land for the majority of peasants. This prompted the Party and Government to socialise land ownership in Ismani. The local people were to resettle into ujamaa villages where they would own land communally and produce maize on a commercial basis.

Since the newly formed ujamaa villages had few agricultural resources other than land and the labour supply of member households as they embarked on commercial maize production, the Government undertook to support them in the 1971/72 season with free agricultural inputs and tractor ploughing services. This support was limited and of short-term duration, and therefore the Government directed the TRDB to support the ujamaa villages with loans. In order to qualify for borrowing, many villagers were registered as multipurpose cooperative units.

The Bank's involvement in Ismani Operations in 1972/73 was experimental as far as an area approach was concerned. The support included financing of mechanisation, agricultural inputs and seeds for the whole group of ujamaa villages. The Ismani programme involved nearly Shs. 1.8 million of a total of about Shs. 20 million loaned to ujamaa villages in 1972/73 (about 9%).

This paper examines the impact of the TRDB credit programme on the Ismani Maize Programme. It is divided into two sections. The first deals with the main characteristics of the programme in which the Bank was involved. The second evaluates the effectiveness of the credit programme and discusses the problems and the possible improvements that could be made in the programme.

THE ISMANI MAIZE CREDIT PROGRAMME

Background Information

Ismani is an administrative division in Iringa District. It covers an area of approximately 625 sq. kilometres and lies at an altitude of 915 to 1,524 metres above sea level. Its soils are primarily red and sticky clay loams derived from ferrisols on sand stones, although in some areas there are patches of black sticky poorly drained soils. Rainfall in the area averages between 510 and 760 mm. per annum and is concentrated in the period between late November and mid April. It is open grassland with scattered shrubs, with patches of thick thorn bushes adorning the valley and hill sides.

The 1967 Census enumerated the population of Ismani at 34,044 persons, which was a population density of 8 persons per sq. km.

Ismani has been an important maize growing area since the 1950s. Its proximity to Iringa Town, the presence of the Great North Road and a landscape suitable for ox-plough and tractorisation contributed to the expansion of maize production on a large scale.

Before 1971 two main types of maize farming predominated: (a) the capitalist and petty capitalist mode on farms which were larger than 15 hectares; and (b) the poor peasant mode on farms which were less than 15 hectares. The capitalists and petty capitalists owned a large proportion of Ismani land. Although they constituted only about 32% of the population, they controlled more than 80% of the land. Nevertheless, average yields were low and had shown a declining trend since the 1950s, from about 35 bags per hectare to 12 bags per hectare in 1971.[1]

The capitalist mode of farming in Ismani was not in keeping with the country's declared socialist policies. Moreover the poor peasants and the labourers who were working on the capitalist farms were agitating for socialisation of the farms so that they too could have some land to use for producing their own food requirements. In keeping with these demands, the Ismani area was declared a place where large-scale farming could be done by ujamaa villages only. The declaration for the Ismani Operation was made in May, 1971.[2] In the following year ujamaa villages were organised, each having about 200 to 400 working adults. For the 1971/72 season the 29 ujamaa villages received assistance from the Government in the form of tractor services and some posho for food supplies.

Before the 1971/72 crop was harvested and an assessment could be made of the impact of Government assistance, the authorities decided to expand the programme. In March 1972 an authoritative speech in

*ERB Paper 75.2.

Ismani called for the registration of the existing 29 ujamaa villages as multipurpose cooperative societies. These societies were authorized to borrow from TRDB since Government and RDF resources were not adequate to meet all the requirements of the villages. The speech also called for modernisation of agriculture by ensuring that each village had proper plans for economic development. Agricultural machinery inputs and fertilizers were considered necessary ingredients in the improvement of agriculture.[3]

Following this TRDB was asked to collaborate with the Iringa Regional authorities in the development of a plan for maize production and to support this plan with a proper credit programme.[4] The main features of the TRDB maize programme were:

(a) Each of the 29 villages was to grow maize in a 240 hectares communal farm.

(b) To enable the villagers to cultivate this large area each village was to receive the following capital inputs:

2 – 60 - HP tractors,
2 – three furrow disc harrows,
2 – sixteen disc harrows,
2 – four row planters,
1 – 4½ ton two wheel tip trailer,
1 – tractor power-driven maize sheller, and
1 – godown.

The cost of these capital costs was estimated at Shs. 120,000 per village. In addition each village was to be supplied with the following recurrent inputs:

600 packets of improved seed,
600 bags of fertilizer (sodium ammoniate), and
600 packets of pesticide (DDT 5%).

The estimated cost was about Shs. 60,364 per village. Because the villages were just commencing their activities, they were to be provided with a loan to cover operating expenses, i.e. to purchase fuel, oil, grease and spare parts. This was estimated at about Shs. 64,270 per village. The production cost per ujamaa village excluding labour costs was as follows:

Capital Costs	Shs.	120,000
Recurrent Inputs	,,	60,364
		180,364

The programme for the 29 ujamaa villages would have cost in excess of Shs. 5 million for the 1972/73 season. It was hoped that successful implementation of this programme would enable expansion of lending to both "repeater" borrowers and new borrowers in subsequent years.

When these proposals were presented for final consideration the Bank wisely decided to introduce the programme in phases. The Bank therefore agreed to provide only Shs. 1,817,692 for the 1972/73 season. This covered tractors and implements for 10 villages, fuel and oil for 10 villages, recurrent inputs (fertilizers, seeds and insecticides) for 30 villages and tractor hire service operation for 20 ujamaa villages which were not provided tractors. The breakdown of the total loan is shown in Table 1.

TABLE 1: UJAMAA VILLAGE LOAN, ISMANI, 1971/72

	(Shs.)
10 tractors and implements	686,771
85 tons of maize seed (30 villages)	25,590
426 tons TSP (30 villages)	391,240
426 tons CAN (30 villages)	291,645
109,000 litres fuel (10 tractors)	117,595
1,885 litres oil (10 tractors)	8,121
60 fuel/oil filters (10 tractors)	3,600
Transport costs	10,530
Tractor drivers	8,100
Tractor Hire Service operating for 20 villages	272,000
	1,817,692

With a reduction in the expected capital and recurrent inputs the total area for maize production was reduced to 120 hectares per village, giving a total maize area under *ujamaa* of 3,600 hectares. If the maize area yielded an average of 25 bags per hectare, each village would produce about 3,000 bags, or 270 tons valued at about Shs. 90,000.

The Programme and the Pre-Existing Local Institutions

The Ismani Maize Credit Programme planned to use the traditional cooperative union to channel maize marketing. The union would also handle the aggregate credit requirements for the participating villages. It was, however, insisted that the members of the ujamaa villages should be involved in planning their own financial requirements. The local regional branch officials of Tanzania Rural Development Bank would visit each village wishing to apply for a loan and discuss with the villagers about their requirements, the effect of the loan on their well being, the loan burden and the responsibility of loan repayment.

A number of other activities related to the Credit Programme also were undertaken: (a) a comprehensive training programme for members of ujamaa villages was to be initiated so that they could assist Kilimo extension staff to become more effective in their work; (b) secretaries of ujamaa villages were to be given additional training in maintaining accurate accounts related to the issuance of loans; and (c) the Credit Programme was to be only part of the larger Ismani Operation where social services such as schools, health facilities and water were to be provided.

The Objectives of the Maize Credit Programme

The objectives of the Credit Programme were threefold:

(a) to replace large-scale capitalist farming by cooperative ujamaa villages;
(b) to raise yields through the application of better husbandry practices and agricultural inputs such as fertilisers, pesticides and improved seeds; and
(c) to improve the Wajamaa farm incomes.

These objectives of the programme had been formulated after it was realised that the initial constraints to improving maize production in Ismani included inadequate finance on the part of villagers, shortage of skills and lack of knowledge of improved farming practices and techniques. By combining in one programme the provision of credit finance and extension service education, the authorities hoped that it would be possible to remove these constraints and pave the way for commercial maize production by ujamaa villages in Ismani.

A close look at the performance of the 1971/72 Ismani Operation, however, suggests that the most critical constraint was not the lack of new inputs but rather the failure of the farmers to adopt such simple husbandry practices as early planting and proper weeding. In a survey of 14 ujamaa villages carried out in 1974, the 1971/72 average yield on communal farms was 595 kgs./ha. On individual farms the average yield was 869 kgs./ha., despite the fact that ujamaa farms applied fertilizers and individual farms applied no fertilizers.[5]

Credit finance was only one of the critical factors in the initial phases of the Ismani Operation. The most critical factor was the utilisation of labour between communal farms and individual farms. The credit plan assumed that available labour would be adequate for the communal farm which usually averaged a hectare per member. However, each villager had an individual farm averaging 1.8 hectares in size.[6]

Selection of Beneficiaries

The identification of finance as the most critical constraint in limiting the expansion of maize production led the plan to the selection of villages that had an unrealistically high acriage as the minimum justification criterion for credit. This criterion was based on the concept of a minimum break-even output that could be sustained even with relatively minor adverse effects from bad weather or a decline in prices.

The Credit Programme covered the 30 ujamaa villages that were registered as multipurpose cooperative societies. Ten of these were granted loans to purchase tractors; the other 20 were given loans to meet tractor hire charges.

Organization and Lending Procedures

The programme was administered by Tanzania Rural Development Bank through its Iringa office. The Iringa Regional Representative in cooperation with the Regional Cooperative Union together with the Regional Authorities were responsible for the implementation of the programme. The Regional Authorities (agricultural, ujamaa and cooperative officials) were involved in making estimates for requirements of ujamaa villages. These material and service requirements were then aggregated by the Iringa Regional Cooperative Union which presented them as a loan application to TRDB through its Iringa Regional Office. The approved loans in the form of materials were passed through the Union for delivery to the villages. The Regional Office kept check of what material and how much materials went to each borrower. The three parties, i.e. the Bank, the IRCU and the Government authorities, often did not coordinate their efforts in meeting the needs of ujamaa villages. This frequently led to delays in the delivery of the wrong type of materials. The IRCU was supposed to recover the debts on behalf of TRDB just as it had borrowed on behalf of the villages, but since the determination of credit requirements was done by Government authorities, there was a communication gap between the Union and the ujamaa villages on whether the materials were delivered on loan or on Government assistance.

The amount of Shs. 1.8 million involved in the programme was a very small proportion compared to the total loan portfolio of Shs. 107,622,068 approved for 1972/73. But its importance lies in the fact that the new approach to financing the programme was to be applied in an integrated way.

Loans for recurrent inputs such as fertilizers, pesticides and improved seeds were short-term loans for the duration of one year. They carried an interest rate of 8½% per annum. Loans for farm machinery were medium-term loans repayable in three annual instalments. They carried an interest rate of 7½%.

Although the TRDB didn't insist on collateral security, loans were issued in the joint names of the Bank and the borrower; and machinery, for example, could be reclaimed if the borrower failed to repay the loan. The Bank's desire that the projects it supported were properly managed in itself was thought to be additional security for the loans extended.

The collection of the loan repayment was to be done by the Iringa Cooperative Union. The Union would collect maize sold from ujamaa villages and deduct the amount of loan for remittance to TRDB. This assumed that all ujamaa villages that had borrowed from the Bank would sell their maize through the Union. This was not the case and there was considerable black marketing. Efforts by a Regional representative to make direct contacts with client debtors produced little effect as he was not involved in the planning stages and was regarded as a distant official.

EVALUATION OF THE ISMANI MAIZE PROGRAMME

Impact of the Programme

The declared objectives of the Ismani Maize Credit Programme were to increase maize production and improve crop husbandry practices in ujamaa villages. Only in 1971 was capitalist maize production stopped in Ismani and land distributed to Wajamaa. The Government did not wish to see a drop in maize production for that would reflect adversely on ujamaa organization, reduce maize supplies and result in a deterioration rather than an improvement in the conditions of the villagers. Hence it wished to marshall for the programme all the credit and non-credit resources required to make the programme a success. On the side of TRDB the Ismani programme was an experimental area credit programme where the geographic area was taken as a whole and its credit requirements were identified.

How did this programme fare? Several variables can be examined to assess the impact of a credit programme. Among them are the following: (a) area cultivated, (b) average yields, (c) average net incomes and (d) assets. For an adequate coverage of these points the programme should have been going on for several years. In this evaluation, data were available for 1971/72 and 1972/73 only.

Area and Average Yields

An initial evaluation of the impact of the credit programme may be obtained by a comparison of ujamaa villages that received tractor loans and another group that did not. Table 2 summarizes acreage and yields data for two groups of villages in Ismani.

TABLE 2: MEAN YIELDS AND CULTIVATED ACREAGE, ISMANI UJAMAA VILLAGES 1972/73

	Members	Hectares	Maize output (bags)	Maize output per member (bags)	Maize yields per hectare (bags)
10 Villages with Tractor					
Loans	351	105	717	2.0	6.8
Range: High	467	120	1,058	3.1	9.8
Low	260	20	180	0.5	4.5
18 Villages without Tractor					
Loans	254	73	344	1.4	4.7
Range: High	450	142	600	2.9	13.0
Low	98	16	56	0.2	0.5

SOURCE: See ERB Paper 75.2, Tables 1 and 2, pp. 15 and 17.

All ujamaa villages were expected to plant 120 hectares of maize. Tractor loans should have ensured that these targets were met. In actuality the 10 villages that were given loans for tractors cultivated an average of 105 ha. of maize, approximately 88% of the target acreage; the 18 villages without loans cultivated an average of 73 ha. or 60% of the target acreage. The failure of the loan villages to meet the planting targets may be due to inefficient tractor maintenance and operation.

The plant population on the ujamaa farms in these villages was uniform and within the recommended populations specified by Kilimo. Differences in yields, therefore, may be due to farm practices such as fertilizer use, weeding, and the quality of ploughing and seedbed preparation. The quality of ploughing depends on the skill of the tractor driver and the supervision by task force leaders. Weeding depends on the participation of the villagers. In the Ismani Ujamaa Villages, such attendance is poor because communal weeding competes with work on individual farms. For this reason ujamaa villages with smaller communal acreage may have higher yields than those with larger communal farms.

Although both groups of ujamaa villages were allowed to apply for loans, the villages with tractor loans used more fertilizer in 1972/73 than the other villages. Seven of the ten villages with tractor loans applied an average of 121 kgs. of fertilizer per hectare and had an average yield of 6.1 bags/ha. A number of individual farms in Ismani that did not apply any fertilizer reported average yields of 10 bags per hectare. Thus there was no observable direct relationship between fertilizer use and yields in the 1972/73 season.

Fertilizer use in Ismani followed a blanket recommendation and took into consideration the levels of output that can be obtained through the application of a given combination at particular levels. No attention is paid to the economically optimum point of fertiliser use in the area.[7]

Ujamaa villages in Ismani began in 1971 with the Ismani Operation and consequently there is no history to examine their use of improved farming techniques. However, villagers in Ismani were either producing maize or working for large-scale maize growers. From records in the area, few Ismani farmers had attempted the application of fertilizers even as late as 1971. The data on maize production in Iringa Region indicate the following:

(a) in 1970/71 one out of 25 respondents used fertilisers;
(b) in 1971/72 three out of 78 used fertilizers; and
(c) in 1972/73 three out of 73 used fertilizers.

The claim is widely voiced that fertilizers are an expensive input without appreciable contribution to farm output and farm income levels. It is recommended that farmers should use about 200 kgs./ha. of CAN and 400 kgs./ha. of TSP. At present prices, a minimum yield of 22 bags per ha. is required merely to cover the costs of fertilizers.

This brings us to an important question of Ismani farmers' readiness to use fertilisers. The Ministry of Agriculture recommends the adoption of such husbandry practices as early planting, adequate weeding and correct plant spacing before the adoption of more complex and expensive technologies. It appears that many elementary problems are still prevalent in the area and these constraints to increasing maize yields must be removed first.

Net Income and Assets

The ujamaa villages which obtained tractor loans had an average of 105 hectares planted in maize. The average yields were around 6.8 bags per hectare per village. On this basis the average income can be calculated in the manner outlined in Table 3. This table shows that the second group of villages is in a relatively better position than the group which has tractor loans. On the whole the credit programme for 1972/73 did not improve the farm income position of ujamaa villages.

TABLE 3: AVERAGE MAIZE INCOME ESTIMATES FOR UJAMAA VILLAGES

	Villages with Loans		Villages without Loans	
	Kgs.	Shs.	Kgs.	Shs.
A. Total Output and Revenue	64,512	25,088	30,942	12,033
Distributed to Shambas	21,934	8,530	10,520	4,091
Reserved for Seeds	3,406	1,324	1,634	635
Sales	39,172	15,234	18,788	7,307
B. Expenditures				
Fertilizer		20,067		12,890
Seeds		750		481
Machinery		11,043		7,673
Maintenance		1,054		—
Depreciation		13,735		—
Interest		6,330		1,819
Transport		351		351
Tractor Driver		810		—
Total		54,139[a]		23,214[a]

[a] If the maize distributed to villagers is considered as a cost of their participation in communal work, then total farm costs should be increased to Shs. 62,669 for villages with loans and Shs. 27,305 for villages without loans.

SOURCE: See ERB Paper 75.2, Tables 5 and 6, pp. 21–22. A sample financial analysis of two villages is illustrated in Appendix 4, pp. 38–40 of the original paper.

Assets of the ujamaa villages include communal buildings, godowns and tractors. The Government and RDF provided the buildings and godowns; the TRDB provided the tractors by means of loans. At this point, these assets only indirectly can be attributed to the Ismani Maize Credit Programme.

The Ismani Maize Credit Programme's objective was to improve maize production through ujamaa villages. The members of these villages who were to manage the communal farms were also owners and managers of their individual farms. If they did not accept certain farm practices on their individual farms, it is hard to see how they would readily embrace those practices in the communal farms. This, therefore, calls for an integrated approach in planning both communal and individual farms for they form a complete system in terms of the utilization of labour resources in the village.[8] An integrated approach then would require the extension of credit facilities to cover individual farms as well.

The Status of the Programme

As it was pointed out earlier the programme was to be financed in phases and therefore its continuation and expansion depended on the progress of the programme. However, the programme was halted as a result of the inefficient performance of the first phase and of the National Maize Programme launched by Government in 1973/74 to subsidise all inputs to ujamaa farmers. Repayment of the 1972/73 loan should have been in the order of Shs. 1,097,220 while maize revenue was around Shs. 348,324. This represented only 32% of the debt owed to TRDB. After much pressure the villagers pledged to repay a total of about Shs. 175,000 or approximately 16% of the required repayment amount.

Many reasons have been advanced for the reluctance of the farmers to repay. First, because of the very low turnover, farmers consider the loan a burden rather than a means to increase their earning power. Second, loan repayment discipline has not been developed in the minds of Wajamaa. Many of the villages had received massive inputs free of charge during the previous season and they considered the 1972/73 loans as another form of free Government assistance.

The arrears began to accumulate as interest payment accrued to unpaid loans. The Wajamaa are in danger of becoming discouraged from producing more as they see a large proportion of their output goes for debt repayment.

PROBLEMS AND POSSIBLE IMPROVEMENTS

Further Issues for Investigation

The ujamaa villages are relatively new economic units which are still grappling with organisational and management problems. In the initial stages they required massive injections of management and technical assistance. The existing arrangements have been for Government and RDF to assist ujamaa villages during the first stages of development. When a village advances to the third stage, characterized by a relatively strong economic base and competent management, a village can then borrow from financial institutions provided that it can meet normal banking credit requirements. In adopting the developmental approach as the criterion for granting a loan rather than an approach based on the credit worthiness of the borrower, TRDB was led to support the Ismani Maize Programme. In addition, TRDB was trusting that the Regional authorities would ensure efficient communal work methods and organization in the ujamaa villages.

The pertinent questions here are whether or not credit was the limiting constraint in the Ismani Maize Programme, and if it was, whether its administration was carried out in such a manner as to ensure that the programme succeeded. There is need to investigate further several issues in relation to the Ismani Maize Credit Programme.

(i) The massive inputs of machinery and fertilizers have not increased maize output. Why has this been so?

(ii) What is the role of simple husbandry practices like proper preparation of seedbed, early planting, adequate weeding and the use of better seeds? Could credit be tailored in such a way that it induces ujamaa villages and individual farmers to adopt these simple practices before the next stage of more sophisticated technologies?

(iii) What type of work methods and organisation can be adopted in ujamaa villages to improve the efficiency of communal work, which is the basis of improved agricultural practices?

(iv) If individuals manage to realise an average of about 10 bags of maize per hectare as against 6.8 bags/ha. in ujamaa villages, which use more inputs, a thorough analysis should be carried out to determine if a better timing of credit and inputs would improve the situation.

Questions on the Implementation of the Programme

(a) The planning of the programme was hastily done and many decisions were based on the historical fact that Ismani was one of the most important maize growing areas in the country. This observation no longer holds true. A re-thinking consequently is needed as improved seeds and fertilizers are offering more attractive yields in the wetter parts of Njombe, Mufindi and Dabaga where risk of rain failure is less than in Ismani. In short, it is doubtful that Ismani should have received the attention it did.

(b) In discussing village plans villagers must be allowed to make appropriate and acceptable decisions. Officials and leaders must communicate with them in simple language that can be understood, such as the number of bags per hectare required to cover costs of inputs. This is more useful than technical terminology such as "internal rates of return."

(c) Future planning of credit needs must take into account the time lag between adoption of new innovations and the full realization of results. This will avoid overestimating a farm's capacity to bear debt burden.

(d) There is need to ensure higher loan recovery by extending loans to clients with a high degree of managerial ability. The risk of non-repayment from doubtful clients not only cripples the financial institution's capacity to expand its business but also impairs the functioning of the defaulting client by overloading it with a loan burden it cannot handle.

(e) Communal farms and individual farms form one economic system and labour demand for one affects the work of the other. It would greatly help and facilitate adoption of recommended practices if there was integrated planning of credit needs of the two types of farms.

(f) Fertilizers used in Ismani follow a blanket recommendation. More work is needed to find out what fertilizer combination and levels of application are suited to Ismani area. Once this fact is known, credit could be limited to such input levels.

The present emphasis by Kilimo has been on the technical efficiency of the use of fertilizers. However, since the farmer is very much concerned with the farm returns and net income, the cost of using that fertilizer combination is important to him. More economic analysis needs to be done to indicate to the farmer the level of fertilizer application which gives him optimum economic yields where his net profit is highest.

Another related question concerns the relative scarcity of fertilizers. Demand in Tanzania for organic fertilizers has been rising, but recent world events including the rise in oil prices and declining of other fertilizer based resources have led to fertilizer production growing very slowly relative to demand. A new approach to fertilizer use must be taken. For example, instead of using the available fertilizers in the country on say 100,000 ha. at present recommended levels, we could reduce the levels so that the available fertilizers would suffice for 150,000 ha.

Coupled with this, people have been encouraged to use composite manure and cow dung. There are ways which must be observed in preparing and preserving these manures to enable them to retain the nutrient values needed by the soils and plants. Experimentation perhaps could start soon on this matter. TRDB credit on a small scale could be extended to enable purchases of cattle manure from owners who don't use it so that it can be sent to places where it can be used effectively.

(g) As noted above, the TRDB Ismani Maize Credit programme was not continued after 1972/73. There is little likelihood that it will be revived in the near future in the same area until additional work is done. However, the Bank may be called on to support similar programmes elsewhere. A frequent criticism of TRDB is that it has tended to support mono-cropping patterns or programmes in isolation. It is called upon to provide credit for integrated programmes so that the impact of its credit can be felt much more in any given area than if it continued financing single projects in isolation. When such an opportunity arises, and there is no reason why the Bank could not on its own initiate such programmes, the Ismani Maize experience could provide some interesting observations which would be worth examining before launching similar schemes elsewhere.

(h) Another item needs to be mentioned, viz., the question of the mechanisation of ujamaa village farms. While this subject has been dealt with in the SFYP, the party's *Kilimo ni Siasa* and the TFYP guidelines, some confusion remains when it comes to planning and applying this agricultural gadget. Tractors do enable the ploughing of large farms but they involve scarce foreign exchange. Moreover, they are expensive to maintain and they require a level of management and care that is sadly lacking in most villages.

Since the early 1960s, experience with the majority of tractor loans in the country is one of failure. Perhaps it is now time to re-evaluate the unplanned use of tractors. The Bank should encourage the use of animal power in ploughing land. Tractors should be restricted to well managed enterprises.

(i) The negligible impact of the Ismani Maize Credit Programme has led to great indebtedness for the majority of loanee ujamaa villages. It has also destroyed the potential for learning the advantages of credit through proper utilisation of loans.[9] This points to the necessity of having periodic re-evaluation of the Bank's credit programmes. All major credit programmes that are implemented for a number of years should have a built-in re-evaluation mechanism.[10]

(j) Food crops marketing arrangements are inadequate and do not ensure a safe recovery mechanism such as exists with cash crops like tea and tobacco. There is an urgent need to develop institutions and proper procedures in food crop marketing so that loan agencies will be attracted to provide credit facilities for the expansion of food crop production which until now has not kept pace with the progress made in cash crop farming.

NOTES

1. A. Awiti, "Ismani and the Rise of Capitalism," *Rural Cooperation in Tanzania*, ed. L. Cliffe, P. Lawrence, *et al.* ,Dar es Salaam: East African Publishing House, 1975, pp. 59–66.
2. A. Awiti, "The Development of Ujamaa in Ismani," in *Rural Cooperation in Tanzania*, p. 418.
3. TRDB, "Ismani Integrated Development Plan," Ismani Ref. No. TYL/B/80/7.
4. *Ibid.*
5. TRDB, "Trends in Maize Production in Ismani and Other Parts of Iringa Region."
6. *Ibid.*
7. TRDB, "Rural Credit Impact: The Case of Ismani."
8. TRDB, "Trends in Maize Production . . . ," *op. cit.*, pp. 25–26.
9. TRDB, "Projected Investment Plans, 1972/73–1978–79."
10. TRDB, "A Manual of Operational Policies and Procedures," p. 2.

The Determinants of Cotton Supply in Tanzania*

KIGHOMA A. MALIMA

THEORETICAL CONSIDERATIONS

Some preliminary assumptions are in order. First, in the ensuing discussion changes in cotton supply and those in cotton production are taken as synonymous. Since there is no reservation demand for cotton among the growers, all that is harvested gets marketed.

Second, the actual cotton output, i.e. the amount harvested and marketed is used as the basis for the analysis of changes in cotton output. A number of studies on the supply response of small farmers has taken acreage under cultivation as the basis for analysis because actual output is usually influenced by weather and by other factors which are beyond the control of the farmers.[1] The problem, however, is that "the elasticity of supply response is certain to be underestimated by the acreage elasticity for those crops which have no "substitute" crops landwise but where production can be increased via application of more inputs."[2] In Tanzania, the character of cotton farming is such that it is almost impossible to obtain reliable figures of cotton acreage. So far no attempt has been made to estimate total cotton acreage; but such data would provide only a cross-sectional picture, and it is more interesting to examine what has been happening to cotton production in Tanzania over time.

An alternative method of estimating cotton output is the use of planting seed requests. This also has its limitations, however, because cotton seed is distributed "free" by the Lint and Seed Marketing Board and nothing prevents cotton farmers from requesting more cotton seed than they actually plant. The Lint and Seed Marketing Board, for instance, claims that in 1966 in the coastal areas alone, the wastage of planting seed distributed free by the Board was over 2,000 tons worth some one million shillings.[3]

No explanation was offered to explain how such a discrepancy occurred, but whatever the causes, the fact remains that planting seed requests are a poor indicator of the planned or desired cotton output. Hence, actual cotton output seems the best proxy for planned or desired cotton production.

The third preliminary assumption concerns the formation of price expectations among cotton farmers in Tanzania. Cotton farmers have some notion of the expected "normal" producer price.[4] They adjust their price expectations in proportion to the difference between the actual price and the expected "normal" cotton producer price in the previous period. Thus,

$$P_t^* - P_{t-1}^* = B(P_{t-1} - P_{t-1}^*) \leq 0 < B, 1 \quad (1)$$

where P_t^* = "expected" producer price of cotton in period t

P_{t-1} = actual producer price of cotton in period t−1.

The above first order difference equation can be rewritten as[5]

$$P_t^* = \sum_{i=0}^{oo} (1-B)^i B P_t - 1 -_i \quad (2)$$

Over the years cotton farmers in Tanzania would become adjusted to relatively stable prices. Consequently, they have come to expect a long-run "normal" cotton producer price which is based on what they have observed in previous years. Small year to year changes in price appear to cause relatively minor changes in their production decisions, and the effect of price changes in output occurs only after a time lag.

In addition to the expected "normal" price, other factors may be assumed to affect production decisions. These assumptions may be formalized in the assertion that in any period t (reasonably demarcated as a cotton growing season consisting of twelve months), cotton output Q_t is directly influenced by the long-run expected "normal" cotton producer price P_t^*, by the number of permanent cotton buying posts in the previous period D_{t-1}, and by the course of time T, i.e.

$$Q_t = F(P_t^*, D_{t-1}, T) \quad (3)$$

The inclusion of such variables as D_{t-1} and T require further explanation. Each year before the cotton picking season begins the Government specified the places in each district where seed cotton will be purchased from the growers. The model asserts that the number of buying posts directly influences cotton production because a greater density of posts in an area reduces the average distance which cotton farmers must travel to sell the crop. Proximity to a buying post reduces average transport costs to the growers and, with given producer prices, results in higher net incomes.

The variable time has been included in the formulation to account for the fact that subsistence households must allocate their labour supply between cotton and food cultivation. The assumption is that such competition diminishes in the course of time as farmers expand output and as the monetisation and specialization of the economy increases. As farming becomes more commercialized, farmers produce crops for cash and begin to use cash proceeds to purchase household food requirements. This presupposes that there are general improvements in marketing, transportation and distribution systems, because the passage of time alone is unlikely to induce cultivators to "take the chance of growing cash crops and of relying on an uncertain market to meet critical food demands."[6] Thus time is taken to include a number of unspecified variables such

*ERB Paper 71.4.

as general economic progress, improved marketing, transportation, communication and distribution systems. In this wider sense, the variable time lumps together a host of additional factors which ideally should be disentangled.

Assuming that the variables which influence Q_t (see footnote 6) enter the formulation multiplicatively, the model can be expressed in logarithmic terms as follows:[7]

$$q_t = a_0 + a_1 p_t^* + a_2 b_{t-1} + a_3 T + U_t, \quad (4)$$

where $q_t = \ln Q_t$
$p_t^* = \ln P_t^*$
$b_{t-1} = \ln D_{t-1}$
U_t = a random error term with zero mean and a constant variance.

STATISTICAL ESTIMATION OF THE MODEL

Model building, as an exercise of the imagination, attempts to specify the relationship which could explain a given phenomenon. The estimation of such a relationship in the model requires the use of statistical data which reflect the environment which is being examined. In the analysis of the determinants of cotton supply, the quantity and quality of available data impinged heavily on the statistical exercise.[8]

Although annual cotton production data from 1925 exist, figures for cotton producer prices are more recent. The Lint and Seed Marketing Board which was established in 1952 has gathered producer price figures since 1942, but because the reliability of these figures before 1952 is questionable, "AR" and "BR" cotton lint are grouped together.

The method followed was to take the official figures on cotton output, cotton producer prices, the number of cotton buying posts and the available labour force for the years 1953 to 1969 in the Lake and Coastal Areas. These time series were converted into centred three year moving averages to smooth out year to year variations and estimate relative long term changes.[9]

The availability of time series data restricted the number of observations to 17, and a time lag of four years for producer prices was thought to be a reasonable approximation for the adjustment of production decisions.[10] This meant a loss of four observations, and left only 13 observations for the actual estimation. With four coefficients to estimate, this implied 9 degrees of freedom which requires relatively higher t-statistics for the estimates of the various coefficients to be significantly non-zero at the 5 per cent level, than if there were 30 degrees of freedom. In spite of these limitations, the use of an econometric analysis would seem to be justified on the grounds that carefully marshalled data with realistically formulated theoretical relationships could provide more fruitful insights than mere casual observations, helpful as the latter sometimes are.

Table 1 reports the statistical results obtained from the formulation (4) using the ordinary least squares method; and Table 2 the results obtained from the following modified formulation:[11]

$$q_t = a_0 + a_1 p_t^* + a_2 b_{t-1} + a_3 \ln L_t + u_6 \quad (5)$$

where L_t is labour force available for period $_t$.

TABLE 1: REGRESSION RESULTS

	Total Cotton Production	Lake Cotton Production	Coastal Cotton Production
Constant	−1.21	−0.54	−10.15
	−(0.37)	−(0.15)	−(1.83)
p_t^*	2.45	2.46	5.98
	(3.23)	(2.88)	(3.06)
b_{t-1}	0.91	0.74	0.49
	(3.05)	(2.47)	(1.25)
T	0.08	0.09	0.06
	(5.76)	(6.39)	(1.68)
$\bar{R}^2$	0.96	0.96	0.64
Durbin Watson	1.22	0.99	1.26

TABLE 2: REGRESSION RESULTS

	Total Cotton Production	Lake Cotton Production	Coastal Cotton Production
Constant	−85.96	−91.95	−72.11
	−(5.64)	−(6.04)	−(1.78)
p_6^*	2.44	2.45	6.02
	(3.27)	(2.89)	(3.10)
b_{t-1}	0.91	0.79	0.48
	(3.08)	(2.49)	(1.22)
$\ln L_t$	5.85	6.53	4.56
	(5.84)	(6.44)	(1.72)
$\bar{R}^2$	0.96	0.96	0.64
Durbin Watson	1.22	0.99	1.25

The figures in the parentheses are the t-statistics for the respective coefficients. The value of $\beta = 0.1$ was selected through a scanning technique.[12] In both formulations the t-statistics for the coefficients for total output and for the Lake Areas cotton output with the exception of the constant terms in the first set of results are all significantly non-zero at the 3 per cent level. The correlation coefficients are significant at the 2 per cent level. For the Coastal Areas, with the exception of the correlation coefficient, only the price elasticity coefficient is significantly non-zero at the 3 per cent level. The other coefficients for the Coastal Areas are not significantly non-zero even at the 5 per cent level. Thus, either non-price variables in the model have little explanatory value in the Coastal Areas or the quality of the data for that region is poor. In view of the high and significant price elasticity and correlation coefficients in the Coastal Areas, the latter reason appears more plausible.

In contrast, the results from a formulation such as, $q_t = a_0 + a_1 p_{t-1} + a_2 b_{t-1} + a_3 T + U_t$, where $p_{t-1} = \ln P_{t-1}$, and P_{t-1} is the actual producer price of the previous period, were either perverse, not significant or both. Thus, while cotton farmers in Tanzania respond positively to price, the relevant producer price is not the actual price but the long-run expected "normal" producer price. The meaning of $\beta = 0.1$, which implies that $(1-\beta) = 0.9$, is that cotton farmers adjust their "normal" producer price expectations over a relatively long time, since it would take some time for the fraction $(1-\beta)^i = 0.9$ to approach zero as it increases. As a corollary, the lack of meaningful results using p_{t-1} instead of P_t^*, suggests that changes in the actual cotton producer price of the previous period have little appreciable effect on immediate cotton supply or production. Producer price changes, however, will be incorporated into expectations of long-run "normal" producer prices with a time lag.

In the Coastal Areas where cotton production increased slowly at about 2 per cent per year,[13] the response to price was significant and positive, with an elasticity coefficient of about 6.0. In contrast in the Lake Areas cotton production increased at about 11 per cent per year between 1953 and 1969, and the elasticity coefficient was about 2.5. Thus, cotton supply appeared to be much more responsive to price in the Coastal Areas than in the Lake Areas. The explanation may be that the long-run downward trend of the producer price in the Coastal Areas was not counterbalanced, as seems to have been the case in the Lake Areas, by significant improvements in non-price variables like the number of permanent cotton buying posts. There also are more alternative economic opportunities in the Coastal Areas than in the Lake Areas.

SOME POLICY IMPLICATIONS OF THE MODEL

Implications of Price Response

The price elasticity of cotton supply

$$e = \frac{\partial(\log Q_t)}{\partial(\log P^*_t)}$$

indicates the speed and magnitude of output adjustments in response to changes in product prices. The reliable estimate of this elasticity parameter is useful in policy formulation because it expresses the ability of producers to adjust their output to a changing economic environment.[14]

Three specific policy implications of the price elasticity of cotton supply should be examined:

(a) Price responsiveness and cotton production policy. Price responsiveness indicates the potential role of price policy in overcoming bottlenecks in agricultural production. It also indicates the potential of altering the composition of agricultural output by changing the relative prices of individual crops.[15] Development plans which specify production targets for different crops also should consider the kind of changes in the respective producer prices that are consistent with the targeted output increases.

In assessing the role of price policy in increasing cotton output, it is well to recall that the transformation of traditional agriculture cannot be brought about only or mainly by price movements. Nevertheless, the required techno-organisational efforts can be retarded or accelerated by price policy.[16] Thus although a positive price policy is a necessary adjunct to a rational agricultural production policy, by itself it cannot bring about the desired agricultural development.

(b) Supply response and pricing policy. In Tanzania cotton prices for producers are established primarily with attention to the world cotton market situation. But with output responsive to price, the effect of these prices on future output should be considered as well.

Theoretically producer prices should be high enough to bring about the desired output levels without encouraging high cost producers. Prices based on transport and marketing cost differentials would discourage cotton production in higher cost areas. Although other commercial crops might be grown in place of cotton, it is possible that cotton might be the only feasible money crop in an area and its cultivation should be encouraged on the grounds of balanced regional growth.

At the same time, relatively higher cotton prices will tend to divert resources from other crops to cotton. Here the relative prices of alternative crops become important. In theory a general equilibrium approach which established producer prices at levels consistent with the achievement of output targets for the several crops is possible. In practice the determination of such price levels is difficult. In Tanzania different marketing boards handle individual agricultural commodities. This problem might be resolved, however, if a central organisation were set up to review the producer prices fixed by the various marketing boards and thereby to ensure that they did not effectively neutralize output targets for the different crops. Alternatively the marketing board system could be reorganised in such a way that in each geographical and ecological region of the country a single marketing board would be responsible for establishing the producer prices of all the crops in the region. One advantage of this latter approach is that it could utilize the experience and personnel of existing marketing boards.

What therefore emerges is that cotton producer prices must be fixed with regard for the effect that such prices will have on the production of other crops. In other words, cotton pricing policy must take into account the mutual interdependence of the various agricultural crops in order to establish consistent agricultural output targets.

(c) Price responsiveness, price and income stabilization, and public finance. An important aspect of price policy is to stabilize producer prices and hence, incomes. In Tanzania cotton producer prices have been stabilized both intra-seasonally and inter-seasonally, and cotton producers have responded positively by a substantial increase in output. It has been observed in South Asia that large seasonal and cyclical fluctuations in agricultural prices are a major reason why farmers are reluctant to specialize and "rationally choose to grow sufficient food for home consumption."[17]

If the aim of price policy is not simply to increase cotton output but also to increase total agricultural output, measures to stabilize cotton prices and income must be implemented with consideration for their overall impact on the growth of other agricultural crops in the respective areas.

In the case of public finance producer prices often are used as one means of generating revenue for the government. The important point is that the more the government taxes farmers by reduced producer prices, the less income remains available to them. The effect of this type of taxation has to be assessed. Taxes on agricultural commodities like cotton can have two interrelated effects. In the first place, high taxes discourage farmers from expanding their cotton production and encourage the diversion of resources into other activities. In the second place, high agricultural taxes leave the farmers with a smaller profit margin, which may prevent them from undertaking further innovations and investment. Thus, in the long run the effect of high agricultural taxes is to slow the growth of agricultural output. If the tax proceeds are used, however, for rural modernization and for services which the peasant farmers otherwise would have to provide for themselves, then the adverse effects of the tax in part are counterbalanced.

This brief analysis of the implications of the price elasticity of cotton supply indicates some of the factors which authorities should consider in fixing producer prices. They must evaluate not only the world cotton market situation but also the impact of producer prices on future cotton production. They also must consider the effect of prices on intra-and inter-regional specialization, the role and importance of cotton in the economy, the comparative costs of production in the various cotton growing areas of the country, price and income stabilization, public finance, and overall agricultural output targets.[18]

Implications of Supply Response to Non-price Variables

The statistical results derived from the econometric model above indicate that cotton output is positively responsive to some non-price variables. The degree of this responsiveness allows us to make two interrelated propositions: (a) given the opportunity, cotton farmers in Tanzania respond positively to economic incentives; and (b) the problems of agricultural development "appear to be less a matter of farmer motivation and more a problem of reducing uncertainty and of improving the organisation of agricultural services."[19]

The slow growth of agricultural production in the less developed countries may be due to the lack of economic opportunities, as is widely asserted, but it remains true that economic opportunities to expand production are much greater in some areas than in others. The reasons seem to be related to economic as well as to sociological and political factors. Thus the slow commercialization of the marketing system may be due to inadequate marketing facilities combined with poor transportation infrastructure.

The response of cotton production to the number of permanent buying posts and to the time trend vindicates this assertion. In the econometric model the positive and significant coefficient for cotton buying posts suggests that providing buying posts close to the farmers stimulated an increase in production. The implication of this evidence for policy is two fold: (a) cotton buying posts not only are a means of collecting the "present" crop but also influence positively future production decisions; and (b) the example of cotton indicates that total agricultural output will increase if farmers have convenient access to markets. In other words, both reasonably stable prices at remunerative levels and adequate marketing channels and facilities are among the basic requirements which enable market demand to provide production incentives.[20]

The provision of marketing facilities, however, is closely linked to the problem of adequate means of transportation, and these two factors are important and often complementary ingredients in "rational" agricultural development policy and planning. In Tanzania the phenomenal increase in cotton production occurred during a period which appears to coincide with a significant increase in government expenditure on roads. The development of roads, however, should affect all crops equally, and the greater response of cotton output suggests that other factors, such as research, marketing and prices also contributed to the rapid growth in cotton output.

Cotton output in Tanzania exhibited significantly non-zero and positive coefficients with respect to time, a variable which indicates monetisation and improved systems of distribution, and labour force. Two interrelated policy implications for agricultural development follow: (a) measures to develop a modern and dependable system of distribution for food and other goods must be an important component of any policy designed to bring about rapid agricultural transformation; and (b) the degree of monetisation is an important factor in agricultural specialization and consequently agricultural development.

In recent years it has become recognized that subsistence food crops should be given as much attention in research and extension programmes as export crops. Only in this manner will subsistence farmers eventually be able not only to meet their own food requirements but also to produce a surplus for sale. Furthermore, specialization among farmers in the cotton growing districts and in the country as a whole should mitigate the labour limitation problem which faces most cotton growers in Tanzania. This specialization will result from concerted efforts to speed up the monetisation of the economy and the development of a reliable distribution system.

NOTES

1. Jere R. Behrman, *Supply Response in Underdeveloped Agriculture*, Amsterdam: North-Holland Publishing Company, 1968. Raj Krishna, "Farm Supply Response in India-Pakistan: A Case Study of the Punjab Region," *Economic Journal*, Vol. LXXII, No. 291, September, 1963. Marc Nerlove, *The Dynamics of Supply: Estimation of Farmers' Response to Price*, Baltimore: The Johns Hopkins Press, 1958.

2. Jagdish N. Bhagwati and Sukhamoy Chakravarty, "Contributions to Indian Economic Analysis: A Survey," *American Economic Review*, Vol. LIX, No. 4, Part 2, Supplement, September 1969, p. 40.
3. Tanzania Lint and Seed Marketing Board, *The Annual Report* 1966–67, Dar es Salaam, 1968, p. 16. (Figures in square brackets are translations of the original figures which were given in the former East African pound).
4. Marc Nerlove, "Estimates of Elasticities of Supply of Selected Agricultural Commodities," *Journal of Farm Economics*, Vol. XXXVIII, No. 2 May 1956, p. 500. ——, "Distributed Lags and Estimation of Long-run Supply and Demand Elasticities: Theoretical Considerations," *Journal of Farm Economic* Vol. XL, No. 2, May, 1958 p. 310. ——, *The Dynamics of Supply: Estimation of Farmers' Response to Price*, Baltimore: The Johns Hopkins Press, 1958, pp. 52–53.
5. $P_t^* = B P_{t-1} + (1-B)P_{t-1}^* = BP_{t-1} + (1-B)BP_{t-2} + (1-B)^2BP_{t-3} + \dots = \sum_{i=0} (1-B)^i B P_{t-1-i}$. Note that $P_t^* \to 0$ as $i \to 00$.
6. Walter P. Falcon, "Comments on Krishna's Contribution," in H. M. Southworth and B. F. Johnston, eds., *Agricultural Development and Economic Growth*, New York: Ithaca, Cornell University Press, 1967, p. 541.
7. Although equation (4) appears complicated by the fact that variable P_t^* contains a summation sign, for the case of a linear equation this can be eliminated by the Koyck method of transformation. However, it is well to note that the ordinary least squares method generally yields in this case inconsistent estimators. For the details of such derivation, see the original ERB paper, p. 6.
8. The data used in the estimation of the model are available in the appendix of the original study.
9. For the three year moving averages of the respective variables, see the original paper, pp. 8–9.
10. The "expected" cotton price is then given by $P_t^* = B\ P_{t-1} + (1-B)BP_{t-2} + (1-B)^2B\ P_{t-3} + (1-B)^3\ BP_{t-4}$.
11. The use of a Cochrane-Orcutt transformation instead of OLS did not really improve the results.
12. I am grateful to Ray C. Fair for suggesting the use of this technique, by taking values for $\beta = j$ ($j = 0.1, \dots, 0.9$) since $0 < \beta < 1$, and then choosing the value of β which produced maximum R-squared and meaningful and significant coefficients. Also see, Zvi Griliches, "Distributed Lags: A Survey," *Econometrica*, Vol. 35 (1), January 1967, pp. 16–17.
13. For the Coastal Areas:

$$\text{Log } Q_t = \underset{(46.54)}{9.54} + \underset{(0.85)}{0.02T}; \quad R^2 = 0.05$$

and for the Lake Areas:

$$\log Q_t = \underset{(108.86)}{11.27} + \underset{(9.86)}{0.11T}; \quad R^2 = 0.87$$

the figures in parentheses are the t-statistics and T = time.
14. L. G. Tweeten and C. L. Quance "Positivistic Measures of Aggregate Supply Elasticities: Some New Approaches," *American Economic Review*, vol. LIX, No. 2, May 1969, p. 175.
15. Walter P. Falcon, "Farmers Response to Price in a Subsistence Economy: The Case of West Pakistan," *American Economic Review*, Vol. LIV, No. 3, May 1964, pp. 589–90.
16. Raj Krishna, "Agricultural Price Policy and Economic Development," in Southworth and Johnstone, eds., *op. cit.* p. 517.
17. Walter P. Falcon, *op. cit.* p. 541.
18. One way in which this could be accomplished is through the use of a non-linear programming model of agricultural pricing. The objective function to be maximized could be either producer incomes or foreign exchange earnings for the country. Among the relevant constraints would be the requirements that output targets of certain important agricultural crops be met and that marketieg boards be financially solvent.
19. Walter P. Falcon, *op. cit.*
20. J. C. Abbott, "The Development of Marketing Institutions," in Southworth and Johnston eds., *op. cit.* p. 365

Bananas and the Dar es salaam Market*

S. M. MBILINYI, and

A. C. MASCARENHAS

Introduction

The increasing importance of bananas in the diet of the people of Dar es Salaam and its predominance at the Kariakoo market led to the decision to make this study. In addition to these two factors, the organization of the banana market is in contrast with that of oranges which we have discussed in another paper.[1]

The main aims of this paper are to examine the sources of supply of bananas, the people involved in the trade, the flow and demand of this crop, price fluctuations and finally of to analyse the economics of the crop in relation to the city to government and the people involved in the trade. Problems pertaining to the marketing of the crop will also be looked into and some suggestions regarding the city marketing policies will be made.

The emphasis in this study of bananas will be put on cooking bananas, although ripe bananas will be discussed in much less detail. The distinction between the two types of bananas is not very clear. Some of the cooking bananas can in fact be consumed as fruit bananas when they ripen. However, the producers' decision to market bananas as cooking bananas is a decisive factor for categorising the bananas into one or the other group. This paper is guided by the following considerations:

(a) at Kariakoo bananas meant for consumption as fruit are sold at a separate place from those meant for cooking;

(b) even when the sale of some cooking bananas is delayed and they ripen, they still are sold as they were originally meant, i.e. as cooking bananas.

A more sophisticated study would have attempted to make a distinction among the banana varieties, separating those which ripen and can be consumed as fruit, and those used exclusively for cooking. Alternatively, a percentage of cooking bananas which ripen and are consumed as fruit could be established. Both of these approaches were beyond the scope of this study.

SOURCE AREAS

The Dar es Salaam market is supplied with bananas from over 130 localities scattered in three major regions: Coast, Morogoro and Tanga. Occasionally, bananas also come from Bukoba and Moshi/Arusha areas. The quantities brought to the Dar es Salaam market for sale range from 3 bunches from some localities per year to over 36,000 bunches from other localities. The most important area however is on the foreland of the Uluguru mountains roughly some 150 miles from Dar es Salaam. This area contains Mkuyuni, Kinole on the eastern flanks and Turiani on the northern periphery. These three localities are the most important producing areas for the Dar es Salaam market, but Kidodi, Kilombero and Ifakara in the valley of the great Ruaha some 210–270 miles away from Dar es Salaam have recently begun supplying the city with bananas. The rate of new planting in this area is also increasing. Other areas of importance include Matombo near Mkuyuni, Handeni in the Tanga Region and Mgeta near Morogoro. Further afield, the Moshi area which is over 380 miles away also attempts to supply the city with bananas, and two arrivals of bananas were recorded from Bukoba just under 1,000 miles away from Dar es Salaam. Rufiji in the south and Bagamoyo in the north are also significant producers. The other potential source area for bananas will be the strip of land 1 to 3 miles deep on either side of the Morogoro road and stretching about 45 miles from the city. This area is developing rapidly and hundreds of banana stools can be seen from the road when one drives along it. The important locatities producing cooking bananas are shown in map 1.

ASSEMBLING AND TRANSPORT COSTS

The most crucial factors affecting assembly of any crop, and especially perishable crops, are the people involved or the marketing institutions and the efficiency of the transport system in terms of road conditions, frequency of lorries or buses on these roads and availability of transport. In the absence of formal marketing institutions, the efficiency of marketing of bananas depends on the individuals, groups of individuals and some semi-organizations involved in the collection and transportation of bananas from the producers to the consumers. In attempting to be logical in presentation, these two factors will be examined at two levels in the market channels: (a) at the rural market and (b) at the urban market.

THE RURAL MARKET

The rural market in the context of this paper has the primary meaning of a meeting place between the producers and the middlemen. The meeting places in the rural areas range from an individual farm and/or a roadstand to an organised rural district market. The former category is more predominant than the latter. During the period of this survey, there were two well organised rural district markets, Turiani and Mkuyuni, both in Morogoro region. The two markets are the major supply sources for the Dar es Salaam

*Edited version of ERB paper 69.14 and later published in East African Journal of Rural Development, 1973.

MAJOR BANANA PRODUCING LOCALITIES

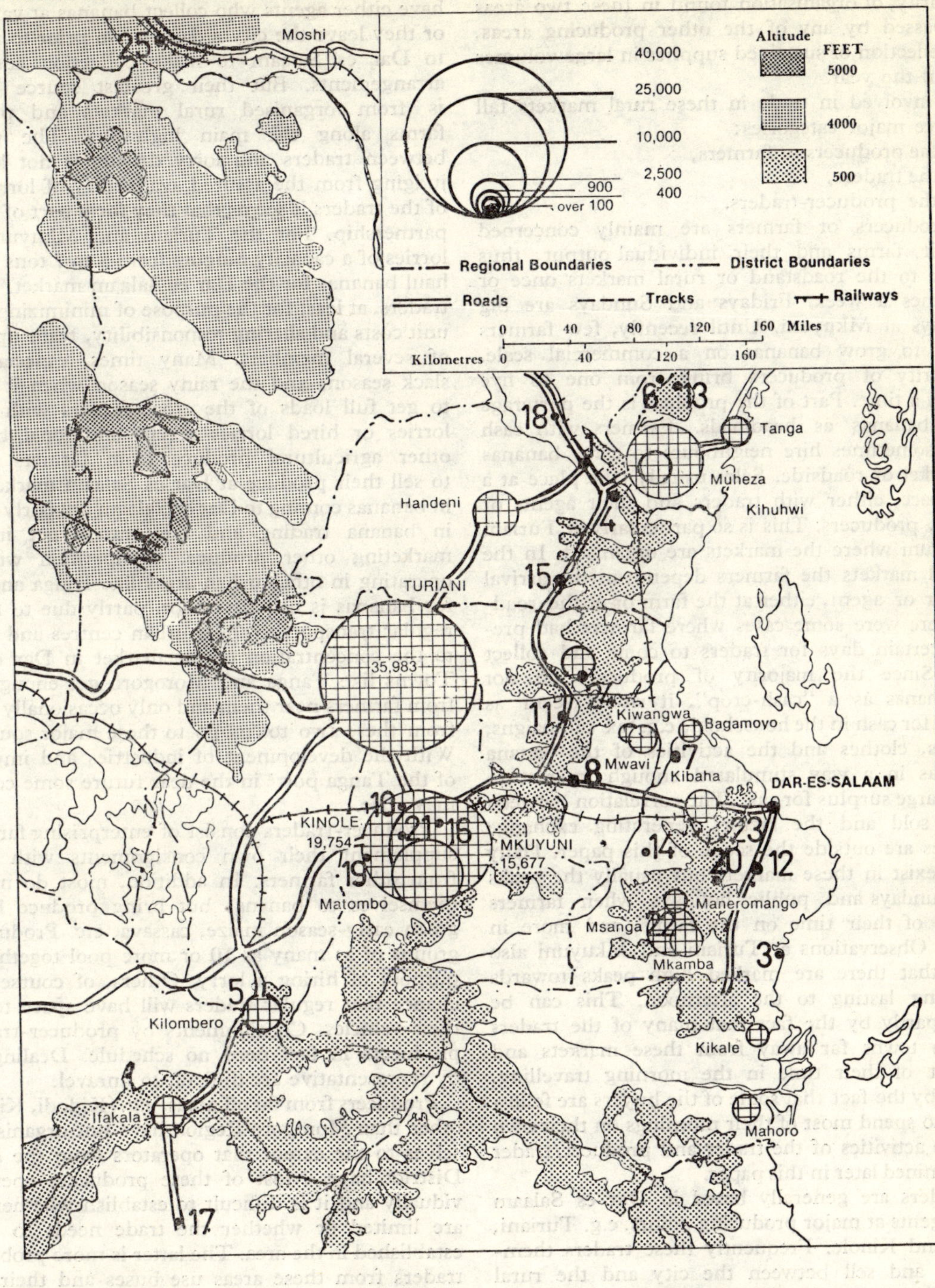

1. Korogwe
2. Kwamba-Mwakinzi-(Tanga)
3. Kisiju
4. Kabuku (Segera)
5. Kidodi (Kilosa)
6. Maramba (Tanga)
7. Yombo (Bagamoyo)
8. Chalinze
9. Kwedikazu-(Handeni)
10. Morogoro
11. Mzata (Bagamoyo)
12. Mkuranga
13. Lugongo (Tanga)
14. Mzenga
15. Mkata (Handeni)
16. Kiroka
17. Ulanga (Mahenge)
18. Makuyuni (Tanga)
19. Mlali (Morogoro)
20. Masaki
21. Tangeni (Morogoro)
22. Malui
23. Kisarawe
24. Hondogo (Miano)
25. Arusha

market, both in terms of quantity and regularity. The maturity, of organisation found in these two areas is unsurpassed by any of the other producing areas, and is a reflection of sustained supplies in large volumes throughout the year.

People involved in trade in these rural markets fall under three major categories:

(a) the producers or farmers,
(b) the traders,
(c) the producer-traders.

The producers or farmers are mainly concerned with heir farms and their individual output; thus they come to the roadstand or rural markets once or several times a week. Fridays and Sundays are big market days at Mkuyuni. Until recently, few farmers attempted to grow bananas on a commercial scale. The majority of producers bring from one to five bunches at a time. Part of the problem is the porterage of these bananas as headloads. Farmers with cash resources sometimes hire neighbours to carry bananas to the market or roadside. Sales usually take place at a leisurely pace, either with traders and their agents or with fellow producers. This is so particularly at Turiani and Mkuyuni where the markets are organised. In the other rural markets the farmers depend on the arrival of a trader or agent, either at the farm or at the road-stand. There were some cases where farmers had pre-arranged certain days for traders to come and collect produce. Since the majority of producers do not regard bananas as a "cash-crop", it would seem as if the need for cash in the household, e.g. tax campaigns, school fees, clothes and the activities of the banana traders, has in a way stimulated enough interest to provide a large surplus for sale. The correlation between quantities sold and the factors generating exchange propensities are outside the scope of this paper. Daily variations exist in these markets but usually the peaks are on Sundays and public holidays when farmers spend less of their time on the farms, and more in marketing. Observations at Turiani and Mkuyuni also indicated that there are marked high peaks towards mid-morning lasting to the afternoon. This can be explained partly by the fact that many of the traders came from towns far away from these markets and spent most of their time in the morning travelling, and partly by the fact that some of the buyers are fellow farmers who spend most of their mornings on their own farms. The activities of the trader and producer/trader will be examined later in this paper.

The traders are generally based in Dar es Salaam and have agents at major producing points, e.g. Turiani, Mkuyuni and Kinole. Frequently these traders themselves buy and sell between the city and the rural markets. Their manner of collecting bananas varies, depending on the mode of transport used. If traders use their own transport, their consignments are bought partly from an organised rural market and partly from the farm. If there is still room in the lorry or pickup on the way to the city, loads of bananas or any other crop may be picked up on the way. Traders travelling on public transport, e.g. buses and railways usually have either agents who collect bananas at various points or they leave the city a day or two prior to their return to Dar es Salaam to make collection and transport arrangements. But their greatest source of bananas is from organised rural markets and pre-arranged farms along the main highways. The relationship between traders and lorry drivers is not known, but judging from the assured availability of lorries to most of the traders it seems that they form part of the trading partnership. For the Turiani and Mkuyuni markets, lorries of a capacity ranging from 5 to 7 tons are used to haul bananas for the Dar es Salaam market. Frequently traders, at least for the purpose of minimizing individual unit costs and sharing responsibility, team up in groups of several members. Many times, especially during slack seasons and the rainy season when it is difficult to get full loads of the crop, traders with their own lorries or hired lorries accept additional bunches or other agricultural produce from farmers who wish to sell their produce at Dar es Salaam market. Traders in bananas coming to Dar es Salaam are fairly specialised in banana trading and they rarely get involved in marketing other produce. Competition with traders operating in other urban areas like Iringa and Dodoma for bananas is usually minor, partly due to the lack of regular transport to these urban centres and partly due to the concentration of the market in Dar es Salaam. Towns like Tanga and Morogoro get enough supplies from farmers near them and only occasionally do traders from these two towns go to these major source areas.[4] With the development of industries and improvement of the Tanga port[5] in the near future some competition may arise.

Producer-traders consist of enterprising farmers who supplement their own consignments with purchases from other farmers. In addition, most do not restrict themselves to bananas but bring produce like yams, green early-season maize, cassava, etc. Producer-trader groups of as many as 10 or more pool together for the purpose of hiring a lorry. Others, of course, take the chance that regular traders will have space to spare in their vehicles. Consignments by producer-traders and producers in fact need no schedule. Dealing in sales by representative are difficult to unravel.

Producers from far off areas, e.g. (Kidodi, Kilombero,) other than Morogoro Region have not organised themselves to the extent that operators from the Morogoro District have. Most of these producers operate individually and it is difficult to establish whether supplies are limited or whether the trade needs to be firmly established in the area. The latter is more probable since traders from these areas use buses and their consignments are usually small.

Producers closer to the city, from places such as Kiwangwa and Mnavi, sell directly at Kariakoo; in fact this urban market is their primary market; Fairly large scale producers bringing 40 or more bunches can afford to hire pickups while small quantities are transported by buses.

TRANSPORT COSTS

The general discussion on the physical layout of roads, modes and costs aspects are to be described elsewhere. This section will discuss mainly the relationship between distances, market-channel, quantities and the transport costs.

There is a direct correlation between the quantity of bananas brought by each group and the means of transport and distance transported. The producer-traders and producers that bring in small to medium size loads usually travel by bus or casual lorry rides, especially from long distances, e.g. Turiani, Mkuyuni, Kidodi, etc. Traders on the other hand hire lorries for similar distances. For shorter distances all the groups tend to hire pick-ups or try to get rides on buses and lorries.

The capacities of lorries vary. A seven ton lorry can carry as many as 250 bunches of bananas. If the banana loads are not big enough to warrant a lorry trip, other staple crops such as the ones mentioned earlier are added to make a full load. In such cases it is almost impossible to allocate the costs of transport to each crop. Pick-ups which usually operate at distances within 70 miles radius can carry 40–50 bunches of bananas as full load, representing a tonnage equivalent to $1\frac{1}{2}$ to $2\frac{1}{2}$. Table 1 shows the various modes of transport in relation to channels.

Just as there is a great variation in the quantity fo bananas carried for different trips, there is also a similar variation in the average charges per bunch of bananas coming from the same place. The main factors that influence the charges are:

(a) the modes of transport,
(b) the distance from the city,
(c) bargaining skills, and
(d) passenger loads in the buses.

From the data available one can cautiously say that the hired lorry mode of transport rather than buses is much cheaper for bananas coming long distances. This is measured in terms of costs per bunch and bunch mile. The greatest bottleneck is that it requires substantial capital to hire a lorry. Pick-ups and vans, on the other hand, are cheap on distances not exceeding 50 miles. Buses and lorry-rides do not give any definite trend and depend on other factors. The common modes of transport and their costs are shown in Table 2.

Distance from the city determines the choice or mode of transport rather than the transport cost which people involved are charged. If the mode of transport was the same for short and long distances, then transport costs could have been compared. This is not the case, because within short distances pickups are used and for long distances hired lorries are frequent. The only modes that bridge the other two transport methods

TABLE 1: CHANNEL AND COMMON MODES OF TRANSPORTATION

Channel	Common Mode of Transportation	Usual distance from Dar es Salaam
Rural Market		
Producer to producer	1. Family or hired labour (head-loads)	less 10 miles
Producer to trader		
Producer to roadstand		
City Market		
Producer to city	1. Bus	over 100 miles
	2. Lorry Rides (casual)	over 100 miles
Producer-trader city	1. Bus	over 100 miles
	2. Lorry Rides (casual)	over 100 miles
	3. Pickup/van rides (casual)	under 60 miles
	4. Pickup/van hires	under 40 miles
Producer groups	1. Bus	over 100 miles
	2. Lorry rides	over 100 miles
	3. Lorry hired	over 100 miles
	4. Pickup/van rides	under 60 miles
	5. Pickup/vans	under 100 miles
Traders	1. Hired lorry	over 100 miles
	2. Hired pick-up and van	under 60 miles

which extend beyond the distances hired lorries cover are usual rides in lorries and scheduled buses. The range of prices charged for the latter mode is so uniform as to make any meaningful statement impossible. Charges per bunch for bananas coming from Kilombero 212 miles away are Shs. 1/50 to 2/50, while those from Mkuyuni 140 miles away are Shs. 1/- to 2/50. Similar discrepancies are observed for lorry rides.

The inconsistency in charges revealed above can partly be explained by the bargaining ability of individual traders or producers and partly by the seasonal nature of the volume of passengers in buses. In regard to the former, good bargainers usually pay less than the "non-bargainers". Occasionally frequency of travels by traders on the same buses result in fare cuts or discounts. The seasonality of the number of passengers in buses was noted during peak travel seasons; drivers fail to have room in the luggage rack. For whatever little room they have, they charge higher prices than usual.

TABLE 2: TRANSPORT COSTS TO DAR ES SALAAM FOR SELECTED SOURCE AREAS

Source Areas	Distance from Dar es Salaam	Mode of transport	Rates @ Lorry bunch (shs)
Turiani	175	Hired lorry	300–550
		Bus	2.00
		Lorry ride	1.00–2.00
Mkuyuni	139	Hired lorry	300–500
		Bus	1.00–2.00
		Lorry ride	1.50–2.00
Kinole	140	Lorry ride	250–600
		Bus	1.00–2.00
		Lorry ride	1.50–2.00
Muheza	210	Lorry hired	400–600
		Bus	1.20–2.50
		Lorry ride	n.a.
Handeni	200		
	via Mandera	Lorry hired	n.a.
		Bus	1.00–2.50
		Lorry ride	0.70–2.00
Kilombero	212	Lorry hired	450
		Bus	1.00–2.00
		Lorry ride	1.50
Msanga	79	Lorry ride	none
		Bus	0.50–1.50
		Pick-up ride	
		Van ride	1.00
Bagamoyo	45	Lorry hire	none
		Bus	uncommon
		Pick-up/ Van hired	n.a.

The condition of roads does not seemingly have much influence on the charges of goods carried. The range of fares and charges for commodities tend to be the same in the wet and dry seasons.

URBAN MARKET AND ITS OPERATION

According to the city regulations and by laws all the fresh farm produce marketed in the city area should first go to the Kariakoo market[6] where it is auctioned at a wholesale stand and then retailed in various ways. In comparison with the orange auctions, the auctions for bananas are, on the whole, successful.

The people who are the suppliers or sellers in the Dar es Salaam city market are those buyers or producers of the rural market whom we have described above. The buyers in the city at the wholesale auction fall under the following categories:

(a) individuals,
(b) shopkeepers,
(c) stall owners in the city market systems,
(d) food suppliers/contractors to institutions,

Stall owners are by far the most important group of buyers.

Individuals are usually from the high and medium income brackets who have large families and many dependants and often originate from the banana culture area of Kilimanjaro, Bukoba and Tukuyu. They come to the market and enter the bidding at the auction. Buyers in this group are not very regular at the market, and probably account for less than 10% of the trade. Most of the bananas bought by these individuals are consumed as cooking bananas.

THE STALL HOLDERS

These are regular and professional businessmen who have rented stalls in the city market systems. the majority deal exclusively in cooking bananas, and They absorb most of the bananas offered for sale. Stall holders buy their bananas mainly from the auction and then retail them either as single bananas or in heaps of three or five bananas. The stall holders do not always buy their supplies from the auction. Occasionally some stall holders have direct contact either with farmers or traders who supply them with bananas at pre-agreed prices.[6] The latter constitutes black marketing and the city loses the money it collects as market dues. It was impossible to determine the magnitude of this black market trade in bananas. Small traders seem to work very closely with the stall-holders and assist them by credit sales. This is a very complex system of transaction, and the people involved in it are often reluctant to discuss it. Nevertheless, on the whole, the stall holders are the main buyers of bananas coming into Dar es Salaam.

Shopkeepers are actually those dealing in general merchandise with a bias towards food selling. These shopkeepers are mainly "duka" owners located in high population density and low to medium income residential areas. Their main line of selling however is ripe bananas. The quantity of cooking bananas they buy and sell is very low.

Suppliers and Contractors are important groups of buyers which include contractors and suppliers to institutions, e.g. schools, police, prisons, hotels, etc. Some hotels buy their supplies direct from the auctions and the smaller ones buy from stalls. There is one farmers' co-operative association which deals in fresh foodstuffs and their operations are similar to those of suppliers and contractors to institutions. The green grocers and super-markets in the city do not seem to carry much stock of either cooking or ripe bananas. Supermarkets are supplied by licensed and unlicensed hawkers who trade at the entrance of the supermarkets.

The banana marketing structure in Dar es Salaam generally meets the requirements of the city laws. In part, this can be explained by the quantities arriving and in part by the marketing channels. Bananas arrive in large consignments and once they are arranged for inspection there can be little confusion since the main channels for marketing are limited to the few outlined above.

There is some inhibition towards stocking without the process of the auction because detection would be easy. Traders and trader-producers from long and medium distances can afford the time to wait and sell their consignments.

However, a varying amount of bananas get to the consumers without ever complying with all the regulations. For instance, some of the traders have places where they retail some of the cooking bananas on a part time basis by using cronies or close relatives. Producers from the area near to Dar es Salaam who bring supplies and speculate on prices are also tempted to sell directly to the consumers. The greater proportion of them are old established producer-traders and retailers who know the responses of the market. In the final analysis, however, the check is again the stall holders, who are quick to report such irregularities, unless one of their members is involved in these transactions. There seems to be a gentleman's agreement between all stall holders in the banana business which is quite contrary to that in the orange market.

TRANSPORT AND TRANSPORT COSTS IN THE CITY MARKETS

The main transport modes in the city markets are pick-ups and "Mkokoteni" (push-carts). Sometimes head-loads, bicycles and taxis are used, but these are used mainly by small hawkers who deal mainly in ripe or fruit bananas. The charges vary according to the mode of transport used and the distance travelled. For most pick-ups and vans the charges are from Shs. 5/- to 15/- within the city limits. Mkokoteni charges are a little less than those of pick-ups. Taxis usually charge the normal rate of personal taxi hire plus Shs. 0/50 to Shs. 1/- per bunch. Bicycles are usually owned by hawkers themselves.

In summary the people who are concerned with bananas in the rural markets are the producers or farmers who sell their bananas to the traders, other farmers, and the farmers themselves individually selling their crops to the urban population. The buyers and producers in the rural market are the suppliers in the urban market and their customers are individuals, stall holders in the city market system, the shopkeepers and the food suppliers/contractors.

SUPPLY AND DEMAND

The people who are involved in the banana production and trade, the source areas and the various modes of transportation and the costs for the latter have been discussed. Two important questions which need considering next are those of supply in terms of frequency and demand in terms of capacity of absorbing the supply by the Dar es Salaam market.

Cooking bananas arrive in Dar es Salaam almost daily. The quantity delivered daily varies in accordance with the road conditions, which in turn depend on weather, distances from the source areas, the availability of transport and to a lesser extent the demand for other staple and subsidiary staple crops coming to the Dar es Salaam market.

Earlier we mentioned that road conditions do not affect transport costs very much, but do affect deliveries immensely. Most if not all feeder roads to the major banana producing areas are either murram or simply dusty roads. During the rainy season some of the roads are sometimes impassable because either they are flooded or bridges have been washed away. These problems were very acute in the months of March to May, 1968. In 1969, one of the bridges on the Morogoro trunk road was washed away and supplies from Morogoro and Tanga regions could not reach Dar es Salaam. The implications of bad roads are that supplies to the Dar es Salaam market are cut off and there is no carry over stock for most perishables in Dar es Salaam. As a result the city markets run short of stocks of perishables within a day or two. The other implication is that as soon as it is known that the stocks are dwindling the prices of most perishables rise rapidly. For a week in 1969, the prices of tomatoes went up from cents 80 a pound, to Shs. 3/- a pound. Prices of bananas also went up but not to the extent of tomatoes. Prices twice above the usual level were not unusual.

Distances from source areas are a factor affecting supply. This is tied in with the mode of transportation. There are regular daily buses to Dar es Salaam from most of the smaller source areas, but sometimes during the month there are too many passengers so that there is no room to carry bananas. Thus, traders who would like to bring their bananas in the market daily have to wait until they get a place on the buses. As buses are the major means of transport, this factor cuts off some of the supplies coming to Dar es Salaam.

There are times when there is competition for transport among the different staple and subsidiary staple food crops. Thus in the Kisarawe areas, when the orange season is on, most lorry and bus drivers pick up orange 'tengas' (may be they are handier to carry, leaving banana sellers stranded.

The frequencies of supply of bananas are shown in graph 1. The frequency is presented on a weekly basis and is based on computed volume from an observation of 2 and 3 days every week, on alternate weeks respectively (see also Appendix II).

VARIATION IN SUPPLIES

Bananas are usually harvested throughout the year, but the quantity harvested per acre or per stool varies according to the seasons. Thus during the dry season the total quantity of bananas harvested declines and the reverse is true when the rains come or during a period immediately after the rains. There is thus a general tendency mildly revealed in the graph above, to have two high peaks in the quantity of bananas arriving in Dar es Salaam. These peaks correspond to some

GRAPH 1: COMPUTED ARRIVALS, PRICES, AND TOTAL VALUE. COOKING BANANAS - DAR-ES-SALAAM 1968/69

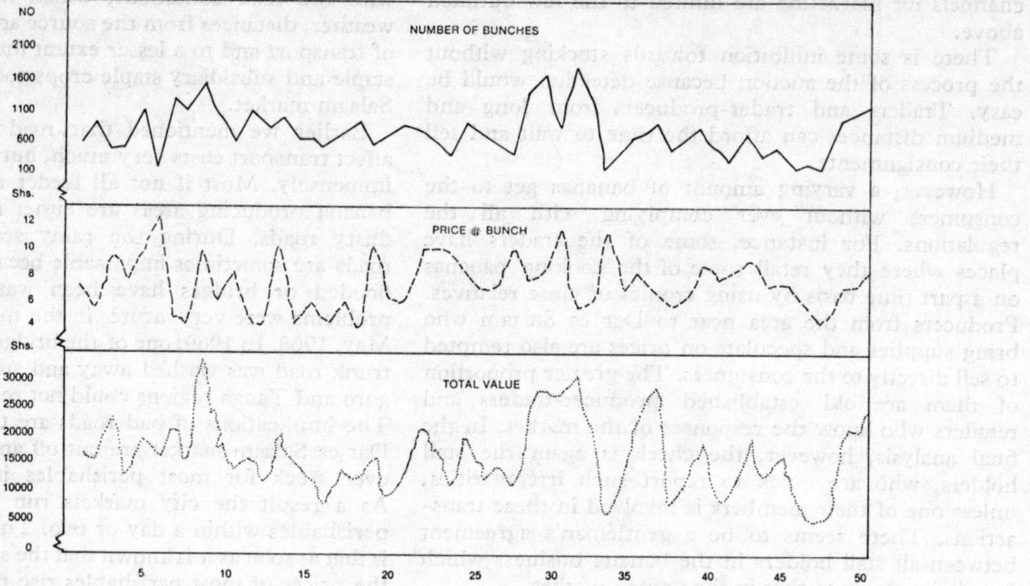

Source: From Appendix II

extent to the short and long rains respectively. The two major troughs observed between weeks 20 to 29/30 and again between week 42 and 48/49 correspond to the dry seasons prevailing prior to these periods.

Abnormal supplies are also recorded in some months The graph above shows large quantities of bananas arriving in weeks 30–34, followed by a sharp decline of deliveries in week 35. Weeks 30–34 fall between the end of November and second half of December. This period coincides with the month of Ramadhan when the Muslim Community fasts. Bananas make a special dish called 'futari' and it features predominantly in the evening and morning meals of those who do the fasting.[7] The sharp decline following this high peak can mainly be explained by the slack in farm business (especially deliveries to town) due to the fact that this is the end of Ramadhan and people were celebrating both Idd El Fitr and Christmas at almost the same time. In addition to celebrating, there was a lot of movement of people going in both directions. The rural people come to town to celebrate and town people go directly to the rural areas to see their relatives. These movements of people affect the availability of space in buses plying between town and the source areas, etc. Other smaller variations are due to the factors discussed earlier.

Demand for cooking bananas in Dar es Salaam seems to be steady. This is reflected in the quantity of arrivals and the high percentage of sales. Almost all cooking bananas that arrive at the market are sold at the auction, unlike oranges where the percentage of sales to total arrival is often less than sixty.

WHOLESALE PRICE VARIATIONS

The graph above shows the weekly fluctuations of prices also at the wholesale level in the Dar es Salaam market. The graph also shows that price fluctuations are not as great as reflected in the quantity of arrivals and the average weekly total values of the crop. This price fluctuation is due partly to the fact that cooking bananas enjoy two distinct markets—a cooking or/and roasting banana market and the fruit or ripe banana market-and partly to the steady minimum quantity of bananas available at the market.

The availability of substitutes such as cooking cassava, green maize, sweet potatoes and yams may contribute to the minimum fluctuations in the wholesale prices. Cassava can be roasted or used as 'futari'. The end use of these crops and their substitutability are summarised in table 3.

TABLE 3: END USE OF SELECTED SUBSTITUTES FOR BANANAS

Boiling	Futari	Roasting
Bananas	Bananas	Bananas
Cassava	Cassava	Cassava
Sweet Potatoes	Sweet potatoes	
Yams	Yams	
Green maize		Green maize

The patterns of price fluctuations follow very closely the supply available. Thus when the supply is plentiful prices tend to be depressed and the reverse is true when the supply is small. In other words in Dar es Salaam the banana is generally price elastic.

There are however some exceptions to this generality. In the 42nd and 48/49th weeks the quantity of bananas arriving in Dar es Salaam was small and yet the prices were still depressed. This is because there was a carry-over stock from the previous days and because the purchasing power of the people is low in the period January to end of February. Most people use their January and February salaries to pay up for the festivities in December. Business starts picking up again in March and April.

TOTAL VALUES

Appendix table II and graph 2 give the weekly values of cooking bananas that arrive in Dar es Salaam through the official channels. It is noted that some bananas go directly to the consumers without going through the market. It is very difficult to quantify the amount but it is estimated to be about 10% to 15% of the official arrival values.

The weekly values range from Shs. 5,594 to Shs.28,620. The total value for the period May 1968 to April 1969, i.e. in a one year period, is Shs. 849,756. If

GRAPH 2: BANANA MARKET CHANNELS, DAR-ES-SALAAM

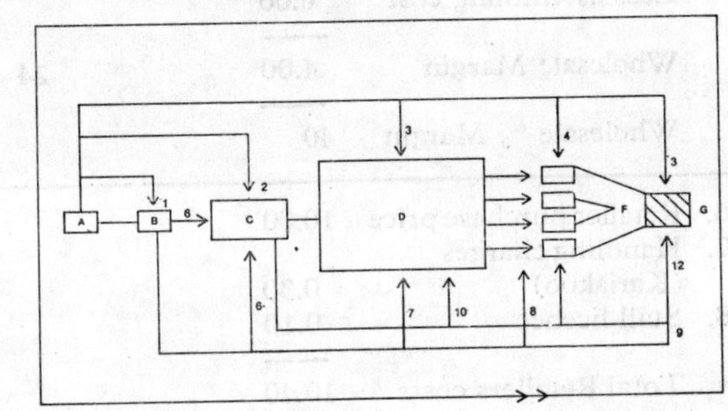

Key:

A. FARMER (PRODUCER) can sell to:
1. Producer Trader (B)
2. Trader in Rural Market (C)
3. Dar-es-Salaam City Market (Auction) (D)
4. Occasionally to (F), i.e. city submarkets (a), shopkeepers (b), food suppliers/ contractors (c). direct to stallholders (d).
5. Consumer (G)3

B. PRODUCER/TRADER can sell to:
6. Traders in Rural Markets (C)
7. Dar-es-Salaam City Market (D) (Auction)
8. Any of the groups (a), (b), (c) and (d) (F)
9. Consumers (G)

C. TRADERS (OCCASIONALLY PRODUCER/TRADER) IN RURAL MARKET can sell to:
10. Dar-es-Salaam City Market - Auction (D)
11. Any of the groups (a), (b), (c) and (d) (F)
12. Very small amounts to consumers (G)

D. THE MAIN KARIAKOO MARKET and the main buyers are:
(a) Traders from city submarkets (Ilala, Magomeni, Temeke, etc.) F (a)
(b) Shopkeepers F (b)
(c) Foodsuppliers/Contractors F (d)
(d) Stallholders at Kariokoo Market F(d)

the 10–15% of unofficial deliveries are added to this annual figure, the cooking banana business in Dar es Salaam can safely be estimated at a million shillings a year.

RETAIL TRADE

Earlier in this paper the people involved in retailing cooking bananas were discussed. The discussion on retail prices and price fluctuation was left until the supply, demand and the wholesale transactions had been discussed.

It is rather difficult to get a clear picture of prices a retailer gets for selling his bananas. These difficulties arise *first* from the change in the units used. In the wholesale transaction the unit used is a bunch while in the retail trade the unit is a single banana. The number of bananas in each bunch varies considerably, from 4–5 (in Mkono wa Tembo variety) to about 200 bananas in the larger bunches of the Kiguruwe variety. *Secondly,* the retail trade is conducted on a variety basis and there is some rudimentary form of grading which is not adhered to strictly at the wholesale level. The most popular varieties and larger bananas fetch higher prices. In grading bananas for retailing the most important factors that are considered are variety, size of the bananas and stage of maturity.

To alleviate the problem of units only a few of the most common varieties in Dar es Salaam market were selected for a sample study. These varieties included Mshale, Kiguruwe (short), Kiguruwe (long) and Dosa. All these varieties have a range of 60–200 bananas on a bunch with a mode at 90 bananas. The average was 120 bananas to a bunch.

Sample of prices per heap and number of bananas per heap were taken and recorded.

The results are shown in table 4 below:

Due to variation of bunch sizes and the number of bananas per bunch the revenue realized per bunch varies from Shs. 10/ to Shs. 25/. Occasionally some bunches (especially those originating from Bukoba which rarely come to Dar es Salaam official market) retail as high as Shs. 40-45 per bunch. For analysis purposes, the calculations shown in table 4 above where the average price per bunch for all varieties is Shs. 17/10 will be used.

A very common feature among retailers of practically all commodities sold in heaps is the attempt to keep the price constant and vary the quantities involved. There are times when a heap of tomatoes (say 3 tomatoes weighing 1 lb.) will retail at Shs. 0.80 and other times the heap will contain one or two tomatoes that weigh less than 1 lb and still sell for Shs. 0.80. In the banana

TABLE 4: RETAIL PRICES OF SOME SELECTED VARIETIES OF BANANAS

Variety	No. of bananas in heap	Price per heap Shs.	Price per banana Shs.	Equivalent price per bunch of 120 bananas
Mshale	3	0.50	0.17	20.40
Kiguruwe (short)	5	0.50	0.10	12.00
Kiguruwe (long)	3	0.50	0.17	20.40
Dosa	4	0.50	0.13	15.60
Average	4	0.50	0.14	14.10

trade these manipulations of heaps are rare. The reasons for these rare occurrences are not known but the most likely ones are that the margins at wholesale and retail are fairly high and stable and also damage due to rotting is less severe than in the case of other perishables.

PRICES PAID TO GROWERS (IN THE RURAL MARKET)

Prices paid to growers vary from place to place. The major factors affecting these prices are variety of bananas, size of bunches, ripening stage and maturity. If the bunches are small the price will be lower, if the bunches are near ripening or immature the prices will also be lower. Besides the above factors the unusual demand due to speculation of bad weather and difficult transport conditions, plus the art of bargaining which most traders use to advantage over farmers, contribute effectively to the price a grower gets for his crop.

Prices also vary in accordance with distance from Dar es Salaam and the time of the day when bananas are offered for sale. An observation made at Turiani showed that morning prices ranged from Shs. 2/50 to Shs. 4/- per bunch while in the afternoon the range was Shs. 1/50 to Shs. 4/- per bunch.

The average prices growers received in selected localities of source areas for 1968/69 are presented in table 5.

TABLE 5: BANANA GROWERS' PRICES IN SELECTED LOCALITIES; 1968/69

Locality	Average price Shs. @ bunch	Range Shs. @ bunch
Turiani	3.00	0.50–6.00
Mkuyuni	3.20	0.75–6.00
Ifakara	2.50	0.40–4.50
Muheza (Tanga)	2.50	1.50–4.00

The major dilemma in the rural areas is that there are very few established rural markets and much of the rural buying and selling is done either at the farm or anywhere along the road side. Places nearer to Dar es Salaam, e.g. Kibaha and Bagamoyo have hardly any rural markets. Growers transport and sell their crops direct to the Dar es Salaam market.

PRICES PAID TO TRADERS (WHOLESALE AT DAR ES SALAAM MARKET)

Prices received by traders at the wholesale or auction dealings in Dar es Salaam depend on the same factors that influence prices in the rural areas, e.g. size of the bunch, variety, ripening stage, maturity, conditions of demand and supply and the time of day the bananas arrive in the city.

Bananas sold through unofficial channels constitute a black market operation and represent a loss of revenue to the city. Black market operations are usually conducted by farmers who live nearer Dar es Salaam and speculate on prices. The nature of their dealings are secret but these people tend to be professional traders, they know their market and tend to specialize in banana trade. The average prices they get is a little higher partly because they know where to sell and partly because they avoid the market levy or dues.

TABLE 6: PRICE STRUCTURE OF COOKING BANANAS—DAR ES SALAAM (1969)

Description	Price per bunch shs.	% of whole-sale price	% of retail price (Kariakoo)
1. Prices paid producer	3.20	32	18
2. Transport costs	2.00	20	11
3. Handling costs	0.20		—
4. Market dues 6% of Auction Price	0.60	—	—
Total assembling costs	6.00	60	30
5. Wholesale price at DSM Auction	10.00	58	
Less assembling cost	6.00		
Wholesale Margin	4.00		24
Wholesale % Margin	40		
6. Retailer purchase price	10.00		
7. Handling charges (Kariakoo)	0.30		
8. Stall licence	0.10		
Total Retailers costs	10.40		
9. Retail price	17.00		
Less Retailers cost	10.40		
Retailers Margin	6.60	66	
Retailers % Margin (Kariakoo Market)	38		
Handling charges (b. submarkets)	0.80		
Stall licences (b. submarkets)	0.10		
Total costs (b. submarkets)	10.90		
10. Retail price (Submarkets)	17.00		
Less costs	10.90		
Submarkets margin	6.10		
Submarket % Margin	35.00		

There is no guarantee, however, that these speculators make profits each time they try these operations. There are two setbacks which they can encounter. The first one is they are not sure when a truck load of bananas from other areas will arrive; and if a load of good quality bananas arrives before they return from the rural areas the chances are they will get very low prices. The second setback is that there is a tendency for producers to harvest premature bananas which fetch lower prices.

Examples of these setbacks have been recorded. The prices paid to traders ex-Bagamoyo on 8th May, 1968 averaged Shs. 1/50 per bunch for the lowest bid and Shs. 1/75 per bunch for the highest. The trader finally refused to sell his bananas. What really happened was that the trader left town earlier that morning after convincing himself that there was scarcity of bananas in town. On his return to the city he found that a big auction had just taken place before he returned from Bagamoyo. In early April on the other hand a Bagamoyo trader realized the lowest and highest bids of Shs. 4/30 and Shs. 13/85 per bunch respectively just because a truck with 200 bunches from Turiani arrived too late for the auction that day.

The average daily prices at the Dar es Salaam wholesale auctions average about Shs. 10/00 per bunch.

COSTS AND MARGINS

In the rural areas the costs involved are those of assembling the bananas which can be measured by the time foregone by the farmer in doing other farm work, or an equivalent wage per hour, and the time spent by growers or producers for assembling or marketing. The costs involved at this level are those of ransport, fare, packages and handling charges only for those growers who decide to sell in Dar es Salaam.

Handling charges are averages and these are normally the amount of money paid for labour for either loading or off loading or both. In the rural areas these charges vary from about 5 cents to 25 cents per bunch. For Kariakoo market the normal charges for off loading and carrying to the auction floor is 30 cents per bunch. Retailers who have their stalls in other parts of the city, e.g. Magomeni, Ilala, Mkunguni and Temeke have to pay 50 cents per bunch transportation fees.

MARGINS OR PROFITS

An attempt was made to get margins by variety and grade of bananas and also cost the grading itself. The task was so complicated that the idea was abandoned. The complications arose from the lack of trained enumerators who could distinguish the various varieties (300 in the world!!) and also the reluctance of the stallholders to answer detailed questions.

In general, however, the margin is highest at the wholesale level, and higher at Kariakoo retail stalls than at the sub-market stalls in the city.

Costs and margins are shown in table 6 above. It is interesting to note that for each shilling that a consumer pays for bananas the farmer gets only about 30–25 cents. The rest is taken by marketing costs plus a small amount for taxes.

Some people may argue that the high return by wholesalers and retailers is justified because of the perishable nature of the crop. This may be true to a very limited degree but there is hardly any quantity of cooking bananas that is thrown away because of spoilage. For fruit bananas spoilage is high. The only major threat of spoilage of cooking bananas is mishandling the crop thus causing bruising in the bananas, a phenomena that can reduce prices considerably.

CONCLUSION

The banana trade in Dar es Salaam and in Tanzania has very particular features. The most important ones are the marked widespread distribution of sources of supply, irregular supplies, unorganised systems of collection, transport and market intelligence and above all a complete lack of specialised and organised traderst

Besides the above features bananas as a product is no. a homogeneous one. There are hundreds of varieties which vary in flavour and end use. The exact number of varieties in Tanzania is not yet established.

A country wide urban supply study is needed to establish areas of surplus and areas of deficits. The data collected by the existing institutions do not throw much light as to how much banana trade is going on in the country. Besides identifying surplus and deficit areas such a study would also help government, parastatals and cooperatives to try to find means and ways of solving the problems listed above and also to set up processing industries.

The other concern in this trade is that the farmer has to be educated in the trade. The people who benefit

APPENDIX 1: HARVESTED AND MARKETED PRODUCTION BANANAS/PLANTAIN 1968 (Tons)

Column 1 Region	Harvested	Marketed	% of 3 over 2
Arusha	61,500	2,250	3.76
Coast	2,300	300	13.0
Dodoma	1,000	700	70.0
Iringa	2,550	2,000	78.4
Kigoma	60,000	12,000	20.0
Kilimanjaro	184,000	49,000	37.5
Mara	6,650	3,800	37.1
Mbeya	107,600	7,900	7.3
Morogoro	10,000	5,000	50
Mtwara	1,100	935	85
Mwanza	6,000	4,000	66.7
Ruvuma	—	—	—
Shinyanga	200	4	2
Singida	100	80	80
Tabora	2,250	1,025	45.5
Tanga	35,000	30,000	85.7
West Lake	470,000	33,300	7.1
Total	950,250	152,294	16.0

APPENDIX II: WEEKLY ARRIVALS AND VALUES OF COOKING BANANAS: DAR ES SALAAM MARKET

Month	Week	Observed arrivals bunches	Computed arrivals bunches	Wholesale Price @ bunch Shs.	Value based on computed arrivals Shs.
1968					
May	1	661	2,314	7.30	16,938
	2	1,146	2,674	5.70	15,269
	3	674	2,359	9.40	22,104
	4	692	1,615	7.65	12,355
	5	1,306	1,828	9.95	18,189
June	6	372	1,302	11.90	15,507
	7	1,579	3,684	5.50	20,041
	8	1,274	2,973	4.70	13,973
	9	1,870	3,273	9.40	30,733
July	10	1,190	2,777	6.15	17,051
	11	733	1,710	8.00	13,680
	12	1,324	3,089	5.10	15,816
	13	1,031	2,406	4.65	11,188
	14	1,130	1,978	9.75	19,246
August	15	874	3,059	4.85	14,867
	16	901	2,102	6.05	12,696
	17	650	1,517	5.05	7,676
	18	973	2,270	9.95	13,529
September	19	1,195	2,788	4.45	12,434
	20	666	1,554	9.80	15,229
	21	775	1,356	6.20	8,407
	22	1,014	2,366	6.20	14,646
October	23	904	2,109	9.60	20,267
	24	715	1,668	10.10	16,847
	25	491	1,146	9.30	10,646
	26	1,032	2,408	7.90	18,999
	27	875	1,531	7.70	11,819
November	28	595	2,083	7.05	14,706
	29	445	1,038	10.20	10,577
	30	1,554	3,626	7.20	26,071
	31	1,907	3,337	8.20	27,363
December	32	1,088	2,352	11.00	25,849
	33	2,093	4,884	5.85	28,620
	34	1,413	3,297	5.95	16,617
	35	143	501	11.20	5,616
	36	710	2,485	6.75	16,724
1969					
January	37	851	2,979	8.10	24,130
	38	1,149	4,022	6.95	27,953
	39	582	1,358	5.80	7,876
	40	829	2,902	6.40	18,573
	41	953	2,224	8.90	19,794

February	42	316	1,106	7.55	8,350
	43	433	1,516	8.30	12,583
	44	880	2,053	8.90	18,272
	45	474	1,659	7.20	11,945
March	46	664	2,324	7.50	17,430
	47	378	1,323	6.75	8,930
	48	444	1,036	5.40	5,594
	49	364	1,274	5.25	6,689
	50	1,151	2,686	7.35	19,742
April	51	1,263	2,714	7.50	20,355
	52	1,331	3,106	8.45	26,245
Annual Total	52	47,977	117,750	—	849,756

most in the cooking banana industry are the traders, wholesalers and retailers, and to some extent the transporters. It is high time that something is done to get banana producers and indeed all perishable crop producers organized so that they can have an institution that can bargain fairly with traders and that consumers receive supplies required at fair prices.

NOTES

1. A. C. Mascarenhas and S. M. Mbilinyi, "The Orange Trade of Dar es Salaam: A Case Study of Risk Taking Among Peasant Food Producers", *East African Journal of Rural Development*, Vol. 4, No. 1, 1971, Department of Rural Economy, Makerere University, Kampala.
2. Cash-crop is defined as a crop produced mainly for sale.
3. It would be interesting to note the development rate of the banana industry and indeed other subsistence crops in view of the 1969/70 tax structure whereby the local rate has been abolished.
4. Tanga has got fertilizer, steel mill and sisal pulp industry.
5. There is talk that Tanga port may be expanded to serve a greater hinterland than it does now.
6. These arrangements are usually secret because such transactions are illegal. Economically, though, this practice shows that there is some limited amount of forward selling transaction.
7. Futari is either a root crop or bananas cooked with either coconut oil/milk or other seasonings. The dish is very popular during the Ramadhan fast.

Section VII

Human Resources and Development

INTRODUCTION

Tanzania's approach to development is based on human equality and dignity, as the Arusha Declaration makes clear. Because of the emphasis on balanced rural development, Tanzania has largely avoided many of the problems that characterize most other low income countries, problems which are manifest in the unequal distribution of incomes and opportunities, high rates of rural to urban migration, uncontrolled urban growth and increasing visible unemployment.

The readings in this section focus more specifically on those topics that often are termed human resources. These include the composition of the labour force, conditions of work, wages and salaries, education and health. The first three papers present some of the results of a national survey of urban migration, employment and incomes carried out by the Economic Research Bureau in the early 1970s. In the first reading Bienfeld examines the occupational structure and sectoral distribution of the industrial labour force and describes the relationship which exists between occupations and the educational background, age and sex of the working force.

Sabot then considers in some detail the functionings of urban labour markets. His findings must be qualified in light of the increased importance that manpower planning has assumed as the country seeks to transform its productive forces to meet more adequately the basic needs of the population. In a second paper Sabot analyzes the extent of urban unemployment and underemployment, and he develops a simple model for a more precise specification of "marginal" employment in the Tanzanian urban context.

The next two papers look at some of the institutional features of the organisation and participation of workers. Mapolu briefly recounts the history of workers' councils and their role in management decisions following the Presidential Circular of January 1970 (*Mwongozo*). The development of a labour-management sector has encountered many difficulties, and Mapolu raises important questions of both a theoretical and practical nature for the further development of worker participation in a socialist society.

Fortmann in turn examines the role of women in development. Her brief survey article provides a helpful review of recent literature and serves to document her position that women in Tanzania, as in most other societies, are both overworked and overlooked, at a great cost to society.

The final paper summarizes Gottlieb's detailed examination of the health care sector in Tanzania. This topic is particularly relevant in the context of the present debate over the choice of means that will best ensure adequate health care to a largely rural population. Other aspects of human resources and development also are of great urgency at the moment in Tanzania, but these readings selectively point to some of the important issues that will remain priorities in Tanzania's efforts to develop a humane and just society.

Occupational Structure and Industrial Distribution of Wage Earners*

M. A. BIENEFELD

OCCUPATIONAL STRUCTURE

The occupational classification of the labour force is designed to indicate the relative proportions of the labour force performing certain functions in the course of their work. Unfortunately such classifications inevitably are crude as descriptive, and ambiguous as analytical tools. Meaningful description is hampered by serious problems of definition, while the analytical usefulness of such data is limited both by the lack of a clear relationship between occupational structures and other significant factors, such as the degree of industrialisation or GDP per capita on one level, and by the often close and almost tautological relationship between occupation and income or education on another level.

It follows that an occupational classification is not only an objective functional classification of workers and their jobs, but also reflects the social structure of that society, as well as its value system. In analysing such classifications, one must bear these constraints in mind. The discovery that occupations are related to education and to income is therefore often merely a tautology, reflecting the fact that these variables were implicitly or explicitly used to define the occupations in the first place. This is not to speak of the additional complication that the present education of members of an occupation may not represent the education "required," any more than that their present earnings necessarily reflect their members' contributions to society. Both quantities of course already depend on the social status and political power of the group.

With all of these difficulties, any attempts to describe the occupational pattern of any one place at any one time or to make comparisons over time or between countries are clearly extremely hazardous. If it is therefore advisable to be careful regarding the significance one attaches to differences in occupational structures that may appear from inter-country or inter-temporal comparisons; it is equally important to be very clear about the purpose of such comparisons.

The occupational data concerning Tanzania's urban wage earners are, therefore, presented here primarily to describe the existing situation, although this also may provide a basis against which future changes can be compared, so long as problems of definition are dealt with adequately at that time.[1] The data are based on surveys undertaken in the principal urban areas in 1971.

TABLE 1: SEVEN TOWNS: ADULT WAGE EARNERS BY SEX: OCCUPATIONAL DISTRIBUTION

Occupation	Males %	Females %	Total population %
a – Prof., tech., managerial, administrative	4.8	9.4	5.5
b – Clerks, typists, steno's, telephonists	15.1	28.7	17.0
c – Sales Workers	4.4	5.2	4.5
d – Domestics, cooks, ayahs, dobis, gardeners,	16.6	6.5	6.6
e – Drivers	5.2	—	4.5
f – Messengers, Watchmen, cleaners, sweepers	8.4	5.5	8.0
g – Pub. Servants, Police, nurses, social workers	2.6	8.1	3.4
h – Hotel workers, waiters, barmaids, porters	4.5	16.5	6.2
i Semi-technical, lab. asst., draughtsmen, surveyors, med. assts., health inspectors	4.6	3.5	4.4
j – Skilled, mechanics, foremen, electricians	10.4	1.6	9.2
k – Craftsmen, tailors, carpenters, masons	10.3	2.3	9.1
l – Machine operators and process workers	6.3	4.5	6.1
m – Unskilled labourers	16.4	8.4	15.2
	100	100	100

Table 1 shows the occupational distribution of urban wage earners by 13 categories, ranging from the largest, "Clerical," with 17 per cent of total employees, to the smallest, "Public Servant," with only 3.4 per cent.

---

* This paper is a summary of material that appears in *The National Urban Mobility, Employment and Income Survey of Tanzania*, Vol. III, "The Wage Employed." Economic Research Bureau, University of Dar es Salaam, 1972, pp. 21–52.

Not unexpectedly, the distribution among occupations is very different for males and females. More than half of all male wage earners are found in four categories, including "Skilled" workers, "Craftsmen" and "Unskilled" workers, and "Clerical" employees. Females are even more concentrated in certain occupations, with more than 45 per cent working either as "Clerical" staff or as "Hotel" employees and "Barmaids."

If one discounts the absolute size of various categories, and the fact that in absolute terms males make up the bulk of all the categories, it is of interest to compare the relative likelihood of finding males or females in particular occupations. Such a comparison shows males to be most heavily over-represented among "Skilled" and "Unskilled" workers, "Craftsmen," "Drivers" and "Messengers, Watchmen, etc." Females on the other hand are relatively most concentrated in the categories of "Professional, Technical, etc.," "Clerical," "Public Service," and "Hotels and Bars."

Table 2 shows wage earners distributed among four major occupational groups. These groups do not follow ISCO practice, but rather reflect combinations of sub-groups based on similarities of function, responsibility and status, and in particular, similar educational requirements. The least satisfactory distinction is that between "Service workers" and "Unskilled." In fact, these are both unskilled, and the distinction is that the former are engaged in personal service, while the latter tend to be engaged in production of various kinds, with many of them in construction. These two unskilled groups make up about 40 per cent of total employment; and although patterns for males and females are very dissimilar, for both it remains true that about 40 per cent are found in these two unskilled groups.

TABLE 2: SEVEN TOWNS: ADULT WAGE EARNERS BY SEX: OCCUPATIONAL DISTRIBUTION BY MAJOR GROUPS

Major Occupational Groups	Males (%)	Females (%)	Total population (%)
White Collar[a]	27.1	49.7	30.3
Production related[b]	32.2	8.4	28.9
Service[c]	23.9	33.7	25.3
Unskilled[d]	16.4	8.4	15.2
	100	100	100
Total Number[e]	1,880	310	2,190

[a] includes a, b, g, i (Table 1)
[b] includes e, j, k, l
[c] includes c, d, f, h
[d] includes m
[e] these numbers can be used with the percentages of Table 1 to calculate the number in each occupation in the sample.

SOURCES: Table 1 and ST 191/001, 002/ — /001, 002: Q5–1, 2.

Wage earners as a whole are fairly evenly divided among the four basic groups, with "White Collar" employees and "Production related" workers accounting for slightly more than a quarter each, while "Unskilled" make up about 15 per cent. The same pattern prevails for males alone, though here "Production" workers outnumber "White Collar" employees. For females the pattern is dramatically different, with almost 85 per cent concentrated in "White Collar" and "Service" jobs.

It is worth noting that in terms of the basic occupational patterns one would expect from a non-industrialized economy, this structure is rather unexpected. This stems from the fact that it relates to the urban wage employed only and hence excludes the bulk of the population engaged in agriculture. The figures suggest that the urban economy of Tanzania has generated a considerable industrial base.

As has already been suggested, these major groups can be further combined into two: the "White Collar" and "Production" workers who are educated and skilled; and the "Service" and "Unskilled" workers who are neither. It follows that if there is such a thing as a "labour aristocracy," it will be either found within or circumscribed by these top two categories.

OCCUPATION AND EDUCATION

Table 3 shows the relationship between occupation and education and the extent to which individual occupational categories are educationally specific. This in turn reflects the homogeneity of each category and the extent to which experience is an acceptable substitute for formal education. In evaluating the results, it should be borne in mind that much of the observed educational homogeneity, especially of the four major groups, arises because the definition of occupation contains an educational element. Nevertheless these observations are useful in describing more concretely the particular attributes of various occupational groups in the Tanzanian context.

The educational patterns within the detailed groups suggest, first of all, that educational selectivity exists, at least to the extent that there are very few occupations where one finds significant numbers of workers with no education and workers with post-primary education. Hence, in 10 of the 13 categories, more than 95 per cent of all employees are found either in the bottom three or in the top three educational categories. Of the three exceptions, sales workers are clearly a heterogeneous and rather ill defined category; and skilled workers and machine operators perform tasks which either are/or formerly were accessible through experience to those without formal education, while at the same time being prestigious enough to attract a significant number of those with post-primary education.

A further indication of the extent of educational selectivity can be gathered from the proportion of any occupation found in any two adjacent educational categories. This yields the very interesting result that the only four groups with more than 88 per cent of their

TABLE 3: SEVEN TOWNS: ADULT WAGE EARNERS OCCUPATION BY EDUCATION

	White Collar					Production					Service					
	Prof. Management	Clerical	Semi-Technical	Public Service	Total White Collar	Skilled	Machine Operators	Craftsmen	Drivers	Total Production	Domestic	Messenger Cleaner	Hotel Bar	Sales	Total Service	Unskilled
	%	%	%	%	%	%	%	%	%	%	%	%	%	%	%	%
None	2.5	3.0	4.2	4.0	3.2	10.8	18.0	20.0	26.8	17.7	33.1	42.3	34.6	22.4	34.4	35.4
Std. 1–4	5.0	3.5	7.3	4.0	4.4	19.7	18.0	34.0*	36.1*	26.4	46.5*	26.1*	25.6*	27.6*	31.5	27.4*
Std. 5–8	20.8	38.4	33.3	72.0*	38.3	55.2*	55.6*	44.0	34.0	48.5	20.4	29.0	36.8	35.7	29.9	34.1
Post-Primary	71.7*	55.1*	55.2*	20.0	54.1	14.3	8.3	2.0	3.1	7.4	—	2.8	3.0	14.3	4.2	3.0
Total	100	100	100	100	100	100	100	100	100	100	100	100	100	100	100	100
Number	120	372	96	75	663	203	133	200	97	663	142	176	133	98	549	328

* Denotes group in which media lines.

SOURCES: CR 334/ —/001 to 007/001, 002.

total number in two categories also make up the "White Collar" category. All of these are concentrated in the upper two educational levels. No less interesting is the discovery that the five occupations with 70 to 80 per cent of their number concentrated in two adjacent educational groups include all four occupations that make up the major category of "Production" workers, plus domestic servants. The remaining occupations are less concentrated and have less than 70 per cent of their numbers in contiguous educational groups.

This pattern suggests a situation where white collar jobs are restricted to those with a relatively high level of education and this restriction is quite rigidly observed. Production jobs are to a very large extent filled by those with some education up to Standard 7, although a number of people with no education also are found in this type of work. Table 4 shows clearly that those with no education are predominantly older workers, who presumably began their job when educational selectivity was not yet possible in these jobs, due to a shortage of "qualified" applicants. Thus while 22 per cent of all production workers are 40 years of age or older, no less than 47 per cent of those production workers without education are in this age group. The remaining occupations in the service and unskilled groups are predominantly done by people with little education, and the lesser educational homogeneity of these groups suggests the possibility that people with Standard 5 to 8 education have been forced to accept work in this sector as the number of educated applicants has increased. This possibility is also supported by the data in Table 4 which show that 54 per cent of all service workers (excluding domestic servants) were under 30 years of age, while the corresponding figures for those with Standard 5 to 8 and post-primary education were 75 and 74 per cent respectively. It appears therefore that a process of up-grading is taking place, and that in production jobs this has proceeded to the point where those with no education have been reduced to a relative remnant. Service jobs are less advanced, having progressed roughly to the stage where the number with Standard 5 to 8 education nearly equals the number in each of the lower two educational categories.

Although this emerges from an investigation of the educational pattern within the basic occupational groups, it appears useful to comment on the relative educational homogeneity of the major groups. White collar workers are the most highly educated, followed by production workers and then by service and unskilled employees, who are virtually indistinguishable in terms of educational attainment. This difference in major group educational patterns is clearly shown in Figure 3, but since this refers simply to the aggregate pattern of the members of the major group, it is necessary to look also at the extent to which each occupational sub-group conforms to this aggregate pattern. The evidence suggests that

TABLE 4: SEVEN TOWNS: ADULT WAGE EARNERS OCCUPATION BY AGE

Age in Years	White Collar		Production		Service*		
	Only those with Stand. 5 to 8 %	All White Collar %	Only those with no education %	All production %	Only those with Stand. 5 to 8 %	Only those Post-Primary %	With All Service %
14–19	9.8	7.9	—	4.3	22.4	4.3	11.3
20–24	32.7	33.7	11.5	25.0	26.9	43.5	21.6
25–29	20.9	22.5	10.6	21.5	25.4	26.1	20.6
30–34	12.6	12.3	12.5	14.5	7.5	8.7	13.1
35–39	10.2	9.7	18.3	12.5	9.0	4.3	11.8
40–49	9.8	9.7	25.0	14.4	6.7	13.0	11.1
50 & Over	3.9	4.2	22.1	8.1	2.2	—	10.6
Total	100	100	100	100	100	100	100
Number stated	254	661	104	633	134	23	398
n.s.	—	2	8	8	1	—	11

* Excluding domestic service.
SOURCE: CR 334/—/001 to 007/001, 002.

there is indeed a high degree of conformity between all of the component parts of the major groups, with the exception of the sales category, which deviates considerably from the other service jobs.

The major significance of this finding is that the high degree of homogeneity within the major categories makes it feasible to use these major categories for the comparison of occupation with other socio-economic variables.

To summarise our findings for the educational patterns of the major groups: (1) white collar work is done primarily by those with secondary school education, although it also involves a substantial number of people with Standard 5 to 8. These people do not appear to be older people, slowly being displaced, since only 14 per cent of them are over 40 years of age, compared with 15 per cent for all white collar workers; (2) three quarters of production workers have some primary school education, with most of the remainder having no education, and of these most are older workers working as drivers or craftsmen; (3) service and unskilled workers are about evenly divided among those with no education, with Standard 1 to 4, and with Standard 5 to 8; those with Standard 5 to 8 tend to be younger, suggesting that a process of up grading is taking place.

INDUSTRIAL DISTRIBUTION OF WAGE EARNERS

The industrial distribution of wage earners reflects the fundamental structure of the economy, although from certain points of view it may overstate the economic importance of some low productivity sectors. Once again the significance of the structures is a matter of some controversy.

The spectrum of views on the subject might be said to begin with those who believe totally in the benefits of international specialisation and attach little or no importance to structural aspects of the individual economies involved. This position is often accompanied by a definition of development as growth in Gross National Product per capita. As one's concept of development extends to a concern about excessive exposure to and dependence on exogenous and hence uncontrollable economic or political developments, one moves along this spectrum to a position which recognises the need for diversification, although in its simplest form this position is satisfied with some diversification of crops or primary production in general.

A further step along the spectrum is taken by those who believe that such diversification is insufficient protection against the vicissitudes of the international economy and that it exposes these economies to factors which affect primary products as a group. Such views lead to a demand for diversification that includes the establishment of manufacturing industry. In its simplest form this view is satisfied with "any kind of industry," which in practice usually means import substituting industries. The other end of the spectrum is reached by those who argue that industrialization must extend to the production of capital goods, since their terms of trade are less difficult to control and they are crucial to the development of technological capabilities. At the same time industrialization must extend to the production of mass consumer goods, since an economy that is amenable to internal policy decisions must have a broad, internal demand base.

In our view the latter end of this spectrum is most realistic, and therefore some importance must be

TABLE 5: ALL ADULT WAGE EARNERS IN TANZANIA[a]: INDUSTRIAL DISTRIBUTION

	Survey: 1971	C.S.B. 1968	Dar es Salaam Wage Earners	
	Seven Towns	All Tanzania*	Survey (1971)	C.S.B. (1968)
Major Industrial Category:	%	%	%	%
Manufacturing	22.0	15.0	22.2	22.1
Construction	11.2	20.0	12.4	15.0
Public Utilities	4.0	4.1	3.7	3.3
Commerce/Finance	12.5	9.1	12.8	12.5
Transport/Communications	18.3	13.4	19.3	20.4
Services	32.1	38.5	29.6	26.6[1]
	100	100	100	100
Total Number stated	2,168	2,36,377		

[a] excluding Agricultural and Mining Quarrying.
[b] comprises the sub groups: Textiles, Manufacturing: Fibres. Manufacturing: Minerals,
[c] Construction, Comworks.
[d] Public Utilities.
[e] Retail and Wholesale Trade,
[f] Commerce and Finance (Parastatals). East African Customs and Harbours, East African Railways, Transport, and Communications, other transport.
[g] Government, Local Government, Domestic Service, 'Hotels, Bars, etc.[2], other services.

SOURCES: ST 171/001, 002/—/001 to 003= "Employment and Earnings", 1966, Central Statistical Bureau, Government of Tanzania.

attached to industrial structures and particularly to the size and composition of the manufacturing sector.

Discussion of the results of the Survey is best preceded by a reminder that the "structure" that is being discussed relates only to the economies of seven urban areas. Hence, industries like agriculture and mining and quarrying are virtually excluded from the calculations. But even among the remaining categories, there are distinctly different patterns for urban and rural areas. This difference is clearly visible in Table 5, which compares the industrial distribution of our sample population with that of the whole wage earning population, excluding agriculture and mining and quarrying, as it appears in the Survey of Employment and Earnings, 1968. The comparison suggests that non urban wage employment is heavily concentrated in services, especially government, and in construction, since these are substantially over represented in the series relating to urban and rural areas. A comparison of only the Dar es Salaam figures, from both the Survey and the Central Statistical Bureau publication, confirms that the previously observed differencc is almost certainly due to the urban-rural difference. The two sets of figures relating to Dar es Salaam are almost identical. The only two non-trivial differences appear in construction, where the high figure of the Government report suggests

TABLE 6: SEVEN TOWNS: ADULT WAGE EARNERS: INDUSTRIAL DISTRIBUTION BY SUB-GROUP

		Proportion of Wage Earners (%)
MANUFACTURING		21.6
Textiles	7.2	
Manufacturing: Fibres	7.6	
Manufacturing: Minerals	6.7	
CONSTRUCTION		11.0
Construction	7.2	
Comworks	3.8	
PUBLIC UTILITIES	3.9	3.9
COMMERCE		12.2
Retail and Wholesale trade	6.4	
Commerce and Finance (Parastatal)	5.8	
TRANSPORT/COMMUNICATIONS		17.9
E.A.C. & H	5.1	
E.A.R.	5.2	
Transport/Communications	4.4	
Other transport	3.3	
SERVICES		31.4
Government	8.6	
Local Government	2.8	
Domestic Service	6.4	
Hotels, Bars, etc.	4.6	
Other Services	9.1	
OTHER	1.9	1.9
	100	100
Total Number:	2,210	

SOURCE: ST 171/001, 002/..................../001 to 003

the very sharp rise in construction employment experienced in 1968, and in services, where the higher figure of this Survey indicates primarily the inclusion of domestic servants, who are excluded from the C.S.B. statistics. The great similarity between the 1968 and 1971 statistics for Dar es Salaam comes as somewhat of a surprise. Possibly, however, it obscures the increase in the proportion of wage earners found in manufacturing, which may have taken place over those three years. This possibility exists, because the 1971 Survey includes businesses of all sizes, while the 1968 statistics undercounted employees in very small establishments.

TABLE 7: SEVEN TOWNS: ADULT WAGE EARNERS/EMPLOYMENT BY INDUSTRIAL SECTOR AND SIZE OF FIRM

		Total Number	Proportion of employees in small firms[a]	Major Industrial Groups:	Proportion of employees in small firms
Industrial Sub Groups:			(%)		(%)
Domestic Service	(S)[b]	139	97.1	COMMERCE	43.9
Retail, Wholesale	(C)	141	73.0	SERVICES	37.5
Hotels, Bars, etc.	(S)	95	66.3		
Other Transport	(T)	71	22.5	MANUFACTURING	12.2
Other Services	(S)	196	21.4	TRANSPORT	6.4
Manufacturing Minerals	(M)	149	16.1		
Manufacturing Fibres	(M)	169	14.2	CONSTRUCTION	4.6
Commerce, Finance	(C)	128	11.7	PUBLIC UTILITIES	2.3
Construction	(Con)	155	7.1		
Transport/Comm.	(T)	96	7.3		
Government	(S)	188	6.9		
Textiles	(M)	159	6.3		
E.A.C. & H.	(T)	112	1.8		
Local Government	(S)	59	1.7		
Comworks	(Con)	82	—		
E.A.R.	(T)	114	—		

[a] Small firms are firms with 20 employees or less.
[b] Refers to the major industrial group to which the sub-group belongs.

SOURCE: CR 284/—/001, 002.

Since such small enterprises are found mainly in commerce and services, an adjustment of the 1971 figures to make them exactly comparable to the 1969 Survey would likely indicate a small increase in the proportion of wage employees working in manufacturing industries.

Table 6 shows a more detailed industrial breakdown of employees derived from this Survey. The urban areas have built up a significant manufacturing industrial base, which employed 22 per cent of all wage earners, a substantial proportion of them in industries producing mass consumer goods. One third are employed in the textile industry alone, although more detailed investigation also reveals a virtual absence of a capital goods sector. There is also a large service sector, which employed about one third of all wage employees, the bulk of whom are found in government administration and "other services," comprising primarily public services such as police, schools, and hospitals. It also shows a high 18 per cent employed in transport and communications, reflecting the fact that five of the seven towns surveyed were major railway depots, and two of them were in addition the nation's major ports. Thus 10 per cent of all wage earners surveyed were employed by the Railways or the Harbours Corporation. Finally, the relatively low proportion of wage earners found in commerce reflects both the nationalisation of most financial institutions, which prevents duplication of services, and, more generally, the limited role played by the private capital market in the economy.

Most of the analysis of employment in different industries will be done in later sections, when incomes and job stability are analysed, but certain aspects of the nature of employment in the various sectors will be discussed briefly here.

The average size of firm in an industrial sector is related to the characteristics of employment in that sector. The results of the NUMEIST Survey are presented in Table 7, which gives the proportion of employees in each industrial sector working in establishments with less than twenty employees, hence referred to as "small firms".[3] The most striking feature of these data is the dramatic disparity between constituent parts of the same major industrial group. Although aggregates based on these major categories obscure much that is of interest and must be used carefully, it is clear, even at this level of aggregation, that only Commerce and Services have a substantial proportion of their employees in small establishments. This is not unexpected. A more detailed look reveals that only in domestic service, retail and wholesale trade, and hotels and bars, do a majority of employees work in small firms. The only other sub-groups that have more than twenty per cent of their employment in such establishments were "other transport" and "other services", which by definition grouped odd little enterprises which did not fit into one of the specified categories. It is also worth noting that much of the disparity between sub-groups comprising a major group exists because some of the sub-groups are defined synonymously with

TABLE 8: SEVEN TOWNS: ADULT WAGE EARNERS/INDUSTRIAL EMPLOYMENT BY OCCUPATION

Industrial Sub-Groups

Major Occupational groups:	Group A[a]						Group B[b]				Group C[c]						Industrial Major Groups					
	Govt. (inc. Loc. Govt.)	Other Service	Commerce	Hotels, Bars	Retail, Wholesale	Domestic Service	Textiles	Mnfrg. Min.	Mnfrg. Fib.	Construction	E.A.C. & H.	Transport Communications	Other Transport	E.A.R.	Comworks	Public Utilities	MANUF'NG.	CONSTRUC-TION	COMMERCE	SERVICE	TRANSPORT	PUBLIC UTILITIES
	%	%	%	%	%	%	%	%	%	%	%	%	%	%	%	%	%	%	%	%	%	%
White Collar	74	61	56	5	22	—	17	14	19	11	18	43	28	25	21	26	17	14	38	45	28	26
Production	6	14	9	4	15	1	62	52	47	56	24	26	39	36	59	40	53	57	12	7	31	40
Service	15	21	28	88	61	99	3	9	9	4	8	20	10	20	5	15	7	4	46	45	15	15
Unskilled	5	5	6	3	2	1	17	26	25	30	50	11	24	18	15	20	23	25	4	4	27	20
	100	100	100	100	100	100	100	100	100	100	100	100	100	100	100	100	100	100	100	100	100	100
Proportion in largest two major occupational groups	89	82	84	93	83	100	79	78	72	86	74	69	67	61	80	66	76	82	84	90	59	66

[a] Most occupationally specific.
[b] Moderately occupationally specific.
[c] Least occupationally specific.
SOURCE: CR 275/—/001, 002.

one major firm or institution. A final comment concerns the substantial 12 per cent of manufacturing employees who were found to be working in small firms. This finding reflects the considerable importance of the scattered "vehicle repair" enterprises and, more generally, the existence of a small scale crafts sector.

An examination of the occupational structure of each industrial category again reveals a high degree of heterogeneity. Naturally this reflects the definitions used. It is obvious that "occupational" categories, such as domestics or hotel service workers, are largely based on, and at times almost synonymous with, a particular industrial sector. Hence employment in many industrial sectors is heavily concentrated in one or two major occupational groups. Table 8 shows the nature of this relationship.

The service and commerce industries are heavily concentrated in the white collar and service occupations, with more than 80 per cent of their employees in these two occupational groups. Government administration, other services, and banking and finance employ primarily white collar workers, while the others, namely hotels, etc., and retail and wholesale trade are largely made up of service workers. Domestic service is of course a special case, where the industrial category and the occupational group are identical, so that all domestic workers are at the same time service workers. These industrial categories are the most occupationally specific.

The next group of industries employs primarily employees classified as production or unskilled workers. In each sector the proportion of employees found in these two occupations ranges from 72 to 86 per cent. This group includes the manufacturing industries, construction and the docks.

All remaining industries have white collar and production workers as the two largest occupational categories. These were also the least occupationally specific industries, and all but one had less than 70 per cent of their employees in the two largest major occupational groups. (The exception was Comworks which in some sense belongs with construction in the previous group, but which is included here because as a part of Government it also has an administrative function and hence includes a substantial number of white collar jobs). This group consists of public utilities and the sub-groups constituting the transport and communications sector, with the exception of the above mentioned dock yards. Generally production workers are the most numerous, and only in the sub group "transport and communications" do white collar jobs predominate.

Although there is considerable variety in the occupational structures of the major industrial categories, certain interesting patterns emerge from the data. Disregarding the exceptional cases of Comworks and E.A.C. & H., the six major industrial sectors fall into three groups. Commerce and service industries are most heavily concentrated occupationally, with manufacturing and construction somewhat less occupationally specific, and with public utilities and transport most diffuse in this respect. At the same time, each sector was concentrated in two of the four major occupations:

the first in white collar and service jobs; the second in production and unskilled jobs; the last in white collar and production jobs.

The predominance of certain occupations in particular industrial groups, accompanies a situation where certain occupations are concentrated in a few industries. The four sub groups—Government (including Local Government), other services, banking and finance, and transport and communications—thus account for 31 per cent of total employment, and for 63 per cent of white collar workers. The five sub groups that constitute the major sectors of manufacturing and construction again make up 33 per cent of total employment and include 62 per cent of all production workers. Similarly,

TABLE 9: SEVEN TOWNS: ADULT WAGE EARNERS/CASUAL EMPLOYMENT BY INDUSTRY

Industrial sub-group:	Proportion of Employees engaged on a casual basis
	(%)
Construction	37
Domestic Service	23
E.A.C. & H.	22
Other Transport	18
Transport/Communications	14
Commerce/Finance	13
Manufacturing: Minerals	11
Manufacturing: Fibres	9
Retail/Wholesale	9
Hotels, Bars, etc.	9
Comworks	6
E.A.R.	5
Textiles	5
Government	4
Public Utilities	3
Other Services	2
Local Government	2

SOURCE: CR 285/—/001, 002.

hotels, bars, etc., retail and wholesale trade, and domestic service employ 58 per cent of all service workers, although they account for only 18 per cent of employment. Finally the unskilled are concentrated in the docks (E.A.C. & H.), construction, and the manufacturing sector which cover 65 per cent of unskilled and 35 per cent of total employment. In short, industry and occupation appear rather closely related, though there is no presumption here that these relationships are, or have been, constant over time.

It is worth reiterating that this apparent degree of unanimity between industry and occupation does not extend beyond a comparison of major groups of both occupation and industry. The diversity that exists within these major groups suggests that manpower planning in this context should compute occupational coefficients for relatively narrow industrial categories, if serious aggregation problems are to be avoided.

Different industries are further distinguished by the extent to which they employ workers on a casual or daily basis. Table 9 shows that this is related to the proportion of unskilled workers, as these are most likely to be employed casually. Thus the two industrial sub groups with the highest proportion of unskilled workers, the docks and construction, are among the three groups with the highest proportion of casual employees. The third group, with a large proportion of casuals, is domestic service, where employment generally is rather informal and unregulated, and whose employees are in effect largely unskilled service workers. Beyond this there seems to be little more detailed connection between the occupational characteristics of industries and their propensity to employ casual labour. Indeed the irregularity of demand that characterizes the three industries at sub-groups employing many casuals is almost certainly the major factor in determining the employment of casual labour.

NOTES

1. In order to ensure a high degree of consistency in the classification of occupations, enumerators were merely asked to describe more or less fully the tasks performed by any employed person. The classification of these functions by occupation was done at the time of coding, using ISCO categories. It should be pointed out that these categories were not always drawn from the same "level" of specificity. They are all based on ISCO, but different sub-groups of that classification were combined or kept separate, according to the concentrations of employment found in the Survey. It follows that the data can be combined into the ISCO Major Categories quite readily but cannot always be broken down to more detailed levels of ISCO.
2. See original text, pp. 34–35.
3. The Survey did not differentiate the size of firm above 20 employees because of the likely inaccuracy of responses of employees who are asked in a household interview to indicate the number of workers in the establishment where they work. See original text, footnote 13, p. 190.

Education, Income Distribution and Rates of Urban Migration in Tanzania*

R. H. SABOT

Introduction

People living in rural areas who have been to school are far more likely to migrate than people who have had no formal education whatsoever. The more education a person has had the more likely it is that he or she will leave his or her home area, leave the familiar way of life of his parents and ethnic group, leave a future that is directly tied to the land for provision of food and money, and make his or her way to town. This phenomenon has been much the same since the beginning of the twentieth century when educational opportunities first became available and desired by the people.

The aim of this paper is threefold:

(a) to describe in some detail how the various groups influencing the urban labour market, i.e. educated and uneducated migrants, government and private employers and even teachers, have responded to the sharp rise in the annual number of school-leavers that has occurred since independence;

(b) to provide the background for understanding the extent to which the spread of educational opportunities has been a causal factor in the emergence of urban employment problems; and

(c) to develop an analytical framework that can yield insights into the more general issues of rural-urban migration and the nature of its determinants.

EDUCATIONAL SELECTIVITY AND RELATIVE RATES OF MIGRATION

The results of the National Urban Mobility, Employment and Income Survey (NUMEIST) indicate the pattern of educational selectivity on migration; they are summarised in Table 1. The main features can be briefly stated as follows:

(a) There are proportionately 2½ times as many migrants with education as there are educated people among the rural population aged 14 years and over. Rates of migration among the educated are markedly higher than among the uneducated.

(b) The relative rate of migration of the educated is marginally higher to the six major towns than to Dar es Salaam. This holds for both males and females.

(c) Rates of migration among educated women are higher than among educated men. At the same time, rates of migration for uneducated women are higher than for uneducated men. This need not imply, however, that women are more likely to migrate than men, because a higher proportion of rural males have some education.

(d) Rates of migration increase with the level of education. This holds both for all urban areas and for males and females. The increase in the rate of migration for those with more education is markedly higher for females.

(c) Tables 2 and 3 provide insights into changes in the rates of urban migration educational selectivity over time. Not surprisingly, migrants have become better educated. Of male migrants who are currently resident in urban areas and who migrated before Independence, one in three are uneducated. Among migrants who arrived more recently, only one in seven lack any formal education. Only one in 14 of those males who arrived in 1970 have no education. Buċ even these figures underestimate the degree of change in the educational composition of the urban migrant streams.[1] As the data in Table 3 indicate, educational selectivity has been a feature of urban migration for some time, but the degree of positive selectivity has actually decreased with time. Among migrant males 60 years old and older, 52% have some education while among rural males 60 and older, only 13% have any education. In the 14–24 age category the relative difference is not nearly so great—93% of male migrants have education as compared to 58% of rural males. In other words, although the education of migrants has been improving, the rate of migration of the rural population with education has been declining. The decline in the rate of migration holds for sub-categories of the educated population as well.

The rates of migration of those without education have also decreased over time. The proportion of male migrants over 60 without education is one-half the proportion of the rural male population without education, while for 14–24 years olds the proportion of male migrants without education is one-fifth the proportion of the rural male population without education. The declining rates of migration of both the educated and the uneducated appear to be inconsistent with the general finding of a rising overall rate of migration, but the apparent inconsistency is explained by the changing composition of the rural population. The rate of migration of the educated has been and remains much higher than the rate of migration of the uneducated. The fact that the number of educated in the rural areas has been growing faster than the number of uneducated more than compensates for the decline in the rate of migration of those with and without education.

* This paper originally appeared as ERB Paper 72.6. The data represent the results of the National Urban Mobility, Employment and Income Survey of Tanzania NUMEIST See volume III "The wage Employed", Economic Research Bureau, University of Dar es Saalam, 1972.

TABLE 1: RATES OF URBAN MIGRATION BY EDUCATION, SEX AND RECEIVING AREA[a]

Receiving Area	Sex	None	Educational Level Some	Std. 1–4	Std. 5–8	Forms 1–6	University
Dar es Salaam	Males	.37	2.02	.88	3.7	8.9	18.3
	Females	.65	3.14	2.00	6.0	30.0	71.0
	Total	.50	2.48	1.20	4.7	11.0	22.5
Six Towns	Males	.27	2.17	.92	4.2	8.9	20.0
	Females	.59	3.50	1.80	8.3	30.0	43.0
	Total	.44	2.68	1.16	5.7	11.0	21.0
Total	Males	.34	2.05	.89	3.9	8.9	18.6
	Females	.62	3.28	1.90	7.0	30.0	57.0
	Total	.48	2.56	1.17	5.0	11.0	22.5

[a]Rate of Migration = MPi/MP ÷ RPi/RP, where
MPi = Migration population of education sub-group i;
MP = Total Migrant population;
RPi = Rural population of education sub-group i; and
RP = Rural population, age 14 and over.

TABLE 2: MALE MIGRANTS: EDUCATION BY TIME OF ARRIVAL IN TOWN (PERCENTAGES)

Time of Arrival	None	Education Level Some	Std. 1–4	Std. 5–8	Forms	University
Before Independence	33	67	29	28	9	1
After Independence	14	86	21	44	20	2

TABLE 3: MALE MIGRANTS: RATES OF URBAN MIGRATION BY AGE AND EDUCATION

Age	None	Education Level Some	Std. 1–4	Std. 5–8	Forms 1–6	University
14–19	.15	1.62	.60	2.65	5.00	3.33
25–34	.28	1.88	.81	3.45	11.11	22.22
35–44	.47	2.00	1.00	3.61	11.81	20.00
45–59	.46	2.62	1.63	4.69	15.00	50.00
60 and Over	.55	4.00	2.09	12.10	30.00	—

These differentials in threatres of migration cannot be explained by one factor alone. If the decision to migrate is viewed as depending upon the various costs and returns, monetary as well as non-monetary, that a rural resident faces, then any differential may be explained by one or more of the various components that determine the rural-urban balance and the migrant's evaluation of it. Nevertheless, a good starting point for the analysis is to see to what extent the pattern within each of the cost and return categories is consistent with the overall pattern of educational selectivity. Consider first how monetary returns to migration vary with the level of formal education.

EDUCATION AND THE ECONOMIES OF MIGRATION

The Money Returns to Urban Migration

Only if incomes were equal within urban areas and within rural areas would there be a single rural-urban income differential. The existing range of intra-urban and intra-rural incomes means that there is an entire spectrum of rural-urban differentials. In this section we will examine how the expected urban income varies with the educational level of the potential migrant. In the section that follows on opportunity costs, we will examine how expected rural incomes vary by education and thus establish the framework for an analysis of whether or not differences in the rate of migration of educational sub-groups can be explained by differences in the expected rural-urban income differential for these sub-groups.

Is it realistic to expect to find income differentials by level of education? Consider first the non-wage money income urban sector. In Tanzania, some 11% of urban dwellers, or 22% of those urban dwellers with money income, derive their income from such diverse non-wage activities as owning a small duka (shop), being a freelance craftsman, driving a self-owned taxi, selling peanuts on a street corner and renting rooms. Some people barely earn enough money to support themselves, while others may earn two or three times the minimum wage. Two reasons suggest that a positive correlation exists between the level of income in this sector and education: (a) formal education may enhance entrepreneurial ability, although evidence from elsewhere in Africa indicates that this is a doubtful hypothesis; and (b) the educated are more likely to have access to sources of capital, a more probable hypothesis.[2]

Wage and salary differentials in African cities are extremely high. There are two explanations for this phenomenon. The first relates to market forces. Skilled labour has been scarce relative to demand and to the supply of unskilled labour, and differentials act both as an incentive for others to acquire skills and as a means for allocating people with skills among competing jobs. The second relates to institutional factors which are of even greater significance than market forces. Salaries in the top level colonial civil service posts were frequently higher than for equivalent positions in England. This provided an inducement for young men to join the colonial service and clearly established the expatriates as an elite. Salaries for lower level African civil servants were generally higher than the supply price of qualified and willing personnel. Thus these differentials became part of the process of creating an African elite which embodied "European" values and emulated the European life style—a costly proposition.

The colonial wage and salary structure was not dismantled at Independence for a number of reasons. Higher salaries were still paid as an inducement to expatriates needed to fill non-Africanized posts. Moreover, to do away with what many Tanzanians in the new elite regarded as the fruits of Independence would have been a politically untenable action for the new government.

These wage and salary differentials are likely to be reflected in educational levels because in Tanzania, more than in most countries, education has become the criterion for allocating jobs in the "modern" sector.

Table 4 presents information on average income for educational sub-groups in the urban migrant population. As might be expected, a significant differential in monthly earnings exists between those with and those without education. The average monthly income of urban area migrants without education is Shs. 258, while those with education have average monthly earnings of Shs. 458, or over 1.75 times as high. The fact that there are significant differentials for young and old alike is an indication that even though the scarcity of educated manpower is less severe, a premium on education still exists. However, the differential is clearly less for younger migrants. This may be explained, at least in part, by the fact that the educated are more likely to work in occupations where work experience is rewarded. It also may be due in part to the phenomenon of "filtering down." This finding of higher incomes for people with education is consistent with the general finding that the educated have a higher propensity to migrate than the uneducated. In addition, there are differentials among the educated. Average monthly incomes for Std. 1–4, Std. 5–7, Forms 1–6 and University leavers are Shs. 273,370,804 and 1,637 respectively. These differentials are consistent with the fact that migration rates increase with the level of education. If the other elements of the cost and returns structure are equal, one would expect a higher rate of

TABLE 4: AVERAGE TOTAL INCOME: EDUCATION BY AGE (SHS. PER MONTH)[a]

	14–19	20–24	25–29	30–34	35–39	40–44	45–49	50–59	60 +	Total
None	86	171	204	203	309	323	258	217	216	258
Standard 1–4	117	192	217	296	349	401	319	295	370	273
Standard 5–8	330	254	299	385	425	762	721	1,173	697	370
Form 1–6	342	474	654	1,189	1,551	1,505	2,011	958	1,040	804
University	—	500	1,271	1,977	5,000	1,900	1,667	—	5,000	1,637

SOURCE: NUMEIST. [a]Wage and non-wage incomes are aggregated in the total income figures.

TABLE 5: AVERAGE TOTAL INCOME AND EDUCATION DIFFERENTIALS: DA ES SALAAM AND SIX TOWNS

	Dar es Salaam			*Six Towns*		
	Shs./ Month	Ratio	Ratio	Shs./ Month	Ratio	Ratio
a. None	258	.6	—	214	—	—
b. Std. 1–4	273	b/a 1.06	—	207	b/a .97	—
c. Std. 5–8	370	c/b 1.36	c/a 1.43	359	c/b 1.73	c/a 1.68
d. Form 1–6	804	d/c 2.17	d/a 3.11	763	d/c 2.12	d/a 3.56
e. University	1,637	e/d 2.04	e/a 6.34	989	e/d 1.30	e/a 4.62

migration of sub-groups in the population for whom the returns to migration are higher.

The difference in the pattern of returns to education between Dar es Salaam and the six towns is consistent with the fact of higher educational selectivity in the six towns, as indicated in Table 5. Incomes are higher in Dar es Salaam within each educational category, but income differentials in percentage terms are higher in the six towns.

However, the pattern of current money returns does not explain the decrease over time in the rates of migration of both educated and uneducated. For that, information about the change in incomes within each educational group and the change in differentials among groups is required. Since Independence urban incomes have been rising for all groups and incomes for those at the bottom of the income scale have been rising faster. Rising urban incomes and narrowing income differentials are consistent with decreasing positive selectivity, but they do not appear to be consistent with the increasing negative selectivity. If money returns are rising in both absolute and relative terms for those at the bottom, one would expect an increasing rather than a decreasing proportion of uneducated in the migrant stream.

However, the money returns to migration are a function not only of expected income levels but also of the probability of finding a job. A closely related factor is that educational requirements for jobs at different places on the urban income spectrum may be changing overtime.

This brings us to the important phenomenon of "occupational displacement" or "filtering down" as an influence on migration patterns in Tanzania as well as in other African countries.

Urban labour markets in Africa, like those in the industrialised countries, are differentiated on both the demand and supply sides of the market. Job seekers rank job categories on the basis of such factors as wages, conditions of work and prestige. Employers rank employees by experience, education, and other factors that may predict workers' productivity. Labour markets thus become stratified, in the sense that not all job seekers compete for all jobs.

There is an asymmetry in the functioning of the market in the sense that stratification, formal or informal, limits upward but not downward mobility. Thus, Form 4 leavers have access to occupations that require a higher level of education, but this usually implies a preferential access to jobs that require Std. 7 or less education. This asymmetry is of little significance when labour markets are in "equilibrium". Assuming that school leavers seek the best jobs they can get and employers the best workers they can get, then Form 4 leavers simply slip into occupations that have come to be recognized as Form 4 jobs. But the asymmetry assumes critical importance when the urban labour market is not in equilibrium, and particularly when the supply of sub-categories of labour exceeds the demand within a given occupational grouping. Then the "best qualified" take the best jobs; and when the available "best jobs" are filled, the remaining "best qualified" filter down into the "next best jobs", thereby displacing the "next best qualified" who filter down to the next lower job level and so on. An important qualification here is that filtering down will occur insofar as the rural areas do not have better alternatives which could lead to urban labour market equilibrium, and expectations on the part of those seeking work are flexible. Otherwise unemployment would emerge even at higher educational levels as job-seekers wait until they find the type of job which meets their expectations.

This model of urban labour market behaviour has direct relevance to the changes that have occurred in the pattern of educational selectivity among rural-urban migrants in Tanzania. There are two threads to the story. First, at the time of Independence, Tanzania faced a severe shortage of middle and high level manpower. In 1963 a manpower planning unit was established as part of the central planning apparatus, and 1984 was set as the target date for self-sufficiency at all skill levels. One implication of this decision was that top priority was given to the expansion of secondary and post-secondary educational facilities.[3] Although self-sufficiency at the highest levels won't be achieved until the target date, the output of post-primary schools is beginning to exceed the absorptive capacity of the scheduled occupations. The problem of oversupply appears to be an implementation problem rather than a planning or projection problem.

The second thread concerns Tanzania's decision, subject to resource constraints imposed by the expansion of secondary education, to achieve universal primary education by 1989. No attempt was made to gear primary school outputs to the absorptive capacity of any particular occupational group or to the expansion of wage employment in general.

The consequences of these actions have taken two forms. First, during the 1960s, the ratio of the number of school-leavers at all educational levels entering the labour force in a given year to the number of non-agricultural wage employment openings rose sharply. In 1964, approximately 18,500 school leavers at various levels entered the labour force; there were approximately 15,700 new employment openings. In 1970, there were approximately 64,700 school leavers and 16,100 job openings, a change in the ratio of educated entrants to openings from $\frac{1.2}{1}$ to $\frac{4.}{1}$ Moreover the number of post-primary entrants has risen from 3,400 to 6,400.

The second consequence concerns the process by which available openings are distributed among the applicants. The Survey results indicate that filtering down and displacement have occurred. There is a definite pattern to the relationship among age (which serves as a proxy variable for three factors—time in town, on the job and out of school), education and occupation. Higher paying occupational categories are assumed to reflect a job seeker's preference function ranked in descending order. Moving down the preference scale and within each occupation category, younger migrants are better educated than their elders. Thus, of migrants 40 years and older in the higher level manpower group (professional, technical and management and administration category), 12% have either no education or Std. 1–4, 27% have a primary school education, and 42% and 18% respectively have secondary and university educations. Among younger migrants in the 25–29 age bracket, all have more than Std. 1–4 education, 20% have a primary education, 53% have a secondary education and 27% have university education. High level manpower posts have always had relatively high educational requirements but it is clear that within the last decade the opportunities for those with only primary school or less education have clearly diminished.

The shift in the educational distribution is greater lower down the preference scale. Within the second category (clerical, accounts and sales) the same pattern of displacement is occurring. The proportion of people with secondary education and higher education has more than doubled, from 29% among those 40 years and older to 61% among the 20–24 age group. The same pattern holds for skilled workers. The shift within the semi-skilled category is striking. Of those 40 and older, over 50% have only Std. 1–4 or no education and 8% have secondary education. Of the recent entrants, 24 years and younger, the proportion with Std. 4 or less education has dropped to 16%, and the proportion with secondary education has nearly tripled. Equally striking is the education shift among the unskilled. A few years ago, a primary leaver would rarely have been found doing manual work. Of those 40 years and older, fewer than 10% have primary education and over 55% have no education whatsoever. Of those with primary education, the proportion is five times as high among those 24 and under and some people with secondary education were found doing unskilled manual labour. Those without education are even being displaced from jobs at the very bottom of the occupational ranking. Only 12% of the youngest category of unskilled migrants have no education.

The aspects of the way the actual process of filtering down and displacement works are worth noting. The process can only advance as fast as vacancies occur. Less well educated people are not being thrown out of work, they are simply replaced by better educated people when they leave their jobs. Also, jobs may initially be taken by secondary leavers as a temporary expedient until a better job is found. The overall increase of better educated people in less preferred occupations then becomes a function both of increasing numbers of better educated having to use these as entrance jobs and the increasing length of stay of such people in these jobs as upward mobility within the urban labour market becomes even more difficult.

It should now be fairly clear how this process of filtering down and displacement has affected differentials in the pattern of money returns to migration by education. The probability of finding a job as indicated by the ratio of job openings to educated output has decreased sharply. Discounting potential money returns to migration by ever lower probabilities raises the likelihood that money returns to the educated are falling, a finding consistent with the decrease in positive selectivity. The fact that new employment opportunities for the uneducated in the urban areas have been decreasing until they are virtually non-existent explains the sharp increase in negative educational selectivity. In addition, it is clear that the probability of finding a job increases with education. "Filtering down" means that people within educational categories are now accepting lower ranking jobs and by implication, lower paying jobs, thereby decreasing the money returns to migration and reinforcing the arguments above. (See Table 4).

Opportunity Costs of Urban Migration

The structure of money returns to migration is consistent with virtually every aspect of the pattern of educational selectivity. But it is not, of course, possible to piece together a picture of differentials in the overall structure of costs and returns to migration for education subgroups of the population without considering differential opportunity costs. Expected rural incomes comprise the largest single element of total opportunity costs that potential migrants must consider.

The analysis depends on understanding the logical relationships among intra-urban, intra-rural and rural-urban income differentials. If we make the assumption of a positive rural-urban income differential for those at the bottom of the educational and income ladder then it follows that:

(a) If intra-urban income differentials by education are greater than intra-rural income differentials in percentage terms, then rural-urban income differentials by educational groupings will be greater in both percentage and absolute terms.

(b) If intra-urban income differentials are greater than–intra rural in absolute terms, then rural-urban differentials by education will be greater in absolute though not necessarily in percentage terms.

The reason for specifying these relationships is that the nature of intra-rural differentials must be inferred from various pieces of evidence, as there are no reliable indicators of rural income dispersion in Tanzania. Although the evidence suggests that intra-rural differentials are narrower than intra-urban, it is not possible to specify whether they are narrower in both absolute and percentage terms.

The first piece of evidence is that rural occupational and employment categories differ from those in urban areas. Rural occupations are predominantly agricultural and manual and few professional and skilled positions are required. Second, within agriculture there is no tradition of differential rewards to education, even though a clear income hierarchy among peasants may exist in some areas. Research indicates that better off peasants and their children are better educated than poorer peasants and that the regions with the highest agricultural incomes, e.g. Kilimanjaro and West Lake have the highest number of primary school-leavers relative to population. But the causal relationship is not that better education leads to higher incomes but vice-versa. In the past, higher regional incomes meant a greater appropriation of local and national funds for education, while the better off peasant has found it easier both to gain access to school places for his children and to afford the school fees.[4] There is no place in Tanzania where a primary or even a secondary school-leaver can, by virtue of his education alone, gain preferential access to an already high-yielding plot of land in the same way in which he has preferential access to high income jobs. Within agriculture, the educated, like the uneducated, must start farming on his plot of land, on a plot taken over from his father, or on a plot held within the context of an ujamaa village. The value of education as a means of raising productivity in agriculture must be proven in every instance, rather than simply assumed, as is the case with urban wage structures.

The educated who have been unsuccessful in finding urban wage employment and who have returned to their home areas have not had much success in contributing more to output than other peasants. The consequences for the opportunity cost structure are clear. The large majority of school-leavers who remain in the rural areas must find self-employment in agriculture. Given the structure of the urban labour market, if their potential incomes are no higher than their uneducated fathers' or brothers' they will have a relatively greater incentive to migrate. This is not to suggest that rural income differentials should be increased to urban levels, but it does raise the issue as to why education appears to have been relatively unsuccessful in raising productivity in rural areas.[5]

Psychic Costs and Returns

There is one additional education selectivity differential for which the structure of money returns and opportunity costs has not provided an explanation. In proportionate terms, over twice as many migrants, both men and women, have Standard 1–4 education as have no education. The wage differential between those with no education and those with Std. 1–4 is negligible, and there does not appear to be any distinct preference among employers for job seekers with Std. 1–4. Both groups are predominantly employed in unskilled occupations where literacy or numeracy count for little. Among more recent arrivals to town, 64% of the uneducated and 64% of those with Std. 1–4 are employed in unskilled occupations. The fact that for all migrants, 64% of the uneducated and only 51% of those with Std. 1–4 are in unskilled jobs indicates that in the past employers did give preference to those with education, either in terms of hiring or promotion. But this does not help explain the higher rate of migration of rural residents with Std. 1–4, as the difference between the rates of migration selectivity for those with no education and those with Std. 1–4 has been widening rather than narrowing over time. The situation is similar with opportunity costs. There is certainly no *a priori* reason to believe and no evidence to suggest that those with Std. 1–4 actually earn less in the rural areas than people with no education.

Why then are people with Std. 1–4 more likely to migrate than those without any education? The explanation for this phenomenon appears to lie within the realm of psychic costs and returns. On the one hand, those who attend school are often preselected by the degree of sensitivity to change of their parents, or of their village and area. The regional distribution of education varies widely in Tanzania, from 13% of the adult population with some education in Shinyanga to 50% in Kilimanjaro. In large part, these differences reflect variations in past levels of mission and government educational activity and in levels of eash incomes. But, in part, this reflects the fact that some groups were more open to the type of change which missionary and educational activity represented than others. It is likely that people who are more open to change in the form of education will also be more open to change in terms of migration.

On the other hand, the educational process itself contributes to changes in values and in attitudes. That intra-regional gaps between the rates of migration of the uneducated and those with Std. 1–4 are nearly as high as for the country as a whole supports the latter hypothesis.

Though the distinction is to a large extent arbitrary, it is useful for heuristic purposes to classify the effect of the latter factor on the psychic costs and psychic returns to migration separately. One of the implicit aims of education during the colonial era was attitude and value change. Missionaries wanted to produce "sincere, educated Christians" and tended both to identify Christianity with western civilization and to view it as the necessary precondition of progress.[6] Government schools also did not try to distinguish between education as a means of developing an individual's rational thought process and as a means of socializing Africans into a fundamentally alien way of life. The specialization aspect of education is to a certain extent inevitable. Achievement of the aim of economic development and transformation necessarily implies reordering of values and social modes. The student is exposed to a world where the structures of obligations and commitments in social, economic and political terms are different from those he is familiar with at home. Horizons are widened, and the student becomes aware that education allows greater mobility. To the extent that education makes it easier for the student than for the non-student to conceive of removing himself from the environment in which he is familiar, of extracting himself from the web of traditional supportive relationships and obligations, it reduces the psychic costs of migration.

The socializing aspect of education played a significant role in the process of change of tastes. Education contributed to the process whereby increasing value was placed on European goods, on goods which only money could buy. It thus led to a higher valuation of money income and by implication to a greater appreciation of income differentials. If a given increase in income leads to greater satisfaction for one person than for another, the psychic returns to migration can be said to be higher. Although the fact that "modern" tastes are far more widely diffused than in the past reduces the importance of this factor, it is far from irrelevant.

CONCLUSION

Throughout the colonial era, obtaining a primary school-leaver certificate meant a virtual guarantee of a wage job in town, a release from the necessity of having to eke out a living from the land. School places were scarce and wage employment in the towns was growing steadily if slowly. Education itself was tailored to prepare the young student for the very different life he would be leading in town. He learned to read and to write, he learned punctuality and the "necessity" of wearing western clothes, and he learned to respect the authority of those who would be telling him what to do. Education began the process of socializing him into a new way of life and made it easier to accept the fact that he would be leaving the familiar and supportive atmosphere provided by family and villagers.

For those with schooling, education became the key to the improvement of their lives. Those who did not go to school came to feel that they were being deprived of a valuable opportunity.

After Independence, belief in the value of education for the individual and for the transformation of Tanzanian society was made manifest in the decision to expand the educational base so that by 1984 all the medium and high level manpower positions would be Tanzanianized and by 1989 every child would have primary. education. This decision led to structural change in the supply of educated manpower. The market for wage labour was thrown out of its equilibrium growth position and government had few mechanisms with which to adjust to the new conditions. It could not lower urban wages or salaries enough to encourage school-leavers to remain in their home areas. Neither could it increase urban employment opportunities fast enough to absorb the increased output of the school system.

The principal short-term adjustment mechanism was a rationing mechanism which would distribute urban wage jobs among school-leavers and others who wanted them. For high-level manpower categories this mechanism was imposed by the government on the supply side of the market. Manpower planners adjusted the number of primary leavers to receive further education according to projected needs of the economy in a way not dissimilar to colonial government actions. For the majority of the primary school leavers who would not go on to secondary school, a demand side rationing mechanism was provided by the functioning of the market and by government hiring policy.

The mechanism that actually emerged was a mixture of rationality and expediency. An employer whether government, parastatal, private firm or an individual faced with choosing among many applicants applied an educational criteria. The best educated had first chance at most jobs, then the primary leavers; those applicants with Std. 1–4 or no education took what remained.

The first consequence was that people with primary school certificates were offered less preferred jobs than previously had been available. The second consequence was those with little or no education had a slight probability of finding a job and they were virtually excluded from the urban labour market. A third consequence was that as the number of post-primary leavers began to exceed the employment target levels, secondary leavers began "filtering down" to lower job levels, thereby displacing primary leavers who previously had claimed these jobs; and so on down the line.

This rationing system has worked only because the expectations of school-leavers were flexible. They accepted, albeit unhappily, the lower wage and prestige jobs offered when it became clear that these provided the highest source of income now open to them. In addition, increasing numbers of persons with education either came to urban areas and returned home after a fruitless job search or, aware of the low and decreasing probability of finding a job, remained in their local areas. While today's primary school leaver is far more likely to migrate to town than his uneducated friend, he is also more likely to remain and work in the rural areas than the school-leaver of 1961. The uneducated are far less likely to go to town today than they were eleven years ago. School-leavers and others are realistic; they do not consider manual work as "beneath their dignity," nor do they refuse to work on a shamba.

The results of the Survey suggest that not only are Tanzanians adjusting their expectations when considering potential returns to migration, but they also are adjusting their behaviour to the new and lower expectations of returns to education. This finding of a high degree of flexibility in regard to expectations of occupations, wages and place of residence in Tanzania is consistent with other evidence in Tanzania and from work done in Ghana, Nigeria, Kenya and Uganda.[7]

This relatively smooth adjustment to the new urban labour supply situation does not mean that Tanzania has no school-leaver problem, but that the school-leaver problem is a rural as well as an urban problem. The academic-oriented education that school-leavers absorbed and the very special treatment that they received as children from their families and fellow villagers ill-suits them for agricultural work. Young people who view returning to the land as a sign of failure to get a Form I place or an urban job are not likely to become the progressive farmers that are necessary to show others the way. One aspect of the school-leaver problem in Tanzania is that the social returns to education in the rural areas fall far short of achieving their potential. The educational system for a number of reasons has failed to adjust to the new role it is meant to play in preparing people for their place in rural society. A pattern of circular causation has emerged: the unexceptional performance of school-leavers relative to other farmers increases the desirability of finding an urban wage job, and the students', parents' and teachers' desire to place the primary school-leaver in a secondary school as a means of finding a wage job only makes the student less suited for agricultural work.

Two points should be made about the relationship of the increased supply of educated manpower to problems of urban labour utilization.

First, the fact that employees are being utilized in less productive jobs than used to be the case with people of their educational level is a direct consequence of the expansion of the educational system. It is also clear, however, that this phenomenon is not an appropriate index of underemployment. The deepening of human capital in urban employment also has occurred in the industrialized countries. The fact that the private returns to education and migration for those without post-primary education are declining is not an accurate guide to social returns.

Secondly there is a clear underutilization of urban manpower in two circumstances: when the educated are employed in an urban job such as a sweeper in a factory that could be done by someone with less education while at the same time there are rural jobs for the educated that other people cannot easily fill or, of course, when the educated are unemployed. The expansion of the educational system has made a contribution to these problems by increasing the propensity of rural residents to migrate beyond that stimulated by wider income differentials and by maintaining an urban bias in the content of the education which has constrained the contribution of the educated in raising rural productivity and incomes. More importantly, to the extent that there is underutilization of urban educated labour, the determining factor appears to be distortions in the urban wage structure, the causes of which lie in the entire pattern of development of post-Independence Tanzania.

In regard to the determinants of migration, the findings on education selectivity suggest:

(a) Economic factors clearly play a highly significant role. The differentials in the rate of migration by educational level, by sex, by receiving town, and over time are all consistent with differentials in the money returns to migration. Money returns consist mainly of two factors, relative wages and relative employment opportunities. The response in rates of migration to differences in each of these was clearly detected. Rates of migration are also consistent with the structure of opportunity costs. In other words, a relatively lower net rate of return in strictly economic terms to migration for a sub-group is associated with a relatively lower rate of migration and when the rate of return falls over time for a certain sub-group, so does the rate of migration.

(b) There is evidence that psychic factors are also significant in determining relative rates of migration. The one case where economic factors were not consistent with the evidence was in regard to the Std. 1–4 and no education rate of migration differential. It appears that either because of preselection or because the experience of being a student for as little as four years loosens traditional ties and changes tastes, people with education are more open to the opportunities available in town and more desirous of them.

NOTES

1. The underlying presumption in Table 4 is that the current age of migrants is a workable proxy for time of arrival. This assumption allows the comparison of the Survey and census data on education by age for rural residents.
2. Many of the more renumerative sources of nonwage income are controlled by the Asian Community who overall are better educated than the Africans. To the extent that this is true, non-wage income differentials by education are not an accurate guide to expected earnings for a potential migrant.
3. Robert L. Thomas, "Problems of Manpower Development," in I. N. Resnick, (ed.) *Tanzania: Revolution by Education*, Arusha: Longman of Tanzania Ltd., 1968.
4. J. D. Heijnen, *Development and Education in the Mwanza District (Tanzania)*. Amsterdam, Holland, 1968.
5. See J. K. Nyerere, "Education for Self-Reliance" in *Ujamaa: Essays on Socialism*, Dar es Salaam: Oxford University Press, 1968. Also see Sabot, ERB Paper 72.6, pp. 24–29.
6. J. Cameron & W. A. Dodd, *Society, Schools and Progress in Tanzania*. Oxford: Pergamon Press, 1970.
7. Caroline Hutton, "The Good Life, Attidudes of Peasant and School Leavers towards Agriculture," paper presented at the Conference on Urban Unemployment in Africa, Institute of Development Studies, University of Sussex, 12–16 September, 1971; Margaret Peil, "Education as An Influence on Aspirations and Expectations," paper presented at the Conference on Urban Unemployment in Africa, Institute of Development Studies, University of Sussex, 12–16 September, 1971; J. D. Heijnen, *op. cit.*

Open Unemployment and the Employed Compound of Surplus Labour*

R. H. SABOT

Introduction

Who are the Unemployed?

If unemployment is defined in the conventional way, as the state in which an individual does not hold a money-earning job but is actively seeking one, then the aggregate rate of open unemployment in Tanzania's urban areas is approximately 8 per cent (see Table 1). The boundary between those who are not in the labour force and those who are unemployed is thus defined by the "job-search criterion" applied. The low level of unemployment in part reflects the fact that a rigorous screening procedure has been applied to the 48 per cent of the adult population without a source of money income.

For an individual to be considered unemployed he or she must have taken some formal positive action such as going to a government employment office, waiting in a factory gate job-queue or writing a letter to a potential employer in the week prior to his enumeration. But the job search process in Tanzania is not always so formalised. Individuals frequently rely on information flows generated by the extensive network of employed family members and friends, and in these instances the pounding-the-streets image of job search behaviour is simply not relevant. If the "job search criterion" is relaxed to include among the unemployed all those adults who lack a source of income but who claim to be seeking employment, whether or not they have taken any specific formal action, the aggregate unemployment rate increases by 50 per cent, to a total of 12 per cent (11.6 per cent in Dar es Salaam and 13.6 per cent in the six regional urban centres). For the most part our subsequent discussion will be based on unemployment rates derived by using the looser criterion.

Does 12 per cent represent a high or a low rate of open unemployment when viewed from the perspective of welfare and resource allocation costs? The welfare implications of this rate depend upon how the incidence of unemployment is distributed, on the one hand, among groups of labour force members who have varying degrees of economic responsibility for themselves and their dependents and, on the other, between those who have rural income earning alternatives and those who do not. Similarly the resource costs will depend on unemployment rate differentials among sub-groups with more or less formal education and employment experience.

TABLE 1: SEVEN TOWNS: UNEMPLOYMENT RATES UNDER ALTERNATIVE JOB SEARCH CRITERIA BY SEX AND STATUS IN HOUSEHOLD

	Unemployment Rates	
	Job Search Criterion 1 (Active)	Job Search Criterion 2 (Active & Passive)
Males	%	%
Heads of Household	2.2	2.7
Other Household Members	18.6	23.0
Total	4.5	5.8
Females		
Heads of Household	7.9	13.1
Spouses of Head	27.0	43.8
Other Household Members	34.1	45.0
Total	20.9	32.5
Total	8.0	12.0

SOURCE: NUMEIST, Economic Research Bureau, 1972.

The rest of this section will be concerned with investigating the welfare consequences of unemployment and the determinants of unemployment rate differentials.

UNEMPLOYMENT BY SEX AND DEPENDENCY STATUS

One of the most striking unemployment rate differentials is that between men and women. Table 1 reveals that while only 5.8 per cent of all male labour force members are without employment and seeking it, the rate of unemployment among women is 32.5 per cent or more than five times the rate among men. The male-female differential is roughly the same in the capital city as in smaller urban areas. At first this differential appears to be somewhat surprising, but it must be recorded that women are in a relatively disadvantaged position in the urban labour market. The large majority of women do not have post-primary education, and they earn wage rates considerably less than those earned by males with the same levels of education. Discrimination in hiring also suggests that the job opening rate for women is considerably lower than for men. Given these wage and employment opportunity differentials, the formal model outlined later provides a theoretical basis for the observed phenomenon that the equilibrium

*This paper is adapted from ERB paper 74.4. It is based on The National Urban Mobility, Employment and Income Survey of Tanzania (NUMEIST), ERB, 1972.

level of unemployment is lower among women than among men.

Two closely related reasons explain why female unemployment rates are so much higher than male. On the one hand, the opportunity costs of female unemployment appear to be considerably less than of male. This is not because migrant women earn less income in the rural areas than what migrant men could be earning, but rather because most women come to town primarily to be with their husbands. What they could earn in the rural areas is an irrelevant consideration, implying that the money opportunity cost of urban unemployment is effectively nil. On the other hand, most women labour force members, migrants and non-migrants alike, are economic dependents, in the sense that they depend on their husbands to pay the cost of their next meal and the rent for their rooms.

We would thus expect the rate of unemployment for women who are not economic dependents, but who are responsible for their own support and in some cases for the support of their children, to be lower than for other women. The survey results confirmed this hypothesis. Table 1 reveals that the rate of unemployment for female heads of households is less than one-third that for wives of household heads or other female dependent household members. The results also reported a distribution in regard to dependency status. Not all male labour force members are heads of households. Thus if ability to afford a period without income is a determinant of unemployment rate differentials, higher male unemployment rates would be expected among the 15 per cent of male labour force members who are still dependents and who can rely on economic support from their fathers or other household members. In fact the rate of unemployment among male "other household members" is nine times that among male heads of household.

In Table 2 male and female unemployment rates are disaggregated by marriage rather than by household status. This highlights even more clearly the positive relationship between the unemployment rate and ability of a sub-group to do without a source of income. Unmarried men, with fewer economic responsibilities and a greater likelihood of being able to draw on support from family and friends, have a rate of unemployment nearly five times that of married men. In contrast, the female unemployment rate is highest (40 per cent) among those who are married and thus most likely to be in a dependent situation, and lowest among those who are divorced or separated. The rate of unemployment among unmarried women falls between the rates for the groups that are economically most and least dependent; this may reflect the fact that there is a growing stream of independent female job seekers.

It is worth taking a closer look at the explanation for the unemployment rate differential between married and divorced women. Certainly it is not because unemployed divorced women withdraw from the labour force. On the contrary married women, when faced with the frustration of unsuccessful job searches, have the meaningful choice of withdrawal. They have an alternative source of support to fall back on. Divorced women in town are likely to have nobody to rely on to support themselves or their children and thus cannot withdraw from the labour force. This is borne out by the differential in participation rates between the two groups. The greater need to find a source of income results in a participation rate among divorced women that is nearly twice that among married women.[1]

TABLE 2: SEVEN TOWNS: UNEMPLOYMENT RATES UNDER ALTERNATIVE JOB SEARCH CRITERIA BY SEX AND MARRIAGE STATUS

	Unemployment Rates	
	Job Search Criterion 1	Job Search Criterion 2
	%	%
Males		
Unmarried	9.3	11.9
Divorced/Separated/ Widowed	1.5	2.9
Married	2.0	2.3
Females		
Unmarried	23.2	31.4
Divorced/Separated/ Widowed	14.2	20.2
Married	23.3	20.0

SOURCE: NUMEIST, 1972.

Although a higher proportion of divorced women participate in the labour market, a lower proportion are unemployed. The explanation for the unemployment rate differential does not appear to lie in differential job credentials between the two groups.[2] Rather the need for income appears to lower the reserve price for the labour of divorced women, implying that they will accept a job, wage or non-wage, at a lower income than married women. A se cond and likely more important aspect is that divorced women are free to return to the countryside, where they can obtain a source of income or support from others if they do not find employment within the job search period they can afford.

The positive unemployment rate differential between men and women makes economic sense, and the high rate for women has little effect on the aggregate rate of unemployment because of the low female participation rate. Nevertheless a definitional problem in the measurement of employment has a significantly greater effect on the estimation of female than male unemployment rates. Estimates of unemployment rates have been based on the assumption that all adults, other than those who derive a cash income from wage employment or self-employment, either are not in the labour force or are unemployed. Such an assumption would be grossly unrealistic in the rural areas where a large proportion of output is produced for self-consumption. In urban areas the situation is different; clearly production for self-consumption is far less important. Nevertheless there are areas within city limits or on the immediate outskirts of town where people grow crops to feed their families. In addition a range of non-agricultural goods produced in urban homes never reaches the market. For the most part, women are engaged in generating the urban subsistence income; only 2 per cent of all adult males derived an income in this way, while 14 per cent of women had a non-money source of income.[3]

Whether or not these women should be included among the employed raises the issue of the relationship between intensity of employment and the distribution of the employed between those who are and those who are not part of the pool of urban surplus labour. Excluding from among the employed those who produced only urban subsistence output could certainly be justified on the ground that their activity still leaves them subject to many of the same welfare and resource under-utilisation problems to which the unemployed are subject. We argue below that a proportion of self-employed and wage employed workers whose economic activity does not generate an income above a properly defined minimum should be included as part of the total of urban surplus labour. For now this group is simply counted among the employed. Since we later extend the estimate of the magnitude of surplus labour to low income earners including those with a source of non-money income, for consistency women with subsistence income should be treated in the same way as women whose employment generates only very low levels of monetary remuneration.

Counting subsistence income earners among the employed will lower unemployment rates in two ways. On the one hand some adults among those without money-earning jobs receive some urban subsistence income but continue to seek work. Transferring them from the unemployed to the employed will lower the rate of unemployment. Other adults without a source of money income have an urban subsistence income and are not seeking work. Transferring this group out of the labour force category will not lower the number of unemployed, but it will increase the number of employed and decrease the rate of unemployment. This adjustment has an insignificant effect on the rate of more unemployment, but for females the rate decreases from 32 per cent to 20 per cent. The decrease in the rate of female unemployment lowers Tanzania's aggregate rate of unemployment from 12 per cent to 9.9 per cent, further reinforcing our impression that open unemployment alone does not yet constitute a serious urban problem in Tanzania.

TRENDS IN THE MAGNITUDE AND RATE OF URBAN UNEMPLOYMENT

This adjustment to the unemployment rate now brings the 1971 definitions in line with those used in the 1965 Labour Force Survey, which was the first of its kind in Tanzania, indeed in all of Sub-Saharan Africa. Although the aggregate rate of unemployment has increased over this period, the rate of growth of urban employment opportunities has not kept pace with the rate of increase in the size of the urban labour force. The lack of reliable data prior to 1965 hampers historical analysis, but annual reports from labour commissioners on the condition of labour supply and demand and other evidence on the urban labour market suggest that significant urban unemployment did not exist prior to the late 1950s or early 1960s.[4]

The evidence that there has been a secular increase in the rate of urban unemployment in Tanzania over the past twenty years is consistent with the widening of rural-urban income differentials and the increase in the rate of growth of urban wage employment opportunities. Given the trend towards higher rates of unemployment, the magnitude of the urban employment problem in Tanzania viewed from a dynamic perspective should qualify our static evaluation of the problem's seriousness. The projection of current rural and urban income and employment opportunity trends into the future indicates a continued growth in the magnitude of unemployment. If there is no change in the rate of unemployment over time, the absolute number of unemployed will continue to grow at the same rate as the labour force. From 1965 to 1971 the number of urban unemployed males increased at approximately 8 per cent per year, and the number of openly unemployed workers increased to approximately 21,000 in 1971.

UNEMPLOYMENT BY AGE AND MIGRANT STATUS

The rate of unemployment among non-migrant males, is nearly twice that among migrant males.[5] The explanation once again appears to lie in a differential in the opportunity costs of unemployment. In this case the predominant factor does not appear to be dependency, but rather access to land. In the Tanzanian context a migrant male who is unsuccessful in finding a job almost always has the security of a potential job in the rural areas. This implies that after a certain amount of time searching for a job the mounting costs of unemployment, in the form of rural income foregone, will make it economically sensible to return to the rural areas. The evidence on the rate of urban-rural migration suggested that rural residents who have gone to town and who are unsuccessful in finding employment return to the countryside after only a short period of job search. This finding is corroborated with differentials by length of time in town.

Most migrant males come to town in search of employment and thus enter the urban labour force immediately on arrival. Moreover there is a high degree of stability in employment among migrants who are successful in their job search. Thus among long term male migrants the proportion who are unemployed because they are entering the labour force for the first time or because they have left their urban job is very low. Therefore one would expect the rate of unemployment to be dramatically lower for migrants who arrived in earlier years relative to those who arrived more recently. If the rate declines for earlier arrivals, this can be taken as evidence that migrants return to the countryside if they do not find a job. The NUMEIST study found that the rate of unemployment among migrant males who entered the urban labour market within the six months prior to enumeration was, at 22 per cent, over two and a half times the rate among migrants who arrived in the year before. Among migrants who arrived in 1968–69 the rate was only 3 per cent while the average rate for those who arrived at a still earlier date was only 1.5 per cent. The fact that unemployment rates among migrant women do not decline with length of time in town nearly so rapidly as among men reinforces the conclusion that as dependents they do not have effective rural alternatives and can afford to remain in town unemployed.[6]

The Survey findings suggest that the migrant may return to his home area even though his expected urban income remains above that of his expected rural income. In fact once a migrant arrives in town and becomes familiar with labour market communication channels and hiring practices, his probability of finding a job and hence his expected income may actually rise. The decision to return home may be due to the migrant's inability to finance a still larger investment in the chance of obtaining a job. In other words even though the odds of his winning in the urban job lottery are improving, and continuing to play the urban labour market game may appear to be his most remunerative economic activity, inability to afford the price of a lottery ticket may force him to return home. The savings with which migrants come to town are likely to be limited. The Survey found that 75 per cent of migrant males receive some form of material support from friends and relatives of their arrival in town, but this support is likely to be limited in duration.

Among those born in the city or who came as children, the proportion with an assurance of a rural income is likely to be considerably lower than among migrants. This lack of a rural income earning option appears to explain the higher rate of unemployment among non-migrant than migrant men. The rural opportunity cost of unemployment for most non-migrants is zero. This would tend to lengthen the tolerable period of unemployment for non-migrants. If a non-migrant male is not successful in finding an urban job, and once he has run through his savings or the hospitability of family and friends, he cannot simply withdraw from the labour force, nor can he withdraw from the urban labour market.

Before considering the welfare implications of this differential, a related set of differentials should be considered. First, migration is highly age selective. The concentration of unemployment among recent arrivals implies that the highest migrant male rates of unemployment are to be found among young men. Concentration of unemployment among young non-migrants might also be expected because they enter the labour force at a young age. It is also likely that even if they remain unemployed for a long time, they eventually will find a job while still young, and once they have a job, they are unlikely to leave it except for a better job. Survey findings confirm that this is the case; the rate of unemployment among 14–19 year olds was over five times that among 20–24 year olds, whose rate was double that of the next oldest group. Fully 68 per cent of all the male unemployed are under 24 years of age. This of course is consistent with the findings that the rate of unemployment is highest among unmarried males.[7]

The fact that unemployment is highest among young men who have minimum family responsibilities implies that the welfare costs of unemployment are less than if the unemployed were older and established family heads. There appears to be some substance to the argument that the individual welfare costs of unemployment among the group of newly arrived migrants is zero or even negative. In other words since these migrants come to town with the expectation that they will have to wait for a period before finding a job, their welfare in town even when unemployed is higher than it would be in the countryside because of the psychic income associated with the far higher probability in the town of eventually obtaining one of the scarce high-paying employment positions.

The high unemployment rate among non-migrants however, is cause for greater concern. Non-migrants do not receive the psychic benefits of the rural-urban employment opportunity differential. They are not in town looking for work on speculation, and thus the welfare costs to unemployed non-migrants are likely to be higher than for unemployed migrants. The fact that 49 per cent of Tanzanian male urban unemployed are non-migrants means that the welfare costs of unemployment in the aggregate are likely to be considerably higher than if all the unemployed were migrants. When the unemployed are out of work, not by choice but by force of circumstance, when they have no economic activity options, and when their length of time unemployed is extended, the welfare costs for themselves and for the community (as reflected in a rising crime rate and social unrest) tend to be high. The fact that unemployment among non-migrants is concentrated among the young, however, does imply that welfare costs are lower than they would be if the non-migrant unemployed were older.

THE DEFINITION AND MEASURE OF SURPLUS LABOUR AMONG THE URBAN EMPLOYED

The Survey evidence in 1971 revealed that open unemployment was increasing but was not yet a serious problem in Tanzania. Open unemployment, however, is only one component of the urban employment problem. That a labour force member is employed does not preclude the possibility that he or she is economically deprived or, as a resource, is misallocated and under-utilised. Some low income, low productivity jobs in the urban sector, in terms of their consequences both for the welfare of the individual job holder and for the maximisation of national output, are more similar to unemployment than to the relatively high wage, high productivity urban employment. Enough distinguishing features of this type of employment exist to isolate an urban sub-sector of jobs. The following describes this "marginal" sector:

"Entrance to the occupations in question is open. Most of them require little or no skill, and also little or no capital. They thus provide a natural entry point for migrants from the country, who win a precarious foothold in the urban economy by crowding into petty trade, services and other small-scale activities. Overmanning of these activities contributes to low output and income per worker. . . . Most people manage to work a little and earn a little. . . ."[8]

The evidence supports the existence of such an urban sector in Tanzania, at least in modified form. But to identify that portion of the urban employed which participates in this sector and thus which makes up the total urban surplus labour, an income criterion is essential. This is for three reasons. First, income is the best indicator of welfare, one of the dimensions along which the unemployed and the marginally employed can be aggregated. Second, income, as the best available measure of productivity, provides the basis for estimating the total number of labour force members who are misallocated because of the distortion in the price of labour. A corollary is that income as a proxy for productivity theoretically allows the calculation of the third element of our index of total resource costs of surplus labour, namely, the absolute magnitude of output foregone per unemployed or marginally employed individual.

The appropriate measure of the resource cost of the misallocation of labour between the rural and urban labour force is the difference between what the worker is earning in the city and what he could be earning in the countryside. More precisely, for the unemployed the social opportunity cost of surplus labour per person is the marginal product of labour in the rural areas. For the marginally employed, the social opportunity cost of surplus labour per person is the marginal product in the rural area minus the output the individual actually generates in the urban area. Conversely, any urban labour force member whose product in town is less than his rural marginal product is part of the urban labour surplus. These conclusions are arrived at by generalising the expected income model of migration from a two-sector rural-urban model to a three-sector model comprised of rural employment, urban primary employment, and urban marginal employment sectors.

The third reason for using an income criterion for defining the marginal sector and the employed portion of urban surplus labour is that the alternative criterion frequently used is inappropriate in the Tanzanian context. Before we define our criterion, it is important to consider why the use of the alternative will not, except by sheer chance, yield an accurate estimate of the magnitude of the employed component of urban surplus labour.

THE REJECTION OF A MARGINAL SECTOR-SELF-EMPLOYED SECTOR IDENTITY

Largely due to an absence of data that would permit a more meaningful disaggregation, some analysts measure the magnitude and rate of increase of the urban employment problem in developing countries by the gaps between (a) the total labour force and the number in wage employment, and (b) the labour force and wage employment growth rates.[9] Implicit in this view is that all of the self-employed are participants in the marginal sector while none of the wage employed are. We will now compare Tanzania's urban self-employed sector with our descriptive model of the marginal sector so as to evaluate this hypothesis.

The comparison can begin with the consideration of the distribution of urban non-wage money earners among the range of economic activities open to them. In the hypothetical model, the greatest proportion of participants in the marginal sector are concentrated in petty trading and services or activities. The actual distribution of the urban self-employed in Tanzania differs dramatically from this description. One-third of all non-wage money earners are engaged in directly productive activities. Producers of traditional handicrafts such as pottery, wood and basketry (fashioned for domestic consumption and to a limited degree for tourists) and small scale manufacturers such as tailors, cabinet makers, bakers and brewers make up the greatest proportion of this group.[10]

A second component of the directly productive group are skilled craftsmen who contract for their own services. These include masons, carpenters, roofers, electricians and plumbers, and they play a particularly important role in the small scale building industry which has been responsible for the construction of the thousands of traditional type houses that have sprung up on the outskirts of Tanzania's towns. The last component of the directly productive group are the farmers and fishermen who live near the urban areas and sell their produce on the urban market.

In addition there are rentiers and shop-owners and owners of small bars and restaurants whose activities are frequently on a considerably larger scale than those usually associated with marginal sector petty trading. In some of these activities, as in the directly productive activities, the amount of initial capital required is large relative to the resources available to newly arrived migrants. The small number of independent workers in the professional occupations also cannot be included among those engaged in socially non-productive service activities that are held to typify the marginal sector. The elimination of those engaged in directly productive and relatively large scale service or trading activities leaves approximately 28 per cent of the self-employed in petty street-trading and menial transportation services. Thus the activity distributions of the self-employed and the hypothetical marginal sector clearly do not match.

A second characteristic of the hypothetical marginal sector is that, because of the lack of the sort of barriers to entry that prevail in the high wage sector, marginal activities serve as an entry point for the urban labour market, providing a temporary source of income while the real job of searching for one of the scarce high income employment positions continues. It already has been noted that a considerable proportion of non-wage money earners are in activities where capital constitutes a significant barrier to entry; we will consider evidence of skill and other barriers to entry below. For now we will concentrate on determining whether or not, despite these barriers, the non-wage money sector in urban Tanzania serves as a labour market entry sector for newly arrived migrants.

The Survey established the distribution of male migrants by source of funds during their first months in the urban area. If self-employment provided a means of gaining a precarious foothold in the urban labour market, a significant proportion of migrants would have participated in the self-employed sector when they were new arrivals. The fact is that only 6 per cent of male migrants supported themselves with some form of self-employment. Excluding those who found a wage job soon after arrival, only 9 per cent of new arrivals relied on self-employment as a means of support. This effectively eliminates this sector as a labour market entry point during the migrant's initial adjustment period in town. It is still possible, of course, that after an initial period of unsuccessful job search and after alternative forms of support have been used up, the migrant might turn to self-employment rather than return to the countryside.[11]

If self-employment can be identified with marginal employment in this way, we would expect to find, among migrant non-wage money earners, a high proportion who had arrived in town within, say, the year and a half prior to enumeration. The Survey indicates that this is not the case. Overall only 14 per cent of non-wage money earners had arrived in town within the year and a half period, and fully 60 per cent had been living in town for over four and a half years. Each activity grouping had more than 50 per cent of its participants living in town for four and a half or more years. The migrant members of the self-employment sector displays a higher degree of stability in terms of their length of stay in town than would be expected in any entry sector supposedly made up predominantly of marginal employment positions. However, we should note that two of the three activities with proportions of recent arrivals above the mean, namely street-hawking and transport services, are activities which in our descriptive model are assumed to have a relatively high proportion of marginal jobs.[12]

That the marginal sector will generate only very low incomes for those who participate in it follows from two assumptions. First, assuming no barriers to entry in the form of a set number of job openings and no institutional constraints such as minimum wages or union activity, incomes will be downwardly flexible in a labour surplus situation. The second assumption is that job seekers will participate in this sector while waiting in the queue for relatively high wage jobs. Since we argue that the self-employed sector is not synonymous with the marginal sector and have shown that the self-employed are not predominantly new arrivals and that barriers to entry exist, we would expect to find that incomes among the self-employed are not uniformly low.

Evidence on the distribution of income of non-wage money earners reveals that this is in fact the case. In 1971 the range of the minimum urban wage was Shs. 180. In that year 43 per cent of all non-wage money earners took home at least Shs. 200 per month. This aggregate distribution for the self-employed was not the product of high incomes concentrated in one set of activities and low incomes concentrated in another set, but rather represented a wide range of incomes in each activity. The activity sub-group with income distribution most skewed towards low incomes still had 25 per cent of its members above the Shs. 200 line. It is clear that not all of the self-employed are relatively poverty-stricken in the way that participants in our hypothetical marginal sector are meant to be. In comparing the income distribution of self-employed and wage employed, we find that a higher proportion of the former group is in the highest income bracket of Shs. 1,000 and over.

This is not to say, however, that there are no marginally employed among the non-wage money earners. Rather, the distribution of income of the self-employed, clearly bi-modal in six out of the eight activity sub-groups, is consistent with the hypothesis that there is a component of each activity grouping that can be classified as part of the marginal sector. Approximately 32 per cent of the self-employed were earning incomes below the Shs. 100 per month income line, which was only 55 per cent of the minimum wage. In addition there are greater concentrations of low income earners in those activities normally associated with the marginal sector. Fifty-seven per cent and 67 per cent of menial transport workers and street-hawkers respectively earned less than Shs. 200, while, with the exception of the rental and *shamba* sub-groups, no other activity sub-group was more than 50 per cent in this lower portion of the income distribution. Also the aggregate proportion of the self-employed earning less than 200 shillings (58 per cent) is over twice that of the wage employed.[13]

If we measure the magnitude of the urban employment problem by the gap between the size of the labour force and the number of people in wage employment, our measure is likely to be seriously biased. On the one hand, an upward bias results from the fact that the non-wage money earning sector and the marginal sector are not identical. The findings of our comparison of the defining characteristics of the marginal sector with those of the non-wage money-earning sector are consistent with the hypothesis that the latter sector can be subdivided into two components or sub-sectors, an economically marginal and an economically viable sub-sector. The marginal sub-sector is characterised by an absence of barriers to entry, by flexible and low incomes and an unstable labour force. The viable sub-sector is characterised by skill, capital and market information barriers to entry. Consequently, even though institutional influences on income structures are weak, incomes are not downwardly flexible in response to an excess supply of unskilled labourers who cannot bypass the entry barriers. Incomes and stability of employment are relatively high in the viable sub-sector. Thus by counting the viable sub-sector as part of the urban employment problem we would be overestimating the problem's magnitude.

On the other hand, the income comparison of the non-wage money-earning sector with the wage earning sector has revealed an element of downward bias in the labour force-wage employed gap measure of the employment problem. For, in addition to the quite clearly economically viable component of the wage-earning sector, there also appears to be a marginal component of the sector. Between 10 and 15 per cent of wage employees earn less than the minimum wage. In casual employment, where minimum wage legislation is most easily evaded by employers, there are few barriers to entry and the level of instability is relatively high. Neglecting this group underestimates the problem's magnitude. The net bias resulting from the use of the labour force-wage employed gap proxy measure will of course depend upon which of the two biases is the stronger. The important point is that analytically there is no justification for using the labour force-wage employed gap as a measure of the magnitude of surplus labour.

Our preliminary analysis of the situation has thus suggested that if we divide the employed into two sectors, the wage sector and the non-wage sector, each of these can be further divided into two sub-sectors, the marginal sub-sector and the viable sub-sector. To measure the urban employment problem we need a means of effectively estimating the number of participants in the marginal sub-sectors of both sectors of urban employment. In the next section we outline a model from which we can derive both a more precise definition of marginal employment and surplus labour in the urban labour market and an income criterion to separate the marginal from the economically viable sub-sectors.

A THREE-SECTOR MODEL OF MIGRATION AND URBAN SURPLUS LABOUR

We begin by assuming a two-sector model of rural self-employment and urban money-earning employment (wage and non-wage). In this model the distinguishing characteristic of the urban sector, as represented in the right half of Figure 1, is that wages, which include the incomes of the self-employed, are flexible. This implies that, since the supply of labour is a function of the rural-urban wage differential, there will be no urban unemployment, for an outward shift of the supply curve (due to a decline of rural incomes or population growth) or an inward shift of the demand curve (due to a decline in investment, factor substitution or increases in labour productivity) will result in a decline in wages that will equilibrate the labour market. An important point to note is that, assuming factors are paid their marginal products, labour's equilibrium supply price will equal the marginal product of labour in the rural sector plus a margin to compensate for the direct costs of migration. W_1 is the equilibrium wage when sector A is the only urban sector.

FIGURE 1:

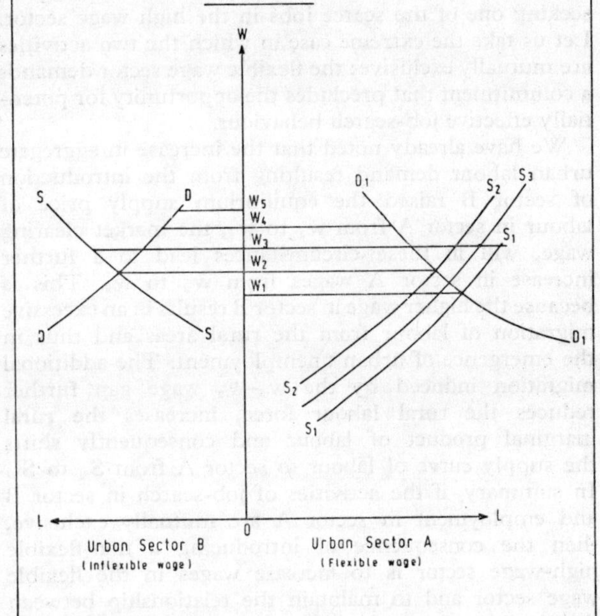

Now we introduce a third sector into the model. This second urban sector, represented in the left side of Figure 1, is characterised by wages that are inflexible in a downward direction and are set, either because of a wage-productivity relationship or institutional factors, at W^5. This is above W_2, equilibrium wage for both urban sectors. W_2 lies above W_1, because the addition of the new sector means that at any given wage the labour forthcoming from the rural areas must be shared between the two urban sectors. In effect this entails a shift inward in the supply curve of labour to sector A as the withdrawal of additional labour from the rural sector results in an increase in rural marginal product.

If there is a positive urban-rural wage differential such that urban wages are in excess of the marginal product of labour in the rural areas plus a cost of moving allowance, and if this differential is not responsive to conditions of excess supply or urban labour, then rural residents will continue to migrate to the urban area even after the probability of obtaining one of the high wage jobs falls below unity. We are particularly interested in the implications of the introduction of this rigid high wage sector for the supply of labour and the level of wages in the flexible wage sector. Note that the only distinction between the two urban sectors is in the level of wages and degrees of responsiveness to changes in labour supply conditions. In other words sectors A and B may have both wage and self-employed components.

The effect on wages and labour supply in the flexible wage sector of the introduction of the new high wage sector and the emergence of urban unemployment depends on the extent to which employment in the flexible wage sector interferes with the activity of seeking one of the scarce jobs in the high wage sector. Let us take the extreme case in which the two activities are mutually exclusive: the flexible wage sector demands a commitment that precludes the opportunity for potentially effective job-search behaviour.

We have already noted that the increase in aggregate urban labour demand resulting from the introduction of sector B raised the equilibrium supply price of labour in sector A from w_1 to w_2, the market clearing wage, will in these circumstances lead to a further increase in sector A wages from w_2 to w_3. This is because the higher wage in sector B results in an excessive migration of labour from the rural areas and thus in the emergence of urban unemployment. The additional migration induced by the w_5–w_2 wage gap further reduces the rural labour force, increases the rural marginal product of labour and consequently shifts the supply curve of labour to sector A from S_2 to S_3. In summary, if the activities of job-search in sector B and employment in sector A are mutually exclusive, then the consequence of introducing a non-flexible high-wage sector is to increase wages in the flexible wage sector and to maintain the relationship between the flexible wage and the rural marginal product of labour such that it will not be economically rational for any migrant to accept employment in sector A at a wage below that which he could be earning in the rural area.

Now let us consider the more realistic case in which holding a flexible-wage employment does not entirely preclude looking for another job. In this case all those employed in the urban flexible wage sector will earn, in addition to their monetary income, a psychic income associated with the positive probability of obtaining one of the scarce high paying sector B wage jobs. If the monetary wage in sector A is at w_3, the total income received (monetary plus psychic) will be somewhat higher, for example w_4. However at w_4 the supply of labour to sector A from the rural areas will exceed the number of employment opportunities available. Since wages in this sector are flexible the total wage per man will be reduced to w_3. This, in turn, implies that the monetary wage will be at a level below w_3, which, we should recall, equals the rural marginal product plus an allowance for the direct costs of migration.

In fact the total wage will be reduced to a level even lower than w_3. This is because a shift in the supply curve of labour in the direction of S_2 and S_1 will result from the fact that a proportion of the excess supply of labour attracted by the high wages in sector B will enter sector A for short term employment as a means of reducing the costs of migration, which include the cost of waiting for a high wage employment position. How high a proportion of the unemployed will enter the flexible wage sector will depend on the degree to which sector A employment interferes with job search and the amount of savings or other sources of support the migrant has available. In other words the migrant's short run supply price may be above the flexible sector wage and below the expected wage in the inflexible wage sector.

The significant point of this downward adjustment of wages in sector A is that the monetary wage earned is likely to be *below* the marginal product of labour in the rural areas. In the case where job search and employment in sector A are mutually exclusive the existence of a high wage sector still leaves the sector A wage at a level, w_3, that will equilibrate the sectoral supply and demand for labour and will be only high enough above the marginal product of labour in the rural areas to compensate for the direct costs of moving. In the present case, in which there is a psychic component to sector A income, if the equilibrium total wage is at w_3 or below, the equilibrium money wage will be at some level below w_3. In other words, the criterion allows a realistic and meaningful assessment of the magnitude of the urban employment problem. It is realistic in that it recognises that the problem is not accurately measured either by the level of open unemployment alone or by the sum of the openly unemployed and the self-employed. Similarly it is realistic in its recognition that arbitrary income criteria, such as the level of minimum wages, are likely to include as part of the problem, workers who are contributing more to national output than they could be elsewhere in the economy and who have fulfilled the aim of their move to town.[14] Such an arbitrary criterion reduces to saying that some people are poorer than others, and opens up the question of what the income distribution should be. Also it inadequately separates the urban employment problem from the development problem as a whole. By contrast, our criterion only includes a worker as part of the problem if wage distortions have led to his misallocation with the result that his employment in the urban sector imposes a cost, in terms of output foregone, on the economy that at least theoretically could be avoided.

AN ESTIMATE OF SURPLUS LABOUR AMONG THE URBAN EMPLOYED

Now that we are clear conceptually about the increasing surplus labour, it is possible to assess the extent to which Tanzania's urban employment problem includes members of the urban labour force who are holding a job. Our model suggests that it is only necessary to determine the proportion of the urban labour force earning less than the rural marginal product. This, of course, poses problems. First, we have no measure of rural marginal product. However, this is not a serious obstacle as land scarcity is not yet widespread in Tanzania. Therefore one can make the reasonable assumption that the marginal rural product equals average rural product and use the latter measure as an index of the opportunity cost of urban employment. Secondly, because of differential resource endowments and market conditions and because of the constraints on labour mobility among areas of agricultural self-employment, aggregating over the entire range of rural incomes would prove misleading.

Therefore we have taken all employed urban migrants, divided them by region of origin, and compared the urban distribution of income for each regional grouping with the average rural income in the region from which the migrants came. Since inter-regional dispersion appears to capture most of the total rural income dispersion, disaggregating in this way will eliminate much of the measurement error that could result from counting an urban resident as part of the problem because his income is lower than the rural average income when in fact, it is higher than the average income in his relatively poor region of origin. It will also eliminate the common error of not counting an urban resident as part of the problem just because his income is above the rural average, even though it is below the average in his relatively rich region of origin.

Among migrant non-wage money earners from each region we have determined the proportion earning less than they could be earning in the rural area of origin. The proportions are then weighted by the proportion of each region in the total urban migrant self-employed labour force to derive an aggregate proportion of surplus migrant self-employed. Approximately 17 per cent of all migrant self-employed by definition are surplus labour.[15] The distribution of non-migrant self-employed earnings are then compared to the aggregate average rural income and 19.8 per cent of this sub-group is found to be surplus labour. The migrant-non-migrant differential parallels that between migrant and non-migrant unemployment rates. Altogether 18 per cent of all non-wage money earners are part of the urban labour surplus.

The proportion of surplus labour among the wage-employed would be expected to be less than among the self-employed, given the previous comparison of income distribution in the two sectors. This is in fact the case. According to the criterion used here, 4.8 per cent of migrants who are wage-employed and 5.2 per cent of non-migrants with wage employment are surplus labour. Overall, 8.4 per cent of the employed and 7.3 per cent of the total labour force make up Tanzania's employed urban labour surplus. This means that transferring 7.3 per cent of the urban employed to rural employment would increase national output. Adding the 12 per cent of the labour force that is openly unemployed to our figure of employed surplus labour yields a total figure of 19.3 per cent of the labour force that constitutes surplus labour.[16] Although the employed labour surplus imposes less significant resource costs on the economy than the unemployed, nevertheless this rather high proportion of the labour force is "misallocated" and forces a reassessment of the magnitude of Tanzania's urban employment problem. When the problem's definition is extended to include low income urban workers it is seen to be considerably more serious than when only the openly unemployed are considered.

There are three further qualifications to this measure of employed surplus labour which suggest it may be an under-estimate. We have assumed that workers in the flexible wage sector are paid their private marginal product and that private marginal product equals social marginal product. However if there are pecuniary negative externalities such that the addition of another shoe-shine boy does not add to the total income of all shoe-shine boys but simply redistributes it so that everyone gets a smaller piece of the same sized pie, then social marginal product is less than private marginal product, and our measurement of urban surplus labour on the basis of private marginal product will yield an underestimate of the magnitude of the urban labour surplus.

Secondly, one might use shadow prices rather than market prices for the valuing of different types of output. For example, a relatively higher price might be placed on export crops relative to urban services because of the premium placed on foreign exchange. In this case, once again there would be a tendency to underestimate the total urban surplus labour.

Thirdly, and perhaps most significantly, no account has been taken of the rural-urban cost of living differential when estimating the magnitude of employed surplus labour. Since there is a strong presumption that the cost of living is considerably higher in town than in the countryside, adjusting for the differential would lower urban relative earnings in real terms and would result in a greater proportion of urban workers earning less than what they could be earning in the rural areas. Thus this measure only establishes a lower bound to the magnitude of Tanzania's urban employment problem.

CONCLUSION

This economic analysis of the determinants of migrant behaviour and of the wage determination mechanism has provided the basis for the generation of a theory of urban surplus labour that is consistent with the empirical evidence from Tanzania. The phenomenon of urban surplus labour certainly cannot be interpreted in the context of a Keynesian, consumer demand insufficiency model. The emergence of urban surplus labour is not accompanied by an increase in excess capacity in industry or a general downturn in economic activity. In addition the phenomenon is neither cyclical nor national. Rather it is chronic and sectoral.

Depending on the interpretation of the generation of the rural-urban wage gap, this theory is either neo-classical or structural or a mixture of the two. If the wage gap is viewed solely as a function of institutional intervention, it is the former. If the wage gap is seen as employer-led and a function of differentials in the relationship of incomes and productivity among the industrial and agricultural wage and the agricultural non-wage sectors, then it is the latter. We have argued that in Tanzania it is a mixture of the two with a somewhat greater weight on the structural component.

In any case the theory is posited on a sectoral income differential that is not narrowed by the mobility of labour from the low to the high income sector. Thus the key components of the theory are wage levels that do not equilibrate the supply and demand for labour in the receiving area, and a labour supply function of migrants of a form such that if wages are above the supply price of labour then it is still economically rational for some source area residents to move to the high income sector, even after a surplus labour situation has emerged and the probability of finding a job has fallen below unity. If these conditions are met, and in Tanzania they have been, then it is the level of surplus in the receiving area that serves as the device equilibrating the demand and the supply for labour.

The theory allows us to predict the precise magnitude of surplus labour only if we have detailed information on the shape of the labour supply and demand functions. Even without this information the theory predicts that the wider the wage gap and the closer the number of job openings to the level that would absorb the labour supply forthcoming in the absence of surplus labour, the higher will be the level of surplus labour required to equilibrate the labour market. In the Tanzanian context we found that the predictions of the theory were consistent with the trend of aggregate unemployment rates over time and with differentials in the rate of unemployment among educational sub-groups. In those cases in which the theory did not adequately explain unemployment rate differentials among demographic sub-groups, it was because differences in their dependency status and in barriers to urban-rural migration consistently altered the level of opportunity costs of unemployment.

Presenting and assessing a theory of urban unemployment was only a subsidiary aim of this paper. The primary aim was to measure the magnitude of Tanzania's urban employment problem. Our theory of the generation of the problem allowed us to define precisely the meaning of surplus labour, namely that portion of the high income sector labour force whose transfer to the low income sector would increase total product. To actually quantify this group posed serious definitional problems and it was necessary, in measuring open unemployment, to consider alternative measures of the total size of the labour force and of that portion of the labour force that is employed. More serious still was the problem of estimating the proportion of the employed group of labour force members to be counted as part of the total urban labour surplus. We rejected that measure which positions an identity between the urban marginal sector and the urban self-employed sector. Rather an extension of our theoretical model allowed us to justify the use of average rural incomes as the income criterion below which the urban employed, both self-employed and wage employed, are included as part of the employment problem.

The conclusion of our analysis is that as a consequence of the rise in urban wages to a level in excess of the equilibrium supply price of labour, Tanzania faces a serious though by no means overwhelming urban employment problem. Altogether a lower limit of approximately 20 per cent of the urban labour force is surplus, in the terms outlined here, and imposes a cost on the economy by decreasing allocative efficiency. The seriousness of the problem is diminished somewhat by the composition of the surplus. Some 8 per cent of the surplus does generate at least some monetary output in the urban areas and in addition the characteristics of the unemployed suggest that the employment problem is not concentrated among the relatively most skilled and most productive members of the labour force.

Our assessment of the welfare costs of surplus labour also somewhat diminishes the seriousness of the problem even though in aggregate a given quantum of surplus labour in Tanzania is likely to have more serious consequences than the same amount of surplus labour in currently industrialised countries, since the government cannot afford welfare schemes to reduce the individual hardship of being without a job. It is partly for this reason that unemployment is a luxury that few urban dwellers can afford. Those unemployed urban dwellers who have access to economic options in the rural areas either find a job or tend to take advantage of those options after only a short time in the urban labour market. For the majority of those who do not have a rural option, most of whom are women, the welfare costs of unemployment are reduced by having an employed labour force members to rely on for support. More generally since our model suggests that migrants included among the labour surplus are in town because it is to their economic advantage to be there, once the psychic income derived from the positive probability of finding a job is taken into account, some grounds exist for claiming that for this group there are no welfare costs. For non-migrants, who comprise nearly half of the unemployed, the situation is more serious.

These qualifications should not, however, be allowed to diminish our assessment of the seriousness of the problem. If the trends in income and employment opportunity differentials continue as they have over the past15–20 years, it will not be long before the problem will be very serious indeed. And even if the rate of urban surplus labour remains constant the number of people in this category will be growing at the rate of the urban labour force. As the relatively faster rate of growth of the urban over the rural labour force is bound to continue for some time, this implies a rapid growth in the number of urban labour surplus and an increase in the national rate of surplus labour. Also, as the proportion of the labour force born in town increases, and as land scarcity perhaps begins to develop, the composition of the labour surplus is likely to be more heavily weighted toward those groups whose welfare costs from surplus labour are relatively high.

NOTES

1. See R. H. Sabot and Bienefield, *National, Urban Mobility, Employment and Survey of Tanzania*, Vol. II, Economic Research Bureau, University of Dar es Salaam, 1972.
2. *Ibid.*
3. *Ibid.*, Ch. 5, Table 5.9.
4. Labour Department, *Annual, Reports*, various years.
5. See R. H. Sabot, original ERB Paper 74.4, pp. 8–9.
6. *Ibid.*, pp. 9–10.
7. *Ibid.*, p. 13, Table 1.7.
8. L. Reynolds, *Relative Earnings and Manpower Allocation in Developing Economies*, New Haven: Yale University Press, 1969, p. 4.
9. For example, see C. Frank, "The Problem of Urban Unemployment in Africa," in *Employment and Unemployment Problems of the Near East and South Asia.* eds. R. Ridker and H. Lubell, Delhi: Vikas Publications, 1971.
10. See Sabot, ERB Paper 74.4, p. 23, Table 1.10.
11. *Ibid.*, p. 25.
12. *Ibid.*, p. 26.
13. *Ibid.*, pp. 27–29.
14. A minimum wage criterion was used to assess the magnitude of the urban employment problem in a recent study of Kenya. While this work represented a step in the right direction it is clear that the criterion defined above is more appropriate. See I.L.O., *Employment, Incomes and Equality: A Strategy for Increasing Productive Employment in Kenya*, Geneva: International Labour Office, 1972.
15. Sabot, ERB Paper 74.4, pp. 36–37.
16. The 12 per cent counts females in subsistence income as not employed. No double counting is involved as our estimate of surplus labour among the employed does not include this group.

The Organization and Participation of Workers in Tanzania.*

HENRY MAPOLU

WORKERS' PARTICIPATION IN TANZANIA

In Tanzania, the idea of involving the workers in the management of enterprises was first substantiated in a Presidential Circular issued in January, 1970.[1]

The circular directed, among other things, that "every Public Corporation or firm employing more than ten workers . . . establish a Workers' Council. . . ." Until then there were already "workers' committees" as well as TANU Branches in enterprises. The boundaries separating the areas of operation of these three organs are not as yet distinct and clear. It is useful therefore to begin with a brief discussion of the TANU Branches and Workers' Committees and then to outline the initial organisation of the Workers' Councils. The final section of this paper presents the results of a case study of workers' participation in Ubungo Farm Implements Manufacturing Co. (UFI, a publicly owned manufacturing enterprise).

TANU Branches

TANU started opening branches vigorously after the proclamation of the Arusha Declaration in 1967. At first the exercise was haphazard; later, however, the National Executive Committee of the Party tried to set up some procedures governing the Party branches in institutions. The functions of these branches in enterprises are supposed to be the same as those of all Party branches. The highest organ at the branch level is the "Branch Annual Conference," whose functions constitute the functions of the Party branch as a whole.[2]

The very broad functions apply to the District and Regional levels, each level recommending to the higher one anything it may see fit to deliberate on. Thus the Party constitution is not much help in finding the intended functions of TANU Branches in industries.

Before Workers' Councils were formed, seminars and workshops throughout the country tried to bring home the idea of workers' participation to the workers. In these seminars, the functions of TANU Branches in the industries were also discussed. A document used in the educational programme states that the duties of Branch and Sub-Branch leaders in corporations and institutions are five-fold:

(i) to explain and interpret the Party policy of socialism and self-reliance to the workers and managers of the industries. These leaders must be conversant with and believe in the policy of socialism and self-reliance;

(ii) to conduct ordinary Party activities (call members' meetings, collect dues, etc.) in industries and corporations;

(iii) to deal with day to day problems of Party members which are not dealt with by the Workers' Committee in accordance with the 1964 Security of Employment Act, No. 62;

(iv) to co-operate with workers' committees in serving the interests of the workers of public industries and corporations; and

(v) the TANU industrial/corporation branch chairman will be a member of the Workers' Council.

In practice, apart from the last duty, it is difficult to pinpoint these duties. These branches cannot assume the functions of discussing, planning, production, sales and such activities, which in fact are within the purview of the Workers' Council. Similarly, they cannot discuss workers' grievances authoritatively—that is a function of the Workers' Committees.

Furthermore, where they have attempted to involve themselves in either planning and production or workers' grievances, they have often been warned against "interference." Reporting on the 1970 Annual National Development Corporation Group Managers' Conference, *Jenga* (the quarterly publication of the N.D.C.) stated that, according to the Minister of Communications, Works and Labour,

> . . . the industrial TANU Branches are not to interfere with other bodies but co-operate with them and provide advice regarding the application of government policies in that particular industry.[3]

When later NDC issued to all its subsidiaries its own "Guidelines" on the establishment of Workers' Councils, it defined the role of TANU Branches in industries in these terms:

> The TANU Branch is the *political* nerve centre in the company. Its role is to arouse the political consciousness of its members and supervise party matters in the organisation. It does *not* deal with disciplinary matters—that is the work of the workers' committee. Nor does it do the work of management. But again, it can be used to good purpose if it is consulted on matters which it is competent to deal with.[4]

The Arusha Declaration, and the TANU Guidelines more emphatically, have called upon the Party to assume leadership in all affairs of the nation:

> The responsibility of leading the masses together with their various institutions in their efforts

*A longer version of this paper appeared originally as ERB Paper 72.1.

to safeguard their freedom so that the Revolution for the liberation of Africa may continue lies in the Party. The duty of a socialist party is to guide all activities of the people. The government, parastatals, national institutions, etc., are instruments for implementing the Party's policies.[5]

Workers' Committees

The Workers' Committee is the trade union organisation at the factory level. It was established in 1964 with the reorganisation of the trade union movement in the country.[6] It is the workers' consultative organ on matters concerning the welfare of the workers.

According to Government Paper No. 1 of 1964, the functions of the Workers' Committees are eight-fold:

(i) to ensure the observance of collective agreements and arbitration awards;
(ii) to safeguard rules of employment including those contained in Bills of general application (such as a disciplinary code);
(iii) to take part in all inspections of employing concerns conducted by any authorities or officials charged by law with that duty;
(iv) to inspect all records of employment including time-and-wage sheets, and to report any non-compliance with the provisions of a wage regulation order to the appropriate labour officer;
(v) to confirm any case of dismissal or termination of employment of any worker which appears justified;
(vi) to confirm an employer's intention to impose any punishment provided for by the Disciplinary Code;
(vii) to hold joint conferences with the employer or his representative, at appropriate intervals, to discuss working arrangements and their improvement if necessary to promote the efficiency and productivity of the establishment in the interests of the economy in general and of the concern and the workers; and
(viii) to hold joint conferences with the employer or his representative in order to keep under periodic review the safety and welfare arrangements in the establishment.

In practice, however, the Workers' Committees have tended to be instruments of the employers for keeping the workers down. It is significant that just as the key word associated with the TANU industrial Branches is "no interference", the key word for the workers' Committee is "discipline." Thus the NDC "Guidelines" referred to above Workers' Committees in these terms:

> The Workers' Committee deals mainly with *discipline*. It does not deal with politics or personnel policy or even with other aspects of management. But it would be wise to consult with the committee on these matters simply because it will help them better to appreciate the implications of their function. Experience has proved that a well-used committee can be a useful tool of good management.[7]

The Workers' Committees are nothing but tools for management! This interpretation may explain why there has been recent agitation for the abolition of NUTA. Since the organisation acquired its parastatal character—its leaders being nominated by Government and getting its funds by compulsory deduction from workers' wages—it has ceased to be the tool of the workers for expressing their interests.

One study of workers' conditions in a privately-owned industry has found that the Workers' Committee is both extremely inefficient and repressive in its dealings with the workers. At a place where racial discrimination is blatant, child labour is practised rampantly and working and living conditions of the people are close to slave conditions, NUTA has just stood by.[8] Yet authorities of the industry are quoted as saying that with the establishment of NUTA industrial relations have become so good "that the company does not need an industrial relations officer" any more. NUTA has assumed that role.

Workers' Councils

The formation of Workers' Councils was first announced in the *Nationalist* of October 9th, 1969. At the time the report stated that the purpose of the Councils would be "to bring the workers close to the management of industries and to promote better industrial relations while giving the workers more say in formulating policies." It was not until January, 1970, however, that some concrete measures were taken in the form of the Presidential Circular.

The Presidential Circular gives basically three underlying principles of workers' participation in the management of enterprises in this country. First, the Circular argues that given a proper work environment, the majority of workers can become more creative and more productive. Second, workers are not just a "factor of production"—they ought to be treated as the very purpose of production. Finally, industrial discipline can be meaningful only when all involved know fully what, why and how production is carried out.

I need point out only the fact that these principles are not those advanced by socialist countries generally. Marxist theory, itself a general theory of society and history, considers workers' management in the context of the total organisation of society and therefore inextricably connected with the overall problems and goals of liberating man. Tanzania's socialism is not based on such a grand theory; it is more a set of pragmatic propositions for solving a limited number of contemporary issues, and thus reflects the practical nature of the notion of workers' participation.

However, it is significant that little emphasis is put on the question of curbing bureaucracy, in spite of the overwhelming evidence provided by the socialist countries, the Soviet Union in particular, that this phenomenon can be a formidable stumbling block.

The Circular seems to assume that "management" generally has interests that coincide with those of workers', so that the real problem is one of occasionally involving workers in management, thereby topping their creativity and increasing production.

It is therefore not surprising that the managers of the parastatals, at their meeting called to discuss workers' participation, viewed the issue as one more technique of manipulating the workers to produce more. Their conference recommended that "workers be invited to take part in decision-making on matters which affected them and the company, *for this was one of the major incentives—above all other techniques.*"[9] (emphasis supplied).

Thus management was given a surprisingly dominant role in the Workers' Councils. When the idea of Workers' Councils was first proposed in 1969, it was stated that these would be headed by the Party chairman in the respective industries. But the Circular later designated the Manager of the enterprise as chairman of the enterprise Workers' Council at least for the first year. Moreover, heads of departments or sections become permanent members of the Council. In fact, the Circular adds that the elected members in any council should not exceed three quarters of the total membership. In addition, management was to appoint the Secretary of the Council.[10]

If my argument that relations between management and workers in the underdeveloped world are generally authoritarian and paternalistic is correct, this does not seem to be a very genuine way of combating bureaucratism and bringing the workers to the fore of decision-making processes in the economic field. It is difficult to envisage how popular pressures can transform management when it is given such a leading role in the councils. In Yugoslavia, to take a different example, not only do workers assume this role, but also a specified percentage of the council's members must be workers actually involved in production directly. This seems to be a particularly good idea in situations like ours where paternalism still plays a part in allocating positions.

The tendency of electing heads of institutions into top Party positions in the respective institutions, for example, can be explained partly by the obvious estrangement of the institution from the workers, partly by the desire of those on top to ensure they control all decision making positions, and partly by the workers' endeavours to win the favours of their bosses.

THE ESTABLISHMENT OF WORKERS' COUNCILS IN TANZANIA

The Presidential Circular directed that all the institutions involved, i.e. "every public corporation or firm employing more than ten workers," should have established a council by the end of 1970. This deadline was put off to the end of May, 1971, to allow an education campaign of the workers to precede the councils' establishment.

However it was not until June, 1970 that the Workers' Education Committee was formed. It consisted of representation from NUTA, NDC, TANU, STC, the Labour Division, the University and the National Institute of Productivity. The committee members numbered about ten, and their duties were to prepare a syllabus for a training programme for cadres who would eventually undertake the direct education of workers in industries and institutions. Eventually this committee constituted the teaching staff of the course.

The 55 cadres subsequently selected from the regions to undergo the course were distributed as follows: Labour (24), Comworks (10), NUTA (16) and TANU (5). The course lasted a month, from 20th July to 18th August, 1970. The course covered the following topics:

(1) Party ideology (Socialism, Self-reliance and the Arusha Declaration, etc.)—12 hours;
(2) Presidential Circular—14 hours;
(3) NUTA—12 hours;
(4) Wages and Productivity Policies—15 hours;
(5) Industrial Relations—10 hours;
(6) Work Safety—10 hours.

It is clear from this coverage of topics that the organizers and teachers mainly sought to explain and justify the work and *modus operandi* of their respective institutions. Not much substance was covered on the underlying ideas of the Council and particularly on the problems of bureaucratism.

Eventually 42 of the 55 trainees were selected to proceed and carry out the educational campaign in the industries. The cadres were organised into seven groups of six cadres so that each group had one specialist on each of the topics covered in the course and was given a "zone" of two to three regions for which it was responsible. According to the *Nationalist* a total of 56,975 workers attended the worker's education seminars conducted by these cadres all over the country and the biggest problem which the cadres faced in their work was "non-co-operation by managements." The councils were formed immediately after the seminars had been completed in a factory. By the end of April, 1971, a month before the official deadline, returns to the Labour Division in Dar es Salaam showed more than a hundred councils operating across the country. The largest number was in the Coast Region (24), followed by Tanga (18), Shinyanga (12) and Morogoro (10).

The following section presents an interesting example of workers' participation as it developed in a specific firm.

THE UBUNGO FARM IMPLEMENTS (UFI): CASE STUDY

The TANU Branch and the Workers' Committee

UFI was officially opened by the Second Vice-President on 5th June, 1970, although production had already been going on for several months. It employs some 200 workers and represents an investment of approximately Shs. 5.5 million.

From the beginning the factory was relatively efficient. In 1970, the first year of production, it managed to produce close to capacity and in 1971 it expected to make a profit. Actual production for 1971 was 274,148 hoes and 3,100 ploughs. At the same time it has had its problems. A few months after it was officially opened, there were attempts to close it on grounds that it was "not feasible." Although the firm produces items that are highly demanded in Tanzania, it has numerous marketing problems because it must compete with products imported by another parastatal.

The labour force is quite young; most of the employees completed primary school and went through the national service before they were recruited. This is an asset for organisational and mobilisational purposes. Moreover, the expertise and capital were provided by the Chinese, and the manager as well as his second-in-command are both former trade union leaders. Together these represent suitable conditions for the firm to be "managed politically," as the personnel officer remarked to me. About half the employees were TANU members and enrolment in the militia was close to 100%.

Needless to say there is both a TANU Branch and a Workers' Committee. However, the Chairman and Secretary of the Party branch, both elected by the members, are the General Manager and his second-in-command, the Personnel Officer, respectively. However well-meaning the incumbents may be, it is difficult to envisage how the party can play a militant role among the workers if it is led by the top bureaucrats.

According to the firm's Party Secretary, the function of TANU is "to see that TANU policies are adhered to in the firm." There are no specific activities the Party carries out, apart from occasional meetings, but the Secretary argued that all activities done there by any organ in the final analysis are TANU functions. Thus TANU does all!

According to the Chairman, i.e. the Manager, the committee has been discussing the possibility of appointing "Party Commissars" in each section. These would undergo some training and then would be charged with "reporting on any problems in their respective sections."

However, workers at UFI do not passively submit to complete manipulation by the leadership of the factory. There are frequent mass rallies at the factory, an unknown thing in most factories. The Manager addresses them in his many capacities as General Manager, Chairman of the Party, Chairman of the Workers' Council, etc. The Workers' Committee is of course in charge of "discipline" as per the Security of Employment Act. Its Chairman is an assistant accountant.[11] Because of the trade union background of the management, the committee has been integrated into the decision making processes so that it does not conceive of itself as an organ of the workers for fighting against the employers.

The UFI Workers' Council

This factory became the first in the country to form its Council on the 16th of October, 1970. At its first meeting on the day following the elections, the Chairman of the Council, i.e. the General Manager, "strongly warned the members of the Council against disclosure of whatsoever is discussed in the meeting to non-members."[12]

For the first time the public's attention was drawn to these councils and several letters were published in the press on the issue. Many people seem to have been baffled by the idea of making the General Manager of the firm chairman of the first Council—not being aware that this is what the regulations required. It was of course paradoxical that the major point raised at the first meeting of the Council should be the question of secrecy, when the very purpose of the Council was the involvement of the workers in all decision making processes.

Thus, a few days after the Council's formation the Party daily newspaper, the *Nationalist*, carried a reader's letter which asked "whose interests the council served." The letter criticised the fact that the Manager was Chairman of the Council, that the Council met only twice yearly, and that the Chairman in the first meeting warned members neither to discuss their personal grievances nor to disclose topics discussed in the meetings to non-members.

Nevertheless, because of the rather political nature of the firm's management, the implementation of the Presidential Circular at the firm has been more flexible than the circular demands. In order to increase the element of democracy and participation, the firm's procedural rules have established that the Workers' Council shall meet quarterly and not twice yearly and that other bodies shall be created to maximise the participation of the workers in decision making.

According to the Chairman of the Council, the experience gained at the factory indicates that it is not easy to work with just one organ, the Council, and that more commitees must be formed to act as standing/working committees of the council. Thus an extra five committees (not provided for in the Presidential Circular) have been set up at UFI to deal with various management for Planning, Production, Education, Canteen Management, and Welfare Activities.

The committees, however, are rather top-heavy with bureaucrats. It is surprising, for example, that no ordinary workers serve on the Planning and Production Committees. Presumably, these committees are considered too "technical" for the workers. Yet the short experience of the UFI has proved that the workers are capable of understanding all matters involving production, a process they themselves carry out any way.

To illustrate, I shall give two outstanding instances. In preparing the annual production plan for 1971, the Planning Committee had endorsed the draft prepared by the "experts." The draft in turn was examined by the Council before being forwarded to the Board of Directors for final approval. The Board is little more than a rubber stamp on such matters. One of the workers suggested that many of the "income" items were grossly underestimated and produced a scheme for increasing such incomes. These were incorporated by the "experts" into the final plan with the result that the estimated income on scrap metal increased fourfold, from Shs. 20,000 to 80,000. Later a group of workers devised a scheme for cutting drastically the firm's expenditure on water by using a pipe system to recirculate the water utilised. The technicians approved the scheme.

This, in my mind, affirms Fanon's view that the workers are capable of understanding the so-called technical matters of their work if given the opportunity and that they can be very creative and innovative if the proper conditions exist.

I shall not attempt to assess the significance and impact of the Council upon production, workers' attitudes and management as a whole. Such assessment is possible only after much more thorough research. Instead, I shall sketch briefly my own impressions of the dynamics of the Council at the factory.

First it seems the multiplication of committees in excess of those demanded by the Presidential Circular makes "participation" more present and dynamic. Of the workers I interviewed, all were aware of the existence of the Council and its duties. However, not all knew who their representatives were. This may be due to the existence of so many bodies, but it may also be due to lack of interaction between the representatives and the workers at large.

The Circular says simply that sections in the factory will elect representatives to the Council, but it does not go into the mechanism of communication. In the case of the UFI Council, in fact, the Council representatives I talked with tended to assume that it was not their duty to inform their constituents of what transpired in Council meetings. It was the duty of the chairman, the General Manager, to call "rallies" to inform the workers of the decisions "they ought to know." Thus every one knew who the Council Chairman was, although at least two out of the fifteen did not know the TANU Branch Chairman.

It appeared that a much better relationship existed between the management and the workers of UFI than is usual in industries generally. This may be because of the trade union background of the two top officials. Workers are more at ease with their bosses than in other industries I have visited, and the manager and his subordinates took part in many of the workers' extra curricular activities.

Yet this should not be overemphasized. The relationship between the managers and the workers remains one of "business boss" and "factory hand." The differences in incomes and the general standard of living as a whole militate against the growth of harmonious comradeship.

CONCLUSION

In Tanzania the concept of workers' participation was introduced as a follow-up to the Arusha Declaration and the nationalisation measures. But while nationalization was based on a philosophical conception of the reorganisation of society at large, the conception of workers' participation was not. It was more of a factory-level phenomenon. Participation at the factory-level was not conceived as a part of a system of new social relations, a method of "democratising the revolutionary process," to use Castro's phrase.

The Presidential directive for the establishment of Workers' Councils underscores this conception. It starts with a long quotation from a speech by President Nyerere in which he urged that workers be given information about the institutions in which they work. Without such information, he said, the workers can neither take "pride" in nor be "enthusiastic" about their jobs.

No attempt has been made to relate factory level participation to the more general forms of democratic control in the socio-political life of the country. Yet in this discussion I have argued that social relations in the broader context determine the relations that ultimately prevail at the micro-level.

It is well-known, however, that subsequent to the policy of Workers' Councils, other factors brought about "Mwongozo," which goes a step further than the Arusha Declaration in arguing for the "democratisation" of social processes in general. Here the question of "participation" is put in a broader context and becomes viewed as a "method of work."

It is widely recognised that the "method of work" prevailing throughout the country is not democratic. The Party, therefore, must initiate the task of instituting the required changes, for "supervising the implementation of goals" is one of its leadership functions. Thus, apart from giving guidance on the structure of the government, the Party should give guidance both on the method of work and how decisions should be reached.

This "guidance" has yet to be given by the Party[13] and we cannot here anticipate the nature it will take. Nevertheless, some issues will be relevant to the implementation of this guidance when it is finally given.

The first concerns the political strategy used in the implementation of socialism in Tanzania. Tanzania's strategy has not gone so far as to identify a "working class" that can be viewed as the chief action-agent of socialist development. The Arusha Declaration envisages a socialist society in Tanzania which is given as "one in which all people are workers." But it adds that even now Tanzania is "a nation of workers and peasants," albeit with "elements of feudalism and capitalism—with their temptations." There are many conceptual difficulties involved in identifying the key categories, difficulties which necessarily are reflected themselves in the attempts to adopt strategies and tactics.

It is obvious that these difficulties are the result of the ideological plane on which development policy in this country is based. Tanzania's "ujamaa" does not emanate from a dialectical class analysis of society. Rather it is very much "an attitude of mind" whose cultivation cannot easily be placed on the pedestal of a strategy for the purpose of analysis and evaluation.

This in my view is at once a cause and a result of the ambiguous role of TANU, particularly at its lower echelons. At the top there have been constant pronouncements that in the context of Africa can only be described as radical, but these have mostly been a result of the orientations of individuals within it, rather than of its organisational strength. At the grass-roots level, therefore, the Party position is even more precarious; activities there depend almostly solely on the qualities of isolated individuals. Party membership is amorphous: one cannot differentiate by any qualitative standard a member from a non-member, and there is not much organisational power within the body. Under these circumstances what role can TANU be expected to play at the factory-level?

As a consequence of the absence of political strategy due to the lack of a class ideological position, there has also been no conception of bureaucracy as a structural phenomenon. The tendency has been to view workers' participation not as a structural mechanism for the control of certain social strata by the class but principally as a wrong attitude which leads to wrong methods of work.

It follows, therefore, that when one reaches the factory-level, participation can only be minimal in substance. Essentially, the tasks of "management" belong to the managers, and the workers can come in only occasionally to "help" in certain fields and to quench their thirst for information on what is going on in the factory as a whole.

At UFI it was felt that the structure of participation had to be widened so as to encompass more people and generally to "democratise" all decision making processes. Such occurrences again depend on the individual traits of managers, but even then they are very seriously limited by the structures within which they have to operate.

In this regard, then, it is difficult to say that there is "control" of managers by the workers in their act of "participation." Perhaps for a long time to come, Workers' Councils will continue to be one of the major incentives and rank above all other techniques in controlling the workers.

NOTES

1. "Presidential Circular No. 1 of 1970," dated 10th February, 1970.
2. For details refer to the constitution of the Tanganyika African National Union (TANU).
3. *Jenga*, No. 8, p. 34.
4. "Guidelines on the Establishment of Workers Councils" by the National Development Corporation.
5. "Mwongozo wa TANU," para 11.
6. See W. Tordoff, *Government and Politics in Tanzania*, Dar es Salaam: East African Publishing House, 1967, pp. 137–158.
7. "Guidelines," *op. cit.*
8. A. P. Mahiga, "The Worker in Private Enterprise," (Political Science Dissertation, University College, Dar es Salaam: 1970).
9. Quoted in the *Standard*, November 9th, 1970.
10. Later it was changed slightly so that management would put forward two names before the Council which would elect the secretary by ballot.
11. Note the tendency of these positions to gravitate to white collor workers.
12. Quoted in the *Nationalist*, October, 1970.
13. At the end of the tenth independence celebrations, the President announed measures for administrative "decentralisation." These are still secret and are receiving their "final touches." This is paradoxical because according to MWONGOZO such measures should have been formulated by the Party and not by a U.S. Company, McKinsey and Company. Moreover in the spirit of MWONGOZO, they should have been publicly discussed by the people.

Women and Tanzania Agricultural Development*

LOUISE FORTMANN

Introduction

The importance of agriculture in Tanzania is obvious. Her major exports—cashews, coffee, cotton, sisal and tea—are all agricultural commodities. Self sufficiency in food and fibre is essential if the people are to be properly nourished, clothed and housed and if scarce foreign exchange is not to be spent in food imports. The vital role of women in agricultural development is recognized by all. The press as well as national and local leaders exhort women to produce more. But only a vague role for women is elaborated, and agricultural development programmes continue to be planned by men, staffed by men, and targeted at men.

The purpose of this paper is to examine the current role and status of women in both food and cash crop production and to identify the factors which affect their participation in agricultural development.

Agricultural development is a multidimensional process, dependent on appropriate technology as well as on adequate physical infrastructure, social organisation, available resources, and the prevailing world economic structure. This paper selectively focuses on the role of women in agricultural development at the level of the village and household units, particularly as they are involved in agricultural production activities. Existing national and international economic structures and relationships are taken as given. This focus seems justified for the following reasons. The immediate and often sole beneficiary of increased or diversified subsistence crop production is the peasant producer/consumer household; hence it is a unit of immediate interest. Second, although 97.8 per cent of economically active Tanzanian women are involved in agriculture, only five per cent of the agricultural employees are women.[1] That is, most women are involved in agricultural production within the village and household units. Moreover, it is at the level of the household and local community that many of the problems of male-female equity have their roots and must be analyzed. At the same time, it is recognized that the liberation of rural women and their assumption of a fuller role in national development requires substantive changes in both national and international economic relationships.

The predominant role of women in African agriculture antedates recorded history. Baumann[2] credits women with the invention of hoe culture. Goody and Buckley[3] in a study of 279 African societies found that women not only did all the household tasks but also performed the major share of cultivation in 45 per cent of them. In 53 per cent of the 232 sub-Saharan societies in the sample, women were the primary cultivators. Boserup[4] reports that female farming predominates in large parts of southeastern and eastern Africa. In Botswana women do nearly 75 per cent of all crop work and are responsible for plowing, weeding, bird scaring, harvesting and threshing activities.[5] Data from Malawi show that in some places women do more work than men on *both* cash and food crops.[6]

Tanzanian agriculture is no exception to this pattern. Women have traditionally played a major role in agricultural production. In a survey including the Hehe, Edgerton[7] found that nearly a third of both men and women agreed that a girl's first useful task is to farm. Swantz[8] reports that among the Zaramo, women grow all the rice. Turu women are responsible for growing food crops and may forbid their husbands to sell these crops.[9] Gogo women produce and control the use of their own grain.[10] Virgin land is traditionally cultivated by Haya women who also weed permanent plantations.[11] The workday of Haya women, often double that of men, includes nearly total responsibility for the foodcrops grown in fields outside the village proper.[12] Among the Wameru, women do most of the work with maize including cultivating, planting, weeding and thinning; they share the harvesting with the men. Among the Waarusha, women plant and harvest maize with the men but do all the weeding themselves. Women are responsible for milking the family cows among the Arusha and the Iraqw. Iraqw women do most of the farm work, although male work parties may weed or harvest in return for *pombe*.

The role of women in agriculture is not limited to food crops. Cash crops are normally considered the property of men. Men control the money received from them although the wives do much of the work.[13] Women are usually assigned the tedious tasks of weeding and thinning. Data from two cotton growing villages in Morogoro Region show that on every occasion a male farmer worked in his shamba, his wife worked with him.[14] Among the Wameru, women do most of the cultivating, weeding and harvesting of coffee. Men do all the selling and keep most of the money. Waarusha women mulch the coffee plants. In the Kilombero Valley women are outgrowers for the local sugar company.

Women are also involved in ujamaa cash crop production, providing most of the labour force. In the tea and tobacco producing villages of Mufindi and Njombe Districts, women comprise as high as 90 per cent of the wajamaa. Over two-thirds of the members in twelve out of twenty-four sample villages were women.[15] Data from other areas suggest that this is a national pattern. According to Bugengo,[16] 57 to 59 per cent of the adult population of Butiama village in Mara Region

*ERB paper 78.4.

were women. Even where male wajamaa outnumber female wajamaa, the women do most of the shamba work, as observed by Mapolu[17] in Mwanza District and Lewin[18] in Matetereka village in Ruvuma Region.

The participation of women, then, is essential to both communal and individual food and cash crop production. But the prevailing image (and also the model from which agricultural project planners apparently work) of female agricultural producers is often that women are ignorant, passive, traditional cultivators. The extent to which this is true would have considerable impact on the kinds of agricultural development programmes which are possible or necessary. Therefore, it is necessary to examine closely the nature of the participation of women, particularly in regard to improved agricultural technology. To this end the following questions are raised: are women using improved farming practices? What do women know about improved farming practices? To what degree are women involved in on-the-farm decision making?

WOMEN IN AGRICULTURE

Are Women Using Improved Farming Practices?

Women are using improved farming techniques. One place they are using them is on ujamaa shambas where they provide most of the labour. In many villages the Bwana Shamba's recommendations are followed on the ujamaa shamba, if nowhere else, as a means of ensuring continued government attention and assistance.[19] In the past inputs have been provided free to ujamaa shambas. Hence female wajamaa are often likely to have had experience with the use of fertilizers, insecticides and even herbicides as well as with proper spacing, improved varieties and so on.

Women's use of improved practices is not limited to village shambas. In a study in Morogoro and Arusha Regions, male and female farmers were compared on a "good maize practices" score which consisted of planting at the proper time, using improved seeds, using fertilizer or manure as recommended, using insecticide as recommended, following the spacing recommendation, and using herbicide or following the weeding recommendation. The farmers were divided into two groups—those who purchased at least one improved input (seeds, fertilizer, insecticide, herbicide) and those who did not. The results, as shown in Table 1,[20] indicate that although there were statistically significant differences between purchasers and non-purchasers, there were no statistically significant differences between male and female farmers in either group. A confidence interval for the difference between means was calculated in an effort to determine (with 95 per cent certainty) the highest possible difference in favour of men. The maximum possible differences of male scores above female scores on a 15 point scale were as follows:

Arusha Purchasers	1.44
Arusha Non-Purchasers	.98
Morogoro Purchasers	2.87
Morogoro Non-Purchasers	1.51

TABLE 1: COMPARISON OF MALE AND FEMALE GOOD MAIZE PRACTICE SCORES (BY REGION AND PROGRAMME PARTICIPATION), N=485

	Average Scores		
Arusha	*Males*	*Females*	*t*
Purchasers	9.88	9.88	0.00008
Non-Purchasers	4.09	4.17	0.125
-statistic	9.38***	7.39***	
Morogoro			
Purchasers	6.81	5.83	0.856
Non-Purchasers	4.08	3.55	0.896
-statistic	4.07***	3.34***	

*** Significant at .001 level

These differences indicate at most a difference in the use of one item out of twelve. Thus the greatest possible difference between men and women compatible with the data is still too small to be of substantial importance. Moreover, in all cases there is a significant possibility that women are actually using more improved practices than men. The approximate probability that women's scores were actually higher than men's was estimated using the normal curve. As shown below, particularly in Arusha Region, it was quite possible that women's scores were actually higher.

Arusha Purchasers	50%
Arusha Non-Purchasers	55%
Morogoro Purchasers	19%
Morogoro Non-Purchasers	18%

The data show neither statistically nor substantively significant differences between the good maize practices scores of men and women. Thus it can be said with reasonable confidence that the male non-purchasers were as traditional as the female non-purchasers, while the female purchasers were as progressive as the male purchasers.

Women comprised only 8 per cent of the purchasers in the sample village.[21] However, as the data presented later in Table 4 show, women are involved in significant numbers in all farming operations. Therefore the wives of male purchasers most probably also utilized the improved technology while working in the household shamba. Data on cotton production also show that women perform the same tasks as men, including "modern" tasks such as applying insecticide and fertilizer.[22]

The ability of women to use these new technologies is demonstrated by a study of Vihiga Division in Western Kenya in which 38 per cent of the farms were managed by women. Not only did these women manage their own farms but they also obtained 6.6 per cent more output at the mean level of input use than the men.[23] There is simply no question but that women are already involved in using new technologies effectively.

What do Women know about Improved Farming Practices?

Some maintain that women are only mechanically doing what their husbands tell them to do without understanding the process. The evidence does not support this. In the maize study described above farmers were asked what the Bwana Shamba recommended about maize production. The comparison of the resulting knowledge scores are presented in Table 2. As expected, there are statistically significant differences between purchasers and non-purchasers. There are also statistically significant differences between male and female non-purchasers (and therefore non-users of most practices). These probably reflect differences in contact with extension agents as discussed below. However, among purchasers (and presumably users) of improved inputs, there were no statistically significant differences between males and females.

TABLE 2: COMPARISON OF MALE AND FEMALE KNOWLEDGE SCORES (BY REGION AND PROGRAMME PARTICIPATION), N=485

	Average Scores		
	Males	*Females*	*t*
Arusha			
Purchasers	4.91	4.81	0.104
Non-Purchasers	2.38	0.96	2.921**
t	5.00***	8.50***	
Morogoro			
Purchasers	4.21	2.93	1.692
Non-Purchasers	1.96	0.85	3.126**
t	5.41***	6.38***	

** Significant at .01 level
*** Significant at .001 level

The largest possible difference of male scores over female scores was calculated to be 1.62 for Arusha purchasers and 2.53 for Morogoro purchasers. The approximate probability that women's scores were actually higher than men's was estimated to be 45 per cent for Arusha purchasers. The notably weaker showing of Morogoro women can probably be attributed to lower extension contact as discussed below.

In an additional sample, one wife of each of 69 male purchasers was also interviewed. The data on knowledge of improved maize practices from these 69 couples are presented in Table 3. A significantly greater number of husbands than wives knew about the weeding recommendation (x^2 significant at .01) and the recommendation for army worm (x^2 significant at .05). Similarly the number of husbands who knew the recommendations for stalk borer and herbicide use was statistically significantly greater than the number of wives who knew. For other recommendations there were no statistically significant differences between husbands and wives. Since other data show that the weeding recommendations are generally followed, only in knowledge about the use of chemical pesticides do the lower scores of women have practical significance.

Traditionally the agricultural knowledge of women was recognized in that it was often the woman who taught her sons and daughters how to farm. The data presented here indicate that many women do know about improved agricultural practices, some women knowing as much or more than their husbands. This is particularly notable since, as will be discussed below, women have fewer contacts with sources of agricultural information.

To What Degree are Women Involved in Farming Decisions?

Although some agricultural practices are dictated by outside factors—government policy, weather, world market prices, availability of resources and so on—there is a wide variety of day-to-day decisions at the village and household levels in which women could be more fully involved.

At the family level although the man is often thought of as the decision-maker, the woman is in fact involved

TABLE 3: A COMPARISON OF HUSBANDS' AND WIVES' KNOWLEDGE OF RECOMMENDED MAIZE PRACTICES, N=69 COUPLES

	Households Where no One Knows	Only Husband Knows		Only Wife Knows		Both Know		Total Knowing	
		No.	%	No.	%	No.	%	No.	%
Planting Time	22	13	27.6	5	10.6	29	61.7	47	100
Variety (seed)	23	6	13.0	2	4.3	38	82.6	46	100
SA/CAN	39	8	26.7	1	3.3	21	70.0	30	100
TSP Use	39	10	33.3	0	0	20	66.7	30	100
Spacing	25	12	27.2	4	9.1	28	63.6	44	100
Weeding	25	17	36.2	2	4.2	25	59.6	44	100
Stalkborer	45	11	45.8	1	4.2	12	50.0	24	100
Army Worm	47	13	59.1	2	9.1	7	31.8	22	100
Herbicide	64	4	80.0	0	0	1	20.0	5	100

TABLE 4: PER CENT OF HOUSEHOLDS IN WHICH AGRICULTURAL PRODUCTION TASKS ARE DONE BY WOMEN

Task	Households where task is done by woman alone	Households where task is done by woman with others	Households where woman does not do task	Total No.	Total %
Maize					
Cultivating	34.9	53.5	11.6	189	100
Planting	42.2	53.9	3.9	180	100
Thinning	40.2	58.5	1.3	159	100
Weeding	40.1	56.5	3.4	177	100
Applying Fertilizer	80.4	19.6	0	46	100
Applying Insecticide	58.6	38.0	3.4	29	100
Harvesting	41.9	53.1	5.0	160	100
Scaring Animals	28.8	45.1	26.1	111	100
Other Crops					
Cultivating	40.6	56.4	3.0	101	100
Planting	41.4	56.6	2.0	99	100
Thinning	40.2	57.7	2.1	97	100
Weeding	41.7	55.2	3.1	96	100
Applying Fertilizer	45.8	54.2	0	24	100
Applying Insecticide	25.0	68.7	6.3	16	100
Scaring Birds	36.9	50.8	12.3	65	100
Pruning	42.1	53.9	4.0	76	100
Harvesting	43.4	52.3	4.3	92	100

in decision making. First of all, she makes many practical decisions in the shamba. The husband may decide to use fertilizer, but the wife in her actions decides how much will be put on what plants and when (see Table 4). In practical terms her on-the-farm decisions are at least as important as her husband's.

Women also make decisions on their own shambas. In addition, heads of households—single women, divorcees, widows, as well as women whose husbands work away from home—make most on-the-farm decisions about agriculture. A rough estimate calculated from the 1967 census would indicate that approximately 25 per cent of Tanzanian women are female heads of households.[24] With the addition of married women whose husbands are absent, this amounts to a large number of female full-time on-the-farm-decision makers who are in need of good agricultural information.

As shown above, many women know as much or more about agricultural practices as their husbands and they make agricultural decisions on a daily basis in the household shambas. Moreover, they are capable of making prompt and firm decisions for the village. A striking example of this occurred in an Iringa village where the women saved the village from an embarrassing court case by raising enough money with pombe brewing to pay a plowing bill unwisely incurred by the men.[25]

Nonetheless, up to now women's involvement in village decision making, including agricultural decision making, has been negligible. In Mapolu's Mwanza study only 13.5 per cent of the villages had more than 30 per cent female committee members, 27.5 per cent had ten per cent or a fewer and 27.5 per cent had none. Those women who did serve on committees were concentrated in "female" areas such as education and culture, health and the community shop.[26] Of 15 Iringa villages, no women served on the village development committee in four villages; and only one in six villages.[27] In a study of five villages in the Usambaras, Sender found that even in villages where women outnumbered the men two to one, no women served on village committees and women rarely attended village meetings.[28] Even where women attended meetings they often do not dare to speak except to agree with their husbands.

This exclusion of women from ujamaa committees and hence from village decision making is a carry over from traditional male-female roles which today embody negative attitudes about women. This exclusion means that much potential talent is wasted at considerable loss to the community.

Women's Enabling Function in Agriculture

In addition to women's major direct involvement in agriculture, their indirect contribution to agriculture in the form of household maintenance often goes unrecognised. Men are free to devote their full attention, should they choose, to income generating activities, including agriculture, because women maintain the household and nurture the children with, at best,

TABLE 5: PER CENT OF HOUSEHOLDS IN WHICH HOUSEHOLD TASKS ARE DONE BY WOMEN

Task	Households where task is done by woman alone	Households where woman works with others	Households where woman does not do task	Total No.	%
Collect Firewood	58.5	33.3	8.2	183	100
Fetch water	57.4	33.9	8.7	183	100
Gather Wood	61.5	32.3	6.2	195	100
Buy Food	58.9	21.1	20.0	180	100
Pounding	71.3	27.1	1.6	129	100
Cooking	71.4	27.8	0.8	126	100
Cleaning	71.5	26.1	2.4	123	100

assistance from older children. As can be seen in Table 5, most household work is done by the women alone.[29] This "enabling function" is often ignored when women's contribution to agriculture is discussed. (For a particularly blatant example, see Spencer).[30]

It has been clearly shown not only that women's labour is essential to both food and cash crop production in Tanzania, but also that significant numbers of women are on-the-farm decision makers either in managing their own shambas or in implementing the decisions of others. An effective agricultural development strategy must include all agricultural workers. Hence, in a productive agricultural plan women's involvement must be given institutional recognition and acted upon. It will be necessary both to identify the factors which prevent women from contributing fully to agricultural development in their own right, not just as the unpaid labourers of their husbands and fathers, and to remedy them. In addition to the more general problems faced by men—unavailability of inputs, low prices, lack of credit, a chaotic marketing system—women face a special set of problems. These can be summed up as limited access to resources—primarily land, labour and information—and the prevailing negative attitudes about women.

ACCESS TO RESOURCES

Land

The problem of access to land is in flux because of changes in traditional practices and the policy of ujamaa being implemented by the Government. However, traditional land rights still have considerable influence. There are notable differences in a woman's traditional right to land among tribal groups. A Luguru woman traditionally had the same right as a man to apply for a piece of land from her lineage.[31] Among the Waarusha, a woman may be given a piece of land by her father, a practice which was absolutely unheard of 20 years ago and which is still rare today. If she is widowed, a Mwarusha woman will receive her husband's shambas to use until she dies, at which time her sons, but generally not her daughters, inherit it. Married women do not have their own shambas. The same holds true among the Wameru, although Meru women do control the kitchen gardens and could in theory sell any surplus produce from it. However, sometimes a sure claim is a function of having a living husband around. For example, among the Haya, wives do not inherit their husbands' land and may be and are thrown off the land by their sons who do inherita[32]. A Zaramo woman, on the other hand, can inherit property from her husband or her parents, although it is not unlikely that some enterprising male relative will find a way of finagling her out of it.[33]

The issue of land is complicated by the customary law regarding permanent crops. If a person obtains land to plant a crop of maize, the land can be reclaimed after the maize is harvested. However, if a person plants a permanent crop such as coffee or coconuts, the trees remain the property of the person who planted them regardless of who owns rights to use the land where they are planted. In the case of a crop such as coffee, this effectively means that the owner of the land has lost all use of it until the coffee trees die or are cut down by the person who planted them. For this reason groups such as the UWT are unable to obtain land on which to grow crops (such as coffee) which would be much more lucrative than the maize or beans for which they can get land. In this way women and women's organizations which do not traditionally have land of their own are effectively excluded from cash crop production.

In theory ujamaa gives women access to land and to other means of production. However, as demonstrated above, it remains male dominated and women do not always benefit from it to the same degree as men. For example, because of the method of earning work points, in some villages men earn more points than women over the course of the year, despite the fact that women contribute the greater share of the work.[34] For married women, it may mean only extra work as the family ujamaa representative without any expectation of getting the benefits.[35] Hence many women express a desire for their own shamba, that is, one controlled by themselves, independent of their husbands. Women who do have land of their own are contributors to the productive effort. As a case in point, sixty-two per cent of a sample of women who purchased inputs in a maize production programme had their own land.[36] Some women have been able to obtain land either through inheritance or from their village, particularly as a result of Operation Vijiji. Other women have been able to clear land for themselves. But for some women, prostitution is the only means of raising money to purchase land, which will provide them with an independent economic base.[37] This is neither an equitable nor a desirable state of affairs. A woman should not have to attach herself permanently to a man in order to have access to the means of agricultural production. Women should have the same rights as men to land both inside and outside the marriage bond.

Labour

The availability of labour has often been identified as a limiting factor in the adoption of improved technology by African peasant farmers.[38] It is certainly a critical problem for women cultivators. Many development projects create a demand for labour, which generally must be supplied by women. It is often forgotten that the much heralded response to fertilizer which occurs in the new crop varieties also occur in weeds. In addition, the expansion of areas under cultivation with new machinery increases the amount of weeding, a task generally done by women. Poultry and livestock projects require more water, generally carried by women.[39] Proper spacing, applying fertilizer, insecticide or herbicide, thinning and pruning all require labour. But labour is not a resource that the average woman has to spare. For example, in two villages in Morogoro District women were working an average of ten hours a day.[40] Reports from other areas indicate that such a workload is typical.[41] Men can add hours to their workday more easily than women simply because their day has a larger component of leisure. A small number of additional hours are a far greater burden to a woman than to a man, a point missed by writers such as Spencer.[42] For a female head of a household, the problem is even greater, because she generally can rely on only the labour of her children at home. Thus it may be difficult for a woman to adopt an "improved" farm practice that demands more labour, whether on her own shamba or her husband's.[43]

Information

Although the Tanzanian Government has made strenuous efforts to get agricultural information to the people, women still largely depend on their husbands for access to that information. In the study of maize production described above, an information contact score was calculated for each farmer. Nine items were included in the score (see Table 7). With the exception of the female purchasers in Arusha Region, women scored significantly lower than men as shown in Table 6. The lower scores were in part due to the fact that the extension service did not reach women to the same extent as men. Only 17 per cent of the sample women in Morogoro Region and 32 per cent of the sample women in Arusha Region had been visited by an extension agent in the past year. In Morogoro Region extension agents visited a significantly larger percentage of the male purchasers (58 per cent) than female purchasers (20 per cent) (x^2 significant at the .01 level).[44]

TABLE 6: COMPARISON OF MALE AND FEMALE INFORMATION CONTACT SCORES (BY REGION AND PROGRAMME PARTICIPATION), N=485

	Males	*Females*	*t*
Arusha			
Purchasers	4.08	3.54	0.68
Non-Purchasers	2.16	1.24	2.27*
t	4.33***	5.73***	
Morogoro			
Purchasers	5.18	2.87	2.52**
Non-Purchasers	4.66**	2.89**	

*Significant at .05 level
**Significant at .01 level
***Significant at .001 level

Even within the same family, women have less contact with sources of agricultural information than do men. Data on contact with sources of agricultural information from the sample of 69 purchasers and one wife of each are presented in Table 7. There were statistically significant differences between husbands and wives for the following items: knows Bwana Shamba's name, attends Bwana Shamba meetings, discusses maize practices with others (x^2 significant at .01 level for all items); attends farming demonstration, reads *Ukulima wa Kisasa*, listens to *Mkulima wa Kisasa* (x^2 significant at .05 level). In the households which had contact with sources of information, the per cent of husbands contacted ranged from 1.3 to 2.8 times greater than the per cent of wives contacted. Likewise in the households where a given recommendation was known, the per cent of husbands knowing the recommendation varied from 1.1 to 5 times the per cent of wives knowing it. The similarity in the magnitude of differences between husbands and wives on these two measures seems to indicate that the reduced contact of women with sources of agricultural information does result in reduced knowledge and presumably in some instances non-use of improved practices. It is evident that husbands are less than one hundred per cent effective in transmitting the knowledge they have to their wives.

It is interesting to note that the cases in which over ten per cent of the contacts were made with the wife only occurred when the item required individual initiative—going to a demonstration, reading the agricultural magazine, listening to the radio, going to see a film. This kind of active search for information by women has been noted in other instances, such as the

TABLE 7: COMPARISON OF HUSBAND'S AND WIFE'S CONTACT WITH SOURCES OF AGRICULTURAL INFORMATION (N=69 COUPLES)

Item	Households with no Contact	Husbands Only No	Husbands Only %	Wife Only No.	Wife Only %	Both No.	Both %	Total with Contact No.	Total with Contact %
Knows Bwana Shamba's Name*	24	24	53.4	1	2.2	20	44.4	45	100
Visited by Bwana Shamba	31	9	23.7	0	0	29	76.3	38	100
Attended Bwana Shamba Meeting*	27	22	52.4	3	7.1	17	40.5	42	100
Attended Farming Demonstration**	35	16	47.0	4	11.8	14	41.2	34	100
Discussed Maize Recommendation*	16	20	37.7	4	7.5	29	54.8	53	100
Demonstration Plot in Village	44	10	40.0	2	8.0	13	52.0	25	100
Listens to Mkulima wa Kisasa**	35	17	50.0	5	14.7	12	35.3	34	100
Reads Ukulima wa Kisasa**	53	11	68.7	2	12.5	3	18.8	16	100
Has Seen Maize Film	51	9	50.0	3	16.7	6	33.3	18	100

*x^2 significant at .01 level
**x^2 significant at .05 level

fact that women comprise 55 per cent of the enrollment in adult literacy classes.[45]

Part of the reason women have little contact with sources of information is that the extension service is almost exclusively male. Hence it is subject to traditional constraints on male/female interaction and conditioned by the prevailing negative attitudes about women. The reason most extension agents are male is that women have not been included proportionately in agricultural training at all levels. (This state of educational affairs has its roots in colonial times when "a policy of training good housewives was pursued."[46]) In addition, those women who are trained are often not sent to the field.

In 1968 women constituted only 3 per cent of the trainees at farmer training courses at Hombolo. In 1969 they made up an estimated 16 per cent of the trainees from Mpwapwa.[47] Even today Folk Development Colleges are built without provisions either for nursing mothers or for child care facilities with which women could more easily attend. Less than 1 per cent of the students sent out of Tanzania for agricultural training from 1966 to 1970 were women. In 1975 only 25 per cent of the graduates of the Agricultural Training Institutes were women. Twenty-five per cent of the women who were enrolled studied at Chakula Bora where they specialized in nutrition, traditionally a "women's subject".[48] With the institution of mature entry into the university, female enrollment at the Faculty of Agriculture and Forestry dropped from a high of 21 per cent in the 1974/75 first year class to a low of 6 per cent of the first year class of 1976/77. This has been somewhat alleviated by the reinstitution of direct university entry for women.

CONCLUSION

It has been shown that women play the primary role in the production of food and cash crops. Yet because of the secondary role of women in society, the organisation of that production is neither efficient nor equitable.

The inefficiency arises from the fact that women, who do most of the work, particularly in food crop production, have limited access to those resources, especially information and land, which would allow them to become more productive. This differential access is based not on ability (indeed, it has been shown that female producers are, other things being equal, at least as able as men), but on accepted social norms and customs. Similarly, the heavy work load already imposed on women often prevents them from adopting improved technology that requires additional labour inputs. Thus the present village and household organisation of labour limits the potential for increasing production. This is reinforced by the fact that often there is little encouragement for men, who often have leisure time, to use it productively.

The inefficiencies noted above stem from the deeply rooted inequities, which the introduction of export crop cultivation has reinforced. It has been shown that women bear a disproportionately large share of the work. Moreover, they are largely excluded from the monetary benefits of their labour and agricultural production in general. They comprise only a small fraction of the paid agricultural labour force. Because of traditional rules of land tenure relatively few women are able to undertake cash crop production in their own right. Those who work on their husbands' cash crops rarely receive a proportionate share of the proceeds. This exclusion from monetary income in turn retards their exercise of independent activity and minimizes any power they might seek to exercise.

The dominant position of men at the village and household level is reinforced by a range of formal and informal institutions which render it relatively impervious to official programmes of change. The durability of the unequal and inefficient organisation of work is indicated by the ability of the system to continue under the policy of ujamaa with its basic philosophical underpinning of human equality.[49]

The Party and Government have made significant efforts to promote the equality of women in Tanzania. However, a number of steps could be taken to alleviate the problems identified in this paper. The first are a series of measures to reduce the inefficiencies in the organisation of production.

If the efforts of women are to be utilized effectively, agricultural development programmes must be addressed directly to women as well as to men and action must be taken to meet women's special problems as producers.

A basic problem which must be addressed, if the other measures are to be efficacious, is the negative attitudes towards women. These attitudes underlie the notion that women should not assert themselves in public, that girls belong at home, that women can not reason as well as men.[50] As a consequence girls are kept out of school, women who assert themselves in village affairs are harrassed, men complain when women are appointed to important political positions, and in general the public role and achievements of women are denigrated. Such attitudes are destructive of persons and impede development. They perpetuate inequitable structures, retard agricultural production and undermine the building of a socialist society. It is not enough to hope that these attitudes will die out with the passing of the older generation. Their elimination requires a concerted effort to change those structures which tend to perpetuate them. Laws have been passed to remove official discrimination against women, but abuses continue. More might be done to correct the most blatant forms of discrimination, and such practices must be vigorously combatted in the press, on the radio and in the schools. If more women were placed in positions of responsibility and influence, their capabilities would be publicly demonstrated.

To provide equal access to information will require major institutional change which will allow women direct access to agricultural information, rather than the present system of indirect access through male intermediaries. A first step could be to increase the number of women enrolled in agricultural training at all levels. A cadre of well trained female agriculturalists, from the level of *Bibi Shamba* to the highest levels of Kilimo, could design and staff agricultural development programmes to be targeted at both men and women.

Tanzanian male agricultural administrators often assert that female extension staff cannot work effectively in the field. There appears too little evidence to support such a view. On the contrary, a programme using female extension agents in Botswana has been highly successful. The women were no less energetic than their male counterparts and were accepted and respected by both male and female farmers.[51]

Tanzanian female government workers and administrators at all levels are convinced that women could work effectively in the extension service. They point out that women from another tribe could be more effective in those areas where women have particularly low status. They feel that men, who have worked with women in positions such as *Katibu Kata*, Area Commissioner and Regional Commissioner, would rapidly adjust to female extension workers. Moreover, they say, women would be able to communicate better with other women and thereby help them to identify and overcome their problems. One of the relatively few Bibi Shambas in Tanzania reported good working relations with both male and female farmers. Farmers of both sexes approached her for advice. In her opinion she communicated with female farmers much better than most Bwana Shambas did, and she was able to work as effectively as a Bwana Shamba with male farmers.[52]

Another useful measure would be to make child care facilities available in the folk development colleges, thereby enabling more women to attend agricultural courses there. A greater emphasis on non-residence courses also would allow more women to learn improved farming practices directly, rather than indirectly through someone else. In addition, agriculturally oriented teaching material (some already exists) could be used in adult literacy classes where women comprise most of the participants.

Until men assume a greater share of the workload, women could ease their burden somewhat by organising their work (both domestic and agricultural) cooperatively among themselves. For example, among the Haya, women's work groups (*vyama*) meet to work on members' shambas on a voluntary reciprocal basis.[53] In an Arusha ujamaa village meals for all shamba workers, male and female, are prepared by the sick and the old, women of course, who cannot go to the field to work. Such cooperative labour forms could be more widely adopted. In addition, the spread of piped water and mechanical grinding mills would ease the workload of women considerably.

In theory the problem of access to land could be resolved if the government policy on the right of all citizens, women as well as men, to the use of land were implemented.[54] In practice this often proves to be difficult. The measures would ensure that the abilities of women were more effectively utilized. Women should become involved in cash crop production either in their own right as independent producers or cooperatively through ujamaa and such organisations as *Umoja wa Wanawake* (UWT). The advantage of cash crop production is that it provides women with cash income, thereby allowing them greater independence and enabling them to meet the needs of their household. This is particularly crucial. Often men contribute little to household expenses such as food, household utensils, school uniforms and medicine.

Thus the women must find some means of obtaining income to meet these needs, and access to a shamba or other means of employment is crucial. The UWT could become directly involved in agricultural production rather than in more traditionally "female" projects such as running hotels and weaving baskets. Some UWT branches have already begun this. Unfortunately production on UWT shambas is often no better (although it is also no worse) than average peasant production. Greater effort must be made to utilize these shambas productively.

The experience and knowledge of women could be more systematically utilized on ujamaa shambas. This could be achieved by stipulating that half of all committee members be women. To ensure that the women members are not weak or silent, female cadres might give them special training to help them gain the confidence required to speak out publicly and to deal effectively with business matters.

The urgency of national development makes it imperative that women's talent and experience be utilized at every level of government decision making. Given the prevailing male attitudes toward women and the role that women play in the household and on the farm, it is essential that women's programmes be planned and staffed by women to ensure that they succeed. Moreover, given the shortage of trained personnel, capable women should be appointed to high level government jobs. They already hold top level posts in many government ministries; there is no reason why they should not also do so in Kilimo.

Many of these measures would alleviate some of the immediate effects of discrimination against women with its consequent inequity and inefficiency. Yet they leave untouched the more fundamental issue of power and control of the means of production. As long as women are systematically excluded from positions of decision making and power at every level of government, there is little hope that they will win greater equity. Legal rights to formal power (e.g. the right to vote and hold office) are meaningless so long as the structures of discrimination and oppression continue. These are an integral part of national and international structures of economic relationships in which the weak and powerless are marginalized.

Changes in the economic relationships in a society are not sufficient in and of themselves to put power into the hands of women and thus raise their status. This has been amply demonstrated in China.[55] Such changes, however, are necessary steps, for without them, other institutional changes (such as increased representation of women in the educational and extension systems) and reform at the household and village levels amount to mere tinkering and will have only minimal impact. Ultimately these relationships of power and the control over the means of production throughout the society must be transformed if women are to have a more effective and equitable role in the processes of development and in the establishment of a socialist society in Tanzania.

NOTES

1. C. Koley, "Agricultural Data", in Bertil Egero and Roushdi A. Henin (eds.), *The Population of Tanzania*, Census Volume t, 1973. Dar es Salaam: BRALUP and Bureau of Statistics, pp. 149–155.
2. H. Baumann, "The Division of Work According to Sex in African Hoe Culture," *Africa*, 1928 1(3), pp. 289–319.
3. J. Goody and J. Buckley, "Inheritance and Women's Labour in Africa," *Africa*, 1973, 43 (2), pp. 108–121.
4. E. Boserup, *Woman's Role in Economic Development*, London: George Allen and Unwin Ltd., 1970, pp. 17–21.
5. C. A. Bond, "Women's Involvement in Agriculture in Botswana," 1974, Mimeo, p. 13.
6. B. A. Clark, "The Work Done by Rural Women in Malawi", *Eastern Africa Journal of Rural Development*, 1975, Vol. 8 (1 and 2), pp. 80–91.
7. R. B. Edgerton, *The Individual in Cultural Adaptation: A Study of Four East African Peoples*, Berkeley: The University of California Press, 1971, p. 145.
8. Marja-Liisa Swantz, *Ritual and Symbol in Transitional Zaramo Society*, Uppsala: Gleerup, 1970, p. 61.
9. H. K. Schneider, *The Wahi Wanyaturu*, Chicago: Aldine Publishing Company, 1970, p. 62.
10. P. Rigby, *Cattle and Kinship among the Gogo*, Ithaca, New York: Cornell University Press, 1969, p. 61.
11. B. Bakula, "The Effect of Traditionalism on Rural Development: The Case of Omurunazi Ujamaa Village, Bukoba," Political Science Paper 6: Dissertation, 1969, University College, Dar es Salaam, p. 5.
12. Marja-Liisa Swantz, "Women's Work Is Double," *Daily News*, 1975.
13. M. J. Mbilinyi, "The State of Women in Tanzania," *Canadian Journal of African Studies*, 1972, 6 (2), pp. 371–377
14. C. D. S. Bartlett, Department of Rural Economy, Faculty of Agriculture and Forestry, University of Dar es Salaam. Unpublished Data.
15. J. DeVries and L. Fortmann, "A Study of Ujamaa Villages in Iringa Region," prepared for the UNDP/FAO Planning Team for the Iringa 3rd Five Year Plan, 1974, Mimeo., pp. 6–10.
16. J. Bugengo, "Ujamaa in Mara Region," in *Proceedings of the Annual Social Science Conference of the East African Universities*, 18–20 December (Dar es Salaam) 1973, p. 3.
17. H. Mapolu, *The Social and Economic Organization of Ujamaa Villages*, Unpublished Masters Thesis, University of Dar es Salaam, 1973, pp. 163–64.
18. R. Lewin, "Matetereka," *Mbioni*, 5 (3), pp. 21–25.
19. J. DeVries and L. Fortmann, "A Study of Ujamaa Villages in Iringa Region," *op. cit.*, pp. 19–92.
20. Tables 1, 2 and 6 are from L. P. Fortmann, "An Evaluation of the Progress of the National Maize Project at the end of One Cropping Season in Morogoro and Arusha Regions." Prepared for USAID/Tanzania, 1976. Mimeo., p. 13. Considerable statistical advice and comments on early drafts of the present paper were provided by Dr. Charles S. Whitmore, Department of Political Science, University of Dar es Salaam.
21. L. P. Fortmann, *ibid.*, p. 29.
22. C. D. S. Bartlett, *op. cit.*
23. P. R. Moock, "The Efficiency of Women as Farm Managers," *American Journal of Agricultural Economics*, 1976, 58 (5), pp. 831–835.
24. United Republic of Tanzania, Bureau of Statistics, Ministry of Economic Affairs and Development Planning. *Statistical Abstract* 1970. Dar es Salaam: Government Printer, 1972, p. 49. This estimate may be biased in that women who did not state their age or marital status were excluded from the calculation.
25. J. DeVries and L. Fortmann, *op. cit.*, p. 66.
26. H. Mapolu, *op. cit.*, pp. 166–167.
27. J. DeVries and L. Fortmann, *op. cit.*, p. 66.

29. J. Sender, "Some Preliminary Notes on the Political Economy of Rural Development in Tanzania, Based on a Case Study in the Western Usambaras," ERB Paper 74.5, University of Dar es Salaam, pp. 34–35.
29. See also J. Willis, "A Study of Time Allocation by Rural Women and Their Place in Decision Making: Preliminary Findings from Embu District," RDR Paper No. 44, Makerere University College, 1967, pp. 14–15, and 28.
30. D. Spencer, "African Women in Agricultural Development: A Case Study in Sierra Leone," OLC Paper No. 9, 1976.
31. R. Young and Henry Fosbrooke, *Smoke in the Hills*, Evanston: Northwestern University Press, 1960, p. 61.
32. Z. K. Bader, *Women, Private Property and Production in Bukoba*. Unpublished Masters Thesis. University of Dar es Salaam, 1975, pp. 40, 134; Marja-Liisa Swantz, "Women's Economic Position in Relation to Marital Status," *Daily News*, 1975.
33. Marja-Liisa Swantz, *op. cit.*, 1970, pp. 96–97.
34. H. Mapolu, *op. cit.*, pp. 167–168.
35. Z. K. Bader, *op. cit.*, p. 121.
36. L. P. Fortmann, "An Evaluation . . .," p. 31.
37. M-L. Swantz, "Women's Economic Position . . .," *op. cit.*
38. C. J. Doyle. "Productivity, Technical Change and the Peasant Producer: A Profile of the African Cultivator," *Food Research Institute Reports*, 1974, 13 (1): 61–7.
39. E. Skjonsberg, "Patriarchy is Alive and Well," *Ceres*, 1975, 8 (2), pp. 61–63.
40. C. D. S. Bartlett, *op. cit.*
41. R. Lewin, *op. cit.*, p. 21; J. DeVries and L. P. Fortmann, *op. cit.*, p. 66; M-L. Swantz, "Women's Work . . .," *op. cit.*
42. D. Spencer, *op. cit.*
43. It should be pointed out in this regard that a technique which is ultimately labour saving, e.g. the application of herbicides using large volumes of water, may add an intolerable volume of work at the time of its use.
44. L. P. Fortmann, "An Evaluation . . .", p. 10, 30.
45. H. Kokuhira, "Towards the Socio-Economic Proportion of Rural Women in Tanzania," *Fikara*, May 1975, p. 9.
46. C. Whybrow, "Education of Africans in Iringa District," Iringa District Book, Microfilm Reel 1/9.
47. D. Z. Mwaga, "The Impact of Farmers' Training in the Rural Area: Mpwapwa," Political Science 7 (2): Dissertations. The University of Dar es Salaam, p. 18.
48. L. P. Fortmann, "The Need for an Expanded Role . . .," *op. cit.*, p. 101.
49. Julius K. Nyerere, *Ujamaa: Essays on Socialism*, Dar es Salaam: Oxford University Press, 1968, p. 78.
50. Marjorie J. Mbilinyi. *The Education of Girls in Tanzania*, Dar es Salaam: Institute of Education, 1969, p. 43; Marja-Liisa Swantz, *op. cit.*, 1970, p. 141; J. DeVries and L. P. Fortmann, *op. cit.*, p. 66–67.
51. C. A. Bond, Personal Communication, 1976.
52. R. Kalinga, Personal Communication, 1977.
53. Z. K. Bader, *op. cit.*, p. 62.
54. Julius K. Nyerere, *op. cit.*, p. 8.
55. For more discussion of the relationship between economic structures and the oppression of women, see M. Mbilinyi, "Women: Producers and Reproducers in Underdeveloped Capitalist Systems," The Twelfth Annual Social Science Conference of East African Universities, 1976, University of Dar es Salaam.

The Health Care Sector in Tanzania*

MANUEL GOTTLIEB

Introduction

In this paper I am primarily concerned with describing the way health care is nowp rovided in Tanzania[1]. Six distinct modes of production (or sectors) of health care are distinguished and they are described in terms of the scope of their activity, the social relationships involved in production, the value of the services rendered and the relationships of each mode to the others and to the people at large whose health interests are served. There however is only one health sector: the facilities and budgets of central government.

HEALTH CARE SECTORS IN TANZANIA: THEIR ACTIVITIES AND EXPENDITURES

The Ministry of Health Sector

The dominant sector of health care services in Tanzania is organised and administered by the Ministry of Health (AFYA), which is financed primarily out of the national budget. Directly under AFYA is a network of 64 hospital institutions with 30 beds or over as of 1970. Including smaller units, as of the end of 1970 these hospitals took care of 304,362 in-patients and 5.2 million new out-patient cases. They employed a clinical and nursing staff of 1,926 persons, not including an important medical mission of Chinese doctors. During 1971 two major new reference hospital facilities with over 600 beds were opened under AFYA control and financing but jointly governed by mission-church and government. By the end of 1971 some ninety rural health centres, with average annual expenditures per centre of around Shs. 90,000 and a staff ranging from a half dozen to thirty persons, were functioning. Joined thereto was a small network of rural dispensaries, research, planning, training, public health, administrative and pharmaceutical facilities. The Ministry altogether employed in 1971/2 some 14,000 persons most of whom of course were non-clinical or nursing personnel engaged in building, maintenance, construction, public health, transport, clerical duties, kitchen and laundry work and the like.

None of these activities produced a revenue except for personal health services rendered to so called "amenity" patients in two grades (I and II formerly called "European" and "Asiatic" grades) who pay or are chargeable for a higher quality of hospital or out-patient services. For the two latest years for which audited accounts are available, some Shs. 5.8 and Shs. 4.3 million were raised by these service charges in 1969/70 and 1970/71. Exclusive of these amenity revenues, the total value of health services rendered by the Ministry (valued at budgeted cost and exclusive of grants to other health sectors or a limited amount of drug sales) for the current year (1972/73) was about 122 million shillings.

Mission and/or Religious Health Sector

The next most important health sector in mainland Tanzania is that provided by mission or religious organisations which originally were staffed, controlled and financed from abroad but which increasingly in recent years have come under the influence of Tanzanian churches. The 65 hospitals with resident doctors in 1970 had a total of 7,917 hospital beds, admitted some 163 thousand patients and treated another 800 thousand persons as out-patients. The total clinical and nursing hospital staff as of end-1970 was 826 persons. Under the supervision of these hospitals were a variety of out-stations which included bedded dispensaries, ordinary dispensaries, maternity units, facilities for leprosy and ante-natal and child welfare clinics. In 1969/70 these out-stations treated over 860 thousand new cases. The total employment of medical personnel, nursing staff, administrative and clerical workers together with orderlies and labourers numbered some 3,141 persons. This did not include some personnel wholly engaged in instructional duties.[2] Mission institutions have launched many important training schemes and provided what high quality medical service is readily available in many rural areas of mainland Tanzania. Total expenditures of mission or voluntary facilities reported for 1970/71 by 52 institutions with 7,643 estimated beds of all descriptions were Shs. 23,126 thousand for purposes of operating health facilities (not including costs of training facilities or capital costs). Of this approximately half was for salaries, a seventh for drugs and the balance for other purposes. For the 52 institutions reporting some Shs. 9.8 million were raised in medical fees and charges to patients (about 42.4% of operating expenditures). A little over Shs. 6.5 million was obtained from central government in the AFYA budget as grants and aid while the remainder was provided by outside gifts and donations.

The Local Government Health Sector

A third important network of medical facilities, the third sector of health care in Tanzania, has been organised by local governments, both urban and rural. In towns the town councils are responsible for public health and sanitation activities. These have been financed about equally from local revenues and central government grants. Since 1970 urban authorities have been receiving

*Edited version of ERB Paper 73.7.

between Shs. 6–8 million yearly on this account. In rural areas the principal form of health care activity has not been in the field of public health but through rudimentary personal health services which were rendered by a network of 1,202 dispensaries (as of end–1970) with 2,491 beds, a paid staff of 1,720 persons and an estimated budget of some Shs. 13 million. In 1970 these health services reported a total of 15 million new out-patient cases.[3,4] Although the rural population was much greater than the urban and although the financial resources of rural governments were inferior to those of urban authorities, the central government provided the rural authorities slightly less by way of grants (Shs. 6.5 million for 1970/71 and 1971/72) than they provided the urban authorities. But since the elimination in 1969 of an independent tax base for rural governments, they have become dependent virtually entirely on grants and transfers so that all of their health expenditures since 1969 have been underwritten by the central government. It is in recognition of this basic fact that under the 1972 "decentralization" programme, the network of rural dispensaries passes completely into the AFYA sector and will be administered and controlled, along with district and regional hospitals and health facilities, under "decentralized" regional and district authorities. These rural facilities for personal health care, often poorly supervised and poorly staffed, have cost on an annual basis between Shs. one and two per person and will embody in future years a potentially great strain on central government budgets.

The Industrial Health Sector

The fourth sector of health care facilities is a network of clinics, dispensaries and hospitals established by plantations and industrial firms primarily for their employees and related family dependents. In Dar es Salaam and in Arusha these facilities are provided by 81 business firms and parastatals operating on a group basis through an association established in 1967. This sector now operates and staffs a network of dispensaries and clinics together with a headquarters building in Dar es Salaam. In 1971 the system took care of 22 thousand in-patient cases and conducted over 300,000 out-patient consultations. It employed three full-time doctors and charged fees per employee averaging nearly Shs. 50 yearly. After 1971 this health service should be expanding its coverage because parastatal and public organisations, which previously had operated private dispensaries and health services, have been ordered to join the group plan or to cease employment of private physicians.[5, 6, 7] Outside Dar es Salaam and Arusha it was common for the larger estates and firms to establish their own medical facilities. At the end of 1969 these facilities included 5 hospitals and 181 dispensaries with a total of 1,028 beds, and they were served by a staff of 463 persons including 35 doctors.[8]

In 1970 the total volume of medical care paid for by 1,068 employing organisations and treated as a business expense affected some 168 thousand regular employees at a cost in 1970 of Shs. 12.1 million and using an investment in medical facilities of Shs. 3.8 million. Including dependents this health service must reach over a half a million persons in both rural and urban areas. The scope of this service has been rising rapidly for it is estimated that in the early sixties health expenditure of this kind involved only Shs. 3 million; and the reported cost of medical outlay nearly doubled between 1969 and 1970.[9]

The Private Health Sector

The fifth sector of health care in Tanzania is operated by a small army of private practitioners—doctors, dentists, retired rural medical aids seeking to capitalize on their acquired medical skills, former dispensare "dressers", nurses of varying degrees of competency and Asiatic practitioners who do not fully qualify for medical practice by western standards. Of western-trained and licensed or registered practitioners, approximately 100 were licensed or registered for private practice in mainland Tanzania at the end of 1970.[10] As a result of further socialist policies taken in 1971, many Asians in the medical field left the country. This meant that by the end of the year the number of registered or licensed practitioners working either privately or for the industrial health service fell off by a third.[11] The larger part of this decline was concentrated in purely private practice, and although emigration subsequently slackened, it has continued to be felt in months that followed.[12] All this indicates that the private practitioner sector of the health services will continue to decline over the coming years.

The shilling expenditure on private practitioners was reported in the Household Budget Survey of 1969, but the coverage of the sample was too limited to yield reliable estimates of an activity with relatively few transactions and a wide range of values.[13] For mainland Tanzania these estimates were Shs. 16.3 million and for urban and rural households Shs. 30 and 4 per household respectively. These estimates appear to be consistent with the relative usage of private practitioners in urban and rural communities. Moreover urban households utilized services of private practitioners up and down the income scale with only a slight tendency for well-to-do urban households to utilize private practitioner services more than poor urban households.[14]

The Traditional Health Sector

The sixth medical sector, the traditional doctors (*Waganga*), is probably the largest in terms of practitioners, in total revenue collected and in number of contacts with the Tanzanian population in both urban and rural areas. A recent painstaking investigation of traditional healers and diviners among the Zaramo population of Dar es Salaam has demonstrated that in the capital city of the country with its relatively high concentration of modernized medical facilities and easy access by public transportation, some 700 fulltime traditional healing methods exist.[15]

Analysis of a single day's case-load of 60 Waganga and discussion with patients waiting in mganga's chambers indicated that healing of hurts and illnesses was the predominant activity. The case-load of the 60 Waganga involved 338 patients who had medical or "illness" problems dealing with a variety of conditions: stomach problems, dizziness, fevers, tuberculosis, menstrual problems and other disorders. Transferring this ratio to an estimated 700 fulltime Waganga in Dar es Salaam leads to the inference that some 4,000 people are treated daily for illness by traditional healers in Dar es Salaam.[16]

These daily visitations to treat illness by thousands of persons involves the exchange of large sums of money. Although practitioners were reluctant to give precise information as to their charges, 29 Waganga gave relatively full information on the scheduling of charges for different medicines and procedures. Very detailed information was however received from 27 clients who listed the payments they had actually made for the treatments they received. The two sources of information corresponded. The lowest price reported for a simple divining procedure to diagnose a problem was from Shs. 2 to 4. The most expensive condition to be treated was for mental illness, presumably because of the more extended visitations required. The 27 clients paid Shs. 46 per case; payments ranged from a low of Shs. 10 to a high of Shs. 160. These fees applied to an entire treatment and not to a single visit, but even so the conclusion is inescapable that the "Waganga practicing in Dar es Salaam are exceptionally wealthy men."[17] The Economic Research Bureau Health Survey indicated similar patterns elsewhere.[18]

The Inter-relationships of the Health-care Sectors

In summary the foregoing accounts of the different sectors of health care in mainland Tanzania indicated the value of the health care provided by each sector (Table 1). For some sectors this value is gauged by budgeted costs for staff services and purchases supplies and equipment (lines 1–4). For the last two sectors, value is estimated by the amounts the people have paid practitioners for services used. For the last listed sector (traditional Waganga) the estimate is minimal and could safely be doubled or even tripled.

TABLE 1: VALUE OF HEALTH CARE, PRINCIPAL SECTORS

	Million Shs.	Year
1. Public Sector (AFYA)	127	72/3
2. Mission Sector	23	70/1
3. District Council Dispensaries and Urban Health Services	27	70
4. Industrial Health Services	12	70
5. Private Modern Practitioners	17	69
6. Traditional Waganga	20	69

If all sector estimates were brought up to the 72/3 level, then the value of health care services would approach Shs. 250 million; and if a fuller estimate of Waganga services were available, our figure would probably approach 300 million. But even as of 1969 our estimate is 80% over the level of health care outlays included in the present national accounts.

The first sector (AFYA) plays a strategic role in a number of ways. It predominates over the others in terms of employed manpower, medical facilities and cost of service. It also provides much of the finance required by the Mission and Local Government sectors and it lays down the standards by which all sectors are governed.

The various health sectors are mutually dependent in many ways. The first five sectors all draw upon a single pool of domestic scarce medical and nursing skills. All the sectors are partly dependent upon the favour of the public which in turn seeks to avoid dependence upon any one sector and seems to favour multiple access to medical care. Of the some 540 surveyed households in the ERB 1972 Health Survey, only 6.3% reported over a two-year period utilizing only one sector of medical service, usually government or mission. Nearly nine out of ten surveyed households (87%) reported use of two *or* three sectors and 6.6% of households utilized four sectors. Even in the surveyed towns with close access to a major government hospital facility with free general medical service, there was reported widespread use of mission facilities, which could be reached only by a long journey, and limited use of private practitioners and of course traditional Waganga.[19] The boundary line between "European illnesses" for which Western medical practice is superior and "African illness" for which Waganga medicines are superior is a commonly reported boundary but a shifting one. Members of the African community seem to be shifting about and experimenting with different forms and combinations of medical treatment from the different sectors, trying first the traditional methods and then the modern or in reverse order, and returning to the traditional when the modern methods seem less successful.[20]

THE MINISTRY OF HEALTH (AFYA) BUDGET

An appreciation of the role of financial limitations in providing for health care in Tanzania requires that we review the principal categories of central government health expenditures. Some necessary background information is set forth in two tables dealing with recurrent and development expenditures separately. In Table 2 estimates for recurrent expenditures for 1972 are distributed by object class of expenditure. In Table 3 a detailed account is provided of actual development expenditures for new facilities or for major improvements to old facilities during two recent years.

Not all of the expenditures brought together in Tables 2 and 3 are reduced to object class. The principal exceptions are the Shs. 21.8 million transferred as subventions and grants to other health care sectors and the development expenditures in Table 3. A little over two-thirds of the subventions and grants are received

TABLE 2: ESTIMATES FOR RECURRENT EXPENDITURE, MINISTRY OF HEALTH FISCAL YEAR BEGINNING 1 JULY 1972, BY MAJOR OBJECT CLASS (IN THOUSAND SHILLINGS)

Item	*Estimates*	*Per cent*
1. Total	154,974	100
2. Personal Emoluments (wages and salaries)	71,924	46.4
3. Hospital Supplies (Chiefly drugs)	32,895	21.2
4. Subventions and Grants (to Mission facilities and Urban councils)	21,821	14.1
5. Purchased Foodstuffs (in-patient diet)	7,724	5.0
6. Travel Allowances	2,449	1.6
7. Maintenance, Replacement and Upkeep (of plant and equipment)[a]	6,615	4.2
8. Office Expenses	4,700	3.0
9. Direct Expenses Training Operations	2,976	1.9
10. Other AFYA	3,870	2.5

Source: United Republic of Tanzania, *Financial Statement and Estimates of Revenue and Public Expenditures . . . Supply Votes and Development Expenditures*, 1972–75, pp. 204–216.

[a]This includes maintenance provided by building division of Comworks responsible for proper upkeep of public buildings and service disposal. This allotment in 1970/71 worked out to 3.6% of the appraised or book value of the property valued at 739 million shillings, while the building expenditure was 26.9 million. On Comworks records AFYA plants in 1969/70 had an appraised value of 70.2 million shillings exclusive of health centres and the two new reference hospitals. With new investment we allowed above for 3.0 million for Comworks building maintenance.

TABLE 3: ACTUAL DEVELOPMENT EXPENDITURES, MINISTRY OF HEALTH FISCAL YEARS 1969/70, 1970/71, BY MAJOR CLASS OF FACILITY (IN THOUSAND SHILLINGS)

	Fiscal Year	
Class of Facility	*1969/70*	*1970/71*
1. Institutional Housing	504	550
2. Out-patient Centres	452	829
3. Obstetric Block Muhimbili	0	2,896
4. Kitchen Equipment and Laundry Units	0	85
5. Other Major Improvements Existing Hospitals	483	1,061
6. Nutrition Services	15	291
7. Rural Health Centres	665	3,509
8. Medical Training Facilities	0	5,142
9. Vaccine Plant	0	545
10. Pathological and Research	0	1,018
11. Total	2,118	15,925

Source: Republic of Tanzania, *Estimates of Public Expenditures Consolidated Fund Services . . . and Supply Votes*, 1971/72, p. 370.

by voluntary missions and the remainder by urban governments. We do not know the utilization patterns of these institutions but it may be presumed that as a composite they are not too different from AFYA as a whole with its responsibilities for curative and preventive services. The outlays for development go to purchase the complex of inputs that go into institutional building: planning and architectural services, building materials and building labour, contracting organisations, and imported equipment and supplies including plumbing and electrical goods.

For most of these object-classes involved in providing goods and services utilized by the AFYA Health Budget it may be presumed that an increase in the AFYA Budget would be met by an increase in the quantity of goods and services utilized by the Budget. That applies above all to object-classes involved in the development budget with their claim on building activity and building resources. Turning to the recurrent budget, the same condition of ready extensibility applies to such object classes as drugs and hospital supplies (21.2% of the budget), purchased foodstuffs (5.0%), maintenance and replacement (4.2%) and travel allowances, training and office expenses (6.5%). But at what cost will this expansion of health care take place? In general terms the answer is clear. In almost all cases the costs will consist of foregoing alternative output or facilities that are ministering to other wants and needs.

FINANCIAL CAPABILITIES FOR MEETING HEALTH CARE NEEDS

What are the financial resources that may be used to finance the actual and impending needs for health care at standards now in current use or within easy grasp? Let us examine first of all the possibilities for increasing the share for health outlays in the central government budget.

We lay out in Table 4 the available record from 1956/57 to 1972/73 central government recurrent health budgets in current shillings and the share which these budgets embodied of the respective total budgets available for all government purposes. In absolute terms the growth of outlays since 1956/57 is considerable, amounting to 4.56 times in current shillings, but some of this growth merely registers inflation of basic wage and price levels. Over the decade 1960–70 for which national income accounts have been calculated, both in current and constant shillings, price slippage was 3 index points a year. If the same rate of inflation is applied to government budgets and extended back to 1956, then the real growth rate of the health budget over the 15 years period was 3.76 times.

On the receipts side the record of major revenues collected by the central government and local authorities for 1964 to 1970 shows that central government revenues have increased in the seven years by 130%, a considerably faster rate than monetary GDP, which rose over the same period by 52.5%. Direct and indirect taxes shared a similar rate of increase over the years though for somewhat different reasons (see original ERB paper, pp. 38–40).

The rise of returns from direct taxes was due to a substantial boost in rates and an acceleration of payment by adoption of pay-as-you-earn schemes for tax collection. The number of persons and firms chargeable for surtax and income tax in Tanzania has fallen since 1960 from 21.7 to 18.4 thousand. The number assessed under the personal tax has also been reduced by increasing the basic exemption so that only some 220 thousand persons are subject to the tax in 1970 compared with 1.7 million in 1961/62.[21] Income tax rates are now declared by knowledgeable observers to be "very progressive", and considering the additional impact of sales and excise taxation aimed at upper income groups, the scope for higher tax rates on upper income groups is limited. The freeze on upper bracket civil service salary schedules and regulation of salary levels in the parastatals will tend to slow up the increase in the number of taxpayers in higher income brackets. The socialization of wholesale trade, the taking over of urban rental property and the socialist orientation of the economy generally, will slow up any increase in taxable corporate profits and business or property income. Therefore, the rate of growth of direct tax revenues may very well be less in the seventies than it was in the sixties.

The increase in indirect tax revenues was continuous and substantial all through the sixties and proceeded at a faster rate than direct tax revenues, accounting in 1970 for 69% of all central government tax revenues. There has been a large absolute increase in import duties. Excise taxes have been extended to items manufactured locally. Many special services and facilities such as operation of a motor vehicle, purchase of electricity, attendance at a theatre, use of a hotel have been taxed. A general sales tax, with rates running between 10 and 20% and with food and most capital goods exempt, was introduced in 1969, partly in replacement of local government personal and product taxes being relinquished. Altogether the sales tax produced in additional revenue about 110 million shillings more than were relinquished in the abolished local levies.

However each round of indirect tax increase makes future rounds more difficult. For some products and services, an increase in excise or sales taxation which widens the gap between selling prices inside and outside of Tanzania stimulates smuggling and illegal border traffic. For other products or services, the increase in tax rates stimulates the rise of small-scale domestic bottle production as of liquors and beer or it fosters consumption of the untaxed products of cottage crafts. Yet again other products and services enter into the cost of living of large numbers of wage-earners or small-holding farmers whose interests must be carefully watched by those who make fiscal policy. For many luxury products and services consumed only by the upper income groups, an increase in already high tax rates can actually discourage purchases and lead to lower and not higher tax yields. All this does not mean that there is no margin in the seventies for raising basic schedules of indirect taxation. It only means that future boosts cannot be as productive in the seventies as in the sixties, that these boosts will be more selective and less general and that they will not produce bonanza returns.

Income from property (from rents, royalties, interest and dividends) and from what are designated as "current transfers" (from socialized enterprises, external gifts, or East African Community Corporations) are revenue sources (see original ERB paper, Table 6, p. 38). These revenue sources may well grow in importance as socialization takes hold and bears fruit.

An important new revenue source for the socialized sector was established in 1971 by the taking over in record time of some 3,000 choice urban properties, mostly combined residential-commercial-office, under the Acquisition of Buildings Act (April, 1971). This produced in the revenue estimates for 1972/73 a "transfer" of some Shs. 42.5 million and an expected "transfer" for the coming year, 1973/74, of Shs. 30 million.[22] But this choice addition to revenue sources will not be entirely a net gain in future budgets since it is subject to three major offsets because of costs for administration and maintenance, reduced income tax payments by persons who have lost their buildings, and some compensation for newer buildings.[23]

The use of domestic borrowing has accelerated in recent years partly due to utilization of the annual reserves accumulated by compulsory saving schemes (such as the National Provident Fund) but partly due to bank credit expansion, the familiar consequence of bank lending on government account. The limit to such borrowing is of course provided by the tendency of increased domestic spending released by the new credit creation running ahead of goods availabilities, generating scarcities and tendencies toward price increase or shortages. This inflationary limit was apparently reached in 1970/71. The increase in the outstanding public debt over the year 1970/71 was

TABLE 4: REVENUE SOURCES FOR THE DEVELOPMENT BUDGET MAINLAND TANZANIA 1968–1972 (MILLION SHILLINGS)

	Fiscal Years			
	1968/69	*1969/70*	*1970/71*	*1971/72*
1. Development Expenditure (excluding Tazara)	461	611	829	770*
2. Financed by:				
a. Surplus recurrent budget	84	50	52	51
b. Local borrowing	230	277	457	386
c. Other internal borrowing	24	62	50	23
d. Foreign loans & grants	123	122	270	330

*Estimate only.

reported at 32%, the debt rising to a level of Shs. 2.4 million. The Central Bank announced a state of alarm, clamped a limit on government borrowing and induced the adoption of measures of fiscal restraint by the Treasury and central planners.

The record for financing development programmes from loans and other more conventional revenue sources is set forth in Table 4. An analysis of these sources has recently been canvassed by Dr. John Loxley and we can do no better than to present his analysis in this short tabular form.

CONCLUSION

The nature of the public finance problem is now very different from what it was only a few years ago. The tax system has been thoroughly overhauled to generate maximum revenue consistent with the changing structure of the economy and with accepted principles of equity, and the nationalisation measures have ensured maximum re-investment of locally generated surpluses. These fundamental changes in revenue structure are, however, once for all measures. In future, extraction of additional revenues in excess of those provided by income growth will be a very difficult process, politically more so than economically.

We suggest a programme which not only widens access to health care financing in Tanzania but also makes it possible for the people who directly or indirectly finance health care to do so via cooperative finance. This programme is based on ability to pay and at the same time it expands the opportunity for participating in decision-making in health facilities.

The programme is based initially upon carefully considered suggestions for the imposition of charges for medical care at strategic points where charges will either promote better use of medical facilities or reduce wastage. In designing this system of charges, I have drawn upon recommendations for charges in two earlier surveys of Tanzania health care needs—that of Sir Eric Pridie in his capacity as Chief Medical Advisor to the Colonial Office in 1949 and the Titmus Committee of able British specialists who reported to Government in 1963 the results of their year-long survey of health facilities in Tanzania (Titmus, Abel-Smith, *et al.*).[24] Unlike these earlier surveys, I have combined a scheme of charges with a parallel programme of cooperative group action to raise local medical funds. These in turn are to be aided and encouraged by a substantial central government subsidy that may well vary with the needs of different cooperative groups, their resources and the health burdens they face. This plan for cooperative group action is modelled after that developed in mainland China especially for rural communities. It represents a form of social security which is not divorced from the life or control of the people and which does not automatically favour urban wage-earners and salary-receivers as do most schemes for organised social security developed in either the Western or Eastern worlds. The great advantage of this form of social security is that it (a) brings people together into cohesive cooperative groups within their capacity to organize and master; (b) it need not be adopted on a nationwide scale; (c) it neither shields people from awareness of the costs of the services which they receive nor builds up illusions of wealth which does not exist; and (d) it promotes participation in decision-making by way of advisory boards which are built up around all public medical facilities utilized by the programme.

NOTES

1. We have utilized in this report some results of a field survey carried out in the summer of 1972 by six students in as many districts. The survey collected information of health care attitudes, experiences, practices and expenditures of selected households. The findings of that survey may be found in M. Gottlieb, *Medical Economic Report No. VI*. The "Report on ERB Health Survey, Summer 1972".
2. The AFYA statistical report on what it designates "voluntary agency medical units utility" (see *AFYA Annual Reports of the Health Division*, 1968–1970) is not quite consistent either in its totals or in reports for individual facilities with the reports of Tanzania Christian Medical Association. The discrepancies are not very great and we have combined information from both sources in the text above.
3. *Annual Report of the Health Division* (Statistics) (treated as Vol. II of item 1 above) until 1967 published as a public document; for later years available in typewritten form, from the statistical officer of the Ministry.
4. Chief Medical Officer, *Annual Report of the Health Division*, Vol. I (until 1967 published as public documents; for 1968–69 in mimeographed, typewritten version 1970).
5. *Nguzo*, Periodical Organ of State Trading Corporation (STC), 1972, 3, p. 33.
6. *The Standard*, Tanzania daily newspaper in English, after 1972 called *The Daily News*. Published in Dar es Salaam.
7. By October 7, 1972 only three parastatals had joined the scheme; others were holding back apparently to obtain some form of preferential service since the group plan is adapted for industrial workers and parastatals employ chiefly office workers and professionals.
8. Chief Medical Officer, *Annual Report of the Health Division*, p. 29.
9. R. H. Titmus, Dr. Abel-Smith, et al., *The Health Services of Tanganyika, A Report to the Government* (London: Pitman Med. Pub. Co., 1964).
10. The AFYA statistical report of practitioners in "private" practice does not distinguish between purely private practice and the industrial practice to which we have alluded above.
11. In July 1971 the Health Minister in his budget presentation said that a "few doctors" had left the country after the measures taken to nationalize buildings but that they were in "private practice" and made "little contribution to the health services of the country." (See Ministry of Health, Budget presentation for the Fiscal Year, 1971/72, p. 6). A few months later the President of the Tanzanian Medical Association in an address to a session of his organisation stated that between April and October 48 practitioners had left the country and that it would be dogmatic to "jump to conclusions" about their "contribution."
12. A storm of controversial comment filled the Tanzanian press after prominent notice was given on 30/5/72 that of 26 Tanzanian MD graduates at Makerere Medical School only 11 reported for their internships in Tanzania. The Health Minister in his July 1972 budget presentation stated that of 24 Tanzanian graduates "only 11 have returned to the country so far." Ministry

of Health, *Budget Presentation for the Fiscal Year*, delivered in Bunge (Parliament): Mimeographed English translation prepared by the Ministry, 1972/73.

13. Gottlieb, Manuel, "The Extent and Character of Differentiation in Tanzanian Agriculture and Rural Society, 1967–1969," paper presented at 1972 Conference of the Social Science Council of the Universities of Eastern Africa meeting, Nairobi, December, 1972, pp. 3–5.
14. If urban households are divided into three income classes (using as a basis statements of cash-income received for a prior 12-months period) and taking incomes of Shs. 500 and 1500 as the breaking points for "low", "middle" and "upper" classes, the mean urban expenditure on private practitioners was Shs. 19, 24, and 32 per year (1969) for the three classes respectively.
15. L. W. Swantz, *The Role of the Medical Man Among the Zaramo of Dar es Salaam* (a Dissertation submitted for the Degree of Doctor of Philosophy in the University of Dar es Salaam, 1972; cited from the Uncorrected Mimeographed Version); L. W. Swantz, "The Zaramo of Dar es Salaam: A Study of Continuity and Change," *Tanganyika Notes and Records No.* 71 (Dar es Salaam 1970) pp 154–164; Marja-Liisa Swantz, *Ritual and Symbol in Transitional Zaramo Society* (Studia Missionalia Upsaliensia XVI; Gleerup: Uppsala, 1970), p. 227.
16. L. W. Swantz, 1972, *op. cit.*, pp. 152–164.
17. *Ibid.*, pp. 145–151.
18. M. Gottlieb, *Medical Economic Report No. VI*, "Report on ERB Health Survey Summer 1972."
19. Reporting for three urban communities, the tabulations showed for 1970–71 a mean number of 37.2 medical visits per household of which 2.05 visits were with traditional doctors, 5.4 with mission establishments, 26.5 with government establishments. In the five surveyed towns the surveyed urban households over the two-year period spent Shs. 105, nearly all of it with the non-government sectors per household. M. Gottlieb, 1972, *op. cit.*
20. Marja–Liisa Swantz reported that "after the people have taken the medicine (of a newly established dispensary) without effect they have an excuse to continue with their traditional methods." Marja–Liisa-Swantz, 1970, *op. cit.*, p. 111; 18% of the Waganga patients interviewed by Mr. Swantz had first gone to the hospital or dispensary for treatment, L. W. Swantz, 1972, *op. cit.* p. 167. See also J. H. Orley, *Culture and Mental Illness: A Study from Uganda* (Makerere Institute of Social Research (EAPH 1970), p. 167. In a valuable investigation of patient behaviour in out-patient departments of Mwanza region hospitals, the different patterns of multiple use of medical facilities were noted.
21. J. Loxley, "The Finance of Government Spending in Tanzania since Independence," *Rasilimali* (Tanzania Investment Bank, 1972), p. 24.
22. United Republic of Tanzania, *Financial Statement and Estimates of Revenue and Public Expenditure . . Supply Votes and Development Expenditures*, 1972/73, p. 72.
23. The expense for administration, maintenance and repair will become more important as the administrative organisation becomes established for management of the buildings distributed over all the major urban communities of Tanzania. The number of properties acquired has not recently been identified but in late 1971 some 3,056 properties were included. (*The Standard*, December, 1977, Former owners of these properties will in whole or in part be taken off the income tax rolls because of the elimination of rental income (which made up 4.5% of net taxable or chargeable incomes in 1969) but also because the net income of many business firms will be reduced, they will in the end need to pay rent for the premises which they formerly owned. Finally procedures for compensation have been established for these properties in February 1973 and some of the revenues produced will now be used to finance com pensation awards which will carry interest back to the time of acquisition (*The Standard*, 14th February, 1973). Compensation is only awarded assuming rapid rates of depreciation of 10% per year so that properties which at the time of acquisition were held for ten years or more were deemed valueless and not worthy of compensation. But the newer properties or properties which had turned over in recent years will be subject to compensation.
24. Titmus, Abel-Smith, et al., *op. cit.*